DONNY

THE OFFICIAL HISTORY OF

DONCASTER ROVERS F.C.

BY
Tony Bluff
&
Barry Watson

Published by:
Yore Publications
12 The Furrows, Harefield,
Middx. UB9 6AT.

© Tony Bluff 1994

....

British Library Cataloguing–in–Publication Data.
A catalogue record for this book
is available from the British Library.

ISBN 1 874427 55 0

Printed by:
BIDDLES LIMITED

Acknowledgements

To all the people who helped in any way to make this book possible.

All the staff at: DONCASTER REFERENCE LIBRARY
                      COLINDALE NEWSPAPER LIBRARY LONDON
                      DONCASTER ROVERS FOOTBALL CLUB

Lorna Parnell at the Football League Headquarters, Lytham St.Annes.
Tom Beardsley for all his help in years past.
Paul Gilligan for supplying action photographs and others.
Chris Worrall for his club shirt colours on the dust jacket.

And to anyone else who we may have forgotten to mention.

Every effort has been made to acknowledge, where applicable, the use of source of items, and to ensure that copyright has not been infringed.

                                               Thankyou all.

Publisher's note:
In many cases originals of illustrations were not traced or are unavailable, and therefore copies of same had to be used. We apologise for the less than perfect reproduction of such items, but considered it best to include, rather than omit them.

Dedication

This book is dedicated to all those players who donned the famous red and white of Doncaster Rovers Football Club.

Also, the club's officials – past and present – for keeping the club afloat, through some turbulent times.

And to all those supporters who have followed the team's fortunes, through the good and bad seasons – past and present.

And to our families who have had to put up with our fascination of the club, and the process of assembling this book.

      – THANKYOU ONE AND ALL –

                    TONY AND BARRY

CONTENTS

Shirt Designs and Colours Over The Years

The shirt designs depicted on the front and back cover (researched and drawn by Chris Worrall), represent those worn by the club during the following periods and/or years.

1. – 1879
2. – Late 1890's
3. – 1900's
4. – 1901 – 1902
5. – 1904
6. – 1900's to early 1920's
7. – 1922 – 1923
8. – 1920's
9. – 1930's to 1940's
10. – Early 1950's
11. – 1955
12. – 1956
13. – 1957
14. – 1958
15. – Early 1960's
16. – Mid–1960's
17. – Late 1960's/early '70's
18. – Early 1970's
19. – 1975 – 1978
20. – 1978/79
21. – 1979 – 1982
22. – 1982 – 1984
23. – 1984 – 1987
24. – 1987 – 1989
25. – 1989/90
26. – 1990 – 1992
27. – 1992/93.

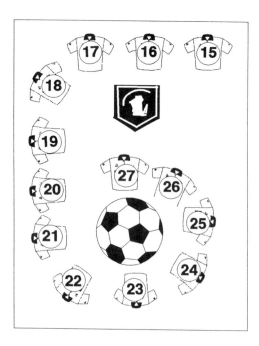

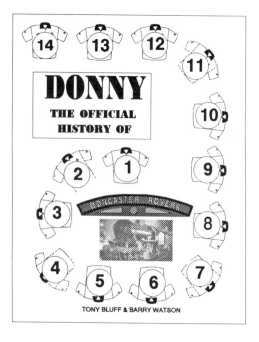

TONY BLUFF & BARRY WATSON

CHAPTER 1

The Early Years

Doncaster, in the mid–nineteenth century, was the main market town for the predominantly agricultural region surrounding it. As the main crossing point over the River Don the town was a major stop–over on the main North to South route, London to Edinburgh, the A1 road of that century. The railway came and not only followed a route similar to the road but brought the Industrial Revolution with it. In the 1850's the Great Northern Railway Co. opened an engine and carriage building works on the edge of the town, known locally as The Plant Works, giving employment to several thousand people. These workers would come from far and wide and push the population of the town up to around the 25,000 mark by the 1870's.

By the late 1870's the industrial boom had established itself, Trade Unions were making their mark and the Saturday half–day holiday was born. Many men would take a rest from their labours but the younger ones still had some energy to spare. Playing cricket was fine in summer but that only covered four months of the year so how could they fill in the rest of the year? Twenty miles away in Sheffield there was this game of football, played in winter, and already well established. Groups of young men thus got together, usually at their place of work, and challenged other groups to a game of football. Teams calling themselves Doncaster Mechanics and Doncaster G.N.R., were already playing matches among themselves and against clubs from Sheffield such as Ellesmere Road Wesleyans and Sheffield Law Students.

South Parade & Hall Cross, Doncaster: The birthplace of the Rovers – The Hall Cross.
Also the Salutation Inn can be seen (on right), which the Rovers used as a Clubhouse and changing–rooms.

On Tuesday evening, August the 19th 1879, a meeting was held at the Guildhall for the purpose of forming an association football club to represent the town. It was resolved that the club would be called the Doncaster Association Football Club and that they would run two teams, one to play on Thursdays and the other on Saturdays. Officials were elected, young men of substance, and plans announced to play on a field at Bennetthorpe.

This was the setting for the entry of the Doncaster Rovers Football Club. Unheralded, an 18 year old fitter at the Doncaster L.N.E.R. works, Albert Jenkins, got together a group of young men to play football against The Yorkshire Institute for the Deaf and Dumb down by the Racecourse, at the request of a master at the school who was a friend of his. So, one day in September 1879, Mr. Jenkins' scratch team played their momentous match at The Deaf and Dumb School. At half–time they were losing 4–0 but a rearrangement of the team enabled them to draw level before the close of play. As they walked back into the town after the match they paused at the Hall Cross for a breather, and after some discussion decided there and then to form a football club giving themselves the title of Doncaster Rovers.

Their first match under this name was at Rawmarsh on October the 3rd 1879, this first historic line-up being:– *W.Walker, A.Jenkins, J.Mitchell, T.Clark, W.Salman, W.Chadwick, W.Bedford, A.Roper, J.Gosling, W.Simpson, W.Titterington.*
The formation of the team was a goalkeeper, two backs, two half-backs and six forwards. The match ended in a draw.

Throughout the eighties they continued to play friendly matches against local clubs, and teams from the surrounding towns of Rotherham, Sheffield, Scunthorpe and Leeds. At first they played on a field provided by the farmer at Intake Farm, which is now occupied by the Fire Station. They also occasionally played on the Town Moor (i.e. the Racecourse) and the Belle Vue playing fields that are now covered by Welbeck Road, Firbeck Road, Sandbeck Road and Danum Road.

Their playing record was by far the best in the district, winning far more than they lost, and quite often by an appreciable margin. Their Headquarters were established at the Rockingham Inn in Bennetthorpe, where on July the 14th 1882 was held their first recorded A.G.M. The officers elected at that meeting for season 1882–83 were:– *Chairman, Mr.T.Pallett; Captain and Secretary, A. Jenkins; Treasurer, T.Clark; Committee, Messrs. Titterington, Bedford and Newbitt.*

For the following season John Mitchell took over as captain with Albert Jenkins becoming secretary and treasurer. The club colours at this time were blue jerseys, white knickerbockers and blue stockings.

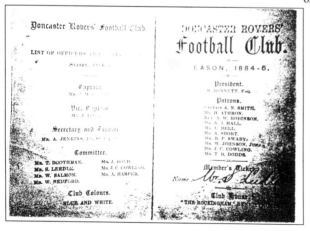

In 1884–85, the club included in their fixture list games against Gainsborough Trinity and Newton Heath (now Manchester United), both clubs of standing at that time. Whilst drawing at home to each club by the same score of 2–2, they lost their away game at Gainsborough by 8–1. This loss was one of only three defeats from twenty games played. Newton Heath must have been impressed because they signed John Mitchell and found him a job in the railway carriage shops of the Lancashire & Yorkshire Railway Company from where the club had originated.

Season 1885–86 saw the Rovers playing on a ground they could call their own. They obtained the use of a field at the rear of the Yorkshire Institute for the Deaf & Dumb, with entry being gained by the side of the school. At first it was known simply as the Deaf & Dumb ground, but by the following season it had acquired the name of the Intake ground. They also entered their first, and indeed were Doncaster's first club to do so, Cup Competition, the Sheffield and Hallamshire F.A.Minor Cup. A change too of colours was made from blue to scarlet jerseys. By now they were the premier club in Doncaster, the club representing the town having disbanded, with a number of their players joining the Rovers club. Thus the Rovers could now run a second team.

Their first foray into competitive football ended in the semi-finals, when they lost to Eckington Works 2nd eleven at Bramall Lane, Sheffield by a score of 3–2. In that team were many players who had grown up with the Rovers, Sol Leedle was captain, George James and Josh Boyd were mainstays of the defence. John Hopwood was a fast raiding winger who had scored one of the goals after a brilliant dribble covering half the length of the pitch. Also in the forward line were James Bilsland who had come from the town club and had played for the Doncaster Mechanics club as far back as 1879, and his younger brother Fred who was still in his teens. Other members of the club were Billy Bridgewater, who went on to play for Rotherham Town and Sheffield United. He later found fame in the 1920's and 30's as a boxing promoter and manager of Roland Todd, a British middleweight champion, and Harry Crossley a British light heavyweight champion; Patrick Stirling, son of the chief locomotive engineer to the G.N.R. Company, was also a member of the Rovers, and became Mayor of Doncaster in 1913, and gave a lifetime of public service to the town.

There were that season, two examples of the creed that the more we make progress the more things stay the same. In a match at Elsecar near Barnsley, on Boxing Day, the Rovers scored a second goal to lead 2–1 after 85 minutes of play. Whereupon the Elsecar team walked off and refused to play any more.

Match ticket of 1887

The Rovers players were subjected to "continuous hooting", a few of them remarking that they would not play there again. Then a month later against Brigg Town at Brigg it was the Rovers turn to walk off the pitch after being subjected to rough and brutal play by the Brigg players and to continuous stone throwing by the spectators. They walked off 20 minutes before time, at which point they were losing 5–0!

The following season they entered the Sheffield & Hallamshire F.A.Challenge Cup besides having an enlarged fixture list of friendlies. The local M.P., Mr.Walter S.Shirley was now the President of the club, with several other dignitaries of the town as Patrons. Albert Pearce was the new secretary and with around a hundred members they decided to run three teams. They went out of the Sheffield Cup after a replay with Sheffield Collegiate, in the first round, but continued to win the majority of their friendly fixtures.

In season 1887–88 they again entered the Sheffield Cup and also the Gainsborough News Charity Cup, as well as playing an increased number of friendly games. But their Cup ambitions were severely dented, losing to Kimberworth 6–3 in the 1st Round of the Sheffield Cup. After beating Gainsborough Ashcroft 12–0, they met Gainsborough Trinity in the next round of the Gainsboro' News Charity Cup and went out, at home, by 3–2. One thing that the secretary, John Fowler, had in common with other club secretaries was the constant ploy of having to find other opponents late in the week because clubs were crying off from their friendly engagements because of Cup games.

This problem led, of course, to the formation of the Football League on April the 17th 1888. But this was way above the heads of the Rovers committee. The club was still making it's way in the larger world outside Doncaster, and had not even entered the F.A.Cup yet. Clubs by now were able to pay players to play, and although there is no direct evidence it seems certain that during the 1887–88 season the Rovers had at least one professional at the club. This was centre–forward Sam Hunt, from Mexborough, who in the two seasons he was with the Rovers certainly knew where the net was.

It is also possible that captain Alex Munro was a professional. A Scot, his previous club had been Glasgow Caledonians, so no doubt he had been found employment at the Plant Works to entice him down to Doncaster where he could also play football for the Rovers. Certainly there was nothing in the balance sheet about payment to players. This showed a credit in hand of £28–2–9½d, more than triple what they had started the season with. As much as £71–16–6½d had been taken in gate money and the members contributions amounted to £24–8–0d. On the expenditure side, the largest sum was £26–13–2d, which had been paid to opponents as their share of gate money. Printing costs came to a total of £12–5–10d, and match expenses to £10–14–11d.

Thus, having a handy balance in the bank, the club embarked upon season 1888–89 by entering the F.A.Cup for the first time, plus the Sheffield Challenge Cup, the Gainsborough News Charity Cup and the Wharncliffe Charity Cup, whilst still making their fixture list up with friendlies. Some of the previous season's profits were spent on ground improvements when a "commodious grand–stand" was erected on the Intake Farm side of the ground, and turnstiles and a ticket office placed at the entrance to the field. The cost of the materials for the stand came to £31 with the labour given free by the volunteers who erected it.

So the Club were set to welcome to the Intake their first F.A.Cup opponents, local rivals Rotherham Town, on October the 6th 1888, in the 1st. Qualifying Round. On the day about 3000 people turned up to witness the match which had the following teams lining up:

ROVERS:- *Wm.Massey in goal; Walter Langton, A.Gray, full backs; George James, A.Munro, the captain and Josh Boyd, half backs; John Fowler, A.Shakespeare, Sam Hunt, John Hopwood and Fred Bilsland, forwards.*

ROTHERHAM:- *A.Hall; F.Turner, H.Taft; A.Sherwood, A.Rodgers, W.Damms; W.Gummer, W.Musson, W.Bennett, G.Medley, and J.T.McCormick.*

In the first 15 minutes Rotherham scored twice through Bennett, thus setting the tone of the game. Medley and Gummer scored two more goals before the Rovers pulled one back through Hunt just before half-time. Although the Rovers attacked continuously in the second half they could not score, but Rotherham could. Five more goals from Bennett (3), Medley and McCormick settled the match in Rotherham's favour with a score of 9-1.

Nothing daunted, the Rovers played their next match at Eckington Works in the Sheffield Challenge Cup and drew 2-2, going on to win the replay, beat Sheffield Clinton in the next round after a replay, only to come up against Rotherham Town in Round 3 at Rotherham. Needless to say they lost this time, too, but only by 6-2. Meanwhile they had beaten Attercliffe 6-1 in the Gainsborough News Charity Cup and were due to play Sheffield Wednesday in the next round. The game should have been played at Doncaster on Monday, January the 21st, but the Rovers had difficulty in playing on that day so eventually it was agreed to play on the Wednesday ground at Olive Grove on Saturday, January the 19th, with the Wednesday cancelling their Club fixture with Grimsby Town. The match turned out to be as one-sided as the score of 10-0 suggests with the Wednesday being seven-nil up at half-time.

The one bright spot for the Rovers, was the report in the Sheffield papers which suggested that Langton was worth a try in the Sheffield F.A. representative team. Their exit from this competition left the club with just the Wharncliffe Charity Cup to play for. They beat Ecclesfield to go into the semi-final against their old rivals from down the Sheffield Road, Rotherham Town. This was the third meeting of the season for these two clubs and this time the Rovers showed they had learned from the previous games.

The game, at Bramall Lane, ended goalless, with the replay at Doncaster finishing at 1-1, when the two captains disagreed as to whether extra time should be played. The second replay at Bramall Lane finished 2-2 after extra time with each club being short of their chief goalscorers, Hunt and Bennett. The pair had been suspended by the Sheffield & Hallamshire F.A. for a breach of the competition rule which forbade professional players playing for more than one club during the same season! The match was finally settled on April the 13th, when Rotherham finally overcame the Rovers by 3-0, with both clubs allowed to play their professional players.

The season ended with a record for all games of, played 36, won 16, drawn 9, lost 11, goals scored 90, goals against 80. Matches had been played against all the leading professional teams in the district. At the A.G.M. a balance in hand was recorded of £54-18-11d – a substantial sum.

Out of 34 matches played in the 1889-90 season only three were competitive games, the others all being friendlies. They went out of the F.A.Cup again to Rotherham Town at the first time of asking losing 2-1 at Rotherham. They also lost at home to Staveley in the Sheffield Cup by 3-0, and on Boxing Day were defeated by the newly formed Sheffield United at Bramall Lane in the Wharncliffe Charity Cup by a goal to nil.

CHAPTER 2

The Midland Alliance and Beyond

n June 1890, at a meeting held at Nottingham *"A football combination under the title of the Midland Football Alliance was formed to consist of ten clubs. The following eight clubs have joined:- Doncaster Rovers, Rotherham Swifts, Notts. Olympic, Notts. Jardines, Newark, Loughborough Town, Heanor Town and Notts. County Rovers".* Thus it was announced to the Doncaster footballing public in the Doncaster Gazette on June the 27th 1890 that the Rovers were widening their horizons. The committee busied themselves by signing a number of new players so that by September the newcomers were, Jim Massey in goal, James Ramsey Gray and Walter Langton (full backs), George James, Bob Pinkerton and McCartney (both from Scotland), brothers Albert and Tom Hoyle, brothers Walter and Albert Attree plus Josh Boyd – half backs. A.Hemingfield from Attercliffe, George Hawksworth and E.R.Herrod – both from Derby St.Lukes – James Gresham from Lincoln City, John Fowler, John Hopwood, A.Shakespeare, were all forwards. They were just about ready to start their first ever league campaign in the ten-club strong Midland Alliance, Grantham Rovers and Sheffield Club having joined the earlier eight clubs.

They opened the season with a couple of friendly games against Matlock and Darlington St.Augustines. Both matches were lost by the odd goal, but the committee had made two more signings after the first match. They had admired the play of Matlock's inside right Frost, and invited him to play for the Rovers, having also signed Tom Kisbey, a centre forward, from Lincoln City. The afternoon of Saturday, September the 20th came with Loughborough visiting the Intake ground for the first game in the new league. The eleven men representing the Rovers were:-

Jim Massey; Ramsey Gray (captain), Walter Langton; Albert Hoyle, A.Hemmingfield, George James; George Hawksworth, Frost, Tom Kisbey, James Gresham, and E.R.Herrod.

The match kicked off at 3.10pm and remained scoreless in the first half, but the Rovers got well on top in the second period and with goals from Herrod, Gresham, Kisbey and Frost ran out worthy winners by 4–0. The Doncaster Chronicle waxed lyrical about the Rovers players, claiming in particular that Frost was the best forward the club had ever had, and that Hemmingfield had been quite outstanding. Unfortunately for the club Frost decided he did not relish playing professional football and decided to go back home to Matlock. Six weeks later Hemmingfield moved on to Sheffield United.

Nevertheless the season progressed with it's mixture of league games interspersed with friendlies and cup matches. The next Alliance match at Grantham was lost, and the Rovers F.A.Cup match at home to Kilnhurst also ended in defeat (5–4), but only after extra time.

This cup-tie on October the 25th was the first occasion that the club used the Salutation Inn on South Parade as their club house. The players changed upstairs there, and walked the few hundred yards to the Intake ground. Entrance to the dressing room was gained via a back staircase leading from the yard, and the dressing room was described as spacious and well heated. November brought three league games – a win over Sheffield, a draw with Notts. Jardines and a loss to Notts. County Rovers (the Notts.County reserve team). It also brought a further defeat when the league committee deducted two points off the club for playing an ineligible player (Frost) against Loughborough, this left the club in 7th place in the league table. Ramsey Gray, the captain, took himself off to Scotland in a search for players, and came back with an inside forward from Johnstone Rangers, J.McCallum.

The first hint of problems with the league system showed themselves in December when Notts. Jardines could not raise a team to come to Doncaster on the 13th, and then Rotherham Swifts failed to turn up for the Christmas Day fixture. In the one league game played the Rovers took a point from Notts. Olympic so that by the end of the year they were showing a record of 4 points from 6 games and were in eighth place, with as many as five games in hand over some of the clubs above them.

New Year's Day 1891 saw the club start on the road to glory. On that day, Thursday, they beat Staveley 2–1 at home in the third round of the Sheffield Challenge Cup. The match had been drawn to be played at Staveley but for a financial guarantee Staveley agreed to switch the venue to Doncaster. Money well spent in view of what the victory led to. However, before the semi-final of the cup competition there were some league matches to play. A loss at Loughborough was followed by a comprehensive 6–0 win over Notts. Olympic and good away wins at Newark and Heanor.

They were running into form and in the semi-final at Bramall Lane they put paid to Ecclesfield Wanderers by 3–1 with goals scored by Langton, recently moved to centre forward from left back to add weight and punch, Herrod and Gresham.

The good form continued with a 7–0 demolition of Newark, a slight set–back at Notts. County Rovers with an odd goal defeat, and then a 6–1 thrashing of Grantham Rovers. This brought them nicely up to the week before their meeting with Sheffield United in the Sheffield Challenge Cup Final at Bramall Lane. While the football fans of Doncaster sent letters to the local papers about the unfairness of the Final being played at the ground of their opponents, the club committee sent the players for a week's special training to Askern, where there was a football ground and the Spa baths.

Saturday, March the 21st 1891 was Cup Final day. True, the Rovers of Blackburn were defending the F.A.Cup that they had won the previous year against Notts. County, at the Oval, and there would be 30,000 fans there to see it, but who cared in Doncaster? Their Cup Final was taking place at Sheffield and so about 1000 fans boarded the special train that the M.S.& L. Railway Co. had laid on, and at 1.15pm left the town together with their heroes, who with the committee, were allocated a saloon carriage. Snow and sleet had fallen intermittently during the morning and the afternoon was dull and cold, but none–theless about 4,000 spectators turned out. With the Rovers supporters making their presence felt and amid cries of "Play up Rovers" the following Rovers players lined up:-

Jim Massey, Harry Parr, Ramsey Gray, Joe Cuthbert, George James, Bob Pinkerton, Tom Kisbey, James Gresham, Walter Langton, J.McCallum and E.R. Herrod

Within 5 minutes a shot from Watson hit a post and Howell from close in put the rebound into the net. The United continued to have the better of the play but could not score even though, after 30 minutes Gray received a kick to his leg which effectively disabled him and necessitated Langton going to left back. Then a few minutes from half–time in a Rovers attack, James put the ball in the net following a melee in the United goalmouth. Half–time came with the score at 1–1. A few minutes after the resumption Gray finally retired from the field of play with a dislocated knee leaving the Rovers to fight it out with 10 men. This they did magnificently, continually thwarting the United forwards who were also guilty of a number of missed chances. Then, five minutes before time, Herrod went down his wing, passed inside to McCallum who passed it on to Kisbey, and with a fine shot the ball whistled past Howlett to put the Rovers 2–1 up.

When the telegram arrived in Doncaster announcing the result there was a large crowd gathered near the fountain, who responded with mighty cheering. The team arrived back at Doncaster Station at 9 p.m., and were met by a surging crowd of excited humanity who gave such a shout when their heroes appeared it must have been heard in Sheffield. The players mounted a couple of buses and a trap, and accompanied by the Volunteer Band playing "See the Conquering Heroes Come", and at least three thousand people, wended their way through town to the Salutation Inn. On reaching there the crowd clamoured for the players, who eventually appeared on one of the balcony.

Each player was made to give a speech, starting with the captain – Ramsey Gray – who acted as prompter to the others who weren't orators. One he didn't prompt was Pinkerton who began by saying *"I have been teetotal for a week"*, a statement greeted by roars of laughter.

Then he confessed as to his intentions that night and much to the crowd's amusement went back inside to carry out his promise. Eventually the crowd went home and the players, after their week's abstinence, together with the other members of the club, spent the rest of the evening celebrating.

But the football season had not yet run it's course. On the Monday after the Cup win, Massey and Langton played for The Sheffield & Hallamshire F.A. against the Berks. & Bucks F.A. Gray had also been selected but could not play because of his injury, which kept him out for the rest of the season. To replace him for the remaining matches the committee brought in a young man from Hexthorpe, Harry Thickett, who went on to greater fame for Sheffield United and England. The team completed their Midland Alliance fixtures by beating Heanor and Sheffield, ending with a record of 17 points from 14 games (Notts. Jardines & Rotherham Swifts having withdrawn), to finish as runner's-up to Notts. County Rovers. The club thus ended their most successful season yet, and they were now ready to move on to greater things.

Their first move was to apply for entry to the Midland Counties League, but at the League meeting called for that purpose they were not elected to any of the three places available – Leicester Fosse, Loughborough and Wednesbury Old Athletic securing the necessary votes. But at the Midland League A.G.M. on June the 6th 1891, the Rovers were voted in to take the place of Sheffield United who had just withdrawn.

With the question of what competition they would be playing in now settled, the committee addressed themselves to the gathering together of a team. Of the Cup winning eleven, Gray had moved on to Grimsby Town and McCallum to Gainsborough Trinity, the rest of the players having signed on again. Adams, an inside forward, came from Wednesbury Old Athletic, William "Micky" Bennett, one of the famous Mexborough family, was signed from Sheffield Wednesday, Burton, a winger, came from Lincoln City and Billy Bridgewater signed from Sheffield United. Charles Waddington, a centre forward, came from Doncaster Wanderers. Together with a number of amateur players, including Albert Attree and John Fowler, the Rovers considered that they had a strong squad to choose from.

The opening game of their first season in the Midland League was at Wednesbury on September the 5th, 1891. The committee put the following team in the field:– *Massey; Parr, Langton; Cuthbert, James captain, Pinkerton; Burton, Kisbey, Bennett, Adams, Gresham.* By half-time the Rovers were three down, with Parr and Langton putting the ball into his own net, but despite a better display in the second half they could only manage one goal in reply, scored by Bennett.

Waddington and Albert Attree replaced the injured Cuthbert and Pinkerton for the following week's match, at home to Burton Wanderers, which gave them their first victory in the Midland League – by 3-1 – Gresham (2) and Bennett getting the goals. Four defeats followed, including one at Lincoln in the F.A.Cup, but it was the fourth defeat, at Loughborough, that raised the eyebrows.

For this match, the captain – James – was out injured and the committee dropped Burton to the reserves. This decision infuriated Burton, and although both Kisbey and Gresham were selected, they refused to play in the match, out of sympathy to Burton. Within fifteen minutes of the start the Rovers were six goals down, seven down at half-time, and eventually lost 11-2. They were now in eleventh place in a twelve club league, with but two points from five games. Burton never played for the Rovers again, but Kisbey and Gresham, although they had asked for their release which was not granted, were suspended for one game then continued – but not for long.

On Monday, November the 23rd, a general meeting of the members of the club was called to consider an application from some of the first team professionals for an increase in the rate of pay per match, and also to be insured against injury. The letter was signed by Massey, Langton, Parr, Pinkerton, Cuthbert, Bridgewater (who was still incapacitated from his recent accident at work in the Plant Works), Gresham, Kisbey, Bennett and Waddington. The demand was for 8 shillings for a defeat, 9 shillings for a draw and 10 for a win, to cover all matches home and away. The existing rates were:– for home matches, 5, 6, and 7 shillings; for away matches 7, 8, and 9. Mr.Musson, the financial secretary, explained the financial situation to the members.

In brief, the situation was that the club could not manage on their present "gates", losing about £3 a game, and it was only the members subscriptions and other fund raising projects that kept the club on an even keel. Although the members gave the committee a mandate to meet the players halfway, the players declined the offer, and also refused to play for the club until some agreement had been reached. The matter of insurance was also voted down, and the players in attendance walked out of the meeting. There was much discussion among the members about the merits of employing professional players or to go back to purely amateurs, but the one thing everyone was agreed on was the continuance of the club. Fortunately for the club their next league match was three weeks away, but they had a friendly game on the Saturday after the meeting, at Darlington St.Augustines, and so from somewhere a team had to be found. They did not want to call upon too many second team players as they were going well in their competitions, so the call was put out to other clubs for assistance.

The team that turned out at Darlington, and gained a 1–1 draw was:–

Fenwick (Sheffield Club); Young and MacDonald (both Newcastle East End);Boyd, James, Attree; Bennett, Fairburn (unknown club), Waddington, Seymour and Fowler. A team made up of four regulars (Waddington and Bennett having made their peace with the committee), three reserves and four players from other clubs.

The following week all the remaining players who were on strike, with the exception of Gresham and Kisbey, resolved their differences with the club and were welcomed back into the fold. Early in December Gresham went to Lincoln City for a fee of £20. The money was needed, since on the night of Thursday December the 10th 1891, the roof of the stand was blown into the Deaf & Dumb School by a gale.

A new and larger stand, at a cost of around £40 was erected in time for the home game against Long Eaton Rangers on Saturday, December the 19th! Alas, the next month, during the Friday night, the 29th of January, another gale blew this stand down.

The club were certainly having a few trials and tribulations in trying to establish a professional football club of quality in the town. Not least with the weather, for not only had the heavy gales destroyed two stands, but the inclement weather had kept attendances down. However, bad as the weather must have been, they had not one match postponed all season. They must have been made of stern stuff these lads! The nearest approach to a postponement had come on the 12th of December, in the match at home to Burslem Port Vale. Two days previously the stand had been blown down and there had been a lot of rain. The ground was saturated and there was a strong wind blowing, but the teams kicked off, only to be then faced with a blinding snowstorm. The match went on for 65 minutes with the Rovers leading 3–1, before the ten Port Vale players, their goalkeeper had missed his train, appealed to the referee to stop the game. The referee ordered them to continue, but the Port Vale players refused and walked off, and the result was allowed to stand.

The Rovers lost their grip on the Sheffield Cup to the team they had beaten the year before, Sheffield United, by 4–0. But gradually a team was welded together that was able to compete, and the end of a traumatic season came with the club finishing in sixth place in the Midland League with 21 points from 20 games. The main players used in the second half of the season were:–
Massey, Langton, Parr, McDonald, Cuthbert, James, Albert Attree, Waddington, Edwards and Shaw who had come from Nottinghamshire, Wilson from Scotland, and Flavill.

The committee set about forming a team for season 1892–93 by re-signing Massey, Langton, Parr, Cuthbert, Wilson, McDonald, the two Attrees, Waddington, Pinkerton, Bridgewater, and Scott who they had signed from Stockton towards the end of the previous season. Among the new players signed were Billy Smith, an inside forward from Derby Junction, Stewart Smith, a centre forward from Arbroath, Townend a forward from Bulwell, Hopewell, a half back from Grimsby Town and McKay an inside forward from the West Manchester club. With a team selected from this squad the club started off by winning their first four Midland League games with a record of 14 goals scored and 6 against. They lost the next match at Gainsborough Trinity and then beat Mansfield Town in the F.A.Cup, their first win in that competition, at the fifth attempt. Two drawn league games were followed by a Cup knockout from Grimsby Town.

The next league match at Mansfield was lost, the Rovers being without Massey who was playing for the Sheffield & Hallamshire F.A. representative team. The goalkeeper selected missed his train so Billy Smith, who was travelling with them but had not been selected because of an injury sustained in the previous match, was pressed into service between the posts. The blame for the one goal defeat was not laid at his door however, since by all accounts he did well. He was to keep goal again some weeks later, over the Christmas period, when the Rovers were ordered by the Sheffield F.A. to replay their Sheffield Cup tie at Eckington where they had drawn the first match against Eckington Works.

This action by the local F.A. caused a lot of ill–feeling towards this body in Doncaster, and among the suggestions at a committee meeting was that they should not play the match and scratch from the competition. The general consensus was, however, that the match should be played as it would lay the club open to a charge of cowardice if they scratched !

The match was played with a below–strength team and to everyone's surprise was won 3–2. Massey should have played in goal and he was waiting at Conisborough station but the train did not stop, so Smith was called into action again. Back in the league in the first match of the New Year they finally won a game when they went to Leicester Fosse and were victorious by 1–0.

Before Christmas the Rovers had signed on three new players. Walter Lester was an inside forward from Derby, whilst Alex Guild, a centre half, and Alex Lee who played at centre forward were both from Scotland. All three settled into the team as they won six out of their last eleven league games.

In between these encounters was the semi-final of the Sheffield Cup in which the Rovers had to meet Sheffield Strollers (Sheffield United Reserves) at Olive Grove, Sheffield Wednesday's ground. This match was drawn 1–1 and the replay, also at Olive Grove, was drawn 3–3. The second replay was played at Doncaster on the date reserved for the final, March the 4th, and was lost 3–1. The Doncaster Chronicle stated that the first and third Sheffield goals were flagrantly offside causing the crowd to get on to the referee. Whilst protesting about the third goal Cuthbert complained of being struck by a Sheffield player, but the referee ignored him. Cuthbert was then sent off for apparently using bad language to the referee, which resulted in the official being attacked by the crowd after the game, and having to be rescued by the police and members of the Rovers committee. It was an hour and a quarter before the referee could leave the ground, and as he was leaving in a waggonette he was hit in the face by a stone thrown by one of the remaining spectators. Both the Doncaster Chronicle and the Gazette, whilst condemning the violent disorder of the spectators, took exception to the handling of the match by "neutral" officials from Sheffield and were strong in their opinions of the Sheffield F.A. and their actions in regard to the Doncaster club who had had the temerity to take the Cup out of Sheffield on one occasion.

Whilst waiting for the verdict of the F.A. in regard to crowd misconduct, the Rovers sent in a protest against Sheffield Strollers claiming that they had played an ineligible player. This protest was upheld and the match ordered to be replayed at Olive Grove where the Rovers finally lost 1–0. A young man named John Morton, of Arthur Street, Doncaster, was summoned for assaulting Mr.Young, the referee, and fined £1 and ordered to pay 26s. costs. The Sheffield & Hallamshire F.A. suspended the Intake ground for three weeks, which happened to include the Easter period.

A Midland League match against Wednesbury Old Athletic had to be postponed because of the lack of time to find another ground, but the Good Friday match against Grantham Rovers and the Easter Monday game against Gainsborough Trinity were played at Askern, in a field placed at their disposal, for a consideration, by Mr.Edwards of the Swan Hotel, Askern. Both matches attracted larger than average crowds of estimated at three to four thousand. There were the unpleasantries, slights and prejudices connected with the Sheffield competition, both during this season and in previous years. In addition the club lost money on every cup game, and with all the replays it disrupted the fixture list, and therefore it is not surprising that Doncaster Rovers did not play in this competition again until 1905.

With a draw, a win and a loss in their final Midland League games the club finished in fifth position, a creditable end to a trying season.

At the A.G.M.of the club on June 2nd 1893, John Musson was elected to the post of secretary in succession to John Hopwood who had resigned. The club had made a loss on the previous season of £2, nothing really compared to the sums of money generated and required to run a team of professional players. But even so there were voices raised as to the amounts paid to players (£233.2s.8d.), the trainer (£17.10s.0d.) and linesmen (who were nominated, and paid £29.0s.7d. by the clubs to assist the referees). Members were also unhappy about the bad attendance record of the players at the practice sessions, so a new code of rules was adopted. The Midland League was now down to eleven clubs, Rotherham Town, the Champions, having gained admission to the Football League, and Derby Junction and Wednesbury Old Athletic resigning. Only one club was admitted, Mansfield Greenhalgh's.

The committee had now to set about building a team. Massey, the goalkeeper, had moved to Sheffield Wednesday, but the following players had been signed:– Walter Langton, Albert Attree, Alex Guild, Alex Lee, Billy Bridgewater, Walter Lester, Billy Smith, J.Radford (goalkeeper), Joe Cuthbert, Andrew Shaw (of Derby) and Charles Waddington. Several amateurs also promised to play, Mr.Richard Fenwick (goalkeeper) previously with Sheffield Club and Sheffield United; Mr.T.Morris (centre half), of York, who had played for the club at the end of the previous season; F.Smith of Conisborough and late of Horncastle; and finally Mr.Billsborough of Frodingham.

The season opened on a warm Saturday afternoon with a Midland League match at home to Burton Wanderers with the team turning out thus:– *Fenwick; Attree, Langton; Cuthbert, Morris, Guild; J.Smith, W.Smith, Lee, Lester.*

A goal by Billy Smith equalised matters and the match ended in a draw due mainly to the excellent goalkeeping of Fenwick, a Leeds solicitor. The Rovers next match was a friendly on the Monday at Woolwich Arsenal, who, even though they were not in the Football League at the time were regarded as equal to that standard. They had offered the Rovers a good guarantee to go down to London and play them, an offer that was willingly accepted. With Morris unable to go Fred Webb came in to an otherwise unchanged team, and the Rovers lost 4–1. This seemed to be a portent of what was to come because their first win did not come until October the 7th in a friendly match at home to Gainsborough Trinity.

They proceeded to lose at home to Grantham Rovers in the F.A.Cup, got hammered 7–1 at Mansfield Greenhalgh's, but the following week – on December the 23rd – recorded their first league victory, beating Kettering 2–1 at home. Walter Attree, elder brother of Albert, had come into the team at centre half, Billy Calder had been signed from Sheffield United to fill the left wing berth,

George Cartwright came in from the reserves at inside right and A.White, a young amateur appeared at inside left. After the victory over Kettering Billy Smith was released from his contract so that he could move back to Derby, for the sake of his wife. Changes came thick and fast, but in January they lost 6-1 at Burton Wanderers and 5-0 at Long Eaton Rangers. Coupled with defeats such as the 5-2 reverse at home to local rivals Mexborough Town, 5-1 at Stockton and 7-1 at home to West Bromwich Albion in friendly matches, it was a most unhappy season and no doubt supporters were glad to see four teams finish below them in the league table at the end of the season. The committee certainly were, because if they had finished in the re-election positions they would have been penalised to the tune of two guineas!

Season 1894-95 presented itself with an increase of clubs in the Midland League. Burton Wanderers, the Champions were elected to the Football League and Leicester Fosse (now Leicester City) withdrew to join the Leicester & Northamptonshire League. Mansfield Greenhalgh's amalgamated with Mansfield Town, but Stoke Swifts (Stoke's Reserves), Derby County Reserves, Ilkeston Town, Heanor Town, Rushden Town and Matlock Town were all elected, to bring the total of clubs to fourteen.

The Rovers also entered the Wharncliffe Charity Cup, normally a straightforward knockout competition, but that season was to be played on a league basis. This would involve Rovers in matches against Barnsley St.Peters (now Barnsley), Sheffield Strollers (Sheffield United Reserves), Sheffield Wednesday Reserves, Mexborough Town and Chesterfield, who all competed in the Sheffield Association League, a stepdown from the Midland League. This would give the club a total of thirty-six competitive matches in the season with the F.A.Cup to be added on, and left very little room for friendly fixtures, when in fact only six were played.

As for the team, well the scouts had been out and had come back with Jack Eggett from Wisbech to keep goal, and had raided Pyebank Rovers in Sheffield for Frank Hulley, a centre half, Harry Hunt, a left back and E.J.Carr, an outside left. All except Hunt, who had to compete with the *"old hoss"*, Walter Langton, for his position established themselves in the team. Albert Attree, George Cartwright, Charles Waddington and Billy Calder remained from the previous season but half a dozen matches into the season Calder went to Barnsley. In November Ike Wright, an inside right, who had been signed on at the beginning of the season but had had to serve a suspension for a misdemeanour committed at Barnsley, at last made his debut as did Gibb, an inside left from the Dundee area. A month later another Scotsman, outside right A.Mackie, who had come down for trials with Sheffield Wednesday was signed on.

His debut was particularly memorable, taking place on December the 15th at Stoke, where the Rovers were crushed 13-1! The Doncaster Gazette on the following Friday described the result as disgraceful and the Chronicle described the scene at the local circus on that Saturday evening, when the figures 13-1 were announced; *"a loud guffaw went the round of the gallery"*.

A week later came a signing that would also be memorable for the service he would give to the club over the next ten years, Ellis Wright, a left half from Ecclesfield. Unfortunately, although they played all season with a fairly settled team, goals were leaked to the extent that only one Midland League club conceded more – Matlock – and they finished bottom. The week before the Stoke match Rushden scored six against the Rovers, Loughborough got six, and Long Eaton Rangers plus Heanor both put five past Eggett in successive weeks. The club went out of the F.A.Cup at the first attempt at home to Mexborough, supposedly a lesser ranked team, but one who proved there wasn't that much difference in stature by winning the Wharncliffe Charity Cup League quite comfortably. The Rovers finished the season third from bottom in the Midland League and third from the top in the Wharncliffe Charity Cup.

The finances of the club were again causing problems, such that on February the 16th, the players actually voted to play at Barnsley without pay. The club ended the season with a deficit of £30.

At the A.G.M.of the Midland League held on May the 25th 1895, the last four teams in the table had to seek re-election - Newark, Doncaster Rovers, Grantham Rovers and Matlock. There were also vacancies caused by the withdrawal of Loughborough Town (elected to the Football League), Stoke Reserves and Derby County Reserves. Would-be applicants were Barnsley St.Peters, Grimsby Town Reserves, Walsall Town Swifts (rejected by the Football League and replaced by Loughborough), Leicester Fosse Reserves, Swadlincote and Wellingborough. Eventually, Newark, Doncaster Rovers, Grantham Rovers, Matlock, Barnsley St.Peters, Walsall Town Swifts and Wellingborough were elected. At a further meeting Dresden United were added, leaving the Midland League with fifteen clubs.

So the Rovers were still in good class football for season 1895-96, but the costs were still high, leaving them with a deficit of £43 on the previous season's workings. Nevertheless, hopes for this new season were optimistic, when three new forwards were signed to add to the bulk of the previous year's players. Two of the three, outside left Bill Linward and inside right W.Fellows came from the Grimsby All Saints club, the third – C.H.McUrich – a centre forward, had played with Kettering for the last three years.

The side settled down straight away losing only once in their first five league games. A win over Mexborough after a replay in the 1st Qualifying Round of the F.A.Cup was followed by two league defeats, then the next round of the F.A.Cup. This latter match was against Second Division Rotherham Town at the Intake ground, and turned out to be quite a game.

Rotherham opened the scoring after five minutes through McCormick, and added another ten minutes later through Bryant. They were so much on top that McCormick added three more before half-time. When the second half started things started to get a bit rough, with the referee repeatedly cautioning players. Eventually Cutts, the Rotherham centre forward went in with a late tackle on Eggett, who took exception to this and kicked Cutts on the legs. The referee immediately sent Eggett off the field.

Waddington of the Rovers and McCabe of Rotherham were soon seen to be swopping punches, and they too were despatched from the field by Referee Howcroft of Redcar. McCormick then scored two more goals for Rotherham, two more players were booked, and Cutts was carried off having been kicked in the stomach. This left both teams at the end with nine men. At the end of the game the crowd pressed around the ropes and some apprehension was felt for the referee, but he managed to escape with just a hooting.

The repercussions were not felt until February, after Eggett and Waddington had been in front of an F.A.-disciplinary committee. This resulted in Eggett being suspended for six weeks and Waddington for four weeks, with McCabe of Rotherham suffering no penalty. So, prior to the game at Walsall on February the 1st, the entire defence of Eggett, A.Attree, Langton, Waddington, Hulley and Wright, had not missed a match of any kind. Alas, they went to Walsall having had to make changes, and were hammered out of sight by 9-1.

The Rovers did not win again until five weeks later, when Eggett returned, coincidentally against Walsall at home. With four wins and a draw from their last seven league games the club finished on a high note, but only tenth in the league. At the A.G.M., on May the 8th 1896, the secretary, Mr.John Musson, announced a profit of £22 on the season just ended. The members voted to increase the secretary's honorarium from £5 per annum to £10 plus 10% of the balance at the end of the season.

At the A.G.M.of the Midland League held on May the 23rd 1896, there was a big change of clubs for the coming season 1896-97. Gainsborough Trinity and Walsall Town Swifts were admitted to the Football League, and so withdrew from the Midland League. Three clubs, Mansfield Town, Newark and Matlock Town, of the four who had to seek re-election, declined

to do so. This left the fourth – Wellingborough Town – to go to the vote alongside seven other clubs for the six places available; Burslem Port Vale (rejected by the Football League), Chesterfield, Mexborough, Finedon, Leicester Fosse Reserves, Glossop North End and Work-sop Town. Finedon and Leicester Fosse Reserves were the clubs to lose out, the others teams being elected.

The Rovers committee set about their team building with gusto, as the majority of the previous season's players re-signed. Newcomers were J.Smith, a strapping centre forward from Darfield Old Club and J. Steers and Billy Longden from the now defunct Rotherham Town. The Rovers first league game was away to near neighbours Mexborough, and in the rain they won with an Ellis Wright goal midway through the second half. The team lined up with Jack Eggett in goal, Albert Attree at right back, Walter Langton at left back, Charlie Waddington at right half, Frank Hulley at centre half with Ellis Wright at left half. The forward line consisted of Billy Longden (outside right), McUrich inside him, Steers at centre forward, Billy Calder at inside left with Billy Linward on the left wing. For the next match, at Dresden United in the Potteries, Smith and Fellows replaced Steers and Calder. The home team won with a goal scored three minutes from time, in a match held up for ten minutes because of a terrific thunderstorm. A win at home to Ilkeston Town followed with Calder replacing Fellows and McUrich, and with Waddington and Longden getting the goals.

October started with a bang, the Rovers going down 5-1 at Kettering with McUrich scoring a consolation goal. For the next match, at home to Heanor Town, George Chester, a local man from Marshgate, came in at inside left to the exclusion of Calder. He made a happy debut, scoring two fine goals in a 4-3 win. The other two goals came from Smith and Waddington, including a shot from all of forty yards by the latter, the goal of the game, which was fitting as it was also his benefit match. In their next match the Rovers suffered their second five goal defeat of the month, losing 5-2 at Burslem Port Vale, after trailing by four goals before half-time. Linward and McUrich pulled two back before the pottery team sealed victory with a fifth goal.

Into November, and the Rovers started with a victory over Chesterfield in a match played in incessant rain. Although Chesterfield scored first, Longden, McUrich (2) and Smith put the issue beyond doubt. Waddington missed this match being replaced by a young reserve, Parr, who also deputised for him in the F.A.Cup at Sheffield against the amateur side, Sheffield Club, a game surprisingly lost 3-1.

December opened with heavy rain and a win for the Rovers at home to Wellingborough Town. Waddington was back in place of young Parr, but Attree had to be replaced by William Dowson. An early goal from McUrich and one from Smith in the second half sealed the win. A fortnight later the team travelled down to Rushden with a new centre forward, Goodison from Kilnhurst, an amateur. A good debut was rounded off with two goals, together with one from Longden, giving them an emphatic away win. On Boxing Day Smith reappeared in place of McUrich, who was away *"keeping Christmas up"*. This match was at Grantham and with a brace of goals from George Chester the Rovers gained the two points, which only kept them in seventh place at this, the halfway stage. This position was mainly due to them only having played ten games compared to the thirteen, fourteen and fifteen of the clubs above them.

Another away game followed on New Year's Day, at Barnsley. Ellis Wright was indisposed, so Smith went to left half with Scott coming in at inside right, from the reserves. The appointed referee did not turn up, so Mr.Musson, the Rovers secretary, was prevailed upon to officiate. Goodison scored twice in the first half to establish a stranglehold on the game, and added his third in the second half after Black of Barnsley had been sent off for deliberately throwing mud into Hulley's face after a tackle.

For the next match, at home to Rushden Town, both Wright and McUrich were back. Played in a snowstorm and on a pitch liberally sprinkled with sawdust because of the mud, the Rovers lasted the pace well enough to romp in as 4-1 winners, with two goals from Wadding-ton, one from McUrich and an own goal. Thus the team were in good heart to tackle the league leaders, Long Eaton Rangers, away, especially as the home team were having injury problems, and amongst other changes, had to play a promising youngster, Ernest Start, at centre forward. So promising, in fact, that he scored a hat-trick! The Rovers could only reply once through Goodison, and Long Eaton remained at the top of the table. The following week, away at Wellingborough, they played in such a heavy blizzard that the snow completely covered the pitch during the game.

But the *"Butterscotch men"* did what no other team had done so far that season, they beat Wellingborough on their own ground. An even more remarkable feat considering the Rovers started the game with ten men, Eggett having missed the train, and Waddington going in goal. The visitors were one up through McUrich before Eggett arrived to give them a full complement. A second goal from Linward before Wellingborough scored a consolation goal gave the Rovers two more points and third place.

A look at the league table now made the fans entertain some hopes of being champions. Heanor Town were on top with 22 points from 17 games, Long Eaton had 22 points from 15 games and the Rovers and Dresden United

had 20 points from 14. The Rovers were to entertain Long Eaton in the next match. A cold, damp Saturday afternoon did not stop 2,000 fans going to the Intake to see McUrich and Goodison rattle in two match winning goals, before Start could answer with only one this time. Now all three teams were at the top with 22 points.

But were the Rovers getting over confident? Their next opponents were Dresden United on the Intake. Dresden were in financial difficulties at this time, and in their last two games had had difficulty in fielding a team, and gave away twenty goals in the process. They duly turned up on the first Saturday in February, an hour late, to play on a pitch that resembled a duck pond, after volunteers had spent the morning clearing away the snow. The Rovers scored first through Chester, but straight from the restart the *"Chinamen"* from the Potteries went down the field and planted the ball into the net. They then scored a second when the ball stuck in a puddle, leaving Eggett stranded, and a third goal before half-time gave the visitors a good lead.

The Rovers captain must have roasted the team at the break, because they came out for the second half and launched attack after attack, forcing corner after corner. At last McUrich headed in from one such kick, and twelve minutes from time Langton played a captain's part by shooting in from thirty yards to secure a point, which put them on the top of the table with a one point advantage. In the next game, at home to Worksop Town (the bottom club with only five points), the Rovers again seemed to think that all they had to do was turn up. Worksop soon jolted them out of that attitude by scoring first, but McUrich equalised before half-time in a match described as the worst Rovers display of the season. This loss of a point let Long Eaton take over at the top, and allowed Glossop North End to move to within a point of them from the same number of games.

March came in and with it came the sun, and two more points in a 2-1 win at Chesterfield. A goalless draw followed at Heanor, and then in a midweek game at Ilkeston from a 2-1 lead at half-time the Rovers slumped to a 4-3 defeat. A return to winning ways came at Worksop, when an own goal and one apiece from Linward and Goodison saw them take the two points. But they were only one point behind Long Eaton with a game in hand, and one point in front of Glossop from the same number of games.

The next match, at home to Burslem Port Vale, which was lost 1-0, was best remembered for the furore it caused. Played in a hurricane the Rovers were 1-0 down at half-time after kicking with the wind in their favour, and Langton having missed a penalty. The second half saw them constantly on the attack but unable to score. The situation was not helped, in one Rover's attack, when the Vale goalkeeper took his overcoat off, and in his haste – on seeing Linward preparing to shoot – dropped it on the goal line. The shot beat the goalkeeper all ends up but was stopped by the coat and cleared by a defender. Despite the protests to the referee about the legality of the shot being stopped by a "foreign body" not associated with the match, the referee refused to award a goal. Despite the Rovers lodging an objection with the Midland League, who passed it on to the F.A. for an adjudication, the result stood. This left them still in third place, only a point behind the new leaders Glossop, who had won their match, and on goal average were above Long Eaton Rangers (who had lost).

The Rovers had six games left to play, five of them at home. The first of these matches was won by a single goal over Kettering. Then on Good Friday they entertained Barnsley St.Peters and completely overran them by 11 goals to 1, with George Chester scoring four and Billy Linward getting three. The following day the Rovers went to the top of the table after beating Mexborough at home. On Easter Monday, as prospective champions they played a *"Rest of the League X1"* on the Intake, in a match to boost the League's funds. The League Xl won 4–2.

The next day, Tuesday, a large number of Rovers supporters travelled to Worksop to see if the local Town club could dent Glossop's hopes. Worksop did, by winning 1–0, and the scorer Uttley, was carried off the field by enthusiastic Rovers supporters. The Rovers were now three points ahead of Glossop from the same number of games. Both clubs had three games to play including home and away against each other. Rumour in the town had it that Glossop were moving heaven and earth to win the Championship, offering a bonus of £2 per man to beat the Rovers. They were also doing a lot of training, and had over the Easter period, met and beat Sheffield United and Blackburn Rovers.

The *"match of the season"* took place on Saturday April the 24th on the Intake, in fine weather with a record crowd numbering about 4,000, in attendance. The special training that the Rovers had undertaken didn't seem to do them any good as it turned out to be one of their poorest efforts of the season. It was also reported to be one of the dirtiest games seen on the Intake all season. Tripping, hacking and other foul tactics were all indulged, the game being a procession of free kicks. Platt, the Glossop centre forward, scored halfway through the first half before aggravating an old injury just before half–time, leaving Glossop with ten men for the rest of the game. This advantage enabled the Rovers to equalise early in the second period, through George Chester. But that was all they got out of this game, leaving the League still to be won.

The return match was played on the following Tuesday, and although the kick–off time was set for 6pm, the match was started just after 5, since the Rovers had to catch the 7 o'clock train! Glossop, who were on a bonus of £10 per man to win the championship, needed a victory to keep their hopes alive. After 20 minutes Longden put the Rovers in front, but then McUrich was carried off with a broken leg after a tackle by McHardie. The Glossop player was remonstrated against by Mr.Balmforth, the Rovers chairman, and replied; *"Yes and I will break another one's leg yet"*. The Rovers were now down to ten men, and Glossop took advantage to equalise after 70 minutes, but the Rovers again went in front with a goal from Smith. With virtually the last kick of the game Glossop drew level again, but it was too late for their championship hopes. The point gained from this match was sufficient to crown the Rovers as Midland League Champions for the first time.

After the match, with feelings running high, mud, stones and tufts of grass were thrown at the Doncaster team as they left the field to go to the dressing rooms at the Station Inn. The referee was also mobbed, and had to stay overnight in Glossop. The Rovers team, some of whom were only partly dressed, had to be escorted to the railway station across the road from the Station Inn, by four policemen.

On arriving at Doncaster station the players and officials got on to a waggonette and preceded by the Volunteer Band, playing *"See the Conquering Heroes Come"*, accompanied by the cheers of the crowds, went to the Three Legs Inn where John Musson, the secretary, spoke a few words to the team. They then followed a route from High Street to Cleveland Street, St.Sepulchre Gate, High Street, Hall Gate, to the Doncaster Arms at Bennet–thorpe, the club house, where congratulatory speeches were made.

The season was rounded off on the Thursday with victory over the wooden–spoonists, Grantham Rovers – who could only muster a reserve team – by 13–1, Goodison scoring 5 goals. A most successful season saw the club acknowledged as Champions with a record of:- Played 28, Won 17, Drawn 5, Lost 6, Points 39. Goals for 77 and goals against 40. The players who receive medals were Jack Eggett, goalkeeper, Albert Attree and Walter Langton the full backs; Charlie Waddington, Frank Hulley and Ellis Wright, half backs; forwards Billy Longden, McUrich, Goodison, Jack Smith, George Chester and Billy Linward. Six more players were used, five of whom played only one game, the other – Billy Calder – appeared in three.

On Monday, May the 24th 1897, a Celebration dinner was held at the Guildhall when 140 sat down, including the Mayor and other dignitaries, to a fine table.

Season 1897–98 saw the Midland League reduced to twelve clubs by teams dropping out because of financial problems. So to supplement their fixture list the Rovers joined the newly formed Yorkshire League in which the Sheffield and Hallamshire F.A. clubs had joined forces with those representing the main towns of the West Riding F.A. This was a missionary effort on the part of the Sheffield area clubs as the area covered by the West Riding F.A. (Leeds and the surrounding textile towns) was a stronghold of the rugby code which had turned professional two years earlier, and was to become the Rugby League. The seeds of Association Football were reasonably successfully sown in the towns of Bradford, Halifax, Huddersfield, Hunslet and Leeds over the next couple of years, but the clubs then representing those towns have no connection with the present day clubs.

Of the previous year's team, only McUrich, with his broken leg, was unavailable. His place at inside right was taken by Arnold Oxspring from Ecclesfield who proved to be a very good signing for the club, and later went on to make a name for himself at Barnsley.

Despite having almost the same side as the previous championship season, and getting off to a cracking start with a 6-0 win over Long Eaton Rangers (Oxspring scoring four goals), the season proved to be a decided anti-climax. The next seventeen Midland League games saw just one win and five draws, and only a goal rush and three wins in their last four games kept the Rovers clear of the bottom spot. They finished in 10th place.

In the F.A.Cup the Rovers played six games, but the run only covered two Rounds. After comprehensively beating Sheffield Club, they were drawn away at Mexborough. This match ended in a goalless draw before a record crowd. The replay on the Intake also ended in a draw, at 1-1. Ellis Wright missed this match because of suspension, having been sent off in October at Hunslet. In the phraseology of the time the Chronicle reported him as; *"Unable to play having transgressed the rules of the Association"*.

The third match at Bramall Lane was abandoned (with the score at 1-1), because of bad light, with only five minutes of extra time left. Finally, at Barnsley, Mexborough came out on top with a 2-1 victory.

The Yorkshire League produced better results with the club winning all but one game against the West Riding clubs, the single defeat coming at home to Hunslet. Only Sheffield Wednesday Reserves did the double over them, but the Rovers still finished in 4th place.

At a meeting of the Midland League on June the 11th 1898, it was decided to allow the Reserve teams of Football League clubs to enter for the coming season. As Barnsley and Burslem Port Vale had been elected to the Football League, and Glossop had resigned and joined the Lancashire League, the Midland League stood at 9 clubs,

therefore this decision made sense. Heanor Town and four reserve teams were admitted to make up a complement of 14 clubs.

Although there were some changes, the complement of the Yorkshire League remained at 10 clubs, so the Rovers would have a full season of fixtures. But this League made a peculiar concession to the two Sheffield clubs, who had asked that their Midland League results in games against clubs in that league (i.e. Doncaster Rovers and Mexborough) should count in both competitions.

With half of the Championship team of two years ago forming the nucleus, hopes were high that the season would be better than the previous one. The committee had been busy looking for new players, and they signed on a number from local clubs, including, A.Turner from Shiregreen, a right back, 'Dutch' Gladwin a centre forward from Kilnhurstand, and C.Woolhouse from Ecclesfield, an inside left. Longden had moved back from outside right to right half and was now captain.

The Midland League campaign was opened on a hot summer's afternoon at the Intake with Derby County Reserves providing the opposition. A 1-1 draw resulted with Gladwin getting the goal, but having a penalty saved. Waddington and Woolhouse were dropped for the next game, Leon Gall, who had joined the Rovers in the previous season after time with Gainsborough Trinity and Needham replaced them. This change brought a win over Sheffield United Reserves at Bramall Lane. For the next match, a defeat at Heanor, Gall replaced Needham at inside left, and Goodison came in on the right wing. This team then produced wins over Ilkeston and Burton Wanderers, but then crashed 5-2 at Olive Grove to Sheffield Wednesday Reserves. The Rovers were in fifth place in the Midland League at this stage.

The defeat at Sheffield was sandwiched between two F.A. Cup-ties in which the Rovers were the victors, with a 6-1 win (Gladwin 3 goals) over Wath, and then a 8-1 crushing (Gladwin and Linward scored three goals apiece) of Parkgate United. In the next round they faced tougher opposition, at home to Barnsley, who ran out winners by 2-1. The Rovers had a goal disallowed five minutes from the end when the referee, Mr. Warde of Derby, blew for a foul on the scorer, Goodison. The Chronicle's comment on the *"eccentricities of referees"*, was that, *"They must be dug up for some of them appear to know as much about the game as a piece of wood and if they possess eyes they do not know why they have been given such valuable possessions"*.

November had brought in three points from matches against Chesterfield and Mexborough, but due to their Cup run they had fallen behind with their Midland League games, and although well down the table had three or four games in hand over the clubs above them.

A visit to Derby County in December caught the local Reserves in unforgiving mood. They were next to the bottom with only one win in thirteen matches, so the management drafted in some new signings from Scotland, and together with players with First Division experience they proved too much for the Rovers, winning by 9-1. The Christmas tour of the Midlands produced losses to Kettering and Wellingborough, with Gladwin being taken ill before the first game on Boxing Day. The travelling reserve, George Chester, took Gladwin's place, and when Langton was taken ill overnight before the next day's game, Walter Attree, the trainer, had to play. The Rovers were now third from the bottom with 10 points from 11 games.

New Year's Eve saw the start of a revival with an emphatic home win over Long Eaton Rangers. This revival would take them through to the end of the season, when they suffered only two defeats in fourteen games. It also coincided with Nelson replacing Goodison at outside right, the rest of the team being largely the same. By the end of January, with two more wins and a draw, they had moved up to 8th place, twelve points behind the leaders, Ilkeston Town, with four games in hand.

Doncaster started February by losing at Chesterfield, but this was only a hiccup, before two more wins took them into March and a visit to the Manor Ground at Ilkeston to take on the leaders. This was Ilkeston's last home game and the last game to be played on this ground, it being required for building purposes. The match was played in a snowstorm, as the Rovers battled to a 2-1 lead with five minutes to go, Robinson and Gladwin scoring the goals. However Ilkeston were not going to give up lightly their chances of winning the championship, and after a period of pressure secured an equaliser, much to the delight of the local crowd. This point lifted the Rovers to 6th place, ten points behind Ilkeston, but with three matches in hand.

A good home win over Sheffield United Reserves was followed by a drubbing at Long Eaton, with the local newspapers lamenting such a result to the extent that it meant waving goodbye to the championship for this season at least. This pessimistic attitude was taken because, although the Rovers were in with a very good chance, it now meant that Kettering and Rushden had more points than the Rovers from the same number of games. But Ilkeston also lost, and the Rovers were only eight points behind them now. The following week, with the Rovers playing a Yorkshire League fixture, Kettering lost at Sheffield Wednesday Reserves and Rushden lost at Burton. The Easter programme followed, which saw the Rovers beat Kettering at home on Good Friday, draw at Rushden on Saturday, and get the better of Burton Wanderers on Easter Monday. The top of the table read thus:-

	played	points
Ilkeston Town (fixtures completed)	26	32
Kettering	25	31
Chesterfield (fixtures completed)	26	31
Doncaster Rovers	24	29

It was going to be a tight finish, with the advantage in favour of Kettering, who had one match left – at Mexborough, and the team at the bottom of the league. The Rovers had two home games to play, versus Sheffield Wednesday Reserves and Rushden, neither of whom were pushovers. Kettering also had the better goal average, in the event of a tie on points.

So the scene was set for the afternoon of Saturday, April the 22nd, the Rovers, at home to Sheffield Wednesday Reserves. Without their goalscoring centre forward, 'Dutch' Gladwin, who had been injured in a Yorkshire League match at Wombwell, the homesters outplayed their opponents, and won convincingly 4-1. Three of the goals came from the foot of Gladwin's replacement, a young man named Norman Clayton, who had been making a name for himself in the local Doncaster League. Pitched straight into the Midland League team from Junior football he had had a storybook game, the sort of game that would make *"Roy of the Rovers"* a byword in football.

Meanwhile, down the road at neighbouring Mexborough, Kettering had a distinct feeling that neighbourliness was being carried to its extreme, as they fought to get the better of the League's wooden-spoonists. Described as the best game seen at Mexborough all season, a big crowd saw Mexborough outplay their illustrious opponents to win 2-1, and end Kettering's hopes of winning the championship, the destination of which rested on the Rovers' last game, at home to Rushden. A win for the Rovers would make them Champions, a draw would hand it to Ilkeston.

Thus an excited crowd of some 3,000 people awaited the start of a game that Rushden had vowed to win for Ilkeston's sake. For fifteen minutes they made a fight of it but by half-time were five goals down, courtesy of goals from the wingers, Linward 2 and Nelson 2 plus one from Clayton. The second half was something of an anti-climax with the result now certain, and the Rovers down to ten men because of an injury to Linward Then in the last minute Clayton received the ball on the half-way line, ran through, and as he shot into the net he was tripped.

Despite the ball going into the net, the referee awarded a penalty which the usual taker, captain Billy Longden, allowed Clayton to take. He shot straight at the goal-keeper but followed up to put the rebound into the net.

19

A 6–0 victory emphasised their right to be Champions of the Midland League, and certainly the crowd thought so as they heartily cheered their heroes.

In the evening the Rovers players and officials were entertained to tea by their chairman, Mr.Samuel Balmforth, at his home in the High Street. At seven o'clock, the committee boarded Steadman's four–in–hand, the players got on a charabanc, and the procession began when they met the Volunteer Band at the Clock. The procession then proceeded along St.Sepulchre Gate, Cleveland Street, Hall Gate and Bennetthorpe, to the Club House at the Doncaster Arms.

Here a private room was provided for the players and officials to attend to; "the wants of the inner man" and for them to listen to the congratulatory speeches by Mr.Balmforth, Billy Longden – the captain – Mr.John Fowler, the secretary, and various other committee men. Each touched on the subject of joining the Football League, but John Fowler counselled caution because he did not think the club's finances would permit the club to go into the higher grade. After all, the Second Division had broken Rotherham Town in 1896, a view with which Billy Longden (who was with that club at the time) fully concurred. The subject was due to be discussed on many occasions.

The return journey was made from the Club House along Hall Gate to the Clock, then to St.Sepulchre Gate, and along Station Road to the railway station. There they met the Reserve team after their return from the Hatchard Cup Final tie against Treeton, played at Carbrook, Sheffield, which they had drawn 1–1 after extra time. They would share the Trophy, each team holding it for six months. Both teams then proceeded along Old Station Road, West Street, Union Street, Cleveland Street and Printing Office Street to High Street where the Party broke up about ten o'clock.

In the Yorkshire League the Rovers had finished second, behind Wombwell, three points adrift with 27 points from 18 games. With double figure and other high scores being run up against most of the West Riding clubs, the competition was obviously too one–sided. At the end of this season, the Sheffield area clubs withdrew, leaving the West Riding F.A. clubs to carry on at their own level.

For the 1899–1900 season, the prospects looked good. All the Championship side had re–signed, except Leon Gall who had moved on to South Shields. Some new signings were made, including Arthur Birch, a right back from Wombwell, and Frank Mawson, an inside left, from Mexborough Town. Unfortunately, Gladwin was destined not to play again for the Rovers after a knee injury suffered against Wombwell in a Yorkshire League match on April the 8th. With a scoring record in the previous season of 13 goals in 22 Midland League

games, and 20 goals in 14 Yorkshire League games, he would be sadly missed. There were only 13 clubs in the Midland League for this season, and no Yorkshire League, so a suggestion came from Mr.Fowler that the Sheffield and Hallamshire F.A. should turn the Wharncliffe Charity Cup competition from a knockout cup to a League format. With ten clubs this would give local teams like the Rovers a full programme of competitive games.

The Midland League campaign started well enough, with only one defeat in the first five matches. In between these was an excellent win at Gainsborough in the F.A.Cup, when they beat Trinity (a Football League Division 2 side) by the handsome margin of 4–1. A further win over Newark in the next round found them matched against another Division 2 side, Grimsby Town, in the Third Qualifying Round. Defeat to the Mariners saw the start of a slump through December, January and February, which left the Rovers third from the bottom of the Midland League. The centre forward position seemed to be the biggest problem, nine players being utilised in this position throughout the season, with varying degrees of success. An unbeaten run of eight games (five wins, including two where they scored eight goals) saw them finish in seventh place. This improvement coincided with the introduction to the side of Len Goodson, at inside left, a local lad from the Marshgate Institute club, who had all the makings of an exceptional player.

The Wharncliffe Charity Cup League, consisted of clubs from the Midland League and the Sheffield Association League, and the Rovers finished in third place behind the two Sheffield clubs' Reserve teams.

On Monday May the 21st 1900, at the A.G.M.of the Football League – held at the Old Boar's Head Hotel, Manchester – the Rovers application for membership was rejected when they received only 5 votes. Barnsley (29 votes), Stockport County (28) and Blackpool (24) were elected, whilst Kettering (12), Loughborough (3) and Stalybridge Rovers (1) were also rejected. Midland League fare was to be the Rovers' lot again, for season 1900–01.

Of the previous season's players Frank Hulley (centre half) did not re–sign and Arnold Oxspring, the inside right and the clubs leading scorer, moved to Barnsley. Among the new signings was Tommy Vail, a centre forward from Gainsborough Trinity who had experience with Bolton Wanderers in the First Division and would also act as coach to the team. An old friend in Leon Gall from South Shields and Harry Crump, a centre half from Tottenham Hotspur were other newcomers.

There were fourteen clubs in the Midland League for this season, and with the Wharncliffe Charity Cup reverting back to a knockout cup format, it meant the fixture list would have to be augmented by friendly matches which by this time had lost a lot of their appeal. The club also entered the Mexborough Montague Hospital Charity Cup.

Having pretensions to gain entry into the Football League, the Rovers started their Midland League campaign with ten straight victories, including a 9-1 win at Coalville, during which period they scored 45 goals and conceded just 11. The chief goalgetters were Vail with 14 goals, Len Goodson with 10 and Gall who netted 8. Billy Linward scored 5 goals in 5 league games, played in the F.A.Cup team – another good run on reaching the 3rd Qualifying Round (before going out to Barnsley) – and played in the Wharncliffe Charity Cup match at Darnall Rovers which was won 9-0. In the latter game, the Darnall outside left Frank Bailey, evidently impressed so much that the Rovers signed him, and replaced Linward with him straight away.

They had also gone to Sheffield United in October and secured a full back, George Simpson, to replace Walter Langton, and in November signed John Murphy, an inside forward, from South Shields and formerly with Notts.County.

Their first loss of points came on Christmas Day, on their Midlands tour when they lost to Rushden and then on New Year's Day they were defeated by their chief rivals, Sheffield United Reserves, at Bramall Lane. Modern players complain of too many games, but the Rovers itinerary for the ten day period over Christmas and the New Year, consisted of six matches, five of which were 'away' games.

This resulted in the players being over absent from home over the Festive season, on their tour of the Midlands, and staying in hotels or boarding houses. They played at Wellingborough on the Saturday, Northampton on the Monday, (Christmas Eve), a visit to Rushden, on Christmas Day and the journey over to Hinckley on Boxing Day, with extensive travelling in between times. They still obtained five points from those four games.

Although they had another 9-1 victory over poor Coalville, their form dipped slightly after this, with defeats at Newark, Worksop, and then at home to the leaders, Sheffield United Reserves. Despite a 7-1 win at Leicester, they lost their final two games, leaving them as runners-up to Sheffield United Reserves, but nine points behind.

The Cup campaigns were reasonably successful, winning more games in the F.A.Cup than ever before losing to 2nd Division Barnsley, who also beat them in the 2nd Round of the Wharncliffe Charity Cup. In the Mexborough Montague Cup, the first team won through the first Round and the semi-final, but the Final was played on Easter Saturday and the first team had to play a Midland League game which took precedence over Charity Cup matches. So the Reserve team took the field against Mexborough Thursday, and ran out easy winners by 5-2. The team consisted of:–

L.Askin; Tom Bann and Walter Langton; Teddy Gregson, Fred Bann and Ernest Dowson; Manny Lindley, Nelson, Charles Waddington, Jagger Hollin and Billy Linward.

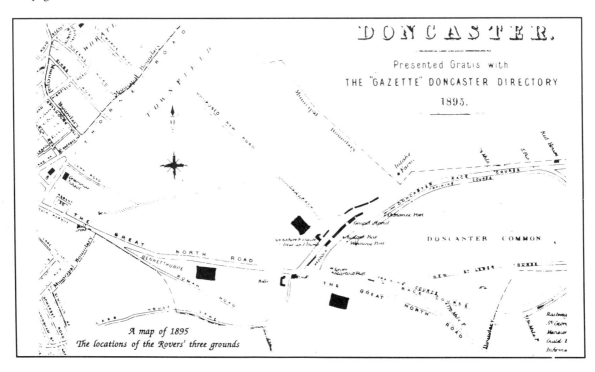

A map of 1895
The locations of the Rovers' three grounds

CHAPTER 3

The Football League 1901-05

t the club's A.G.M. in June 1901, Mr.Balmforth was critical of the need to play friendly matches to eke out the competitive programme. The club had a successful season in 1900-01, and had made a profit, but the attendances at the friendly matches played were minuscule. So, having failed to get into the Football League again, they would play in the Midland League, but had also applied and been accepted into the Lancashire League, for additional competitive matches. The extra income from playing different opposition would offset the higher expenses that would be incurred. The club then applied to the Sheffield and Hallamshire F.A. for permission to play outside the county's boundaries.

As permission was not necessary when they joined the Midland League, or if they joined the Football League, this request seemed to be just a formality. The club received a massive shock when the local F.A., directed by their autocratic chairman Mr.J.C.Clegg, refused permission on the grounds that; *"It was not considered right for the Lancashire League to be allowed to take clubs away from the County Association"* (i.e. the Sheffield and Hallamshire F.A.). In the appeal against the decision Mr.Balmforth explained that the S.& H. F.A. could not provide the class of football that the Rovers desired, but the appeal was turned down. The Lancashire League, however, insisted that the Rovers had been accepted by them and would have to fulfil their fixture list. After the S.& H. F.A.'s decision, this could only be done by playing the matches as friendlies.

Most of the previous season's players had signed on again, among the exceptions being Linward, who had moved to West Ham United (for a wage of £2.10s.a week, reported the Doncaster newspapers incredulously) and Gall, who had signed for Wellingborough. Among the new signings were Ike Marsh, a full back from Newark, formerly with Notts.County, Billy Langham, a right winger from Leicester Fosse, Arthur Jones, a centre half from Tottenham Hotspur and John Price, a centre forward from Watford.

Thus the Rovers opened their Midland League campaign on September the 2nd away to the Champions, Sheffield United Reserves, and performed sufficiently well to come away with a goalless draw. Then came some sensational news. New Brighton Tower had folded, and resigned from the Football League Division 2.

As the club with the most votes among those rejected at the League's A.G.M., the Rovers were invited to replace them and to take over the already prepared fixture list. This decision was communicated to the Rovers on Wednesday, September the 4th, and was readily accepted by the club committee, even though the first home match of the season was on the following Saturday, at home to Burslem Port Vale.

There were other problems as well, with the players on the Rovers books who had played League football and whose League registrations were held by existing League clubs. The Football League gave immediate permission for the Rovers to play these players, pending agreement between the Doncaster and the relevant Clubs. It was October before the League fixed transfer fees for the players in question, namely Simpson at £15 payable to Sheffield United, Murphy and Marsh at £10 each to Notts.County, and Price at a £15 fee to Small Heath. Langham's transfer from Leicester Fosse was also confirmed at this time.

However, the Midland League and the Lancashire League were quite upset by the sudden resignation of the Rovers from their competitions, especially as their season had already started and they referred the matter to the F.A., even though the Midland League had accepted their resignation upon the forfeiture of their £10 affiliation fee. The F.A.eventually decided there was no case to answer.

So, against this chaotic background, the Rovers made their debut in the Football League. The eleven who turned out on a bright, sunny, Saturday afternoon, against Burslem Port Vale on September the 7th were:-
Jack Eggett in goal; George Simpson, captain and Walter Langton, full backs; Billy Longden, Arthur Jones and Ellis Wright, half backs; Billy Langham, John Murphy, John Price, Len Goodson and Frank Bailey, forwards.

A crowd numbering some 2000 saw a goalless first half, but on resuming the Rovers raced into a two goal lead, their first-ever Football League goals and both scored by the local lad, Len Goodson. Nothing daunted, the Vale fought back so well that they put three goals past Eggett to take the lead. But the home crowd saw that their men were not beaten, and 0they were treated to an exciting climax culminating in Bailey getting the equaliser, and giving the Rovers a creditable start to their Division 2 career.

A goalless draw at Chesterfield was followed by their first League win, at home to Gainsborough Trinity, when goals by Bailey, Price and Langham set them up for a comprehensive win. The Rovers' next match brought not only their first defeat but a heavy one (6–0) at that, reminding them that there were teams in this League that were of a class that they had not encountered before, but at a level which they were aspiring to. Apart from another 6–0 drubbing, at Newton Heath, and a 7–0 defeat at Burnley, the team performed creditably recording home victories over the eventual champions West Bromwich Albion, Preston North End – who finished third – and Woolwich Arsenal, fourth in the table, plus comprehensive revenge wins over Newton Heath and Burnley. With a final placing of seventh and an average of a point per game a successful season had ensued, leaving the club in their best ever financial position. The prospects were bright for continued success in the higher sphere.

For the new season, 1902–03, the Rovers, hoping to build on their success of the previous season had to replace Longden, Jones and Bailey who had all left the club. Therefore a number of new signings were made, amongst them George Ratcliffe, an outside left, from West Ham United and James Aston, an experienced centre forward from Small Heath. Others who would come into first team reckoning were Phil Bratley from Rawmarsh, Charles Laverick and Andy Gordon from the Newcastle area, Arthur Pyle from Doncaster St.James, Frank Foxall from Wombwell Town, and Tommy Woodland from Clay Cross. Missing from the final practice match were Arthur Birch, who was taking the waters for rheumatism at Askern, a spa village near Doncaster (which from around 1910 became a mining village), and Len Goodson, who reported as being somewhere on the racing track!

Things were happening off the pitch as well. In August, just before the season kicked off, at a meeting of the Doncaster Council, a special committee had been appointed to select a site for a new ground for the Rovers, as they were unable to build any commodious stands on the privately owned ground at the Intake. The Council, who had been accused of not being willing to promote sport in Doncaster because facilities were lacking for other sports such as cricket, tennis and bowls, made a recommendation that the club be offered – on a yearly tenancy or lease at £2 per acre per annum – about six acres of the Low Pastures adjoining the Great North Road, near the Racecourse. This was subject to no wooden stands being erected which would obstruct the view from the Great North Road across the Pastures. As one Council member, who was obviously a football fan, pointed out, the Racecourse had built stands which obstructed the view across the Common but nobody had objected to that. It took another twenty-one years before this particular move came off.

In the meantime Mr.William Rogerson was granted an occasional license to sell intoxicants on the Rovers ground on Saturdays between 3 and 5 o'clock in the afternoon.

The season got under way with a visit to Burnley. Memories of their 7–0 drubbing the previous season were dimmed when they gained a 1–1 draw, and missed a penalty into the bargain. Unfortunately this creditable start was not maintained, and as the season went on the Rovers struggled in the bottom half of the table. The crowds drifted away so that the club's considerable expenditure on this season was never likely to be pulled back. Part of the costs came in November, when a new stand was put up on the Bennetthorpe side, with accommodation for 1000 spectators standing or 750 sitting. One third of the stand, in the centre, was reserved for members of the committee, officials and season ticket holders, the remainder was open to the public for a sixpenny entrance fee.

Built by Messrs. Mullins & Richardson at a cost of £200, it was a modern construction with windows at the side and was passed by the Borough Surveyor as quite safe. Alas, on Christmas Day night a hurricane-force gale blew the new structure down and completely demolished it. The members of the club must have spent all Boxing Day, Sunday, clearing up, for on the Monday the club were at home to the Second Division leaders, Manchester City. Over 4000 people attended, but of course with the demolition of the stand, the amount of revenue was less than expected.

Doncaster Corporation was approached for a donation towards rebuilding the stand, but on going to the vote it was turned down by 10 to 7. The Doncaster Chronicle obviously disapproved of this action by the Corporation, because they revealed that the Rovers averaged crowds of 1500 to 2000, and if 1000 people travelled to the ground by tram it meant a profit of £4.3s.4d.to the Corporation every home game. If the club folded through lack of support, this income would be lost. With the help of donations, collections and dances, plus the sale of Goodson to Middlesbrough for a substantial sum, the stand was rebuilt.

By the end of March the Rovers were third from the bottom of the League table and in the re-election zone. Matters were not improved on Easter Saturday when they travelled to Birmingham to play Small Heath, and were smashed out of sight by 12–0. Small Heath were in a three-sided fight with Manchester City and Woolwich Arsenal for the two promotion places, and on the previous Saturday had gone down 6–1 at Plumstead, the home of Woolwich Arsenal. The Rovers were obviously the antidote to that particular disappointment, for Small Heath went on to gain second place to Manchester City, and leave Arsenal three points behind in third place.

The season petered out for the Rovers leaving, them third from the bottom, five points clear of Stockport County and Burnley, but all three clubs had to seek re-election.

At the Football League A.G.M. on May the 25th, the Rovers delegation put forward their case for re-election. They received 14 votes but could only finish in fourth place behind Bradford City, with 30, a new club in Stockport County, who received 20, and Burnley with 19. The Rovers felt betrayed, being the highest finisher of the bottom three, and with an altogether better record in the League than Stockport County, who in their three seasons had had to apply for re-election on each occasion. But the fact remained that the Rovers were no longer in Division 2.

It was back to the Midland League in 1903-04 for the Rovers, replacing their reserve team in the competition. Under no circumstances would they apply to join the Lancashire League, since it was the Lancashire clubs that had voted them out of the Football League, stated Mr.J.Shreeve at the club's A.G.M. The club had to put their disappointment behind them and set about carrying on in the coming season by gathering a team together, despite having only £67 in the bank compared to the £552 of a year earlier. Jack Eggett had gone to Woolwich Arsenal, Billy Langham joined Gainsborough Trinity, John Price moved to Brighton & Hove Albion, George Simpson and Tommy Woodland went to Chesterfield and Alonzo Drake, the Yorkshire County cricketer, was transferred to Sheffield United. To replace these players, they went to Sheffield United to sign J.T.Holmes, a goalkeeper, and Tom Bennett, a right half. Also signed were Moran, outside left, from Aston Villa and James Dyer, centre forward, from Barnsley. A number of other signings were made from local junior football, and the club was ready to go.

A 6-0 win over Lincoln City Reserves in the first match augured well, with Dyer grabbing four goals. On October the 10th, they had to compete with 'Buffalo Bill's Wild West Show' taking place across the road on the Racecourse. The attendance for the match with Thornhill United was only meagre at the start, but after half-time had increased considerably, no doubt Buffalo Bill had ridden off into the sunset !

Unfortunately that initial impression of success did not materialise, as the Rovers never reached the top half of the table at any point in the season, eventually finishing eleventh. The sorry tale did not improve in the F.A.Cup as once again only two matches were played.

Even with this indifferent season behind them they applied for admission to the Football League, and succeeded, one suspects because of a sympathy vote, in ousting Stockport County for season 1904-05. Having succeeded in regaining their Football League status, the

next move was perhaps inevitable, incorporation as a Limited Company. There was no opposition to this, so *Doncaster Rovers Football & Athletic Club Ltd.*, was incorporated on July the 1st 1904, with a capital of £1000, which was divided into 2000 ordinary shares of 10 shillings (50p) each. The first directors were Mr.S.Balmforth, Councillor M.Dowson, Mr.H.Athron, Mr.F.Richardson, Mr.R.S.Dawson and Mr.W.E.Rogerson, all prominent businessmen in the town. Mr.John Fowler was appointed secretary with the registered office at 11 Cunningham Road, Doncaster (Mr.Fowler's home address).

At a Public Meeting held in the Guildhall on July the 10th, the public of Doncaster responded so well that about 300 shares were taken up that evening. Improvements were made to the ground, with the playing area being extended and widened. The new stand front was banked and new turnstiles were installed. Season tickets would cost 15 shillings for the Ground and Stands, 10 to the Ground only with Ladies and boys paying just 5 shillings.

On the playing side, Bob Chatt, a former player with Aston Villa, was appointed trainer. A number of players were signed, including Bob Norris, a half back from Nottingham Forest, Len Hyde (forward) from Brighton & Hove Albion, H.Hawkins (full back) from Aston Villa, Harry Davies (full back) from Gainsborough Trinity and formerly with Wolverhampton Wanderers, Jimmy Hanson (forward) from Bolton Wanderers, Laurie Pember (forward) from Aston Villa, Josh Burn (full back) from Newcastle, Billy Law (outside left) from Walsall and Matt Moralee, a Sheffield Wednesday centre half. Added to most of the previous season's team a strong squad seemed assured.

Before the season started John Fowler decided to retire from the secretary's job. The new appointee was Mr.G.Watson with the title 'secretary-manager'. So after all the happenings of the summer the Doncaster Chronicle, in it's football leader came to the conclusion that the "new" Doncaster Rovers was destined to occupy a more prominent position in the world of football than heretofore.

But even after the first match the Chronicle's optimism had disappeared. It wasn't the fact that the Rovers had lost, but the manner of that defeat. The quality of the team in practice had looked good, but in the actual arena of combat was found wanting, and the quality of football from the Rovers was abysmal even by Midland League standards. This was never overcome throughout the season despite changing the team around and signing new players. The season progressed on the back of a string of defeats interspersed with three wins and two draws. A total of 8 points from 34 games, in which 23 goals were scored and 81 conceded, spoke volumes.

The F.A.Cup didn't provide any respite either, the club going out at the first hurdle, after a replay, to Mexborough Town, from the Sheffield Association League.

At the end of March it came to the notice of the F A. that wages had not been paid to the players for some time. They ordered the club to either pay the arrears due to the players or make satisfactory arrangements within 14 days, under penalty of suspension. At a meeting of the directors and players on March the 30th, the players agreed to sign withdrawals of their claims.

The next day Harry Davies was transferred to Hull City. A series of smoking concerts were held throughout March and April to help raise funds for the club. To top off this season of misfortune, the Reserve team finished at the bottom of the Midland League with a record of Played 32, Won 3, Drawn 4, Lost 25, Points 10. With a goal record of 29 to 104. The club were in debt to the tune of £260.

Despite this the club decided to apply for re-election to Division 2, but were firmly pushed out into the cold with only four votes. It was then decided to increase the Football League by four clubs with the voting being restricted to the five clubs not elected in the re-election issue; the Rovers came fifth with twenty votes! The new era of prominence hoped for by the Doncaster Chronicle and others at the beginning of the season was at an end before it had had a chance to take off.

It was back to the Midland League for the Rovers, and a lot of hard work to be put in to get the finances of the club on to a sound footing.

CHAPTER 4

Back To The Midland League 1905–15.

he Rovers entered the 1905–06 season with a new secretary in Mr. William Proctor taking up the post. With only three of the regular team from the previous campaign re-signing for the club, Moralee, Birch and Walter Butler, a recruitment drive was needed to get a team ready for the coming season.

With the decision not to run a second team, it became imperative to come up with the right men to form a squad of players, some of whom would not be likely to play for various periods of time. Whilst some players were signed on from local Doncaster clubs, the local leagues in Sheffield were also raided, including Jack Almond, a centre forward, who was formerly with Sheffield United. In the week before the first match, Len Goodson was also secured from Middlesbrough.

The season progressed reasonably well, although the usual exit was made from the F.A.Cup at the first time of asking, this time to Denaby United. Then the team hit December and trouble. In three successive games at the beginning of that month they conceded twenty goals, eight of which were to the benefit of Leeds City Reserves who had only won one game to that time. There was an explanation for that particular game though, since the club played two first team matches on the same afternoon. For the first time in a decade they entered the Sheffield & Hallamshire F.A. Chal-

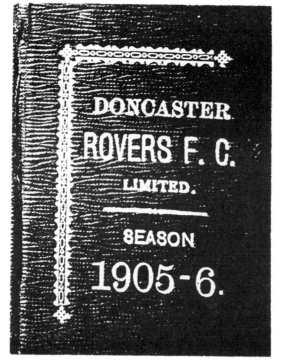

lenge Cup, and the first team played against Sheffield Wednesday Reserves in that competition, and lost. The team for the Midland League match at Leeds was made up of players from the local league.

After the Christmas games the Rovers were third from the bottom, at that time having lost five successive League games and only scoring one goal. They picked up slightly thereafter, but by Easter they were back to

being third off the bottom of the league. Two wins out of their last five games saw them pull up to fourteenth place. Although the season had not been a great success on the field it certainly had financially, even with less revenue from the smaller crowds, and was due in the main to good housekeeping. £80 was knocked off the debts that had piled up during the previous season, and by then stood at £180.

For the 1906–07 season the directors decided to run a second team in the Sheffield Association League, and about thirty players were signed on including the new captain, Harry Roberts, Walter Butler, Jimmy Briggs, Herbert Fretwell and Edward Gyte of the previous season's first team. New signings included Billy Langham from Gainsborough Trinity and Alf "Mick" Butler (cousin to Walter), from Doncaster St.James.

Unfortunately this team was no better than their predecessors, and they started the season with ten defeats in the first thirteen games, which left them at the bottom of the table. In October, Walter Butler was transferred to Preston North End for a fee of £250 which cleared their debts, but presented them with a left back problem which wasn't solved until December, when Walter Wilson was signed from Mexborough Town.

In their fourteenth match they beat the well- placed Nottingham Forest Reserves and were awarded a football by the Sheffield Telegraph for the best performance of the week. But also in December the club were fined 2 guineas for an illegal approach to E.Cawley, the Hallam F.C.goalkeeper.

At the turn of the year the results picked up a bit, taking them up to twelfth place, but this was short lived as they sank to fourth from the bottom – seventeenth – by the end of the season. In March, Langham was transferred to Lincoln City for a fee of £75, but the Rovers only received £25, the other £50 going to Gainsborough Trinity who held his Football League registration.

In the F.A.Cup they again lost out to Denaby United, but only after the third attempt. Their record in this competition was so bad that they had to play in the Preliminary Round, at Morley, which the first team duly won comfortably but the second team, who fulfilled a Midland League fixture at Gainsborough on the same afternoon, were beaten rather comprehensively.

Although the reserves were run at a considerable loss, the directors regarded it as essential to provide players for the first team as and when needed, and in a match fit condition. Due to the transfers of Butler and Langham the club reported a profit for the season of £54.

With the club in the black again after the financial traumas of recent seasons they entered the 1907-08 season in an optimistic mood. The practice matches were very encouraging, and the new players who had been signed on had showed up well. Of these players Teddy Lowe, a right back and Bill Brelsford, centre half, had both signed from Rawmarsh Albion; Fred Charles an inside forward came from the Sheffield area, and Laurie Bramall, an amateur who had played for the Sheffield Club and Sheffield Wednesday (another forward) were the ones to go straight into the first team, with Bramall being appointed captain.

But again the team got off to a losing start, and with the season less than three weeks old a bombshell hit the club. The Secretary of the Sheffield Licensed Victuallers League reported the Rovers club to the Sheffield & Hallamshire F.A. for poaching. The complaint claimed that towards the end of the previous season the Rovers had signed William Jackson, a goalkeeper, and played him in the reserve team. It transpired that he was a registered professional with the Sawmill Tavern F.C., and had not been properly transferred. The S.& H. F.A. convened a meeting on Tuesday, September the 17th, but Mr.Proctor (the Rovers secretary) failed to bring his letter book, stating that it had inadvertently been burned. At the adjourned meeting two days later Mr.Proctor failed to appear, although two directors were in attendance.

It soon became clear that Mr.Proctor had signed Jackson, knowing that he was a professional and had tried to cover his tracks, when the complaint had been made, by making a letter out, pre-dating it and getting Jackson to sign it. Jackson had originally complied with this but admitted the truth at the adjourned meeting. The S.& H. F.A.acted promptly – some said too promptly – by suspending the Rovers club for seven days from the night of that meeting, Thursday, September the 19th., thereby causing problems for the innocent victims, the Rovers opponents for the coming Saturday.

Mr.Proctor was suspended sine die from football and football management, and nine directors, who professed ignorance of what had gone on, were suspended for two months from football and football management. Jackson was also suspended for two months.

Mr.Harry Kerr took over as secretary, running the club almost single handedly until the directors suspensions were over. The F.A.Cup provided no solace either, with the Rovers going out at the first hurdle to Goole Town, albeit after a replay. The club were in trouble again in December, when the first team played a Sheffield Challenge Cup match against Hoyland Town and turned the second team out at Gainsborough that same afternoon in a Midland League game. The Midland League Management Committee frowned upon this slight and fined the club one guinea.

Scoring goals seemed to be the main problem for the Rovers over the previous few years, and after spending all the season next to the bottom of the league, things took a turn for the better in April when they transferred their goalkeeper, Joel Lindley, to Aston Villa, and in return got a cash payment and a centre forward, Ben Jones. Jones played in the last seven games of the season and scored four goals, but the team won five of those matches, and only lost one.

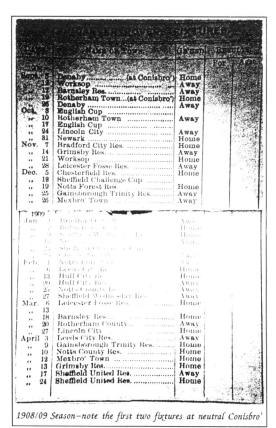

1908/09 Season-note the first two fixtures at neutral Conisbro'

One match was on Easter Saturday against Worksop Town on the Intake, which the Rovers won with an 89th minute penalty from Jones, who was then kicked *"in a very dangerous place"* by a Worksop player after the whistle had gone for full-time. As he was being carried off the field the crowd invaded the pitch and allegedly assaulted the Worksop players before they could reach the dressing rooms. On their, by now regular, visit to the S.& H. F.A.headquarters, their previous record of crowd misbehaviour was taken into consideration, with the result that the Intake ground was suspended for a month from the start of season 1908–09.

The end of an eventful and traumatic season saw the club finish in fourteenth place in the Midland League. However, their appetite for advancement was only slightly diminished as they showed in May 1908 when they sent off an application to the Football League, not for the Second Division, but for a place in the proposed new Third Division. The project was shelved because of the shortage of time, and the necessity for clubs to inform their current leagues of their intentions regarding the forthcoming season.

Due to his business interests, Mr.Samuel Balmforth stood down as club President at the A.G.M., Mr.Stanley Brightmore being elected in his place. The club had only made a profit of £2.17s.0d. on the previous season's workings, a minimal one but at least it was something to work on. Having retained only the best players from the previous season, although Ben Jones, had been transferred to Barnsley, the Sheffield Licensed Victuallers League was again raided for players. Their search for a ground to play both teams September fixtures on was settled when they came to an agreement with the Conisborough St.Peter's club to use their ground at Park Road.

Conisborough, situated at the halfway point on the main Doncaster to Rotherham road and next door to Denaby was ideally placed as a venue for the first team, whose two home matches to be played there were against Denaby United and Rotherham Town. Large crowds, each between three and four thousand, were double their normal attendances, but in both matches the Rovers were beaten. Three weeks into the season Harry Kerr resigned as secretary, and Mr. John C.Nicholson, the Doncaster Conservative Agent, took over with problems on the playing side as the Rovers lost all of their first seven Midland League games and were soundly beaten in the F.A.Cup by Castleford Town, after a replay.

This appeared to prompt Messrs.Stanley Bros., Tailors and Gentlemens Outfitters of High Street, to make an offer of an overcoat to the first Rovers player to score two goals in a match. It also prompted the directors to go out and sign better players than what the Sheffield Licensed Victuallers League could offer. Economy was one thing but in essence you got what you paid for, and

the Sheffield area players were out of their class. William Jex, a goalscoring inside forward and goalkeeper Fred Thompson were signed from Norwich City. Thompson had many years experience in the Football League with both Bury, whom he had won an F.A.Cup Winners medal, and Bolton Wanderers. John Pattinson, another inside forward, was signed from Sheffield United for a fee of £10 in October, won an overcoat for scoring two goals against Chesterfield Reserves on December 5th, and was then transferred on to Gainsborough Trinity for an undisclosed sum. Matt Edwards, a full back who had had League experience with Barnsley, was signed from Crystal Palace. Gradually the results improved so that after bringing back Len Goodson in February from the local Marshgate club, they only lost once in their last thirteen games, to finish a very respectable eleventh in the Midland League. Jex was the main goalscorer with 20 goals in his 27 games.

Members Card

Before the start of the 1909–10 season, John Nicholson resigned as secretary due to pressure of business, and Mr.Fred Keyworth took over. William Jex went to Rotherham Town and Bill Brelsford, a centre half, was transferred to Sheffield United, where he carved out a very long and distinguished career. Joel Lindley was signed from Hull City to replace Thompson in goal, and many other signings were made in an effort to build a successful side.

But once again the Rovers made an inauspicious start to the season, going fifteen games, to the end of November, without a win and with only five draws. In half of those games they had failed to score. Action was needed and taken. Albert Waterson, a centre half was signed from Fulham, Ted Gyte came back from Nottingham Forest as a wing half, Tommy Simons, a centre forward who had played for Clapton Orient was signed on, and the Rovers went to Sheffield United for an outside left, Frank Blank. Even so the usual happened in the F.A.Cup, as once again they went out at the first hurdle, this time to

Mexborough Town, following a replay. They did, however, get some measure of revenge a month later when they went to Mexborough in a Midland League fixture, and with only ten men won 1–0 with Mexborough even missing a penalty.

December in those times always appeared to be a bad period for the Rovers and this season was no exception. With the team being unsuccessful the attendances had dwindled to such an extent that a Public Meeting was called on December the 17th.

DONCASTER ROVERS FOOTBALL AND ATHLETIC CLUB, LTD.

Doncaster's Sporting Reputation in Peril.

How shall we improve our Team?

Those of our supporters who are really anxious for the success of Doncaster's Premier Team, are invited to a

PUBLIC MEETING,

at the

Temperance Hall (Lower Room),

ST. SEPULCHRE GATE.

On Friday, Dec. 17th, at 7-45 p.m.

All suggestions will be welcomed and considered.   5003

The necessity to get support for the team

The President of the club, Mr.Stanley Brightmore, in appealing to the large gathering for help, support and sympathy, stated the situation of the club as being very serious. The small profit of £27 made on the previous season had soon been swallowed up by the signing of players. The directors had kept the club going financially so far, but would appreciate help from other forms of fund raising. But in the short term an appeal was made for true supporters of the club to attend the matches, especially now that the directors had pushed the boat out in signing more experienced players, who would, said Mr.Brightmore, with the backing of the supporters, ultimately be successful.

Whist drives and dances were held to raise funds, attendances improved, and eventually so did the results. With a run of five wins in their final five matches they finished the season on a high note and in fourteenth position. But financially the club, it was reported at the A.G.M., had made an horrific loss amounting to £465, a great deal of money in those days.

Even so the Rovers retained the best of the previous season's players, signed William Jex back from Rotherham Town and exchanged Tommy Simons for Billy Bromage, an outside left, from Sheffield United. Sam Gunton, a right full back, came from Norwich City, Charles Woodruff, outside right, was signed from Tottenham Hotspur and Teddy Wagstaff, a centre half, arrived from West Ham United.

Although they opened their 1910–11 Midland League campaign with three successive defeats, an unbeaten run of nine games took them up the table into sixth place, having only failed to score in one match. This was in direct contrast to previous seasons when goals were hard to come by. All the forwards got amongst the goals, even Laurie Bramall, who having borne the burdens of the poor years was now experiencing the best football of his time with the Rovers, but which was soon to come to an end – in February 1911 – when he sailed out to Canada to join his brother in a farming venture. He was an amateur, and described as a true gentleman, who was treated as such by his fellow players. He was given a great send-off when, in his last match, at Bramall Lane against Sheffield United Reserves, the Rovers won 6–1 with the rest of the team finally helping him to score the last goal, his 14th of the season from 19 Midland League games.

A good run in the F.A.Cup saw them win through three rounds before going out to Denaby United, although they had a scare in the second game, against Grimsby Rovers, when they were leading 4–1 at half-time then sat back thinking they had won it, and were thankful to finish as 5–4 victors.

The team had been strengthened in October by the acquisition of James Taylor, a left half, from Sheffield Wednesday.

E. LOWE.

Ben Jones was signed from Denaby United in January, and then as Denaby United's financial problems increased the Rovers took Ernie Gregory (left back), Shepherd the goalkeeper and Teddy Dyal a centre forward from that ailing club. All these players helped the Rovers in their charge up the table, to reach third place by Easter, their final placing. In only three games had they failed to score, and in fact had managed 106 goals with Jex and Green leading the way with 23 goals apiece, followed by Bramall with 14, Bromage 11, Woodruff 9, Teddy Lowe (full back) with 7 – all penalties – Jones with 6 in 14 games and Dyal who got 5 in 7 games. Jex and Bromage had played in every game with Gunton only missing one. The best season for some time for the club ended with the announcement of a profit on the season's workings of £19, leaving the club still with a deficit of £445.

The club applied to the Football League for election to Division 2 for 1911-12, but despite Mr.Brightmore's eloquent espousal of their cause – the opening up of the coalfields and the subsequent increase of the town's population, together with the railway system of which Doncaster was a focal point – they did not get a single vote. On the playing front, Sam Gunton and William Jex had moved to Gainsborough Trinity in Division 2, Teddy Wagstaff had been signed by Sheffield United, and Ben Jones went to Worksop Town. New signings included Harry Bromage, a goalkeeper from Leeds City and brother of the captain Billy Bromage, Fred Shreeve, full back, from West Ham United, Syd Morrison (centre half), from Croydon Common, Jack Nuttall, another centre half, from Sheffield United, and Tommy Astill, an inside forward, from Leeds City.

A steady start to the season, including the almost inevitable dismissal from the F.A.Cup in their first game in the competition, saw them in 13th place by November. A 7-0 hammering of Rotherham County, with a hat-trick from Green, set them on a run up the table into the top six.

In December "Stewarts, the King Tailors" of Baxtergate, Doncaster, came to an arrangement with the directors to award overcoats to the players for various accomplishments in their matches at home. The first match that an award was in operation was against Barnsley Reserves in the Sheffield Challenge Cup. The Rovers won 2-0 with goals from Green and Billy Bromage. The scorers each received an overcoat with two more being awarded for the win, these going to Teddy Lowe and Charles Woodruffe.

The next home game was against Huddersfield Town Reserves, and the offer was two overcoats for a win, the allocation of the coats to be left to the players. The Rovers duly won 3-0 with a hat-trick from Green. Did the desire to be able to keep warm through the winter prove to be an inducement to win ?

With the signing of two 20 year-olds, a promising centre forward from Denaby United, Harold Buddery, in January, and an inside right, Fred Pagnum from Huddersfield Town, they certainly won enough points to finish in third place at the end of the season. Although Green and Dyal were the ones to make way for Buddery and Pagnum, they still finished at the top of the scorers list; Green with 19 goals in 24 Midland League games, and Dyal getting 12 in 21. Buddery was next with 8 goals from 17 games.

The club did win a trophy though, the Sheffield Challenge Cup, which they had last won in 1891. By March they had battled their way through to the semi-final of the Wharncliffe Charity Cup and the final of the Sheffield Challenge Cup. On the Monday of the second week in March they travelled to Bramall Lane to play Sheffield United Reserves in the Wharncliffe Charity Cup semi-final, but lost 2-0. The following Saturday the two teams met again, this time in the Final of the Sheffield Challenge Cup, at Wath-upon-Dearne. Against all expectations the Rovers had the best of the play and three second half goals, from Taylor and Reed (2), gave them the trophy.

Reed, an 18 year old youth from the Leadmill St.Mary's club in Sheffield had played his first game for the club the previous Saturday, for the Reserves at Rawmarsh where he appeared on the teamsheet as S.O.Else. As a Rovers fan was overheard saying to his mate at the first team match, *"I see the Reserves have got a new centre forward".* Back came the reply *"Yes, they call him Else. He comes from Leeds ". "Is he an amateur". "He must be, they've put his initials in front of his name on the sheet".*(!) He scored three goals that day for the Reserves, and was selected for the Final because Buddery was ineligible and Green was injured. After some initial butterflies he settled down, scored two good goals, one a solo effort and was shouldered off the field at the end by happy supporters. That was his only first team appearance for the Rovers and a few weeks later he was signed up by Birmingham.

For some reason the Cup was not presented at the conclusion of the game and some of the players who did not live in Doncaster went on their way to their respective homes. But there was still enough players on the train upon it's arrival at Doncaster Station to receive a welcome from a large crowd and with a brass band playing *"See the Conquering Hero Come".* The procession went up West Laithe Gate along St.Sepulchre Gate to the Crystal Palace.

The Rovers team consisted of:-
Harry Bromage; Fred Shreeve and Ernest Gregory; Teddy Lowe, Jack Nuttall and James Taylor; Charles Woodruffe, Teddy Dyal, A."Pav" Reed, Tommy Astill and Billy Bromage (the captain).

The United side included two former Rovers players in Tommy Simons and Fred Charles, and in goal was Joe Lievesley, father of two future Rovers players. Of course there was a sting in the tail. The Rovers were fined 10 shillings by the Sheffield & Hallamshire F.A., on April the 9th, for playing Reed without having transferred him from Leadmill St.Mary's as per the regulations.

All the regular players from the previous season signed on again for 1912-13, with the exception of Victor Green, who transferred his abilities to Gainsborough Trinity. Among the crop of youngsters to join was a goalkeeper, Willis Walker, from Sheffield United who was also a cricketer with the Sheffield United Cricket Club. The club were still in financial difficulties but attempts to raise the entrance fee from 4d.to 6d. were defeated at the A.G.M., however, season tickets were increased from previous seasons prices.

The team opened their season with three successive wins but the excessive amount of away matches up to Christmas were not accompanied by a great deal of success. With a preponderance of home matches after the New Year, the club had enough success to finally finish in fourth place. John Pattinson had come back to the club from Manchester City at the end of September, but otherwise it was virtually the same team as the previous year. Buddery topped the scoring list with 14 Midland League goals in 25 games, Pattinson following him with 10 in 25. Once again they did not progress very far in the F.A.Cup, a sore point as a good cup run could well have solved their financial problems which were now, because of poor gates, more acute than ever. The low attendances were instrumental in the admission price finally going up in February to 6d., which in turn did nothing to tempt the spectators back. A loss of £738 was reported for the season exacerbating an already considerable debt.

The majority of the players, who over the past three years had given the club their most successful seasons for a long time, were not re-signed for season 1913-14, due in no small measure to the club's financial situation. Harry Bromage and Fred Shreeve stayed locally with Bentley Colliery, as did Tommy Astill with Mexborough Town, Ernie Gregory moved to Rotherham Town, Charlie Woodruffe went to Grantham, John Pattinson moved to Rotherham County, Harold Buddery joined Portsmouth and Billy Bromage went into local football at Leicester. Only Teddy Lowe, Jack Nuttall and Jimmy Taylor remained together with the previous season's reserve team goalkeeper, Willis Walker. A lot of young players were signed on, but even at the pre-season public practice matches the local papers spoke in tones of guarded and diplomatic optimism.

Their unspoken fears were justified when the club lost their opening four games, having scored only one goal, conceded eleven and used sixteen different players. Jex rejoined the club in late September from Croydon Common, and more players were signed on and discarded just as quickly. Even the Corporation seemed to be against them when, in November, they put the price of the fares to the ground up to sixpence. The first gate after the rise drew receipts of £17 compared to the £100 needed for the club to just pay their way.

In late October, Stewarts the tailors offered an overcoat to any Rovers player who scored two goals in a Midland League match at home, and in addition any spectator brought along by the player would also receive one.

Alas, this time the overcoats stayed in the shop as no player managed to score a brace of goals after the offer was made.

In December an old friend, Laurie Bramall, returned home from Canada on three months holiday and offered his services to the club. They were readily accepted, and he took charge of the team again as captain, and in his first match – at Mexborough in the Sheffield Challenge Cup – the Rovers secured a 4–0 victory. Yet they had only scored eight goals in eleven Midland League matches prior to his arrival. His first two league matches also produced wins, lifting them up to sixteenth place, third from the bottom. But even Bramall could not keep the miracle going when, just before Christmas in an accident at work in the Plant Works, Jex, the chief scorer, badly injured his foot when a loaded trolley ran over it. Even so when Bramall sailed again for Canada on February the 14th, the team had gained two more wins and a draw. Jex returned to the side at the beginning of April to inspire them to gain seven points from the last five matches and pull the club out of the re– election places to finish third from bottom.

Again, the F.A.Cup was looked at briefly, one match sufficing as they went out to Goole Town. The other two cups didn't offer much more solace although they did win a game in each one. In the Wharncliffe Charity Cup the club even waived their right to hold the replay with Sheffield United Reserves at their own ground, in the hope of a better gate at Bramall Lane.

The club used 36 players in all competitions during the season, with no more than nine of them playing in half (20) or more of the games, and only Walker was an ever present. Leading scorer for the club in league fixtures was Jex with 6 goals, followed by Nuttall with 5.

On Thursday evening, May the 14th 1914, at a special meeting of shareholders, which was held in the Old County Court Room, a director of the club – Mr.J.Atkinson – said the meeting had been called because of the critical nature of the situation regarding the financial state of the club. He told the meeting that the club had only a month to live unless someone could come up with some ideas of how to raise the money that was owed. He explained that they had been reported to the F.A.for non–payment of wages to the players, who were owed a total of £120; £45 was owed to the landlord and there were sundry other debts which brought the total to around the £200 mark. There was also an overdraft at the bank of £158, which some of the directors were personally responsible for.

Although the population had greatly increased with the opening of new collieries around the town, and it was said that people would support a winning team, crowds had actually gone down when they had had a winning team previous to last season.

The meeting was adjourned for a fortnight when it was decided to form a new company which would take over the assets of the club, as well as the debts.

At the adjourned meeting it was stated that the Board had found it impossible, with the outbreak of war, to raise sufficient capital to pay the wages claimed by the players. Although certain gentlemen of the town had been found to put money down to keep football going they, were unwilling to take over the debts of the old club. Having taken advice from the highest authority, Councillor Harland submitted a resolution to the meeting that the club be voluntarily wound up. It was passed unanimously. The old club was voluntarily wound up on August the 27th, and an interim committee appointed, with Councillor Harland acting as secretary, to get a team together in time for the new season. Adverts were put out for players, since only Teddy Lowe was retained by the new club. George Cutts, a Doncaster licensee and a former Nottingham Forest player plus Frank Hilton, formerly with Bristol City, volunteered to sift through the players who answered the adverts and then to coach them into some sort of team.

The Midland League season started on Saturday, September the 5th, but it was only on the previous Wednesday evening that sanction for the new club was received from the F.A. The players could only be signed on after that date, and in fact were only officially recruited on the Friday evening. The first game was at home to Bradford Reserves and was duly won 3-0. The line-up was:-
Hustler (ex-Huddersfield Town); Lean, (a Welshman) and Maltby - formerly with Nottingham Forest; Hicks, from Swindon Town, Royston, with Barnsley the previous season and Lowe; Birtles, outside right from Northampton Town and a Yorkshire County cricketer, Tebbutt, (ex-Northampton Town), Brodie, formerly with Liverpool, Hall from Preston North End and Stevens, who had previously played for Chesterfield.

The optimism that this win gave was soon muted as the team showed a remarkable inconsistency, by getting a good result at home and failing away. Albeit, such defeats as 10-0 at Hillsborough, 8-0 at Goole and 7-0 at Bradford were suffered with weakened teams, but even with a full team they only managed five points in total away from home. At Gainsborough in February, due to disrupted rail services, the Rovers started the game with seven men and only had ten when the match finished. At half-time a Lieutenant Tinkler talked to both teams and then signed up Coxon (goalkeeper) and Tebbutt from the Rovers, and Hunter from Trinity, for the Footballers Battalion. With the Rovers four goals down at Goole, Coxon walked off the field after arguing with his own players. Another player was injured, and the Rovers finished the game with nine men. Their final league position was 15th.

On November the 3rd 1914, a new company - *Doncaster Rovers Limited* - was registered to take over the assets and liabilities of the Doncaster Rovers Football & Athletic club. The nominal capital was £500 in 10 shilling shares. The directors were Robert Capes, solicitor, who was to be chairman, F.H.Buckland and G.W.Cutts (licensees), E.J.Dowson, a tailor, E.Goult, an insurance superintendent, S.Morris (wallpaper manufacturer), W.Ward, mineral water manufacturer, and E.Wilburn, a valuer. The secretary was Councillor Joseph Harland. A loss of £290 was reported on the 1914-15 season, due in no small measure to the war and to inclement weather which affected attendances particularly against the more attractive opponents.

At the Midland League A.G.M. held on July the 31st 1915, it was decided that the competition would be suspended until the war was over. A week later a group of clubs formed the Midland Combination. The final count of clubs were the Rovers, Goole Town, Halifax Town, Rotherham County, Sheffield United Reserves, Worksop Town, Silverwood Colliery and Chesterfield Town. The Rovers also entered the Wharncliffe Charity League, and thus had a full fixture list for the season.

Only four of the previous season's first team players reported to the club but with a number of second team players available a team was able to turn out. In October, at half-time in the match against Mexborough Town, the Mayor of Doncaster addressed the crowd and the players, in a bid to gain more recruits for the war. By November he had obviously succeeded because the Rovers were unable to raise a team from their own players and those drafted in from members of the Durham Light Infantry, who were stationed in the town. However, on December the 3rd., the club was stunned to receive a communication from the F.A. to the effect that the club were suspended until such time as they complied with an order, made in March, that they pay outstanding wages to a former goalkeeper, Hustler. The club sorted out their differences with the player, and the suspension was lifted by the F.A. in time for Christmas. Gradually the soldiers began to put some good results together so that the season ended on a fairly buoyant note.

At the A.G.M.of the club in March, even though a loss on the season 1914-15 of £290 was reported, new directors came forward to replace the ones who had gone to the war, and despite all the difficulties attached to running the club in the difficult times ahead it was pledged that the club would be kept going. On July the 22nd 1916, at a meeting of the clubs in Sheffield, on a proposition from Rotherham County and seconded by the Rovers, the Midland Combination was abandoned because of a lack of clubs willing to compete. Councillor Harland, as secretary, was holding the fort and made strenuous efforts to find some fixtures, having obtained promises from quite a few prominent players who were stationed in the district to turn out for the club. Unfortunately he made himself ill with the strain of trying to keep the club going with the result that the club quietly slipped into a state of suspension.

CHAPTER 5

Reformation and The Midland League 1920–23

or the remainder of the war, no attempt was made to play any game of football under the auspices of the Doncaster Rovers Football Club. For one thing their ground at the Intake had been requisitioned by the War Department for use as a military depot, and additionally there was only Councillor Harland available to run things. The war ended and football, like everything else, slowly came back to life. But not Doncaster Rovers!! Rumours abounded in the town that an attempt would be made to revive the club but nobody stepped forward to lead the way. In May 1919 they were even one of the clubs who were sent a circular by Rochdale Town in an effort to form a new Northern League. But there was still no reaction as clubs from towns all around Doncaster, such as Rotherham County who applied for and were accepted into the Football League, and Gainsborough Trinity who were revived to enter the Midland League on it's restart in 1919–20 as did both Mexborough Town and Scunthorpe United. Good class football all around the town but none in it !

During season 1919–20 the football loving public of the town had to go elsewhere to see good class football, and this evidently irked sufficiently for a number of enthusiasts to call a meeting of like–minded souls, on Friday April 30th 1920, in the Cleveland Cafe – a meeting place gladly lent by Councillor Joseph Harland the proprietor. An attendance of about one hundred from the town and surrounding colliery villages was very good considering there had been little advertising. Mr.Arthur E.Porter presided, and Councillor Harland was in attendance to answer any questions on the state of the old club. There was much enthusiasm displayed to revive the club when this was proposed by Mr.G.Trowell, seconded by Mr.Ward, and carried unanimously.

It was also decided to take over the liabilities of the old club, which according to Councillor Harland amounted to about £150. He also thought that the tradespeople of the town to whom the money was owed would probably accept 50% in settlement. A debate raged on a new title for the club before finally settling in favour of the original title of 'Doncaster Rovers'. Several promises of support were made, and offers for shares in a limited liability company abounded from those present at the meeting. It was decided to enter the F.A.Cup and to make an application for admission to the Midland League. Mr.S.Criddle of Woodlands was elected secretary protem, and a provisional committee was formed to implement the decisions taken at the meeting.

The following Friday another meeting was held at the same venue, to further the revival of the old Doncaster Rovers club. It was decided to recommend that the capital of £500 be increased to £10,000, which was to be raised by 10 shilling shares. The Rovers were accepted for the F.A.Cup and for membership of the Sheffield & Hallamshire F.A.. A ground seemed to be the only problem as the Intake was still occupied by the military.

A further meeting a week later, chaired by the newly elected chairman, Mr.S.Criddle and supported by secretary Arthur Porter, were told that because of legal difficulties it was recommended that an entirely new company be formed. The meeting agreed. It was also reported that the Corporation had been approached for assistance in finding a suitable site for a ground.

A week later at another meeting Councillor Harland said that their request for a ground had been put before the Estates Committee. The club committee decided that a deputation should be appointed to meet the Estates Committee to impress upon them the urgency of their need for a playing venue. The secretary also reported that he had attended a meeting in Sheffield regarding the proposed formation of a Third Division of the Football League. If they were to join such a venture straight away, there was an urgent need for funds.

On Tuesday, June the 1st, the club deputation met the Estates Committee and after putting their views across were taken to a field on the Low Pastures, of about six acres extent, which the Committee were prepared to offer the club at a nominal rent. But as it would take some time to get the ground ready the Corporation agreed to allow the club to use the Education Committee's playing fields at Belle Vue, Bennetthorpe, for the forthcoming season – commencing on August the 2nd – the club to share it's use, and the cost, with the Education Committee.

The ground scheme was accepted by another enthusiastic meeting on the Friday and the secretary read out his circular regarding the club's application that was being sent to every club connected with the Midland League. This was approved and at the A.G.M.of the Midland League on June the 12th, the Rovers topped the poll for the election of four clubs from the eleven that applied. The stage was now set for the new company to be floated. On June the 24th the old company was wound up, and the following day a new company was formed, being registered on September the 13th as *Doncaster*

Rovers Football Club (1920) Limited (170192), with a capital of £10,000 in 10 shilling shares. The first directors were: Messrs. Arthur Thomson (contractor),chairman; Joseph Franks J.P., H.G.Fogg, W.A. Curtis and R.W.Merriman. The secretary was Mr.Fletcher Hibbert of Messrs. Newsum & Co. Meanwhile, an old Rovers player, Billy Calder, offered to act as honorary manager and form a team from the numerous applications that flooded in from prospective players.

Eventually, the great day arrived, Saturday August the 28th. The visitors were Rotherham Town, and in front of a large crowd, approaching 5000, and before many local dignitaries, the Rovers turned out the following team: - C.Blakey (goalkeeper, ex–Lincoln City), full backs Arthur Wigglesworth (from Hull City, captain), and Harry Hutchinson (Yorkshire Main). Half backs John Mahon (previously with Gillingham), Harry Newham (from Chesterfield), plus Jimmy Cowen (Bentley United and Sheffield Wednesday). Billy Cox (outside right from the Scottish League club,St.Bernards), Harry Wainwright (Highfields F.C.and Port Vale), Freeman (from Rossington), Gilbert Kemp (ex–Grimsby Town), and George Bromage (from Derby County, brother of former players, Harry and Billy).

A good, fast and even game was decided late in the second half when Rotherham were awarded a penalty, the conversion of which made the final score 2–1 in their favour. Although beaten in this first match the Rovers were far from disgraced, only the failings of the forwards stopped them gaining a victory. This failing was to plague the team throughout the season, although their first win came in the next match at home to Denaby United. Of their thirty–eight Midland League games they failed to score in nineteen, despite using thirty–six players, twenty–three of them being forwards.

Over the New Year they won three matches in succession, but in March they had a run of seven games without scoring a goal, although gaining points in the middle of that run with three consecutive goalless draws. The start of the goalless run was at Gainsborough. On the way to the match their charabanc broke down with engine trouble at Gringley–on–the–Hill. They had to wait for another one to come out and take them to Gainsborough, so that the kick off was three quarters of an hour late. The club were later fined 2 guineas (£2–10p) by the Midland League for taking unnecessary risks in travelling by road! By winning their last two games they had gained sufficient points to finish in sixteenth place.

However, trouble was brewing off the field with regard to a suitable ground for the club. The Board felt that they were not bound by the decisions made by the Provisional Committee – which were agreed before their time – and in January 1921, refused to accept the offer of the Low Pastures. They understood it to be swampy and unsuitable, which would require a large sum of money to make it into a football ground. The Corporation Estates Committee were insisting on the club vacating Belle Vue at Bennetthorpe, at the end of the season. There were public meetings, with the directors putting their views to the supporters. Meetings of supporters, led on April the

8th to the formation of a Supporters Club. There were also meetings between the directors and the Estates Committee. Eventually, on Tuesday the 7th of June, at a meeting of the Doncaster Town Council, the terms of an agreement between the Estates Committee and the Rovers were submitted for ratification. The club had agreed to rent the Low Pastures on a longish lease at a rent of £50per annum and were to be allowed to use the Bennetthorpe ground for the 1921–22 season at the current rent of £26 per annum, until such time as the Low Pastures ground was ready.

Although the club had made a profit in 1920–21 of £438, they were going to need far more than that to get the new ground into shape, so once again the call went out for more finance. With the question of the ground now settled (an application by the club to join the new Division 3 North had been withdrawn because of the uncertainty over a suitable venue), the directors appointed Harry Tufnell, the former Barnsley player and scorer of the winning goal when they won the F.A.Cup, as secretary–manager, on a salary of £7 a week, with a remit to build a team good enough to win the Midland League and gain entry to the Football League. Whilst this was a high figure for wages at that time, the directors felt that to get the best you had to pay for it.

Only Arthur Wigglesworth, Harry Wainwright, Gilbert Kemp, Arthur Tilsley, Percy Ekins, and Alvy, of the previous season's players were signed on again. New players to sign included a number of former Football League players such as Nick Hendry, a goalkeeper from Hull City, Ted Thorpe, a full back from Lincoln City, Billy McLeod, the ex–Notts County centre forward who had scored nearly 200 goals in over 300 League appearances for his previous clubs. Plus George Cooper, centre half, and Walter Butler, forward, both from Leeds United and Bernard Naylor, outside left, ex–Sheffield United.

Even with this wealth of experience the team got off to a bad start and in fact were bottom by the end of October with only five points from nine games. An unbeaten run of four matches through November raised them clear of the bottom, and thereafter they maintained a mid–table position, finally finishing in fourteenth place. Again there was no settled side, and thirty–six players were called on, quite a number of them being ex–League players who had signed halfway through the season, including Billy Boardman, a forward from Leeds United, Percy Reed, a wing half from Chesterfield and previously with Sheffield Wednesday plus Edgar Smithurst, a winger from Chesterfield and previously with Oldham Athletic. But it was all to no avail, and after a disagreement with the directors, Harry Tufnell resigned in March. There was much talk throughout the season of Division 3 North increasing their number from 20 to 22 clubs, with the Rovers applying for one of the extra places.

The directors kept stressing that to go into the Football League and to properly equip their new ground would require more finance. Thus, at a meeting of shareholders in May, it was decided to increase the number of directors to a minimum of seven and a maximum of twelve. The Supporters Club were also urged to raise more money for the club, and indeed to raise £1000 to purchase shares in the club, and thus being allowed to have two of their members on the Board. The application to join the Third Division North went in, but the League decided not to increase their number, and the clubs for re-election, Halifax Town and Rochdale, were overwhelmingly voted back in, with the Rovers in third place. Whilst it was a setback, nobody was too upset. As Arthur Porter, the new secretary-manager said; *"We are going to concentrate our efforts in getting a first class team to win the Midland League, or go very near it, and improve our position all round, and there is not a shadow of doubt that next time we shall walk in."* Prophetic words indeed.

Mr.Porter's words were put into action at the club's A.G.M. in July, after a profit of £97 was reported and when progress on the new ground was going well. Five new directors were elected, including Messrs.J.C.Morris and Frank Tighe,the nominees of the Supporters Club, which took the Board to twelve members. A full-time trainer, Bill Russell, from Brodsworth Main, was engaged to improve the physical training of the players. A former professional sprinter and boxing trainer, he had trained the Brodsworth team for the previous three years. Most of the players were new to the club, only Wigglesworth, Smithurst, Boardman, Rintoul and Jimmy Cowen remained from the previous season. Newcomers included full back George Shaw from Gillingham, Harold Jacklin, a goalkeeper from Leeds United, Bob McLean, a wing half from Alloa Athletic, Dick Ashmore, a centre half from Nottingham Forest and James Bauchop,an ex-Bradford Park Avenue inside forward.

Another landmark in the history of Doncaster Rovers occurred on Saturday August the 26th 1922, when on a brilliant summer's day the formal opening of their new ground on the Low Pastures was performed by Mr.Charles E.Sutliffe of the Football League when he unlocked the gates with a silver presentation key. The opposition for the first match on the ground, which became known as the Belle Vue ground, following the opening ceremony was Gainsborough Trinity in the initial Midland League match of the season. The Rovers team that faced them on this auspicious day was: -
Harold Jacklin; Arthur Wigglesworth, J.Jackson; Bob McLean, Dick Ashmore, James Miller; Edgar Smithurst, Arthur Charlesworth, Billy Boardman, James Bauchop and Robert Rintoul.

In front of around 10,000, the biggest crowd ever to see a football match in Doncaster, the first goal on the new ground took only seven minutes to arrive when Charlesworth headed in a fine cross by Rintoul. This proved to be the only goal of the match but it set the Rovers off on the right foot. After four games they were on top of the table, however two defeats and a run in the F.A.Cup saw them hurtle down to seventeenth place by November, but with a lot of games in hand. The F.A. Cup, at last, provided some measure of success, when they commenced in the Preliminary Round beating Cudworth at the first attempt, but needed two bites at the cherry to dispose of both Denaby United and Mexborough Town. A second game was also required against Wath Athletic, but this time the Rovers lost out. So it was back to the Midland League and matches to catch up on.

This they did in splendid style starting at the end of December with a run of eleven consecutive victories, which took them to second place, and a point behind leaders Sheffield Wednesday Reserves. Two wins in the Wharncliffe Charity Cup during this period, added up to an incredible thirteen successive victories. Championship winning form in anybody's language! The run was stopped at Castleford with a draw on the first Saturday in March, and the following week they were beaten at Worksop Town. But with a settled team they hit back and only lost one more game before the end of the season. Unfortunately that defeat, at Notts. County Reserves in the penultimate game, cost them the Championship. Although they gained 61 points, a total that had won the Championship comfortably in the previous season, that number was still two points behind Sheffield Wednesday Reserves; but if it had come down to deciding the Championship on goal average then the Rovers would have been the winners.

The team did not go empty handed in the silverware department that season. A win over Sheffield United Reserves in the semi-final of the Wharncliffe Charity Cup had pitched them against Scunthorpe United in the Final. Scunthorpe waived their right to play the match on their ground, and the game went ahead at Belle Vue before a crowd of 5,183. An even match was decided in the 89th minute when Lumb crashed a terrific shot into the net from a fine pass by Boardman. The Rovers team lined up:-
Jacklin; Wigglesworth, George Shaw; McLean, Ashmore captain, H.White; Rintoul, Charles Picknett, Stan Lumb, Billy Taylor and Boardman.
After the match, several of the directors, their wives, players and supporters of the club visited the headquarters of the club, the Red Lion Hotel, where the victory was celebrated in time honoured style.

The Rovers success had been down to fielding a settled side which had produced a defence that did not relish giving goals away and was certainly the best in the Midland League. The forward line had also played their part because if the goals were not going in for the opposition then it only took one to go in for themselves. The regular team consisted of Jacklin in goal, an ever-present; Wigglesworth,who only missed one match when his father died, George Shaw, played 38 games at full back; McLean appeared in 40. Ashmore was ever present, Miller and White made up the half back line. Spencer, Boardman, Rintoul, Taylor and Picknett were the forwards. The leading scorers were Boardman with 25 Midland League goals, followed by Picknett with 12 and Taylor 11.

A successful season was blighted when the architect of that success, Arthur Porter, resigned as secretary-manager in May, because of ill-health. However the club went ahead with their application to the Football League for entry to Division 3 North and with the League increasing the numbers to twenty-two clubs, the Rovers and New Brighton were successfully voted in. Arthur Porter's pronouncement twelve month's earlier had come true in every detail. A new era was opening up for Doncaster Rovers.

CHAPTER 6.

The Football League 1923–39.

he Rovers were back where they felt they belonged, in the Football League. The first job was to appoint a new secretary/manager, so there was a maximum amount of time to line up a team capable of playing in the Division 3 North. The man selected for the job, from seventy applicants, was Dick Ray – the assistant secretary and the man in charge of the second team at Leeds United. As a player he had played for Burslem Port Vale, Manchester City, Stockport County, Chesterfield and Leeds City, before becoming the first secretary–manager of Leeds United. He immediately set about his task of finding players to add to the eight that had been retained. A centre half, Sam Cowan, had already been signed on from Denaby United and Ray added Albert Shears, Tommy Keetley, Peter Robertson, Albert Sissons – who had had trials with Arsenal – Robert Harris, David Russell, Grant McEachrane, Robert Benzies and Bill Palmer. With the second team playing in the Midland League a strong reserve squad was necessary to also provide cover for every position in the first team. At the A.G.M., a loss of £307 had been reported on the previous season's working, a shortfall due mainly to the expense in moving grounds and to increased wages and bonuses in providing a team that had done so well the previous season.

Another unforeseen point also arose due to their League elevation, for they had been drawn to play in the early rounds of the F.A.Cup, but as this would disrupt the fixtures, they withdrew from the competition altogether.

On Saturday, August the 25th 1923, the Rovers played their first match back in the Football League, at home to Wigan Borough. Before a record crowd of 10,923, who paid £598 in receipts, the following teams lined up:–
Rovers: *Jacklin: Wigglesworth, Shaw; McLean (captain), Cowan, Lowson; Sissons, Robertson, Keetley, Boardman, Palmer.*
Wigan Boro': *Hunter; Fare (captain), Ward; McGraham, Whitfield, Findlay; Jones, Glover, Armitage, Spencer, Stevenson.*
A fairly even match ended in a goalless draw, but the Rovers gained some comfort from the fact that they had matched Wigan, and really should have scored in the second half when they were awarded a penalty. George Shaw took the kick but put it into the Town end stand. It was left to Peter Robertson to score their first Division 3 North goal on the Monday, at Ashington, when they were three goals down. The Rovers, in the shape of Tommy Keetley, missed another penalty that day.

Their first win came a week later, in the return match against Ashington, but this was followed by four successive defeats which left them at the bottom of the table. In the match against Rotherham County, at home, the Rotherham goalkeeper Sutcliffe, was constantly ridiculed by laughter from the crowd every time he took a kick. In the second half, with Rotherham leading 1-0, the referee from Newcastle stopped the game. He went over to the offending spectators, told them that he thought Yorkshire folk were sportsmen, then re–started the game.

"Rovers' Teams. Season 1922-3."

The spectators ceased jeering the goalkeeper! At this point, with the Rovers at the bottom of the table, their supporters were bemoaning the lack of a goalscoring centre forward. Dick Ray didn't panic but moved Tom Keetley to centre forward. From the next four games, in October, the team took six points including three from second placed Darlington. Ray then went back to Leeds United to sign Welshman Billy Poyntz, a weighty forward. In his first two games the team failed to score, but in his third game Poyntz scored twice to secure a point at Southport, only the second one the Lancashire team had dropped at home.

With a fairly settled side the Rovers continued to pick up points, but without scoring many goals, and by the New Year they were sixteenth in the table. They continued in fine form through January until the game at Walsall, which, because of a railway strike, they travelled to in a fleet of taxis, a four hour journey by road in those days. A 5-2 defeat after a convincing win over the same team the week before suggests that the long journey somewhat cramped their style. This match proved to be George Shaw's last for the Rovers as he was transferred to First Division Huddersfield Town some days after the match. His replacement against the leaders, Wolverhampton Wanderers, the following Saturday was Grant McEachrane, who certainly did not weaken the team. With Benzie having replaced Lowson at left half, the players had settled into a team and were progressing very nicely up the table. In March came a 7-0 demolition of Halifax Town, the Rovers highest score in the League. A hat-trick apiece from Sam Cowan (all headers), and Tom Keetley were the highlights. The final placing of ninth was very satisfactory in their first season against new opposition.

A loss of £46 was reported, with some disquiet expressed at an average gate of 6,500, below the figure they required to break even. The club's creditors were now owed a total of £1,487.

During the summer of 1924 many improvements were made to the ground including the completion of a shelter on the popular side, which was funded by the Supporters Club. Dick Ray was also busy adding to the squad of players retained from the previous season. Among the new signings were Jimmy Hanwell, Tom Gascoigne, Fred Horsman, Fred Emery, Joe Bowman and Harold Keetley, a brother of Tom, so that the club started season 1924--25 with twenty- five signed professional players and two amateurs, to turn out for their two sides.

The team started in a similar fashion to the previous season, and again obtained their first win at home, to Ashington, with a goal rush. They ran riot and scored seven goals, their first goals of the season. But the results remained inconsistent, the only consistency being the maintaining of a mid-table position, with Tom Keetley scoring the overwhelming majority of goals.

The club chairman, Councillor Joseph Franks, entertained thirty-six players and officials to a Christmas dinner at his residence, The Lodge, and the following week, on Friday December the 5th, the players and officials were the guests of the management of the Grand Theatre at the second house show.

The F.A.Cup provided the club with a good run and high attendances. Wins were recorded over non-League Mansfield Town (Sam Cowan getting the winner in the 87th minute with a bullet header from a corner), Rotherham County at Millmoor, and Southport. Norwich City were then drawn at home in the 1st Round proper (equivalent to the 4th round today). A record crowd of 13,042 saw a close match decided by a controversial goal in the 75th minute. A shot by the Norwich inside left Banks, was caught by Jacklin, who then overbalanced. The referee decided he had fallen over the line and awarded a goal, despite the strenuous protests by the Rovers players and crowd. However the goal stood and Norwich held out to move into the next round.

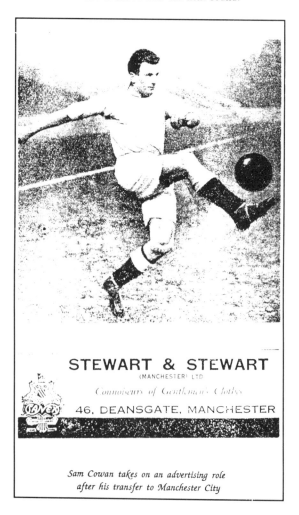

Sam Cowan takes on an advertising role
after his transfer to Manchester City

Sam Cowan missed the Norwich match, having played his last game for the Rovers in the previous round against Southport, before his transfer to Manchester City for a very substantial fee. With them he went on to win F.A.Cup and England honours. In April, Manchester City came back for Benzie, two moves that cost City £3,150. Although supporters expressed their dismay at the sales, the club had little option because of falling gates, the average attendance now being down to 5,690. At the end of the season the club showed a profit of £1,646, reducing the amount owed to creditors to £581.

A week after the F.A.Cup defeat by Norwich City another famous name, Jack Lambert, made his debut for the club at Tranmere. Jack was signed from Leeds United having failed to make any impact there, but he was to prove a very able partner to Tom Keetley, who was the club's leading scorer with 23 League goals, the next highest total being seven from Boardman and Campbell.

The majority of the previous season's players were retained for 1925–26 with the addition of John Ashford, Paddy McConnell, Alwyn Wilks, and Billy Taylor returning to the club, plus George Bromage, son of Harry.

This season also saw an important change in the Laws of the game, when the offside rule was changed from three defenders to two, between the goal and the attacking player. Throughout the season there were many high scores registered right through the League as defenders tried to come to terms with this change. The Rovers were no exception. In their second game they had a 5–2 home win over Crewe Alexandra, beat Southport 6–1 on Boxing Day, hammered Coventry City 8–1 in January, and overcame Accrington Stanley 6–2 in the penultimate game of the season. But it was not all one-sided as they were on the receiving end at Nelson, 5–3, and a fortnight later received a 6–1 hiding at Ashington.

Their goals scored record of 80 was far in excess of the previous season, with Tom Keetley netting 24, Harold Keetley 17 and Jack Lambert 11. Rovers finished in tenth place, averaging a point per game.

Although the team were hit by injuries throughout the season, this gave other players a chance to shine. Among those to do so were Billy Down, who was signed from Leeds United to cover for Jacklin when he was injured. Harold Keetley didn't get in the side until December, after Lambert was injured, before being moved to centre forward with brother Tom moving to outside right. In addition Joe Bowman got his chance, and whose play stamped him as a player for the future who would form a formidable partnership at full back with Jack Buckley in years to come.

Another feature of this season came on February the 20th, when for the match at home to Wigan Borough, there were three Keetley brothers lined up in the Rovers team; Tom at outside right and the provider for the Rovers goal, Harold at centre forward and scorer of the goal and Joe, recently signed from Wrexham and playing at inside left. The only other occasion that these three played together was in the penultimate match against Accrington Stanley. At the end of the season Joe was released, but in June, brother Frank was signed from Derby County.

The F.A.Cup did not provide much in the way of results, although a win over non-League Wellington Town was achieved in the 1st Round. But the next, at home to Rotherham United, was lost in front of a record crowd of 13,764.

Just after the New Year, Councillor Franks, the Chairman of the club since the re-formation, died of pneumonia, aged 59. It was a great loss because he had overseen the rise of the club from the ashes of the First World War, through the Midland League into the Football League, and the move into a new modern stadium. His successor was Councillor Thomson. There was a loss on the season of £625 due mainly to gate receipts going down again, and but for the transfer of the 21 year old outside right Albert Sissons to Leeds United for a substantial sum in October it would have been worse. The Rovers actually cleared their debt in June, although it would not show in the accounts until the following year, when they sold Jack Lambert to Arsenal.

During the close season of 1926 the only players added to the existing squad were Alex Milne, a seasoned player who had had ten years with Stoke City, Frank Keetley, Bobby Whitelaw, (aged 20), Ben Underwood. Frank Whitfield and an 18 year old from Sheffield junior football, Allan Hall.

The way the season started it looked as though they needed all the players they could muster. In the first game, at home to Walsall, centre half John Morgan broke his collar bone and then in the third match, at Nelson, Jack Buckley also suffered the same fate. Other injuries sidelined Underwood, Tom and Frank Keetley, Joe Bowman plus Emery, for various periods, and it was October, the eighth match, before Rovers gained their first win. The first half of the season saw the club firmly fixed in the bottom third of the League table, and with injuries to more players they rarely played the same team twice. During this period they had seven goals scored against them twice, at Rochdale who were third in the table and at Bradford Park Avenue on Christmas Day.

Into the New Year they actually turned the same team out in five successive matches, and gained six points. The tide had been turned now that a settled team could be turned out. On Good Friday they met the leaders, and eventual champions, Stoke City, at Belle Vue before a record crowd of 18,069, who paid record receipts of £973, and the visitors were comprehensively beaten 3–1. The team scored five against Durham City, six against Nelson and seven against Barrow, scoring 81 goals for the season and passing the previous season's total. Tom Keetley netted 36 including four in one match (Barrow), and five hat–tricks. The next best was Len Hargreaves, at outside left, with eight. A finishing place of eighth was acceptable considering the start to the season.

Progress in the F.A.Cup was once again rather stilted. In the 1st Round they were drawn away against opposition from the Northamptonshire League, Desborough Town. Desborough however agreed to play the game at Doncaster, and on the day travelled up by train. They had to leave the train at Sheffield, and travel to foggy Doncaster in taxis, arriving at Belle Vue shortly after two o'clock for a 2.15p.m. kick off. A small crowd of spectators waited outside the ground until ten minutes past two when the fog had lifted somewhat when the gates were opened. On each gate was marked in chalk *"MONEY NOT RETURNED"*. The ground was covered with a hazy mist and from the main stand it was impossible to see either of the goals or the opposite side of the ground. The referee went to the centre of the field and looked at both goals which he could evidently see, for he decided to start the match. Many people in the stand went into the enclosure in front of the stand in order to get a better view.

There were about 2,000 spectators in the ground when the match started five minutes late. After five minutes of the second half the referee sent the players back to the dressing room with instructions not to change. They returned after five minutes, the fog having lifted to such an extent that the goalposts were visible from the enclosure for the first time. But the fog had the last word, coming down so thick that the match was abandoned after 80 minutes with a 0–0 scoreline. The replayed match, on the following Thursday, was won comfortably 3–0, but in the next round Rovers went down at home to Chesterfield.

However, once again the club had had to sell to survive. This time it was Alwyn Wilks, outside right, going to Sunderland in February. The directors cited the poor support for the matches up to that time which had led to a critical financial position. Of course the results in the early part of the season had not been good, but this was 1926 –the year of industrial strife in the coal mines – and they could hardly expect supporters to put the club before their families. Consequently the average attendance for the season was down again, to 5,315.

But curiously the club announced a record profit of £2,012 before tax, due entirely to transfer fees received principally for the sales of Lambert and Wilks, which amounted to £4,531 in total. The directors for the first time in the history of the club were able to announce and receive, a dividend of 5% free of income tax.

In June 1927, Dick Ray accepted the post of manager with Leeds United. The Rovers Board decided to split the positions of secretary and manager, appointing Arthur Porter as financial secretary and David Menzies as manager. Menzies, a Scotsman, started with Raith Rovers as a player before moving to Bradford City where he later became secretary–manager, his last position before joining the Rovers. Meanwhile Len Hargreaves had joined Wilks at Sunderland, and Billy Boardman severed his connection with the club when he went to Crewe Alexandra. The newcomers included John Maughan, George McNestry and John Phillipson.

During the close season the cover on the popular side and the main stand had been extended with money raised by the Supporters Club. They were formally opened at the first game of the season by Mr.Frederick J.Wall, the F.A.Secretary. For this opening game, against Lincoln City, the team contained eight of the players who had played in the previous season's opening game. A 3–0 win gave them their first ever winning start in the Football League. Two successive defeats followed, but a 5–1 hammering of New Brighton sent them on a twelve match unbeaten run that included nine consecutive wins. The ninth win was at Park Avenue, over the leaders Bradford, which resulted in the Rovers taking over as leaders of the Northern Section, their first taste at such a pinnacle. The feat – from goals by the Keetley brothers Tom and Frank – was all the more meritorious in that it was Bradford's first home defeat since Boxing Day 1925.

Tom Keetley, and his 'Barrow' full of goals (he scored 4 in the match, and 36 during the season).

Frank Keetley scores in the home match against Champions-elect Stoke City – Rovers won 3–1 before a crowd of over 18,000. Other Rovers' players, left to right in the foreground: Tom Keetley, Boardman, Frank Keetley, Emery and Harold Keetley.

However, the Rovers were brought down to earth the following Saturday with a considerable bump, when they travelled up to Carlisle, then a non–League club playing in the North–Eastern League, to play the United in the F.A.Cup 1st Round. Carlisle had gained a reputation as cup fighters over the recent years, and in front of a very big crowd they set about proving that they were a match for even the best in the Third Division, a fact that gained them election to the Football League at the end of the season. The Rovers were always chasing the game falling behind after half an hour to a shot from inside left, Ward. McConnell equalised for the League team before half–time, but they were behind again half an hour into the second half when Milne handled in the penalty area, Jepson doing the necessary from the spot. Two minutes from time Tom Keetley had a chance to at least take Carlisle back to Belle Vue, but his penalty kick was well saved by goalkeeper Prout.

Not only had the team's confidence taken a knock at Carlisle, but so had Underwood and Emery, who both missed the next match at Stockport, which the Rovers lost, although they retained their top place – only on goal average – over Bradford. Although they only dropped five points from their six games to the end of the year, Bradford were putting the pressure on, and after the Rovers' loss at Lincoln on New Year's Eve, Bradford took over as leaders, and in fact never relinquished their lead. The Rovers in the meantime gradually lost ground, and although still second to Bradford at the end of March, they were ten points behind, even though they had just completed the double over them.

Injuries now began to take their toll on the players, Milne, Underwood, Morgan, Frank Keetley, McConnell,

Hall and Wilf Bott were all absent at various times over the closing two months of the season. The team did finish on quite a high note though, or at least Tom Keetley did. In two successive matches, after the team had gone four consecutive games without scoring, Tom scored four goals against both Nelson and Tranmere Rovers, bringing his total for the season to 36. The next best being Allan Hall with 18 from 24 games. By losing the last game at Rochdale the Rovers finished in fourth place still ten points behind the Champions, Bradford.

Despite the team falling away from the promotion race in the latter part of the season it had still been a good and profitable one. Gates were up, to an average of 7,400, bringing in more revenue, and good housekeeping had resulted in a profit on the season of £2,493, enabling another dividend of 5% to be paid. For once the directors had been able to refuse offers for players, which they had had in plenty in December, although in March they had let Hall go to Middlesbrough for a fee of £3 500.

Another plus for the club was the call to international duty of McConnell for Ireland, against Wales, in February – the first Rovers player to be capped whilst with the club. Unfortunately for Doncaster he was injured in the match, and having missed one League game, he went on to miss the next.

The close season brought renewed work on the ground with the concreting of the popular side right round to include the Kop. Twenty–three players were retained and seven more signed on, including half backs Joe Wilkinson and Ted Nelson, Tommy Atkin, an outside left, and Ernest Binns (centre forward).

Starting the 1928–29 season with two wins sent shivers of anticipation down the spines of the Rovers faithful. A big crowd turned up to see them play one of the League's perennial losers, New Brighton, but only for the team to go down inexplicably. So, instead of making the running as expected, the Rovers were among the clubs on the fringe of the promotion pack all season, when once again injuries played a big part in the club failing to field the same eleven on a regular basis.

Even Tommy Keetley had a spell out injured for the first time since joining the club, but he caused an even bigger shock when it was announced in October that he had been placed on the transfer list at his own request. The problem appeared to be over the terms of his benefit. Before he would re–sign in the summer, he apparently had offers from clubs in the U.S.A., and wanted the club to give a clear commitment about a benefit for him. The club acquiesced and guaranteed him a certain sum, a match played on September the 10th against Heart of Midlothian. But some differences had arisen between the Board and Keetley, which had prompted him to ask for a transfer.

However, when he was in the team he scored most of the goals, including six in one match At Ashington in a remarkable victory scoreline of 7–4. This match was played on a pitch covered with two inches of snow before 729 spectators. Ashington were at the bottom of the table and indeed, finished the season in that position, and were voted out at the end of the season.

Keetley scored his first goal after only three minutes, and with the Rovers dominating play in the early part of the game he scored again after fourteen. But Ashington fought back three minutes later through Charlton. Tommy Keetley then took advantage of being set up by brother Frank, to run through and score goal number three. Ashington came back again, helped by Underwood being off the field with damaged ribs, and were awarded a penalty which Robson (another famous North–East name) took, but Maughan pulled off a brilliant save. However, he could not stop Johnson scoring for Ashington five minutes from half–time to make the score 3–2 to the Rovers. The visitors, with Underwood at outside right, went straight on to the attack in the second half with the result that Tommy Keetley scored three more goals to put them 6–2 up, and the game out of Ashington's reach. But the North–Easterners were doughty men and hit back with two more goals from Charlton, before Wilf Bott killed them off five minutes from time.

Yet three weeks later, supposedly with their strongest team out, the Rovers went to lowly Accrington Stanley and were pulverised 6–0. The following week Tommy Keetley put his name on the scoresheet, four times, against Hartlepools United, and followed this a fortnight later with a hat–trick against Darlington, but he was to finish the season on the injured list again. He had done his job though. Could figures like this ever be beaten? 40 goals scored in 32 League games in one season!

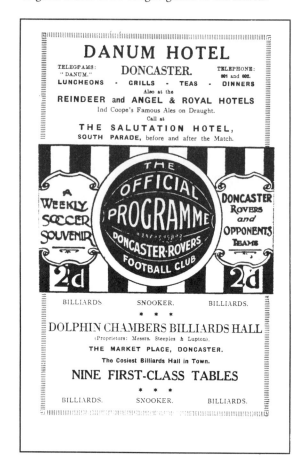

Joe Wilkinson had displaced Morgan at centre half for the Hartlepools match and then kept his place for the next five games scoring the only goal against Rotherham United. His next appearance in the first team was a month later when he lined up against Wigan Borough – as the goalkeeper – and kept his place for the last game at Halifax.

In the F.A.Cup one game sufficed to put the Rovers out. Bradford City, battling for promotion at the time from the Third North and eventually the Champions, beating them soundly by 4–1. The Sheffield County Cup also only took just one round, but three games, before the Rovers bent the knee to Rotherham United. One trophy they did win – or rather half won – was The Scunthorpe Hospital Charity Cup. This was an invitation match against Scunthorpe United which ended with the score at 1–1 after extra time. The clubs held the Trophy for six months each.

Just before the end of the season Ben Underwood was transferred to Leeds United for a four–figure fee, making his debut for them in Division 1 before the close of the season. The Rovers had a final placing of fifth in the League but had never seriously threatened the chief promotion contenders. Even so it was disappointing to see the average gate go down to 6,425, a loss on the year of 1,000 per game, but which was no doubt due to the recession that had put the collieries on short time. The overall financial loss on the season was £1,425, part due to the shortfall at the gates, and also to the fact that the transfer account had not seen any great increase in incoming fees. This was about to be rectified with the move that everybody dreaded, but knew was coming.

Evidently the rift between the club and Tommy Keetley could not be mended, and he refused to re–sign saying he was going to retire to the business that he had recently bought in his home town of Derby. But in July he signed for Notts County, bringing in a fee that the chairman said did not cover the loss on the season just ended, but refusing to divulge any figures because of the League's ruling of confidentiality on such matters. Who was going to replace him at centre forward and where were they going to find another Tommy Keetley ?

David Menzies' choice was an 18 year old Rossington youth, Leslie Lievesley, son of an old Sheffield United goalkeeper, Joe. He made his debut in the first match of the 1929–30 season, at home to Accrington Stanley on a pitch made treacherous by torrential rain. After five minutes he sustained a leg injury which necessitated him leaving the field (and the Rovers with ten men), and it was February before he reappeared in a Rovers shirt. In that period the club tried **nine** players in the centre forward position, including three half backs – Fred Emery, Fred Gregory and Bobby Whitelaw. Lievesley made his comeback against Tranmere Rovers, but it was not until the match at Accrington, ironically, that he opened his scoring account with two fine goals. By the end of an undistinguished League season for the club, they finished in fourteenth place. Lievesley was the brightest star around with a Keetley–like record of 12 goals in 14 League games, the clubs top goalscorer.

The club's chief success in this season was in the F.A.Cup. It took three games to overcome non–League Shildon in the 1st round, the first of which had been at home. In the 2nd round they comprehensively beat New Brighton, but only by 1–0 with a goal from Whitelaw. The next opposition was supplied by Stoke City from Division 2, in front of the biggest crowd at Belle Vue for ten months. The Rovers took the game to their opponents and turned round with a 2–1 lead through goals by Bobby Smith and Bowman. Stoke equalised after 57 minutes, and then a blinding snowstorm descended on the ground. Play continued until the 75th minute, when

Stoke scored again, although Ike Tate in the Rovers goal was to say that he never saw anything. It was at this point that the referee called a halt to proceedings.

The game was replayed on the following Thursday with both teams unchanged, but the attendance was only half of that from the previous Saturday. Stoke made all the running for the first half hour and their task seemed all the easier when Jim Smith, the Rovers left back, was sent off for a foul after 33 minutes. This reverse only seemed to inspire as they took the attack to the opposition. On 66 minutes the goalkeeper was penalised for carrying, and Patterson tapped the free kick to the side for Emery to shoot into the net. Tate was the hero of the hour with a string of brilliant saves, and had to be rescued by the police at the end from the fans who had invaded the pitch.

The 4th round meant a journey into the Lions Den when they were drawn to play another Second Division team, Millwall. Here they got their come–uppance although the result was in doubt right up to the last fifteen minutes, when a second goal to Millwall seemed to knock the stuffing out of them. They had, however, given a good account of themselves, but the main disappointment was the lack of a successful goalscorer.

The Sheffield & Hallamshire F.A., in their wisdom, had seen fit not to invite the Rovers to participate in the County Cup, a far cry from more modern times when non–participation meant a hefty fine.

In November, Frank Keetley was transferred to Bradford City, and in March 18 year old Fred Gregory, the centre half, was transferred to Manchester City – as understudy to Sam Cowan – for a fee of £2000. This was necessitated by the financial state of the club at the time, and economies dictated the disposal of players. As the economic state of the country got worse so did the attendance figures, which by then were down to 4,479, which had been provoked by the sales of the club's star players. These transfers enabled the club to report a profit of £170 on the season's workings.

Due to the financial situation, a number of players were not retained for 1930–31, and few new players were signed. One who had left was long serving Bob McLean, now coming to the end of his playing career, who journeyed across the Irish sea to Waterford Celtic. The newly signed players included John Moody, John Vickers and Wilf Shaw – who came from Rossington – the brother of George, who was now with West Bromwich Albion. A more aesthetic alteration was in the matter of the club strip, which was changed from red and white vertical stripes to red and white hoops.

The Rovers opened their campaign with a visit to newly named Gateshead, known previously as South Shields, at their new ground, Redheugh Park. This venue was formally opened by the vice president of the League Management Committee, Mr.Charles E.Sutcliffe. Gateshead christened their new ground with a 2–1 win, with the Rovers goal coming from Lievesley, who charged the goalkeeper as he jumped to catch the ball and then put the loose ball into the net. Four points were all that had been gathered from the first six games, when the Rovers went to Lincoln to play the leaders. Unfortunately the team bus developed engine trouble, and they did not reach Sincil Bank until three o'clock, the scheduled kick off time. The players had changed on the bus so the delay in kicking off was minimalised to five minutes, but they lost 1–0.

The team dropped down to eighteenth place, with Menzies ringing the changes amongst his players. Then suddenly in November, off the back of three successive defeats, George Gladwin was switched from left half to inside left, and the team went goal crazy with a 6–1 demolition of Accrington Stanley, Lievesley getting three goals. The following week they went to Rochdale for a 5–3 win, this time Wilf Bott getting a hat–trick, then Bobby Smith got both goals in a win over Crewe Alexandra, and a fortnight later Bott managed another hat– trick in a 6–0 thrashing of second placed Tranmere Rovers. Nineteen goals – plus another win in the F.A.Cup, over Rochdale – gave the team five wins in a row.

Equally as sudden came the loss to Notts.County (and Tommy Keetley) in the 2nd round of the Cup, without scoring a goal, followed by two goalless draws in the League. The run of League points had lifted them to fourteenth place, and things were looking up. But then came a slide which included their heaviest defeat in the Third North, 8–2 at Hull, after being 2–0 down at half-time. This defeat prompted the management to go out and recruit a centre forward, Fred Castle from Ireland, although he had previous League experience. He played eight games and scored three goals, all in one game against Wigan Borough. The club finished fifteenth after a troubled season.

Early in March Wilf Bott was transferred to Huddersfield Town for a substantial fee, again the financial situation dictating such a move by the club. Gates were now down to an average of 4,050 against a figure of 8,000 required to break even. Financially it was the most disastrous season since the club had reformed with the balance sheet showing a loss of £2,139. Sixteen players were retained for season 1931–32, with four newcomers – Ernest Pattison, Billy Atherton, James Rorrison and local lad Frank Beresford from Owston Park Rangers. But a surprise was in store for supporters in the very first match when 17 year old Cliff Parker, from Mexborough, was selected at outside left after showing up very well in the practice games.

The team were soon struggling though, with heavy defeats at Rotherham and Carlisle. October and November saw a run of seven successive defeats, four at home, which put them in the bottom four. Better form before the end of the season left them in fifteenth place out of twenty– one clubs, Wigan Borough having withdrawn in October through financial difficulties The F.A.Cup didn't provide much relief, although they did go down in the record books when it took four games, a total of seven and a half hours, to decide their tie in the 1st round against Barrow. Having finally overcome the Cumbrians, they were in action again three days later in the 2nd round at Brighton, where they lost heavily. In a fourteen day period they had played five F.A.Cup ties and a League game.

At the A.G.M.it was reported that the gate receipts were the lowest on record, causing a loss on the season of £238. Attendances had averaged 3,815, and only the transfers of Jim Smith, Joe Bowman, Les Lievesley and John Moody had kept the deficit down to a manageable figure. The chairman, Mr. Fletcher Hibbert, asked for increased attendances, but said that at the moment the position of the club was satisfactory, since although £1,230 was owed at the bank it was covered by the directors guarantee. Otherwise they did not owe a penny.

F. EMERY, the Doncaster captain.

Before the start of the season 1932–33, long serving full back Jack Buckley was surprisingly transferred to Lincoln City. Equally long serving Fred Emery was appointed as the captain, being one of the fifteen players retained.

Among the new signings were Billy Walker, Harold Schofield, Len Hargreaves – returning to his old club – Dan Kelly, Jack Beynon, Archie Waterston and Albert Hunter.

A better season was experienced with the club having found a regular goalscorer in Waterston, who finished the season with 24 League goals including two hat-tricks, despite being out injured for the last six games. Although they finished in sixth place, being unbeaten at home for the first time in the League, they actually had an adverse goal record, scoring 77 goals but conceding 79. With that number of goals around no wonder the attendances went up, giving an average of 5,399.

The 3rd round of the F.A.Cup was reached again with an easy victory over Gainsborough Trinity, and a hard fought win at Northampton Town, who had not been beaten at home thus far that season. Halifax Town were their 3rd round opponents, and hopes were high for further progress, for the Rovers had home advantage and Halifax were struggling in the Third North. Atherton was injured in the first half, followed by Flowers in the second – and was off the field for a spell – but both carried on although they were little more than passengers. With this advantage Halifax wore down the Rovers defence, scoring three goals in the last twenty minutes.

They did have one other shot, in April, at winning a trophy when they were invited to play Barnsley for the Sheffield Invitation Cup at Belle Vue. Again the Rovers were hit by injury with Bobby Smith having to go off, leaving the team to battle on with ten men for fifty minutes. Barnsley gained a 2–2 draw with a penalty in the 82nd minute, Schofield for the Rovers missing one in the next minute. An own goal and a goal from Parker had put the Rovers in front. The replay was fitted in two weeks later, to be played on a Monday after playing a League game on the Saturday with two more to come on the Thursday and the following Saturday. Little wonder that the Rovers turned out a team containing eight reserves, that were outplayed in the second half having held Barnsley to 1–1 at half time with a goal from Jack Martin four minutes before the interval. A final score of 4–1 represented Barnsley's first win over the Rovers during this season, having twice lost in the League.

The club retained nineteen of the previous season's players, more than usual, but they seemed to think they had the nucleus of a good side. Additional players signed included James Imrie, Albert Turner, John Green, Ronnie Dodd and Arthur Rodgers.

After the second game Waterston was out injured, giving Dodd, from North-Eastern local football with Usworth Colliery, his chance which he seized with both feet, scoring 24 League goals including four at home to Gateshead.

With a settled team they reached eighth position by December, when Cliff Parker was transferred to Portsmouth. His replacement, Albert Turner, proved more than adequate as he rattled 14 goals, in only 22 League games.

In January McHale was injured and replaced by John Green – like Dodd he had signed from Usworth Colliery – so successfully that he never lost his place. Then in February, as the Rovers started an unbeaten run of eight games, Frank Beresford was transferred to Preston North End. George Gladwin moved from right half to replace him at inside right with George Flowers coming in to the half back line. Ike Tate had also replaced Imrie in goal at the beginning of February, but none of these changes affected the Rovers' form unduly, as they finished the season in fifth place, nine points behind the champions, Barnsley.

In the F.A. Cup they lost to old adversaries, Barrow, this time at the first time of asking. Even in the new Division 3 North Cup they only played one game, with Chesterfield. But they did reach the final of the Sheffield County Cup after beating Sheffield United, only to lose to their neighbours, Wednesday, by three clear goals.

It had been Doncaster Rovers' most successful season on the field for some three years, reflected in an increased average attendance to 5,798. But once again players had had to be sold to keep the finances on the right side. Although a profit of £209 was reported it was due entirely to outgoing transfers.

Optimism was running high that the coming season, 1934–35, would be the club's most successful yet. So convinced were the management that they had a successful team that they had retained eighteen players, and paid them summer wages, not something done too often in previous seasons. Only three additions were made, in John Rennie, Ted Vaux and Joe Hall.

After a good start away from home they received a shock at their first home game, when Stockport County were always in front, running out winners by 4–3 in front of over 10,000 expectant fans. But this was the only hiccup from their first eleven games which took them to fourth place.

Then, again at home they came off second best to Chestefield and the following week lost their first away game, at Mansfield. The team were going through a sticky patch at this time, and lost at home to lowly Barrow for the second season in succession, in the 1st Round of the F.A.Cup. Only fourteen players had been used, and David Menzies evidently decided something needed changing, so for the game at Lincoln he went out and bought Reg Baines from Sheffield United.

"HERE WE ARE AGAIN."

1934

A snap at Belle Vue on Tuesday when Doncaster Rovers resumed training. Left to right; Cave, Vaux, Tate, Emery, and Smith (W.).

Ike Tate had been injured at Carlisle and was replaced by Imrie, Joe Hall was brought in for Green, and Baines replaced Dodd. The same team played for the next nineteen games, with the exception of four games in the middle of the run, when Dodd first replaced the injured Gladwin, and then Bobby Smith. This successful run took them to top place, on goal average, when they scored in every game and ran up a total of fifty-five goals including two fives and one seven. Baines had a hat-trick against Gateshead, and indeed scored in thirteen of the nineteen games. Turner netted three at Accrington, and then put five past New Brighton at Belle Vue.

In April the Rovers played Tranmere Rovers, another team going for promotion, at home on a Thursday afternoon, before a record crowd of 23,238. Green came in for the injured Hall, and with goals from Turner and Bobby Smith they ran out winners by 2-0. On the Saturday, in front of thirteen and a half thousand people at Belle Vue, the Rovers, with Tate coming in for the injured Imrie, looked jaded and although they went in front early in the game, they were beaten 3-1 by Lincoln City, an unexpected result.

The following weekend was Easter, usually a make or break time for teams going for promotion. So it proved for the Rovers. On Good Friday they were at home to middle of the table Rotherham United, their neighbours from down the Sheffield road, in a sensational match played before a new record crowd of 27,554. In a fast but grim and dour affair, the Rovers were two up through Baines and Burton. After forty minutes they were 3-1 in front, with another goal from Burton, but a couple of defensive blunders let Rotherham go in at half time, level

at 3-3. The second half with Emery and Burton limping, was immediately taken over by Rotherham with two goals in the first five minutes, and eventual winners by 5-3. Whilst this win dented the Rovers hopes they were still in the driving seat with games in hand.

On Easter Saturday they travelled to Tranmere to play a side fading out of the promotion picture. Emery and Burton were replaced by Dodd and Bint, with Gladwin going back to left half. Harold Lievesley, who had played at centre-half against Rotherham, was also replaced by Green. Two goals by Baines and Dodd gave Doncaster a much desired win.

A record crowd of 20,357 was at Rotherham to see the Rovers complete their Easter programme. Revenge was gained with goals from Baines, Bint and Dodd giving the Rovers a 3-1 win and a lead at the top of the table of one point over Chester with three games to play, whilst Chester had only one. Saturday, April 27th was to be decision time.

Chester, their only challengers, played their last game of the season at Lincoln in the afternoon. Rovers were to play Wrexham at Belle Vue in the evening. But by kick off time the Rovers were already champions, Chester having lost at Lincoln City. The Rovers, with the pressure off, played just well enough to gain a 2-1 win to confirm their status as Champions. Their remaining two games, both against Halifax Town, were something of an anti-climax, reflected by the scorelines, 1-0 in each game to the opposition. These four points enabled Halifax Town to move from fourth to runners-up place. But who cared, the Rovers were back in Division 2 after a gap of thirty years and some said they had regained their rightful place. The championship shield and medals were presented to the Rovers by Mr.A.Brooke Hirst, chairman of Huddersfield Town and a member of the League Management Committee.

Nineteen players had been used in the League campaign, fourteen of whom received medals. Albert Turner led the goalscoring list with 25, a splendid figure for a winger, with Baines, Burton and Dodd also reaching double figures.

The optimism shown at the beginning of the season had been well founded in view of the club's ensuing success. A profit was reported of £1,753 on the season with the balance sheet showing the club to be clear of debt and with a sum in hand of £656. No players had been transferred due to attendances nearly doubling, with the average attendance rising to 10,681.

The club retained the entire championship side with Menzies making some judicious new signings; Norman Wharton, Claude Sharp, Hugh Jacobson, Les Turner, Tommy Dutton and Charlie Johnston. But the team that turned out at Blackpool, in their first Second Division match for thirty years was the championship side being given their big chance – *Imrie; Wilf Shaw and Rodgers; Flowers, Joe Hall and Emery; Burton, Gladwin, Baines, Bobby Smith and Albert Turner.*

Fred Emery, the Rovers' Left-half.

The Rovers soon made their mark with a goal from Burton after seven minutes. Then Blackpool took charge with four goals before half–time, two of them after going down to ten men when their outside right was injured. A gentleman by the name of Peter Doherty, the Blackpool inside left, also got his name on the scoresheet. A final score of 5–2 gave the Rovers some food for thought, emphasised by their first home game against Southampton, who went away with the two points.

Their first win came in the next home game against Charlton Athletic, the champions of Division 3 South. Only a superb goalkeeping exhibition from Sam Bartram kept the score down to 2–0, with goals from Baines and Albert Turner. Southampton completed the double over the Rovers, but now they had found their feet and apart from one blip at Leicester City, when they conceded six goals, they surged up the table.

By Christmas, they were second, on goal average only, to Leicester City. But the matches over the festive period changed their season. Emery and Hall were injured in a goalless draw at Nottingham, but Forest romped to a 6–2 victory in the return encounter. This was followed by six successive losses, with only one goal scored, and a drop down to tenth place.

Two successive wins in February seemed to have stemmed the rot. The first was over Leicester City, and the second was by 6–1 over Hull City, the team with the leakiest defence in the Second Division and firmly entrenched the City at the bottom. A hat–trick from Baines, two goals by Johnston, with one from Albert Turner emphasised the Rovers' superiority.

Only five points, all draws, were gained from the re-mainder of the season, so by the end they were only five points above the relegated clubs, in eighteenth place. The second half of the season had produced only two wins and nine points but at least they were still in Division 2. They also had a new attendance record when on Good Friday they entertained Sheffield United before a crowd of 28,560, who witnessed a goalless draw. In February David Menzies resigned as secretary–manager to accept the manager's job at Hull City. His replacement was Fred Emery, who carried on as a player until the end of the season, when he retired from the field of play to carry on in his managerial role.

The F.A.Cup didn't provide any joy either. Entering in at the Third Round stage, the Rovers faced their Christ-mas tormentors, Nottingham Forest, at Belle Vue before a record Cup attendance of 19,409. Forest continued their hold over the Rovers by winning 2–1. The season did end on a winning note however, when they won the Sheffield County Cup for the first time, beating the F.A.Cup Finalists Sheffield United with two goals from Baines, against his old club, with only one in reply.

The club's first venture into a wider sphere came in early December when they entertained one of the Continent's best teams, F.C.Austria of Vienna. The Austrians surprised everyone with their skill and accuracy of passing, with the Rovers having to get used to "not charging", especially on the goalkeeper, a policy not employed in the English game for some years to come. After five minutes some smart passing resulted in the Austrians taking the lead through Jerusalem. Albert Turner equalised from a penalty after a full back had acted as goalkeeper to keep out a shot by Dodd. Turner had another chance to score from a penalty in the second half, but he hit a post, the ball going behind. With three minutes left, Molzer, the outside right, met a ball from the left to win the game for F.C.Austria. A crowd of 3,700 on a Monday afternoon would hardly have paid the guarantee for the visitors, but it was certainly an experi-ence for players and fans alike.

The Rovers team lined up as:– *Imrie; Wilf Shaw and Jacobson; Gladwin, Hall and Emery; Bint, Bobby Smith, Dodd, Dutton and Albert Turner.*

In March, at Valley Parade Bradford, George Flowers, the Rovers reserve anticipated a restful afternoon watching the match. But the referee, Mr T.Firth, did not arrive so the senior linesman had to take over. Flowers was pressed into service as a linesman, and received as compensation, the official's fee of £1.11s.6d.

The club reported a profit of £2,579, and for the first time for a number of years, shareholders received a dividend of 5%. An average attendance of 14,077 had helped the club to pay transfer fees for players without having to sell anyone to survive.

So there was a certain amount of optimism when the 1936–37 season kicked off under new manager Fred Emery. Having retained nineteen players – one released was George Flowers – new players were signed, including Mick Kilhourhy, George Bradshaw, Tom Wildsmith and Reg Keating, all experienced men.

Opening the season with games against newly promoted Coventry City and Southampton, a good start was made with a draw and a win. Four defeats followed however, including heavy losses at Plymouth (7–0) and Chestefield (5–1). An inside forward, Albert Malam, was secured from Huddersfield Town at a club record fee, making his debut in a win over Aston Villa before over 23,000 spectators at Belle Vue, which produced the Rovers' last victory before the end of December.

Before the game at Barnsley, towards the end of November, two new signings were made in Ted Perry, for a record fee from Fulham plus Cyril Smith from Brentford. With goal scoring at a premium the plunge for Perry, a Welsh international centre forward, was regarded as a good move. But results did not improve, the team remained at the bottom of the table, and were eventually relegated together with Bradford City, whose manager was former Rovers' man Dick Ray. They did however cause one upset at the end of the season, when they went to Blackpool and held the Seasiders to a draw, thereby depriving them of the Second Division Championship.

In February Manchester United came in for George Gladwin, paying the Rovers a fee in excess of that received for Allan Hall, and a new club record.

The F.A.Cup again only produced more heartache. Drawn to play at Chester, leaders of the Third North, they were well and truly beaten by 4–0. They lost to Sheffield Wednesday in the 1st round of the Sheffield County Cup, but were invited to play Midland Leaguers Grantham Town, for the Grantham Hospital Cup. Including two former Grantham players, Syd Bycroft and

Eric Bott, the Rovers won 1–0 with a goal from Albert Turner early in the second half.

On October the 21st 1936, the Rovers made club history by accepting an invitation to play the Dutch National XI at the Sparta Rotterdam Stadium, the first time the club had played abroad. A rough crossing over the North Sea did not augur well, with most of the players suffering seasickness. The Dutch, preparing for a match against Austria, won 7–2 with centre forward Bakhuys scoring five goals. But the Rovers forwards were the least effective force for the visitors, not capitalising on good approach work. The Rovers were not too impressed by the referee, claiming that two of Backhuys goals were offside, and that a disallowed goal by Albert Turner was a legitimate one. One Dutch newspaper was not impressed with the Rovers display, calling it "Holiday football", and the players a bunch of comedians from the English Second and Third Division. The Rovers also had their first taste of substitute players when Kilhourhy replaced the injured McMahon at half time. The team for this historic encounter was:– *Bradshaw; Wilf Shaw and Rodgers, captain; Gladwin, Bycroft and McMahon; Keating, Malam, Dodd, Bobby Smith and Albert Turner.*

A month later the Rovers entertained Gradjanski F.C. from Zagreb, Yugoslavia, who were bolstered by several international players from other clubs in Yugoslavia. The Rovers, with several reserves, won an exciting exhibition match 6–4, after leading 2–0 at half time. This, result coming only two days after losing 7–0 at Newcastle United.

Although the season was a disaster from the playing point of view, the club still returned a profit of £119 on the season. For once the club paid out more in transfer fees, £6,285, than the £5,500 they had received. But by careful management of the finances even a drop in the average gate to 11,697 had not had too detrimental an effect.

It was back to the Third North for the Rovers in 1937–38. Due to two northern clubs being relegated from Division 2, there was a vacancy in the Third South. The Rovers decided to apply for a transfer to the Third South because of the attraction of the new clubs that it would provide. This enterprising idea, alas, came unstuck when Mansfield Town were deemed to be the southernmost club in the northern section, and so were transferred to the South.

Fred Emery decided that he would have a clear out putting Baines, Albert Turner, Johnston and Hall on the transfer list, and giving Eric Bott, Bobby Smith, Les Turner, Jacobson, Payne and Monaghan free transfers. He then went out and signed Ron Morgan, Bobby McFarlane, Ralph Pedwell, Vic Potts, Ernie Vincent and Albert Allen, so that the Rovers started the season with twenty–five full–time players, the most they had at the beginning of a season. The first game was at home to fellow relegation team, Bradford City, which the Rovers won comfortably by 4–0, with two goals from Pedwell and one apiece from Malam and Perry. Unfortunately, it was achieved at a price when four minutes from time Pedwell, who had a fine game and showed excellent form, was carried off with a broken leg. He never played for the Rovers first team again.

Two wins and two defeats followed, but then a run of six games undefeated took them up to fifth place and a challenge for the promotion place. A defeat at Wrexham, then another six–game unbeaten run, took them to Christmas and second place, one point behind the leaders Oldham Athletic. A double loss over the New Year knocked them back to seventh place. A settled team with few changes, and only then because of injury, was proving successful. Goals were coming from Perry, Kilhourhy and Malam, with the defence only occasionally failing. February proved to be the low point of the season when three successive matches were lost.

From then to the end of the season one defeat in fifteen games saw them challenging really hard for the top place. The last game of the season had them playing host to prospective champions Tranmere Rovers, who were one point in front but with a superior goal average. In fact, to take the championship away from Tranmere the Rovers had to win 8–0. In the event the match ended all square at 1–1, the Rovers finishing in second place two points adrift of the Champions.

Three home draws were the Rovers lot in the F.A.Cup. The first game against Blyth Spartans was won comfortably 7–0 with Mick Kilhourhy getting four goals. Another comfortable win in the next round over Guildford City, in which Bob McFarlane opposed his brother, took them to a meeting against Sheffield United, promotion contenders from Division 2. A record Cup crowd of 23,280 saw a disappointing match, from the Rovers point of view, as Sheffield United's defence kept a tight grip on the Rovers forwards. A goal late in each half from Barton and Pickering gave the United their passport to the 4th round.

Earlier, in October, the Rovers had overwhelmed Sheffield United – fresh from a League victory over their neighbours Wednesday – by 5–1 in the semi–final of the Sheffield County Cup. The final, played at the end of the season, was a typical end–of–season game. A goal by Kilhourhy after 78 minutes finally settled the issue and gave the Rovers some silverware for the season. They also reached the semi–final of the Third North Cup with victories over Lincoln City, 7–2 (Morgan scoring three goals), Halifax Town 4–1 (Harry Brooks getting three), and at Barrow where less than a thousand people turned out to watch.

The semi–final at Valley parade, against Bradford City, went to extra time before the Rovers capitulated.

A successful season from the playing side and on the financial front was reported. An average attendance of 13,040 showed that a successful team could be accommodated in the town. A profit of £465 was the end result of the season's workings, and optimism was high that the club could go one better in 1938–39.

Most of the previous season's players were retained, new signings bringing the total to twenty–six full time professionals to start the season with. The Rovers paid £2,000 to Chelsea for William Barraclough, and swapped Arthur Banner for Fred Dell and Albert Walker from West Ham United.

The season started in the same way as the previous one with a win, a draw and a loss. Early in September Stan "Dizzie" Burton was transferred to Wolverhampton Wanderers with George Little taking his place in the Rovers side. Billy Gold was badly injured at Wrexham, Imrie taking over. In October a draw at Barnsley took away their 100% home record, and then by beating Oldham Athletic, the Latics were knocked off the top spot, whilst the Rovers moved into fifth place, and into contention with the leading pack of clubs. The Barnsley game was the start of an unbeaten run of twelve games that took the Rovers to third place, one point behind Southport but eight behind the clear leaders, Barnsley. The run began to lose it's momentum over the Christmas and New Year period when only four points from four games were gained, two of them goalless draws.

In November, Charlie Leyfield had been brought from Sheffield United to fill the problem outside left position, made his League debut at Barrow and scored two goals in a 4–4 draw. So well did the Rovers play that day that letters of congratulations on the football played arrived at the Rovers office from Barrow supporters and directors.

The end of January saw the club regain it's momentum with four successive victories that took them into second place with the next match being a home game against the leaders, Barnsley. A crowd of 34,046 turned out for this top of the table duel, easily a record for the club. The Rovers gave a debut to Leslie Owens, who they had signed during the week from Charlton Athletic, at centre forward, Perry being out through injury. Barnsley's forwards took some holding giving the Rovers defence a hard time. With the Rovers forward line not being too effective it was no surprise when Barnsley ran out 3–1 winners with goals from Steele and Asquith (2). The Rovers reply came from Malam after thirty minutes, so that they went in at half–time only 2–1 down. This win put Barnsley eleven points clear at the top with Southport pushing Rovers into third place on goal average.

Syd Bycroft

like Joe Mercer, Tommy Jones, Ted Sagar, Tommy Lawton and Wally Beyes. Two of the Rovers team, Malam and Leyfield, were former Everton players.

With four trainloads of supporters shouting them on, the Rovers gave as much as they got for thirty–four minutes. Then Boyes, after a solo run, shot Everton in front, scored again three minutes from half time and Lawton added another two minutes later. Lawton scored a fourth after forty–eight minutes, but the Rovers continued to fight against the odds, until fifteen minutes from time. Four goals in that last fifteen minutes swamped the Rovers to a final total of 8–0. The Rovers would remember their first ever encounter in the F.A.Cup against First Division opposition.

After a successful season on the playing side it was a bit disappointing to report that attendances were down overall to an average of 11,629, although it didn't help with a runaway winner. However, a profit of £546 was reported due to making a profit on transfer dealings. A dividend of 5% was paid to shareholders, for the fourth time.

The 1939–40 season started amid the clouds of war looming on the horizon. Some former first team players were not retained, James Imrie and Arthur Rodgers being two, but newcomers added to the twenty–two who were retained including Ambrose Buckley, Ernest Phypers, Jimmy Heal and Ted Embleton.

For this season the League brought in the numbering of players on the back of their shirts. The season opened on a scorching summer's day with a match, in aid of the League Jubilee Fund, at Millmoor against neighbours Rotherham United.

The Rovers treated the match as an exhibition with Rotherham wanting a competitive match, and going 3–0 up with ten minutes to go when Kirkaldie, after a brilliant dribble past three defenders, scored a consolation goal. At half–time the Rovers made a substitution when Stirland replaced Mitchell at right half, but then Owens received a foot injury which was to keep him out of the first two League games.

For the first match against Rochdale, Ted Perry replaced George Burditt and Fred Dell came in for the injured Owens. Two goals from Leyfield gave them a win but in their next two matches, both away, they came away without any points. It all proved to be academic though, because the day after the New Brighton match, war was declared on Germany.

After this game the Rovers lost only two games out of the fourteen to the end of the season. Although four games ended goalless they also scored plenty of goals in the other matches. Perry came back to hit the goal trail, Owens scored eight goals in eleven games, and at the end of April Jack Kirkaldie was brought from Coventry City. He only scored once but the team managed nine in the last two matches. This good form over the last stretch left them clear in second place, but eleven points behind the Champions, Barnsley. The fifty–six points that the Rovers had gained would have been enough in previous seasons to ensure promotion, but this particular one had seen Barnsley in splendid form whilst equalling the Third North record for points gained.

For the second season in succession Syd Bycroft was an ever–present in the League side, the only one of the twenty–three players used to do so. The goals were shared round with six players reaching double figures and Perry leading the way with fifteen.

The F.A.Cup provided some cheer, in the first three rounds anyway, when they progressed at expense of New Brighton, Gainsborough Trinity and Southport – the latter after a replay. The 4th round took them to eventual League Champions Everton, to play against internationals

CHAPTER 7

The War Years 1939–46

hree days after the declaration of war the Football League suspended their competition.

All players contracts were also suspended with the result that all the Rovers' players dispersed to their various work of National importance to which they had been assigned. Syd Bycroft, for instance, joined the Doncaster County Borough Police Force, and Mick Kilhourhy joined the staff at the A.R.P. Headquarters in the town. Charlie Leyfield went back to his trade as a joiner, Albert Walker and Wilf Shaw worked for a builder, George Little and Joe Johnson got positions in works in the town, whilst Bob McLean, the trainer, did hospital work as did Billy Gold; Ted Wynter, the assistant, trainer joined the Forces.

Ten days after the suspension of all football, the Rovers directorate met and decided they would carry on as a football club. A friendly match was arranged against Bradford P.A. for the following Saturday, September 16th. Fred Emery rounded a team up, turning out the following:-
Gold; Wilf Shaw, Walker; Mitchell, Vincent, Stirland; Little, Owens, Burditt, Kilhourhy, Bilton.

All were registered Rovers players. A keen game ensued with the players showing an element of competitive spirit, but the match ended goalless. During the following week the F.A., after consultation with the Home Office, decided to support the organisation of both friendly and competitive matches on Saturdays and public holidays provided they were based on a local and district group of clubs and did not interfere with National war work.

The Rovers continued to play friendly games until the Football League organised regional leagues for the clubs. The Rovers were placed in the East Midlands League, their furthest journeys being East to Grimsby Town, South to Nottingham Forest, and West to Barnsley, whilst they were the Northern extremity of the group.

The Football League decreed that travelling should be limited to a radius of fifty miles, professionals were to be paid a limit of 30s. per match with no bonuses, and registered players were permitted to play for another League club within reasonable distance of his home or place of work. The minimum charge for spectators was a shilling (5p), members of the Forces (in uniform), plus women and boys excepted. Points were to be awarded and league tables compiled but no trophies would be available.

As the East Midlands League only contained eleven clubs, providing twenty competitive matches, a number of friendlies were also arranged. The League started on October the 21st. With a final game being played as late as June the 1st. The Rovers record of winning seven out of twenty games speaks for itself as they finished sixth. A number of guest players were used, including ex-Rovers' Burton, Dodd, Beresford and Les Lievesley, together with some junior players from the Reserves such as 17 year old Clarrie Jordan.

The Rovers reported a loss on the first war-time season of £1,505. Whilst making money was not the object in war-time football, clubs still needed the staff to carry on. The problem was that receipts were divided on a F.A. Cup rules fifty – fifty basis, and they had paid out 50% more to visiting clubs than they had received on their travels. They had calculated at the start that with crowds of 3,000 they could survive and, in fact, the East Midland League attendances had averaged 3,319. On the grounds of economy, Fred Emery's services as manager were dispersed with in July 1940, after a sixteen year connection with the club.

For the 1940–41 season the Football League re-organised the competition. The Rovers were placed in the League North with thirty-five other northern clubs. Playing against clubs from within the prescribed limit – in Yorkshire, Lincolnshire and the North Midlands – they played twenty-nine games plus three Sheffield County Cup ties, winning fifteen of them and drawing seven. With such a large number of clubs and not being able to play each other, the placings were decided by goal average. The Rovers goal average of 77 for and 74 against, worked out at an average of 1.04, placing them in nineteenth place. In the Sheffield County Cup they beat Sheffield Wednesday, Sheffield United and then Rotherham United in the Final. The League War Cup, played on a two leg basis, saw the club go out in the first round to Grimsby Town.

As increasing numbers of their own players went into the Forces the Rovers, had to call more upon guest players to fill out the team, hardly ever turning the same eleven out twice. A total of thirty-two players were used during the season. On Christmas Day they had played two League games, at Belle Vue against Lincoln City in the morning, and at Sincil Bank against the same opposition in the afternoon, after a light lunch and a journey by road. Lincoln used the same eleven players but the Rovers made two changes, Wilf Shaw, home on leave, and Stirland, replacing Walker and Sinclair.

DONCASTER ROVERS F.C. (1920) LTD.
OFFICIAL PROGRAMME
SATURDAY, 19th September, 1942.   ONE PENNY

ROVERS v. CHESTERFIELD

The games to date have hardly produced the results desired, for it is some time since we opened with three defeats in a row. Although there is, however, some grounds for optimism for the future. The latest departure is Head, whose absence at full back will be missed. The chief trouble appears to be that while certain players are available one week, they have difficulty in getting away for the next time, and therefore an established eleven is almost out of the question. Nightingale is now unable to travel, and has been given permission to play for Grimsby again. To-day we are introducing Attwell, the West Ham half-back, whose experience should help to compensate for the absence of Bycroft, and Leeman, a youngster who has been doing well with the Reserves. Chesterfield have also introduced youngsters with good results and to-day's return encounter should be an enjoyable one. The Sheffield County Cup draw has meant the Rovers travelling again, for they are due to play the winners of the Sheffield Wednesday—Rotherham United game on the winner's ground. We would like to appeal to our supporters to attend the Reserve games, as we feel sure that our youngsters are worth watching. They have had a double win at the expense of the R.A.F., and shown fine form in each game. Brodsworth Colliery have now withdrawn from the League, and so the already scanty fixtures are further reduced.

Doncaster Rovers
(Red and White Hoops, White Knickers)

Right   Left

FERGUSON

WALKER (A.)   WOOLDRIDGE
2   3

STIRLAND   ATTER   ATTWELL
4   5   6

HUBBARD   LEEMAN   SUTHERLAND   DRURY   SINCLAIR
7   8   9   10   11

Linesmen:
Referee: Mr. H. ROWLEY
                                                  (Doncaster)   Red Flag
Mr. W. D. STONE   Mr. J. L. DAVIES
(Moorends)   (Hatfield)   Blue Flag

MILLER   PRINGLE   LINACRE   COLLINS   HARPER
11   10   9   7

SOUTHALL   LEVENE   HARTLEY
6   5   4

ALDERSON   MILBURN
3   2

MIDDLETON

Chesterfield
(Blue and White Stripes, Black Knickers)

Left   Right

SATURDAY NEXT, Sept. 26—ROVERS v. LINCOLN CITY
Saturday, October 3—Reserves v. Brooklands (Don. Senior League)
Kick-offs 3-15 p.m.

Chronicle Co., Printers, Scot Lane, Doncaster

Unhappily, in the week before Christmas, the secretary of the club, Frank Wass, died at his desk. The Rovers reported a profit of £86 on the season, having covered the season's expenses with income from match revenue. An average attendance of 2,200 attended games throughout a difficult year.

For 1941–42 the League North was again re-organised. The Rovers were to meet nine other teams, mostly on a local basis. This gave them eighteen matches in what was called the First Championship. These games were completed by December the 25th; the Rovers won six and drew two. This put them in twenty–seventh place out of the thirty–eight clubs in the League North.

The War Cup started in the New Year and was played with a qualifying competition first. Each club played five other clubs on a home and away basis. Due to the weather, the Rovers only managed to play eight matches, winning two. Only the top thirty-two clubs qualified for the Competition Proper, and the Rovers were not one of them.

All the cup games and the Sheffield County Cup matches also counted towards a Second Championship, covering the second half of the season.

But, with the exception of the County Cup game against Rotherham United, this season finished at the end of March, the club being unable to arrange any other fixtures. Again, a number of guest players were used but youngsters like Brough and Micky Walker also came through, Clarrie Jordan by now was already a regular member of the side.

As the situation worsened, it became difficult to get new kit without the required amount of clothing coupons, and footballs were also difficult to obtain so existing ones had to be used as long as possible. A ban was put on using petrol for pleasure, as one Rovers supporter found out. He was on his was to Belle Vue from out of town when he was stopped by the police and asked for the nature of his journey. Telling them he was going to watch the Rovers he found himself in court and fined. But for football clubs it meant using trains or travelling by service bus.

The League in 1942–43, as far as the North of England was concerned, was organised on the same lines as the previous season. During the first half of the season, which ended on Christmas Day, the Rovers played only seventeen of their scheduled eighteen matches, the last match – at home to Grimsby Town on December the 25th being cancelled because Grimsby had difficulty in getting transport. Of their seventeen games, three were won and three drawn, and in the overall table they finished forty–seventh of fortyeight clubs. At Chesterfield play had to be held up for seven minutes whilst the referee was revived, having been knocked unconscious by the ball. At Halifax, Rovers travelled with ten men and made up a full team with a soldier, R. Wilson, who was picked up at the ground.

The Cup Qualifying Competition started on Boxing Day with the Rovers at York. York started the game with nine men whilst efforts were made to find two substitutes. By the end of February, Doncaster had played their ten games, of which only two were won and two drawn. Again, they did not qualify for the competition proper.

A Second Championship was played, comprising the Cup Qualifying matches, League games played in March and April and Sheffield County Cup games. Of seventeen matches, five were won and three were drawn, which left them in fortysecond place of fifty–four clubs in the overall table.

Guest players like Freddie Steele, the English international centre forward from Stoke City, ex-Rovers' Arthur Banner, George Gladwin, Dizzie Burton, Jimmy Harkin and Fred Gregory, plus players with local connections like Harold Bodle and Jack Thorogood, were all used. In fact, of the forty-eight players used, at least thirty-two were connected with other clubs.

A profit of £570 and average gates of 2,454 were reported at the A.G.M. This was due entirely to the directors being very careful about cutting their coat according to the cloth.

The improving war situation led many to think that the hostilities could be over in the immediate future. The F.A. had discussed the post-war situation, and the Rovers were equally optimistic. Bob McLean was appointed full-time trainer and groundsman, and Jimmy Geary became part-time second team trainer. Fred Gregory, the old Rovers player, was signed from Crystal Palace and arrangements were made with twenty-four players for season 1943-44. The Football League often complained of clubs abusing the guest system but little appeared to be done about it.

The League North was again run as in previous seasons. But with a more settled team, the Rovers gave the best account of themselves since the war started. Only losing two of their eighteen First Championship games, they were placed fourth out of fifty clubs in the overall table.

In the War Cup Qualifying competition, the Rovers started well but faded and did not qualify for the competition proper. On New Year's Day they played Grimsby Town, at Blundell Park, the first time in three years that Grimsby had used their own ground, having shared Scunthorpe United's Old Showground during that period. The Mayor and Mayoress of Grimsby were in attendance, when with the match petering out to a 1-1 draw, the referee ordered Hall, the Grimsby captain and right half, off the field for misconduct. Hall refused to go off so the referee abandoned the game, eighty-five minutes having been played. In February the Rovers had great difficulty selecting a side because of frequent calls on players for Army representative matches so that it was a case of waiting to see who turned up before the match before they knew what team to put on the field.

The Second Championship was comprised of the War Cup Qualifying matches, some League games and the Sheffield County Cup, a total of seventeen matches of which nine were won and three drawn. Overall, the Rovers were placed in twenty-second place out of fifty clubs.

In April, during the week before the season's last game, Billy Marsden, the former Sheffield Wednesday and England half-back, was appointed manager. Although starting at a difficult time, the prospects were good with a substantial profit, £1,281, made on the season and an average gate of 6,305 recorded, far in excess of anything thus far during the war.

Mr. Fletcher Hibbert, the chairman, showed the way people were thinking at this stage, in the summer of 1944, when he talked about the possibility of returning to normal in 1945-46.

Billy Marsden had been busy checking the local talent and the reserve strength in preparation for 1944-45. The League North programme started with a bang, at Hull, where the City were making a start after being closed down for most of the war years. The Rovers were well on their way to winning the match when Hull had two players injured in the second half leaving the visitors to run riot, and Jordan getting a hat-trick. Only two guest players were used, Bodle and Thorogood, the rest of the team being home grown young players with the exception of Bycroft, the only Rovers player from pre-war days. A home win over Hull City was followed by five successive defeats. But then came an incredible run of ten wins out of their last eleven League games, the one being lost at home to Chesterfield. The only guest players used in this period, apart from the two already mentioned, were Robinson, Banner, Attwell, Woodburn, Heydon, Mitcheson, Williams and Massarella. The bulk of the side were the Rovers own signed players. A record of twelve wins out of eighteen games gave them seventh place in the overall table.

DONCASTER ROVERS F.C. (1920) LTD.

OFFICIAL PROGRAMME

Saturday, October 21, 1944.   Three Halfpence

ROVERS v. NOTTS COUNTY

The win over Sheffield United was very pronounced and actually the "Blades" were fortunate to escape so lightly. It was not a good day for football, but the exchanges were fast and exciting, and all the eleven pulled their weight. Williams, the Southampton player, who was introduced at inside right, did well, as did Heydon, the Derby half-back. The latter is playing in the Northern Command team to-day and so we miss his services. As Stirland is also unfit, the position of right half was not filled at the time of going to press. Also included in to-day's side is Beedall, who has been doing well with the Reserves. Notts County, now under the management of Major Buckley, are to-day's visitors, and have two amateurs. Hepworth, the right back, is the Bradford player, while Clack and Davie have also considerable experience. The teams should be well matched and the Rovers have hopes of going further ahead after their bad spell.

The Reserves lost at Bramall Lane by the odd goal of three, after scoring first. The game was an excellent one and opportunity was given to try out two new youngsters. Hemmings was the Reserves scorer.

Doncaster Rovers
(Red and White Hoops, White Knickers)

Right   Left

ROBINSON
1

STEVENSON   WOOLDRIDGE
2   3

A. N. OTHER   BYCROFT   BEEDALL
4   5   6

TINDILL   PETERS   JORDAN   BODLE   THOROGOOD
7   8   9   10   11

Referee: Linesmen:
Mr. L. DALE   Mr. J. SHERLOCK
(Sheffield)   (Sheffield)   Red Flag
                                   Mr. S. FOX
                                   (Barnsley)   Blue Flag

PIERCEY   STEPHENSON   DAVIE   WOOD   EDWARDS
11   10   9   8   7

MORRAD   BARTON   SOUTHWELL
6   5   4

POMPHREY   HEPWORTH
3   2

CLACK
1

Left   Right

Notts County
(Black and White Stripes, Black Knickers)

Saturday Next, Oct. 28—Reserves v. R.A.S.C.
Saturday, Nov. 2—Reserves v. Chesterfield Res.   Kick-offs 3-15

Chronicle Printers, Rent Lane, Doncaster

The War Cup Qualifying competition also proved a success for the Rovers young team. With the addition of the Everton and England right half, Cliff Britton, they won seven of their ten games to qualify for the competition proper. Goals were plentiful with Bodle getting four against Lincoln City and Jordan with a hat-trick against Grimsby Town and four goals at Hillsborough.

In the competition proper each round was played on a two-leg basis. Getting by Bradford P.A. in the 1st round, their next opponents were the cup favourites, Derby County, a very strong combination. The first leg, at home before 23,899 excited spectators, was an even game with the only difference being Raich Carter, the Sunderland and England inside left, who was the architect behind the one goal lead that Derby took home. That difference was apparent the following week at the Baseball Ground when Carter was away playing for England against Scotland.

The Rovers got off to a terrific start when straight from the kick off the ball was sent down the middle for Jordan to chase. He reached the ball at the same time as Nicholas came in to tackle, the ball shooting up and into the net like a rocket. All square on aggregate and the game barely a minute old. The Rovers then took the game to Derby, outplayed them and scored further goals through Jordan and Bodle (2). A consolation goal for Derby ten minutes from the end did nothing to inspire them, as the Rovers went through on aggregate to meet Manchester United in the last eight of the competition. The first leg, at home, before a big crowd of 29,177 saw the United strike twice in the first half-hour through Smith and Bellis, and then sit back on their lead. Jordan pulled a goal back four minutes into the second half but despite constant pressure could not pierce the United's defence again. The return match, played at Maine Road because Old Trafford had suffered bomb damage, was an anti-climax for the Rovers who were well beaten by a much better side.

It proved to be the last match of a successful season. With an average gate of 9,104, a substantial profit was made enabling the club to look forward to the new era that would open up following the end of war.

But there was sadness as well for the club and its supporters, when in October came the news that 21 year old Sgt.Glyn Jones had been killed in action over Germany. He had last played for the Rovers in 1943-44. In March, Wilf Shaw was killed in action on the Western Front.

Season 1945-46 was a transitional season between the end of the war and the time that it would take to demobilise all the players from the Services, with a return to full normality set for 1946-47. Clubs were only allowed to play three guest players from November placing the emphasis on the clubs using their own available players. Billy Marsden and his assistant Jackie Bestall had gathered a good crop of young players together and continued to look around to build the squad up.

The League was re-organised for this season so that, as far as the Rovers were concerned, the pre-war Division 3 North was divided into sections with the Rovers in the Eastern Section containing ten clubs. A programme of eighteen games, eight won and four drawn, gave them fourth place. New players at the club were Ken Hardwick, Paul Todd and Bill Archer. Gradually the players in the Services came back to the club and were introduced into the side, namely McFarlane, Kilhourhy, Kirkaldie and Little. Ralph Maddison was signed from the Forces on the recommendation of Todd.

The War Cup was replaced by the F.A.Cup and a supplementary competition, the Division 3 North Cup. The F.A. Cup, for this season, was played on the two-leg system, the Rovers opponents in the 1st Round being Rotherham United, who won both games for an overall aggregate win of 3-1. The qualifying competition for the Division 3 North Cup comprised of home and away matches against five other clubs. The Rovers finished at the top of their section thereby qualifying for the competition proper. Their first opponents were Stockport County, and the first leg at home ended level at two goals each. The second leg at Stockport, the following week (March the 30th), was to go down in the record books as the longest match ever played.

Kicking off at 3 o'clock, Stockport took the lead after five minutes with a penalty, the Rovers through Maddison equalised after 25 minutes and went ahead a minute later through Todd. Eighteen minutes from the end Shaw made it all square again. The rules of the competition stated that in the event of a draw after ninety minutes, extra time would be played. If the scores were still level at the end of normal extra time, play would continue until one side scored a goal. This is exactly what happened.

There were some amazing scenes in the play which followed the normal extra time. The teams did not change ends; there was no interval; and at the end, when approaching darkness and the smoky haze from the railway made further play impossible, players were collapsing from exhaustion. Three of the Doncaster team – Swallow, Marriott and Jordan – had worked the night before, and Jordan, who was a mineworker, had worked a double shift in order to be able to travel to Stockport and play. Stirland, the Rovers' right-half, had been in bed the previous week with 'flu' and a touch of pleurisy.

When the game finally ended, it was all the players could do to hobble off the field. On hearing the final whistle, Swallow sat down in the middle of the pitch, unlaced his boots, and walked in stockinged feet to the dressingroom.

A 1945/46 season line-up: (Back) Heydon, Swallow, Archer, Harwick, Wooldridge, McFarlane. (Front) Todd, Jordan, Mitcheson, Maddison, Kirkaldie.

An exceptionally hard ground and one of the hottest days of the year combined to make playing conditions even more arduous.

Despite the shocking fatigue of both teams, the crowd towards the finish was appealing to the referee to stop the game, and there were some exciting moments in the closing stages. It was mostly Stockport's game, with the Rovers packing the goal and the home forwards shooting all over the place. After 173 minutes Cocker raced through, to bustle the ball into the net. Immediately the Stockport "fans" rushed onto the field, and were preparing to carry him off in triumph, but the persistent whistle of Mr.A.Baker, the Crewe referee, indicated that he had not missed Cocker's hand on the ball as he beat Hardwick.

Two minutes later the referee himself collapsed and rolled over in agony, with his leg muscles knotted in cramp. After attention by the trainer, and a douse with the magic sponge, he resumed, and the game went on. The replay took place the following Wednesday at Belle Vue, and was a personal triumph for Ralph Maddison, who scored three of the four goals, Todd being the other scorer, and he also shot wide from a penalty kick.

The only change in the Rovers side was Kirkaldie for Little. The following Saturday they met Rotherham United in the 2nd round in a goalless first leg, eventually going out on aggregate 2-0. Eight times they had met Rotherham in various competitions during the season and only once had they won, therefore the two goalless draws could be counted as successes.

At the end of February, manager Billy Marsden resigned after a difference of opinion about the status of the job. The directors were determined to get together a first class team and felt that the manager's job would have to be full-time. Marsden, a Sheffield hotel licensee, felt that he had managed perfectly over the previous two years and could carry on doing a good job without giving up his outside livelihood. Of course, there is only one winner in these circumstances and Jackie Bestall was appointed as his successor.

A profit of £435 on the season gave the club a firm base to pursue their ambition of higher-grade football. Jackie Thompson was recruited from Sheffield Wednesday, Bestall considering that he had now sufficient players both in the first team and in reserve to be successful.

CHAPTER 8

The Road To Division 2

he list of fixtures used in 1946–47 were those that were abandoned in 1939–40. Thus, on August the 31st, the Rovers played Rochdale at Belle Vue in the first match of a season that was normal fare before the war. The team that they turned out only included one pre–war player, Bob McFarlane, although George Little, Syd Bycroft, Jack Kirkaldie and Les Owens were all signed players. The line–up for this match was:– *Archie Ferguson; Ernie Swallow and Jim Wooldridge; Cec Stirland, Bill Archer and Bob Mc–Farlane; Bert Tindill, Jackie Thompson, Clarrie Jordan, Paul Todd and Ralph Maddison.*

A thunderstorm broke just before the game but a crowd of some 8,000 turned up to see the Rovers get the season off on the right foot with a win, Maddison doing the necessary, scoring both goals.

Bycroft and Owens replaced Archer and the injured Todd for the midweek evening game at Chester. Goals from Jordan, Thompson and Tindill gave them a well deserved win. With Todd replacing Owens for the match at New Brighton an excellent display, and three goals from Tindill, set them on their way to a resounding 5–2 victory. Two days later, at Stockport, a brace of goals from Jordan helped them to another win, three goals to one. The same team gave a poor display against Halifax Town, but still brought off a victory with goals by Thompson and Tindill. A great start to the season with a hundred per cent record after five games, but the Rovers were brought down to earth when Stockport County paid them a return visit, when Todd, Thompson and Stirland were out injured. Owens, the replacement for Todd, scored after three minutes but was then injured, and remained a passenger for the rest of the game. Although they battled away, the previous week's scoreline was reversed in favour of Stockport.

This loss turned out to be their only defeat until the turn of the year. Victory followed victory as the goals flowed, particularly from the feet of Clarrie Jordan, who scored three hat–tricks in four games in October. It was in October that Syd Bycroft decided to resign from the Doncaster Borough Police and become a full–time footballer. Jack Kirkaldie had replaced Tindill at outside right, otherwise the team remained unchanged. Although Darlington took a point off them at the beginning of November they returned to winning ways, and by the end of that month the table showed the Rovers at the top with a lead of two points over Chester, with Rotherham United two points further behind.

The Saturday before Christmas brought Rotherham United to Belle Vue. In icy conditions before around 21,000 spectators a hard fought game ended with a goal apiece, Owens having scored in the second half to equalise a first half goal by Jack Shaw. The three matches over the Christmas period produced maximum points; Corbett had replaced the injured Wooldridge and Owens, Heydon, Mitcheson and Marriott came in for other injured players.

The New Year opened, at Belle Vue, with that rare type of game, a goalless draw, to one of the bottom clubs – New Brighton.

Clarrie Jordan – prolific scorer.
Rovers' record number of 42 League goals
1946/47 season.

The next League game also surprised the Rovers' supporters when another lowly club, Halifax Town, surprisingly beat the Rovers by scoring four goals – the only time during the season that the club conceded that many in one match. Swallow put through his own goal to give Halifax the lead after two minutes, but Maddison equalised twenty minutes later after Thompson had missed a penalty. Todd put the Rovers in front five minutes after half–time, but in the last half hour the Rovers were hit for three goals, although Swallow had been injured.

This defeat seemed to inject renewed life into the team. They went to Crewe and came away with a clear three goals victory and followed that up with a real thumping of Carlisle United. Nine goals were put past the poor unfortunate Jones in the Carlisle goal, six of them in the second half. All the forwards got among the goals with Jordan leading the way with three. February brought snow and ice ruling out the playing of any games during that month.

In March the Government requested that the F.A. cut out mid–week games in the interests of the industrial drive following the end of the war. With no floodlights, all mid–week matches were played in the afternoon thereby causing some people to take time off from work. Whilst the clubs feared that all their efforts would come to nought if the F.A. cancelled promotion and relegation by insisting on the season finishing on the original date of May the 3rd, the F.A., in their wisdom, extended the season until June the 14th. Relief all round!

The Rovers resumed playing on the 1st of March, at Birkenhead, outplaying Tranmere Rovers to the tune of five goals to three. But scorelines can be deceptive, for although outplayed for most of the game, Tranmere actually led three times and were leading 3–2 with only five minutes left, the Rovers having scorned innumerable scoring chances. But it all came right in those last five minutes as first Todd, then two minutes later, Kirkaldie with a header, and finally in the last minute, Maddison, all made amends for earlier missed chances. Two games during the following week gave the club's fans a goal feast as first five were put past Darlington, and then eight versus Barrow, without a reply from their opponents. All the forwards scored against Barrow, the second time this had happened during the season. So the Rovers rolled on, putting win after win behind them, but they could not fully shake off Rotherham United, their only worthwhile challenger.

Late in March there was an unfortunate incident after the home game with Gateshead when the crowd gathered round the players' tunnels at the end of the game to congratulate the team as they left the pitch. A perimeter wall collapsed injuring the referee, Mr Porter and ten year old Ralph Scotting. Both were taken to Doncaster Infirmary whilst the boy's elder brother, William, also collapsed and had to receive treatment. Two Rovers players, Maddison, his right leg injured by the falling brickwork, and Stirland, his right forearm injured, also had to be treated. It was only twelve months since the Burnden Park disaster at Bolton, yet the authorities took no action.

Jordan won this heading duel with two of the Crewe defenders,

From the three games over Easter, the Rovers gained five points, dropping one at home to Crewe Alexandra. But with a twelve point lead over neighbours Rotherham United, the Rovers' promotion now seemed assured, although mathematically it was not over, nine points still being required from their last seven games as a guarantee. Rotherham had three games in hand, with the Rovers having to visit Millmoor.

Ferguson went down with tonsillitis, so that Bill Lambton had to play in the Easter matches, and some players had other niggling injuries. But the same team played in five of the last seven games, with Swallow replacing the injured Harry Tomlinson for the last two games.

A home point was lost to Lincoln City and Rotherham United won. The Rovers went to Southport and hit them for five with two goals from Jordan equalling Tommy Keetley's record of forty goals in a season previously set in 1928-29. Rotherham only drew at Rochdale leaving them twelve points in arrears. But the next match was the big one, at Millmoor. An all- ticket crowd of 20,000, including 5000 from Doncaster, saw an even game that looked like ending in a draw of two goals each, when in the last minute Ferguson let a harmless-looking shot from Jack Shaw slip through him into the net to give Rotherham the victory. Although this "four pointer" put Rotherham ten points behind, they were running out of matches as the Rovers only needed four points from their last four games, with their superior goal average being worth a point.

Clarrie Jordan scored the goal that beat Keetley's record, in the next match - against Chester - with Tommy Keetley himself being there to see it, and to congratulate Clarrie on the feat after the match. Rotherham were still hanging on with a win over Wrexham but the Rovers wrapped the Championship up with a two goal win over Southport to give them a new record points total for the Division of 69. Two points from Bradford City meant they had beaten Tottenham Hotspur's Football League record of 70 points.

The final game of the season, at home to York City, was perhaps an anti-climax. A large crowd gathered, hoping to see the team score the six goals needed to beat the all-time scoring record for a season of 128 goals.

But it was not to be, in fact, there were no goals at all, only the second time the Rovers had failed to score throughout the season. At half-time Mr.W.C. Cuff, the League President, presented the Division 3 North Championship Shield to Paul Todd, and medals to all the players.

The Rovers consistency throughout the season had been amazing, only twelve points being dropped throughout a campaign that was played out in every conceivable weather condition. Truly, the players could be classed as men for all seasons! Only twenty players were used, thirteen of them qualifying to receive medals. Bob McFarlane and Ralph Maddison were the only ever-presents, but Syd Bycroft and Clarrie Jordan each only missed one game. Jordan set up a new club record by scoring 42 League goals and the team also set a new one by scoring 123 goals.

The League records beaten by the club for the 42 game season were:-
1. Most points – 72. 2.
Most successive Away League wins – 7 (from Jan 22 to April 19).
3. Most away wins in a season – 18.
4. Smallest number of defeats – equalled with 3.
5. Most wins in a season – 33.

The F.A.Cup had also provided some thrills for the club. Accrington Stanley surprised everyone when they came to Belle Vue in the 1st Round and took a two goal lead after fifty-two minutes.

Mr. W. C. Cuff, President of the Football League, presents the Third Division (Northern) championship shield to Paul Todd, Doncaster Rovers' captain.

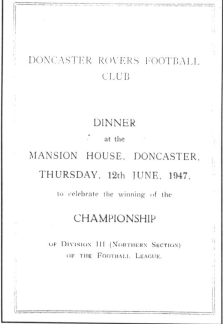

DONCASTER ROVERS FOOTBALL CLUB

DINNER
at the
MANSION HOUSE, DONCASTER,
THURSDAY, 12th JUNE, 1947,
to celebrate the winning of the

CHAMPIONSHIP
OF DIVISION III (NORTHERN SECTION)
OF THE FOOTBALL LEAGUE.

Thompson pulled one back after seventy–one minutes but there was only three minutes left when Todd got the equaliser. In the midweek replay the Rovers put Stanley firmly in their place with a hat–trick from Kirkaldie and one goal apiece from Todd and Jordan. A win at Oldham, who missed a penalty just before time, with goals from Jordan and Maddison, after they had been one goal down, gave them a home tie with First Division Portsmouth. The Rovers were always behind, going two goals down in the first eighteen minutes. Fighting back, Kirkaldie got one back before half– time, but Jack Froggatt's second goal of the match gave Portsmouth a third after an hour, but still fighting, Todd scored a second for the Rovers thirteen minutes from the end. Despite constant pressure from the homesters the Pompey defence held out to move into the next round.

With an average League attendance of 15,260, easily a record for the club, the portents were for even bigger crowds in Division 2. This would hopefully, give the club more purchasing power in the transfer market, and enable them to compete in the higher sphere. A profit of £4,635 was made on the season, and the directors declared a dividend of seven and a half per cent should be paid.

Jackie Bestall spent the summer of 1947 travelling thousands of miles throughout the country, and even to Ireland. But every player he enquired about was overpriced, the usual fee to be quoted being £10,000 (the record fee at this time being £15,500 that Derby County paid to Morton for Billy Steel). This figure was way above the Rovers' capabilities, so the outcome was that no new players were signed to add to the twenty–nine retained from the previous season.

The same team that played in the last two Third North games opened the season in Division 2, a Maddison goal giving them a point against Southampton.

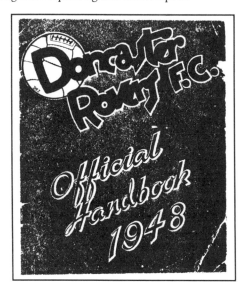

Two defeats away from home followed before the return game against the other promoted side, Cardiff City, gained them another point in a two–all draw. Three wins from the next four games gave some confidence that the team had found their feet. But six defeats from seven games from late September to early November – the other a goalless draw – without the team scoring a goal plummeted them down to the relegation zone. Twice they had finished games with ten men, when Jordan and then Wooldridge were injured. The form of the players who had won the Third North Championship so convincingly had been extremely disappointing. Paul Todd was one to be dropped leading to him, and Owens, asking for transfers, requests that were refused on the grounds that all the players were required.

Meanwhile a win was recorded over West Bromwich Albion, one of the better teams, with two goals from Frank Mitcheson. The next home game, against Plymouth Argyle, was also won with goals from Mitcheson and Todd after the introduction of a new player, Alf Calverley, who had been signed during the week from Preston North End for a club record fee. The second half of this match was broadcast on the radio to a wider audience – a first for the Rovers.

December brought only three points from five games. It also heralded their heaviest defeat of the season, 6–1 at Southampton. A youngster signed from the R.A.F., Pat Gillespie, made his debut at centre forward, Jordan being injured. The newcomer scored the Rovers' only goal and never played in the first team again during the rest of the season. At Christmas, Ken Hardwick replaced the injured Ferguson and kept his place for the rest of the season. Into the new Year and a loss to Bury brought changes. Dave Miller was signed from Derby County and made his debut at West Ham United, whilst in the same game, Harry Tomlinson made his first team comeback after his serious injury the previous May. This match was also lost and drastic changes were implemented. Bycroft was dropped, Swallow was swapped for Walter Bennett from Barnsley, Jack Hodgson was signed from Grimsby Town, and negotiations were started with Sheffield Wednesday for the transfer of Jordan. A one goal victory over Chesterfield ensued, scored by Bennett. The transfer of Jordan went through a few days later, the Rovers getting Arnold Lowes and a fee in return.

February opened with a one goal defeat at Millwall, the bottom club, Lowes missing a penalty that would have gained Doncaster a point. Three points from games against the 'Spurs and Leeds United seemed to give some hope of better things to help move them away from the relegation area. The team started March two points ahead of Millwall and three behind Nottingham Forest and Brentford, but only six points were gained from the last eleven games. Relegation was confirmed after the Plymouth Argyle match, and only 6,000 turned up for the last home game, against Luton Town. The team that played the second half of the season was an altogether different line-up to that of the first half.

The F.A.Cup reflected the Rovers season, for the only match was lost without reply, at Fulham, an average Second Division side, who took two of their chances. Sixteen of the twenty-two League matches at Belle Vue attracted crowds of over 20,000, an aggregate of 467,493 for an average of 22,261. All club records, but the team had been relegated!

Only twenty players were retained for the 1948-49 season. The departure of McFarlane (a pre-war player), Ferguson, Wooldridge, Kirkaldie, Lambton, Corbett, Heydon and Wands paved the way for new faces to be brought in. They were not the only departures, for Mr.Fletcher Hibbert, the chairman for many of his twenty-seven years on the Board, resigned during the summer and was replaced by Mr.H.Butler. Bob McLean, the trainer, also departed and was succeeded by Jimmy Milne, the former Preston North End, half back.

Syd Goodfellow was signed from Chesterfield, Ken Reeve from Mansfield Town, Len Hainsworth from Rotherham United and Jack Jones from Wrexham, to fill some of the gaps left by the summer clear out. A steady start was made to the season, although the goalscoring department was once again not the best part of the team. Bert Tindill was given his chance taking it with both feet, his introduction coinciding with a run of twelve games without defeat. This time it was Hull City and Rotherham United setting the pace at the top, and the Rovers had already recorded a new record attendance when Hull City, with Raich Carter as player-manager, visited Belle Vue on October the 2nd.

A crowd of 37,099 turned up to see Hull lose their first point of the season in a goalless draw. Halfway through this run, in late October, George Antonio was bought from Derby County and replaced Bennett. He scored on his debut at Darlington adding to a hat-trick from Reeve and a goal from Todd, as the Rovers went 'nap', before Darlington's record crowd, with both teams fighting to keep up with the leading pack.

January and February saw the club lose ground in the promotion race as Hull City and Rotherham United forged ahead on their own leaving the rest trailing in their wake. A late run of success from the middle of March, including a win at Hull, put the Rovers in third place at the end of the season, twelve points behind Rotherham United, who in turn were three behind Hull City.

The F.A. Cup once again only lasted one round, when the team went to Valley Parade. Calverley gave the Rovers the lead after a quarter of an hour, but two goals in three minutes gave Bradford City a lead at half-time. Hawksworth extended the lead two minutes after half-time, but a brilliant solo goal by Antonio reduced the arrears with Reeve equalising a quarter of an hour from the end. Finally a late penalty, after Hodgson handled, gave the final result to Bradford City.

Early in April 1949 a momentous announcement was made to the football world at large – and to the Rovers' supporters in particular – by Mr W.G.Dickinson, the club secretary, to the effect that they had agreed a fee of £8000 with Huddersfield Town for the transfer of Peter Doherty, the Irish international. He would take over as manager from Jackie Bestall on May 18th and also carry on playing.

DONCASTER ROVERS

DOHERTY

In early May came sadder news, from Italy, when word came through that on May the 4th, whilst returning from a match in Portugal, the plane carrying the Torino team had crashed at Superja, in the hills above Turin. Among the many dead was Leslie Lievesley, their coach, the same Rossington man who started his career with the Rovers.

Thirty-one players were retained for 1949–50, almost the entire professional staff, because it was felt that Doherty would want to see what talent was available, and as the retained list had to be out before he took over, this seemed reasonable. Two of the five not retained were Jones and Archer.

A loss of £7,066 was reported for the season mainly due to the club being a buyer, rather than a seller of players. But even so, Mr.Butler promised that should Peter Doherty need money it would be found. However, Doherty started with a team of players already on the books, for the first game at Valley Parade. A goal down at half-time, Doherty scored his new club's first goal of the season with Antonio getting a winner to give the player-manager a winning start. In fact they won five of the first seven games, the other two being draws, before going to Darlington, where they lost a hard-fought game by the odd goal. They also lost their place at the top of the table to Gateshead, on goal average.

Meanwhile Doherty, who had suffered a cracked shoulder-blade at Southport and was therefore unable to play, had gone over to Ireland looking for players. He came back with Len Graham, a twenty-three year old full back from Brantwood F.C. of Northern Ireland.

In October two successive goalless draws led to calls for a goalscorer to be signed, for although the team commanded the midfield play, nobody seemed to be able to finish off the fine approach work with any regularity; whilst the defence kept conceded goals to a minimum, goals at the other end were required to win the extra points. Already the team had drawn half of their games.

Doherty was now back to fitness and returned to score the two goals that beat Mansfield Town at Field Mill, and then guided the team to a good win over Accrington Stanley, to take the team back to the top of the Division with a two point lead over Crewe Alexandra. George Antonio, now getting on in years, was then sold to Mansfield Town for a fee around £7000, money that would be useful when it came to further acquisitions.

Early in November, Doherty went back to Ireland to sign twenty-two year old Bert Anderson from Derry City, and the Rovers kept picking up the points to keep their nose in front at the top of the table. Christmas proved to be a lean time though, when only two points were gained (from draws) from the three holiday games. At this stage, Doherty decided to move for an experienced goalscoring forward and plumped for Ray Harrison, a centre forward from Burnley, for a record fee. He made his debut on New Year's Eve, against Southport, and contributed a goal to add to the two apiece from Todd and Doherty.

The next League game – following a fine F.A.Cup win at Reading – produced one of the best attendances of the season, and saw Doherty score a hat-trick to gain the points from Stockport County. The following week nearly 31,000 turned up to see a goal from Harrison send Rotherham United back to Millmoor empty-handed.

Peter Doherty by this time had organised nursery sides throughout South Yorkshire and in the Newcastle area of the North-East, to keep a constant supply of young talented footballers flowing to Belle Vue. Obviously it was a long term policy, but he vigorously pursued it whilst carrying on the short term aim of gaining promotion. He was also ahead of his time in regard to a form of loan players. He decided to release some of the younger professionals, letting them go to a Midland League team, on condition that when he wanted them back they would be free to return to the Rovers. This enabled a player to gain experience, and also profited the receiving club. The first one released under this scheme was Charlie Spedding, who went to Newark until the end of the season.

The Rovers were now at the top of the Division, and they did not relinquish this top spot for the rest of the season.

The Rovers' may not have won Cup glory (losing at Blackpool), but they won the greatest prize – promotion!
.......despite a last minute 'hiccup' at home to Lincoln City

Only once were they caught, when they lost at home to Mansfield Town. Gateshead reached their points total of fifty-one but the Rovers had two games in hand so there was no danger of them falling away. They did, however, only get four points from their last four matches, but finished two points ahead of Gateshead. They had drawn (17) nearly as many as they had won (19) but promotion had been gained, in the first season with Peter Doherty at the helm. Their reward was a civic reception at the Mansion House and then a fortnight's tour of Ireland, where they were to play five matches.

In the F.A.Cup the Rovers enjoyed a good deal of success. Starting with a resounding win over New Brighton, they received a visit from Mansfield Town. A second goal from Todd put them into the 3rd Round and a visit to Reading, and new territory for the Rovers. A great start by the Rovers, with a goal by Todd in the first minute, gave them the edge until half-time. Three minutes after the break, Doherty increased the lead, but Reading fought back in great style to equalise with two goals in five minutes from their centre forward, Blackman. But it only took another five minutes for Todd, after good work by Doherty, to give the lead back to the Rovers, who then held out to the final whistle for a well deserved victory.

Blackpool was the next venue. Not for a holiday, but to tackle the First Division club with their collection of international stars – Farm, Matthews, Mortensen and the rest. The Rovers set about their task with gusto, taking command for the first twenty minutes, but the first goal went to the home team on the half hour when McIntosh, through sheer persistence, chased a long ball to the goal-line, and hooked it past Hardwick. Nothing daunted the Rovers proceeded to give as good as they got, but on the hour McKnight picked up a loose ball and shot in to put the Tangerines two up. The Rovers at this juncture threw everything forward, eventually gaining a penalty when Goodfellow was fouled. Doherty, the penalty-taker, seldom missed and put the Rovers back in with a chance, with eighteen minutes to go. But Blackpool's defence held out as they had done throughout the game, apart from conceding the earlier penalty. A Blackpool newspaper congratulated the Rovers on their football and the fact that a Third Division team could present such a magnificent show against a top-class club.

At the end of the season a party of fifteen players with Directors and officials left on Friday May the 5th, for Bray in the Republic of Ireland. After a weekend of sightseeing they faced their first match on the Monday, against Shamrock Rovers at Dalymount Park, Dublin. Goals by Todd and Harrison gave the Rovers a win by two goals to one. It was the first match that Shamrock Rovers had lost to a touring side. Two days later they met the League of Ireland Cup Winners Transport F.C., at Bray.

Having suffered a few injuries, the Rovers turned out a side with a number of changes that saw Goodfellow at centre forward. Although on top for a large part of the game, the Rovers missed many chances paying for it late in the game when Transport scored the only goal of the game. Travelling up to Belfast they met Glentoran on the Saturday. Being Peter Doherty's old club, there was the biggest crowd of the tour – approaching 12,000 – to see the 'old boy' score two goals, plus one from Tindill, as the Rovers ran out 3-1 winners. On Monday, they tackled Coleraine, coming away with a 4-1 victory with goals from Todd (2), Calverley and Harrison. Their final game, on Thursday, was at Londonderry against a representative North-West of Ireland XI captained by Kevin Doherty, Peter's brother. Kevin scored a goal for the Irish, but the Rovers replied with three from Todd and one apiece from Tindill and Harrison. The Rovers party arrived home on Saturday, May the 20th, after a pleasant and successful tour.

The battle for promotion had been achieved at considerable cost, both in wages and transfer fees. The average attendance had been good at 17,901 but Peter Doherty was asking for 20,000 to help pay for his plans with the nurseries, and the advancement of the club. A loss of £4,450 was reported on the season putting the club in debt to the tune of thirteen and a half thousand pounds. There had also been considerable expenditure on a new ground at Thorne for the 'A' and 'B' teams, who were operating in the Yorkshire and Doncaster Senior Leagues.

The professional staff had been cut by a third when the retained list came out, only twenty-three players being kept on. Among those released were Arthur Stevenson and Harry Tomlinson. But Doherty had no intention of running two professional teams with such a small staff, and the first legacy of the tour to Ireland came with the signing of Chris Giles and Kit Lawlor from Drumcondra. Bobby Herbert was recruited from a junior club in Scotland, Walter Jones from Blackpool, Tommy Martin from Stirling Albion and Alan Wakeman from Aston Villa. Evidently, to pay for all this activity, Paul Todd was allowed to go to Blackburn Rovers, plus Jackie Bestall, in July, for a fee of £10,000.

The start to their Second Division life could not have been harder. Of the first nine games seven were away. However, undaunted they set about their task under the captaincy of Doherty, with splendid intention. They were unfortunate to lose the first game at Leeds United but of their next eight games, two at home, they won three and drew five. This put them in seventh place coming to the end of September. A magnificent return from a difficult programme, achieved with a minimum of changes in the team. Herbert Rouse had started the season at right back but was replaced by Hainsworth, Tommy Martin was injured against West Ham United thereby paving the way for Kit Lawlor to make his mark in English football.

The tenth game, at home to second placed Blackburn Rovers, was lost by the odd goal. Then, a week later they met the leaders, Manchester City, at Belle Vue, one of Doherty's former clubs. Almost thirty–three thousand people packed into the ground, and saw a magnificent match in which Manchester City had a superb first half scoring three times through inside left, George Smith. The Rovers had hardly troubled Bert Trautmann, the City's German goalkeeper, but within six minutes of the start of the second half Harrison hit a first–time shot past him. A minute later the goalkeeper was again picking the ball out of the net as Lawlor shot in.

The crowd were now on their mettle and got behind the team. Four minutes later, the Rovers were awarded a penalty when Rigby handled. Doherty, as sure as ever, made no mistake. Another four minutes and unbelievably, the Rovers were in the lead, when Doherty placed a shot from twenty–five yards wide of Trautmann. Four goals in nine minutes and more could have followed so much on top were the Rovers. But the match ended with a 4-3 scoreline in favour of the Rovers, and dropped the City to second place. A remarkable fact of the game was that all seven goals were scored at the Rossington end – the Spion Kop.

Yet, in the next three games the team only gained one point, from Cardiff City, when Arnold Lowes was badly injured, so badly as it turned out, that he never played football again. This brought Walter Jones into the team, a place he secured for the rest of the season.

November displayed their Jekyll and Hyde character perfectly. A home win over next to bottom Grimsby Town, plus an away victory at promotion–chasing Birmingham City – with Bert Anderson making his debut in place of the injured Len Graham – followed. But a loss at home to one of the bottom clubs, Chesterfield, came next, which pushed the Rovers down to tenth place, followed by a trip to London where they beat middle–of––the–table Queens Park Rangers.

A heavy defeat at Preston was followed by an eight goal thriller against Leeds United, with the goals equally shared between the clubs, and Leeds missed a penalty; for the Rovers, Doherty scored a hat–trick. Fifteen goals in total in two matches, and yet the next one – at West Ham United – was goalless, with Ken Hardwick getting rave notices. A double over Barnsley during a foggy Christmas, left the Rovers in eighth place.

A preponderance of home games to the end of the season was not utilised to any degree, when only half of the matches were won. The chief benefit to the club was the introduction at right back of a young man from Rossington, Brian Makepeace. He replaced Hainsworth at Blackburn, did so well that he kept his place to the end of the season, with the result that Hainsworth was released. Three weeks earlier Doherty had suffered a broken leg in the home game against Swansea Town, which put him out for the rest of the season. Another fightback at Manchester City from a two goal deficit at half–time ended in a three–all draw. A five–two defeat of Luton Town on Good Friday actually promised a bid for the promotion places, but two defeats over the rest of the holiday period put paid to that.

All told, a finishing place of eleventh was a fine result upon their return to the higher sphere. The gates averaged a very encouraging 22,799, and the scene was set for further progress.

In the F.A.Cup 3rd Round, they faced Rotherham United and an all–ticket crowd of 22,000 at Millmoor. They quietened the homesters after twenty minutes with a Dave Miller penalty, but Rotherham, who were going great guns at the top of Division 3 North, fought back to score twice through Danny Williams and Jack Shaw and so restrict the Rovers to just one cup game. The Rovers did reach the final of the Sheffield County Cup however, with wins over Barnsley and Rotherham United, only to narrowly lose to Sheffield Wednesday, a relegated team from the First Division.

The season was wound up with a game played under the Festival of Britain title. A series of matches for all League clubs was arranged against a variety of foreign clubs, to celebrate the Festival of Britain which was being held to show the rest that Britain had recovered their place in the industrial world. The Rovers opponents were to be Racing Club de Bruxelles of Belgium and Floriana of Malta. The match with Racing Club was called off because of the weather but the match against Floriana produced an emphatic win by five clear goals, three of them from Harrison.

An outstanding feature of the season was the international recognition given to four of the players. Northern Ireland chose Peter Doherty for the last of his caps, and Len Graham for his first; the Republic of Ireland capped Chris Giles and Kit Lawlor.

A profit of £1,552 for the season was reported, but Peter Doherty now upped his demands on the supporters with a call for average gates of 30,000, although he appreciated the support given already. But money was needed for his progressive policies and that had to come through the turnstiles.

Having retained thirty–one of his thirty–four professionals, Doherty evidently thought he had the making of a successful team. He added Jimmy Doherty from Airdrieonians and Jimmy McKee and Tommy Ewing, both from junior football in Scotland. Doherty had been successful so far in management but he was now seeing the other side of the coin.

Rovers started the new season at Sheffield Wednesday, with virtually the same players that had finished the previous season, and whilst the defence was only adjusted because of injury, the forward line saw many changes, not only due to injuries but loss of form as well. Dissatisfaction soon reared its head when Doherty asked for a transfer back to Scotland in early October, and although he had a run in the side through the next two months, he was transferred to Third Lanark at Christmas for a fee of £5000. Kit Lawlor went home to Dublin in October and started job hunting, insisting he was not coming back to Doncaster.

Giles followed suit early in November because the club refused to give him home leave to see his sick wife. He failed to turn up for the match at Coventry City in which he had been selected to play, and turned up in Dublin saying he had taken "French Leave". The club imposed a suspension on both players, effectively stopping them playing football anywhere else. On December the 3rd both players returned to Doncaster and resumed their careers, the whole episode being quietly swept under the carpet.

Meanwhile, the club had been playing football with a fair modicum of success. In a division in which all five South Yorkshire clubs were competing they faced stiff local competition. Newcomers Sheffield Wednesday and Rotherham United were fighting with Sheffield United and others for the top places, whilst the Rovers and

Barnsley occupied middle of the table places. From the first eighteen games the Rovers gained twenty points, but a disastrous spell of twelve matches with only one win saw them drop into the relegation area. Their fighting spirit then came to the fore, to gain twelve points from the next eight games, and guarantee Division 2 football in sixteenth place, but only four points above the relegated club.

Doherty's policy of using home-grown talent was coming to fruition with young players coming through. Tommy Brown deputised for Jones, Bill Paterson replaced Syd Bycroft, and Arthur Adey, Bobby Herbert, Tommy Ewing and Jack Teasdale were all given a run.

For the first time in their history the Rovers reached the 5th Round of the F.A.Cup. A hard won victory over Cheshire League team, Buxton, in the 3rd Round was followed by a resounding 4-1 win at Ayresome Park over First Division Middlesbrough. A second minute goal by Lawlor let the Rovers take command, with further goals coming from the same player, plus Harrison and Tindill. Middlesbrough's reply was scored in the last minute. A visit to a top First Division club, Portsmouth, came in the 5th Round, but here the Rovers met their Waterloo with a defeat by four clear goals.

During the season the club upgraded their training floodlights to match standard, by installing four towers with twelve lamps on each, thereby covering the whole playing area. They hoped to recoup the cost of around £2,000 by playing attractive friendly games. On March the 4th the Rovers made modern football history by becoming the first club in the North, and the first outside London, to stage a floodlit game, when the Scottish club Hibernians visited Belle Vue. A crowd of 18,474 saw an entertaining game end in a win by three goals to the Scots.

During the close season of 1952 the Rovers again paid a visit to Ireland. Wins were recorded over Drumcondra and Cork City, and a three-all draw resulted with Waterford, whilst the last match against Glentoran was lost by the odd goal in five.

Giles and Lawlor failed to report back to Belle Vue for the coming season. Giles was never to return, but the Rovers retained his registration, before eventually transferring him to Aldershot in August 1953. Thirty-two players were retained for 1952-53 the most notable absentee being Syd Bycroft, who was given a free transfer. But, in fact, he retired from playing and joined the backroom staff at Belle Vue as chief coach. A bad start by the team, three defeats in the first four games, saw them struggling at the bottom of the table from the beginning.

An Agreement

An Agreement made the **First** day of **July** 19**53** between **William Geoffrey Dickinson** of **27, Hall Gate,** **Doncaster** in the COUNTY OF **York** the Secretary of and acting pursuant to Resolution and Authority for and on behalf of the **Doncaster Rovers** FOOTBALL CLUB of **Belle Vue Ground, Doncaster.** (hereinafter referred to as the Club) of the one part and **Kenneth Hardwick** of **108, Shadyside, Hexthorpe, Doncaster,** in the COUNTY OF **York.** Professional Football Player (hereinafter referred to as the Player) of the other part **Whereby** it is agreed as follows :—

1. The Player hereby agrees to play in an efficient manner and to the best of his ability for the Club.

2. The Player shall attend the Club's ground or any other place decided upon by the Club for the purposes of or in connection with his training as a Player pursuant to the instructions of the Secretary, Manager, or Trainer of the Club, or of such other person, or persons, as the Club may appoint. [This provision shall not apply if the Player is engaged by the Club at a weekly wage of less than One Pound, or at a wage per match.]

3. The Player shall do everything necessary to get and keep himself in the best possible condition so as to render the most efficient service to the Club, and will carry out all the training and other instructions of the Club through its representative officials.

4. The Player shall observe and be subject to all the Rules, Regulations and Bye-Laws of The Football Association, and any other Association, League, or Combination of which the Club shall be a member. And this Agreement shall be subject to any action which shall be taken by The Football Association under their Rules for the suspension or termination of the Football Season, and if any such suspension or termination shall be decided upon the payment of wages shall likewise be suspended or terminated, as the case may be.

5. The Player shall not engage in any business or live in any place which the Directors (or Committee) of the Club may deem unsuitable.

9. In consideration of the observance by the said player of the terms, provisions and conditions of this Agreement, the said **William Geoffrey Dickinson** on behalf of the Club hereby agrees that the said Club shall pay to the said Player the sum of £ **10. 0. 0.** per week from **1st July, 1953.** to **31st July, 1953.** and £ **12. 0. 0.** per week from **1st August, 1953.** to **1st May, 1954.** and £10. per week from the 2nd May, 1954. to 30th June, 1954.

10. This Agreement (subject to the Rules of The Football Association) shall cease and determine on **30th June, 1954.** unless the same shall have been previously determined in accordance with the provisions hereinbefore set forth.

Fill in any other provisions required

The player shall receive £2. extra when playing in the First Team and shall receive all bonuses allowed by the football League.

As Witness the hands of the said parties the day and year first aforesaid

Signed by the said **William Geoffrey Dickinson** and **Kenneth Hardwick**

In the presence of

(Signature)

(Occupation) **Assistant Secretary,**

(Address) **Belle Vue Ground, Doncaster.**

Kenneth Hardwick (Player)

(Secretary)

A Football Player's lot in 1953 (part of a Rovers' Agreement)

In the match against Swansea Town, Alf Calverley was injured, this eventually necessitated his retirement from the game. The next match, at Lincoln City, Herbert Rouse broke a leg and Paterson injured an ankle that kept him out for all of September. Changes were made that did not bring much change of fortune. In fact, at the end of September a heavy defeat at Everton, for whom Tommy Eglington scored five times, rooted them securely in twenty-first place. Tommy Martin had moved to Nottingham Forest in October for a club record fee of £16,000, but the return of Kit Lawlor in November compensated. Gradually the team settled down and began to gain some points, and a lift up the table. In January a goalkeeping crisis hit the club when Hardwick contracted tonsillitis. Harry Gregg deputised against Blackburn Rovers but dislocated an elbow, and with no other goalkeeper available they signed an amateur, Freddie Kingshott, from Eastbourne, who played in two games until Hardwick was fit to take over.

The turn of the year saw a decided improvement in the results. Poor finishing had been their main problem throughout the season and in an effort to improve it Eddie McMorran was signed from Barnsley in March. Injuries to various players continued to dog them to the end of the season but the team finished the season in thirteenth place, a fine placing considering their start to the season.

The F.A.Cup sent the team to Highbury in front of the biggest crowd that a Rovers side had ever played before, 57,443. The occasion eventually proved too much for the players since although they were on top for the first twenty minutes, Arsenal ran out eventual winners by four clear goals.

Three floodlit friendlies were played against an International XI, Celtic and Djurgaardens from Sweden. Excellent crowds witnessed these games and generated revenue for the club, especially needed as the average attendance slumped to 15,324 for the season. A profit of £1,907 was shown in the balance sheet, which was due entirely to transfer fees received.

The retained list had thirty-five names on it with free transfers being given to Alf Calverley – retired – and Jack Hodgson, who joined the backroom staff as a coach. New signings included Johnny Mooney from Hamilton Academical, Paddy Gavin from Dundalk and Reece Nicholson.

The Rovers set off the new season at a cracking pace winning six of the first seven games plus one draw. Only one point dropped put them at the top of Division 2 for the first time in their history. Their away form, with a young winger Maurice Robinson showing up well, was tremendous with big wins at Notts.County and Brentford. Their gallop was stopped at Goodison Park however, before an enormous crowd of 58,110, where Everton overwhelmed them by four goals to one, after Rovers had first taken the lead. Doncaster continued to head the table until three defeats – at Bury, at home to Rotherham United, and away to Leicester City – knocked them down to fifth. Three successive wins then put them back into second place where they remained until Christmas, when a double defeat by Blackburn Rovers initiated a gradual slide down the table to a finishing place of twelfth; an average of nearly a point a game. One win and six draws from the last sixteen games was certainly a distinct contrast to their first half of the season form. Only twenty–two players were used, the defence being particularly stable until late in the season when Graham and Teasdale were injured and out for a lengthy spell. Peter Doherty did not play in any competitive match, which thereby signalled the end of his playing career.

Alick Jeffrey

In the F.A.Cup the Rovers reached the 5th Round again, without playing at home. The 3rd Round pitted them against First Division strugglers, Sunderland.

Against a team that included internationals Jimmy Cowan, Stan Anderson, Ray Daniel, George Aitken, Billy Bingham, Len Shackleton, Tommy Wright and Billy Elliott, the Rovers took command with two goals in the first half hour from McMorran and continued to press to the end of the game. A well merited win put them on the road to Plymouth for the 4th Round. Again, a double strike, this time by Tindill, gave them the win and a visit to Third Division South Leyton Orient in the 5th Round. This game was new territory for the Rovers never having played the Londonners in competitive football. It proved to be a disaster for the club, for although they held a fifteenth minute lead until half–time, through McMorran, they played from the second minute with Graham injured, and from the thirtieth minute with injuries to both Makepeace and Teasdale. Len Graham stayed on the pitch for the rest of the game with torn knee ligaments. Imagine that situation today! With such a depleted team the Rovers defence cracked three times under the pressure.

A number of floodlit friendlies were played including one against Wacker Sportklub from Vienna. Unfortunately fog put paid to the game after twenty–eight minutes. It had attracted a gate of over 17,000 but in general the novelty was beginning to wear off unless, the opponents were a top team.

Their good form in the League over most of the season ensured an increase in attendances to an average of 16,919. Dave Miller, Ray Harrison, Walter Jones, Arthur Adey, Tommy Brown and Maurice Robinson all left the club, with the only newcomer for 1954–55 being Jimmy Walker from Linfield.

The opening game was at Anfield against the relegated club, Liverpool. Before a near 50,000 crowd the Rovers held a half–time lead through Kit Lawlor, but were pegged back before Lawlor restored their lead three minutes later. Two goals from Rowley, to give him a hat–trick, in the last four minutes snatched some well–deserved points from the Merseysiders. In the home game against Fulham, Peter Doherty occasioned some surprise when he included fifteen year old Alick Jeffrey in the team, and a four–nil win made it a happy debut. Jeffrey, from Rawmarsh near Rotherham, although not yet sixteen, was a well built, strong lad who had been holding his own in the Midland League side, let alone the Junior side.

After the Bury game in October, Bill Paterson was transferred to Newcastle United, his replacement being Jim Lawlor, until the New Year when Charlie Williams was given his chance. Until the New Year the defence was shipping goals with a seven and four fives against them, and finished the season conceding a total of ninety five goals, one less than the worst record produced by Liverpool.

A new winger, Geoff Walker, was brought from Middlesbrough in December to improve the supply to the forwards. In the home game against Rotherham United there was the unusual spectacle of three Walkers in the side, although none of them were related, but the trio soon became familiar to the Rovers supporters. Also in December Kit Lawlor was transferred back to Ireland, letting Alick Jeffrey back into the side. A final placing of eighteenth was not what was looked forward to at the beginning of the season.

The F.A.Cup provided the main interest of a disappointing season. A good win at Watford in the 3rd Round, with two goals from Herbert Tindill, gave the team a tie at home to First Division Aston Villa. Alick Jeffrey, on his sixteenth birthday, could not provide the finish required on the day as the tie finished goalless.

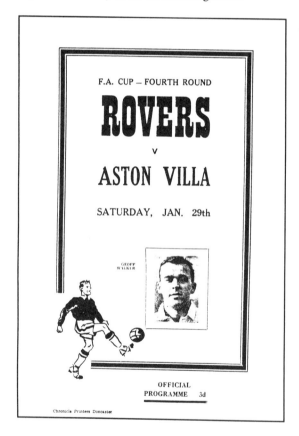

F.A. CUP – FOURTH ROUND

ROVERS

v

ASTON VILLA

SATURDAY, JAN. 29th

GEOFF
WALKER

OFFICIAL
PROGRAMME   3d

Chronicle Printers Doncaster

In the replay at Villa Park the Rovers led after eighteen minutes through Tindill, but the Villa went into the lead ten minutes after half-time. A goal from Mooney took the game into extra time, but no further goals came. The following Monday the teams met up again, at Maine Road Manchester. A goal from Jeffrey a minute before half-time gave the Rovers the lead, but an equaliser from Thompson took it into extra time again, and yet again no further addition to the score.

A week later they met one more, this time at Hillsbrough, Sheffield. Again the teams could not be separated and could not even score a goal between them, the match being abandoned at the end of ninety minutes because of bad light.

On the following day, at The Hawthorns, West Bromwich, the Rovers lasted the pace better taking a two goal lead after fifty minutes, through Jeffrey and Geoff Walker. The Villa got one back fourteen minutes from time but Jeffrey finally settled the matter with three minutes to go. Five hundred and ten minutes to split two teams, for the honour of playing Birmingham City in the 5th Round, four days later, at St. Andrew's. The Rovers may well have outlasted the Villa but all those games had taken their toll. They gave Birmingham a game, though, with a goal from Mooney sandwiched between two from Brown, for Birmingham, in the period ten minutes either side of half-time.

The only floodlit game to attract a decent crowd was the visit of Newcastle United, when Bill Paterson made his debut at centre half, under the Rovers' new floodlights. Even with names like Scoular, Milburn, Broadis, White and Mitchell, Newcastle found it hard to contain the home team, who ran out winners by seven goals to two, with Mooney getting a hat-trick.

At this time there was a decline in attendances throughout the League, and the Rovers were hit by a serious decline, down to an average of 12,385. Finances were getting tight.

An interesting aside during the season was Ken Hardwick's selection for the England Under-23 side - at the age of 30! Recognition was long overdue for him, but this situation was somewhat ridiculous.

With the success of Hungary over England, the televising of the World Cup from Switzerland, and the start of the European Cup, the continental influence invaded the English game both with tactics and fashion. The Rovers began the 1955-56 season with a new continental style strip of red shirts with a 'V' neck collar.

The Rovers started the campaign with the same players that finished the previous season. Results also followed a similar line so that only a decent home record kept them out of trouble. Results on their travels were horrendous, with sixty-six goals conceded, including one six and four fives, for an average of three goals per match. One bright spot was the double accomplished over promotion contenders Liverpool, at Easter. But the last six games after this period produced five defeats, which dropped them down to seventeenth place in the final table, well clear of the relegation places, but with only thirty-five points.

Only twenty-three players were used throughout the season. Harry Gregg had taken over in goal by the end, but the bulk of the defence stayed much the same throughout, with Jimmy Kilkenny and Morgan Hunt sharing one of the wing half positions with Bobby Herbert. The only serious injury victim was Jimmy Walker, who suffered his at Middlesbrough in mid-November, which led to him giving way to Eddie McMorran. A number of young players were blooded during the season, which seemed to augur well for the Rovers future because it was becoming clear that they could no longer compete in the transfer market for ready-made players. Another sign of the future was the use of floodlights becoming accepted by the authorities for competitive games. The Rovers first evening match under the 'lights at Belle Vue was against West Ham United in March.

A Second Division match
Doncaster Rovers versus Liverpool !

Despite their poor League form at the turn of the year, the Rovers summarily dismissed Nottingham Forest from the F.A.Cup by three clear goals, in order to meet the conquerors of League Champions Manchester United, Bristol Rovers at Eastville. Doncaster fought hard on a heavy ground to come away with a one-all draw and bring Bristol Rovers back to Belle Vue. The replay took place on an ice-bound pitch at below freezing temperature under floodlights, but nevertheless over 22,000 people attended to see Bert Tindill score the winning goal only three minutes from the end. This gave the Rovers a home tie against the Danny Blanchflower led team of Tottenham Hotspur. On a day of wind and snow the 'Spurs scored two goals in the first quarter of an hour in front of over thirty thousand spectators, and comfortably held on to their lead for the rest of the game.

One trophy came the team's way however, when they beat Rotherham United in the semi-final of the County Cup, and went on to a four goal victory over Sheffield United, the first time they had won the trophy since 1938.

Peter Doherty continued as manager of the Northern Ireland team with Eddie McMorran and Len Graham gaining more caps. Alick Jeffrey was capped for the England Amateur team, Barry Staton captained the England Youth team, and Jack Teasdale toured South Africa with an F.A.XI. Unfortunately, Teasdale suffered a bad knee injury on the tour that eventually finished his career at 27 years of age. The average attendance during the season was 12,414, thus halting the dramatic slide in crowds drifting away from the club.

The 1956-57 season saw an improvement all round. The team scored more goals, conceded fewer, gained more points and finished in fourteenth place. An experienced campaigner in Tommy Cavanagh was signed to captain the young team whilst departures included Bobby Herbert and Herbert Rouse. Two of the first three games were lost, but a run of nine games unbeaten put in fourth place. The run was halted at Swansea Town, but in the thirteen games played to that date, Alick Jeffrey had only missed scoring in two, and amassed fifteen goals.

Prospects for success were very bright, but then came disaster – for Jeffrey, for the Rovers, for England and ultimately for football. On October the 17th, playing for England Under-23 against France, at Ashton Gate, Bristol, Jeffrey's leg was badly broken. So badly that he was eventually paid off by insurance, with his career in the Football League at an end. Disaster for football? Certainly, for in the opinion of many who have seen all the stars of the post-war era, he would have become as great as Jimmy Greaves in the goalscoring stakes, and as big a star with a top club, as Duncan Edwards.

The Rovers home record kept them in the top half of the table, but their away form was non-existent, until the end of the year. Then from the turn of the year to the end of the season even their home results deserted them, and points were hard to come by – ten only coming from the last sixteen games. Twenty-two players were used during the season, six of them mostly youngsters not reaching double figures, and Jeffrey not adding to his early season games. So, remarkably, only fifteen players played during the bulk of the season. Alick Jeffrey's fifteen League goals still made him the club's top scorer, with Bert Tindill whose efforts came from thirty-one games.

In the F.A.Cup the team were drawn at home to the 1954 Cup Winners, West Bromich Albion. Tommy Cavanagh gave the Rovers a lead after ten minutes which they held for half an hour, before Bobby Robson equalised for the First Division side. The replay was won comfortably by the Albion with two goals from Ronnie Allen.

The support for the team remained on a constant level, being 12,389 for the season. Gregg and McMorran were capped by Northern Ireland, Jeffrey for England Under-23, and Barry Staton plus Mike Connolly for the England Under-18's. Departures from the club included Ken Hardwick, George Bell and Geoff Walker. The only newcomer of note was Walter Kelly from Bury, who started the season with ten of the previous season's players.

The first match at Millmoor was lost, and the first home game against Leyton Orient was won – with Billy Mordue making his debut, deputising at centre half for Asian 'flu victim, Charlie Williams. However, the next five matches ended in defeat, with Middlesbrough putting five past Gregg. The Rovers had only managed four goals during these first seven games, but the return game with Middlesbrough provided them with an odd goal in five win. An innovation this season was that floodlights could be used for the second half of matches, enabling clubs to kick-off at three o'clock during the winter instead of a quarter past two, as in past years. The next three months brought moderate success but the club were struggling at the wrong end of the table.

After the defeat at Ipswich in December, Harry Gregg was transferred to Manchester United for a club record fee of £25,000, and indeed the biggest fee ever paid for a goalkeeper. Ted Burgin was hurriedly signed from Sheffield United to replace Gregg, making his debut in a home win over local rivals Rotherham United. Both Christmas matches were lost to Charlton Athletic but Francis Callan, recently signed from Dundalk, made his debut at Huddersfield Town earning the Rovers a point with two goals. Jimmy Kilkenny went down with 'flu before this game, and it was mid-April before he was fit enough to come back.

At this stage the Rovers were next to bottom in the table. The next League game brought in a point from a draw against Grimsby Town in which Ted Burgin broke his collar bone.

Doherty went to Sheffield Wednesday and signed Dave McIntosh in time for the game at Stoke City. But consternation reigned among the Rovers supporters when it was learned that Peter Doherty was not at the Stoke City match, and had in fact resigned. This was made official on the Monday when a statement was made to that effect. No official explanation of the reasons for his departure were ever given, but various people spoke out and rumour abounded of a clash of personalities between Doherty and certain directors. The immediate repercussions lent some credence to the rumours when the secretary, of seventeen years, Geoff Dickinson, resigned on the day of the official announcement. The following day the honorary surgeon and director, J.Paterson Semple, followed suit.

The Board were now down to only eight members; assistant-secretary Derek Bestall took over the secretarial duties and Jack Hodgson and Syd Bycroft were put jointly in charge of the team until the end of the season. Their first match in control was against Bristol City, a fortnight later, managed by .... Peter Doherty. The Rovers won this confrontation by the odd goal in three, but then went twelve games without a victory, the twelfth being against bottom club Lincoln City, who had won their last match. The City team also won at Belle Vue, which put them one point behind the Rovers, who in turn were five points behind Notts County. The following week they went to Meadow Lane to meet the third club fighting relegation, Notts County, and came away with a win by five clear goals. The Rovers were still in with a chance if Lincoln City and Notts County slipped up with their games in hand. The Rovers only got a point in their last game against Ipswich Town, and Notts County got three points from their final two games. Incredibly, Lincoln City had actually won all their last six games, and by one point escaped relegation, a fate which had seemed a certainty at Easter. The two clubs going down to the new Division 3 were Notts.County and the Rovers.

The F.A.Cup provided the club with a chance to play the only League club that they had not met in competition, Chelsea, at Belle Vue. But they were no match for the First Division team, even though Cavanagh had a penalty saved, and the homesters lost by two goals. A number of new players had been signed in a late bid to escape from the relegation zone with a number having left, including Eddie McMorran, Bert Tindill (to Bristol City) and Walter Kelly. The average attendance dropped, as could be expected, to 11,132. The challenge now was to fight their way out of the new National Third Division, which was composed of former Third South and North clubs.

nly twenty–two players were retained for the club's first season in Division 3, ten were given free transfers and three, Roy Brown, Morgan Hunt and Reece Nicholson, were put on the transfer list. The chairman – H.A.Butler – together with fellow director Stanley Dixon resigned, leaving the board with only six members. Jack Hodgson and Syd Bycroft were to be relieved of their positions, as soon as a new manager was appointed. This was the aftermath of the drop into Division 3.

Jack Garnham took over as chairman of the Board, but there were no new members joining. Their first choice of manager fell to George Swindin, the manager of non–League Peterborough United, but he turned the post down. Despite the drop in status the board decided that they would pay top wages, £20 a week, to the first team players during the season, and £17 during the close season.

On June the 16th the appointment of 48 year old Jack Crayston the former Arsenal manager, was announced by the club. Syd Bycroft and Jack Hodgson reverted back to their old jobs of coach and trainer respectively, although Wally Ardron who had been appointed trainer towards the end of the previous season was also retained in that position. Early in the season Jack Hodgson was dismissed "as an economy measure".

Only one player of note, Malcolm Stephens, was signed in the close season. A good start was made to the season with three wins out of the first four matches, but misfortune wasn't far away as September and October brought a run of eight successive defeats. In six of these games the Rovers were goalless, but one game – at home to Plymouth Argyle – produced ten goals; unfortunately for the Rovers, six of them went to Plymouth. The four goals that the Rovers got were scored in the first half, to give them a four–two lead, but Plymouth took over after half–time putting four goals past Nimmo without reply. A week later Jim Fernie and Ron Sharp were signed from Arbroath for a combined fee of around £8,000. A win over Colchester United arrested the decline but six more consecutive defeats in November landed them in real trouble. Albert Minton was signed from Scunthorpe United to add some pep to the attack.

The second half of the season produced a better return of points, but not nearly enough to keep them out of the bottom four. So a second successive relegation (with Notts County) took them down to Division 4.

Not surprisingly the attendances plummeted, giving an average of 6,652, an unheard of low over the previous thirty years.

The F.A.Cup began at the 1st Round stage, and a meeting with non–League Consett, who were easily overcome by five clear goals. The 2nd Round took them to Tranmere Rovers where goals from Callan and Kilkenny gave them the advantage. Their next opponents – Bristol City – included old friends Tindill and Gordon Hopkinson, for their visit to Belle Vue. An injury to Makepeace reduced the Rovers to ten men for seventy minutes, with the result that the tie was lost by two clear goals.

In March 1959 Jack Crayston was appointed secretary–manager, when Derek Bestall left the club. Jackie Bestall, who had been chief scout, was then appointed team–manager.

A mass exodus of players took place in the close season, as Crayston and Bestall set about the task of building a side to get out of the bottom division. A number of new signings included experienced players Albert Broadbent, Tony Leighton and Lol Chappell.

A reasonable start was made to life at their new level, although they lost their first match, at Torquay United. Some topsy– turvy results were recorded during the first two months, but a heavy defeat at Gateshead led them into a lean time when ten games were lost out of fifteen played. Only a five–one hammering of wooden–spoon–ists Hartlepools United provided any relief. The New Year saw matters take a turn for the better, for a succession of wins and a fair number of goals was the result as the season wore on. Tony Leighton had a hat–trick against Carlisle United, and Peter Clark scored four goals at Hartlepools. This revival in the second half of the season pulled them away from the bottom four re–election places to a respectable final position of seventeenth.

The F.A.Cup brought old rivals to Belle Vue, when Gainsborough Trinity visited in the 1st Round. A thrilling match was only made palatable to Rovers supporters when the Rovers fought back after going three goals down with twenty–minutes to go. Two goals by Fernie and one by Chappell, the last with five minutes left gave them another chance. In the replay that chance came in the very first minute when Ronnie Walker shot in. No more goals were scored, and so the Rovers went through to meet Darlington in the 2nd Round. This match was decided in the first twenty–five minutes when

when all the five goals were scored. Sharp put the Rovers two up in two minutes and Chappell added a third on seventeen minutes. Darlington hit back to score two goals in two minutes, but were unable to add further to their total. The 3rd Round saw the Doncaster pitted against Bristol Rovers at Eastville. A goalless draw brought them back to Belle Vue, where, before the largest crowd of the season the Rovers of Bristol proved too strong for the locals.

With attendances going down again, to an average of 5,251, economies were the order of the day. The accent was placed on a successful Youth Policy, by grooming their own players, for the club were no longer able to afford fees.

Paddy Gavin, Peter Clark, Tony Cope and Ron Sharp were the players of note to leave the club at the end of the season. With only nineteen retained, several new men were signed, including Jack Haigh from Scunthorpe United and Carl Wilson from Gateshead.

A disastrous start to the season, in losing the first two games by an odd goal, led the club to appoint the Sheffield Wednesday left back, Norman Curtis, as player–manager.

Football League Division IV v PETERBOROUGH UTD. Tuesday, Sept. 20, 1960

His first match in charge, albeit at short notice, was even more disastrous, a 5–1 home defeat by Crystal Palace. Bottom of the entire League, and the signs were not good. A few changes in the team brought two away points from Southport and York City, and a home win over Exeter City raised the hopes of the supporters, but these were dashed by the return of only two points from the rest – six in all – of the September matches. The biggest humiliation was the double loss to newcomers Peterborough United, losing by an odd goal at home, but crashing badly away when losing six goals with only two in reply. They had now dropped back into the bottom four. A reasonable spell of success followed to the end of the year spoilt only by five goal defeats at Aldershot and Crystal Palace. But at least they were out of the danger zone at this stage.

The revival continued during the second half of the season to such an extent that four away wins were recorded, an unusual occurrence during the years of that period. In February, John Ballagher was signed from Sheffield Wednesday, in exchange for John Meredith, and the newcomer made an immediate impact on the forward line, climaxed by the last game of the season when he scored a hat–trick in a six clear goal win over Crewe Alexandra.

This rounded the season off and left the club in eleventh place with almost a point per game. Barry Swallow, son of Ernie of 1946–47 fame, Ray Veall and Tony Wales – all products of the club's Youth Policy – were introduced to the side during the latter part of the season and proved their worth.

In the F.A.Cup 1st Round, the Rovers were leading Chesterfield by three goals to one, at Saltergate, with eight minutes to go. Then a Chesterfield fightback was rewarded with two goals in two minutes to take the tie to Belle Vue. Unfortunately, home advantage didn' do the Rovers any good as they went down to a goal by Foley.

A new competition, the Football League Cup, was introduced during this season. The Rovers, coming in at the 2nd Round stage, drew Second Division Stoke City at home, took command of the game and ran out comfortable winners. Their next opponents, Chelsea, provided stiffer opposition and inflicted a severe defeat – by seven clear goals – on an outclassed Rovers side that was starting its revival in the League. One consolation though was a crowd approaching 10,000.

With the average attendance falling even further, to a crippling 4,754 per game, further economies had to be made. The first victim was the Reserve team which was disbanded for season 1961–62, leaving the Northern Intermediate League team as the only available back-up to the first eleven. The snag here was the fact that the Juniors were limited to, maximum aged, nineteen year–

olds. Although the playing staff was much reduced in numbers, the question arose of keeping non-regular players match-fit.

No doubt these happenings had a bearing on player-manager Curtis' decision to resign in July. Jack Crayston also left the club during the summer, with Tom Garnett from Crewe Alexandra taking over as general manager-secretary. At the beginning of August Danny Malloy took over as player- manager, having been secured from Cardiff City for a fee of £10,000.

Long-service players Brian Makepeace, Ron Walker, Billy Mordue, Jimmy Kilkenny and Maurice White also departed the scene as did more recent signings Lol Chappell and Tommy Hymers, plus a number of junior professionals. The replacements were signings Bobby Lodge from Sheffield Wednesday and Harold Bratt from Manchester United.

Another momentous happening in football came into force at the beginning of the 1961-62 season, when the abolition of the maximum wage came into force. How this would affect the smaller lower division clubs would only become apparent with time, but the previous paragraph seems to indicate Doncaster's reaction.

The nucleus of the side was formed by some of the previous season's players, with Malloy, Bratt and youth product Fairhurst being the newcomers in the team for the first match of the season at Gillingham. Three points from the first six matches was not an auspicious start, but suddenly they clicked into gear with six successive victories, including a five goals to one win at Exeter City, followed by a 6-1 home win over Tranmere Rovers. This run rocketed the Rovers from the bottom four to sixth place by the beginning of October. Philip Robinson, signed from Huddersfield Town, was brought into the side at outside right during this successful period.

Inexplicably the team then lost six games in succession, pushing them back to the brink of the re-election places. They continued to live dangerously in twentieth place throughout the season, until early March when suddenly the twentieth place became one of the last four places when Accrington Stanley resigned from the League. Only later did the Football League announce that only the last three clubs would face re-election. Even this and the acquisition of a number of experienced players for considerable transfer fees, namely Larkin, Benson, Younger and Parry did not inject any success in keeping clear of the bottom three places. Of the ten games played after the withdrawal of Accrington Stanley, the Rovers lost seven, thereby dropping to twenty-first place, eight points behind the nearest safe club.

The Rovers met Chesterfield, for the second successive season, in the 1st Round of the F.A.Cup, this time at Belle Vue. It also ended the same way but this time the Rovers lost by four clear goals. Earlier, they had defeated Grimsby Town in the 1st Round of the League Cup, by the odd goal in five, before going out at Rochdale in the next round by four clear goals.

During the season Ray Veall was transferred to Everton for a fee of £7,500 and Albert Broadbent moved to Lincoln City. Danny Malloy left the club at the end of the season and was replaced as manager by Oscar Hold, who had been coaching in Turkey prior to this appointment. Numerous players left the club, including eleven who had played some first-team games during the previous season. This meant new players were required, and almost an entire team was signed for the new season. Trainer Wally Ardron also left the club, his successor being Lew Clayton, a former Barnsley and Brighton player, with Frank Marshall becoming his assistant. Attendances again fell, to an average of 4,470, but the board decided to run a reserve team in the North Regional League for season 1962-63.

Only two of the previous season's players started the season, against Brentford - Tony Wales and Phil Robinson. With the money spent and the complete overhaul of the playing staff hopes were high for some success. But, once again, these were soon dashed when only one point was gained from the first six matches, even though Colin Booth was secured from Nottingham Forest for a £10,000 fee for the second game at Chesterfield. He was bought to add some thrust to the front line and scored the Rovers only goal on his debut. A couple of one goal victories followed, Booth getting both plus the one against Stockport County in the next match which was lost. Three hours before the kick off against Oxford United, John Nibloe was signed from Stoke City for a fee of £5,000, and then turned out and scored on his debut. His role was to take the weight off Booth as a typical centre forward. A good run up to Christmas with a minor hiccup in November put them in the centre of the table.

The New Year brought the big freeze and snow which caused a near total close down of football for two months. The Rovers managed to play one game at Belle Vue on February 9th, when the players and various helpers cleared over a thousand tons of snow and ice from the pitch to enable the match to be played. Their thanks from Stockport County, who then went on to win the game, was to protest about having to play the game. The season 're-started' on March the 2nd with a visit to Torquay United, and the Rovers managed to take a point back home. Of the remaining nineteen games only six were lost, but only five were won. Fourteen games were drawn during the season and whilst that represented a point gained, it also meant a point lost thus leaving them in sixteenth position at the conclusion.

The success story of the season related to Colin Booth and his scoring touch. He did not miss a game after signing for the club and achieved the best individual scoring figures since Clarrie Jordan. His thirty- four League goals in forty-five games was over fifty per cent of the team's total.

The F.A.Cup provided another 1st Round game against non-League opposition when the club went to South Shields for a goalless draw, and a second chance at Belle Vue, thanks to a great display by goalkeeper Fred Potter. In the replay South Shields went one better by taking the lead in the first half, only to see the Rovers come back in the second half with goals from Booth and Billings. The 2nd Round paired them with Tranmere Rovers at Belle Vue before a good crowd of nine and a half thousand. Goalless at half-time, the match was marred when Tony Conwell, the Doncaster left back, broke a leg. The Rovers from Tranmere progressed in the competition with a four to one victory. In the League Cup, the Rovers took a two goal lead in the first half at Valley Parade in the 1st Round, but Bradford City came back to equalise and take the match to Belle Vue for a replay. A goal in each half from Booth and Billings put the Rovers into the 2nd Round and a tie at First Division Birmingham City. The eventual winners of the League Cup ran out clear winners by five goals.

During the season Bobby Rooney was signed from Sheffield United and three months later was exchanged for Albert Broadbent from Lincoln City. Two more players signed in mid-season, John Wallace and Willie Purvis, together with Tony Wales and Eric Thompson, all left at the end of the campaign.

The comparative success of the team at least inspired supporters to attend matches, the average attendance of 6,305 showing a healthy rise. Talked about as the big spenders of Division 4 with all the transfer dealings over the previous year, general manager Tom Garnett announced in June 1963 that the club was prepared to outlay more money by doubling the incentive bonuses for 1963–64. A top four place was worth a bonus of £6, in the top eight it would be £4 and in the top twelve £2. They were also paying the best wages in Division 4, so much was expected from the club in the coming season.

The close season kept Oscar Hold busy as he brought in more players, including Brian Westlake, Dennis Crompton, Alan Haspell, Colin Lambton and Brian Moore, all on free transfers. John Nibloe had completed his National Service and was now available full-time.

A good start was made to the season, seven points out of eight being gained from the first four matches. The expectancy of success increased the attendance to over nine thousand for the match with Oxford United. Unfortunately, Oxford did not stick to the script and won with a single goal. In the period up to Christmas only fifteen points were added to their initial total, less than a point per game. After the festivities, for the match against Southport, came the return of the prodigal son Alick Jeffrey. He had been playing his football in Australia and with Skegness Town, having been paid compensation in England. After coming to an agreement with the F.A., the Football League and the insurance companies, he was signed by the Rovers to resume his League career at the age of twenty-four.

The high point of the season came at the end of January when Darlington were the visitors. By half-time, the Rovers were six goals up through Booth (2), one from Ripley and a hat-trick from Alfie Hale. Although they relented a little in the second half they still added four more goals through Windross, Hale, Ripley and Broadbent. This was a club record for a League victory but it didn't herald any spectacular charge up the table. In fact, two months later, they were heavily beaten by six clear goals at Carlisle and, although they won the last match of the season, they had lost the previous four. This had dropped them to fourteenth place with the same number of points as the previous season. Colin Booth again led the scoring list, with twenty-three goals, followed by Alfie Hale with twenty-.

The F.A.Cup gave the club a shot in the arm with victories over Tranmere Rovers, and Notts County at Meadow Lane, having first drawn at Belle Vue. In the 3rd Round they had Bristol City as opponents, at home. Atyeo put City in front after two minutes with the equaliser coming after fifty-five minutes from Taylor. Then came a furious finish to the match when Keith Ripley put the Rovers in front with two minutes left. Celebrations among the crowd were cut short, though, when City got the equaliser a minute later. The replay at Ashton Gate was lost by two goals. The League Cup was a non-event as they went out in the 1st Round to York City after a replay, without scoring a goal.

Despite not coming up to expectations attendances rose slightly, the highest being for the return of Alick Jeffrey. An average of 6,360 was considered satisfactory. as the board looked elsewhere for the man to bring success. They eventually obtained permission from Manchester City to appoint Bill Leivers, as player-manager.

A massive clear-out was instituted at the club at the end of the season, only Fred Potter, Bob McMinn, Keith Ripley, Alick Jeffrey, Albert Broadbent, Alfie Hale, John Billings, Freddie Taylor and John Fairhurst remained. Chief goalgetter, Colin Booth, was transferred to Oxford United for a substantial figure, representing a profit on the trade. Bill Leivers therefore had a big job to do to bring in sufficient players to form a squad. The season began on a very inauspicious note when the Rovers, including former English international winger, Colin

Facts & **Fixtures**
Figures

Doncaster Rovers Football Club Ltd

OFFICIAL HANDBOOK
SEASON 1964-65

The League Cup also served up some thrills for the Belle Vue supporters as the club reached the 3rd Round with a home draw in every round. Meeting Bradford in the 1st Round just ten days after losing the first match of the League season to the same team, they gained a narrow victory with a single goal from Henderson. Three weeks later came a visit from Second Division Preston North End, who also went away with a (Jeffrey) goal against them. This brought Bradford City to Belle Vue in a keenly contested game. City gained the edge in the second half to go away with a three goals to two victory. The Rovers got to the Final of the Sheffield County Cup after beating Rotherham United in the semi-final, but ran up against First Division Sheffield United in full flow, after escaping relegation. Four goals without reply put paid to the Rovers hopes of a trophy in front of 11,000 of their own supporters.

During the season John Billings, Freddie Taylor and Ken Oxford left the club, with only Brian Kelly coming in from Bradford City. Others who left, at the end of the season, included David Raine and Alex Tait, with John Henderson and Alfie Hale transferred in the summer. One sad note to the season came at the end of November 1964 when John Nibloe, transferred to Stockport County in July, was killed in a car crash travelling home from a game.

Grainger, visited Park Avenue Bradford, only to crash by five goals to two. As the team included six newcomers perhaps they had not had sufficient time to knit together. Gradually they did get it together when they put five into Southport's net and got six against Darlington, Jeffrey helping himself to four goals.

October was a bad month, the team suffering three successive defeats, but this period was overcome as they kept themselves in the top half of the table. Whilst never challenging for promotion the season was reasonably successful, if only for the fact that Alick Jeffrey realised his potential and took over the goalscoring mantle. An everpresent he scored thirty-six times, the next best being Alfie Hale with thirteen.

In the F.A.Cup the club reached the 3rd Round again. They overcame Bradford at Park Avenue in the 1st Round and then met stiff opposition at Belle Vue against a Scarborough side containing two former Rovers players, Billy Mordue and David Cade. A goalless encounter took the Rovers to Scarborough for a replay and nearly eight thousand people came to see the Rovers edge out the Midland Leaguers by two goals to one. The 3rd Round brought Second Division Huddersfield Town to Belle Vue. On a cold winter's day, nearly twenty-thousand turned up to see the Rovers push the Town all the way. A goal scored in the first half gave Huddersfield the victory but they were considered fortunate to hold out.

Leivers now considered he had the nucleus of a decent side and to strengthen it he brought in Trevor Ogden, Andy Wilson, Paul Durrant and Lawrie Sheffield, all forwards. A pre-season match was played at Skegness as a thankyou to that club and their manager, George Raynor, for the part they had played in getting Alick Jeffrey back to the standard of fitness required for English football. Taking only their expenses the Rovers let Skegness Town keep the bulk of the receipts of the match. Jeffrey played in the match with a broken nose sustained the previous day in training but still scored two goals for the Rovers to run out winners by four goals to one.

The 1965-66 season saw an historic decision by the Football League come into force, when a substitute was allowed to be used, but only as an injury replacement.

Rovers started the season with two four goal wins, the second at home to Hartlepools United was played in torrential rain on a Tuesday evening under their new floodlights which had cost the club £15,000. The next game, at Southport, produced the team's first defeat, and also became the first match where the Rovers had to use a substitute, when Keith Ripley came on after half-time for the injured Sheffield. After five games they were in second place, but four defeats in the next five dropped them to halfway in the table. At the end of October, Doncaster went to neighbours Barnsley, four places above them, and came away with a five goals to one victory.

This was the start of a seven game unbeaten run which took them through to Christmas in a challenging position to the top four clubs. The last match of this run, against Tranmere Rovers – the leaders – was won with a hat-trick from Jeffrey. There was a bit of a stutter over Christmas against Barrow. In Cumbria on Christmas Monday, Dawson the goalkeeper suffered a dislocated shoulder, Ricketts having to replace him, and Watton coming on as substitute. This match was lost by the odd goal in three, all scored in the first half. With both Potter and Dawson injured the Rovers needed a goalkeeper for the following day's return game. Two hours before kick-off they signed Roger Chapman from Rotherham United.

Several players had been signed during the first half of the season, and were introduced into the team, namely John Nicholson, from Port Vale, Bobby Gilfillan (£40,000) from Southend United and Tony Coleman from Bangor City. This allowed crowd favourite Albert Broadbent to be transferred to Bradford at the end of September for a fee of £5,000.

Doncaster born Alan Finney was signed from Sheffield Wednesday for a £5,000 fee, in January and made his debut for the club at Colchester United. Although it ended in defeat they were only to suffer that indignity three more times before the end of the season. On February the 10th, Bill Leivers announced his resignation, for "personal reasons". What a time to leave a club managerless! They were sixth in the Division, going well as a team, and were confident of filling one of the four promotion places.

Trainer Frank Marshall and chief scout Jackie Bestall were put in temporary charge, and in fact, saw the season out with the Board deciding not to appoint a new manager until the summer. Instead of losing momentum at the loss of their manager the team actually gathered it, and continued to gain on the leaders. Harry Fearnley was signed after they had lost four goals at Wrexham, making his debut against bottom club Bradford, the forwards having a field day with six goals. This win put them in fourth place. The pace was hotting up now as there were at least seven or eight clubs in with a chance of gaining one of the four promotion places. Nothing daunted they faced one of the front runners, Torquay United, at Plainmoor and came away with a point in a goalless draw.

Then came Easter, the barometer of 'who wins what and goes where'. Easter Saturday brought fellow promotion chasers, Chester, to Belle Vue. A goal from Jeffrey finally gained the Rovers a point. On Easter Monday they travelled North to Darlington, dark horses in the promotion race, with games in hand. Darlington got the verdict with an odd goal in five victory. The Rovers gained ample revenge the following day when they met

at Belle Vue. Running up a three-nil scoreline by half-time, the Rovers had a hard fight of it in the second half but always had their noses in front. The crowd saw six goals shared in this half to give the Rovers a six goals to three victory. Trevor Ogden got a hat-trick, Laurie Sheffield two and Brian Kelly weighed in with the other goal.

The fight had certainly hotted up and Easter had not solved any situations at all. There were still seven clubs in the running with four points covering them. Colchester United had 51, Chester 49, The Rovers 48, Tranmere Rovers 48, Torquay United 48, Darlington 47, and Luton Town 47. The following Saturday the Rovers gained the points at Port Vale, while Colchester United, Chester and Luton Town only gathered one point; Darlington picked up a brace. Darlington hit the top spot on April 25th, with the Rovers in second place a point behind, meanwhile Tranmere Rovers and Chester had dropped back. Promotion was on now but whose championship was it going to be? A great win at Chester, while Darlington beat Luton Town, and Torquay United won at Colchester United had them leading the rest, although the others were not out of it yet.

The Rovers went to the top on May the 3rd after overcoming Barnsley, then on the Saturday were beaten at home by Notts. County. An unsavoury incident in this match involving Tony Coleman led to him being suspended for twenty-eight days by the F.A. He was sent off by the referee, Jack Pickles, but before leaving the field he swung a punch at him. Although he apologised to Mr.Pickles after the match the matter was reported with the aforesaid conclusion. This defeat did not affect their position at the top, even though Darlington had the same number of points, since the Rovers had by far the better goal average.

On the Monday, Torquay United went a point in front, only for the Rovers with their win at Crewe Alexandra on the Wednesday to retake the number one position. Tranmere Rovers had finished their programme with 56 points and had to sit back and wait to see if it would be enough for promotion, Colchester United had two games left and were on 56 points also. Chester had lost three games in a row and with three games left were on 50 points and virtually out of the race. Torquay United were in second place with one game left and 57 points, Darlington had two games left and 56 points, and Luton Town were on 53 points with four games to play. The Rovers had one game to play at Valley Parade and were on 58 points but still not certain of promotion.

They gained a draw at Bradford City to stay at the top with 59 points, Darlington beat Colchester United to go second on 58 points, Torquay United without a game were still on 57 points while Colchester United's loss kept them on 56 points.

Luton Town lost at Halifax Town and stayed on 53 points with three games to play, but the following Thursday beat Barrow. Saturday the twenty–first decided the championship when Darlington played host to fellow aspirants Torquay United. Sharing the points from a drawn game it left the situation thus:– the Rovers 59 points, Darlington 59, and Torquay United 58, all having finished their programme. Luton Town could also total 59 points if they won their last two games, but to oust the Rovers they would have to score a lot of goals. They lost their next match at Newport County on May 25th, so the Rovers could now truly be crowned Champions of Division 4.

The race to be chief goalscorer was won by Laurie Sheffield with twenty––eight goals in the League campaign, with Alick Jeffrey scoring–twenty–two. No other player reached double figures. The

Success brought its rewards with increased attendances, the average rising to 10,594. But the most pressing matter was to appoint a manager as soon as possible to give him time to assess the needs of the club and players. But the matter was left on the table with Bestall and secretary Tom Garnett selecting the team and Frank Marshall as coach.

Several players left the club including Colin Grainger, Keith Ripley and Fred Potter. Replacing them were John Flowers, at a cost of £10,000 from Stoke City, Keith Webber from Wrexham, Keith Lindsey from Scunthorpe United and Martin Ferguson from Barnsley.

A good start was made to the League campaign with a three all draw at Peterborough United and a win over Torquay United. But their joy was short lived when on Thursday September the 1st 1966, whilst driving his car along the A630 between Conisborough and Warmsworth, John Nicholson was badly injured – along with his passenger Alick Jeffrey. The car was involved in a crash with a lorry and ended up in a field. Early on the following Sunday morning John Nicholson died, never having regained consciousness. He was to be badly missed not only in the defence but as the captain. Jeffrey, already on the goal trail, would also be out for three months and be badly missed.

The tragic month of September had it's effect on the field when a four goal hammering at home to Darlington was followed by six goal thrashings at the hands of Queens Park Rangers and Oxford United. More heavy losses followed including an incredible home defeat of six goals to four by Mansfield Town. A seventeen year old goalkeeper, Dave Cromack, made his debut in this match, and Trevor Ogden got a hat–trick, only to finish on the losing side.

F.A.Cup was a let–down for everybody. A draw at home to non–League Wigan Athletic was followed by defeat four days later at Springfield Park, with the Rovers consolation goal only coming two minutes from time. As this was around the time of the start of their climb up the League table, it was most probably a blessing in disguise.

The League Cup, played early in the season, paired the Rovers with Barnsley in the 1st Round at home. Two goals from Ogden gained them a draw after Jeffrey had to go off with an ankle injury. The replay a week later gave the Rovers a win, and a visit from high flying Burnley of the First Division.

A measure of their attraction can be appreciated with the crowd figure of 24,988, the best in eight years, which brought in record receipts of £5,023. This talented team gained a victory by four clear goals.

The natives were getting restless now over the paucity of good results and were calling for the heads of chairman Hubert Bates and his board, or at least to do something about the situation. Even the players complained when Laurie Sheffield was sold to Norwich City (for £12,000), before Alick Jeffrey was fit enough to replace him in the team.

In December the board finally made a move for a manager. They wanted a non-player this time, and approached Keith Kettleborough of Newcastle United with a view to him taking over the managerial reins and hanging up his boots. Having recently paid £20,000 from Sheffield United, Newcastle wanted a fee of £15,000 from the Rovers, who offered £8,000. They eventually paid £12,000 and got themselves a player-manager!

In his first match for the Rovers the team gained a welcome win, over Peterborough United, with a hat-trick from Jeffrey in his second comeback match. This was followed by another win versus Grimsby Town on the Friday night before Christmas. But Boxing Day set the trend for the 1967 half of the season. Only ten points were gained until the end of the season, three wins and four draws, and indeed the Rovers lost their last eighteen away games. Kettleborough soon upset the supporters by dropping Alick Jeffrey, claiming he was unfit. He did bring him back for one game, then promptly dropped him again. Jeffrey claimed he was being made the scapegoat for the lack of goals and asked for a transfer. This possibility raised some interesting questions because if the Rovers let him go for a fee they would have to pay back the £13,000 insurance payment they had received eight years previously. The only way Jeffrey could move to another club was on a free transfer, and his request was refused.

Norman Sykes was bought from Stockport County to stiffen the defence but there were more positions than centre half causing concern. The forwards cause was not helped either, when in March, Tony Coleman was transferred to Manchester City for a £12,000 fee. Goals continued to go past the goalkeepers with astonishing regularity, eventually creating a new club record for goals conceded, a total of 117, more than any other team in the entire League. The season ended with the blooding of some of the junior players, Dennis Leigh, Alan Warboys and Arthur Ashmore, with seventeen year old Graham Watson already a regular. Relegation after one season came as a bitter blow.

The F.A.Cup saw the team go out at home to Fourth Division Halifax Town, having earlier forced a draw at the Shay ground. These games, of course came in November when the Rovers were struggling. But in the League Cup the 1st Round was played at the beginning of the season. With John Nicholson and Alick Jeffrey in the team the Rovers earned a draw at Valley Parade, with

Bradford City missing a penalty. In the replay the Rovers got five of the seven goals scored, the Sheffield – Jeffrey partnership getting four between them. The 2nd Round took them to Darlington and a draw again brought the tie back to Belle Vue. The Rovers (overcoming a six-nil League defeat at Q.P.R. two days earlier) went out and won the cup match with two goals from Sheffield and Webber. A 3rd Round tie at home to fellow Third Division side Swindon Town brought a one-all draw, three days after they had gone to Swindon in the League and gained their only away win of the season. The replay saw Swindon Town take a two goal lead in the first half, only for the Rovers to fight back in the second period with two goals by Laurie Sheffield, to send the match into extra time, Swindon Town getting another brace to clinch the result.

Attendances held up remarkably well until after Easter when the fans voted with their feet at the prospect of relegation, and gates dropped to the three thousand mark, knocking the overall average down to 7,908. The end of the season brought the sack for Kettleborough although he was retained as a player. There was also a shake-up in the boardroom with Hubert Bates stepping down as chairman, and handing over to Frank Wilson. A number of players departed the scene including All three goal-keepers.

In June 1967 sixty year old George Raynor was appointed manager of the club. This was his first post in England with a senior club, although he had made a name for himself as a coach abroad, especially with the Swedish National Team, taking them to the Final of the World Cup in 1958.

His first job was to find a goalkeeper and he went to Aston Villa for John Gavan. The Rovers made a poor start losing their first two games. Their first point, at Hartlepools United, ended a run of nineteen away games without one. After obtaining only got three points from the first five games Raynor decided that he had given the previous season's players their chance and it was time to find replacements. Gordon Morritt was signed from Rotherham United and former England international Graham Shaw from Sheffield United. Things picked up slowly but the team never rose above mid-table. Kettleborough became a target for the boo-boys and was transferred in November to Chesterfield for a fee of £6,000, a big loss to the club both as a player and as a business transaction. John Flowers replaced him and at last began to show his potential.

In February came a sensational move when Tommy Docherty, at Rotherham United, took Dennis Leigh and Graham Watson to Millmoor, and let the Rovers have Harold Wilcockson, Colin Clish and Chris Rabjohn along with £8,000 in return. A year earlier Rotherham had turned down offers of £50,000 for each of them.

Rod Johnson came from Leeds United at the end of February and initiated a run of five wins in March. Just two defeats to the end of the season gave some satisfaction and hope that a successful team was in the process of being built, for they finished in tenth place, just seven points behind the fourth placed team.

A run to the 3rd Round of the F.A.Cup provided some excitement and some controversy. A Jeffrey goal at York saw the City off and brought Workington to Belle Vue in the 2nd Round. A one-all draw required a replay at Borough Park. Before setting off for Workington the chairman called all the players together and gave them a dressing down in front of a reporter who had been invited to sit in. This brought a censure from Cliff Lloyd, secretary of the Players Union. But it certainly seemed to work the oracle as the players went out at Workington and fought back after going a goal down to score the winning goal in extra time. Jeffrey was dropped for this match and replaced by Warboys. The club went out of the League Cup at the first time of asking.

The average attendance held up very well at 7,852 and there was a lot of hope among supporters that things were looking up. Several players departed from the club in the summer, but the main transaction was the transfer of Alan Warboys to Sheffield Wednesday. Brian Usher made the return journey and David Stainwright was signed from Nottingham Forest.

The Rovers started 1968–69 in fine fettle getting six points from their first five games. Five successive victories followed putting them into second place. A meeting with Darlington, the only unbeaten club in the League, drew a crowd of over twenty–two thousand to Belle Vue, only to see Darlington take the points with a goal just after half–time. John Regan, the Rovers centre forward, was substituted after seventy minutes and left the field with anger and dissention displayed for all to see. He was severely disciplined afterwards by the club. Some poor results followed which led to George Raynor being relieved of his post in November. Laurie McMenemy, coach at Sheffield Wednesday, was appointed manager–coach of the club.

The team was still in the top five despite indifferent results through December. But, beginning with a goalless draw at Darlington on Boxing Day, they then went twenty–games undefeated, although twelve were drawn, seven of which were goalless. A seven clear goal victory over Aldershot in February put them on top of the Division on goal average, displacing their defeated opponents. By the time they had a five goal victory over Brentford they were leaders by a clear five points, but a week later the same team inflicted the only defeat on the Rovers in the second half of the season. The end of the campaign saw them crowned as Champions for the second time in four seasons, with a two point lead over

their nearest rivals. Consistency was the Rovers strong point with the defence playing a leading part, having conceded only thirty– eight goals, the best ever return by the club. Alick Jeffrey was the leading scorer with twelve goals even though he left for Lincoln City in January. During the season John Regan and Steve Briggs joined the club and played their part in the scoring department. Only twenty–three players were used, three of whom came from Rotherham United, John Haselden, Mick Harrity and Graham Watson.

In the F.A.Cup the Rovers got through the 1st Round with a late goal by Jeffrey against Notts County. A header four minutes from the end by Robertson gave them a winning goal over Southport that gained them a 3rd Round game at Anfield against Bill Shankly's Liverpool. The Rovers gave a good account of themselves keeping a blank scoresheet until twenty–minutes from the end, when first Hunt and then Callaghan gave the First Division team a hard earned win. The League Cup rewards were as usual, minimal, the club going out in the 1st Round to Peterborough United after a replay.

DONCASTER ROVERS
FOOTBALL CLUB
SHEFFIELD COUNTY CUP — SEMI-FINAL TIE
Season 1968-69

WEDNESDAY, 7th MAY, 1969

Rovers
versus
Rotherham United

———

Official Programme — Sixpence

A degree of success also came in a Cup competition. The semi-final was won, the Final drawn, but the replay lost to Sheffield United - nearly one year later!

Success brings the crowds in as this season proved, the League games averaging 10,212 per game and the fans feel entitled to expect success to continue.

Season 1969–70 started at an earlier date than ever before. This early start was agreed to by the Football League to allow England's international players to have a rest between the end of season and the 1970 World Cup. This second Saturday in August brought temperatures in the seventies when they visited the South coast to play Torquay United. Unlucky to lose this opening game, they replied with wins over three neighbouring clubs, Mansfield Town, Rotherham United and Barnsley, and gained a point at Shrewsbury where Clish broke a leg and Regan missed a penalty. A good display at Reading was negated when Ogston presented the home team with the winner. Eight games undefeated followed this loss, taking the club up to eighth place and a challenging position for the promotion places.

But in the game at Orient they had Regan and Watson injured, actually finishing the match with ten men. The loss of points was bad enough but losing players was a big blow when there was only a small squad. With both these players missing the following week against bottom club Stockport County it came as a shock when the visitors went away with a one goal victory. Laurie Sheffield returned from his travels when he rejoined the Rovers from Norwich City and made his presence felt straight away with a goal on his debut at Walsall. Clish came back early in December but his partner, Wilcockson, was exchanged for Sheffield Wednesday's Ian Branfoot and Archie Irvine. Christmas was a decidedly un–festivelike occasion when Rotherham United and Barnsley gained revenge for their early season defeats, both coming out on top with an odd goal in three victory. Two more defeats followed in the New Year as the second half of the season failed to match the promise of the first. The final placing of eleventh at an average of a point per match came as a relief, after dropping down to sixteenth in February, although there was never any real danger of becoming embroiled in the relegation struggle.

Rovers played four games in the F.A.Cup but only two rounds, both against Fourth Division teams. A home tie in the 1st Round against Crewe Alexandra went to a replay before the Rovers came through with a goal from Robertson. The 2nd Round took them to Chester where Johnson gave them the lead. An equalising goal fifteen minutes before time brought the tie back to Belle Vue, where a goal by former Rover Keith Webber, before nearly eleven thousand spectators, set Chester on the way to a two goal win.

A goal after two minutes by Robertson led to a two goal victory over Fourth Division Grimsby Town in the 1st Round of the League Cup. A visit to Second Division

Blackburn Rovers followed where the Rovers of Doncaster, after taking the lead through Briggs, were eventually overcome by four goals to two. Two interesting friendlies were played during the season. On October the 28th, the American team Dallas Tornadoes faced the Rovers and showed that they were no pushovers when they held out for a one all draw. At the end of the season, Lazio of Italy visited England to play in the Anglo–Italian Cup, and fitted in a friendly game at Belle Vue. Although the Rovers gave it all they had the Italians strolled through the game scoring four second half goals without reply.

The success of the first half of the season brought in more spectators, culminating in nearly twenty–thousand attending the Rotherham United match on Boxing Day. But with a loss of form as the season wore on the crowds dwindled down to the three thousand mark. An overall figure of 8,561 was down on the previous season and causing concern in the boardroom.

John Flowers quit the club and football at the end of the season to take over a hotel, but returned in September on a part–time basis. Glenn Johnson was signed from Arsenal and some of the young players, Roy Young, John Adamson and Peter Kitchen from the Juniors were signed on professional forms. Confidence was high within the club that they could carry on where they had left off the previous season.

The season started badly, their first victory not coming until the tenth match, seven of which had been lost. Two more victories followed but the promised revival never materialised. Six successive defeats through December and into the New Year left them in trouble in the relegation zone. Without the finances to buy players the club had to use the loan system to bolster their existing staff, which was shrinking as players were transferred and not replaced. Gray, Sheffield, Rod Johnson, Regan, Marsden and finally John Bird were all transferred. With goals seemingly hard to come by eighteen year old Peter Kitchen was pitched into the team. His return of six goals in thirteen games augured well for the future, which with the way things were going, was going to be in Division 4. This was confirmed when they lost their last four games.

The Cups provided no relief in a sorry season. After a goalless draw at Crewe Alexandra in the 1st Round of the F.A.Cup the team was well beaten at home in the replay. The same pattern was followed in the League Cup with the Rovers held to a one all draw at home to Darlington then going down in the replay.

Towards the end of the season Frank Wilson, who had been replaced as chairman during the 1969–70 season by Ben Bailey, resigned from the board.

At the end of the season Lawrie McMenemy was dismissed as Team Manager and replaced by the former Manchester United wing half Maurice Setters. The sudden plunge of attendances to an average of 4,479, less than half of two years previous was a matter for some concern. Finances were tight so the manager had to be quite a juggler in the transfer market.

Just before the start of the 1971-72 season John Flowers was transferred to Port Vale, but newcomers to the club were Harold Wilcockson, returned from Sheffield Wednesday, and Paul Gilchrist from Charlton Athletic.

The Rovers started with a fine win over Newport County, but three defeats followed. September proved a happier month and gradually their fortunes picked up on the field. Welsh international Graham Moore, from Charlton Athletic, was brought in to add some experience to a side containing a number of young players produced by the youth team – Stan Brookes, Steve Uzelac and Mike Elwiss. In fact only twenty–players were used all season and that included Don Beardsley, brought on loan from Hull City for the last two months. A notable win over Grimsby Town, champions of the Division, was achieved at the end of the season in front of the best Belle Vue crowd of over twelve thousand.

Paul Gilchrist impressed sufficiently for Southampton to pay out £30,000 for him in March 1972. But Mike Elwiss was the find of the season, scoring fifteen goals in thirty– five League games. The season ended on a winning note but only two thousand people turned up to see a thrilling win over Bury, just four days after the Grimsby Town match; from the highest attendance to the lowest in a matter of days. Attendances were a major topic of discussion, particularly among the lower division clubs, many of who were struggling financially. An average of 4,126 was the Rovers lowest since joining the League. A finishing position of twelfth at an average of a point a game just about summed up an average season.

The Cups didn't help much either, the club going out in both competitions in the 1st Round. A source of much needed revenue and a revival of interest was therefore extinguished at the earliest stage.

The transfer market was virtually out of bounds to manager Setters, so the only men signed were Brian Joy from Tranmere Rovers and nineteen year old Charlie Morrison on trial from Chelsea. Steve Wignall, from the junior team, was also added to the professional list.

Five of the first six games were lost, the first Rovers win coming at home to Southport, and around this time Graham Watson was transferred to Cambridge United. Points were picked up on an ad hoc basis from this point on. In February the team at last ran into form going six matches without losing, four of them away from home.

A five goals to one win over Exeter City gave a paltry crowd of 1,800 something to cheer about as attendances fell to an all time low. A fortnight later Rovers were themselves hammered for five goals, at Bury, followed three weeks later, on Easter Saturday, by a five goals to one defeat at home to promotion chasing Newport County. Two more defeats over the Easter period dropped them down from a mid–table position to a finishing place of seventeenth.

Of the twenty–two players used, eight formed the nucleus of the team, playing over thirty–five matches. Goals were fairly scarce to come by which led to John Haselden being moved up to striker for a number of games. His success can be gauged when it is seen that he finished second to Elwiss in the goalscoring list by only one goal. Ernie Hunt, from Coventry City and Dudley Roberts, from Mansfield Town were both brought in on loan to pep up the attack, with only relative success – not in the goalscoring stakes but in the results.

The F.A.Cup brought some success after a few years of early exits. Round 3 was reached after the defeat of Bury in the 1st Round and overcoming Scarborough at their seaside home in the second. The reward was a trip to fellow Fourth Division members Reading. Postponed on the Saturday date because of the weather, it was played on the following Wednesday before a crowd of over ten thousand. A tough match with five bookings eventually ended in Readings' favour by two clear goals. The League Cup campaign lasted just one match, at Hartlepool, with a loss by a single goal.

Attendances were again the bane of the lower division clubs, dropping to new record lows. When the highest attendance in a season is for a pre–season friendly, against Stoke City, then matters have reached an uncomfortable point. The highest League crowd was on the opening day, three and a half thousand, so that an average per game dropped to a new all time low at 2,258.

Glen Johnson, Harold Wilcockson, Brian Joy, Chris Rabjohn, Brian Usher and Steve Briggs were all released at the end of the season. A number of new signings were made including Alan Murray from Brentford and Ray Ternent from Southend United. Because of the ongoing financial difficulties, fed by poor support, Setters options were limited in the extreme. Basically the club had to produce their own players through the Youth team. This season would see some more come through.

The 1973/74 season started more promisingly than other years, but the end of September saw a glut of goals in three successive matches both for and against. Visiting Peterborough United, the pacesetters at the top, the Rovers were five goals down after seventy–five minutes, and only a penalty three minutes from time converted by Murray gave the Rovers anything to talk about.

The following Saturday they played host to fellow strugglers Workington, but were not too hospitable as they put five past Regan, the Workington goalkeeper; Kichen getting two, O'Callaghan two, and Higgins one. Workington actually held the lead twice but the Rovers went in at half-time level at 2-2. A crowd of just fifteen hundred saw this seven goal feast.

One week on, and the Rovers were at Gillingham, coming under the cosh themselves to the tune of five goals, Kitchen getting a consolation goal. Their inconsistency showed in the next match when they overcame Peterborough United, in revenge for their heavy defeat a fortnight earlier. December brought four successive defeats and landed them at the bottom of the League. Yet they took on leaders Colchester United and beat them fair and square in the first League match to be held on a Sunday at Belle Vue. Whilst playing on a Sunday is quite common in the nineties, it was only as a result of the miners strike bringing the power workers out that the Government ordered power to be saved. This cut off the use of floodlights, and because of the four day week imposed on workers, it meant Saturday was treated as a normal working day. Sundays were therefore sanctioned for playing, provided both clubs agreed. Entry was by programme only, given to you when you paid the normal entrance fee at the turnstile!

The following week six thousand turned up to see the Rovers lose the points to Rotherham United. With Book injured, John Turner was secured from Derby County to make his debut at Workington, fellow strugglers with the Rovers. Although he saved a penalty in the first half he failed to keep the Workington forwards out as they ran in three goals, and then gave the Rovers a consolation goal. After the five goals to nil defeat at Reading, Mike Elwiss was transferred to Preston North End for a club record fee.

At last, in March, things got back to normal and a memorable match at Millmoor on a Tuesday evening gave the Rovers a tremendous lift when they came away with full points after a gutsy performance. Higgins gave them the lead in the first half – in which four players were booked, three of them from the Rovers. The second half was only ten minutes old when Steve Wignall was sent off for a second bookable offence. Nothing daunted, the Rovers defended doggedly and amazingly went two goals up after eighty-two minutes through Murray. Rotherham pulled a goal back with the last kick of the match, but a well merited victory and two points went to the Rovers in their attempt to get away from the re-election zone.

Three days later they gained two more points with a two goal victory over Newport County at Belle Vue, but a new low in attendances was reached when just eleven hundred were present.

The team continued to pick points up but not in sufficient quantity to save themselves from having to seek re-election. Fortunately they were re-elected, almost unanimously.

DONCASTER ROVERS FC

DONCASTER ROVERS
VERSUS
NORTHAMPTON TOWN

Official Programme

Whilst the 'Town' went up, the 'Rovers' only just stayed in!

Whilst the Rovers were struggling in the League, the Cups gave them a sight of life on the other side of the tracks. The F.A.Cup 1st Round was won by a Murray penalty against Lincoln City, giving them a home tie against Third Division Tranmere Rovers. The Rovers were two up after fifteen minutes, with both goals coming in a three minute spell from Kitchen and Woods. With five minutes to go Elwiss flicked in a third goal from a pass from seventeen year old substitute Terry Curran.

The 3rd Round paired them with League Champions Liverpool at Anfield, the toughest task to ask of anyone from the basement of the League. Liverpool took the lead after four minutes through Doncaster born Kevin Keegan. But the Rovers hit back within three minutes, when Kitchen put the ball into the back of their net. Twelve minutes after half-time Keegan again put the Champions in front and again the Rovers hit back almost immediately, this time through O'Callaghan.

Withstanding immense pressure, the Rovers held out and indeed, nearly won it in the last minute, to bring Liverpool back to Belle Vue three days later. With a 2 p.m. kick off, a crowd of 22,499 was a tremendous turn-out. But Liverpool were not League Champions for nothing. Despite an icy, blustery wind they set about putting everything they had learned on the previous Saturday into practice, and set Rovers firmly in their place with a goal in each half from Heighway and Cormack.

The League Cup also created some excitement when at the start of the season they went to Second Division Notts County in the 1st Round and took the lead after seven minutes through Kitchen. Early in the second period Elwiss ran through to shoot in goal number two. County pulled one back minutes later only for Kitchen to restore the two goal advantage after sixty-two minutes. However County were not going down without a fight and hit back two minutes later with Randall's second goal. Then twelve minutes later they were level, centre half Stubbs doing the necessary. But with only seconds left, Kitchen completed his hat-trick and sent the Rovers into the 2nd Round, and a visit to another First Division side, Newcastle United.

Alas and alack, the Rovers held out for half-an-hour before Malcolm MacDonald set to work and within three minutes had put two goals past Kim Book. The second half saw the Magpies run riot with two goals from 'Pop' Robson, one from MacDonald to complete his hat-trick, and a final nail in the coffin from full back Frank Clark.

Although the League attendances were only slightly better at an average of 2,397 the two Cups produced some excellent crowd figures for the Rovers to share in. The end of the season saw the departure of John Haselden, Kim Book and Graham Moore. But some exciting youngsters had come through from the juniors with Brendan O'Callaghan, Steve Reed, Terry Curran and Rob McLuckie making the first team.

With the club struggling financially, only free transfer players were signed including goalkeepers Chris Wood and Graham Brown. Because of injury Brendan O'Callaghan was unable to start the season. Unable to replace him adequately from the small squad at his command, Setters used the loan system to bring in Bob Lee, a young reserve forward from Leicester City. Lee stayed for two months, showing up very well, and although the team started the season reasonably well, by the time he returned to his club in the middle of October they had slid down the table to the edge of the re-election zone.

November brought only one point from six games, with Setters being suspended on full pay, a euphemism for dismissal. By the end of the year the team were stuck in twenty-second place with just sixteen points, and only Workington and Scunthorpe United below them. Attendances had dropped to the twelve hundred mark, and players could not be brought in, although the board did sanction the signing of Les Chappell just before Christmas. His presence certainly added a measure of strength to the side as they drew three of their games in January.

They started February by visiting second placed Shrewsbury Town, scored four goals, yet finished as the losing team. The Rovers were two down at half-time with no indication of what was to come. Four minutes into the second half Kitchen pulled one back, yet fifteen minutes later the Rovers were five-two down, four goals coming in seven minutes with Reed getting the Rovers' goal. Then came two goals in two minutes from Curran and Kitchen to bring the deficit down to one goal, with fifteen minutes left. But the scoring didn't stop there as Shrewsbury put the ball past Brown twice in the last three minutes to complete an incredible match of eleven goals. This left the Rovers next to bottom, and seemingly odds-on to go cap-in-hand to the League again. However, the board acted by appointing Stan Anderson, a former manager of Middlesbrough, as manager

Anderson made an immediate impact as the team won their first five games under his leadership, lost at Rotherham United, then won two more, to lift the club up to sixteenth place and relative safety. They obtained sufficient points to the end of the season to stay out of the re-election zone, so much so that Anderson felt able to play two young amateurs – Billy Miller and Nigel Long – in the last match of the season at Darlington.

Cup success was short lived in the early part of the season when they only reached the 2nd Round in both competitions. The F.A.Cup saw them get past the non-League hurdle of Oswestry Town before going down to Chesterfield. A home victory over Mansfield Town in the League Cup sent them to Bury where they went under by two goals.

The revival under Stan Anderson, from February, brought in better support with the best attendance of the season turning up for the visit of leaders Mansfield Town. With an average of just under three thousand per game, the season ended on a far happier note than looked likely at the half way stage, when attendances had again dropped to a new all-time low.

Archie Irvine and Andy Crellin were released at the end of the season, the squad being augmented with the signing of Chris Balderstone from Carlisle United and Denis Peacock from Nottingham Forest on loan. At the end of the first week of the 1975–76 season Terry Curran was transferred to Nottingham Forest in exchange for Ian Miller and Denis Peacock plus a cheque for £50,000.

Undreamed of riches for the club at this time, although little of it could be used for the purchase of players.

Having started the campaign with only one point from the opening two games the team gradually began to put some decent results together. With Balderstone able to play once his cricket duties were over, and the introduction of Fred Robinson, from Rotherham United, in the left back position, the team went on a run of six unbeaten games that lifted them into fifth place. Balderstone in fact created some sort of record on September the 15th, when he spent a day in the field for Leicestershire at Chesterfield, and then made a dash up the motorway to Belle Vue to play in the evening match against Brentford.

Goals were also forthcoming, the O'Callaghan – Kitchen pairing – fed from the wing by Miller and from behind by Les Chappell plus Balderstone – was proving a prolific one. Kitchen had a hat–trick against Southport, O'Callaghan one at Valley Parade and Miller got in on the act with a trio against Newport County.

It was after the Newport game that the team stuttered, with seven defeats from nine matches including all three Christmas games. This tumbled them down to mid–table, having lost their early season impetus. To bolster the defence Peter Creamer and Brian Taylor were brought in from Middlesbrough, these additions coinciding with their disastrous run. But a run of eight games without defeat, six of them won, from the end of January to early March kept them on the fringe of the promotion race. The run ended with a heavy home defeat at the hands of leaders Northampton Town. The season ended in disappointing fashion with three successive defeats and no goals scored, but Anderson had taken the opportunity to blood some youngsters, promotion having passed them by earlier in the month. Tenth place was their final position, but with a better home record – they lost seven games – promotion would have been attained because on their travels they were certainly good enough.

Rovers went out of the F.A.Cup at Bury, but only after a stiff fight. Going into the match with Kitchen and Balderstone not fully fit, Bury gained the initial advantage with two goals in the first thirty minutes, but Uzelac scored with a header just before half–time. Bury restored their two goal advantage early in the second half, but were then pegged back by constant Rovers attacks which produced another headed goal from Uzelac. Throwing everyone forward Bury hit them on the break in the last minute to settle the tie.

The real Cup excitement for the Rovers came in the League Cup. A two leg overall victory versus Grimsby Town gave them a home tie against another Third Division team, unbeaten Crystal Palace. O'Callaghan, with his fourth goal of the competition, gave the Rovers a tenth minute lead, and went further ahead in the second half through Chappell. Although Palace pulled a goal back two minutes later, the Rovers held out for a well–merited win. An away tie against fellow Fourth Division club Torquay United in the 3rd Round produced a terrific fightback by the Rovers after they had gone a goal down. The onslaught finally brought an equalising goal in the eighty–second minute, from Steve Reed.

A brilliant display in the replay, when O'Callaghan gave the Rovers the lead after forty–eight seconds, put them in the last sixteen for the first time, with a home game against Hull City from the Second Division. A crowd of over twenty–thousand turned up to see Kitchen give the Rovers a tenth minute lead. Hull equalised after half an hour and gradually took command of the game but without getting the goals. Instead midfielder Ray Ternent produced a diving header to a cross from O'Callaghan to put the Rovers in front again. Peacock pulled out all the stops to keep Hull out leaving the Rovers just two steps from Wembley.

Their reward was a visit to White Hart Lane to face Tottenham Hotspur, twice the winners of the League Cup in the previous five years. Nothing daunted the Rovers had the effrontery to score first through Alan Murray, but the Spurs hit back to lead by two goals to one at half–time. Kitchen levelled the scores after fifty–two minutes only for skipper Chappell to divert a Perryman pass into his own net within minutes. This seemed to inspire the Spurs and demoralise the Rovers because the floodgates opened as the defence failed to cope with some rampant forwards and Spurs rammed in four more goals. Class told in the end but it was a long time coming due to a great fight from the Fourth Division team.

The Rovers quest for a trophy was rewarded in the Sheffield County Cup when after beating Barnsley in the semi–final they faced Sheffield United, relegated from the First Division, at Bramall Lane. A goal in each half from Kitchen, either side of one from the United gave the Rovers the County Cup for the first in eight years.

Anderson had done a good job in his first full season. He had made money in the transfer market and had provided a team that had done well on the field after some poor seasons. Consequently attendances had been given a welcome lift, averaging 6,083, more than double the previous season. Big things were expected in the coming season of 1976–77.

Chris Balderstone, by then in the English cricket team, had his contract terminated by mutual consent and Les Chappell was among several players released by the club. Joe Laidlaw, an experienced player with First Division experience, was signed from Carlisle United, but Peter Kitchen asked for a transfer, ambition being his reason. It was granted but nobody came in for him until the end of the season.

A poor start inspired Anderson to ask Nottingham Forest for the loan of a young winger, Tony Woodcock. In his first game for the club he inspired them to a crushing victory over Darlington, and scored on his debut. His play on the left wing allied to the clever play of Miller on the right provided the Rovers' supporters with some thrilling moments during his loan period. He did so well in fact that Brian Clough recalled him after his month was up and put him into the Forest first team. The following season saw him win a Championship medal followed by a European Cup medal and England caps. And the Rovers could have had him at the beginning of his loan period for £15,000, but couldn't afford it!

A defeat by six clear goals at Halifax Town forced Anderson into making changes in his defence by bringing in two players on loan, Ian Bailey from Middlesbrough and Paul Walker from Sunderland. Three successive wins followed as the team at last found it's feet. A ten game unbeaten run including six successive victories brought them into contention for promotion. The run ended in a crushing defeat by fellow contenders, Watford, and their promotion hopes were finally put to rest at Cambridge United. The club again finished the season with three successive defeats as they gave a taste of first team football to some of their young players.

Peter Kitchen led the goalscoring list with twenty-three goals, followed by O'Callaghan with fifteen. Kitchen had spent all season on the transfer list at an asking price of £75,000. Only Orient, at the end of the season, came in for him so he moved down to London. Other departures included Steve Wignall to Colchester United, leaving his brother David at Belle Vue. Uzelac, Brookes, Ternent and Murray also left the club.

The F.A.Cup provided two exciting and entertaining games when Shrewsbury Town came to Belle Vue in the 1st Round. Shrewsbury, third in Division 3, were fortunate at the end to earn a replay as the Rovers hammered away at the Shrewsbury goal. Kitchen gave the Rovers a ninth minute lead but goals by Ian Atkins and Paul Maguire put Shrewsbury in front. But the Rovers came back through Kitchen in the fifty-sixth minute and continued to press to the final minute. The replay was a classic Cup-tie, with Miller giving the lead to the Rovers after five minutes. A minute later Shrewsbury were level then took the lead. Peacock kept the Rovers in the game until just before half-time, when Kitchen scored an equaliser. Just after the break, Maguire completed his hat-trick, but four minutes later Reed put the Rovers level again. Although shaken, Shrewsbury scored what turned out to be the winning goal five minutes later. The Rovers just couldn't come back a third time.

The League Cup saw the Rovers draw three times with Lincoln City, home and away and finally at the City ground, Nottingham. After extra time they were still level, but the Rovers won through on penalties to receive First Division Derby County in the 2nd Round. The Rovers took a first half lead through Kitchen before nearly 15,000 people, but the County, a team with eight international players on view, came good in the second half with goals from Charlie George and Bruce Rioch for the visitors to make further progress in the competition.

A number of new signings were made including Chris Jones, Bobby Owen, David Bentley and Ted Hemsley, with a number of the juniors also being signed on as full time professionals. After the previous season's Cup triumphs the lack of any success in the succeeding season caused a big drop in attendances, to around the four and a half thousand mark on average.

With the 1st Round of the League Cup being played before the League campaign started the Rovers were out of one competition in the first week. Two heavy defeats over the two legs to Sheffield Wednesday did not augur very well for the coming season.

A poor start to the League campaign for 1977-78, with only two points from five games and just three goals scored, prompted Anderson to fork out £10,000 to bring in Dick Habbin from Rotherham United. The response was instant with a victory over previously unbeaten Brentford. At the end of September they again upset an unbeaten team when they beat Southend United. A win over Barnsley took them into the top half of the table, but three successive defeats dropped them back, only for the inconsistent Rovers to follow up with four consecutive victories taking them up to eighth place and a possible stake in the promotion hunt. If they had been inconsistent to this point, the tide turned up to the end of the season, in drawing fourteen of their remaining games. This gave them a final mid-table position, averaging a point per game.

A disappointing season was rounded off by the F.A.Cup sortie, when they met Shrewsbury Town in the 1st Round for the second successive season. The end result was the same too, but this time at the first time of asking with Shrewsbury getting the only goal of the game.

Just before the transfer deadline in March, Stoke City paid £50,000 for Brendan O'Callaghan who had been on the transfer list all season. The most interesting point over the previous months was the introduction of young players to the side, like Glynn Snodin and Kevin Olney. Ian Miller went to Swindon Town in the close season in exchange for Micky French and cash. Jack Lewis from Blackburn Rovers and Pat Lally from Swansea City were also signed.

Season 1978-79 again started with the League Cup 1st Round as an opener, with Sheffield Wednesday providing the opposition. Each club gained a one goal win on their opponent's ground which necessitated a replay, the Rovers winning the toss for choice of venue. The pattern continued with the away team gaining a one goal victory.

The League season opened with better form than in previous years but this proved deceptive. The loss of Kitchen and O'Callaghan over the previous two seasons, without being adequately replaced led to a lack of firepower up front. In November Stan Anderson resigned to take up the post of assistant manager at Bolton Wanderers, leaving the Rovers in the re-election zone. His successor, Billy Bremner, was appointed five days later. He had been playing with Hull City in the twilight of a career spent at Leeds United, and was now being given his first chance in management. His first League game in charge brought a victory over Rochdale, but the team were unable to break out of the bottom four until February, when a disastrous result at Bournemouth (7–1) sparked off three successive wins to move them up to mid-table. It didn't last, however, when five consecutive defeats plunged them back into trouble.

The Rovers were unable to avoid the necessity of seeking re-election, although a four goals to three win at second placed Grimsby Town in the last match of the season when, Jack Lewis got a hat-trick against his old team, gave the club a measure of satisfaction. But finishing twenty-second meant asking the rest of the League clubs to vote them back into the League for the following season, and this they did quite comfortably. The scarcity of goals, particularly in the last few months, was a big factor in the team's lack of success, and would occupy Bremner's thoughts during the close season as he reflected on his apprenticeship in management, and prepared for his first full season in charge.

A number of players left the club at the end of the season, their replacements including Alan Warboys from Hull City, Ian Nimmo and Hugh Dowd from Sheffield Wednesday plus John Dowie and Billy Russell from Celtic. Les Cocker, a former England trainer became Bremner's assistant, and Roger Reade took over as secretary. Changes all round in the Rovers one hun-

DONCASTER ROVERS FOOTBALL CLUB
(FOUNDED 1879)

100 YEARS ON

OFFICIAL HANDBOOK
CENTENARY SEASON 1978/79

FACTS - FIGURES - FIXTURES
PHOTOS

Published by Doncaster Rovers Supporters Club
Printed by B. & B. Press (Parkgate) Limited

25p

dredth year, could they now round it off by gaining some measure of success?

The average attendance had dropped again, to the three thousand mark, not surprising with the team struggling all season, but over eleven thousand turned out for the 'derby' match against Barnsley when the match was televised by Yorkshire Television.

Starting the season with the League Cup 1st Round, the Rovers shrugged aside Third Division Sheffield United over the two legs, and moved on to the League in good heart to start with a victory over Northampton Town. A home leg win over Exeter City in the league Cup 2nd Round gave them a two goal advantage for the second leg, which at the end of the normal ninety minutes left the aggregate scores level. In extra time Exeter took the honours and moved into the 3rd Round. Meanwhile, in the League, the Rovers had lost two games without scoring, which prompted Bremner to call for more goals from his forwards. They answered him in fine style against Torquay United putting five goals past the Torquay goalkeeper, Turner, the last two coming eight minutes before time, after Torquay had pulled back to three all.

October brought tragedy when on the 4th of that month, after taking a training session, Les Cocker collapsed and died. He was 55. On the brighter side it also brought an eight game unbeaten run – two draws and six successive wins – including one over the leaders, Portsmouth Their run was stopped at Northampton Town, but they came back to complete a double over York City, to reach sixth place, only two points behind Bradford City in fourth.

A tremendous win at Port Vale in the F.A.Cup 1st Round, when they came from behind to win comfortably by three goals to one kept the impetus going. But December proved their undoing as a home defeat in the 2nd Round of the Cup, to Mansfield Town, was followed by three successive League defeats over the Christmas period. During the Boxing Day match at Walsall, Bremner had an argument with the referee and was reported to the F.A. The F.A.charged him with *"bringing the game into disrepute"*. He was fined £200 and warned as to his future conduct.

During the winter the club found it difficult to train properly because the club had no indoor facilities and there were few options in the town. The club had used the facilities at nearby R.A.F.Finningley when they were available, and they were negotiating for the use of a hangar, owned by the Doncaster Aero Club, that stood behind the Rossington end. This situation came about after the entire playing staff had to queue up at the entrance to the town's only leisure centre, while Bremner paid for them to use the gymnasium for their morning's indoors workout!

The second half of the season only brought five wins, but a modicum of draws kept them in or around mid-table so that a finishing place of twelfth was acceptable. A

Another promotion in 1981 – under manager Billy Bremner

number of teenagers were introduced into the side throughout the season with Daral Pugh, Steve Lister and Glynn Snodin coming to the fore. Ian Snodin came in late in the season and David Harle was also given a game at Port Vale. Bremner himself played in one match because of injuries, against Bournemouth, helping his team to a one goal win. He acquired Alan Little from Barnsley just before Christmas and signed Willie Boyd from Hull City enabling him to transfer Dennis Peacock to Bolton Wanderers for a fee of £70,000.

The comparative success of the team brought a 50% increase in attendances. Among the departures at the end of the season was Jack Lewis, Dave Bradley and Keith Ripley, with Dave Bentley moving on to the coaching staff.

An air of confidence pervaded the corridors of Belle Vue as manager Bremner prepared his strategy for the new season. Mick Bates, a former Leeds United colleague of Bremner, was signed from Walsall and John Saunders came from Lincoln City to bolster his small squad. Finances were not in the best of shape as the club struggled to keep afloat, only the sale of their best players keeping the wolf from the door.

After a disappointing start – in which they lost three of their first four matches – the team responded in September by winning all six games played, gaining Bremner the Fourth Division Manager of the Month award. October was less successful only one win being achieved and five of the games goalless on the Rovers side.

November was only marginally better with an average of a point per game, even though they suffered a five goal defeat at Darlington. From December onwards only three games were lost as the Rovers gathered momentum up the table. It was March before they established a place in the top four positions and from then on there was a steely determination to succeed. Promotion was assured in the last home game against Bournemouth, when old favourites Jack Buckley, Clarrie Jordan and a few more were introduced to the large crowd.

The scenes of jubilation at the end were easy to understand as the club shrugged off a decade of non-achievement. A point in the last game at Mansfield Town eased them past Wimbledon into third place, a good distance behind Southend United and Lincoln City, but they were all going the same way. Promotion had been achieved with a small squad of players, including many teenagers, making it one of the youngest teams in the League. Ian Snodin and David Harle gained regular places and at the end of the season Russell Wilcox and Glenn Humphries were introduced into the side.

Ian Nimmo led the scoring list with eighteen goals outstripping everyone else, the next best being midfielder Alan Little with seven. Mick Bates left the club in November and only Richard Dawson on a free transfer and Carl Swan, for a small fee, were signed during the season.

The League Cup was over before it began for the Rovers, with their exit in the 1st Round over the two legs to Mansfield Town. But in the F.A. Cup they reached the

The F.A.Cup 4th round took Rovers to Norwich in 1982
But Steve Lister can only look on as the City score.

3rd Round with wins over non–league Sutton Coldfield Town and Third Division Blackpool. The 3rd Round tie at Hull City provided another instance of one club having a majority of possession only to be dumped out of the competition because the other side scored the goal that matters. Hull got the goal and progressed to the 4th Round.

Whilst the average attendance increased to the five and a half thousand mark it was still not enough to keep the club going. A figure of ten thousand was required to break even. The Supporters Club and the Development Association both had a job to do in trying to supply the club with extra funds through totes, lotteries, raffles and the like. For season 1981–82 shirt and match sponsorship, plus sponsorship of the family stand helped to bring in fresh money.

Cyril Knowles, the Youth team coach, went to Middlesbrough in a similar capacity with David Pugh replacing him, and a young man from Celtic – Colin Douglas – was the only player signed during the close season. The campaign opened with a new competition, the Group Cup, in which the Rovers were in a group of four with Sheffield United, Chesterfield and Grimsby Town. A win over Chesterfield but defeats against the other two left the Rovers out in the cold. The League Cup followed with a 1st Round tie against Chesterfield. Both legs ended in a draw but the Rovers having scored in their away game took the tie on the away goals rule.

Meanwhile the 1981/82 League campaign started with a new points system in operation – three points for a win

and one for a draw. Opening with just one point from the first two games, they followed up with five wins on the trot that put them on top of the table.

The first leg of the 2nd Round tie in the League Cup was played at Belle Vue against Second Division Crystal Palace before nearly eight thousand spectators. A first half goal from Stewart Mell won the game and enabled the team to go into the second leg with a lead. After a plucky fight they lost by two clear goals in London to go out of the competition.

In the League there was better luck through October with three wins and a draw from the five games played thus keeping them in the top group. However November brought the start of a disastrous sequence of three draws from eleven games which plunged them down the table until a win over Chester stopped the rot. But not for long, for three points from the next five games put them in relegation danger. Even the signing of former Leeds United and England left back Terry Cooper could not halt the slide as injuries to players like Dowd, Nimmo and Warboys – which kept them out for long periods – decimated the small squad of players available. Bremner himself turned out as the substitute against Newport County. So, just before the transfer deadline in March, Bremner signed Graham Cawthorne from Grimsby Town, Garry Liddell from Heart of Midlothian and Clive Wigginton – on loan – from Grimsby Town. This injection of new blood saw the team lose only two games out of the last thirteen and gain sufficient points to pull away from the relegation places to the safety of nineteenth place and a cushion of three points.

Rovers on the attack again, in the incredible 12 goal thriller versus Reading.

Their second consecutive season in Division 3 started with one point from three games, each one goalless for the Rovers. Then came the craziest five weeks in the clubs history as it rained goals, particularly at Belle Vue, where the crowds saw thirty- six in four games. This goal spree started on a Friday evening in September when the Rovers beat Exeter City 6-1, having gone three goals up in the first fifteen minutes. A 3-2 defeat followed at Southend United then Reading visited Belle Vue, when an incredible match followed.

Interrupting their decline in the League the team gained relative success in the F.A.Cup when they went to Mansfield Town in the 1st Round and put them out with an early Douglas goal. Non-League Penrith came to Belle Vue next and despite a gallant fight the superior quality of the League team shone through with two goals from Warboys plus one from Little in between. Second Division Cambridge United were the next visitors to Belle Vue and were a goal down in eight minutes through the misfortune of one of their own players. Although they levelled the score after half an hour, a goal from Warboys settled the tie a minute before half-time. In the 4th Round the Rovers had to visit promotion chasing Second Division Norwich City, and giving them a fright by scoring the first goal after eighteen minutes. Their lead only lasted two minutes and a further goal ten minutes into the second half put paid to the Rovers hopes of further progress.

An average attendance of 5,234 was only a slight drop from the previous season but perhaps more could have been expected because of the step up in the League. But could a team be found to give the crowds something to come in and cheer?

Terry Cooper left to take the job of manager at Bristol City, David Harle moved to Exeter City, and Steve Humphries refused the terms offered to him. Other departures were Pat Lally and Richard Dawson, the leading scorer from the season just ended. The incoming signings included Dennis Peacock, re-signed from Bolton Wanderers, and Tommy Graham as a non-contract player.

Colin Douglas put the Rovers in front after just two minutes with a glancing header, but Kerry Dixon equalised a minute later. Ian Snodin put the Rovers in the lead with a penalty on seven minutes, and Billy Russell increased the advantage after eleven with a fierce twenty-yard shot. Fifteen minutes went by without a goal, until Dixon shot in from the edge of the area. Ian Snodin then made the score 4-2 after twenty-nine minutes only for Dixon to put away a penalty seven minutes later.

After thirty-eight minutes it was the Rovers turn to have a penalty, the third of the match, which Ian Snodin comfortably dispatched. Half-time came with the score 5-3 in favour of the Rovers. It took only five minutes of the second half before Dixon netted his – and his side's – fourth goal.

Eight minutes later Tommy Graham got on the scoresheet with a spectacular overhead kick following a corner. Score 6-4. Robinson got a fifth for Reading on seventy-one minutes, only for Glyn Snodin, eight minutes later, to hit an indirect free kick from thirty yards which the goalkeeper touched on it's way into the net. A crowd of just over three thousand went home breathless and hoarse. The Rovers were now in thirteenth place.

However, more was to follow, when on the Tuesday evening Wigan Athletic were the visitors. Four and a half thousand decided to come and see what the team could produce this time. Ian Snodin took only two

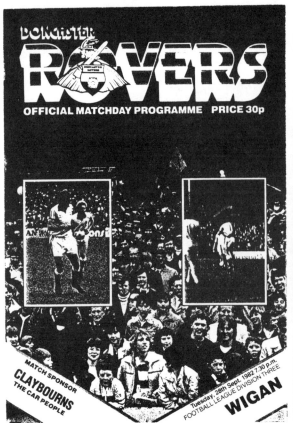

Contrasting programme covers from the early 1980's

minutes to put the Rovers in the lead, but two goals in a minute from Methven – after ten minutes – and Houghton, put Wigan in the lead. O'Keefe added a third after twenty–six minutes with Colin Douglas getting one back two minutes later for the Rovers. Six minutes before half–time Bradd put Wigan 4–2 up. Glyn Snodin then scored after sixty–two minutes and with the Rovers going for the equaliser Houghton struck twice in five minutes in the last quarter of the game. The final score, an incredible 6–3 to Wigan Athletic. Twenty–one goals seen in total in three days!

A one goal defeat at Orient put the Rovers in twenty–second place and in trouble. The following week at Lincoln City the Rovers crashed by 5–1 and were at the bottom of the Division. The next game, at home to Brentford ended in a 4–4 draw, after the Rovers had gone 4–1 up on the hour. Between the Reading and the Wigan Athletic games Daral Pugh moved to Huddersfield Town in exchange for Terry Austin, who was viewed as a replacement for the injured Warboys. Then between the Lincoln City and Brentford games Alan Little was exchanged for Clive Wigginton from Torquay United. The moves were initially controversial, and when they didn't work out in the Rovers' favour they drew considerable criticism. At this juncture Tommy Graham also left the club, but Stuart Robertson – a midfielder – was

signed from Exeter City. The club now had only fifteen fit players to choose from, of which two were goalkeepers. Therefore advantage was taken of the loan system with first Garry Watson and Gordon Owen coming in, then later Winston Campbell and Colin Walker. The team's next win after the Reading match had to wait until December 18th, and from then until the end of the season only six more victories were recorded. The club never got out of the relegation zone and failed to score in about half of the games. In fact Glynn Snodin, ostensibly a left full back (the best in the Third Division said Bremner), topped the goalscoring list with twelve goals, followed by Douglas with seven.

With the general lack of success throughout the season even the Cups didn't bring much joy and the failure of the club to consolidate a place in Division 3 was most disappointing to everyone concerned with the club. With attendances dropping to the three and a half thousand mark the club had to work on strict cash limitations, limiting the options in finding good experienced players to put alongside the youngsters coming through the Youth Scheme. Warboys and Nimmo had both had to call it a day because of injuries and a number of other players left the club. Newcomers, all free transfers, included Bill Green and Andy Kowalski from Chesterfield, Ernie Moss from Port Vale, John Breckin from Bury and Mark Miller from Gillingham.

The club made a good start to season 1983–84, the best for some years, by winning three of the first four matches, but then followed up with just one win in the next four games. Early in October David Harle was brought back from Exeter City, but later that month Green was injured and missed most of the rest of the season. Nonetheless, from October the 8th to March the 6th, the Rovers played twenty-five matches losing just once – on December the 3rd at Swindon Town. This run put them into second place behind York City from New Year's Eve. Although they slipped slightly early in April to third place, they soon resumed their good form, and finished in second place, thus returning to the Third Division at the first attempt.

Injury restricted Breckin from playing regularly so Steve Yates was signed from Southend United. Les Mutrie was brought in on loan from Hull City over the Christmas and New Year period, whilst Harle was out with an injury. But the introduction of Mr.Peter Wetzel to the board proved beneficial to the club when he provided the money to go into the transfer market, just before the deadline in March, and hence clinch promotion. John Philliben, a young defender from Stirling Albion was signed for a club record fee of £60,000, Jim Dobbin – a midfielder from Celtic cost £25,000 – and Alan Brown, a proven goalscorer, cost £35,000 from Shrewsbury.

Several good performances were recorded during the season, one such being the visit of leaders York City to Belle Vue. With York two goals in front, the Rovers fought back splendidly to score the brace necessary to gain a point. Another such match came when Colchester United were the visitors and were leading by three goals to two after an hour's play. The fight to get something from the match eventually brought the Rovers a penalty two minutes from time which Ian Snodin converted.

In April, on the way down to Northampton, the Rovers coach broke down some fifty miles away from their destination. The players changed while parked at the roadside and were picked up and transported to the match by supporters travelling down to the match in cars. The start was delayed by eleven minutes, but it all came right for the Rovers as they went on to win by 4-1.

The leading scorers were veteran Ernie Moss and his partner Colin Douglas, both with fifteen goals. Playing alongside the ageless Moss could only have benefitted Douglas who was still learning his trade. Glyn Snodin was also to the fore with thirteen goals from midfield. The total of eighty-two goals was the highest total scored by the club for some years.

The F.A.Cup saw an exit in the 1st Round at the hands of Mansfield Town. In the League Cup (now the Milk Cup due to sponsorship), they reached the 2nd round, but were beaten in both legs by Fulham.

A new Cup, the Associate members Cup for Third and Fourth Division clubs, saw the Rovers win at Lincoln City, then beat Preston North End before going out in the regional quarter-final to Burnley. With gates down to an average of 3,778, and losing money every week, the club reported a debt of £170,000.

During the close season of 1984 the Rovers paid £30,000 for John Buckley from Partick Thistle, and signed Aidan Butterworth from Leeds United, these being the only additions to the playing staff of which big things were expected.

The League campaign opened at Preston North End with a two goal defeat, but three successive wins showed the Rovers in fourth place in the Saturday night *Green 'Un*. The successes included their first away win at Reading, who had previously gone undefeated at home for thirty-three games. A hat-trick from Alan Brown, after Reading had taken a four minute lead, put the skids under the Royals whose night was completed when their captain and centre half, Hicks, was sent off for a foul on Brown.

This victory ended a week in which the Rovers had been dumped out of the League (Milk) Cup by York City quite emphatically. York had gained a one goal lead in the first leg after the Rovers had taken a two goal advantage in the first quarter of an hour. But in the second leg the Rovers capitulated to the tune of five goals. The win at Reading was the antidote and the week as a whole symbolised the Rovers whole season – inconsistent. They continued to flirt with the top half of the table, pushing themselves into promotion contention by the end of November when they comprehensively beat Swansea City at Belle Vue on a filthy, rainy afternoon. I wasn't to last though, for in the very next match a Davison hat-trick for Derby County sent the Rovers home pointless, a state of affairs that applied to five of the next eight games, and dropped them down to mid-table.

Then came Boxing Day and a visit to Valley Parade to meet the leaders of the Division Bradford City, who had a five point lead and were unbeaten at home. Playing with Ian Snodin as a sweeper the Rovers defence held firm against a lively attack. After sixty-six minutes a free kick thirty yards out was awarded to the Rovers. Glynn Snodin stepped up and drilled his shot through to the net for the only goal of the game. For the last few minutes of the match the Rovers were down to nine men. First Butterworth – after only eighteen minutes on the pitch as substitute – was sent off in the eighty-fifth minutes for talking out of turn to a linesman when Peacock was injured. Two minutes later Harle was given his marching orders for another bookable foul.

New Year's Day exemplified the team's fighting spirit when they went a goal down after 19 minutes to Walsall at Belle Vue. It took them another three-quarters of an hour to find their way through the Walsall defence, but once having done so they slotted three more goals in for a well deserved victory to maintain their mid-table position.

The inconsistency of the team's displays showed in the next League match, when, after beating First Division Queens Park Rangers in the F.A.Cup, they crumbled a fortnight later at home to Reading, although in mitigation they had a number of players missing through injury and suspension. With Alan Brown being on the long term injury list a goalscoring forward became a necessity. Derrick Parker had come in on loan over the Christmas and New Year period but someone was needed permanently. Eventually, in March, Bremner signed nineteen year old Ray Deans from Clyde for a £40,000 fee.

Injuries and suspensions throughout the season were a constant problem necessitating many team changes. Ian Snodin was badly missed when he was out, Alan Brown was to retire through his injury, and Jim Dobbin also spent some time out injured. David Harle was sent off three times and cautioned eleven times during the season.

The only consistent period during the second half of the season showed their position in the League, which barely fluctuated, and fourteenth place was their final position. Good wins were achieved at Burnley, Rotherham United and Lincoln City, whilst poor performances at Bolton Wanderers and Wigan Athletic and at home to Bradford City, showed up the inconsistency of their season.

The Lincoln City game was definitely a triumph over adversity. The Imps were battling against relegation when the Rovers paid them a mid-week visit. After nine minutes the referee, Howard Taylor, sent Ray Deans off for dissent. Four minutes later Douglas put the depleted Rovers team in front following good work by Buckley. Never a dirty game, the Rovers were down to nine men after thirty- our minutes when Glynn Snodin was sent off for the first time in his career, after he was fouled and retaliated by throwing the ball at the offender. With their backs to the wall the Rovers surprised everyone when Ian Snodin was hacked down in the penalty area and from the resultant penalty gave them a two goal lead after sixty-six minutes. Five minutes later Lincoln were awarded a penalty. Redfearn took it but hit the crossbar, leaving the Rovers to hold out to the end of the game and keep a clean sheet.

The F.A.Cup also provided much excitement beginning with a relatively easy victory at Rochdale, then going to Gola League leaders Altrincham, and overcoming them. A home tie against First Division Queens Park Rangers was their reward and a tremendous display was crowned ten minutes from time when Harle struck a left foot shot from twenty-yards past the goalkeeper for the only goal of the game.

Having reached the 4th round for the first time in twenty-nine years, the Rovers found their next opponents were Cup holders Everton at Goodison Park. A plucky display meant they were not disgraced as they held the First Division leaders and eventual Champions to two first half goals. Attendances were up slightly to just over the four thousand mark, but disappointment was rife in the club and among the supporters, for the club – at various times in the season – were in a position to make a challenge for promotion only to falter. The hope was for Bremner and team to get it right in 1985–86.

The season past ended on a catastrophic note with the month of May being a month of disasters. On the 11th came the Bradford City fire in which fifty-six people died. Then on the 29th.at the European Cup Final in the Heysel Stadium, Brussels, came the ultimate in soccer violence as Liverpool fans rushed at the Juventus supporters, leaving thirty-nine people dead under a pile of debris. The reactions by Government to these disasters led to long reaching effects on football and football clubs. The immediate effect on clubs was that their stadia had to come up to new regulations and be licensed to operate. Clubs like the Rovers had to spend money they could ill afford on making old wooden stands fire resistant to comply with the new standards.

The Rovers were criticised in early August by the South Yorkshire County Council for dragging their feet over the implementing of the improvements required by the new laws, and threatened to close the ground to spectators if they were not done before the start of the season. Local contractors worked round the clock to put fire cladding on the Main stand, installing emergency lighting and putting in a new PA system. Terracing improvements were carried out at the Rossington end, and the old North stand at the Town end of the ground was demolished. The total cost would be around £450,000 when it was finished, with the Rovers having to find a quarter of it, and a new ground capacity of 9,900. Having satisfied minimum safety standards the relative licence was granted in time for the opening game of the season.

Some of the fringe players were released the previous May, followed by the transfers of the saleable players. Ian Snodin was transferred to Leeds United for £200,000, and his brother Glynn went to Sheffield Wednesday for £115,000. Steve Lister and Billy Russell refused new contracts and were transferred to Scunthorpe United. With all this traffic out of the club some new blood was required to fill the gaps. Dave Cusack was signed from Millwall for £40,000, Brian Caswell was secured from Walsall for £19,000, and Dave Rushbury came in from Gillingham.

On Sunday August the 25th came some tragic news. Roy Cork, the Youth team manager, was stabbed to death in the early hours of that morning by a neighbour, after an argument between Cork's son and the neighbour. He was forty-four years old.

The season started quite well with an unbeaten run of seven games, including four draws, that promised much for the months ahead. All this was achieved without the services of Alan Brown and Ray Deans because of injuries received the previous season. Although both attempted to play again they eventually had to admit defeat and retired from football – in Deans' case at the age of twenty. Suspensions carried over from the previous season kept Philliben, Cusack and Harle out of action for the first match, so that Bremner gave a debut to sixteen year old Micky Nesbitt.

Three defeats followed this run, but the ship was steadied by two wins, the second at Wolverhampton Wanderers with Douglas getting both goals. Then the unthinkable happened, when Leeds United dispensed with the services of their manager and decided that Billy Bremner was the man for the job. Although on contract the club did not stand in his way, although it caused an upheaval within the club when Dave Bentley – the assistant manager – and Dave Blakey – the chief scout – went with him. Cusack, after being put in charge temporarily, was given a permanent appointment a fortnight later, on Bonfire Day, making him at twenty-nine the youngest manager in the League.

Cusack's first signing had to be a goalkeeper because Peacock was out with an injured back and Bremner had loaned Trevor Swinburne from Leeds United. He had been recalled by Leeds United so that in Bremner's last match in charge, against Bristol Rovers, Paul Allen had played. Andy Rhodes, Doncaster born, was secured from Barnsley at a cost of £20,000.

Late in November Cusack accepted a second bid from Leeds United for Brian Caswell, and although criticised at the time, to receive double the fee paid for him surely was good business. Micky Stead from Southend United was the replacement, for a third of the fee received for Caswell. Stead also became coach. The other member of the backroom staff was Steve Beaglehole, who was appointed manager of the reserve and youth teams.

When Tony Brown was injured at Cardiff, Brian Flynn was recruited from Cardiff City on a free transfer and was able to bring a vast amount of experience to the team. Although not scoring many goals the team continued to pick points up, such that on New Year's Day, after a successful programme of maximum points from three games, the club stood fourth – just two points behind second placed Derby County who were nineteen points behind runaway leaders Reading.

Unfortunately the Rovers were unable to capitalise on this position. A steady loss of points, mainly due to the inability to put away the chances that they created, saw them slip down the table to eleventh place in the table at the end of the season. Although this was the highest position for sixteen years, it was also disappointing after being so well placed at the half way mark. Only four clubs conceded fewer goals than the Rovers, with fifty-two, but only one club – bottom of the table Swansea City – scored fewer than the Rovers total of forty-five goals. Those facts spoke for themselves.

The Cups didn't bring any success or extra revenue either. In the F.A.Cup, at Wigan Athletic, with six first choice players out, the Rovers scored first after six minutes, but a mistake by Rhodes after half an hour let Wigan in and they proceeded to win handsomely. In the Milk Cup, their tie with Notts. County ended level after two legs, but County went forward on the away goals rule. The Freight Rover Trophy was also a non-event as far as the Rovers were concerned, for they went out after the first round of games.

At the club's A.G.M. which was held in February 1986, it was announced that a record profit of £40,674 had been made on season 1984–85, but that the club were still in debt. A new director, Mike Collett (an airline executive) would join the board, replacing Nigel Taylor, a local farmer, who had died in November. Ian Jones, the chairman, told the meeting that despite dwindling attendances and spiralling wage costs he remained optimistic about the club's future. The accounts showed that Peter Wetzel had loaned the club nearly £90,000 in 1984–85 to buy players in addition to a previous loan of £140,000. But, the meeting was told, he was not prepared to go on propping up the club year after year. They had to reduce operating costs and get back in the black.

In May, the club announced that painful measures would have to be taken to ensure the club's survival because of pressure from the bank to reduce a massive overdraft. On May the 7th, the entire playing staff, except Cusack and Stead, were put on the transfer list. A fortnight later, a public meeting was held at the Main Line club to discuss the club's future. Over three hundred people were present to hear Ian Jones and Dave Cusack talk in general about the club. The conclusion was that there would be two teams, first and reserves, with hopefully a sponsor to keep the Junior team going. It was also decided to extend the 3-2-1 lifeline to 1,500 members for a chance to win £1000 for a £2 outlay.

CHAPTER 10

...And The Fall 1986–93

eason tickets for 1986–87 were offered at a cut-price if purchased before May 31st, and there was a staggering response, with around £10,000 coming in to help the club's summer cash flow; a figure representing half of the previous season's total sale. An appeal was also made to the townspeople to contribute fifty pence each to a fund.

Against this background Cusack had to get a team together to go on the field. A number had been released at the end of the season and several more had moved on. Colin Douglas, at the end of his contract, wasn't offered an increase on his wages and went to Rotherham United for a fee of £12,000, John Buckley moved to Leeds United for £40,000, and Brian Flynn went to Bury. Replacements brought in were Colin Russell from Bournemouth for a five figure fee, Neil Redfearn from Lincoln City for a tribunal fixed fee of £17,500, and Gary Clayton from Burton Albion for £6,000. One unwelcome outlay was a fine of £1,000 from the F.A. for the club's disciplinary record, of which £500 was suspended.

The Rovers started the season by winning a trophy. An unexpected and cryptic statement, but the Trophy in question was the Sheffield County Cup. The Final of the 1985–86 competition had been held over to this, the next, season and was played as a pre-season game. Before 638 paying spectators the Rovers beat Rotherham United by a goal from Neil Woods in the second half.

Having spent what money was available, the League season started with four wins and a draw from the first seven games to put the team in fourth place. Heady heights indeed after a traumatic summer. But still the wheeling and dealing of players carried on. At the end of August Steve Burke was brought in from Queens Park Rangers, a week later John Philliben was transferred to Motherwell for around £30,000, and at the end of September Jim Dobbin went to Barnsley for £35,000. With all the problems surrounding the club Ian Jones admitted the strain was getting to him, and resigned as chairman, but kept his seat on the board. Bernie Boldry, a director since 1980, took over as chairman.

Back on the field the Rovers lost four of their next six games, but November proved a good month, taking them back to the fringe of the promotion group. Early in December the bank put pressure on the club to bring some money in, so top scorer Neil Woods was sold to Rangers for £130,000 plus two players; Colin Miller, a

Canadian international, came down to Doncaster straight away but it was well into January before Stuart Beattie signed for the Rovers. December also saw Tommy Gaynor brought over from Eire club Limerick City for a small fee.

Into January the club started to slide, winning just one game from the twenty-five played, including a record equalling run of fifteen games without a win, taking them to the brink of the relegation places. But three successive victories got them away from that possibility, and although they lost their last match, at home to promoted Middlesbrough, they finished in a very respectable thirteenth place with fifty-seven points.

On the day before this last match, safety experts closed the Popular stand at Belle Vue after discovering serious subsidence problems, thereby cutting the capacity of the ground to 4,859. Attempts to postpone the match or switch it to another venue were blocked by the Football League. The match went ahead with three and a half thousand spectators present, but at the end the Middlesbrough fans invaded the pitch, to celebrate the victory and promotion. Unfortunately the hooligan element took over, causing damage to one of the crossbars and fighting broke out with the home fans. A total of thirty-six arrests were made inside and outside the ground.

On the financial front, in January, the club had asked the local council for permission to raise money by taking a street collection. The council refused on the grounds that the Doncaster Rovers was not a charity, and only a limited number of such organisations were allowed to collect money on the streets of the town. In any event, the local authority – it was stated – had already given a substantial grant following the Bradford tragedy. At the end of that month another director, architectural designer Graham Smith, left the Board after six years because of increased business commitments.

March brought the staggering news that things had got so bad for the Rovers support-wise that the Dons, Doncaster Rugby League Club – the traditional chopping blocks of Rugby League – were actually drawing larger crowds than the Rovers, as they challenged for promotion to Division 1 of the Rugby League. The Rovers chairman appealed to the stay-away supporters to write to him and tell him the reasons for their desertion of the club, so that the Board could take stock of what the fans wanted. Many did write in but only the Board know if any of their comments were taken aboard.

High-flying Brian Deane - later to on to greater things...
in the opening match of the 1887/88 season versus Grimsby.

The Cups, traditional means of gaining much needed revenue, were not of much help to the Rovers in this particular season. In the Littlewoods Cup they were dismissed in the 1st Round by neighbours Rotherham United. The F.A.Cup took them to Whitby, where the local Town club gave them a hard game and felt that they should have won. Russell gave the Rovers the lead just after the half hour, but Whitby hit back following the break, scoring two goals in six minutes to go into the lead on the hour. There were only ten minutes left when Deane got the goal that took the tie to Belle Vue.

The replay again showed that Whitby Town, managed by a former Rovers player – Peter Creamer – were a tough nut to crack. The Rovers took a two goal lead in the first twenty minutes through Woods and Stead. Whitby got one back just before half–time when Humphries put into his own net trying to clear. Immediately after half–time the Rovers regained their two goal cushion when Redfearn put away a penalty, but Whitby didn't give up and were rewarded with a second goal three minutes from time. This win took the Rovers to Chester City in the 2nd Round, where they held out for fifty–five minutes, then gave the home side three goals, but only managing one for themselves.

The Freight Rover Trophy saw them lose at Middlesbrough and, wanting a three goal win to make progress, only achieved a goalless draw at home to Chesterfield.

The accounts for the year ending May 31st 1987 showed an overall deficit of £27,084 making their overdraft £276,127. The club had cut their operating costs by over £100,000 in bringing down the wages bill, and cutting the spending on travelling and accommodation by half. The loss would have been much more but for a record profit of £153,525 on transfer dealings. With the average gates down to 2,408 and the club losing up to £5,000 a week they needed to sell players to survive.

Dave Cusack had a busy close season chasing players to replace Redfearn – transferred to Crystal Palace for £100,000 –Tony Brown, to Scunthorpe United for £10,000, and Gary Clayton who moved to Cambridge United for £6,000. Cusack enquired after numerous players, but either the fee asked was too high, or the player did not want to make the move. The only players signed before the season started were Brian Flynn on a short term agreement, and Neville Chamberlain on a year's contract. Neither of whom had cost a fee.

A new director, Ken Chappell, a farmer and former British ploughing champion, joined the Board and was given the job during the close season of supervising the digging up of the centre of the pitch. Once rated one of the finest pitches in the country, damage had been done during 1986–87 when a special chemical compound had been applied to the pitch to prevent frost setting in. It did ease freezing problems but it destroyed the turf and stopped surface water draining away. The Rovers successfully claimed compensation against the chemical manufacturers. The Popular side stand was also pulled down and the terracing was re-concreted, but that part of the ground was not re-opened to spectators until well into the season.

This season saw the League introduce the use of two substitutes. For the opening match against Grimsby Town, Cusack gave a League debut to Mark Rankine, captain of the successful Youth team, principally since he could only raise twelve players from his first squad, the others being injured. A win got the season off to a good start, but four successive defeats followed to leave the team in the relegation places. Three wins lifted them up the table, but a run of five defeats dropped them right into the thick of the relegation fight.

Still the transfer dealings went on. Early in October Tommy Gaynor was transferred to Nottingham Forest for a fee of £30,000, Colin Russell went to Scarborough – initially on loan – and Glenn Humphries, late in the month, moved on to Bristol City for £22,000. Their replacements were John Buckley, on loan from Leeds United, Garry Kimble, signed for £10,000 from Cambridge United, and early in November Lee Turnbull from Aston Villa for £17,500. In September goalkeeper Andy Rhodes received a cracked jaw at Wigan. His deputy was untried Youth team goalkeeper Mark Samways, but after medical advice Rhodes continued to play.

In October the club found themselves in trouble with the Football League when they called off their match at Chester City on October the 10th because their squad had been decimated by illness. Under new Football League regulations on postponements they had two points deducted, since although eleven players were unavailable due to a stomach virus, the League felt they could have turned out a team. Upon appeal the two points were restored.

Early in December Dave Cusack was dismissed as manager and Dave Mackay, the former Derby County manager, appointed in his stead, along with Joe Kinnear as his assistant. Both Cusack and Stead, relieved of his coaching duties, were retained as players but Cusack was soon given his release, and around Christmas time was appointed manager of Rotherham United.

Whilst the appointment of Mackay generated interest around the town it did not improve the success rate on the field. He saw only three League victories before the end of the season, which left the club in bottom place and relegated to Division 4. Even York City, at one stage fourteen points behind the Rovers, leapfrogged them on the last day. A total of thirty-three players were used during the season, including several members of the Youth team who had been called up.

At the end of February all the players had been placed on the transfer list. The first to go was Andy Rhodes to Oldham Athletic for £55,000 with £20,000 of that going to Stockport County a few weeks later for the acquisition of Les Robinson. Eight players were given free transfers at the end of the season, including Miller, Kinsella, Stead, Chamberlain, Joyce and Nesbitt.

The Cup record showed hardly any difference to the previous year or so. Meeting local rivals Rotherham United in the F.A. Cup 1st Round, they could only get a one-all draw, before going down by two goals in the replay. In the Littlewoods Cup they met League newcomers Scarborough. Losing the first leg at Seamer Road, to a goal by central defender Steve Richards, they went a goal down at Belle Vue in twenty minutes, and two goals down on aggregate. In the second half the Rovers got their act together and in an eleven minute spell on the hour they put three goals in the Scarborough net to go on and meet the mighty Arsenal, the holders, in the 2nd Round.

The first leg, at Belle Vue, before a five and a half thousand crowd was easily won by Arsenal with three second half goals. The Rovers, with seventeen year old Steve Raffell making his debut in the centre of the defence, were outclassed. In the second leg the Rovers gave a brave performance with Rhodes again in fine fettle, only losing by a goal from Rocastle seconds before half-time. The Freight Rover Trophy was hardly worth the effort, each match being lost by a single goal, to Mansfield Town and Hartlepool United. The attendance at Hartlepool was 782 !

The only success surrounding the Rovers Football Club came from the Youth Team in the F.A. Youth Cup, when they reached the Final for the first time. Starting in the 1st Round at Preston North End with an excellent victory by four goals to one, they progressed with home wins over Port Vale (1-0) and Sheffield Wednesday (2-1). An incredible victory by six goals to three at Plymouth Argyle put them in the quarter final, and up against the big guns of Manchester City. A crowd of two and a half thousand at Belle Vue cheered the local youngsters on to a two-one win. The semi-final was played on a two leg basis with the Rovers at home first, against Tottenham Hotspur.

Before a crowd of over five thousand they gained a one goal lead with goals by Mark Rankine and Paul Raven. The second leg at Tottenham went to extra time before Rankine notched the goal to take them through to meet the Arsenal Youth team in the Final. Again the Rovers gained home advantage for the first leg and six and a half thousand turned out to see these lads. Unfortunately they came up against a goal machine called Kevin Campbell, who scored three of the five goals that Arsenal netted without any reply.

(Top) Pre–1988/89 season 'warmer', the Yorkshire & Humberside Cup match v. Sheffield United... new signing Colin Douglas gets in a tackle. (Bottom) Dobson scores from the 'spot' in the League match v. Exeter

The second leg four days later saw a much improved display, with the Rovers unlucky to only get a one all draw from the encounter, with a goal from Andy Peckett on the half hour. Doncaster Council recognised their exploits by giving them a Civic reception at the Mansion House.

The lads who played in the Final, and gaining a runners up medal were: *Lee Lamont, Mark Hall, Rufus Brevett, Steve Raffell, Paul Raven, David Snowball, Andy Peckett, Mark Rankine, Neil Morris, Andy Winship, Steve Gaughan, Robbie Stewart and Lee Slingsby.* Only Lamont, Snowball, Winship and Slingsby failed to play for the Rovers in the Football League, although Slingsby did so for Scarborough.

Gates were down to below the two thousand mark at an average per game of 1,893. Finances were now extremely tight with no money coming in during the close season. The success of the Youth team however prompted Doncaster Council to loan the club £90,000 to ensure that the club could kick off season 1988–89. Chairman Bernie Boldry said the money would go towards ground improvements and team rebuilding.

Brian Deane, the leading scorer, refused the offer of a new contract and was transferred to Sheffield United for a total of £40,000. Mackey made only four signings in the close season of 1988, bringing Colin Douglas back from Rotherham United for £15,000, signing ex Manchester United and Republic of Ireland midfielder Gerry Daly from Stoke City. Paul Dobson came from Torquay United for £20,000 and Paul Holmes plus goalkeeper Paul Malcolm signed on a free transfer from Barnsley. Hopes were high that with a mixture of youth and experience the team would be able to make a bid for promotion and go back to Division 3.

The League campaign got off to a bad start at Rotherham United when Malcolm was sent off for kicking an opponent in the 41st minute. A penalty for the incident was also awarded to Rotherham, giving them their first goal as they went on to beat the ten men with two further goals. Two wins followed this defeat, including their first away victory. A run of three successes in October took the Rovers to sixth place in the table, but was ended by an amazing match, when on a Friday evening, Halifax Town – who were in the bottom four – came to Belle Vue.

Dobson challenges in the match versus Hartlepool – his former club.

A staggering spell of four goals in four minutes by the visitors in the first quarter of an hour effectively won the match for them. Although Ronnie Robinson pulled a goal back two minutes from half-time, Halifax held out comfortably to take the points. Apart from a capitulation at Grimsby Town, the Rovers kept in touch with the play-off positions into the new Year.

Experienced central defender Jack Ashurst was secured for a £15,000 fee in November to play alongside the youth of Raven, Raffell and Beattie. But chief scorer, Paul Dobson, on being dropped to substitute against Peterborough United, immediately asked for a transfer. Eventually, in January, having asked again, he went to Scarborough for £40,000, Mackay reiterating that anyone who wasn't happy was no good to the club. This left the goalscoring department a bit short with Turnbull being injured – playing in midfield prior to his injury – and the burden fell on nineteen year old Mark Rankine. Gary Jones, a prolific scorer in local football for Rossington Main, was signed as a non-contract player.

In the meantime, in December, the Inland Revenue pounced on the club when they presented them with a winding-up petition regarding a tax debt of £86,000. It hadn't been settled by the statuary month after presentation, so the case had to go before the Royal Courts of Justice in London on January the 18th. The directors then decided they would dig into their own pockets to pay the debt instead of having to sell any of the players. The unpaid tax demand was eventually cleared in February, removing from the club, the spectre of closure.

Although Vince Brockie was obtained on loan from Leeds United and Rufus Brevett at last came back from injury, results gradually got worse. A winless February, losing five out of seven games – with goals getting scarcer by the minute – set the club on a slide down the table. The high hopes of the first half of the season were now shattered as fear set in about the prospect of going out of the League.

On March the 17th, the day before the home match against Colchester United, Dave Mackay resigned claiming that financial pressures had forced the club to begin considering offers for the top young players, and also that money promised for strengthening the side had not been forthcoming. However, although his resignation was *"reluctantly accepted"*, he was persuaded to stay on for another fortnight until his successor was appointed. The next day the team went out and beat bottom club Colchester United with two goals from Rankine and one from Gary Jones, the most goals in a single match they had scored since New Year's Day.

The club then released a statement saying that they were making losses of £3,000 a week, and were £500,000 in debt. With the transfer deadline date in sight they were set to sell some of their prized youngsters, but there was a snag. As one condition of the £90,000 loan during the previous summer, the local council had stipulated that half of any fees received went to them as a repayment.

Monday March the 20th 1989, was a day of comings and goings – a day of tremendous activity. The chairman announced that Joe Kinnear had been appointed the manager of the club on a contract to the end of 1989–90 – much to the despair of the supporters – and Mr.Wetzel resigned from the Board declaring that he had no desire to have any further involvement with the club. As the major shareholder and backer this was a big blow. Both the supporters club and Mr. Wetzel had backed the return of Billy Bremner, out of a job since September when he was dismissed by Leeds United.

The following day youth team coach Steve Beaglehole resigned, believing that the youth project was being undermined. Meanwhile, Kinnear's first day in charge was hectic to say the least. His first job upon his appointment was to finalise the sale of Paul Raven and Ronnie Robinson to West Bromwich Albion for a combined fee of £200,000. At the same time he paid out £15,000 to Leeds United to keep Vince Brockie at Belle Vue. Two days later he appointed Dave Bentley, Bremner's assistant when he was manager of the Rovers, as youth development officer and reserve coach.

After all this upheaval the team got down to playing football again, but not to much avail in the way of points. With eleven games to play under Kinnear they won one and drew three, only scoring eight goals, with the result that the team slid down to twenty-third place, with only Darlington below them (to be relegated to the Vauxhall Conference). But the fear of relegation had gone by the penultimate game when a point against Tranmere Rovers ensured the Rovers' safety. It had been a close thing.

Early in April had come another blow for the Rovers when Stuart Beattie announced his retirement from the game at the ripe old age of 21. He had finally given up the struggle against the back injury that had plagued him.

In the Littlewoods Cup, the club went out in the 1st Round on aggregate to Darlington. The F.A.Cup gave them new opponents in the 1st Round when they drew North-Eastern side Brandon United at Belle Vue. The Rovers, with seven first team players injured or suspended, could only get a goalless draw. Having persuaded the non-leaguers to play the replay at Belle Vue, the Rovers eventually won with two goals in three minutes from Dobson just before half-time; Brandon's former Rovers youth captain, Neil Richardson having missed an eleventh minute penalty. Although Brandon got the goal that they deserved six minutes before time, it was only a consolation.

In the 2nd Round Rovers faced Third Division Sheffield United, in front of six and a half thousand supporters, with Sheffield United complaining about the Rovers' refusal to switch the tie to Bramall Lane. Played on a Sunday afternoon, Sheffield United – with Brian Deane leading their attack – took command with two goals in the first half and ran out comfortable winners, by three goals to one. In the Sherpa Van Trophy (formerly the Freight Rover Trophy), the team went out in the preliminary Round, before a gate of only 681 at home to Grimsby Town, the lowest ever attendance for a first team competitive game at Belle Vue.

Just before the end of the season, Doncaster Council served the Rovers with a High Court writ to recover a balance or £52,000 owing on the £90,000 loan. The Council considered that the Rovers had broken the terms of the agreement and were seeking immediate restitution. The Rovers, of course, were in the same position as when they received the loan a year previously, namely at the end of a season with little revenue coming in during the summer months. Amazingly enough, although this was the worst ever season in the Rovers' history, the average gate had increased to over two thousand (2,135) but the club made a loss of £18,297 over the period, despite making a record profit on transfers of £232,500 and marginally reducing their overdraft.

It was not to be a quiet summer for the club. On June the 30th came the news that Joe Kinnear had been dismissed by the club upon returning from a holiday, having been assured by the chairman before going away that his job was safe! The chairman – Bernie Boldry – also resigned, and made way for a new consortium, which was made up of airline owner Mike Collett (chairman), major shareholder Peter Wetzel (vice-chairman), and wealthy businessman John Ryan joining the board. A new issue of 300,000 shares was planned, with Mr.Collett promising a cash injection and a five year plan to reach the Second Division. But their first real decision was to appoint Billy Bremner as the new manager. He in turn brought in Steve Beaglehole as his assistant and Dave Blakey as general manager.

Bremner inherited seventeen professionals from his predecessor, but to bring in fresh faces he needed to move others on. Paul Gorman, Garry Kimble and Andy Peckett had already been released by Kinnear at the end of the season, and Bremner put Mark Hall and Lee Lamont on the transfer list. Gerry Daly was given a free transfer although he had a year left on his contract. The new manager's first signings were John Stiles from Leeds United, Grant Morrow from Rowntrees Macintosh at York, and Justin Sumner – a former junior with Leeds United and York City.

April 1989 of course saw the Hillsborough disaster, and more legislation governing football stadia. Following the recommendations made by the Taylor inquiry the standing areas capacity were reduced by fifteen per cent, reducing the ground capacity at Belle Vue to 7,294. Some good news though was the erection of a cover on the Popular side. Covering a length of ninety yards, the steel roofing cost around £50,000, and was in use for the DAF Cup game against Grimsby Town on November the 28th.

The season started with the Yorkshire and Humberside Cup, but the Rovers didn't get past the group matches, beating Scunthorpe United but losing at Leeds United and versus Scarborough. The Littlewoods Cup didn't provide any thrills either, the Rovers going out on aggregate in the 1st Round to Huddersfield Town.

The League campaign started with three defeats in four matches, with the first win coming away from home at Scarborough. Two more losses followed, then came an astonishing result at bottom of the table Hartlepool United. In seven League games to that date, the Rovers had managed just three goals, despite some impressive approach work. But against Hartlepool they came good and ran riot with six goals without reply. Scoring three in each half they simply overwhelmed poor Hartlepool, and could have scored more. Lee Turnbull helped himself to a hat-trick, Les Robinson chipped in with a couple, leaving Steve Gaughan to get the other goal.

October brought a return to the losing habit and a drop in the table to the bottom three. The tide turned in November when Kevin Noteman was secured from Leeds United for £10,000, and David "Bruno" Jones was signed on a free transfer. Both made their debut at Rochdale with Jones getting a hat-trick to give the Rovers a good win. Five wins followed from the next six games, lifting the team up to a respectable fifteenth place. But after beating the League leaders, Exeter City, in mid-January the Rovers slumped, losing six of the next seven games. Hit by injuries and suspensions, Bremner was prompted into signing the Beazer Homes League top scorer John Muir from Dudley Town for a £5,000 fee, plus David Harle – for the third time – from Peterborough United, and Neil Grayson from Rowntrees Macintosh.

In the meantime the Rovers were enjoying a Cup run, not in the F.A.Cup having gone out in the 2nd round of that competition to Grimsby Town, but in the Leyland DAF competition, formerly the Freight Rover Trophy. Coming through the group matches with Huddersfield Town and Grimsby Town, they met Bury in the 1st Round of the North Section. A splendid win was capped in the 2nd Round, when on a filthy, wet January night at Wigan Athletic, they produced a fighting display on a pitch that became a swamp in the torrential rain, to eventually win through after extra time with goals by Turnbull and David Jones. Their next opponents were Halifax Town in the North Section semi-final which was to be played at Belle Vue. Despite their poor League form in February, they produced a fine commanding display with Muir making his debut in place of the suspended Jones. Goals by Brockie, Turnbull and Noteman sent the five and a half thousand success-starved spectators wild with delight.

This win put the Rovers one step from a Wembley appearance against the winners of the Southern section. First, however, there was a two leg Northern final to play against Tranmere Rovers, the Third Division leaders. In the first leg at Prenton Park the Rovers kept the home crowd quiet for the first half hour with an attacking display that was not rewarded with the goals required, including a clear case for a penalty. Against the run of play Tranmere went ahead, yet although they then came more into the game they were never sure of ultimate victory. Noteman failed to make sure when he sidefooted the ball towards an empty net and it was cleared off the line, proving to be a costly miss, when ten minutes from time Tranmere scrambled a second goal to take a good lead into the second leg. The match at Belle Vue, in front of a six and a half thousand crowd, was something of an anti-climax with the onus being on Doncaster to go all-out on attack. After a goalless first half the stalemate was broken shortly after half-time when Tranmere scored to make the Rovers task even more formidable. They got an equaliser through Jones, but could not make any further impact, leaving Tranmere to go on to Wembley as aggregate winners.

The Cup run provided the impetus required to gain some points in the League. Points were needed, since although Colchester United were adrift at the bottom, a good run-in – and a poor return from any of the half dozen clubs above them – could change the situation dramatically. As one of the clubs within Colchester's range, the Rovers needed points. A home win over promotion chasing Chesterfield was most welcome, and a point was gained at fellow strugglers Wrexham.

Then came a home game against next-to-the-bottom Halifax Town, who were three points behind the Rovers. The homesters took a three goal lead in the first half hour with goals from Turnbull, Muir and Grayson, and were so much on top that they should have scored even more before half-time. But the second half took a different slant when Halifax scored after two minutes, then went on to score three more goals, without ever taking command of the game.

This setback for the Rovers left them coupled on 48 points with Halifax Town, Wrexham and Hartlepool United, with Colchester United at the bottom with 40 points. All these clubs had three matches to play, so the Rovers needed at least one point to escape the drop. They didn't get it in the next match at Colchester, which increased the pressure on themselves.

But an all-out attacking performance gained a big win in their penultimate game against Rochdale, and safety was assured in twentieth place, eight points clear of relegated Colchester United.

Although the return of Bremner and his brand of attractive football had increased the average gate for the season to 2,706 the team had not achieved much success on the field except in the DAF Cup. With finances still tight, wheeling and dealing in the transfer market was necessary if the club was to achieve it's aim of promotion. Among the free transfers granted at the end of the season, thirty-five year old Jack Ashurst, Steve Gaughan and Steve Raffell left.

The main topic of conversation during the summer of 1990 was the decision of the club to hold talks with Doncaster R.L.F.C. and the Council on the prospect of ground sharing, either at one of the existing stadiums or at a purpose built new venue. This topic was to run and run.

Turnbull, Brevett and Rankine all expressed a desire to further their careers elsewhere, and were placed on the open to transfer list. But Douglas signed a new three year contract, and Jones, Morrow and Samways all renewed their contracts. To replace Ashurst, Bremner went back to Leeds United to snap up Brendan Ormsly on a free transfer. Two more fee-free men were also signed – twenty-one year old Andy Holmes from Stoke City, and Eddie Gormley from Tottenham Hotspur.

Once again the Yorkshire and Humberside Cup opened the season, with the Rovers losing to Rotherham United by the only goal, getting a goalless draw at Barnsley and beating Huddersfield Town in a best of five goals game, but it wasn't enough for them to progress any further. The renamed League Cup, now sponsored by Rumbelows, opened the season proper with another tie against Rotherham United over two legs. The first leg at Belle Vue was hardly a game to remember from the Rovers viewpoint as Rotherham ran riot, in winning by six goals to two. At half-time Rotherham had just shaded the play and led by three goals to two, having scored the first goal in just thirty-five seconds! They took command in the second half to add three more goals, as each side finished the match with ten men after each centre half had been sent off – Ormsly for a professional foul, and Law for elbowing Muir. The second leg resulted in a hard fought victory for Rotherham United by two goals to one, and a comfortable aggregate win.

The League campaign started in a different vein altogether. Five successive victories, three of them away from home, equalled a club record for the start of a season. But an injury to Jones, when he suffered a broken bone in his neck, seemed to have a detrimental effect on the Rovers – already without Ormsly through suspension – as they suffered from four consecutive defeats. Then an excellent win at Cardiff City got them back into the groove and kept them in the top four. Although they lost the next match at Chesterfield, when John Muir received his marching orders, the team then embarked on a nine match unbeaten run that took them to the top of the table on Boxing Day. This run coincided with the return to the club on a non-contract basis of Jack Ashurst to cover for the long term absence of Holmes, who had a stress fracture of the shin.

Rovers held top spot going into the New Year, but were knocked off by Darlington on the first Saturday of 1991. They continued to keep up with the top four promotion pack, despite a poor return of points in February. Although the month ended with a great win over Burnley, after being a goal down until twelve minutes from time, when two goals in three minutes from Brockie (with a penalty), and Muir gave them the victory. But the victory was achieved without Lee Turnbull, transferred to Chesterfield for £35,000, and Rufus Brevett, who had moved on to Queens Park Rangers for a club record fee of £275,000. These moves had more or less been forced upon the club as a result of a six figure unpaid tax bill. The club did not wish to go down the same road as before, when the Inland Revenue had issued a winding-up order.

With Turnbull gone and Jones still having injury problems Billy Whitehurst was obtained on loan from Sheffield United, and was eventually transferred to the club. But goals seemed to be hard to come by in this latter part of the season, although the goals against column remained as solid as ever, despite losing Brevett from left back – Kevin Noteman having to move back to that position. Paul Smalley came from Leeds United to take over from Rankine at right back, so that the latter could move back into midfield.

The club's away record had been enough to make them promotion contenders, so all that was required was to keep their home form going. However, Scunthorpe United came and gained their first away win of the season, and this was followed by Scarborough taking the points, after the notorious Jim Parker had sent off both Ashurst and Noteman. Rovers were still in with a chance of a place in the play-offs at the end of April, but a last minute goal by Burnley took the points, and in the next two home games Chesterfield gained a win for the first time in many years at Belle Vue, and Torquay United went away with a draw. A disappointed Bremner had seen his side go the last eight games without a victory, and after being in the top echelon for most of the season it was with dismay that he, and the supporters, saw the team fade out of the play-off picture at the end. A finishing position of eleventh was still a considerable advance for the club, considering they were operating on a shoestring.

During the season they had also suffered badly from injuries, when on some occasions there had been as many as eight first-teamers unavailable through injury and suspension.

A good cup run into the later rounds, when the 'big boys' come in, always helps the smaller clubs to survive with the additional revenue. But this avenue was closed to the Rovers at the first attempt in the F.A.Cup when they did the hard work getting a draw with Chester City at Macclesfield, only to lose the replay at home, albeit to a disputed goal in extra time. In the Leyland DAF Cup they came through the group round against Chesterfield and Scunthorpe United, only to meet Scunthorpe United again in the 1st Round of the knock-out competition at Belle Vue. On a cold January evening, and a frost bound pitch – like a skating rink – the match went ahead, and ended goalless after extra time. Penalties were then the order of the day, and Scunthorpe proved more adept at scoring from the spot when netting with all four of their kicks. The Rovers' first two penalties, from Brevett and Ashurst, were saved, and although Turnbull and Ormsby both scored theirs, it was to no avail in the end.

Colin Douglas, voted Player of the Year for 1990-91, a record third time, is presented with the Eddie Ward Memorial Trophy by Rovers Supporters Club President Dr. William Erskine. Colin also receives an inscribed carriage clock.

Towards the end of May Mike Collett stepped down as chairman, and was succeeded by long-serving director James Burke, with Ken Chappell as vice-chairman.

Despite a record profit on transfer dealings, the club still announced a loss of £123,989 on the season.

On the playing side Bremner made just two signings during the summer. Much travelled Tommy Tynan, aged 35, was signed from Torquay United on a free transfer, with a view to utilising his scoring skill that had brought him over two hundred and fifty goals in his long career. At the other end of the age scale came 18 year old Andy Crosby signed on a free transfer from Leeds United. On the way out were Jack Ashurst, who had not been retained, and John Stiles who had refused to sign a new contract or even to operate on a week to week basis.

With the Yorkshire and Humberside Cup having fallen by the wayside because of the withdrawal of the top clubs, the Rovers were restricted to friendlies against local clubs in their build up to the new season. In their opening League game against Carlisle a number of the more experienced players were either on the injured list or suspended, so that the thirteen players selected contained five teenagers and only three over the age of twenty-four. Beaten by three clear goals, Bremner's reply was to go to Leeds United and obtain the loan of left back Dylan Kerr, and also to resign Jack Ashurst on a year's contract. However, the first four League games were lost as well as the two legs of the Rumbelows League Cup against Crewe Alexandra.

Not only had all six matches ended in defeat, but twenty-two goals had been conceded. The defensive qualities of the previous season were nowhere in evidence. At last the run was broken by a win over Wrexham, but that was the only bright spot in the first half of the season as the team went sixteen League games without a win. By New Year's Day they had only nine points from twenty-two matches, and were five points adrift of the next club, Aldershot.

In the meantime there had been changes at management level, when on the eve of the match at Mansfield Town, Billy Bremner resigned, along with Dave Blakey. This landed Steve Beaglehole with the job of holding the fort, and after gaining two draws in his first two matches in charge, he was given the manager's job on a three year contract. However, at the end of November, Lincoln City went away from Belle Vue with a five-one win, prompting Beaglehole to show his dismay by putting all the players on the transfer list.

Goalscoring was proving a problem for the club. Injury prone 'Bruno' Jones went to Bury on a free transfer in September, Tynan had only scored once and didn't figure in the new manager's plans, and Muir had not regained his scoring touch after his ankle injury.

Another blow to the club came in September when Vince Brockie had to retire at the age of twenty-two with a knee injury. Offsetting this was the signing on professional forms of 18 year-old Jon Cullen, and Nicky Limber who was 17.

The New Year opened with the Rovers in a perilous position at the bottom of the League, but even worse news was to come when the Inland Revenue served the club with a winding-up petition for a tax bill of £200,000; the PFA were also called in to pay the wages of the players. With the High Court hearing set for February the 5th, money had to be raised quickly. Manchester City provided £75,000 when they stepped in and signed Nicky Limber late in January. Now able to make a down payment on the debt, the club came to an agreement with the Inland Revenue over arrears, and the petition was dismissed when the hearing came up. But the club were still in trouble since the payments had to be met.

A Fighting Fund was set up with supporters doing their bit in raising money by the various means at their disposal. More famous names joined in too, with Paul Daniels – the TV magician – pledging his support and sponsoring a section of the pitch, and idea which the fans also supported, and which raised £6,000 within a month. Charlie Williams the comedian, and a former centre half for the Rovers, also did his bit when he starred in a fundraising night at the Belle Vue Social Club that raised about £2,000. Meanwhile a grant of £10,000 was received from Jewsons, the builders merchants, that was used to upgrade the toilet facilities and to modernise the community room. In February, Mark Rankine was transferred to Wolverhampton Wanderers for a fee of £100,000 and John Muir went to Stockport County for £10,000.

The saddest news came in March, when the brass name-plate taken from a 1936 steam engine named after the club which had hung at the entrance to Belle Vue for some thirty years, was sold for a sum of £10,212. This sale plus donations from the directors enabled the players' again overdue wages to be paid. To cap all the difficulties, a crack was found in one of the floodlight pylons at the Town end. Unable to undertake an immediate replacement, it too was going to cause problems.

During all these happenings there was some football played! On the first Saturday in January a splendid win was achieved at mid-table Walsall, but the loss of Limber and Rankine led to four more defeats in the next five games. To replace Limber, Steve Prindiville was signed on a non-contract basis upon his return from Greece. Then, early in March, a number of local firms joined forces to finance the wages necessary to obtain twenty-year old centre forward Mike Jeffrey on loan from Bolton Wanderers. His first match for the Rovers at Hereford United brought a one goal win, Noteman scoring, which moved the Rovers off the bottom rung, and above Aldershot. Jeffrey's worth came with three goals in the next four matches as the team picked up four more points.

But the last week of March brought a number of points to the fore. Another PFA loan was necessary to pay the wages, then came disaster as Aldershot withdrew from the League. When their record was expunged it left the Rovers at the bottom, nine points behind the next club Carlisle United. Then came transfer deadline day with Kevin Noteman going to Mansfield Town for £25,000, Mark Samways on loan to Scunthorpe United, John Stiles on loan to Rochdale and Billy Whitehurst going to Crewe Alexandra on a free transfer.

On the last day of March, a Tuesday, the team were due to play high-flying Barnet with an evening kick off of 7.30 pm, but the damage to the floodlight pylon prevented the match taking place. Barnsley stepped in and offered the Rovers the use of their Oakwell ground, but the Football League put a stop to that idea. The police stepped in when the Rovers arranged for a five o'clock kick-off, saying it would clash with the rush hour traffic on Bawtry Road, so the eventual outcome was for the match to kick off at two o'clock in the afternoon. This was a throwback to the pre-floodlight era, or more recently the three-day weeks of 1974. Expecting the lowest ever attendance, the club were pleasantly surprised when 1,247 people turned up to urge the Rovers on to victory, when a solo effort from Jeffrey in the first half proved to be the only goal of the game. They were now six points adrift of the next team.

Although there would be no relegation at the end of the season due to the disappearance of Aldershot, it was important to the club, the manager, the players and the supporters to get off the bottom of the table. This was achieved with one point to spare over Carlisle United, after a tremendous effort in the last six games resulted in four wins, whilst the Cumbrian team could only muster one win and two draws.

Mike Jeffrey played eleven League games and scored six goals, a great return in anybody's language, but he also had a promising partner in six of those games in seventeen year old new professional Gavin Worboys, grandson of a pre-war Rover, Ted Vaux. Worboys missed the last match of the season when he was transferred to Notts County for £100,000.

Fundraising was still an important feature in the effort to provide some funds to help the Rovers. Karaoke nights were held and a collection in the town raised over £600. On April the 30th, a 'Save The Rovers' pro-celebrity darts competition, organised by Doncaster businessman Alan Critchlow and held at The Dome, was hoped to raise around £20,000. A number of personalities from the darts world and from showbusiness and other sports gave their services free. Darts celebrities present were Mike Gregory – the World number two – who travelled up from Bristol, former World Champions Jocky Wilson, John Lowe, the Crafty Cockney Eric Bristow, Denis Priestley (from nearby Mexborough), the current World Champion Phil Taylor, and English internationals Cliff Lazarenko and Denis Hickling. Showbiz people in attendance included stars from Coronation Street and Emmerdale Farm, Paul Shane of Hi-de-Hi fame, and Duncan Norville. Other sports stars included boxers Bomber Graham and Barry McGuigan.

In the financial report for the year ending May the 31st 1992 the club reported a loss of £105,094 on the year's trading, even with income from transfers amounting to £290,000. With an average attendance of 2,058 all the above activities would continue to be necessary with, hopefully, more sponsorship. But sponsors like successful teams, and the Rovers were far from being that.

The Board decided, as an economy measure, to dispense with the Reserve team for season 1992–93, but were evidently well satisfied with Steve Beaglehole's handling of the team in a very pressurised situation, when his attention was – of necessity – taken away from playing matters and focused on monetary affairs. They rewarded him with a new three year contract. His end of season free transfer list included Jack Ashurst, Brendan Ormsby, David Harle, Tommy Tynan and Max Nicholson, with John Stiles retiring from professional football to become a financial consultant. On the incoming side Beaglehole was busy persuading the Board to find £20,000 to secure the permanent services of Jeffrey, and then to build a team ready for the new season. Some half a dozen free transfer players were signed on, together with a loan signing from Scunthorpe United, Stuart Hicks.

In the week before the start of the new season, Maidstone United went out of business leaving the new Third Division – the original First Division having broken away to form the F.A. Premier League – with twenty-two clubs. The season opened with what was fast becoming the norm, that is losing in the 1st Round of the Coca-Cola (League) Cup, and then going on to lose the opening three games of the League campaign, two of which were at home. However, with signs of the team knitting together, there being so many new players in the team, they gained their first win, against Barnet, and went on to lose just one game in the next nine. This took them up to sixth place with thoughts of staying in the play-off places. The acquisition of Kieron Brady, a Republic of Ireland Under-21 international midfielder on loan from Sunderland, helped to compensate for the loss of Jeffrey through a groin injury. When Sunderland called him back after refusing to extend the loan, it was quite a blow, for the team then went eight matches without a win.

The victory that stopped the rot came in an incredible match against Scarborough, who took a seventeenth minute lead only for Douglas to equalise seven minutes later. Four minutes from half-time Prindiville shot the Rovers into the lead, but Scarborough equalised three minutes after half-time. Just after the hour came three goals in four minutes when Winston White and Gormley put the Rovers in front with goals either side of one from Scarborough. That was the end of the scoring but the issue was in doubt right to the end as both teams continued on attack.

Unfortunately this burst of goalscoring was like an oasis in the desert, as once again the goals dried up with Jeffrey not showing his pre-injury form until the last month of the season. His popularity and worth to the team, according to the fans, can be gauged by the fact that when it became known that he was having trials with Sheffield Wednesday and Liverpool, the telephone in the Rovers office was inundated with people ringing up to urge the club not to sell. A run of eleven games through March into April saw the team plunge down to eighteenth place, just four points above the bottom club Torquay United. Once again a late effort was required to get away from the danger area. Ten points from the last five matches ensured that the Rovers were well clear of the relegation zone as they finished in a respectable sixteenth place.

The Cups once again did not provide much in the way of additional revenue as they went out in the 1st Round of both of the major competitions, albeit somewhat unluckily in the F.A.Cup to Hartlepool United. The Autoglass Trophy provided the best chance of glory, but after getting through the preliminary group they lost out to Huddersfield Town.

Of course, the state of the finances was the main talk throughout the season. With the collapse of Aldershot and Maidstone United, the fear among a majority of the lower division clubs was that they might be next. In the Rovers' case, despite all the assistance from a vast array of efforts from many people, they were still in financial trouble. Early in October the directors decided to increase the company's share capital to £450,000, by a new issue of 300,000 shares at 50p each. This proposal was put to the AGM at the end of that month and was

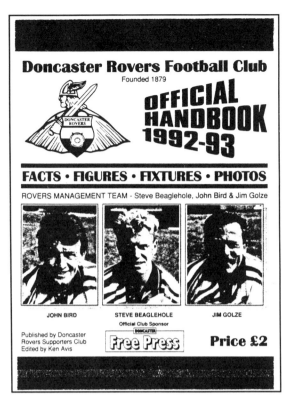

surprisingly defeated by a large majority. Apparently there was the fear that one person could acquire all the new issue, leaving the need to only obtain a small percentage of existing shares to take control of the club. At the same time it was announced that the Rovers had agreed to sell the Belle Vue Social Club to the Town Moor Golf Club.

The share issue was raised again before Christmas when it was made known that the Rovers still owed a substantial sum of money, amounting to five figures, to the Inland Revenue. At a special shareholders meeting early in the New Year, it was approved unanimously when the Board revealed that the Inland Revenue had issued a winding-up petition on the club for payment of an outstanding debt of £70,000. An agreement was reached with the Revenue in which they paid £30,000, with the balance due in March.

On March the 10th 1993, James Burke – the Rovers chairman – announced that the club had been taken over by Dinard Trading Company, who were based in the Isle of Man, and had acquired a 52% controlling interest. Their representative, Ken Richardson, a wealthy businessman, was formerly president of Bridlington Town, building them into a thriving, successful club.

However, the Rovers were taken to the High Court again at the end of March since the balance due to the Inland Revenue had not been paid. An adjournment was granted due to the club being in the process of being taken over. But shareholders at a special meeting on April the 1st wanted to know why the tax debt had not been paid off, after all that had been the reason why the issue in January had been voted through. It emerged that a Board meeting had voted in favour of the directors being allowed to convert their loans into shares, a common practice at many clubs. This practice, however, did not put any fresh money into the club.

The tax bill was finally settled in May. At the end of that month Dinard announced that after a thorough investigation of the Rovers accounts they were ready to commit themselves to the club. The accounts showed debts of over £360,000, so a commitment of that extent augured well for the future of the club. A new era dawns.........!

CHAPTER 11

The Grounds

 hen the Rovers were formed in 1879 the whole area between Thorne Road and the Racecourse was farmland, not densely built on as today. They played their early matches on a field loaned to them by the farmer at Intake Farm, which stood where the Fire Station now stands on Leger Way. They also played on the Town Moor, or to non-locals – the Racecourse – and occasionally on the Belle Vue playing fields used by the Rugby club.

These playing fields are now covered by Welbeck Road, Firbeck Road, Sandbeck Road and Danum Road.

THE INTAKE GROUND 1885–1916

The Intake Ground c. 1900.

For season 1885–86 the Rovers obtained the use of a field at the rear of the Yorkshire Institute for the Deaf and Dumb. It is still used today by the Institute as a sports field. Initially known as the Deaf and Dumb ground, it was not until November 1886 that the name, 'Intake ground', was first used. There were no facilities on the ground at that time, the teams having to change at the Rockingham Inn and then walk the four or five hundred yards to the ground. The 1886–87 season brought a change of clubhouse to the Doncaster Arms but the walk was still the same distance.

A commodious grandstand was erected on the Intake Farm side of the ground for season 1888–89, with turnstiles and a ticket office placed at the entrance, which was at the rear of the Deaf and Dumb buildings off what is now Town Moor Avenue. Materials cost £31 for the materials with the labour given free

by volunteers. For season 1890–91 press facilities were provided in the shape of a shed next to the grandstand. On October the 25th 1890, for the F.A. Cup-tie against Kilnhurst, the Salutation Hotel was first used as the club house.

They used an upstairs room as changing rooms with access by stairs from the outside courtyard. Duckboards were spread around the ropes encircling the ground for the spectators to stand on, particularly useful in bad weather when the surrounds were churned into mud.

On the night of December the 10th 1891, the roof was blown off the stand, and landed in the Deaf and Dumb Institute's yard. Yet the scheduled Midland League match against Burslem Port Vale still went ahead, but with very few spectators. A week later a new enlarged stand costing £40 had been erected, and

106

*The F.A.Cup – November 1909 – Rovers v. Mexboro' at the Intake Ground
Looking towards Town Moor Avenue, showing dressing rooms and Press Stand.*

was by December the 19th, for the match against Long Eaton Rangers. Unfortunately six weeks later, on Friday, the 29th of January 29th, another gale blew the stand down! This in turn was rebuilt with donations from members and other fundraising activities, so that the club only contributed £20.

For the Easter period of 1893, the Intake ground was under suspension, so the Rovers – who had two Midland League home games to play on Good Friday and Easter Monday – played on a ground at Askern, which had placed at their disposal for a consideration by Mr. Edwards of the Swan Hotel, Askern. The exact location of this 'ground' has not been identified, but for both games the Rovers attracted nearly 4,000 spectators, more than the numbers that had been attending the Intake matches.

The fiasco of the Newark match in April 1900, when a visiting player was harassed by the crowd at the end of the game, resulted in the club being ordered to provide dressing accommodation on the ground which was necessary in any event if Doncaster were to be admitted into the Football League. The structure built provided changing facilities, and was located at the northern, or town end, of the grandstand on the Town Moor Avenue side. Meanwhile the tenancy at the ground was precarious, with the club restricted in the accommodation they could provide for spectators, and Doncaster Council were approached for assistance in providing a site for a new ground. They offered six acres of land at the Low Pastures, where the present ground is sited, on a yearly tenancy or a lease of £2 per acre, subject to no wooden stands being erected that would obstruct the view from the Great North Road across the Pastures. This restriction rendered the whole object of the Club's request useless, and eventually they came to terms with the landlord and stayed at the Intake ground. The ground evidently came up to any standards that the Football League set, if any, because they were allowed to join Division 2.

The attendance record was set on Good Friday 1902, when the leaders, Middlesbrough came to town. The Committee arranged for a temporary stand and enclosure, at a cost of £50, to accommodate 1,200 people on the Bennetthorpe side of the ground for this match. Over 6,000 attended the match, a figure never equalled.

In November 1902 an up-to-date, handsome, new permanent stand was constructed on the Bennetthorpe side of the ground at a cost of £200. It could accommodate 1,000 people and had windows at the side. It was passed as safe by the Borough Surveyor, but unfortunately a hurricane on Christmas Day evening blew the stand down. Two days later the Rovers were hosts to Manchester City, a promotion contender. The loss of the stand kept the crowd down to around 4,000, and therefore the results of the weather represented a loss on two fronts. It was eventually rebuilt at a cost of £132 to the club, the balance being donated by members and other supporters.

On Easter Saturday, April 18th 1908, at the end of the match against Worksop Town, the crowd invaded the pitch and allegedly assaulted some of the Worksop players. The Sheffield and Hallamshire F.A. suspended the Intake for the whole of the following September – the first month of the next season. The Rovers had difficulty in finding a ground to play their two home matches on, but eventually they came to an agreement with Conisborough St.Peter's to use their ground at Park Road, Conisborough, which is now built over by houses.

During the First World War, after the club had suspended operations in 1916, the ground was requisitioned by the War Department as a military depot. With the Rovers not re-starting immediately after the war, when the military moved out the tennis club took over. At some stage the ground reverted to its present owners, the Yorkshire Institute for the Deaf and Dumb, and is still used for sports.

The 'White Swan' Askern today. Two matches were played here, it is believed, on the field behind.

THE BENNETTHORPE GROUND 1920–22

When the Rovers re-formed in April 1920 they needed a ground and approached Doncaster Council for assistance in finding a suitable venue. Eventually, after much tooing and froing the club accepted the Council's offer of a six acre site at the Low Pastures. But it would take time for a ground to be prepared on this site, and the Corporation agreed to allow the club the use of the Education Committee's playing fields at Belle Vue, Bennetthorpe, the same Belle Vue that the club had used some forty years previously when the Rugby club used it. This ground was enclosed, and new turnstiles were put in to provide an entrance from Back Lane. Originally the club was only granted the use of the ground for one year, but the directors, upon taking over the club from the Provisional Committee, refused to accept the Low Pastures because of the money required to make it into a football ground.

At last, in June 1921, the club accepted the offer of the Low Pastures with a long lease at a rent of £50 per annum, and would also be allowed to use the Bennetthorpe ground for season 1921–22 at the same rent as the previous season – £26 per annum – until the Low Pastures ground was ready. A stand had been erected on one side of the Bennetthorpe ground in the summer of 1921, and would held 1,000 people. This structure is familiar to anyone who has visited Belle Vue up to recently; the stand that stood at the Town End of the present Belle Vue ground was that very structure! The record attendance at the Bennetthorpe ground was 7,219, the number that attended the opening game of the 1921–22 season against Gainsborough Trinity.

THE BELLE VUE GROUND 1922–93

Belle Vue – 1924/25 season.

This ground was opened on Saturday, August the 26th 1922 by Mr. Charles E.Sutcliffe of the Football League. The opposition was provided by Gainsborough Trinity in the opening Midland League match of the season, a match watched by about ten thousand people.

The initial levelling of the ground required five hundred loads of earth to be removed, and 50,000 loads of ash to form the foundation of the pitch and the banking around it. The main stand was built to seat 4,000 people, but would be extended to seat 6,000 as and when the necessary finance was provided. In front of the main stand was terracing for 3,000 spectators. During the summer of 1924 a shelter was completed on the popular side, and then in the close season of 1927 this was extended, as was the main stand, with funds supplied by the Supporters Club. These extensions were formally opened by the F.A. Secretary, Mr.Frederick J.Wall, at the first game of the season against Lincoln City. Also at this time, the Main Stand at Bennetthorpe was jacked up and moved on rollers to become the Town End stand at Bell Vue. The Supporters Club again provided the funds in the summer of 1928 to concrete the popular side right round to include the Spion Kop.

In the close season of 1935, with Division 2 football looming, the club spent £182 on turnstiles, fencing and gates, with another £600 on extensions and other improvements. During that first season in the Second Division they spent £787 on additional stand accommodation, and a further £287 on banking and terracing. The summer of 1937 saw the Supporters Club providing the funds to concrete 1,600 lineal yards of terracing on the popular side. Then a year later the popular side shelter was taken down, rebuilt further back, and raised. It also required about two miles of concrete on the new terracing, that would accommodate another five thousand spectators, bringing the capacity of the ground to about 40,000.

In September 1938 the club negotiated a new lease on the ground to run for the next twenty-one years, then in that fateful summer of 1939, the club built a concrete wall running the whole length of the popular side, and also laid down a running track for the players.

During the next ten years or so only essential repairs were allowed to be carried out unless a building licence could be obtained.

Belle Vue – 1949/50 season. (Note the Bennetthorpe Stand on the left)

In March 1950 the lease of the ground was re-negotiated and one for sixty years was granted. For the first nine years, the unexpired portion of the previous lease cost £50 per year, and for the next ten years the figure was £100 per year with the rent reviewed after this nineteen years period.

The ground was now the ground that everyone who has visited Belle Vue between the Second World War and 1985 knows. The uncovered Kop was raised quite steeply and had sixty two steps giving an almost aerial view of the ground, and when the play wasn't very interesting you could always turn round and watch the aircraft on the local airfield behind the ground! In the 1970's the capacity was reduced to 21,150, including 2,010 seats, around seven hundred of which were in the Town End Stand.

The Rossington End, formerly the Spion Kop – but now looking more like a prison yard with its heavy metal fencing, formed a pen along half of the terracing, which had the top third sliced off to form an all-weather five-a-side pitch.

The Valley Parade Fire and the Safety of Sports Grounds Act of 1985 changed everything, reducing the capacity at a stroke to around the 10,000 mark, since the Town End (North) Stand – used for some years as a Family Stand – was demolished under the terms of the Act. The Main Stand alone required over £100,000 spent on firecladding before the start of the 1985-86 season.

Plans were afoot in 1985 to rebuild the stadium, but these were overtaken by the events at Heysel and Bradford. Emergency lighting and a new PA system were also installed, and around £450,000 was spent on improvements, seventy five per cent of it provided by the Football Grounds Improvement Trust. The capacity was then set at 9,900. During the summer of 1986 extensive repair work to the terracing at the Town End was carried out by the Junior Rovers with the concrete donated free of charge by the local firm, Steerley's.

A massive blow to the club struck in May 1987 when it was discovered that the Popular side terrace had been hit by mining subsidence. This side was closed, reducing the capacity to 4,859. The cover was taken down and the top third of the terracing taken away, with the remainder re-concreted, and was re-opened as an uncovered terrace.

In October 1988, the Rossington End pen was extended to cater for 2,000 visiting supporters, which increased the capacity of the ground to 8,259. This cost £50,000 but was funded by the Football Trust.

Then, of course, came Hillsborough in April 1989. The response of the authorities in regard to Belle Vue was to cut the capacity to 7,294, by reducing all standing area limits by fifteen per cent. The maximum capacity for the main stand terrace became 2,125, for the Popular side 1,700, the pen for away supporters was 1,700 and on the Town End terrace 510. The main stand seating capacity was set at 1,259. Extra stewards, thirty four in all, had also to be provided. In November 1989, a ninety yard long cover was built on the Popular side at a cost of £50,000.

The 1990's have brought many meetings between the Rovers, Doncaster RLFC, and Doncaster Council with a view to providing a ground to be shared by the two clubs.
The talk originally centred around one of the grounds being improved and shared, then came the idea of a single new ground being built for the two, but the Council eventually knocked this idea into touch because of government rate-capping. Whilst these ideas are still talking points in 1993, there has been no action in three years of negotiations. It is to be hoped that now the club is under new ownership, and a new era beckons, that this will also include the provision of a modern stadium.

Belle Vue as it is today

Sequences and Records

Major Honours:

Champions Division 3 North:	1934/35, 1946/47, 1949,50.
Champions 4th Division:	1965/66, 1968/69.
County Cup Winners:	1890/91, 1911/12, 1935/36, 1937/38,
	1955/56, 1967/68, 1975/76, 1985/86.

F.A.Cup – Furthest in competition – 5th round:

23/2/52: 0–4 v. Portsmouth	19/2/55: 1–2 v. Birmingham City
20/2/54: 1–3 v. Leyton Orient	18/2/56: 0–2 v. Tottenham Hotspur

Football League Cup – furthest in competition – 5th round:
3/12/75: 2–7 v. Tottenham Hotspur

Attendances at Belle Vue:
Highest: 37,099 v. Hull City (League) 2/10/48.
Lowest: 613 v. Blackpool (Autoglass Trophy) 17/12/91

Record Transfer Fees:
Received: Ian Snodin – £200,000
Paid: John Philliben – £60,000

Most League Goals in one season:

Scored: 123 – 1946/47	Conceded: 117 – 1966/67

Youngest League player: Alick Jeffrey – 15 years 229 days
Oldest League player: Mitchell Downie – 40 years 252 days

Most League wins in a season: 34 (in 42 games) – 1946/47
Most League defeats in a season: 28 (in 34 games) – 1904/05

Most points: 72 – 1946/47 (2 points for a win)
Least points: 8 – 1904/05

Largest victory:

League – 10–0 v.Darlington (h) 25/1/64	F.A.Cup – 7–0 v.Blyth Spartans (a) 27/11/37

Largest defeat:

League – 0–12 v. Small Heath (Birmingham) (a) 11/4/03	F.A.Cup – 0–8 v. Everton (a) 21/1/39

Most Capped player: Len Graham – 14 (Northern Ireland)

Most (League) Goals:

In a match: 6 – Tom Keetley v. Ashington (a) 16/2/29	In a season: 42 – Clarrie Jordan 1946/47

Most Football League Appearances:

1. F.Emery – 417	2. C.Douglas – 404	3. H.Tindall – 401

Most League Goals:

1. T.Keetley – 180	2. A.Jeffrey – 127	3. H.Tindall – 124

Players' of the season:

1970/71 – Brian Usher	1978/79 – Pat Lally	1985/86 – Tony Brown
1971/72 – Archie Irvine	1979/80 – Alan Warboys	1986/87 – Neil Redfearn
1972/73 – Archie Irvine	1980/81 – Alan Little	1987/88 – Ronny Robinson
1973/74 – Mike Elwiss	1981/82 – Glyn Snodin	1988/89 – Jack Ashurst
1974/75 – Peter Kitchen	1982/83 – Glyn Snodin	1989/90 – Colin Douglas
1975/76 – Ian Miller	1983/84 – Colin Douglas	1990/91 – Colin Douglas
1976/77 – Ian Miller	1984/85 – Ian Snodin	1991/92 – Eddie Gormley
1977/78 – Bobby Owen		1992/93 – Eddie Gormley

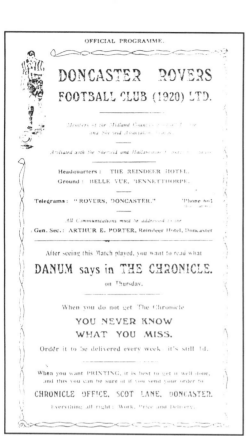

PROGRAMME

Doncaster Rovers Football Club

OFFICIAL PROGRAMME
·
Saturday, 27th August, 1966
·
Rovers v. Torquay Utd.
·

FOOTBALL LEAGUE — DIVISION III

PRICE
SIXPENCE

DONCASTER ROVERS FC

ROVERS
v
BARNSLEY

Official Programme

PARADE

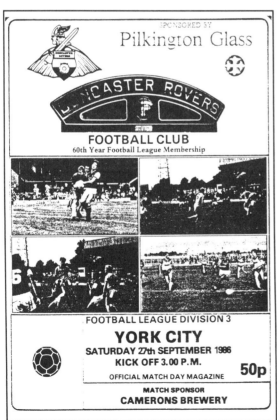

SPONSORED BY
Pilkington Glass

DONCASTER ROVERS
FOOTBALL CLUB
60th Year Football League Membership

FOOTBALL LEAGUE DIVISION 3
YORK CITY
SATURDAY 27th SEPTEMBER 1986
KICK OFF 3.00 P.M.
OFFICIAL MATCH DAY MAGAZINE
50p
MATCH SPONSOR
CAMERONS BREWERY

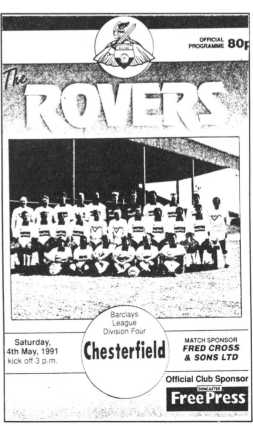

OFFICIAL
PROGRAMME 80p

The ROVERS

Barclays
League
Division Four

Saturday,
4th May, 1991
kick off 3 p.m.

Chesterfield

MATCH SPONSOR
*FRED CROSS
& SONS LTD*

Official Club Sponsor
DONCASTER
Free Press

Complete League Record

1890-91 to 1992-93

	HOME							AWAY							TOTAL								
	P	W	D	L	F	A	PTS	P	W	D	L	F	A	PTS	P	W	D	L	F	A	PTS	POS	Ave.Att.
								MIDLAND LEAGUE															
1890-1891	7	6	0	1	32	6	12	7	3	1	3	11	13	7	14	9	1	4	43	19	19	2nd	
1891-1892	10	6	2	2	18	9	14	10	2	3	5	11	25	7	20	8	5	7	29	34	21	6th	
1892-1893	12	6	2	4	26	19	14	12	5	2	5	21	25	12	24	11	4	9	47	44	26	5th	
1893-1894	10	5	2	3	19	15	12	10	0	2	8	9	32	2	20	5	4	11	28	47	14	8th	
1894-1895	13	6	5	2	23	17	17	13	0	1	12	8	46	1	26	6	6	14	31	63	18	12th	
1895-1896	14	9	4	1	34	16	22	14	1	2	11	10	40	4	28	10	6	12	44	56	26	10th	
1896-1897	14	10	3	1	52	18	23	14	7	2	5	25	22	16	28	17	5	6	77	40	39	1st	
1897-1898	11	5	4	2	26	10	14	11	0	2	9	6	25	2	22	5	6	11	32	35	16	10th	
1898-1899	13	12	1	0	41	11	25	13	2	4	7	15	36	8	26	14	5	7	56	47	33	1st	
1899-1900	12	7	4	1	36	14	18	12	2	2	8	15	28	6	24	9	6	9	51	42	24	7th	
1900-1901	13	12	0	1	59	14	24	13	5	2	6	28	18	12	26	17	2	7	87	32	36	2nd	
								DIVISON 2															
1901-1902	17	12	3	2	39	12	27	17	1	5	11	10	46	7	34	13	8	13	49	58	34	7th	4,000
1902-1903	17	8	5	4	27	17	21	17	1	2	14	8	55	4	34	9	7	18	35	72	25	16th	5,800
								MIDLAND LEAGUE															
1903-1904	17	10	3	4	42	21	23	17	3	2	12	16	34	8	34	13	5	16	58	55	31	11th	
								DIVISON 2															
1904-1905	17	3	2	12	12	32	8	17	0	0	17	11	49	0	34	3	2	29	23	81	8	18th	3,000
								MIDLAND LEAGUE															
1905-1906	17	9	3	5	35	19	21	17	1	3	13	12	58	5	34	10	6	18	47	77	26	14th	
1906-1907	19	8	5	6	34	23	21	19	2	2	15	18	59	6	38	10	7	21	52	82	27	17th	
1907-1908	19	9	2	8	26	18	20	19	5	2	12	25	48	12	38	14	4	20	51	66	32	15th	
1908-1909	19	12	3	4	28	19	27	19	6	0	13	22	40	12	38	18	3	17	50	59	39	11th	
1909-1910	21	10	7	4	33	18	27	21	4	4	13	18	48	12	42	14	11	17	51	66	39	14th	
1910-1911	19	14	3	2	63	24	31	19	9	1	9	43	39	19	38	23	4	11	106	63	50	3rd	
1911-1912	18	14	2	2	52	15	30	18	7	4	7	27	27	18	36	21	6	9	79	42	48	3rd	
1912-1913	19	15	2	2	38	13	32	19	6	5	8	29	30	17	38	21	7	10	67	43	49	4th	
1913-1914	17	9	0	8	19	18	18	17	3	2	12	11	34	8	34	12	2	20	30	52	26	16th	
1914-1915	19	12	2	5	42	13	26	19	2	1	16	16	69	5	38	14	3	21	58	82	31	15th	
1915-1916	8	4	2	2	29	10	10	8	0	0	8	8	19	0	16	4	2	10	37	29	10	7th	
								(1st World War)															
1920-1921	19	9	5	5	25	19	23	19	2	5	12	13	35	9	38	11	10	17	38	54	32	16th	
1921-1922	21	11	2	8	29	28	24	21	6	4	11	24	38	16	42	17	6	19	53	66	40	13th	
1922-1923	21	16	4	1	40	6	36	21	10	5	6	32	22	25	42	26	9	7	72	28	61	2nd	
								DIVISION 3 NORTH															
1923-1924	21	13	4	4	35	17	30	21	2	8	11	18	36	12	42	15	12	15	53	53	42	9th	7,285
1924-1925	21	12	5	4	36	17	29	21	2	5	14	16	47	9	42	14	10	18	52	64	38	18th	5,380
1925-1926	21	11	7	3	52	25	29	21	5	4	12	28	47	14	42	16	11	15	80	72	43	10th	5,190
1926-1927	21	13	4	4	58	27	30	21	5	7	9	23	38	17	42	18	11	13	81	65	47	8th	5,334
1927-1928	21	15	4	2	59	18	34	21	8	3	10	20	26	19	42	23	7	12	79	44	53	4th	7,574
1928-1929	21	14	3	4	39	19	31	21	6	7	8	37	43	19	42	20	10	12	76	62	50	5th	6,733
1929-1930	21	13	5	3	39	22	31	21	2	4	15	23	47	8	42	15	9	18	62	69	39	14th	4,652
1930-1931	21	9	8	4	40	18	26	21	3	4	14	23	47	10	42	12	12	18	63	65	36	15th	4,176
1931-1932	20	12	3	5	38	27	27	20	4	1	15	21	53	9	40	16	4	20	59	80	36	15th	3,903
1932-1933	21	13	8	0	52	26	34	21	4	6	11	25	53	14	42	17	14	11	77	79	48	6th	5,262
1933-1934	21	17	1	3	58	24	35	21	5	8	8	25	37	18	42	22	9	11	83	61	53	5th	6,000
1934-1935	21	16	0	5	53	21	37	21	10	5	6	34	23	25	42	26	5	11	87	44	62	1st	10,761
								DIVISION 2															
1935-1936	21	10	7	4	28	17	27	21	4	2	15	23	54	10	42	14	9	19	51	71	37	18th	14,122
1936-1937	21	6	6	9	18	29	18	21	1	4	16	12	55	6	42	7	10	25	30	84	24	22nd	11,697
								DIVISION 3 NORTH															
1937-1938	21	15	4	2	47	14	34	21	6	8	7	26	33	20	42	21	12	9	73	47	54	2nd	12,373
1938-1939	21	12	5	4	47	21	29	21	9	9	3	40	27	27	42	21	14	7	87	48	56	2nd	11,587
								(2nd World War)															
1946-1947	21	15	5	1	67	16	35	21	18	1	2	56	22	37	42	33	6	3	113	38	72	1st	15,359

DIVISION 2

Season	P	W	D	L	F	A	Pts	P	W	D	L	F	A	Pts	P	W	D	L	F	A	Pts	Pos	Att
1947-1948	21	7	8	6	22	19	22	21	2	3	16	17	46	7	42	9	11	22	39	65	29	21st	22,261

DIVISION 3 NORTH

Season	P	W	D	L	F	A	Pts	P	W	D	L	F	A	Pts	P	W	D	L	F	A	Pts	Pos	Att
1948-1949	21	10	8	3	26	12	28	21	10	2	9	27	28	22	42	20	10	12	53	40	50	3rd	13,284
1949-1950	21	9	9	3	30	15	27	21	10	8	3	36	23	28	42	19	17	6	66	38	55	1st	17,901

DIVISION 2

Season	P	W	D	L	F	A	Pts	P	W	D	L	F	A	Pts	P	W	D	L	F	A	Pts	Pos	Att
1950-1951	21	9	6	6	37	32	24	21	6	7	8	27	36	19	42	15	13	14	64	68	43	11th	22,799
1951-1952	21	9	4	8	29	28	22	21	4	8	9	26	32	16	42	13	12	17	55	60	38	16th	21,066
1952-1953	21	9	9	3	26	17	27	21	3	7	11	32	47	13	42	12	16	14	58	64	40	13th	15,324
1953-1954	21	9	5	7	32	28	23	21	7	4	10	27	35	18	42	16	9	17	59	63	41	12th	16,919
1954-1955	21	10	5	6	35	34	25	21	4	2	15	23	61	10	42	14	7	21	58	95	35	18th	12,236
1955-1956	21	11	5	5	45	32	27	21	1	6	14	24	66	8	42	12	11	19	69	98	35	17th	12,420
1956-1957	21	12	5	4	51	21	29	21	3	5	13	26	56	11	42	15	10	17	77	77	40	14th	12,389
1957-1958	21	7	5	9	34	40	19	21	1	6	14	22	48	8	42	8	11	23	56	88	27	22nd	11,132

DIVISION 3

Season	P	W	D	L	F	A	Pts	P	W	D	L	F	A	Pts	P	W	D	L	F	A	Pts	Pos	Att
1958-1959	23	13	2	8	40	31	28	23	1	3	19	10	58	5	46	14	5	27	50	89	33	22nd	6,652

DIVISION 4

Season	P	W	D	L	F	A	Pts	P	W	D	L	F	A	Pts	P	W	D	L	F	A	Pts	Pos	Att
1959-1960	23	13	3	7	39	23	29	23	3	7	13	29	52	13	46	16	10	20	68	75	42	17th	5,251
1960-1961	23	15	0	8	52	35	30	23	4	7	12	24	45	15	46	19	7	20	76	80	45	11th	4,754
1961-1962	22	8	5	9	34	27	21	22	3	2	17	26	55	8	44	11	7	26	60	82	29	21st	4,470
1962-1963	23	9	10	4	36	26	28	23	5	4	14	28	52	14	46	14	14	18	64	78	42	16th	6,305
1963-1964	23	11	8	4	46	23	30	23	4	4	15	24	52	12	46	15	12	19	70	75	42	14th	6,360
1964-1965	23	13	6	4	46	25	32	23	7	5	11	38	47	19	46	20	11	15	84	62	51	9th	8,557
1965-1966	23	15	6	2	49	21	36	23	9	5	9	36	33	23	46	24	11	11	85	54	59	1st	10,594

DIVISION 3

Season	P	W	D	L	F	A	Pts	P	W	D	L	F	A	Pts	P	W	D	L	F	A	Pts	Pos	Att
1966-1967	23	11	6	6	40	40	28	23	1	2	20	18	77	4	46	12	8	26	58	117	32	23rd	7,908

DIVISION 4

Season	P	W	D	L	F	A	Pts	P	W	D	L	F	A	Pts	P	W	D	L	F	A	Pts	Pos	Att
1967-1968	23	12	8	3	36	16	28	23	6	7	10	30	40	19	46	18	15	13	66	56	47	10th	7,852
1968-1969	23	12	9	2	42	16	33	23	8	9	6	23	22	25	46	21	17	8	65	38	58	1st	10,212

DIVISION 3

Season	P	W	D	L	F	A	Pts	P	W	D	L	F	A	Pts	P	W	D	L	F	A	Pts	Pos	Att
1969-1970	23	13	4	6	31	19	30	23	4	8	11	21	35	20	46	17	12	17	52	54	50	11th	8,561
1970-1971	23	8	5	10	28	27	21	23	5	4	14	17	39	14	46	13	9	24	45	66	35	23rd	4,479

DIVISION 4

Season	P	W	D	L	F	A	Pts	P	W	D	L	F	A	Pts	P	W	D	L	F	A	Pts	Pos	Att
1971-1972	23	11	8	4	35	24	30	23	5	6	12	21	39	16	46	16	14	16	56	63	46	12th	4,126
1972-1973	23	10	8	5	28	19	28	23	5	4	14	21	39	14	46	15	12	19	49	58	42	17th	2,258
1973-1974	23	10	7	6	32	25	27	23	2	4	17	15	58	8	46	12	11	23	47	83	35	22nd	2,297
1974-1975	23	10	9	4	41	29	29	23	4	3	16	24	50	11	46	14	12	20	65	79	40	17th	2,975
1975-1976	23	10	6	7	42	30	26	23	9	5	9	33	38	23	46	19	11	16	75	64	49	10th	6,083
1976-1977	23	16	2	5	47	25	34	23	5	7	11	24	40	17	46	21	9	16	71	65	51	8th	4,500
1977-1978	23	11	8	4	37	26	30	23	4	9	10	15	37	17	46	15	17	14	52	63	47	12th	3,228
1978-1979	23	8	8	7	25	21	24	23	5	3	15	25	50	13	46	13	11	22	50	71	37	22nd	3,072
1979-1980	23	11	6	6	37	27	28	23	4	8	11	25	36	16	46	15	14	17	62	63	44	12th	4,403
1980-1981	23	15	4	4	36	19	34	23	7	8	8	22	29	22	46	22	12	12	58	48	56	3rd	5,411

DIVISION 3

Season	P	W	D	L	F	A	Pts	P	W	D	L	F	A	Pts	P	W	D	L	F	A	Pts	Pos	Att
1981-1982	23	9	9	5	31	26	27	23	4	8	11	24	44	16	46	13	17	16	55	70	43	19th	5,263
1982-1983	23	6	8	9	38	44	20	23	3	3	17	17	55	7	46	9	11	26	55	99	27	23rd	3,004

DIVISION 4

Season	P	W	D	L	F	A	Pts	P	W	D	L	F	A	Pts	P	W	D	L	F	A	Pts	Pos	Att
1983-1984	23	15	6	2	45	22	36	23	9	7	7	36	31	25	46	24	13	9	81	53	61	2nd	3,729

DIVISION 3

Season	P	W	D	L	F	A	Pts	P	W	D	L	F	A	Pts	P	W	D	L	F	A	Pts	Pos	Att
1984-1985	23	11	5	7	42	32	27	23	6	3	14	29	40	15	46	17	8	21	71	72	42	14th	4,103
1985-1986	23	7	10	6	20	21	24	23	9	6	8	25	30	24	46	16	16	14	45	51	48	11th	2,822
1986-1987	23	11	8	4	32	19	30	23	3	6	14	21	41	12	46	14	14	18	53	60	42	13th	2,402
1987-1988	23	6	5	12	25	35	17	23	2	4	17	15	48	8	46	8	9	29	40	83	25	24th	1,893

DIVISION 4

Season	P	W	D	L	F	A	Pts	P	W	D	L	F	A	Pts	P	W	D	L	F	A	Pts	Pos	Att
1988-1989	23	9	6	8	32	32	24	23	4	4	15	17	45	12	46	13	10	23	49	77	36	23rd	2,166
1989-1990	23	7	7	9	29	29	28	23	7	2	14	24	28	23	46	14	9	23	53	57	51	20th	2,710
1990-1991	23	12	5	6	36	21	41	23	5	9	9	20	24	24	46	17	14	15	56	45	65	11th	2,835
1991-1992	22	7	2	13	22	35	23	22	3	7	12	19	30	16	44	10	9	25	41	65	39	21st	2,079

DIVISION 3 (Old Division 4)

Season	P	W	D	L	F	A	Pts	P	W	D	L	F	A	Pts	P	W	D	L	F	A	Pts	Pos	Att
1992-1993	21	6	5	10	22	28	23	21	5	9	7	20	29	24	42	11	14	17	42	57	47	16th	2,411

Complete record against Football League teams
(up to and including 1992/93 season)

TEAM	HOME						AWAY						TOTAL					
	P	W	D	L	F	A	P	W	D	L	F	A	P	W	D	L	F	A
ACCRINGTON STANLEY	19	15	3	1	63	16	19	5	6	8	26	36	38	20	9	9	89	52
ALDERSHOT	20	13	4	3	42	19	20	1	5	14	15	39	40	14	9	17	57	58
ARSENAL	2	1	0	1	1	1	2	0	0	2	0	4	4	1	0	3	1	5
ASHINGTON	6	6	0	0	19	9	6	2	1	3	12	17	12	8	1	3	31	26
ASTON VILLA	2	2	0	0	3	1	2	0	1	1	3	4	4	2	1	1	6	5
BARNET	2	2	0	0	3	1	2	0	0	2	0	3	4	2	0	2	3	4
BARNSLEY	26	12	9	5	41	31	26	6	8	12	29	42	52	18	17	17	70	73
BARROW	25	13	8	4	48	24	25	3	8	14	28	45	50	16	16	18	76	69
BIRMINGHAM CITY	7	3	1	3	6	12	7	2	1	4	7	23	14	5	2	7	13	35
BLACKBURN ROVERS	9	1	3	5	9	18	9	0	3	6	13	26	18	1	6	11	22	44
BLACKPOOL	11	5	3	3	14	16	11	0	2	9	8	29	22	5	5	12	22	45
BOLTON WANDERERS	4	2	1	1	6	5	4	1	0	3	2	7	8	3	1	4	8	12
BOURNEMOUTH	13	6	6	1	19	11	13	4	3	6	16	26	26	10	9	7	35	37
BRADFORD CITY	30	12	11	7	48	36	30	7	6	17	26	53	60	19	17	24	74	89
BRADFORD PARK AVENUE	15	11	2	2	35	16	15	2	3	10	19	40	30	13	5	12	54	56
BRENTFORD	21	10	4	7	34	24	21	4	8	9	23	28	42	14	12	16	57	52
BRIGHTON & HOVE ALBION	6	3	2	1	8	5	6	0	2	4	1	11	12	3	4	5	9	16
BRISTOL CITY	14	6	4	4	20	15	14	1	3	10	13	39	28	7	7	14	33	54
BRISTOL ROVERS	14	7	2	5	25	22	14	2	2	10	12	33	28	9	4	15	37	55
BURNLEY	11	7	0	4	16	12	11	3	2	6	9	22	22	10	2	10	25	34
BURTON UNITED	3	1	1	1	4	4	3	0	1	2	1	3	6	1	2	3	5	7
BURY	22	9	7	6	30	22	22	4	4	14	32	62	44	13	11	20	62	84
CAMBRIDGE UNITED	8	2	4	2	8	9	8	0	4	4	7	16	16	2	8	6	15	25
CARDIFF CITY	9	1	4	4	7	11	9	2	2	5	7	14	18	3	6	9	14	25
CARLISLE UNITED	23	12	5	6	48	29	23	7	6	10	23	37	46	19	11	16	71	66
CHARLTON ATHLETIC	2	1	0	1	3	2	2	0	0	2	0	5	4	1	0	3	3	7
CHESTER CITY	26	13	10	3	48	28	26	9	6	11	34	41	52	22	16	14	82	69
CHESTERFIELD	35	17	7	11	40	43	35	6	12	17	35	57	70	23	19	28	75	100
COLCHESTER UNITED	13	10	1	2	24	15	13	3	2	8	11	25	26	13	3	10	35	40
COVENTRY CITY	5	3	2	0	12	3	5	1	1	3	4	10	10	4	3	3	16	13
CREWE ALEXANDRA	38	20	9	9	72	35	38	13	11	14	43	62	76	33	20	23	115	97
CRYSTALL PALACE	2	0	0	2	1	3	2	0	0	2	1	9	4	0	0	4	2	12
DARLINGTON	41	27	3	11	96	43	41	9	15	17	54	76	82	36	18	28	150	120
DERBY COUNTY	5	2	0	3	6	9	5	0	1	4	2	12	10	2	1	7	8	21
DURHAM CITY	5	4	1	0	16	3	5	1	1	3	6	9	10	5	2	3	22	12
EVERTON	3	2	1	0	8	3	3	0	1	2	3	12	6	2	2	2	11	15
EXETER CITY	17	12	3	2	37	17	17	6	1	10	17	24	34	18	4	12	54	41
FULHAM	14	6	4	4	23	18	14	3	4	7	14	29	28	9	8	11	37	47
GAINSBOROUGH TRINITY	3	1	1	1	3	5	3	0	0	3	1	9	6	1	1	4	4	14
GATESHEAD	2	2	0	0	3	1	2	0	0	2	1	3	4	2	0	2	4	4
GLOSSOP	3	2	0	1	7	4	3	0	0	3	1	8	6	2	0	4	8	12
GILLINGHAM	21	7	6	8	28	26	21	1	4	16	15	46	42	8	10	24	43	72
GRIMSBY TOWN	15	6	3	6	21	23	15	2	4	9	16	33	30	8	7	15	37	56
HALIFAX TOWN	36	14	11	11	63	37	36	15	9	12	41	49	72	29	20	23	104	86
HARTLEPOOL UNITED	39	21	12	6	78	41	39	8	13	18	46	61	78	29	25	24	124	102
HEREFORD UNITED	10	8	1	1	20	6	10	5	2	3	16	12	20	13	3	4	36	18
HUDDERSFIELD TOWN	10	5	1	4	17	18	10	3	1	6	11	21	20	8	2	10	28	39
HULL CITY	16	8	3	5	31	19	16	4	4	8	19	39	32	12	7	13	50	58
IPSWICH TOWN	2	0	2	0	2	2	2	0	0	2	1	7	4	0	2	2	3	9
LEEDS UNITED	7	2	3	2	10	7	7	0	3	4	3	11	14	2	6	6	13	18
LEICESTER CITY	12	4	6	2	17	12	12	1	0	11	10	36	24	5	6	13	27	48
LEYTON ORIENT	7	3	2	2	12	8	7	0	1	6	3	17	14	3	3	8	15	25
LINCOLN CITY	44	17	13	14	61	63	44	9	12	23	51	85	88	26	25	37	112	148
LIVERPOOL	5	2	2	1	8	7	5	1	0	4	5	12	10	3	2	5	13	19
LUTON TOWN	9	4	2	3	13	12	9	2	0	7	14	24	18	6	2	10	27	36

TEAM	HOME						AWAY						TOTAL					
	P	W	D	L	F	A	P	W	D	L	F	A	P	W	D	L	F	A
MAIDSTONE UNITED	3	2	1	0	7	1	3	1	1	1	3	3	6	3	2	1	10	4
MANCHESTER CITY	2	1	0	1	5	5	2	0	1	1	4	7	4	1	1	2	9	12
MANCHESTER UNITED	4	1	2	1	6	3	4	0	1	3	0	16	8	1	3	4	6	19
MANSFIELD TOWN	20	7	3	10	25	29	20	4	6	10	24	41	40	11	9	20	49	70
MIDDLESBOROUGH	8	4	1	3	13	11	8	0	1	7	6	26	16	4	2	10	19	37
MILLWALL	8	4	2	2	13	5	8	2	2	4	6	10	16	6	4	6	19	15
NELSON	7	4	3	0	19	6	7	2	0	5	10	21	14	6	3	5	29	27
NEW BRIGHTON	17	11	5	1	35	10	17	6	5	6	31	27	34	17	10	7	66	37
NEWCASTLE UNITED	3	0	1	2	3	7	3	0	0	3	1	11	6	0	1	5	4	18
NEWPORT COUNTY	21	8	8	5	29	27	21	6	2	13	25	36	42	14	10	18	54	63
NORTHAMPTON TOWN	16	9	3	4	25	22	16	4	3	9	13	23	32	13	6	13	38	45
NORWICH CITY	3	1	0	2	4	3	3	0	0	3	2	7	6	1	0	5	6	10
NOTTINGHAM FOREST	9	2	2	5	6	13	9	0	3	6	12	27	18	2	5	11	18	40
NOTTS COUNTY	17	9	3	5	31	27	17	7	3	7	34	33	34	16	6	12	65	60
OLDHAM ATHLETIC	11	6	5	0	17	8	11	3	4	4	13	15	22	9	9	4	30	23
OXFORD UNITED	6	2	2	2	9	8	6	1	1	4	6	16	12	3	3	6	15	24
PETERBOROUGH UNITED	12	5	2	5	17	21	12	2	3	7	14	27	24	7	5	12	31	48
PLYMOUTH ARGYLE	14	6	6	2	29	24	14	4	6	4	16	25	28	10	12	6	45	49
PORTSMOUTH	4	1	1	2	4	5	4	0	1	3	1	8	8	1	2	5	5	13
PORT VALE	15	9	2	4	25	14	15	3	2	10	14	33	30	12	4	14	39	47
PRESTON NORTH END	8	5	1	2	15	7	8	1	0	7	5	27	16	6	1	9	20	34
QUEENS PARK RANGERS	4	2	1	1	7	3	4	2	0	2	5	10	8	4	1	3	12	13
READING	16	2	6	8	22	33	16	3	1	12	13	33	32	5	7	20	35	66
ROCHDALE	42	29	9	4	92	32	42	14	7	21	60	77	84	43	16	25	152	109
ROTHERHAM COUNTY	2	1	0	1	4	2	2	1	0	1	3	5	4	2	0	2	7	7
ROTHERHAM UNITED	32	12	12	8	38	38	32	9	6	17	38	58	64	21	18	25	76	96
SCARBOROUGH	5	3	1	1	11	9	5	1	1	3	4	7	10	4	2	4	15	16
SCUNTHORPE UNITED	15	6	4	5	24	16	15	2	8	5	12	14	30	8	12	10	36	30
SHEFFIELD UNITED	8	3	4	1	9	7	8	0	2	6	5	20	16	3	6	7	14	27
SHEFFIELD WEDNESDAY	3	0	2	1	3	4	3	0	0	3	3	10	6	0	2	4	6	14
SHREWSBURY TOWN	5	2	1	2	6	7	5	1	1	3	9	11	10	3	2	5	15	18
SOUTHAMPTON	7	3	2	2	7	5	7	0	3	4	6	15	14	3	5	6	13	20
SOUTHEND UNITED	11	5	2	4	10	11	11	1	2	8	8	26	22	6	4	12	18	37
SOUTHPORT	31	20	5	6	67	23	31	7	13	11	50	56	62	27	18	17	117	79
STOCKPORT COUNTY	38	21	9	8	64	40	38	11	5	22	43	64	76	32	14	30	107	104
STOKE CITY	6	3	1	2	11	7	6	0	4	2	5	11	12	3	5	4	16	18
SUNDERLAND	1	0	0	1	0	2	1	0	0	1	3	3	2	0	0	2	1	5
SWANSEA CITY	21	12	5	4	37	19	21	5	5	11	23	42	42	17	10	15	60	61
SWINDON TOWN	5	3	2	0	8	2	5	1	3	1	5	5	10	4	5	1	13	7
TORQUAY UNITED	22	12	2	8	29	23	22	4	4	14	23	42	44	16	6	22	52	65
TOTTENHAM HOTSPUR	3	1	2	0	4	3	3	0	0	3	1	7	6	1	2	3	5	10
TRANMERE ROVERS	29	19	9	1	67	21	29	8	7	14	35	48	58	27	16	15	102	69
WALSALL	22	11	6	5	35	24	22	5	2	15	21	40	44	16	8	20	56	64
WATFORD	5	2	1	2	3	4	5	1	0	4	5	18	10	3	1	6	8	22
WEST BROMWICH ALBION	3	2	0	1	4	2	3	1	1	1	6	9	6	3	1	2	10	11
WEST HAM UNITED	11	7	1	3	20	12	11	3	4	4	14	18	22	10	5	7	34	30
WIGAN ATHLETIC	8	1	4	3	14	17	8	2	2	4	8	13	16	3	6	7	22	30
WIGAN BOROUGH	8	5	2	1	24	8	8	1	3	4	9	15	16	6	5	5	33	23
WIMBLEDON	4	2	0	2	4	6	4	1	1	2	6	7	8	3	1	4	10	13
WOLVERHAMPTON WAND	2	0	0	2	0	2	2	1	0	1	2	2	4	1	0	3	2	4
WORKINGTON	14	7	5	2	28	15	14	2	4	8	14	25	28	9	9	10	42	40
WREXHAM	32	15	14	3	57	35	32	9	8	15	37	52	64	24	22	18	94	87
YORK CITY	30	16	6	8	48	35	30	10	10	10	47	48	60	26	16	18	95	83

Friendlies and other (non-Cup) matches 1890/91 to 1992/93

(Attendances where given are approximate when noted *)

Friendlies 1890-91:

Date	Opponent	Result	Scorers	Att.
Sep 6 h	Matlock	L 0-1	Kisby.Herrod.	
13 a	Darlington St Aug	L 2-3	Gresham(2).Herrod.Hawksworth.Unknown.	800*
Oct 4 h	Kilnhurst	W 5-0	Gresham.Gresham.	
18 h	Darlington St Aug	D 2-2	Kisby.Gresham.	
Nov 8 a	Notts Jardines	L 2-6	Herrod.Gresham.	
22 a	Darlington	L 0-3		
Dec 6 h	Stockton	D 2-2	Langton.Gresham.	1.500*
13 h	Gainsboro Wanderers	D 2-2	Langton.Gresham.	800*
26 h	South Bank	W 4-1	Gresham(3).Langton.	
27 a	Stavely	D 3-3	Gresham.Langton.	
Jan 2 h	Boston	W 4-0	McCallum.Gresham.Langton.Herrod.	
24 a	South Bank	L 1-5	Unknown.	1.000*
Feb 5 a	Stockton	L 2-3	Kisby.Gresham.	
Mar14 h	Eccelsfield Wand	W 5-0	Herrod(2).McCallum.Kisby.Cuthbert.	800*
27 h	Darlington	L 1-2	Gresham	2.000*
28 h	Rotherham Town	W 2-1	Langton.Herrod.	3.000*
30 h	Crewe Alexander	W 2-1	Herrod.Langton.	
April11 a	Stavely	W 13-0	Gresham(4).Kelly(3).Herrod(2).Langton(2),Cuthbt,o.g.	1.200*
25 a	Rotherham Town	L 0-2		3.000*
29 a	Lincoln City	L 3-9	Unknown.	

Friendlies 1891-92:

Date	Opponent	Result	Scorers	Att.
Oct24 h	Mansfield Green	W 8-2	Waddington(3).Kisby(2).Bridgewater.Gresham,Langton.	500*
Oct31 h	Stavely	W 2-0	Bridgewater(2).	800*
Nov14 h	Grantham Rovers	W 2-0	Kisby.Bridgewater.	600*
21 h	South Bank	D 0-0		600*
28 a	Darlington St Aug	D 1-1	Waddington.	
Dec 5 a	Nelson	L 1-3	Waddington.	
25 h	Attercliffe	W 7-0	Edwards.Cuthbert.Parr.	400*
Jan 1 a	Darlington St Aug	W 5-0	Shaw(4).Fowler.Bennett.Edwards.	1.000*
9 h	Preston N.E. 2nd	W 5-3	Wilson(2).James.Edwards.Unknown.	
Feb 6 h	Bolton Wand res	W 3-2	Edwards(2).Wilson.	1.000*
13 a	Bootle	L 1-3	Waddington.	
Mar21 h	Royal Scots Guards	W 5-4	Bridgewater(2).Waddington.Flavill.Cuth't 800*	
28 h	Lincoln City	L 1-2	Parr.	600*
Apr 2 a	Attercliffe	D 2-2	Unknown.	
11 a	Rotherham Town	L 0-3		2.000*
16 a	Kettering	L 1-7	Waddington.	
23 a	South Bank	L 0-3		
28 h	Rotherham Town	L 1-6	Flavill.	800*

Friendlies 1892-93:

Date	Opponent	Result	Scorers	Att.
Oct 8 a	Northwich Victoria	L 3-4	S Smith(2).W Smith.	
Nov19 h	Greenhalghs Incorp	L 1-4	Cuthbert.	
26 h	Maccelsfield	W 3-0	Lester.Hill(2).	
Dec24 h	1st Royal Scots	W 5-0	Unknown.	3.000*
Apr 1 a	Maccelsfield	W 3-2	Bridgewater(2). og.	
4 h	Attercliffe	W 3-0	Unknown.	
8 a	Attercliffe	D 2-2	Waddington.	

Friendlies 1893-94:

Date	Opponent	Result	Scorers	Att.
Sep 4 a	Woolich Arsenal	L 1-4	Shaw.	3.000*
7 a	Grimsby Town	L 0-3		
9 a	Gainsboro Trinity	L 0-3		
Oct 7 h	Gainsboro Trinity	W 3-2	Lees.Calder.Guild.	1.000*
14 h	1st Royal Scots Gd	W 5-0	Smith W.Calder.Dawson.(2) Unknown.	800*
30 h	Stockton	D 3-3	Lees(2).Smith W.	
Dec 2 a	Mexborough	D 1-1	Lees.	
9 a	Lincoln City	L 0-3		
25 a	Rotherham Town	L 1-3	Lees.	1.000*
26 h	Middlesbrough	W 3-2	Unknown..Cartwright.	1.000*
Jan 1 h	Rotherham Town	W 3-2	White(2).Cartwright.	1.500*
Feb 3 h	Sheff Wed res	L 0-1		
24 h	Mexborough	L 2-5	Cartwright.Chester G.	600*
Mar10 h	Stockton	W 3-1	Langton(2).Cartwright.	
17 a	Stockton	L 1-5	Phillips.Waddington.	2.000*
26 h	Grimsby Town	W 2-1	Unknown.	2.000*
31 h	West Bromwich Alb	L 1-7	Unknown.	600*
Apr14 h	Lincoln City	L 1-2	Langton pen.	
28 a	Middlesbrough	L 1-2	Unknown.	

Friendlies 1894-95:

Date	Opponent	Result	Scorers	Att.
Sep 1 h	Gainsboro Trinity	W 2-1	Calder.Carr.	800*
8 a	Gainsboro Trinity	L 1-3	Unknown.	
Nov 3 h	East Ardsley	W 2-1	Waddington.Whitt.	300*
24 a	Gainsboro Trinity	L 0-2		
Dec25 a	Rotherham Town XI	W 4-0	Mackie(2).Carr.1 Unknown.	1.500*
31 h	Rotherham Town	W 3-0	Gibb.2 Unknown.	

Friendlies 1895-96:

Date	Opponent	Result	Scorers	Att.
Sep 2 h	Rotherham Town	L 0-2		500*
Nov23 h	Grimsby All Saints	W 7-2	Mackie(2).Lang'n.Hul'y.Bul'k.Fell's.McUr'	300
Dec25 a	Barnsley St Peters	W 2-1	Linward..McUrich.	1.100*
Jan18 a	Grimsby Town	W 1-0	Unknown.	300*
Feb29 h	Millwall Athletic	L 1-4	McUrich(3).	
Mar21 a	Gainsboro Trinity	L 0-2	Calder.	
Apr 7 a	Norfolk FA	W 2-1	Woodward og.Fellows.	500*
11 h	Mexboro Town	W 2-1	Waddington.McUrich.	3.000*

Friendlies 1896-97:

Date	Opponent	Result	Scorers	Att.
Sep 9 h	Mexboro Town	W 1-0	Longden	2.000*
19 h	Chesterfield	W 1-0	Longden.	2.000*
Oct10 a	Chesterfield	D 2-2	Unknown.	800*
31 a	Millwall Athletic	L 1-3	Chester.	600*
Nov14 a	Sheepbridge	L 1-2	Longden.	
28 h	The Black Watch	D 0-0		
Dec12 a	Gainsboro Trinity	L 1-3	Linward.	
28 h	Leeds	W 5-2	Longden.Linward.Chester(2),1 Unknown.	1.000*
Feb27 h	Barnsley St Peters	W 6-1	McIlrich.Longden.Good'n.Wadd'ton.O.G..1? Unknown.	1.000*
Mar22 a	Mexboro Town	D 0-0		
Apr 3 h	Sheepbridge	W 2-0	Goodison.Attree.	
19 h	Rest Of Mid Lge	L 2-4	Waddington.Goodison.	4.000*

Friendlies 1897-98:

Date	Opponent	Result	Scorers	Att.
Feb19 h	Stalybridge Rovers	D 1-1	Oxspring	800*

Friendlies 1898-99:

Date	Opponent	Result	Scorers	Att.
Apr 4 a	Norfolk County	W 4-1	Linward(2).Gall.Oxspring.	500*

Friendlies 1899-1900:

Date	Opponent	Result	Scorers	Att.
Mar28 a	Gainsboro Trinity	D 2-2	Goodson.Oxspring.	3.000

Friendlies 1900-01:

Date	Opponent	Result	Scorers	Att.
Nov17 a	Stockton	D 1-1	Vail.	
Dec15 h	Hunslet	W 3-0	Vail(2).Gall.	
Jan 5 h	Sheff Wed res	D 1-1	Gall.	
Feb19 a	Sheff Wed res	W 2-1	Goodson.Gall.	
Mar16 h	Bolton Wanderers	W 4-2	Goodson(2,ipen).Nelson.Vail.	
30 h	Stockton	W 4-0	Goodson(3).Linward.	
Apr10 a	Gainsboro Trinity	L 2-7	Murphy.Vail.	500*
27 h	Gainsboro Trinity	W 3-0	Goodson(2).Bailey.	

Friendlies 1901-02:

Date	Opponent	Result	Scorers	Att.
Sep 2 h	Sheff Utd Res	D 0-0		3.000*
Dec14 a	Watford	W 4-1		
Apr24 h	Sheff Wed	L 0-1		1.500*

Friendlies 1902-03:
Oct20 a Aberdare   L 2-5
Nov15 a Lincoln City   L 0-4
Jan15 h Doncaster Old Boys   W 4-1
Apr25 h Doncaster District   W 8-3   Richards(4).Price(3).Roberts.

Friendlies 1903-04:
Oct17 a Middlesbro res   D 3-3   Moran.Murphy.1 pen Unknown.   1.000*
Mar12 h Middlesbro res   D 2-2   Bennett.Roberts.   1.000*
Apr 2 a Selby Mizpah   W 2-1   2 Unknown.

Friendlies 1904-05:
Sep 1 a Bradford City   L 2-5   Carnegie(2).
Jan26 h Doncaster Thursday   W 8-3   Carnegie(3).Shinner(3).Pember.Hyde.
Feb 2 h Hull City   L 0-3

Friendlies 1905-06:
Nov 4 h Coldstream Guards   D 1-1   Bradney og.
Jan25 h Doncaster Thursday   W 3-2   Smith.Gyte.Fretwell.
Feb17 a Goole Town   D 2-2   Fox.Gyte.
Mar17 h Goole Town   W 3-1   Goodson.Simms.Gyte.

Friendlies 1906-07:
Nov 3 h 18th Royal Hussars   D 1-1   Roberts.
Feb 2 a Castleford Town   W 2-1   2 Unknown.

Friendlies 1907-08:
Oct19 h Selby Mizpah   W 4-0   Robinson(3).Charles.   500*
Apr30 h Doncaster Thursday   W 4-0   4 Unknown.

Friendlies 1908-09:
Oct17 a Goole Town   W 3-0   Rogers(2).Lister.
Apr26 h Doncaster Rov Past   W 3-2   Jex(2)(1 pen).Taylor.

Friendlies 1912-13:
Apr10 h Teddy Lowe's XI   Unknown.

Friendlies 1915-16:
Sep11 h Scunthorpe Utd   L 0-2
Oct16 a Scunthorpe Utd   L 2-4   Allen.Rippon pen.
Dec 4 h Ranks Durham Army   L 0-9
Apr 1 a Goole Town   L 0-3
  21 h York City   W 3-1   Brown(2).Stevenson.
May 6 h Donc Dist Lge XI   W 5-2   Unknown.

Friendlies 1920-21:
Jan 8 h Heanor Town   D 2-2   W Cowen.Wainwright.   4.000*
Feb26 h Darlington   D 0-0   5.000*

Friendlies 1921-22:
Dec 3 h Accrington   L 0-3   4.000*
Jan14 h Man Utd res   L 0-3
Feb25 h Rotherham County   L 2-3   White.Boardman.   5.000*
May 4 h Halifax   L 2-4   Boardman.Dent og.

Friendly 1923-24:
Feb 2 h Hull City   W 2-1   T Keetley.Harris.   4.000*

Friendly 1924-25:
May 2 h Stoke City   L 2-3   Gascoigne(2).   3.000*

Friendlies 1925-26:
Sep15 h Ex Rovers XI   D 1-1   Taylor.   3.000*
Apr29 a Grantham Town   W 4-2

Friendly 1926-27
May 2 h Derby County   L 1-2   T.Keetley   1.894

Friendly 1928-29:
Sep10 h Hearts   L 2-3   McConnell.   3.887
Jan12 a Sheff Wed res   L 2-4   Patterson.Binns.
Apr13 h Motherwell   L 1-2   Patterson   3.487

Friendly 1929-30:
Apr14 h Leeds Utd   L 0-5   2.886

Friendly 1930-31:
Apr13 h Man City   L 0-3   2.650
  30 h Sheff Wed   L 2-6   C Price.Emery.   4.000*

Friendlies 1931-32:
Oct12 a Frickley Colliery   L 1-2   R Smith.   1.000*
Apr23 h Doncaster FA   W 8-2   Wadsworth(3).Potter(3).R Smith.Atherton
  25 a Thorne Dist XI   W 2-1   Potter(2).

Friendlies 1933-34:
Oct 7 h Doncaster FA XI   W 11-0   Atherton(6).Kelly(3).Turner(2)   2.000*
Dec 9 h Watford   W 3-2   Dodd(2).Burton.   3.000*
Apr26 h Leicester City   L 1-2   Burton.

Friendlies 1934-35:
Dec 8 a Luton Town   1-2   R Smith   3.000*

Friendlies 1935-36:
Dec 9 h FC Austria   L 1-2   A Turner pen.   3.700
Apr30 h Grimsby Town   L 1-3   Burton.   3.316

Friendlies 1936-37:
Oct21 a Dutch XI   L 2-7   Malam.Dodd.   (Rotterdam)   18.000*
Nov16 h Gradjanski   W 6-4   A Turner(2).Dodd(2).Malam.Killourhy.   3.000*

Jubilee Match 1938-39:
Aug20 h Rotherham Utd   D 3-3   Killourhy(2).Morgan.   6.325

Friendlies 1938-39:
Apr24 h Leeds Utd   L 0-2   4.130

Silver Jubilee Fund 1939-40:
Aug19 a Rotherham Utd   L 1-3   Kirkaldie.   3.000

Friendlies 1940-41:
  h Lincoln City   L 1-2   Bodle.

Friendlies 1942-43:
Apr26 h Nottm Forest   D 3-3   Bodle(2).Killourhy.

Friendlies 1948-49:
Dec12 h Crystal Pal   L 0-1   4.042
Feb12 h Chesterfield   L 1-3   Antonio.   5.751
  26 a Grantham   W 2-0   Lowes.Robinson og.

Friendlies 1949-50:
May 8 a Shamrock Rovers   W 2-1   Todd.Harrison.   6.000*
  10 a Transport FC   L 0-1   2.000*
  12 a Glentoran   W 3-1   Doherty(2).Tindill.   12.000*
  15 a Coleraine   W 4-1   Todd(2).Calverley.Harrison.   4.000*
  18 a N.Wireland XI   W 5-1   Todd(3).Tindill.Harrison.
Jan   h Halifax Town

Friendlies 1950-51:
```
Oct16 h Racing of Brussels      (Never Played) Fog.
Apr18 h Third Lanark        D 2-2 Tindill,Lawlor.
   23 a South Liverpool     W 3-0 Giles,Tindill,Dubois.            16.041
   28 a Stirling Albion     W 2-1 Harrison,Giles.
May10 h Floriana (Malta)    W 5-0 Harrison(3),Herbert,Giles.
```

Friendlies 1951-52:
```
                                                                  13.399
Mar 4 h Hibernian           L 0-3
Apr 1 h Scottish XI         W 8-0 Brown(5).                       18.474
   24 a Grantham Town       L 1-3 Doherty                          6.351
May 9 a Drumcondra          W 2-1 Lawlor,Tindill
   11 a Waterford           D 3-3 Harrison(2),Tindill
   17 a Cork Ath            W 3-0
   20 a Glentoran           L 2-3
```

Friendlies 1952-53:
```
Oct21 h International XI     D 1-1 Tindill.                        21.572
Nov18 h Celtic              W 3-2 Lawlor(2),Tindill.              14.841
Mar17 h Djuurgarden         W 3-0 Tindill,Lawlor,McMorran.
   30 a Eastbourne Utd      W 2-1 Walker,Tindill.
May 1 a Denaby Utd
```

Friendlies 1953-54:
```
Oct 5 h Falkirk             W 5-2 Robinson,Lawlor,McMorran,Tindill,og.   13.898
Nov 9 h Hearts              L 1-3 Lawlor.                          11.940
   19 h Sportklub Wacker    D 0-0 (Abandoned after 28mins fog).    17.326
Mar17 h Past International   W 4-3 Lawlor(2),Adey,McMorran.        15.575
   22 a Millwall            L 0-1
Apr 5 h Rotherham Utd       W 2-0 Mooney,Hardwick.                 5.085
   27 a Denaby Utd
```

Friendlies 1954-55:
```
Sep 9 h St Ledger Jockeys   W 1-4 Mooney                          10.000*
Oct 5 a Falkirk             W 7-2 Mooney(3),Walker(2),Tindill,Jeffrey.   16.479
   18 h Newcastle Utd       L 2-4 Mooney,Herbert.                  1.206
Nov16 h Linfield            W 5-0 Doherty(2),Walker J(2),Tindill.  6.602
   29 h RAF Bomber Command  L 0-1                                  5.487
Mar28 h International XI     W 2-0
```

Friendlies 1955-56:
```
Oct31 h International XI     W 4-3 Tindill,Walker R.                8.218
Nov 8 a Carlisle Utd        D 2-2 Mooney,Tindill.                 12.000*
Mar12 h Spandauer           W 6-0 McMorran(4),Tindill(2).          6.470
```

Friendlies 1956-57:
```
Oct15 h Past & Present      D 7-7                                  3.240
   23 a Carlisle Utd        W 3-0 Walker R(2),McMorran.            4.014
Jan26 a Lincoln City        D 2-2 Mooney,Tindill.                  2.970
Feb18 a AccringtonStanley   D 3-3 Walker J(2),Connelly.            2.650
Mar 5 a Stockport County    D 0-0                                  4.924
```

Friendlies 1957-58:
```
Feb15 h Airdrieonians       D 3-3 Kelly,Cavanagh(2).               5.463
May 2 a Services Cranwell   W 11-3
```

Friendlies 1958-59:
```
Feb14 h Blackburn Rovers    L 0-2                                  6.060
```

Friendlies 1959-60:
```
Aug15 h 1st XI v 2nd XI
May 6 a Frickley Coll
```

Friendlies 1960-61:
```
Aug16 h Rotherham Utd       L 1-2
```

Friendlies 1962-63:
```
Aug 7 a Cambridge City
   22 a Kings Lynn          L 3-4 Booth(2),Johnson.                1.343
Feb19 a Barnsley
```

Friendlies 1963-64:
```
Nov 6 a Kings Lynn          D 3-3 Broadbent,Ripley,Nibloe.
Apr28 h Select XI
```

Friendlies 1964-65:
```
Aug13 a Skegness Town
May 5 h Stockport County
```

Friendlies 1965-66:
```
Aug13 a Skegness Town       W 4-1 Jeffrey(2),Broadbent,Ogden.      5.408
Oct 4 h Nottm Forest        L 1-6 Jeffrey.                         6.494
Nov 9 h Wormatia Worms      W 1-0 Jeffrey.                         7.027
Jan19 h Sheffield Wed       W 6-5 Coleman(3),Gilfillan,Ogden,Hardy.
```

Friendlies 1966-67:
```
      a Chelmsford Town
      a Gateshead
Aug 6 a Burton Albion
Oct31 h Liverpool           D 1-1 Watson
Jan27 h Stockport county
```

Friendlies 1967-68:
```
Jul29 a Altrincham
Aug 5 a Cambridge City      L 0-2                                  1.376
Feb24 a Grantham Town       W 4-0 Ormrod,Gray,Warboys,Slater.
Apr18 h Minden Youth        W 6-1 Warboys(3),Robertson,Gray,Jeffrey.   2.778
May13 h Rotherham Utd
```

Friendlies 1968-69:
```
Jul27 a Scarborough         W 3-0 Rabjohn(2),Robertson.            1.787
Aug 3 a Cambridge Utd       D 1-1 Usher.
Apr29 h Werder Bremen       W 2-1 Briggs,Johnson.                  8.239
```

Friendlies 1969-70:
```
Jul28 a Bishop Auckland     W 6-2 Watson(2),Briggs(2),Rabjohn,Wilcockson.
Jul30 a Shildon             W 2-0 Watson,Rabjohn.
Aug 1 a South Shields       W 5-1 Clarke(2),Regan.   (2 unknown)   5.667
Oct28 h Dallas Tornadoes    D 1-1 Rabjohn.
Feb13 a Gainsboro Trin      W 2-1 Watson,Sheffield.
Mar18 a Queen Of The South  W 2-0 Briggs,Marsden.                  3.090
May 5 h Lazio (Italy)       L 0-4
```

Friendlies 1970-71:
```
Jul27 a Peterborough Utd    W 4-0 Regan(2),Briggs,Irvine. (closed doors)
Aug 1 a Macclesfield Town   W 2-0 Briggs,Watson.
Aug 5 h Burnley             D 2-2 Robertson,Briggs.
    8 h Arsenal XI          W 5-0 Marsden(2),Bird(2),Johnson R.    4.899
   11 h Leeds Utd           L 1-2 Johnson R.                      15.797
Nov29 a Gainsborough Trin
Jan20 a Chesterfield
```

Friendlies 1971-72:
```
Aug 3 h Rotherham Utd       W 4-1 Kitchen,Briggs,Watson,O.G.,      1.624
    7 h Cowdenbeath         W 3-1 Usher,Briggs,Wilcockson          2.230
    9 h Man City            L 0-2
```

Friendlies 1972-73:
```
Jul29 h Stoke City          L 1-2 Kitchen.                         6.214
   31 a Leeds Utd           L 0-3
Aug 4 a Bradford PA         D 2-2 Kitchen,Morrison.
    7 a Hatfield Main       W 4-0 Briggs(2),Rabjohn,Ketley.         400*
```

```
Friendlies 1973-74:
Aug  6 h Stoke City              L 1-4
    11 a Sutton Town             W 1-0
    15 h Leeds Utd               L 0-2

Friendlies 1974-75:
Aug  3 h Dunfermline             D 1-1                                        1.298
     5 a Sutton Town             W 3-0
    10 h Huddersfield Town       D 1-1                                        1.443
    12 a Halifax Town            L 0-4

Friendlies 1975-76:
Aug  5 h Leeds Utd               L 1-2 O'Callaghan.
    11 h Man Utd res             W 2-1 Kitchen,Curran.

Friendlies 1976-77:
Jul31 h Rotherham Utd            L 1-2                                        4.661
Aug  9 h Southampton             D 2-2                                        749
Dec10 h Tranmere Rovers
      a Barnsley

Friendlies 1977-78:
Aug  4 h Chesterfield            D 0-0 Taylor,Owen,Jones C.
     6 h Coventry City           L 3-4
     9 h Leeds Utd               W 2-1 Laidlaw,O'Callaghan.

Friendlies 1978-79:
Aug 15 a Harworth Coll           D 1-1 Habbin.                               1.976
Sep  1 h Bolton Wand             W 1-0 Lewis.                                1.120
     4 h Chesterfield

Friendlies 1979-80:
Aug  2 h Sheffield Wed           L 0-1
     4 h Barnsley                L 0-4
     7 a Sheffield Wed           D 2-2 Lewis,Bradley.                        2.530

Friendlies 1980-81:
      h York City                D 0-0
      a Rotherham Utd            L 0-3
      a Denaby Utd               W 3-0 Warboys(2),Lister.
      a Frickley Coll            D 2-2 Nimmo,Warboys.

Friendlies 1981-82:
Aug  8 a Winterton Rangers       W 1-0 Warboys.                             50
    11 a Southport               W 1-0 Warboys.                             168

Friendlies 1982-83:
Aug  7 a Denaby Utd              W 2-1 Mell,Snodin G.
    11 a Burton Albion           D 2-2 Liddell,Graham.
    14 a Middlesbrough           W 1-0 Douglas.                 (closed doors)
    16 a Gainsborough Trin       W 4-0 Douglas,Lister,Liddell,Snodin G.     529
    21 h Leeds Utd               L 0-1
Mar20 a Teignmouth               W 6-1 Snodin G(2),Walker,Russell,Boyd.     4.950
May  9 h Sheffield Wed           D 4-4 A Graham,Glavin,G Snodin,Russell.    1.007

Friendlies 1983-84:
Aug  1 h Leeds Utd               L 0-1
     9 h Scunthorpe Utd          W 1-0
    12 h Sheffield Utd           L 0-1
    17 h Notts County            L 1-3

Friendlies 1984-85:
Jul31 a Motherwell               D 1-1 Snodin G.
Aug  2 a Stirling Albion         D 0-0
     8 h W.B.A.                  D 3-3
    14 a Denaby Utd              D 1-1 Harle.
    18 h Wolves                  L 0-2
    21 h Chelsea

Friendlies 1985-86:
Aug  3 h Sunderland              L 1-2 Russell pen.                         1.462
    10 h W.B.A.                  L 2-3 Woods,Dobbin.                        405
    13 a Worksop Town            W 5-0 Woods(2),Buckley,Dobbin,Russell.     670

Friendlies 1986-87:
Jul29 h Leeds Utd                L 1-2 Woods.
Aug  6 h Hull City               L 0-1
     9 h Barnsley                L 1-2 Clayton.
    15 h Sunderland              D 0-0
Nov25 a Lincoln Utd              D 1-1 Redfearn.                            250
Dec  2 h Notts Forest            D 2-2 Woods,Douglas.                       2.303
Feb  9 a Whitby Town             D 0-0

Friendlies 1987-88:
Jul24 a Scunthorpe Utd           L 1-4 Joyce.                   (closed doors)
    28 a Harworth Coll           W 5-2 Kinsella(2),Gaynor(2)(1 pen),Joyce.  230
    30 h Stockport County        W 2-0 Peckett,Russell.                     133
Aug  1 a Armthorpe Welfare       W 1-0 Gaynor.                              357
     7 a Barnsley                W 1-0 Russell.                             545
    10 h Millwall                D 2-2 Russell pen,Deane.                   280

Friendlies 1988-89:
Jul25 a Truro City               W 4-2 Dobson,Daly,Rankine,Gorman.
    30 a Shepshed Charter        W 5-1 Gorman(2),Turnbull,Dobson,Robinson L. 230
Aug  3 a Mexborough Town         W 5-0 Dobson pen,Turnbull,Kimble,Gorman,Robinson L.
     5 a Gainsborough Trin       W 3-0 Dobson,Kimble,Turnbull.             192
     9 a Armthorpe Welfare       W 3-0 Dobson,Rankine,Gorman.              350

Friendlies 1989-90:
Jul22 a Thorne Coll              W 3-0 Turnbull,Brockie pen,Robinson L.    500
    28 a Mexborough Town         W 5-2 Ashurst,Turnbull,Robinson L,Warren(2). 250
    28 a Gainsborough Trin       W 2-1 Brevett,Turnbull.
May  7 h Barnsley                W 7-3 Gas'ne(3),Turn'l(2),Adams,Brem'r(p.) 2.914

Friendlies 1990-91:
Jul31 a Grantham Town            W 1-0 Harle pen.                          300
Aug  4 h Bremners XI             W 6-3 Turnbull(2),Gormley(2),Stiles,Rankine 831
     8 h Reading                 D 1-1 Jones.                              561

Friendlies 1991-92:
Jul24 A Fricklet Coll            W 1-0 Pickering own goal.       (closed doors)
    27 a Tadcaster Albion        W 7-0 Tynan(3),Whitehurst,Muir,Bennett,Redhead pen.
    31 h Barnsley                D 2-2 Tynan pen,Muir.                     529
Aug  3 a Goole Town              W 2-1 Tynan,Redhead.
     7 a Burton Albion           W 4-0 Morrow(3),Noteman.                  309
Mar26 a Goole Town               W 3-0

Friendlies 1992-93:
Jul13 a Harrogate Railway        L 0-2
    20 a North Ferriby           W 3-0
    25 a Thorne Colliery         W 5-0 Jeffrey(2),Heritage,Douglas,Crosby.
    31 a Matlock Town            W 3-1 Tallon,Prindiville,Jeffrey.
Aug  4 h Newcastle Utd           D 1-1 Jeffrey.                            3.951
     7 h Derby County            W 2-0 Jeffrey(2).                         2.250
Sep29 a Armthorpe Welfare
```

Other Cups 1890/91 to 1992/93

(Attendances where given are approximate when noted 'c')

Sheffield Challenge Cup 1890-91:
3	Jan 1	h	Staveley	W 2-1	Gresham(2).	2.000c
SF	Feb 7	a	Ecclesfield	W 3-1	Langton(2),Gresham.	5.000c
F	Mar21	a	Sheff Utd	W 2-1	James,Gresham.	4.000c

Sheffield Challenge Cup 1891-92:
| 3 | Jan23 | a | Sheff Utd | L 0-4 | | 3.000c |

Sheffield Challenge Cup 1892-93:
3	Dec 3	a	Eckington Works	D 1-1	Unknown.	1.000c
3R	27	h	Eckington Works	W 3-2	Unknown.	6.000c
SF	Jan28	†	Sheffield Strollers	D 1-1	Lee.	2.000c
SFR	Feb18	†	Sheffield Strollers	D 3-3	Langton,Bridgewater,Guild.	
SFR	Mar 4	h	Sheffield Strollers	L 1-3	Waddington. +	3.000c
SFR	13	†	Sheffield Strollers	L 0-1		

† Matches played at Olive Grove. Sheffield.   + Match ordered to be replayed

Wharncliffe Charity Cup 1894/95:
	Dec24	h	Mexborough Town	L 0-1		
	29	h	Barnsley St Peters	W 5-1	Mackie(2),Cartwright,Langton,Carr.	
	Feb 2	h	Sheff Utd res	W 4-1	Cartwright(2),Carr,Mackie.	700c
	9	a	Barnsley St Peters	D 1-1	Gibb.	
	26	a	Mexborough Town	D 2-2	Wright I,Gibb.	
	Mar 9	h	Sheff Wed res	D 1-1	Langton.	1.000c
	18	a	Sheff Wed res	L 0-5		1.500c
	Apr 6	a	Sheff Utd res	W 2-0	Unknown.	1.000c
	13	a	Chesterfield	L 1-2	Mackie.	
	20	h	Chesterfield			

Wharncliffe Charity Cup 1899-1900:
	Sep23	a	Wath Athletic	L 1-3	Cutts.	
	25	a	Sheff Utd res	L 1-3	1 Unknown.	
	Oct21	h	Mexborough Town	W 3-1	Robinson,Oxspring,Lee.	
	Nov 4	h	Wath Athletic	W 5-0	Cutts(2),Robinson,Hulley,Linward.	
	Dec16	h	Worksop Town	W 3-1	Oxspring,Ray,Booth og.	
	Jan 1	h	Wombwell Town	W 4-1	Ray,3 Unknown.	
	6	a	Attercliffe	L 0-1		
	13	h	Attercliffe	W 2-1	Robinson,Linward.	
	Feb24	h	Sheff Wed res	D 1-1	Langton.	
	Mar10	h	Sheff Utd res	L 1-2	Nelson.	
	17	a	Wombwell Town	L 1-2	Linward.	
	Apr 2	a	Sheff Wed res	L 0-3		
	17	a	Worksop Town	W 4-1	Lindley(2),Nelson,Hulley.	
	26	a	Sheffield Club		Unknown.	
	30	a	Mexboro Town	W 3-1	3 Unknown.	600c

Mexborough Montague Charity Cup 1900-01:
1R	Sep29	a	Bolton-On-Dearne	W 4-0	Vail(2),Linward,Meakin.	
SF	Feb 9	a	Denaby Utd	W 2-0	Vail(2).	
F	Apr 6	a	Mexboro Thursday	W 5-2	Hollin(3),Lindley,linward.	

Wharncliffe Charity Cup 1900-01:
| 1 | Nov10 | a | Darnall Rovers | W 9-0 | 9 Unknown. | |
| 2 | Jan10 | a | Barnsley | L 0-2 | | 300c |

Sheffield Challenge Cup 1905-06:
| 1R | Dec16 | h | Sheff Wed res | L 0-4 | | |

Sheffield Challenge Cup 1906-07:
| 1R | Dec15 | a | Sheff Utd res | L 0-3 | | |

Sheffield Challenge Cup 1907-08:
| R1 | Dec14 | h | Hoyland Town | W 2-0 | Roberts,Murphy pen. | 100c |
| R2 | Jan18 | a | Sheff Wed res | L 0-6 | | 500c |

Sheffield Challenge Cup 1908-09:
R1	Dec12	h	High Green Swifts	D 1-1	Brelsford.	600c
R1R	17	a	High Green Swifts	W 4-1	Jex,Roberts,Bramall,Charles.	3.218
R2	Jan23	h	Sheff Utd res	D 1-1	Bramall.	3.600c
R2R	25	a	Sheff Utd res	L 0-2		

Sheffield Challenge Cup 1909-10:
R1	Dec11	h	Mexboro Town	W 1-0	Simons.	
R2	Jan22	a	Barnsley res	D 2-2	Walt Taylor,Simons.	500c
R2R	27	h	Barnsley res	L 0-3		

Sheffield Challenge Cup 1910-11:
| R1 | Dec10 | a | Mexboro Town | L 1-2 | Green. | |

Sheffield Challenge Cup 1911-12:
R1	Dec 9	h	Barnsley res	W 2-0	Green,W Bromage.	2.000c
R2	Jan27	a	Wath Athletic	W 2-1	Green,Astill.	3.000c
SF	Feb17	a	Rotherham County	D 1-1	Woodruff.	
SFR	22	a	Rotherham County	W 3-0	Taylor,Green,Astill.	
F	Mar16	a	Sheff Utd res	W 3-0	Reed(2),Taylor.	6.000c

Wharncliffe Charity Cup 1911-12:
R1	Nov18	h	Mexboro Town	W 3-0	Green,Dyal,W Bromage.	
R2	Dec28	h	Hickleton Main	W 8-0	Bromage W(2),Astill(2),Cowan(2),Green(2).	
SF	Mar11	a	Sheff Utd res	L 0-2		6.000c

Sheffield Challenge Cup 1912-13:
| R1 | Dec 7 | h | Rotherham County | D 1-1 | Pattinson. | |
| R1R | 16 | a | Rotherham County | L 0-3 | | 2.907 |

Wharncliffe Charity Cup 1912-13:
R1	Nov14	h	Hickleton Main	W 2-0	Bates,Buddery.	
R2	Jan25	h	Silverwood Colliery	W 4-2	Shackleton(2),Buddery,W Bromage.	
SF	Mar17	a	Sheff Wed res	L 0-1		

Sheffield Challenge Cup 1913-14:
| R1 | Dec 6 | a | Mexboro Town | W 4-0 | Bramall,Westwood,Jex,Plumb. | |
| R2 | Jan24 | h | Rotherham County | L 1-3 | Rhodes. | |

Wharncliffe Charity Cup 1913-14:
R1	Nov27	h	South Kirkby	W 7-3	Westwood,Taylor,Jex(2),Curran,Williams,Bates.	
R2	Feb23	a	Sheff Utd res	D 1-1	Hawthorn.	
R2R	Mar23	+	Sheff Utd res	L 0-3	+ Played at Bramall Lane	2.000c

Mexborough Montague Cup 1913-14:
| | Nov 1 | a | Mexboro Town | W 3-0 | Loughran,Taylor,Lowe pen. | |

Sheffield Challenge Cup 1914-15:
| R1 | Dec12 | a | Bentley Colliery | W 3-1 | Stevens(2),Brodie. | |
| R2 | Jan28 | a | Barnsley res | L 1-2 | Lean pen. | |

Wharncliffe Charity League 1915-16:
(Competition supplemented Midland Combination - see 1915/16 statistics)

Sheffield Challenge Cup 1920-21:
R1	Dec11	h	Maltby Main	W 2-0	Docherty,W Cowen.	6.000c
R2	Jan15	h	Wombwell	W 1-0	W Cowen.	5.000c
SF	Feb12	a	Barnsley res	L 1-2	Sharpe.	

Sheffield Challenge Cup 1921-22:
| R1 | Dec10 | a | Wath Athletic | L 2-3 | Hollins,Butler. | |

Sheffield Challenge Cup 1922-23:
| R1 | Dec 9 | h | Frickley Colliery | D 1-1 | Rintoul. | 2.700c |
| R1R | 14 | a | Frickley Colliery | L 0-1 | | |

Wharncliffe Charity Cup 1922-23:
R1 Jan11 a Monkton Athletic   W 5-4 Boardman(3).Slicer.Cooper.
R2 Feb15 h Worksop Town   W 5-1 Board'n(2).Taylor.Picknett.Shaw pen.   2.000c
SF Apr16 h Sheff Utd res   W 1-0 Boardman.   4.000c
F   24 h Scunthorpe Utd   W 1-0 Lumb.   5.183

Sheffield County Cup 1926-27:
R1 Sep27 a Rotherham Utd   L 1-2 T.Keetley.   5.000c

Sheffield County Cup 1927-28:
R1 Oct17 h Rotherham Utd   D 1-1 T Keetley pen.
R1R   24 a Rotherham Utd   L 2-6 T Keetley.Hall.   3.000c

Sheffield County Cup 1928-29:
R1 Sep24 h Rotherham Utd   D 0-0
R1R Oct22 a Rotherham Utd   D 0-0 aet
R1R Dec 3 a Rotherham   L 2-3 Atkin.Emery.   (At Sheff Utd)   4.000c

Scunthorpe Hospital Charity Cup 1928-29:
F Apr29 a Scunthorpe Utd   D 1-1 T Keetley. aet   (Cup shared)

Sheffield County Cup 1930-31:
SF Oct27 a Barnsley   L 2-3 Bott.Lievesley.   1.500c

Sheffield County Cup 1931-32:
PR Oct 5 a Rotherham Utd   L 0-2

Sheffield Invitation Cup 1932-33:
F Apr 6 h Barnsley   D 2-2 Henderson O.G..Parker.   2.023
FR   24 a Barnsley   L 1-4 Martin.   1.544

Chesterfield Hospital Cup 1933-34:
F May 7 a Chesterfield   L 1-3 Dodd.   1.000c

Sheffield County Cup 1934-35:
SF Sep17 h Sheff Wed   L 1-3 Rennie.   2.520

Sheffield County Cup 1935-36:
SF Nov25 a Barnsley   W 3-0 Dutton.Dodd(2).
F May 4 h Sheff Utd   W 2-1 Baines(2).   5.607

Grantham Hospital Cup 1935-36:
F Apr20 a Grantham Town   L 1-2 A Turner.

Sheffield County Cup 1936-37:
PR Sep28 a Sheff Wed   L 0-3   1.423

Grantham Hospital Cup 1936-37:
F Apr26 a Grantham Town   W 1-0 A Turner.

Sheffield County Cup 1937-38:
SF Oct18 h Sheff Utd   W 5-1 Perry(2).Killourhy(2).Burton.   2.281
F May14 h Barnsley   W 1-0 Killourhy.   5.135

Sheffield County Cup 1938-39:
R1 Oct 3 h Barnsley   W 3-1 Perry(2).Killourhy.   1.130
SF   31 h Sheff Utd   L 0-3

Sheffield County Cup 1940-41:
PR Jan11 h Sheffield Wed   W 4-0 Bodle(3).Jordan.   3.000
SF   18 h Sheffield Utd   W 5-1 Bodle(2).Jordan.Nightingale.Sinclair   1.592
F Mar29 h Rotherham Utd   W 3-2 Bodle pen.Jordan.Burton.   1.743

Sheffield County Cup 1941-42: (N.B. Treated as League fixture - see 1941-42 statistics)
   Apr18 a Rotherham Utd   L 0-3   2.000

Sheffield County Cup 1942-43: (N.B. Treated as League fixtures - see 1942-43 statistics)
   Apr17 h Rotherham Utd   W 3-1 Bodle.Jordan.Hanson og.   1.000
      24 a Rotherham Utd   L 1-5 Gregory.   1.500

Sheffield County Cup 1943-44: (N.B. Treated as League fixtures - see 1943-44 statistics)
   Mar18 h Barnsley   D 1-1 Attwell.   3.866
      25 a Barnsley   L 0-1   6.359

Sheffield County Cup 1944-45: (N.B. Treated as League fixture - see 1944-45 statistics)
   Mar10 a Sheffield Wed   L 0-1   8.827

Sheffield County Cup 1945-46:
SF Apr25 a Barnsley   L 2-4 Tindill.Jordan.

Sheffield County Cup 1946-47:
SF May17 a Rotherham Utd   L 1-2 Owens.

Sheffield County Cup 1948-49:
PR Jan29 a Barnsley   L 1-3 Barritt.   15.388

Sheffield County Cup 1949-50:
SF May 1 a Sheffield Utd   L 0-3

Sheffield County Cup 1950-51:
PR Feb10 h Barnsley   W 3-2 Lawlor(2).Holmes.   13.727
SF May 7 h Rotherham Utd   W 3-1 Giles.Tindill.Harrison.   16.057
F May12 a Sheffield Wed   L 1-2 Henry O.G.

Sheffield County Cup 1951-52:
SF Apr22 a Rotherham Utd   L 1-4 Addey

Sheffield County Cup 1952-53:
SF May 4 a Sheffield Wed   L 1-2 Harrison

Sheffield County Cup 1953-54:
PR April3 h Barnsley   L 1-2 Adey   2.135

Sheffield County Cup 1954-55:
SF Oct25 h Sheffield Wed   L 1-3 Walker   13.549

Sheffield County Cup 1955-56:
SF Mar 5 h Rotherham Utd   W 2-1 Tindill.Kilkenny.   5.007
F May10 h Sheffield Utd   W 4-0 Walker R(2).Mooney.Jeffrey.   3.058

Sheffield County Cup 1956-57:
SF Dec12 h Rotherham Utd   D 1-1 Mooney.   3.767
SFR Apr29 a Rotherham Utd   L 1-3 Tindill.

Sheffield County Cup 1958-59:
PR Apr 6 h Rotherham Utd   W 3-1 Meredith.Callan.Fletcher.
SF   28 a Sheffield Wed   L 2-5 Walker R.Sharp.

Sheffield County Cup 1959-60:
PR Oct27 h Rotherham Utd   D 2-2 Walker R.Meredith.   2.758
PRR Apr25 a Rotherham Utd   L 0-4

Sheffield County Cup 1960-61:
SF Nov29 a Sheffield Wed   L 0-3   4.100

Sheffield County Cup 1961-62:
SF Jan22 a Rotherham Utd   L 1-2 Balagher   6.000

Sheffield County Cup 1964-65:
SF Nov30 a Rotherham Utd   D 3-3 Hale(2).Tait.   3.937
SFR Apr29 h Rotherham Utd   W 3-2 Ripley(3). aet.   5.704
F May 3 h Sheffield Utd   L 0-4   11.001

Sheffield County Cup 1965-66:
SF May18 h Rotherham Utd   L 1-6 Ogden   5.383

Sheffield County Cup 1966-67:
SF Apr17 a Sheffield Utd   L 1-6 Ricketts.   3.749

Sheffield County Cup 1967-68:
SF May15 h Sheffield Utd   D 1-1 Jeffrey.   5.135
SFR 17 h Sheffield Utd   W 3-1 Webber.Flowers.Jeffrey   4.501

Sheffield County Cup 1968-69:
F+ Oct29 h Barnsley   W 1-0 Barratt. + (1967-68 Final)   8.325
SF May 7 h Rotherham Utd   W 1-0 Watson.   5.408
F   9 h Sheffield Utd   D 0-0   8.793

Sheffield County Cup 1969-70:
SF Apr17 h Rotherham Utd   L 1-2   2.846
FR+ 20 a Sheffield Utd   L 0-2 + (1968-69 Final)   5.612

Sheffield County Cup 1970-71:
SF May 4 h Barnsley   D 3-3 Watson.Briggs.Young. aet   979
SFR a Barnsley   L 0-1   1.301

Sheffield County Cup 1972-73:
PR Sep5 h Barnsley   W 2-1 Elwiss(2)   935
SF Apr17a Sheffield Utd   L 2-4 Wignall S..Elwiss

Sheffield County Cup 1973-74:
PR Oct30a Rotherham Utd   L 0-1

Sheffield County Cup 1974-75:
PR Feb 4 a Sheffield Wed   D 1-1 O'Callaghan.   2.100
PRR 18 h Sheffield Wed   L 0-2   4.207

Sheffield County Cup 1975-76:
SF Apr12 a Barnsley   W 3-2 Miller.Jones.O'Callaghan.   1.618
F   May 7 a Sheffield Utd   W 2-1 Kitchen(2).   4.602

Sheffield County Cup 1976-77:
SF Dec20 h Barnsley   W 4-2 O'Callaghan(3).Laidlaw.   679
(According to Sheffield and Hallamshire records the Final was never played)

Sheffield County Cup 1977-78:
SF Jan 7 a Sheffield Wed   D 1-1 Habbin.   1.972
SFR 13 h Sheffield Wed   W 2-0 Habbin.Bailey.   1.572

Sheffield County Cup 1978-79:
F+ Sep18 a Sheffield Utd   L 1-4 Bradley. + (1977-78 Final)   2.992
SF Nov14 h Sheffield Wed   W 2-1 French.Cork.   1.580

Sheffield County Cup 1979-80:
SF May 5 a Sheffield Utd   L 1-6 Mell.   826

Sheffield County Cup 1980-81:
SF Dec 8 a Sheffield Utd   L 2-4 Snodin I.Little.   656

Sheffield County Cup 1981-82:
SF May17 a Sheffield Wed   L 1-9 Dawson.

(N.B. Sheffield County Cup not competed for 1982/3 to 1984/85)

Associate Members Cup - Northern Section 1983-84:
R1 Feb22 a Lincoln City   W 2-0 Woods.Harle.   1.941
R2 Mar13 h Preston N E   W 2-1 Miller.Woods.   2.098
R3 20 h Burnley   L 1-3 Snodin G.   (aet)   3.052

Freight Rover Cup - Northern Section 1984-85:
1R1Jan22 h York City   D 0-0   1.892
1R2Lfeb 5 a York City   L 0-2   4.397

Sheffield County Cup 1985-86:
F+ Aug11 h Rotherham Utd   W 1-0 Woods. + (1985/86 Final)   638

Freight Rover Trophy - Northern Section 1985/86:
PR Jan16 a Notts County   L 0-1   1.642
PR 21 h Mansfield Town   W 1-0 Flynn.   1.584
PR Mar17 a Mansfield Town   L 2-4 Cusack. Woods   2.896

Freight Rover Trophy - Northern Section 1986-87:
PR Nov24 a Middlesborough   L 0-3   3.978
PR Dec 9 h Chesterfield   D 0-0   1.079

Sherpa Van Trophy - Northern Section 1987-88:
PR Oct13 h Mansfield Town   L 0-1   1.280
PR Nov24 a Hartlepool Utd   L 0-1   782

Sheffield County Cup 1987-88:
F   Feb23 h Rotherham Utd   L 1-2 Turnbull.   723

Yorkshire & Humberside Cup 1988-89:
PR Aug13 h Rotherham Utd   D 1-1 Dobson.   1.394
PR 16 h Sheffield Utd   L 1-3 Rankine.   1.736
PR 20 a Bradford City   L 0-1   2.462

Sherpa Van Trophy - Northern Section 1988-89:
PR Dec 6 h Grimsby Town   L 1-2 Ashurst.   681
PR 13 a Rotherham Utd   L 1-2 Dobson.   1.775

DAF Cup - Northern Section 1989-90:
PR Nov 7 a Huddersfield Town D 2-2 Rankine.Adams.   1.714
PR 28 h Grimsby Town   W 1-0 Robinson L pen.   1.551
R1 Jan 9 h Bury   W 2-0 Stiles.Jones D.   2.547
R2 30 a Wigan Ath   W 2-1 Turnbull.Jones D.   aet   2.757
SF Feb20 h Halifax Town   W 3-0 Brockie.Turnbull.Noteman.   5.754
FiL Mar12 a Tranmere Rovers   L 0-2   10.004
F2L Apr 3 h Tranmere Rovers   D 1-1 Jones D.   6.670

Yorkshire & Humberside Cup 1989-90:
GPA Aug 5 H Scunthorpe Utd   W 1-0 Turnbull.   1.084
GPA 8 a Leeds Utd   L 0-2   3.502
GPA 12 h Scarborough   L 1-2 Stiles.   936

DAF Cup - Northern Section 1990-91:
PR Nov 6 a Chesterfield   D 1-1 Grayson.   2.757
PR 27 h Scunthorpe Utd   W 1-0 Muir.   1.394
R1 Jan15 h Scunthorpe Utd   D 0-0 aet (Rovers lose 2-4 on pens.-Turnbull,Ormsby)   1.635

Yorkshire & Humberside Cup 1990-91:
PR Aug11 h Rotherham Utd   L 0-1   1.572
PR 15 a Barnsley   D 0-0   1.510
PR 18 h Huddersfield Town   W 3-2 Muir.Stiles.Gormley.   1.119

Autoglass Trophy - Northern Section 1991-92:
Pr Nov19 a Burnley   L 0-2   2.590
Pr Dec17 h Blackpool   D 2-2 Rankine.Limber.   613

Autoglass Trophy - Northern Section 1992-93:
R1 Dec 1 h York City   W 2-1 Prindiville.Hine.   1.419
R1 15 a Hull City   L 1-2 Crosby.   1.716
R2 Jan20 a Huddersfield Town   L 0-3   1.535

Sheffield County Cup 1992-93:
F   May 4 a Barnsley   L 2-3 Hine.Jeffrey.   466

(Secretarys)

1879 (Formed by) Albert Jenkins	1898 – 1903 J.H. Fowler
1880 – 1884 Albert Jenkins	1904 G. Watson
1885 – 1886 Albert Edward Pearce	1905 – 1907 W. Proctor
1887 – 1889 J.H. Fowler	1908 H.V. Kerr
1890 – 1892 J. Hopwood	1909 F. Keyworth
1893 – 1897 J. Musson	1915 J. Hapwood

(Managers)

1920 – 1922 W. Calder	1964 – 1965 W. Leivers
1923 – 1926 R.Ray	1966 T.Garnett/K.Kettleborough
1927 – 1935 D.L. Menzies	1967 – 1968 G. Raynor
1936 – 1940 F. Emery	1969 – 1971 L.McMenemy
1944 – 1945 B. Marsden	1972 – 1974 M. Setters
1946 – 1948 J.G. Bestall	1975 – 1978 S. Anderson
1949 – 1957 P. Doherty	1978 – 1985 W. Bremner
1958 W.J.Crayston	1985 – 1987 D. Cusack
1959 J.G. Bestall	1987 – 1988 D.McKay
1960 N. Curtis	1989 J. Kinnear
1961 J.G. Bestall	1990 – 1991 W. Bremner
1962 – 1963 O. Hold	1991 – S. Beaglehole

STATISTICS: 1879 – 1993 KEY

The statistics pages that follow have been designed for easy reference and are generally self explanatory, however the following notes explain various specific details.

League match numbers are shown in the left hand column, and are repeated in the column after the attendances. Fixture dates, Results (Doncaster score first plus), and (Doncaster) Goalscorers are self-explanatory. 'W' denotes a Doncaster victory, etc. 'Att' shows the attendance (where known), and an attendance with a 'c' (circa), is an approximate figure. Under 'Scorers', '(pen)' refers to a goal scored by a penalty, and 'O.G.' an own goal – generally the name of that scorer is also given. 'h' signifies a Doncaster home game, and 'a' an away game; neutral venues are also given. All players that have appeared for the Club in League and/or major Cup matches are entered at right angles to the general details, and their appearance(s) are shown by a number (their position) for the appropriate match. For pre-war matches (numbered shirts were not used), the number shown refers to the normally accepted position for the period; e.g. '1' = goalkeeper, '2' = right back, '11' = left winger, etc. Substitutes, where they made an appearance during the appropriate game are included, as '12' and/or '14'. Substitute number 12 replaced the player suffixed * (e.g. 8*), and number 14 replaced the player suffixed + (e.g. 10+).

Major cup match details are also given (abbreviated statistical details for minor games, and pre-league friendly matches are given in separate sections). The left hand column indicates the round of that Cup match, e.g. PR = Preliminary round, 4Q = 4th qualifying, R1 = 1st round, S/F = semi-final, 1R2L = 1st round second leg, R3R = 3rd round replay etc. A.E.T. = the result 'After extra time'.

During the 2nd World War years, the details are similar, however in view of the large number of players used each season, the players and positions are reversed in these tables, i.e. the players' positions are shown at the top, and the players' names are shown in the main section of the table.

The statistical facts have taken 15 years detailed research by the Authors. Information has been taken from old Doncaster newspapers, (from 1880), and most attendances and substitute details were taken from the records of the Football League at Lytham St.Annes.

Friendlies 1879–80

No	Date	V	Opponents	F-A	Scorers
1	Oct 3	a	Rawmarsh		

Friendlies 1880–81

No	Date	V	Opponents	F-A	Scorers
1	Oct23	a	Deaf & Dumb Inst	D 3-3	
2	Nov13	a	Bentley Trinity	W 3-0	Roper(2).Mitchell.
3	20	a	Deaf & Dumb Inst	D 1-1	
4	Dec1	h	Hexthorpe Wand	L 0-1	
5	Feb19	a	Market Star	L 0-1	

Friendlies 1881–82

No	Date	V	Opponents	F-A	Scorers
1	Oct22	a	Frodingham & Scun	W 5-0	Mitchell(3).Pallett.White.
2	Dec10	h	Great Northern	W 6-0	
3	Jan21	h	Frodingham & Scun	W 5-0	Bedford.
4	Feb 4	h	Sheffield Clar	L 1-4	Symington.
5	18	h	Epworth	W 2-0	
6	Mar18	a	Epworth	W 2-1	

Friendlies 1882–83

No	Date	V	Opponents	F-A	Scorers
1	Oct 7	h	Frodingham Town	W 5-1	
2	14	a	Tickhill	L 1-2	
3	Nov 4	h	Eastwood Wanderers	W 7-0	
4	11	h	Knottingley	W 1-0	
5	Dec 2	a	Kimberworth	L 0-3	
6	Jan 6	a	Doncaster Rutlands	W 1-0	
7	Feb 3	a	Knottingley	W 4-1	
8	Mar 3	h	Sheffield Clar	W 4-1	
9	24	h	Kimberworth	W 6-1	

Friendlies 1883–84

No	Date	V	Opponents	F-A	Scorers
1	Aug25	a	Donc El	W 6-1	Symington.
2	Sep22	h	Meersbrook Ra	W 3-1	
3	29	a	Massborough	W 4-2	Smith.Symington.Fowler.Bedford.
4	Oct13				
5	20				
6	27	h	Doncaster El	W 5-0	
7	Nov 3	a	Knottingley		cancelled
8	10	h	Tickhill	L 1-2	
9	17	a	Kimberworth		
10	24				
11	Dec 1	h	Stourton Rov	W 6-0	Symington(3).Smith(2).Whitley.
12	8	h	Massborough	W 4-1	
13	15	a	Doncaster El	W 3-0	
14	29	a	Oulton Vic	W 4-0	
15	Jan 1	h	Aston Hall	W 4-0	
16	5	h	Knottingley		
17	12				
18	19	a	Sheff Clar	L 0-2	
19	26	h	Kimberworth		
20	Feb 2	a	Epworth		
21	9	h	Oulton Vic		
22	16				
23	23	h	Epworth		
24	Mar 1				
25	8	a	Tickhill	L 0-1	
26	15	h	Sheff Clar	W 2-0	
27	22	a	Stourton Rov		
28	Gd Fr	a	Meersbrook		

Friendlies 1884–85

No	Date	V	Opponents	F-A	Scorers
1	Oct 4	a	Kilnhurst Ch	W 3-0	Boyd.Harper.Smith.
2	11	h	Conisborough	W 1-0	Boyd.
3	18	a	Gainsboro Tr	L 1-8	
4	25	h	Oak Street SS		
5	Nov 1	a	Knottingley	W 4-0	Pearce.Harper.
6	8	h	Don Gr School	W 1-0	
7	15	a	Stourton	W 6-1	Smith(5).Boyd.
8	22	a	Lockwood Bros	L 0-1	
9	29				
10	Dec 6	a	Don Gr School	W 5-0	Boyd.Symington.
11	13	a	Kilnhurst	W 2-0	Boyd.Bedford.
12	20				
13	27				
14	Jan 1	h	St Bartholmews	W 4-1	
15	10	a	Conisborough	W 3-2	Pearce.
16	17	h	Lockwood Bros	D 1-1	Pearce.
17	31	h	Knottingley	W 1-0	
18	Feb 7	h	Newton Heath	W 2-0	
19	14	a	Sheff Clar	D 1-1	Smith.
20	21	h	Stourton	L 0-1	
21	Mar 7				
22	14	h	Scunthorpe		cancelled
23	21	h	Sheff Clar	W 1-0	Whitley.
24	28	a	St Bartholmews	W 4-1	
25	Apr 4	h	Gainsboro Tr	D 2-2	Smith.Pearce.

Friendlies 1885-86

No	Date	V	Opponents	F-A	Scorers
1	Oct24	h	Ryecroft	W 3-0	Boyd,Fowler,Thrush.
2	31	h	Brigg Town	W 3-0	Harper,Leedle,Pearce
3	Nov21	a	Retford	D 1-1	Hopwood.
4	Dec12	a	Kilnhurst		
5	19	h	Peterboro GNR		
6	26	a	Elsecar	W 2-1	Fowler,Boyd.
7	Jan 1	h	Sheff Clar	W 3-0	Wyatt,Whitley(2).
8	2	h	Rawmarsh Utd	W 1-0	Boyd.
9	9	a	Mexborough	L 2-3	
10	16	h	Retford	W 5-0	Boyd,Bridgewater,Bilsland,Fowler(2).
11	23				
12	30	a	Brigg Town	L 0-5	
13	Feb 6	h	Leeds Assoc	W 8-0	Fowler(2),Hopwood(2),Whitley,Bilsland,Brdgwtr
14	13	a	Leeds Assoc		
15	20	h	Kilnhurst	L 1-8	
16	Mar 9	h	Attercliffe		
17	13	a	Rawmarsh	W 4-0	Bridgewater(2),Fowler,Millard.
18	27	h	Newton Heath		
19	Apr17	a	Newton Heath		

Sheffield Challenge Cup

No	Date	V	Opponents	F-A	Scorers
R1	Oct10	h	Park Grang	W 2-1	Mosby,Whitley.
R2	Nov 7	a	Heeley 2nd XI	W 1-0	Bilsland.
R3	28	a	Sheff Wed	W 2-1	James,Bilsland.
R4	Feb27	a	Eckington 2nd	L 2-3	Hopwood.

Benefit Match

No	Date	V	Opponents	F-A	Scorers
20	Mar20	h	Mexborough	L 1-5	Marshland,og.

Friendlies 1886-87

No	Date	V	Opponents	F-A	Scorers
1	Sep18	h	Sheff Club	W 1-0	
2	Oct 2	h	Rawmarsh & Pk	L 0-2	
3	9				
4	11	a	Hull	W 4-1	
5	16	a	Retford	W 5-1	
6	30	h	Kilnhurst		
7	Nov13	h	Barnsley	D 1-1	
8	20	a	Bethel Reds	D 1-1	
9	27	h	Rawmarsh & Pk	W 3-0	
10	Dec 4	h	Retford	W 5-3	
11	11	a	Kimberworth	W 5-3	
12	18	a	Barnsley	W 2-0	
13	25	h	Kimberworth	W 1-0	
14	27	a	Wombwell		
15	Jan 1	a	Rotherham		
16	8	h	Wombwell		
17	15	h	Kilnhurst		
18	22	h	Bethel Reds		
19	29	a	Holmes		
20	Feb 5	a	Rotherham		
21	12	a	Leeds		
22	19	h	Gainsboro Tr		
23	26	h	Holmes		
24	Mar12	h	Kilnhurst		
25	19	a	Kilnhurst Ch		
26	26	h	Newton Heath	W 2-0	
27	Apr 9	h	Sheff Clowns	W 4-2	

Sheffield Challenge Cup

No	Date	V	Opponents	F-A	Scorers
R1	Nov 6	h	Sheff Coll	D 2-2	
R2	13	a	Sheff Coll	L 1-5	

Benefit Games

No	Date	V	Opponents	F-A	Scorers
28	Dec31	a	Oak St	D 1-1	
29	Mar 5	h	Mexborough	L 0-2	
30	Apr 2	h	Rotherham	W 2-0	
31	11	a	Mexborough	L 2-6	

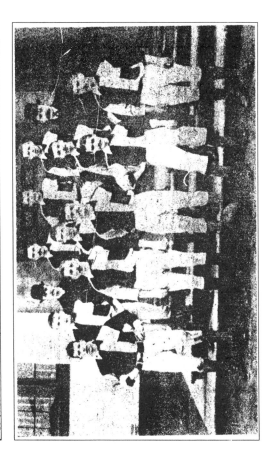

The oldest known (unnamed) team group of
Doncaster Rovers – Season 1884/85

Friendlies 1887-88

No	Date	V	Opponents	F-A	Scorers
1	Sep24	h	Sheff Wed 2n	W 4-2	
2	Oct 1	h	Rawmarsh	W 8-0	Webb.
3	15	h	Gainsboro Tr	D 2-2	
4	22	a	Lockwood Bro	W 6-2	
5	29		Retford		
6	Nov12	h	Rotherham	W 4-0	
7	19	h	York City	W 6-0	
8	26	a	Gainsboro Tr	D 0-0	
9	Dec 3	h	Rotherham		
10	17	a	Newark		
11	24	h	Morton St Pl	W 4-1	
12	26	h	Attercliffe	W 8-2	
13	27	a	Bethel Reds		
14	31	a	Attercliffe	L 2-5	Hunt(2).
15	Jan 2	h	Sheff Wed 2n	W 4-0	Hunt(2),Mosby(2).
16	7	a	Retford	L 4-6	
17	14	h	Newton Heath	D 3-3	
18	21	a	Rotherham res	D 3-3	
19	28	h	Lockwood Bros	W 7-1	Fowler(3),Hunt(2),Munro(2).
20	Feb 4	a	Rawmarsh & Pk		
21	18	h	Newark		
22	Mar 3	h	Lincoln Ramb	W 4-2	Whitley,Munro,Hunt,Fowler.
23	10	h	Retford	W 2-0	
24	17	h	Owlerton	W 7-1	Bilsland,James,Boyd,Fowler(2),Hunt(2).
25	30	h	Nth Wales Wa	W 6-1	Hunt(2),Hopwood(2),Fowler
26	31	a	Lincoln City	W 2-1	Hunt(2).
27	Apr 2	a	York		
28	14	h	Carbrook Ch	W 5-1	Hunt(3),Fowler,Bilsland.
29	21	a	Sheff Wed		
30	28	a	Sheff Wed	L 1-3	Bilsland

Sheffield Challenge Cup:1887-88:

31	Oct 8	a	Kimberworth	L 3-6	

Gainsborough News Charity Cup:1887-88

32	Nov 5	h	Gainsboro Ash	W 12-0	
33	Feb11	h	Gainsboro Tr	L 2-3	

Benefit Match:

34	Mar24	h	Sheff & Hal	W 4-1	Hunt(2),Kelly,Fowler.

Friendlies 1888-89

No	Date	V	Opponents	F-A	Scorers
1	Sep. 8	h	Walkley	W 3-1	Hunt(2),Fowler.
2	12	h	Sheff Wed	L 1-3	
3	15	h	Park Grange	W 4-2	Fowler(3),Hunt.
4	22	h	Retford	W 6-0	
5	29	a	Rotherham Sw	D 2-2	
6	Oct20	h	Rotherham Sw	W 4-2	Shakespear(2),Hunt,Fowler.
7	Nov17	a	Attercliffe	W 6-1	
8	Dec 1	h	Barnsley St P	W 6-0	
9	8	a	Sheffield Club	D 1-1	Shakespear.
10	15	h	Owlerton	W 3-0	Munro(2),Hopwood.
11	22	h	Park Grange		
12	24	h	Lincoln Ramb	W 7-1	
13	29	h	Gainsboro Tr	L 1-3	
14	Jan 5	a	Grimsby Town	L 1-6	
15	12	a	Gainsboro Tr	L 0-4	
16	26	h	Ecclesfield	W 4-1	Shakespear(2),Hunt,Fowler.
17	Feb 2	a	Grantham Town	L 1-2	Hunt.
18	9	h	Newark	D 2-2	Langton(2).
19	16	a	Lincoln City		
20	23	a	Ecclesfield	D 3-3	
21	Mar30	h	Sheffield Club	W 3-2	
22	Apr 6	h	Sheff Clinton	W 4-0	Hunt(2),Munro(2).
23	19	h	Manchester As	W 2-1	
24	20	h	Derby St Lukes	W 3-1	Hopwood,Boyd,Shakespear.

F.A. Cup

25	Oct 6	h	Rotherham Town	L 1-9	Hunt.

Sheffield Challenge Cup

26	Oct13	a	Eckington Wks	D 2-2	Hunt,Munro.
27	27	h	Eckington Wks	W 2-0	Hunt,Munro.
28	Nov 3	h	Sheff Clinton	D 3-3	Hunt(3).
29	10	a	Sheff Clinton	W 4-3	Hopwood(3),Hunt.
30	24	a	Rotherham Tn	L 2-6	

Gainsborough News Cup

31	Nov17	a	Attercliffe	W 6-1	
32	Jan19	a	Sheff Wed	L 0-10	

Wharncliffe Charity Cup

33	Dec26	a	Ecclesfield	W 3-0	
34	Mar 2	a	Rotherham Tn	D 0-0	
35	16	h	Rotherham Tn	D 1-1	Munro.
36	23	a	Rotherham Tn	D 2-2	
37	Apr13	a	Rotherham Tn	L 0-3	

Benefit Match

31	Mar 9	h	Grantham Tn	L 3-4	
32	May 4	h	Notts Olympic	L 0-1	

Friendlies 1889–90

No	Date	V	Opponents	F-A	Scorers
1	Sep 7	h	Sheff Club	D 2-2	Mosby,Musson.
2	14	h	Retford	W 4-1	
3	21	a	Gainsboro Tr	L 0-3	
4	28	h	Leeds Albion	W 1-0	
5	Oct12	h	Rotherham Sw	D 0-0	
6	26	h	Grimsby H Rov	W 4-1	Wood(2),Shakespear,Flavill.
7	Nov 2	a	Sheff Utd	L 0-3	
8	9	h	Heeley	W 3-0	Fenn(2),Shakespear.
9	16	a	Matlock	W 2-1	
10	23	h	Ecclesfield	W 4-1	Scarlett,Wood,Parr,Fenn.
11	30	h	Attercliffe	W 1-0	Gray.
12	Dec14	h	Staveley	W 3-1	Fowler,Flavell,Parr.
13	25	h	Gt Lever Dr	W 9-2	
14	28	h	Sheff Utd	W 2-0	Bell(2).
15	Jan 1	h	Wigan	L 1-2	
16	4	h	Boston	W 2-1	Shakespear,Wood.
17	11	a	Boston	D 2-2	
18	25	h	Notts Olympic	L 2-4	
19	Feb 1	h	Newark	W 8-0	
20	15	a	Attercliffe Sw	L 0-4	
21	Mar 1	a	Attercliffe	W 4-1	
22	8	h	Sheff Clinton	W 8-0	Wood(2),Langton(2),Shakespear(2),Flavell,
23	15	h	Rotherham Sw	W 3-0	Fenn,Wood,Langton.
24	22	a	Darlington	D 2-2	Shakespear,Flavell.
25	29	h	Sheff Utd	D 1-1	Howell.
26	Apr 4	h	Rawtenstall	W 3-0	
27	5	h	Scarboro	W 6-2	Langton(2),Wood(2),Fenn,Flavell.
28	7	h	Gainsboro Tr	D 2-2	Procter,Fenn.
29	19	a	Darlington	L 0-2	
30	26	a	Scarboro	L 1-2	

F.A. Cup

No	Date	V	Opponents	F-A	Scorers
31	Oct 5	a	Rotherham Tn	L 1-2	

Sheffield Challenge Cup

No	Date	V	Opponents	F-A	Scorers
32	Dec21	h	Staveley	L 0-3	

Wharncliffe Charity Cup

No	Date	V	Opponents	F-A	Scorers
33	Dec26	a	Sheff Utd	L 0-1	

Friendlies

No	Date	V	Opponents	F-A	Scorers	
31	May 1	h	Rotherham Town	W 2-1	Flavill.	(Benefit).

Midland Alliance League 1890–91

No	Date	V	Opponents	F-A	Scorers	Att
1	Sep20	h	Loughboro	W 4-0	Herrod,Gresham,Kisby,Frost.	
2	Oct11	a	Grantham Rovers	L 0-3		2,000
3	Nov 1	a	Sheffield Club	W 1-0	Herrod.	
4	15	h	Notts County Rovers	L 0-2		
5	Dec20	a	Notts Olympic	D 2-2	McCallum,Unknown.	2,000
6	Jan 3	a	Loughboro	L 0-3		
7	10	h	Notts Olympic	W 6-0	McCallum(2),Langton(2),Kisby,Boyd.	
8	17	a	Newark	W 2-1	Langton,Herrod.	
9	31	a	Heanor	W 4-1	Langton(2),Gresham,Kisby.	
10	Feb14	h	Newark	W 7-0	Herrod(2),McCallum(2),Langton(2),Kisby.	1,000
11	21	a	Notts County Rovers	L 2-3	Langton,Kisby.	500
12	28	h	Grantham Rovers	W 6-1	Kisby(2),Herrod(2),Langton,Gresham.	1,500
13	Apr 4	h	Heanor	W 5-1	Herrod(2),Kisby,Gresham,Langton.	
14	18	h	Sheffield Club	W 4-2	Herrod,Gresham,Kisby,Kelly.	1,000

	P	W	D	L	F	A	PTS
HOME	7	6	0	1	32	6	12
AWAY	7	3	1	3	11	13	7
TOTAL	14	9	1	4	43	19	19

F.A. Cup

No	Date	V	Opponents	F-A	Scorers
2	Oct25	h	Kilnhurst	L 4-5	Herrod(2),Gresham,Hoyle.A.

All attendances are approximate

Midland League 1891-92

No	Date	V	Opponents	F-A	Scorers	Att
1	Sep 5	a	Wednesbury Old Ath	L 1-3	Bennett.	
2	12	h	Burton Wanderers	W 3-1	Gresham(2),Bennett.	
3	19	h	Rotherham Town	L 0-2		2.000
4	26	a	Burslem Port Vale	L 0-4		1.500
5	Oct10	a	Loughboro	L 2-11	Bridgewater.Adams.	
6	17	h	Wednesbury Old Ath	W 4-1	Waddington(3),Bennett.	2.000
7	Nov 7	a	Derby Junction	W 2-1	Waddington.Unknown.	
8	Dec12	h	Burslem Port Vale	W 3-1	Bennett.Edwards(2).	200
9	19	h	Long Eaton Rangers	W 3-1	Parr.Edwards.Bennett.	800
10	26	h	Leicester Fosse	W 1-0	Edwards.	1.800
11	Jan16	a	Grantham Rovers	L 0-3		
12	30	a	Gainsboro Trin	L 0-0		
13	Feb27	h	Loughboro	D 0-0		1.000
14	Mar 5	a	Rotherham Town	L 1-2	Parr.	3.000
15	19	a	Long Eaton Rangers	D 1-1	Parr.	1.200
16	26	H	Derby Junction	D 2-2	Parr.Bridgewater.	
17	Apr 9	a	Burton Wanderers	W 4-2	Pinkerton.Cuthbert.Shaw.Flavill.	2.000
18	15	h	Grantham Rovers	W 2-0	Waddington.Shaw.	3.000
19	18	h	Gainsboro Trin	L 0-1		3.000
20	30	a	Leicester Fosse	D 0-0		3.000

(Staveley withdrew from league).

HOME							AWAY							TOTAL							
P	W	D	L	F	A	PTS	P	W	D	L	F	A	PTS	P	W	D	L	F	A	PTS	POS
10	6	2	2	18	9	14	10	2	3	5	11	25	7	20	8	5	7	29	34	21	6th

F.A.Cup

1	Oct 3	a	Lincoln City	L 1-3	Bennett.	2.000

All attendances are approximate

Midland League 1892-93

No	Date	V	Opponents	F-A	Scorers	Att
1	Sep 3	a	Grantham Rovers	W 2-1	Cuthbert.Smith W.	1.000
2	10	h	Burton Wanderers	W 4-2	Langton.Waddington.Smith W.Smith S.	1.500
3	17	a	Loughboro	W 4-1	Bridgewater(2).Smith S.Smith S.	
4	24	h	Mansfield Town	W 4-2	Scott(2).Smith S.Smith W.	2.000
5	Oct 1	a	Gainsboro Trinity	L 0-2		
6	22	a	Burton Wanderers	D 1-1	Unknown.	2.000
7	Nov 5	H	Kettering	D 2-2	Smith W(2).	1.000
8	12	a	Mansfield Town	L 2-3	Unknown.	
9	Dec10	a	Wednesbury Old Ath	D 1-1	Hill.	
10	17	h	Leicester Fosse	L 0-1		1.000
11	26	h	Loughboro	L 1-3	Waddington.	
12	31	a	Long Eaton Rangers	L 1-3	Unknown.	
13	Jan 7	a	Leicester Fosse	W 1-0	Smith W.	4.000
14	14	h	Newark	W 1-0	Smith W.	1.500
15	21	a	Rotherham Town	L 3-6	Lee.Lester.Smith W.	
16	Feb 4	a	Derby Junction	W 5-4	Orme og.Bridgewater.Waddington.Attree.SmithW	4.000
17	11	h	Derby Junction	W 6-1	Boyd.Bridg'r.Lester.Wadd'n.Smith W.+	1.500
18	25	h	Rotherham Town	L 0-1		3.000
19	Mar11	a	Newark	W 1-0	Bridgewater.	
20	31	h	Grantham Rovers	W 3-2	Lester(2).Lee.	
21	Apr 3	h	Gainsboro Trinity	L 1-3	Smith W.	4.000
22	15	h	Wednesbury Old Ath	D 2-2	Parr.Scott.	
23	22	h	Long Eaton Rangers	W 2-0	Smith W.Cartwright	3.000
24	29	a	Kettering	L 0-3		

HOME							AWAY							TOTAL							
P	W	D	L	F	A	PTS	P	W	D	L	F	A	PTS	P	W	D	L	F	A	PTS	POS
12	6	2	4	26	19	14	12	5	2	5	21	25	12	24	11	4	9	47	44	26	5th

F.A.Cup:

10	Oct15	h	Mansfield Town	W 2-0	Lester.Smith S.	500
20	29	a	Grimsby Town	D 1-1	McDonald. (abandoned 108 mins.)	3.000
20	Nov10	h	Grimsby Town	L 1-2	Smith S.	2.000

Final League Table 1891/92 (Top six positions only)	P	W	D	L	F	A	Pts
Rotherham Town	20	13	1	6	70	41	27
Gainsborough Trinity	20	12	2	6	49	31	26
Burslem Port Vale	20	11	1	8	49	33	23
Wednesbury Old Athletic	20	9	5	6	49	41	23
Burton Wanderers	20	10	2	8	48	32	22
Doncaster Rovers	20	8	5	7	29	34	21

Final League Table 1892/93 (Top 6 positions only)	P	W	D	L	F	A	Pts
Rotherham Town	24	19	3	2	80	28	41
Burton Wanderers	24	15	4	5	49	33	34
Loughborough Town	24	15	3	6	64	30	33
Leicester Fosse	24	12	3	9	50	37	27
Doncaster Rovers	24	11	4	9	47	44	26
Gainsborough Trinity	24	12	1	11	51	34	25

THE SHEFFIELD CHALLENGE CUP WINNERS, 1891.
Back row—Cuthbert, Mr J. Le Brun (Committee), Massey, McDonald (Trainer), Grey, Mr. W. Reid (Committee), Parr, James, Mr. J. Musson (Secretary), Pilkington.
Front row—Kirby, McCullum, Langton, Herd, Gresham.

Midland League 1893-94

No	Date	V	Opponents	F-A	Scorers	Att
1	Sep 2	h	Burton Wanderers	D 1-1	Smith W	1,000
2	16	a	Grantham Rovers	L 2-3	Lester.Lees.	700
3	23	h	Mansfield Greenhal	D 3-3	White.Lees.Calder.	
4	30	a	Kettering	D 0-0		
5	Oct21	a	Newark	L 2-3	Guild.Lees.	1,000
6	28	h	Long Eaton Rangers	L 0-1		
7	Nov11	a	Mansfield Town	D 0-0		2,000
8	18	a	Leicester Fosse	L 1-2	Cartwright.	
9	Dec16	a	Mansfield Greenhal	L 1-7	Lees.	
10	23	h	Kettering	W 2-1	White.Lees.	600
11	Jan 6	a	Burton Wanderers	L 1-6	Unknown.	1,000
12	13	h	Newark	W 2-0	White.Calder.	1,500
13	20	h	Leicester Fosse	L 1-2	Lees.	
14	27	a	Long Eaton Rangers	L 0-5		
15	Feb10	a	Loughboro Town	L 1-3	Lees.	
16	17	a	Gainsboro Trinity	L 1-3	Unknown.	
17	Mar 3	h	Mansfield Town	W 5-3	Hoyle.Cartwr't.Langton.Dawson.Frogson O.G.	500
18	23	h	Grantham Rovers	W 1-0	Phillips.	2,000
19	Apr 7	h	Gainsboro Trinity	W 3-1	Calder.White.Langton.	1,000
20	19	h	Loughboro Town	L 1-3	Dawson.	

	P	W	D	L	F	A	PTS	POS
HOME	10	5	2	3	19	15	12	
AWAY	10	0	2	8	9	32	2	
TOTAL	20	5	4	11	28	47	14	8th

F.A. Cup

20	Nov 4	h	Grantham Rovers	L 1-2	Cartwright.	1,500

All attendances are approximate

Final League Table	P	W	D	L	F	A	Pts.
Burton Wanderers	20	17	3	0	82	12	35
Leicester Fosse	20	15	2	3	49	13	32
Loughborough Town	20	12	6	2	52	22	30
Grantham Rovers	20	9	4	7	35	33	22
Mansfield Greenhalghs	20	9	3	8	43	54	21
Long Eaton Rovers	20	7	4	9	43	44	18
Newark	20	6	2	12	28	55	14
Doncaster Rovers	20	5	4	11	28	47	14
Kettering	20	4	5	11	28	46	13
Gainsborough Trinity	20	5	1	14	28	46	11
Mansfield Town	20	2	4	14	27	54	8

Midland League 1894-95

No	Date	V	Opponents	F-A	Scorers	Att
1	Sep15	h	Long Eaton Rangers	W 2-1	Cartwright(2).	700
2	22	h	Stoke Swifts	D 2-2	Dawson,White.	1,000
3	29	a	Kettering	L 1-2	Hoyle T.	2,000
4	Oct 6	a	Loughborough	L 1-6	Beck-Bessinger.	1,500
5	20	h	Heanor Town	W 1-0	Cartwright.	
6	27	a	Grantham Rovers	L 0-1		2,000
7	Nov10	a	Ilkeston Town	L 0-1		
8	17	a	Mansfield Town	L 0-1		600
9	Dec 1	h	Mansfield Town	L 0-2		1,000
10	8	a	Rushden Town	L 0-6		
11	15	a	Stoke Swifts	L 1-13	Unknown.	1,000
12	26	h	Derby County res	D 1-1	Mackie.	
13	Jan 5	a	Long Eaton Rangers	L 1-5	Carr.	
14	12	a	Heanor Town	D 2-2	Pears,Carr.	
15	19	h	Matlock Town	W 4-2	Mackie(3).Cartwright.	800
16	Feb16	h	Ilkeston Town	L 0-4		
17	23	a	Gainsboro Trinity	D 2-2	Carr.O.G.	700
18	Mar 2	h	Kettering Town	D 1-1	Mackie.	
19	16	a	Matlock Town	L 1-3	Wright I.	
20	21	a	Derby County res	D 2-2	Wright I.Milnes O.G.	800
21	23	h	Newark	L 2-3	Unknown.	
22	30	a	Newark	W 4-2	Wright I(2).Mackie.Carr.	2,000
23	April 2	h	Grantham Rovers	W 2-0	Langton.Wright I.	2,000
24	15	h	Gainsboro Trinity	W 1-0	Carr.	
25	20	h	Rushden Town			
26	27	h	Loughborough Town	W 1-0	Carr.	600

	P	W	D	L	F	A	PTS	POS
HOME	13	6	5	2	23	17	17	
AWAY	13	0	1	12	8	46	1	
TOTAL	26	6	6	14	31	63	18	12th

F.A. Cup

R1	Oct13	h	Mexborough Town	L 1-2	Cartwright.	1,000

All attendances are approximate

Final League Table	P	W	D	L	F	A	Pts.
Loughborough Town	26	19	4	3	84	25	42
Stoke Swifts	26	14	7	5	90	33	35
Gainsborough Trinity	26	14	4	8	55	36	32
Derby County Res.	26	13	6	7	46	27	32
Kettering	26	12	8	6	59	45	32
Ilkeston	26	13	5	8	53	46	31
Mansfield Town	26	12	5	9	46	37	29
Heanor Town	26	9	5	12	49	48	23
Rushden Town	26	10	3	13	47	70	23
Long Eaton Rangers	26	7	5	14	41	55	19
Newark	26	6	6	14	37	63	18
Doncaster Rovers	26	6	6	14	31	63	18
Grantham Town	26	5	7	14	27	59	17
Matlock	26	3	7	16	37	92	13

Midland League 1896-97

No	Date	V	Opponents	F-A	Scorers	Att
1	Sep 5	a	Mexborough Town	W 1-0	Wright.	1,000
2	12	a	Dresden Utd	L 0-1		1,000
3	26	h	Ilkeston	W 3-2	McUrich.Waddington.Longden.	1,500
4	Oct 3	a	Kettering	L 1-5	McUrich.	
5	17	h	Heanor Town	W 4-3	Chester(2).Smith.Waddington.	1,000
6	24	a	Burslem Port Vale	L 2-5	Linward.McUrich.	500
7	Nov 7	h	Chesterfield Town	W 4-2	Longden.Smith.McUrich(2).	
8	Dec 5	h	Wellingboro Town	W 2-0	McUrich.Smith.	800
9	19	a	Rushden	W 3-0	Longden.Goodison(2).	
10	26	a	Grantham Rovers	W 2-0	Chester(2).	
11	Jan 1	a	Barnsley St Peters	W 3-0	Goodison(3).	3,000
12	9	h	Rushden	W 4-1	Waddington(2).McUrich.Willey O.G.	500
13	16	a	Long Eaton Rangers	L 1-3	Goodison.	
14	23	a	Wellingboro Town	W 2-1	Linward.McUrich.	800
15	30	h	Long Eaton Rangers	W 2-1	Goodison.McUrich.	2,000
16	Feb 6	h	Dresden Utd	D 3-3	Chester.Langton.Goodison.	
17	20	h	Worksop Town	D 1-1	McUrich.	1,000
18	Mar 6	a	Chesterfield Town	W 2-1	Goodison,1 Unknown.	3,000
19	13	a	Heanor Town	D 0-0		800
20	16	a	Ilkeston Town	W 3-0	Linward.Goodison.Allsop O.G.	1,000
21	20	a	Worksop Town	W 1-0	Linward.	
22	27	h	Burslem Port Vale	W 1-0	Linward.	2,000
23	Apr10	h	Kettering	W 1-0	Linward.	3,000
24	16	h	Barnsley St Peters	W11-1	Chstr(4).Lnwrd(3).Gdisn.(2).Lngdn.McIl	
25	17	h	Mexboro Town	W 3-1	Goodison.Hulley.Linward.	
26	24	h	Glossop North End	D 1-1	Chester.	4,000
27	27	a	Glossop North End	D 2-2	Smith(2).	2,000
28	29	h	Grantham Rovers	W13-1	Gdsn(5)Chstr(2)Lgdn(2)Hlly.Smth.Lngt.OG	

```
HOME                        AWAY                       TOTAL
P  W  D  L  F  A  PTS        P  W  D  L  F  A  PTS       P  W  D  L  F  A  PTS POS
14 10 3  1  52 18 23        14 7  2  5  25 22 16       28 17 5  6  77 40 39  1st
```

F.A. Cup
```
3Q  Nov21  a Sheffield Club   L 1-3 Unknown.                300
```

All attendances are approximate

Final League Table	P	W	D	L	F	A	Pts.
Doncaster Rovers	28	17	5	6	77	40	39
Glossop North End	27	15	4	8	67	39	36
Long Eaton Rangers	28	15	2	11	55	39	32
Chesterfield	28	13	6	9	74	53	32
Kettering	28	13	5	10	51	40	31
Wellingborough Town	28	11	9	8	52	46	31
Burslem Port Vale	28	14	3	11	62	56	31
Heanor Town	28	12	6	10	55	47	30
Ilkeston Town	28	12	5	11	60	57	29
Dresden United	28	12	5	11	48	63	29
Barnsley St. Peter	28	10	4	14	57	71	24
Rushden	28	9	5	14	43	53	21
Mexborough	28	7	7	14	39	50	21
Worksop Town	28	6	5	17	27	63	17
Grantham Rovers	28	6	3	18	26	76	15

Midland League 1895-96

No	Date	V	Opponents	F-A	Scorers	Att
1	Sep 7	a	Gainsboro Trinity	D 1-1	Unknown.	
2	14	h	Mansfield Town	W 3-0	Mackie.Kay.Linward..	1,000
3	21	h	Dresden Utd	D 1-1	Fellows.	
4	28	a	Grantham Rovers	L 1-3	Fellows.	400
5	Oct 5	h	Rushden Town	W 3-0	Bullock.Fellows.McUrich.	1,000
6	19	a	Newark	L 0-1		
7	26	a	Barnsley St Peters	L 1-3	Bullock.	
8	Nov 9	a	Mansfield Town	D 1-1	Mackie.	
9	16	h	Newark	W 3-2	Bullock.Langton.Linward..	500
10	Dec 7	a	Long Eaton Rangers	L 1-2	Bullock.	
11	14	h	Wellingborough	W 3-1	Mackie(2).Linward..	
12	21	h	Matlock	W 5-1	Bullock.McUrich.Mackie.Langton.O.G.	
13	26	a	Ilkeston	L 0-4		
14	Jan 4	a	Heanor Town	L 0-6		800
15	11	h	Long Eaton Rangers	D 1-1	Bullock.	
16	25	a	Dresden Utd	L 0-3		
17	Feb 1	a	Walsall	L 1-9	Bullock.	
18	8	h	Kettering	L 1-3	McUrich.	
19	15	h	Grantham Rovers	L 1-3	Linward.	
20	22	a	Rushden Town	L 1-3	Bullock.	
21	Mar 7	h	Walsall	W 3-2	Fellows(2).McUrich.	1,000
22	14	a	Kettering	L 0-3		
23	28	h	Heanor Town	W 2-1	Hulley.Linward..	
24	Apr 3	h	Barnsley St Peters	W 4-0	McUrich(2).Bullock.Fellows.	2,000
25	4	a	Matlock	W 3-0	Calder.Linward.McUrich.	
26	6	h	Gainsboro Trinity	D 1-1	Calder.	2,500
27	8	a	Wellingborough	L 0-1		1,200
28	18	h	Ilkeston	W 3-2	Laurence.Linward..Fellows.	

```
HOME                        AWAY                       TOTAL
P  W  D  L  F  A  PTS        P  W  D  L  F  A  PTS       P  W  D  L  F  A  PTS POS
14 9  4  1  34 16 22        14 1  2  11 10 40 4        28 10 6  12 44 56 26  10th
```

F.A. Cup
```
1Q   Oct12  a Mexboro Town     D 1-1 Fellows.                       3,500
1QR  17     h Mexboro Town     W 4-1 Fellows(2).McUrich, 1 Unknown. 1,500
2Q   Nov 2  h Rotherham Town   L 0-7                                2,500
```

All attendances are approximate

Final League Table	P	W	D	L	F	A	Pts.
Kettering	28	20	5	3	74	28	45
Gainsborough Trinity	28	17	6	5	59	26	40
Walsall	28	17	6	5	91	47	40
Long Eaton Rangers	28	18	3	7	68	46	39
Rushden	28	14	4	10	61	45	32
Heanor Town	28	12	7	9	70	45	31
Ilkeston Town	28	12	6	10	62	52	30
Barnsley St. Peters	28	13	3	12	62	64	29
Grantham Rovers	28	11	5	12	64	56	27
Doncaster Rovers	28	10	6	12	44	56	26
Dresden United	28	9	6	13	44	49	24
Wellingborough Town	28	10	4	14	44	71	24
Mansfield Town	28	7	6	15	35	68	20
Newark	28	6	1	21	38	78	13
Matlock Town	28	0	0	28	9	130	0

1896/97 Season (Midland League Champions)

(Back): S.Balmforth (Chairman), Waddington, Wright, Smith, J.Musson (Secretary),
Attree, Eggett, Hulley, R.Thompson (Trainer)
(Front) Longden, McIlrich, Langton, Chester, Linwood

1901/02 season (First in the Second Division)

(Back) Dowson, Attree (Trainer), Birch, Eggett, Marsh, Wright,
Goodson, Simpson. (Front) Langham, Drake, Price, Murphey, Bailey.

Midland League 1897-98

No	Date	V	Opponents	F-A	Scorers	Att
1	Sep 4	h	Long Eaton Rangers	W 6-0	Oxspring(4),Linward,Longden.	
2	11	a	Chesterfield	D 3-3	Goodison,Chester,Linward.	3.000
3	18	a	Kettering	L 0-1		
4	25	h	Chesterfield	D 0-0		2.000
5	Nov 6	a	Long Eaton Rangers	D 1-1	Gall.	
6	13	h	Barnsley	L 1-3	Gall.	3.000
7	Dec18	h	Burton Wanderers	W 1-0	Oxspring.	
8	25	a	Rushden Town	L 0-1		2.000
9	27	a	Wellingborough Tn	L 1-3	Robinson.	2.000
10	Jan 1	h	Kettering	D 1-1	Gall.	2.000
11	3	a	Burslem Port Vale	L 0-4		2.000
12	8	h	Burslem Port Vale	D 0-0		
13	15	h	Ilkeston Town	L 1-2	Ward.	3.000
14	22	a	Barnsley	L 0-2		2.000
15	29	a	Glossop North End	L 1-5		1.500
16	Feb 5	a	Burton Wanderers	L 0-4		1.000
17	Mar 5	a	Mexboro Town	L 1-2	Langton pen.	2.500
18	16	a	Ilkeston Town	L 0-1		
19	Apr 2	h	Glossop North End	W 4-1	Oxspring(2),Robinson,Linward.	
20	8	h	Rushden Town	W 7-0	Linward(2),Rbson(2),Needham(2),Hulley.	3.000
21	11	h	Wellingborough Tn	D 3-3	Needham,Goodison,Langton.	
22	28	h	Mexboro Town	W 2-0	Goodison,Longden.	

HOME							AWAY							TOTAL							
P	W	D	L	F	A	PTS	P	W	D	L	F	A	PTS	P	W	D	L	F	A	PTS	POS
11	5	4	2	26	10	14	11	0	2	9	6	25	2	22	5	6	11	32	35	16	10th

F.A. Cup

3Q	Oct30	a	Sheffield Club	W 4-0	Oxspring(2),Linward,Chester.	500
4Q	Nov20	a	Mexboro Town	D 0-0		3.125
4QR	25	h	Mexboro Town	D 1-1	Oxspring.	2.000
4QR	Dec 2	a	Mexboro Town	D 1-1	Langton.(Aband 115 mins).	1.500
4QR	6	a	Mexboro Town	L 1-2	Chester.	2.000

All attendances are approximate

Final League Table	P	W	D	L	F	A	Pts.
Mexborough	22	15	3	4	53	30	33
Barnsley St. Peters	22	14	4	4	47	29	31
Chesterfield	22	11	7	4	54	39	29
Ilkeston Town	22	9	6	7	37	33	24
Burslem Port Vale	22	10	3	9	46	32	23
Rushden	22	9	5	8	35	44	23
Kettering	22	7	5	10	19	28	19
Long Eaton Rangers	22	7	5	10	26	44	19
Glossop North End	22	8	2	12	41	47	18
Doncaster Rovers	22	5	6	11	32	35	16
Burton Wanderers	22	5	5	12	31	44	15
Wellingborough Town	22	5	3	14	21	48	13

Midland League 1898-99

No	Date	V	Opponents	F-A	Scorers	Att
1	Sep 3	h	Derby County res	D 1-1	Gladwin.	2.500
2	10	a	Sheff Utd res	W 3-1	Oxspring,Linward,Longden.	
3	24	a	Heanor Town	L 1-2	Gladwin.	
4	Oct 1	h	Ilkeston Town	W 2-0	Gladwin(2).	2.000
5	8	a	Burton Wanderers	W 3-2	Oxspring,Gladwin,Linward.	
6	22	a	Sheff Wed res	L 2-5	Oxspring,1 Unknown.	
7	Nov12	h	Chesterfield	W 3-2	Gall(2),Gladwin.	2.000
8	26	a	Mexboro Town	D 1-1	Hulley.	1.500
9	Dec17	a	Derby County res	L 1-9	Oxspring.	1.200
10	26	a	Kettering	L 1-2	1 Unknown.	3.000
11	27	a	Wellingborough	L 0-5		1.200
12	31	h	Long Eaton Rangers	W 4-0	Goodison,Gladwin,Linward,Oxspring.	
13	Jan 7	h	Mexborough	W 3-0	Oxspring,Nelson,Gladwin.	3.000
14	14	a	Leicester Fosse res	D 1-1	Gall.	2.000
15	21	h	Leicester Fosse res	W 5-1	Gladwin(2),Linward,Langton,Oxspring.	1.000
16	Feb 4	a	Chesterfield	L 0-2		3.000
17	11	h	Welligborough	W 2-0	Oxspring,Nelson.	
18	25	h	Heanor Town	W 3-2	Linward(2),Gladwin.	
19	Mar 4	a	Ilkeston Town	D 2-2	Robinson,Gladwin.	
20	18	a	Long Eaton Rangers	L 0-4		3.000
21	22	h	Sheff Utd res	W 2-1	Gall,Oxspring.	
22	31	h	Kettering	W 3-1	Nelson(2),Gladwin.	3.000
23	Apr 1	a	Rushden	D 0-0		1.500
24	3	h	Burton Wanderers	W 3-2	Nelson,Linward,Gall.	1.500
25	22	h	Sheff Wed res	W 4-1	Clayton(3),Gall.	2.000
26	29	h	Rushden Town	W 6-0	Nelson(3),Clayton(2),Linward.	3.000

HOME							AWAY							TOTAL							
P	W	D	L	F	A	PTS	P	W	D	L	F	A	PTS	P	W	D	L	F	A	PTS	POS
13	12	1	0	41	13	25	13	2	4	7	15	36	8	26	14	5	7	56	47	33	1st

F.A. Cup

2Q	Oct15	h	Wath Athletic	W 6-1	Linward(2),Gladwin(3),Gall.	2.000
3Q	29	h	Parkgate Utd	W 8-1	Linward(3),Gladwin(3),Goodison,Oxsprg.	1.500
4Q	Nov19	h	Barnsley	L 1-2	Gladwin.	3.000

All attendances are approximate

Final League Table	P	W	D	L	F	A	Pts.
Doncaster Rovers	26	14	5	7	56	47	33
Ilkeston Town	26	15	2	9	55	37	32
Kettering	26	12	7	7	47	32	31
Chesterfield	26	14	2	10	59	42	31
Wellingborough Town	26	11	6	9	49	34	28
Burton Wanderers	26	11	5	10	49	38	27
Rushden	26	12	3	11	44	42	27
Derby County Res.	26	10	5	11	61	45	25
Sheffield United Res.	26	9	7	11	45	45	25
Sheffield Wednesday Res.	26	10	5	11	42	52	25
Heanor	26	8	5	13	35	53	21
Leicester Fosse Res.	26	9	2	15	34	58	20
Long Eaton Rangers	26	9	2	15	33	54	19
Mexborough	26	8	3	15	33	54	19

Midland League 1899-00

No	Date	V	Opponents	F-A	Scorers	Att
1	Sep 2	h	Derby County res	W 3-1	Nelson(2).Oxspring.	2.000
2	9	a	Lincoln City res	L 0-1		2.000
3	16	h	Ilkeston Town	D 1-1	Nelson.	2.000
4	21	a	Barnsley res	D 1-1	Linward.	800
5	Oct 7	h	Heanor Town	W 3-0	Cutts.Oxspring.Robinson.	2.000
6	Nov11	a	Burton Wanderers	L 0-2		
7	25	h	Kettering	W 3-2	Clayton.Oxspring.Heskin O.G.	1.300
8	Dec 2	a	Derby County res	L 1-3	Clayton.	1.000
9	9	h	Leicester Fosse res	D 0-0		1.000
10	23	h	Wellingborough	L 1-2	Ray.	3.000
11	25	a	Kettering	L 1-2	Ray(2).	600
12	26	a	Rushden Town	W 2-1	Lee.Ray.	1.000
13	Jan13	a	Leicester Fosse res	L 1-6	Lee.	
14	27	a	Ilkeston Town	L 1-3	Brooks.	
15	Feb 3	h	Barnsley res	L 1-3	Brooks.Oxspring.	
16	10	a	Northampton Town	L 2-2	Oxspring.Linward.	
17	Mar 3	h	Wellingborough	D 2-2	Oxspring.Linward.	
18	24	a	Newark	W 3-1	Nelson(2).Linward.	
19	31	h	Rushden Town	W 8-1	Goodison(3).Oxspring(2).Lnwrd(2).Nlson.	1.500
20	Apr 7	a	Heanor Town	D 1-1	Robinson.	
21	13	h	Northampton Town	L 1-1	Oxspring.	
22	14	h	Lincoln City res	W 3-0	Goodson(2).Oxspring.	
23	16	h	Burton Wanderers	W 8-2	Lnwrd(2).Oxsprg(2).Nlson(2).Ldley.Gdson.	
24	28	h	Newark	W 3-1	Goodson.Linward.Nelson.	

HOME								AWAY								TOTAL							
P	W	D	L	F	A	PTS		P	W	D	L	F	A	PTS		P	W	D	L	F	A	PTS	POS
12	7	4	1	36	14	18		12	2	2	8	15	28	8		24	9	6	9	51	42	24	7th

F.A. Cup

No	Date	V	Opponents	F-A	Scorers	Att
10	Sep30	a	Gainsboro Trinity	W 4-1	Cutts.Nelson.Robinson.Mawson.	2.000
20	Oct14	h	Newark	W 3-1	Cutts(2).Oxspring.	
30	28	h	Grimsby Town	L 1-3	Hulley.	3.000

All attendances are approximate

Final League Table	P	W	D	L	F	A	Pts.
Kettering	24	16	5	3	57	24	37
Wellingborough Town	24	16	4	4	64	38	36
Northampton	24	16	2	6	66	36	34
Derby County Res.	24	11	5	8	63	46	27
Lincoln City Res.	24	11	3	10	45	46	25
Heanor	24	9	7	8	31	36	25
Doncaster Rovers	24	9	6	9	51	42	24
Ilkeston Town	24	9	6	9	43	44	24
Newark	24	10	1	13	51	50	21
Burton Wanderers	24	6	6	12	40	62	18
Rushden	24	7	2	15	38	56	16
Barnsley Res.	24	6	3	13	39	68	16
Leicester Fosse Res.	24	3	3	18	34	74	9

Midland League 1900-01

No	Date	V	Opponents	F-A	Scorers	Att
1	Sep 1	h	Worksop Town	W 5-1	Vail(2).Linward.Goodson.Turner O.G.	1.500
2	8	h	Derby County res	W 5-2	Vail(2).Linward(2).Goodson.	
3	15	h	Leicester Fosse res	W 2-1	Linward.Gall.	
4	Oct13	h	Ilkeston Town	W 6-2	Goodson(3).Vail(2).Linward.	
5	27	h	Burton Wanderers	W 5-3	Nelson2).Vail.Langton.Lowe O.G.	
6	Nov24	h	Wellingborough	W 8-1	Vail(3).Gall(3).Goodson(2).	1.000
7	Dec 1	a	Coalville	W 9-1	Gall(4).Goodson(2).Murphy(2).Vail.	
8	8	a	Ilkeston Town	W 2-0	Vail.Goodson.	
9	22	a	Wellingborough	W 1-0	Murphy.	1.000
10	24	a	Northampton Town	W 2-0	Vail(2).	2.000
11	25	a	Rushden Town	L 1-2	Nelson.	
12	26	a	Hinckley Town	D 2-2	Goodson.1 pen.1 Unknown.	
13	29	h	Lincoln City res	W 2-1	Longden.Murphy.	
14	Jan 1	a	Sheff Utd res	L 0-1		4.000
15	19	h	Newark Town	W 5-0	Murphy(2).Vail(2).Goodson.	
16	Feb16	h	Coalville	W 9-1	Murphy(3).Lindley(3).Goodson(2).Gall.	1.000
17	23	a	Newark Town	L 0-2		700
18	Mar 2	h	Rushden Town	W 4-1	Goodison(2).Bailey(2).	1.200
19	9	a	Lincoln City res	D 2-2	Vail.Gall.	
20	23	a	Worksop Town	L 0-1		
21	Apr 5	a	Northampton Town	W 3-0	Vail.Gall.Murphy.	
22	6	h	Hinckley Town	W 5-0	Goodson(2).Murphy(2).Vail.	4.000
23	13	h	Sheff Utd res	L 0-1		
24	13	a	Leicester Fosse res	W 7-1	Gall(2).Vail(2).Murphy(2).Goodson.	4.000
25	20	a	Derby County res	L 1-3	Bailey.	2.000
26	25	a	Burton Wanderers	L 1-3	Birch.	

HOME								AWAY								TOTAL							
P	W	D	L	F	A	PTS		P	W	D	L	F	A	PTS		P	W	D	L	F	A	PTS	POS
13	12	0	1	59	14	24		13	5	2	6	28	18	12		26	17	2	7	87	32	36	2nd

F.A. Cup

No	Date	V	Opponents	F-A	Scorers	Att
PR	Sep22	h	Rotherham Town	W 6-1	Nelson(2).Goodson(2).Vail.Crump.	
10	Oct 6	a	Attercliffe	W 2-0	Vail.Goodson.	2.000
20	20	a	Worksop Town	D 0-0		
20	Rep 25	h	Worksop Town	W 2-1	Linward.Unknown.	2.000
30	Nov 3	a	Barnsley	L 1-2	Gall.	4.000

All attendances given are approximate

Final League Table	P	W	D	L	F	A	Pts.
Sheffield United Res.	26	21	3	2	78	23	45
Doncaster Rovers	26	17	2	7	87	32	36
Northampton	26	13	7	6	65	43	33
Derby County Res.	26	14	4	8	74	45	32
Hinckley Town	26	12	6	8	55	44	30
Newark	26	13	2	11	56	50	28
Wellingborough Town	26	12	4	10	44	44	28
Ilkeston Town	26	10	4	12	70	50	24
Leicester Fosse Res.	26	11	1	14	60	64	23
Lincoln City Res.	26	11	1	14	46	49	21
Rushden	26	8	5	13	35	61	21
Worksop Town	26	8	4	14	50	75	20
Coalville Town	26	5	2	19	30	102	12
Burton Wanderers	26	4	3	19	33	99	11

League Division 2 1901-02

No	Date	V	Opponents	F-A		Scorers	Att
1	Sep 7	h	Port Vale	D	3-3	Goodson(2),Bailey.	2,000
2	14	a	Chesterfield	D	0-0		2,000
3	21	h	Gainsboro Trinity	W	3-0	Bailey,Price,Langham.	
4	28	a	Middlesbrough	L	0-6		10,000
5	Oct 5	h	Bristol City	W	3-0	Langham,Murphy,Bailey.	1,500
6	12	a	Blackpool	L	1-3	Langham.	1,000
7	19	h	Stockport County	W	2-0	Bailey,Murphy.	2,000
8	26	a	Newton Heath	L	0-6		7,000
9	Nov 9	a	Burton Utd	D	1-1	Price.	
10	23	h	West Bromwich Alb	W	2-0	Price,Bailey.	4,000
11	30	a	Woolwich Arsenal	L	0-1		10,000
12	Dec 7	h	Barnsley	L	0-1		3,000
13	21	a	Preston North End	L	0-3		2,000
14	25	a	Lincoln City	D	0-0		5,000
15	26	a	Leicester Fosse	L	0-1		
16	28	a	Burnley	L	0-7		1,000
17	Jan 4	a	Port Vale	D	2-2	Price(2).	
18	11	h	Chesterfield	W	4-1	Marsh(3),Price.	
19	18	a	Gainsboro Trinity	L	1-4	Goodson.	3,000
20	Feb 1	a	Bristol City	L	0-3		4,000
21	8	h	Blackpool	W	4-3	Price,Longden,Jones,Goodson.	2,000
22	15	a	Stockport Co	W	2-1	Drake,Price.	2,000
23	22	h	Newton Heath	W	4-0	Murphy(3),Langham.	3,000
24	Mar 1	a	Glossop	L	1-3	Langham.	1,000
25	8	h	Burton Utd	W	2-0	Drake,Longden.	2,000
26	15	h	Lincoln City	D	1-1	Price.	3,000
27	22	a	West Bromwich Alb	D	2-2	Langham,Price.	6,000
28	28	h	Middlesbrough	D	0-0		6,000
29	29	h	Woolwich Arsenal	W	1-0	Langham.	3,500
30	31	h	Glossop North End	L	1-2	Drake.	3,000
31	Apr 5	a	Barnsley	L	0-3		1,000
32	12	h	Leicester Fosse	W	2-1	Price,Drake.	2,000
33	19	h	Preston North End	W	4-0	Price(2),Drake,Bailey.	2,500
34	26	h	Burnley	W	3-0	Langham(2),Drake.	2,000

Player columns: Bann, Drake, Pepper, Birch, Dowson, Lindley, McKenzie, Langton, Bailey, Goodson, Price, Murphy, Langham, Wright, Jones, Longden, Marsh, Simpson, Eggett

App 34 33 25 31 21 31 30 34 32 27 22 22 20 2 1

	HOME							AWAY							TOTAL						
	P	W	D	L	F	A	PTS	P	W	D	L	F	A	PTS	P	W	D	L	F	A	PTS
	17	12	3	2	39	12	27	17	1	5	11	10	46	7	34	13	8	13	49	58	34

F.A. Cup

						Scorers	
3Q	Nov 2	a	Royston Utd	W	3-1	Marsh,Jones,Price.	
4Q	16	a	Lincoln City	L	0-1		

All attendances are approximate

League Division 2 1902-03

No	Date	V	Opponents	F-A	Scorers	Att	Roberts	Nettleton	Parker	Richards	Petitt	Stables	Foxall	Pyle	Gordon	Robinson	Langton	Drake	Woodland	Bratley	Birch	Goodson	Ratcliffe	Aston	Price	Langham	Wright	Marsh	Murphy	Laverick	Simpson	Eggett
1	Sep 6	a	Burnley	D 1-1	Price.	1,000																11	10	9	8	7	6	5	4	3	2	1
2	13	h	Preston North End	L 1-2	Ratcliffe.																	11	10	9	8	7	6	5	4	3	2	1
3	20	a	Port Vale	L 0-3		2,000																11	10	9	8	7	6	5	4	3	2	1
4	27	h	Barnsley	W 2-0	Langham.Price.	3,000							5						11	2		6	10	9	8	7			4	3		1
5	Oct 4	a	Gainsboro Trinity	L 0-3		3,000							11						10	5		6		9	8	7			4	3	2	1
6	11	h	Burton Utd	D 1-1	Goodson.	2,000													10			11		9	8	7	6	5	4	3	2	1
7	18	a	Bristol City	L 2-4	Aston.Langham.	6,000																11	10	9	8	7	6	5	4	3	2	1
8	25	h	Glossop	W 4-1	Ratcliffe(2).Aston.Goodson.	2,500																11	10	9	8	7	6	5	4	3	2	1
9	Nov 8	h	Stockport County	W 2-0	Ratcliffe.Langham.											5						11	10	9	8	7	6		4	3	2	1
10	22	h	Woolwich Arsenal	L 0-1												5		9				11	10		8	7	6		4	3	2	1
11	29	h	Chesterfield	L 3-4	Langham.Ratcliffe.Murphy.											5		9			2	11	10		8	7	6		4	3		1
12	Dec 6	a	Lincoln City	L 2-4	Price.Pyle.	2,000								10				9			2	11			8	7	6	5	4	3		1
13	13	h	Small Heath	W 1-0	Langham.	3,000								10				9			2	11			8	7	6	5	4	3		1
14	20	a	Leicester Fosse	W 1-0	Pyle.									10				9				11			8	7	6	5	4	3	2	1
15	25	a	Blackpool	L 0-4										10				9				11			8	7	6	5	4	3	2	1
16	27	h	Man City	L 1-2	Simpson(pen)	4,000								10				9				11			5	7	6	4	8	3	2	1
17	Jan 1	a	Man City	L 1-4	Simpson(pen)	20,000												9				11	10		5	7	6	4	8	3	2	1
18	10	a	Preston North End	L 0-5														9				11	10		5	7	6	4	8	3	2	1
19	17	h	Port Vale	W 3-2	Foxall(2).Drake.	4,000							10				3	9				11			5	7	6	4	8		2	1
20	24	a	Barnsley	L 0-2		4,000							10				3	9				11			5	7	6	4	8		2	1
21	31	h	Gainsboro Trinity	D 0-0		4,000							10				3	9				11		4	5	7	6		8		2	1
22	Feb 7	a	Burton Utd	L 0-1									10				3	9				11		4	5	7	6		8		2	1
23	14	h	Bristol City	D 0-0		2,500							10				3	9	11					4	5	7	6		8		2	1
24	24	a	Glossop	L 0-3									10				3	9				11		4	5	7	6		8		2	1
25	28	h	Man Utd	D 2-2	Price.Langham.	3,000									10		3	9				11		4	5	7	6		8		2	1
26	Mar 7	a	Stockport County	L 0-1											10		3	9				11		4	5	7	6		8		2	1
27	14	h	Blackpool	W 3-0	Ratcliffe(2).Langham.												3	9				11	10	4	5	7	6		8		2	1
28	21	a	Woolwich Arsenal	L 0-3		8,000				8			11				3	9					10	4	5	7	6				2	1
29	28	a	Chesterfield	D 1-1	Parker.	2,000			8	9			10				3					11		4	5	7	6				2	1
30	Apr 4	h	Lincoln City	W 2-1	Murphy.Nettleton.	2,000		11					10				3	9						4	5	7	6		8		2	1
31	10	h	Burnley	W 2-1	Murphy.Aston.	4,000							11				3	9						4	5	7	6		8		2	1
32	11	a	Small Heath	L 0-12		9,000	1			8	10	9					3							4	5	7	6		11		2	
33	13	a	Man Utd	L 0-4		6,000	1			8		9					3							4	5	7	6		11		2	
34	18	h	Leicester Fosse	D 0-0		2,500	9			8							3							4	5	7	6		11		2	1
						App	9	1	2	7	1	1	12	5	12	5	25	15	4	3	4	23	11	27	30	32	32	8	28	8	31	33
						Gls		1	1			1	2	2				1				2	7	3	4	7			3		2	

HOME								AWAY								TOTAL						
P	W	D	L	F	A	PTS		P	W	D	L	F	A	PTS		P	W	D	L	F	A	PTS
17	8	5	4	27	17	21		17	1	2	14	8	55	4		34	9	7	18	35	72	25

F.A. Cup

No	Date	V	Opponents	F-A	Scorers	Att
3Q	Nov 1	a	Gainsboro Trinity	L 0-1		4,000

All attendances given are approximate

Midland League 1903-04

No	Date	V	Opponents	F-A	Scorers	Att
1	Sep 5	h	Lincoln City res	W 6-0	Dyer(4),Lovatt,Bennett.	
2	12	a	Sheff Wed res	L 0-1		
3	19	h	Nottm Forest res	L 1-2	Bennett.	
4	26	a	Chesterfield res	D 1-1	Bennett(pen).	1,000
5	Oct 3	a	Gainsboro Tr res	W 3-2	Dyer(2),Lovatt.	
6	10	h	Thornhill Utd	W 2-1	Moran(2).	
7	24	a	Worksop Town	L 0-1		1,000
8	Nov 7	h	Whitwick White Cr	W 3-0	Bennett,Moran,Murphy.	
9	21	h	Worksop Town	W 2-0	Bennett,Moran.	
10	26	a	Nottm Forest res	L 1-2	Bennett(pen).	
11	28	a	Thornhill Utd	L 1-4	Dyer.	1,000
12	Dec 5	h	Denaby Utd	D 1-1	Roberts.	
13	12	a	Whitwick White Cr	L 0-1		
14	19	h	Gresley Rovers	L 1-2	Moran.	
15	25	a	Barnsley res	L 2-5	Dyer(2).	2,000
16	26	h	Derby County res	D 0-0		
17	Jan 2	h	Gainsboro Tr res	W 7-0	Moran(3),Murphy(2),Roberts,Bennett.	
18	9	a	Grimsby Town res	D 1-2	Moran.	
19	16	h	Hinckley Town	W 4-2	Bradley(2),Tomkins,Murphy.	
20	23	a	Denaby Utd	W 2-1	Dyer,Roberts.	
21	30	h	Rotherham Town	D 3-3	Murphy(2),Roberts.	
22	Feb13	a	Lincoln City res	L 0-2		
23	20	a	Rotherham Town	L 1-2	Moran.	3,000
24	27	h	Sheff Wed res	W 3-1	Tomkins,Roberts,Moran.	
25	Mar 5	a	Newark Town	L 0-4		
26	10	a	Hinkley Town	W 2-1	Bennett,Moran.	
27	19	h	Grimsby Town res	L 2-3	Roberts(2).	1,200
28	26	h	Sheff Utd res	L 0-4		
29	Apr 1	h	Chesterfield res	W 4-1	Gordon,Dyer,Murphy,Bradley.	
30	4	h	Barnsley res	W 2-1	Murphy,Roberts.	
31	9	a	Derby County res	D 1-1	Bennett	2,000
32	11	a	Sheff Utd res	L 0-1		
33	16	a	Gresley Rovers	L 1-3	Bennett(pen).	
34	23	h	Newark Town	W 1-0	Bennett(pen).	

	P	W	D	L	F	A	PTS	POS
HOME	17	10	3	4	42	21	23	
AWAY	17	3	2	12	16	34	8	
TOTAL	34	13	5	16	58	55	31	11th

F.A.Cup

| 3Q | Oct31 | h | Belper Town | W 2-0 | Lovatt,Bennett. | |
| 4Q | Nov14 | h | Gainsboro Trinity | L 0-1 | | 2,000 |

All attendances are approximate

Final League Table	P	W	D	L	F	A	Pts.
Sheffield United Res.	34	26	4	4	101	24	56
Sheffield Wed. Res.	34	25	5	4	104	28	55
Newark	34	17	5	12	64	45	39
Nottingham Forest Res.	34	15	9	10	57	50	39
Chesterfield T. Res.	34	14	10	10	57	50	38
Rotherham Town	34	15	8	11	67	49	38
Derby County Res.	34	15	6	13	63	53	36
Barnsley Res.	34	16	2	16	66	70	34
Grimsby Town Res.	34	15	4	15	56	62	34
Hinckley Town	34	15	4	15	61	73	34
Doncaster Rovers	34	13	5	16	58	55	31
Thornhill United	34	10	9	15	49	58	29
Gresley Rovers	34	10	8	16	61	84	28
Denaby United	34	8	11	15	40	75	27
Whitwick White Cross	34	10	6	18	47	67	26
Worksop Town	34	10	6	18	57	83	26
Gainsborough Trin. Res.	34	7	9	18	52	89	23
Lincoln City Res.	34	7	5	22	48	92	19

League Division 2 1904-05

No	Date	V	Opponents	F-A	Scorers	Att		Thorpe	Hawkins	Davies	Gordon	Moralee	Norris	Hyde	Hanson	Carnegie	Pember	Law	Burn	Roberts	Howard	Harling	Birch	Wright	Raby	Bedford	Shinner	Tompkins	Crowcroft	Russell	Daw	Butler	Whittaker	Gould	Magee	Flowitt	Wilkinson	Bradley	McIntyre
1	Sep 3 h Lincoln City			L 0-2		3.500	1	1	2	3	4	5	6	7	8	9	10	11																					
2	10 a Leicester Fosse			L 2-3	Law.Davies.	5.000	2	1		3	4	5	6	7	8	9	10	11	2																				
3	17 h Barnsley			W 2-0	Moralee.Hanson (pen)	3.500	3	1		3	4	5	6	7	8		10	11	2	9																			
4	24 A West Bromwich Alb			L 1-6	Hanson.	5.000	4	1		3	4	5	6	7	8		10	11	2		9																		
5	Oct 1 h Burnley			L 0-2		2.000	5	1		3	4	5	6	7	8	9	10	11				1	2																
6	8 a Grimsby Town			L 1-2	Carnegie.	3.000	6	1			5			7	4	9	10	11	2					6	8														
7	15 h Blackpool			D 0-0		3.000	7	1		3		5	6	11	4	8			2							10	7	9												
8	22 a Bolton Wanderers			L 0-2		11.000	8	1		3	4	5	6	11	7	8	10		2								9												
9	Nov 5 h Burton Utd			L 1-3	Tompkins.	2.000	9			3		5	6	7	8				2								9	10	11	1	4								
10	12 a Burton Utd			L 0-1			10	1		3	4	5	6	7	8				2								9	10	11										
11	19 h Port Vale			D 2-2	Shinner(2)(1 pen)	1.500	11	1		3	4		6	7	8			11									10	5		9										
12	26 a Bristol City			L 1-4	Carnegie.	5.000	12	1		3		5	6	7	8	9		11									10	4												
13	Dec 3 h Man Utd			L 0-2		4.000	13	1		3		5			8			11					2	6			9	4				7	10						
14	10 h Bolton Wanderers			L 0-4		2.000	14	1			5			8			11	3				2	6			9	4				7	10						
15	17 h Chesterfield			L 0-2			15	1		3	4	5		7				11		9			2	6			8	10										
16	24 a Bradford City			L 1-4	Shinner.	8.000	16	1		3	4	5		7		9	10	11	2					6			8												
17	26 a Gainsboro Trinity			L 0-2			17	1		3	4	5		7		9	10	11	2					6			8												
18	31 a Lincoln City			L 0-3		3.000	18	1		3	4	5		7		9	10	11	2					6			8												
19	Jan 7 h Leicester Fosse			W 3-0	Moralee.Hyde.Magee.	2.000	19	1		3	4	5		7		9		11	2					6										8	10				
20	14 a Glossop			L 0-2			20	1		3	4	5		7		9		11	2					6										8	10				
21	21 h West Bromwich Alb			L 0-1		3.000	21	1		3	4	5		7		9		11	2					6			8								10				
22	28 a Burnley			L 3-4	Carnegie.Norris(2).	1.000	22	1		3	9	5	10	7		8		11	2					6				4											
23	Feb11 a Blackpool			L 0-1		3.000	23	1		3	9	5	10	7					2	6								4						8		11			
24	25 h Gainsboro Trinity			L 1-5	Norris.		24	1		3	9	5	10	7				11	2					6				4						8					
25	Mar11 h Liverpool			L 1-4	Magee.	2.000	25	1		3	4	5	10	7					2					6										8		9	11		
26	18 a Port Vale			L 0-2		1.000	26	1		3	4	5	10	7					2					6										8		9	11		
27	25 h Bristol City			L 0-2		1.600	27	1		3	4	5	9	7					2					6										8			11	10	
28	Apr 1 a Man Utd			L 0-6		9.000	28				4		9	7			5	11	2				3	6						1				8				10	
29	8 h Glossop			W 2-1	Roberts(2).		29	1			4	5		7			6	11		9			2								3			8				10	
30	15 a Chesterfield			L 1-4	Magee.	3.000	30	1			4	5		7			6	11		9			2								3			8				10	
31	21 a Liverpool			L 0-1		14.000	31	1			4	5	9	7			6	11					2				8				3							10	
32	22 h Bradford City			L 0-1		3.000	32	1			4	5		7			6	11					2				9				3			8				10	
33	24 h Grimsby Town			L 0-2		3.000	33	1			4	5	9	7			6	11					2				8				3							10	
34	25 a Barnsley			L 1-2	Law.	2.000	34	1			4	5	9	7			6	11					2				8				3							10	

	HOME						AWAY							TOTAL						
P	W	D	L	F	A	PTS	P	W	D	L	F	A	PTS	P	W	D	L	F	A	PTS
17	3	2	12	12	32	8	17	0	0	17	11	49	0	34	3	2	29	23	71	8

App 31 1 26 28 32 21 12 14 14 17 26 19 4 1 1 16 17 2 1 12 15   3 2 7 2 2 11 3 2 4 8
Gls   1   2 3 1 2 3   2   2   3 1   3

F.A. Cup							FAC:																											
PR	Oct29 h Mexboro Town			D 0-0		4.000	PR	1		3	4	5	6		7	9	10	11	2								8									
PRR	Nov 3 a Mexboro Town			L 1-3	Tompkins.		PRR			3	4	5	6	7	1		8		2								9	10	11							

Doncaster gain only 8 pts.Lowest ever on record ! All attendances are approximate.

Midland League 1905-06

No	Date	V	Opponents	F-A	Scorers	Att
1	Sep 2	h	Lincoln City res	W 3-0	Bridon(2).Fox.	1,000
2	9	a	Newark	W 1-0	Simms.	
3	16	a	Denaby Utd	L 1-3	Almond(pen).	3,000
4	30	a	Sheff Utd res	L 0-4		4,000
5	Oct14	h	Notts Co res	W 2-0	Bedford.Briggs.	1,000
6	19	a	Nottm Forest res	L 1-2	Fox.	700
7	21	h	Gainsboro Tr res	D 1-1	Roberts.	
8	28	a	Gresley Rovers	D 1-1	Almond.	
9	Nov11	h	Sheff Wed res	D 0-0		
10	18	h	Sheff Utd res	L 0-1		
11	25	h	Grantham Avenue	W 3-1	Almond.Fox.Butler.	
12	Dec 2	a	Lincoln City res	L 1-5	Almond.	
13	9	h	Nottm Forest res	L 0-7		
14	16	a	Leeds City res	L 0-8		2,000
15	25	a	Barnsley res	L 0-2		
16	26	a	Worksop Town	L 0-2		1,500
17	30	h	Leeds City res	W 5-0	Goodson(2).Roberts(2).Fox.	
18	Jan 1	h	Worksop Town	D 2-2	Goodson.Rogers.	
19	6	a	Mexborough Town	L 0-6		200
20	13	a	Grantham Avenue	D 1-1	Roberts.	
21	20	h	Grimsby Town res	L 0-3		
22	27	h	Newark	W 3-1	Smith(3).	2,000
23	Feb 3	a	Rotherham County	L 1-2	Almond.	
24	10	a	Gainsboro Tr res	D 3-3	Almond.Gyte(2).	
25	24	a	Grimsby Town res	L 0-4		1,000
26	Mar 1	a	Notts Co res	L 2-8	Gyte.Simms.	
27	10	h	Gresley Rovers	W 8-0	Fretwell(2).Simms(2).Gyte(2).Almnd.Gdsn.	1,000
28	31	a	Sheff Wed res	L 0-5		
29	Apr 7	h	Rotherham County	W 2-0	Gyte(2).	2,000
30	13	h	Mexborough Town	L 0-2		
31	14	h	Barnsley res	W 4-0	Haigh(2).Gyte.Almond.	
32	16	a	Rotherham Town	L 0-2		1,000
33	17	h	Denaby Utd	W 2-0	Fretwell.Moralee(pen).	4,000
34	21	h	Rotherham Town	L 0-1		

HOME								AWAY								TOTAL								
P	W	D	L	F	A	PTS		P	W	D	L	F	A	PTS		P	W	D	L	F	A	PTS	POS
17	9	3	5	35	19	21		17	1	3	13	12	58	5		34	10	6	18	47	77	26	14th

F.A. Cup

PR	Oct 7	a	Denaby Utd	L 2-4	Moralee (2pens).	2,000

All attendances are approximate

Midland League 1906-07

No	Date	V	Opponents	F-A	Scorers	Att
1	Sep 1	h	Rotherham Town	D 2-2	Gyte(2).	2,000
2	8	h	Rotherham County	L 1-2	Peate.	2,000
3	15	a	Lincoln City res	L 2-3	Hibbins.Peate(pen).	500
4	20	a	Worksop Town	L 1-5	A.Butler.	
5	22	a	Gainsboro Tr res	L 0-5		
6	29	h	Barnsley res	W 2-1	Langham.Mover.	
7	Oct13	h	Notts Co res	W 5-2	Kernick(2).Gyte.Fretwell.A.Butler.	1,200
8	25	a	Nottm Forest res	L 0-5		
9	27	a	Rotherham County	L 0-1		2,000
10	Nov10	h	Sheff Utd res	L 0-2		
11	17	a	Denaby Utd	L 2-3	A.Butler.Fretwell.	500
12	24	a	Barnsley res	L 1-5	Langham.	
13	Dec 1	a	Sheff Utd res	L 0-5		
14	8	h	Nottm Forest res	W 3-0	Peate.Murphy.Craig O.G.	
15	13	a	Notts Co res	W 4-2	Gyte(2).Peate.A.Butler.	
16	22	h	Chesterfield res	W 3-2	Gyte(2).Murphy.	
17	24	h	Worksop Town	D 1-1	Langham.	
18	25	a	Leeds City res	W 2-0	Peate.Morris O.G.	3,000
19	26	a	Mexboro Town	L 1-2	Clamp.	2,500
20	Jan 1	h	Grimsby Town res	L 1-2	Langham.	3,000
21	5	a	Gainsboro Tr res	W 2-1	Langham.Brookes.	
22	12	h	Newark	L 1-2	Peate.	
23	19	a	Grimsby Town res	L 0-7		800
24	26	h	Denaby Utd	D 0-0		
25	Feb 9	a	Chesterfield res	D 1-1	Murphy.	
26	16	a	Hull City res	L 2-3	Peate.A.Butler.	2,000
27	23	h	Grantham Avenue	W 7-1	Langham(4).Peate.Roberts.A.Butler.	
28	Mar 2	h	Lincoln City res	D 0-0		
29	9	a	Grantham Avenue	L 0-2		800
30	16	a	Newark	L 0-4		
31	23	a	Sheff Wed res	L 1-3	Shackleton.	
32	29	h	Mexboro Town	W 1-0	Shackleton.	1,000
33	30	h	Sheff Wed res	L 1-3	A.Butler(pen).	3,000
34	Apr 1	a	Leeds City res	W 3-0	Hardy(2).Shackleton.	2,000
35	6	a	Rotherham Town	L 0-2		
36	13	a	Bradford City res	D 1-1	Halliday O.G.	3,000
37	20	h	Bradford City res	D 1-1	Shepherd.	
38	29	h	Hull City res	L 0-1		1,000

HOME								AWAY								TOTAL								
P	W	D	L	F	A	PTS		P	W	D	L	F	A	PTS		P	W	D	L	F	A	PTS	POS
19	8	5	6	34	22	21		19	2	2	15	18	59	6		38	10	7	21	52	82	27	17th

F.A. Cup

PR	Sep22	a	Morley	W 4-1	Gyte(2).Peate.A.Butler.	
1Q	Oct 6	a	Denaby Utd	D 0-0		3,000
1QR	11	h	Denaby Utd	D 2-2	Kernick.Gyte.	3,000
1QR	15	a	Denaby Utd	L 1-3	Roberts. (played at Mexboro)	2,000

All attendances are approximate

Midland League 1907-08

No	Date	V	Opponents	F-A	Scorers	Att
1	Sep 2	a	Chesterfield res	L 0-2		
2	7	h	Mexboro Town	L 0-1		3.000
3	11	h	Newark	D 3-3	Robinson,Shackleton,Charles.	2.000
4	14	a	Leicester Fosse res	L 1-4	Roberts.	3.000
5	28	h	Leeds City res	W 1-0	Robinson.	2.000
6	Oct12	a	Lincoln City res	W 1-0	Robinson.	
7	26	a	Newark	L 2-3	Robinson(2).	
8	Nov 2	h	Grantham Avenue	W 2-0	Robinson,Bramall.	1.500
9	9	a	Worksop Town	L 2-7	Robinson,Parramore O.G.	1.000
10	16	h	Sheff Wed res	L 3-5	Charles,Robinson,Bramall	1.000
11	21	a	Nottm For. res	L 1-2	Bramall.	
12	23	a	Bradford City res	L 0-3		1.000
13	30	a	Sheff Utd res	L 2-3	Shepherd(2).	
14	Dec14	a	Gainsboro Tr res	L 0-6		
15	21	h	Rotherham County	W 4-1	Bramall(2),Shepherd,Priestley.	
16	25	h	Grimsby Town res	W 2-0	Priestley,Murphy.	1.000
17	26	a	Rotherham County	W 2-1	Bramall(2).	
18	28	a	Mexboro Town	D 2-2	Bramall,Murphy(pen).	2.000
19	Jan 1	h	Barnsley res	D 0-0		
20	4	h	Sheff Wed res	L 1-3	Charles.	1.000
21	11	h	Denaby Utd	L 0-1		2.000
22	25	h	Leicester Fosse res	L 0-1		2.000
23	Feb 8	a	Grantham Avenue	L 0-1		
24	15	a	Denaby Utd	L 2-5	Murphy,Charles.	
25	22	H	Rotherham Town	W 3-1	Bramall(2),Murphy.	
26	29	a	Hull City res	W 2-1	Bramall,Priestley.	
27	Mar 3	a	Leeds City res	L 0-2		
28	7	h	Chesterfield res	W 1-0	Charles.	2.000
29	14	h	Nottm For. res	L 0-1		
30	21	h	Lincoln City res	W 2-0	Bramall,Brelsford(pen).	2.000
31	Apr 4	h	Hull City res	L 1-2	Sharman.	
32	11	a	Rotherham Town	D 1-1	Murphy.	2.000
33	13	h	Bradford City res	W 2-0	Jones(2).	15.000
34	17	h	Grimsby Town res	L 0-1		3.000
35	18	h	Worksop Town	W 1-0	Jones(pen).	2.000
36	20	h	Gainsboro Tr res	W 2-0	Stubbins,Dobson.	2.000
37	21	h	Sheff Utd res	W 2-0	Stubbins,Sharman.	
38	25	a	Barnsley res	W 4-2	Jones,Roberts,Bramall,Stubbins.	3.000

	P	W	D	L	F	A	PTS	POS
HOME	19	9	2	8	26	18	20	
AWAY	19	5	2	12	25	48	12	
TOTAL	38	14	4	20	51	66	32	15th

Abandoned Match
Feb 1 h Notts Fo res L 2-4 Priestley,Shepherd.

F.A. Cup
1Q	Oct 5	h	Goole Town	D 1-1	Charles.	3.292
1QR	10	a	Goole Town	L 1-2	Robinson.	2.000

All attendances are approximate

Midland League 1908-09

No	Date	V	Opponents	F-A	Scorers	Att
1	Sep 5	h	Denaby Utd	L 1-2	Wilson.	4.000
2	12	a	Worksop Town	L 1-2	Rogers.	2.000
3	17	a	Barnsley res	L 1-3	Bramall.	
4	19	h	Rotherham Town	L 0-4		3.000
5	26	a	Denaby Utd	L 0-1		
6	Oct10	a	Rotherham Town	L 1-5	Thackeray.	5.000
7	24	a	Lincoln City	L 0-7		
8	31	h	Newark	W 2-1	Charles.Brelsford.	2.000
9	Nov 7	h	Bradford City res	D 1-1	Pattinson.	
10	14	a	Grimsby Town res	L 0-1		1.000
11	21	h	Worksop Town	W 2-1	Brelsford.Pattinson.	3.000
12	28	a	Leicester Fosse res	L 1-4	Jex.	5.000
13	Dec 5	h	Chesterfield Tn res	W 2-1	Pattinson(2).	3.000
14	19	h	Notts Fo res	L 1-2	Jex.	2.000
15	25	a	Gainsboro Tr res	L 0-3		2.500
16	26	a	Mexboro Town	L 3-4	Jex(2).Roberts.	2.000
17	Jan 1	a	Bradford City res	L 1-3	Roberts.	3.000
18	2	h	Rotherham County	W 1-0	Jex.	3.000
19	9	h	Sheff Wed res	W 2-0	Jex.Roberts.	1.200
20	16	a	Newark	W 2-0	Jex(2).	800
21	30	a	Chesterfield Tn res	L 0-1		
22	Feb 4	a	Notts Fo res	W 3-2	Jex(2).Brelsford.	
23	6	h	Leeds City res	W 4-0	Jex(3)(1pen).Fretwell.	4.000
24	13	h	Hull City res	W 3-2	Goodson.Jex.Brelsford.	4.000
25	20	a	Hull City res	L 0-1		
26	25	a	Notts Co res	W 2-0	Goodson.Jex.	
27	27	a	Sheff Wed res	W 1-0	Bramall.	
28	Mar18	h	Barnsley res	W 1-0	Taylor.	
29	20	a	Rotherham County	W 2-0	Jex(2).	2.000
30	27	h	Lincoln City	D 0-0		4.500
31	Apr 1	h	Leicester Fosse res	W 2-1	Bramall(2).	2.500
32	5	a	Leeds City res	W 3-1	Jex(2.1pen).Bramall.	
33	9	h	Gainsboro Tr res	W 1-0	Jex.	4.500
34	10	h	Notts County res	W 3-2	Jex (pen).Thackeray.Bramall.	4.000
35	12	h	Mexboro Town	W 1-0	Taylor.	4.000
36	13	h	Grimsby Town res	L 0-1		1.200
37	17	a	Sheff Utd res	W 2-0	Taylor.Charles.	4.500
38	24	h	Sheff Utd res	D 1-1	Taylor.	3.500

	P	W	D	L	F	A	PTS	POS
HOME	19	12	3	4	28	19	27	
AWAY	19	6	0	13	22	40	12	
TOTAL	38	18	3	17	50	59	39	11th

Abandoned Match
Mar 6 h Leicester Fo res D 1-1 Bramhall.

F.A. Cup
PR	Oct 3	h	Castleford Town	D 1-1	Charles.	3.000
PRR	7	a	Castleford Town	L 1-4	Charles.	3.000

All attendances are approximate

Season 1907/08

(Far back): Attree (Trainer), (Directors) Jones, F.Richardson and W.Richardson, Kerr (Secretary)
(Players back): Lowe, Pinder, Lindley, Brailsford, Dobson, Wilson,
(Front): Murphy, Charles, Robinson, Brammall, Shepherd.

Season 1912/13

(Back): Pearce (Trainer) (Players) Lowe, Shreeve, H.Bromage, Gregory, Nuttall, Taylor.
(Front): Woodruff, Dyal, Reed, Astil, W.Bromage.

Midland League 1909-10

No	Date	V	Opponents	F-A	Scorers	Att
1	Sep 1	a	Gainsboro Tn res	D 2-2	Green(2).	1.000
2	4	h	Denaby Utd	D 1-1	Walt Taylor.	
3	11	a	Denaby Utd	L 0-2		
4	18	h	Lincoln City res	D 1-1	Evans.	2.000
5	25	h	Leeds City res	L 0-1		2.000
6	27	a	Notts Co res	L 1-3	Green.	
7	Oct 2	a	Leicester Fosse res	L 0-3		5.000
8	9	h	Chesterfield Town	L 0-2		1.500
9	16	a	Grimsby Town res	L 1-3	Walt Taylor.	
10	23	a	Sheff Wed res	D 2-2	Hutchinson(2).	
11	28	a	Hull City res	L 0-3		2.000
12	30	h	Nottm For res	L 0-2		
13	Nov 2	a	Bradford P.A res	L 0-5		2.000
14	6	a	Chesterfield Town	L 0-5		
15	13	h	Bradford City res	D 1-1	Simons.	
16	27	h	Worksop Town	W 2-1	Phillips.Evans.	
17	Dec18	h	Rotherham County	D 3-3	Wood.Blank.Simons.	1.000
18	25	a	Castleford Town	W 3-0	Simons.Bramall.McMillan O.G.	4.000
19	27	a	Rotherham Town	L 0-1		
20	28	a	Mexboro Town	W 1-0	Fretwell.	
21	Jan 1	a	Castleford Town	D 1-1	Lowe(pen) - (only 10 men)	
22	8	a	Bradford City res	L 0-4		
23	15	h	Grimsby Town res	W 2-1	Wood.Simons.	1.500
24	20	a	Nottm For res	L 1-4	Simons.	
25	Feb 5	a	Sheff Utd res	L 0-1		
26	9	a	Leeds City res	L 0-1		
27	12	h	Notts Co res	W 1-0	Bramall.	3.000
28	19	a	Lincoln City res	L 0-4		1.500
29	26	a	Worksop Town	D 1-1	Simons.	
30	Mar 5	h	Sheff Wed res	W 1-0	Simons.	2.000
31	12	h	Leicester Fosse res	W 4-1	Lowe(pen).Simons.Wood.Evans.	1.500
32	19	h	Mexboro Town	W 3-0	Wood.Evans.Murray O.G.	
33	25	h	Gainsboro Tr res	W 2-0	Simons.Lowe.	4.000
34	26	h	Rotherham Town	W 2-1	Simons.Evans.	3.000
35	28	h	Huddersfield Town	L 0-1	Lowe.	
36	29	h	Hull City res	D 1-1	Green.	
37	Apr 2	a	Huddersfield Town	D 1-1	Green.	2.000
38	9	h	Sheff Utd res	W 3-0	Simons(2).Evans.	2.000
39	14	h	Barnsley res	W 3-0	Simons.Evans.Blank.	
40	16	h	Rotherham County	W 2-0	Green(2).	1.500
41	18	a	Barnsley res	W 3-2	Simons.Green.Lowe(pen).	
42	23	h	Bradford P.A.res	W 3-0	Green(2).Bramall.	

HOME								AWAY								TOTAL								
P	W	D	L	F	A	PTS		P	W	D	L	F	A	PTS		P	W	D	L	F	A	PTS	POS	
21	10	7	4	33	18	27		21	4	4	13	18	48	12		42	14	11	17	51	66	39	14th	

F.A. Cup

No	Date	V	Opponents	F-A	Scorers	Att
4Q	Nov20	h	Mexboro Town	D 0-0		4.000
4QR	25	a	Mexboro Town	L 1-2	Wm Taylor.	

All attendances are approximate

Midland League 1910-11

No	Date	V	Opponents	F-A	Scorers	Att
1	Sep 1	a	Huddersfield res	L 1-2	Brooks.	2.500c
2	3	h	Hull City res	L 2-3	Bromage.Green.	2.500c
3	10	a	Leicester Fosse res	L 0-1		5.000c
4	19	a	Denaby Utd	W 5-1	Bramall.Jex.Bromage.Woodruff.Lowe(pen)	2.000c
5	24	a	Chesterfield Town	L 1-2	Poppleton.	4.000c
6	Oct 8	h	Sheff Wed res	W 3-2	Bromage.Bramall.Jex(pen).	2.282
7	22	a	Worksop Town	W 2-1	Jex.Bramall.	1.500c
8	29	h	Leicester Fosse res	W 2-0	Bramall.Bromage.	1.880
9	Nov12	h	Barnsley res	D 2-2	Bramall(2).	1.800c
10	19	h	Worksop Town	W 4-1	Green(3).Jex.	1.620
11	23	a	Leeds City res	W 4-1	Green(2).Bramall.Jex.	
12	26	h	Sheff Utd res	W 5-2	Lowe(pen).Woodruff.Bramall.Green.Jex.	1.920
13	Dec. 3	h	Rotherham County	W 4-2	Lowe(2pens).Bramall.Green.	3.000c
14	17	a	Rotherham Town	W 3-2	Bromage.Bramall.Green.	2.000c
15	19	a	Notts Co res	L 1-6	Bromage.	
16	27	a	Mexboro Town	W 5-4	Jex(3).Bramall(2).	
17	31	h	Chesterfield Town	W 2-1	Green(2).	3.860
18	Jan 7	h	Denaby Utd	W 4-1	Jex(2).Bromage.Woodruff.	2.801
19	14	h	Notts Co res	W 5-2	Jones(3).Jex.Bramall.	2.920
20	19	a	Nottm For res	W 2-1	Bromage.Green.	2.500c
21	21	a	Rotherham County	L 1-3	Lowe(pen).	6.000c
22	28	a	Hull City res	D 3-3	Wagstaff.Jones Jex(pen).	3.000c
23	Feb 4	a	Sheff Utd res	W 6-1	Jex(3).Taylor.Bromage.Bramall.	4.312
24	11	h	Leeds City res	D 0-0		4.065
25	15	a	Castleford Town	L 1-3	Woodruff.	1.000c
26	18	a	Barnsley res	L 0-1	Jex.	1.500c
27	25	h	Huddersfield Tn res	W 5-0	Green(2).Jex.Jones.Gibbons.	3.564
28	Mar 4	a	Gainsboro Tr res	L 1-2	Jones.	1.200c
29	11	a	Lincoln City res	W 3-1	Green(2).Bromage.	1.500c
30	18	h	Grimsby Town	L 0-3		4.845
31	25	h	Nottm For res	W 3-1	Green.Lowe(pen).Freebury O.G.	1.811
32	30	h	Castleford Town	W 6-0	Jex(3).Dyal(2).Green.	2.314
33	April4	h	Lincoln City res	W 5-0	Green(2).Bromage.Dyal.Woodruff.	3.701
34	15	a	Grimsby Town	L 2-3	Woodruff.Lowe(pen).	5.000c
35	17	h	Gainsboro Tr res	W 5-2	Woodruff(2).Wagstaff(2).Dyal.	3.387
36	18	h	Mexboro Town	D 1-1	Woodruff.	2.775
37	22	a	Sheff Wed res	L 1-2	Dyal.	4.000c
38	29	h	Rotherham Town	W 5-1	Green(3).Jex(2).	1.800c

HOME								AWAY								TOTAL								
P	W	D	L	F	A	PTS		P	W	D	L	F	A	PTS		P	W	D	L	F	A	PTS	POS	
19	14	3	2	63	24	31		19	9	1	9	43	39	19		38	23	4	11	106	63	50	3rd	

F.A. Cup

	Date	V	Opponents	F-A	Scorers	Att
PR	Sep17	h	Hull Day St O.B.	W 7-0	Green(2).Jex(2).Bromage.Brmll.Pppltn.	1.161
1Q	Oct 1	h	Grimsby Rovers	W 5-4	Jex(3).Brookes(2).	2.000c
2Q	15	h	Mexboro Town	W 1-0	Woodruff.	3.100c
3Q	Nov 5	a	Denaby Utd	L 1-2	Bramall.	4.000c

c - attendances are approximate

Midland League 1911-12

No	Date	V	Opponents	F-A	Scorers	Att
1	Sep 2	a	Leicester Fosse res	L 0-3		4.000c
2	9	h	Leicester Fosse res	W 4-0	Dyal(3),Tonkinson(pen).	3.000c
3	16	a	Mexboro Town	W 3-1	Dyal,Woodruff,Tonkinson(pen).	
4	23	a	Worksop Town	W 4-1	Woodruff(2),Dyal,Green.	1.000c
5	Oct 7	a	Rotherham County	L 0-1		5.000c
6	14	h	Barnsley res	L 2-3	W Bromage(pen),Green.	
7	21	a	Rotherham Town	L 3-4	Dyal(2),Tonkinson.	
8	28	h	Worksop Town	W 5-0	Taylor(2),Green(2),Dyal.	2.800c
9	Nov 4	a	Barnsley res	L 2-3	Green(2).	1.000c
10	11	h	Rotherham County	W 7-0	Green(3),Dyal(2),Taylor,H Brmage(pen)	3.717
11	25	h	Rotherham Town	D 2-2	Gregory,Lowe(pen).	2.900c
12	Dec 2	h	Notts County res	W 2-1	Dyal,Lowe(pen).	
13	16	h	Huddersfield T res	W 3-0	Green(3).	
14	23	h	Hull City res	L 1-2	Lowe(pen).	
15	25	a	Gainsboro Tr res	W 4-2	Woodruff,Astill,Green,Lowe(pen).	3.500c
16	26	a	Huddersfield T res	D 0-0		
17	30	h	Sheff Utd res	W 3-1	Green(2),Astill.	
18	Jan 1	a	Chesterfield Town	D 2-2	Green(2).	
19	6	h	Grimsby Town res	W 5-1	Astill(3),Woodruff,Shreeve.	
20	13	h	Chesterfield Town	D 1-1	Shreeve(pen).	
21	20	h	Denaby Utd	W 6-0	Buddery(2),Cowen(2),Green,Shreeve(pen).	
22	Feb 3	a	Hull City res	W 1-0	Green.	
23	10	a	Sheff Utd res	D 1-1	Dyal.	
24	24	a	Leeds City res	L 0-2		
25	Mar 2	h	Castleford Town	W 2-1	Buddery,Taylor.	3.000c
26	9	a	Grimsby Town res	D 1-1	Buddery.	
27	21	a	Notts County res	L 1-3	Astill.	
28	23	a	Lincoln City res	W 2-1	Astill,Buddery.	
29	30	a	Denaby Utd	W 2-1	Pagnum,Buddery.	
30	Apr 5	h	Gainsboro Tr res	W 1-0	Pagnum.	3.767
31	6	h	Sheff Wed res	W 2-1	Pagnum,Buddery.	3.078
32	8	h	Mexboro Town	W 3-1	Woodruff,Buddery,W Bromage.	2.627
33	9	h	Lincoln City res	W 1-0	Nuttall.	2.000c
34	13	a	Sheff Wed res	W 1-0	Nuttall(pen).	
35	20	h	Leeds City res	W 2-1	Nuttall(2).	
36	24	a	Castleford Town	L 0-1		

	P	W	D	L	F	A	PTS								POS
HOME	18	14	2	2	52	15	30								
AWAY	18	7	4	7	27	27	18								
TOTAL	36	21	6	9	79	42	48								3rd

F.A. Cup

1Q	Sep30	a	Castleford Town	L 0-1		4.000c

c - attendances are approximate

Midland League 1912-13

No	Date	V	Opponents	F-A	Scorers	Att
1	Sep 7	a	Halifax Town	W 2-1	Cook,W Bromage.	1.000c
2	11	h	Chesterfield Town	W 5-2	Buddery(3),Astill,Nuttall(pen).	
3	14	h	Denaby Utd	W 2-0	Dyal,W Bromage.	3.000c
4	18	a	Gainsboro Trinity	L 0-1		
5	21	h	York City	W 1-0	Nuttall.	2.938
6	Oct 5	a	Rotherham County	D 2-2	Nuttall,Cook.	5.000c
7	19	a	Chesterfield Town	L 2-3	Cook,Pattinson.	
8	26	a	Goole Town	W 2-0	Dyal,Pattinson.	
9	Nov 2	h	Goole Town	D 0-0		
10	9	a	Hull City res	L 2-3	Buddery,W Bromage.	
11	16	a	Scunthorpe Utd	W 3-1	Pattinson,Cook,Bates.	
12	23	h	Grimsby Town res	W 1-0	W Bromage.	
13	30	a	York City	L 1-3	Cook.	
14	Dec14	h	Rotherham County	W 2-0	W Bromage,Cowen.	1.500c
15	21	a	Lincoln City res	L 0-3		
16	25	a	Sheff Utd res	D 1-1	Pattinson.	
17	26	a	Mexboro Town	L 1-3	Dyal.	
18	30	a	Sheff Wed res	W 3-2	Cowen,Nuttall,Buddery.	4.000c
19	Jan 1	a	Rotherham Town	D 0-0		
20	4	h	Worksop Town	W 1-0	Pattinson.	
21	18	h	Notts County res	W 4-1	Buddery(2),Cowen,Nuttall.	
22	Feb 1	h	Lincoln City res	W 4-1	Cowen(2),Pattinson,Buddery.	
23	8	a	Worksop Town	L 1-2	Astill.	
24	15	a	Denaby Utd	W 5-2	Astill(2),Pattinson(2),Buddery.	
25	22	h	Castleford Town	W 3-2	Taylor(2),Buddery.	3.000c
26	Mar 1	a	Grimsby Town res	W 2-0	Pattinson,Nuttall.	
27	8	h	Scunthorpe Utd	D 2-2	Woodruffe,Astill.	
28	15	h	Mexboro Town	W 1-0	Ward.	2.000c
29	22	h	Halifax Town	W 2-0	Buddery(2).	
30	24	h	Sheff Utd res	W 2-0	Nuttall,W Bromage.	
31	25	a	Notts County res	D 2-2	Astill(2).	
32	29	a	Castleford Town	L 0-1		
33	Apr 3	h	Rotherham Town	W 3-1	Bates,Buddery,Woodruffe.	
34	5	h	Sheff Wed res	D 0-0		
35	11	h	Leeds City res	D 0-0 * Abandoned at half time		
36	12	h	Hull City res	W 2-1	Nuttall,Pattinson(pen).	
*						150
37	17	h	Gainsboro Trinity	L 1-2	Buddery.	
38	19	h	Leeds City res	W 2-0	Woodruffe,Gregory(pen).	

	P	W	D	L	F	A	PTS								POS
HOME	19	15	2	2	38	13	32								
AWAY	19	6	5	8	29	30	17								
TOTAL	38	21	7	10	67	43	59								4th

F.A. Cup

1Q	Sep28	a	Denaby Utd	W 2-1	Cook,Pattinson
2Q	Oct12	a	Castleford Town	L 0-2	

c - attendances are approximate

Midland League 1913-14

No	Date	V	Opponents	F-A	Scorers	Att
1	Sep 3	a	York City	L 1-5	Nuttall.	
2	6	h	Goole Town	L 0-2		
3	13	h	York City	L 0-1		
4	20	a	Worksop Town	L 0-3		
5	Oct 4	a	Goole Town	W 2-1	Taylor(2).	
6	18	a	Castleford Town	W 2-1	Nuttall,Jex.	
7	22	a	Gainsboro Trin	L 1-4	Jex	
8	25	h	Worksop Town	L 1-2	Nuttall	
9	Nov 8	h	Halifax Town	L 0-3		
10	15	h	Sheff Wed res	W 1-0	Jex.	
11	22	a	Sheff Wed res	L 0-2		3,000
12	Dec13	h	Castleford Town	W 1-0	Plumb.	
13	20	h	Lincoln City res	W 2-1	Nuttall,Lowe(pen).	
14	25	a	Mexboro Town.	L 0-1		
15	26	a	Grimsby Town res	L 1-2	Leneghan.	
16	27	h	Chesterfield Town	W 1-0	Smith.	
17	Jan 1	a	Halifax Town	L 1-3	Bramall	
18	3	h	Rotherham County	L 0-3		
19	10	h	Leeds City res	W 3-0	Leneghan,Plumb,Westwood.	
20	17	a	Leeds City res	L 0-4		
21	31	h	Hull City res	D 0-0		
22	Feb 7	h	Sheff Utd res	L 1-3	Richardson O.G.	
23	14	h	Scunthorpe Utd	W 2-0	Lowe(pen),Williams.	
24	21	a	Scunthorpe Utd	L 0-1		
25	28	a	Chesterfield Town	L 0-3		
26	Mar 7	h	Hull City res	W 2-0	Leneghan,Hawthorn.	
27	14	a	Rotherham County	L 0-1		
28	21	h	Gainsboro Trinity	L 0-1		
29	28	a	Shef Utd res	L 0-2		
30	Apr 4	a	Rotherham Town	D 1-1	Leneghan.	
31	10	h	Mexboro Town	L 1-2	Jex.	
32	11	h	Rotherham Town	L 1-2	Jex.	
33	13	h	Grimsby Town res	W 2-0	Jex,Shackelton.	
34	25	a	Lincoln City res	W 2-0	Jex,Lowe(pen).	

HOME								AWAY								TOTAL							
P	W	D	L	F	A	PTS		P	W	D	L	F	A	PTS		P	W	D	L	F	A	PTS	POS
17	9	0	8	19	18	18		17	3	2	12	11	34	8		34	12	2	20	30	51	26	16th

F.A. Cup

PR	Sep27	a	Goole Town	L 1-2	Tudor	4,000

All attendances are approximate

Midland League 1914-15

No	Date	V	Opponents	F-A	Scorers	Att
1	Sep 5	h	Bradford PA res	W 3-0	Maltby,Hall,Stevens.	
2	7	h	Rotherham Town	L 1-2	Lowe(pen).	
3	12	h	Lincoln City res	W 4-0	Brodie,Stevens,Tebbutt,McFadden O.G.	1,300
4	14	a	Rotherham Town	L 1-4	Stevens.	
5	19	a	Heckmondwyke	W 3-1	Stevens(2),McSpadden.	
6	21	a	Sheff Utd res	L 0-2		
7	Oct 3	a	Lincoln City res	W 1-0	Brooks.	
8	8	h	Sheff Utd res	L 0-1		
9	29	a	Halifax Town	L 1-4	Hall.	
10	31	h	Heckmondwyke	W 3-0	Tebbutt(3).	
11	Nov 7	a	Chesterfield Town	D 0-0		
12	21	h	Castleford Town	W 3-0	Jones(2),Hall.	
13	28	h	Gainsboro Trinity	W 2-1	Stevens(2).	
14	Dec 5	a	Rotherham County	L 0-4		
15	19	a	Sheff Wed res	L 0-10		
16	25	a	Mexboro Town	L 0-3		
17	26	a	York City	L 1-2	Jones.	
18	29	h	Worksop Town	L 0-1		
19	Jan 2	a	Bradford PA res	L 0-7		
20	9	a	Leeds City res	L 2-4	Stevens,Birtles.	
21	16	h	Halifax Town	W 2-1	Stevens,Tebbutt.	
22	23	h	Goole Town	W 2-0	Royston,Birtles.	
23	30	h	Hull City res	W 5-0	Birtles(2),Tebbutt(2),Hall.	
24	Feb 6	a	Chesterfield Town	L 0-2		
25	13	h	Leeds City res	L 0-3		
26	20	a	Castleford Town	L 1-2	Wright.	
27	27	a	Gainsboro Trinity	L 0-2		
28	Mar 6	h	Sheff Wed res	W 3-0	Carey,Wright,Lean(pen).	
29	20	h	York City	D 1-1	Poppelton.	
30	27	a	Worksop Town	D 3-3	Brookes(2),Dudley.	
31	Apr 2	h	Mexboro Town	W 6-0	Stevens(2),Hall,Royston,Tebbutt,Brkes.	
32	3	a	Scunthorpe Utd	L 2-3	Birtles,Stevens.	
33	5	h	Scunthorpe Utd	W 2-0	Brookes,Lean(pen).	1,600
34	6	a	Hull City res	L 1-5	Tilsley.	
35	10	h	Rotherham County	L 1-2	Tebbutt.	
36	15	a	Goole Town	L 0-8		
37	17	a	Grimsby Town res	L 0-3		
38	24	h	Grimsby Town res	W 4-1	Tebbutt,Brookes,Lean,Birtles.	

HOME								AWAY								TOTAL							
P	W	D	L	F	A	PTS		P	W	D	L	F	A	PTS		P	W	D	L	F	A	PTS	POS
19	12	2	5	42	13	26		19	2	1	16	16	69	5		38	14	3	21	58	82	31	15th

F.A. Cup

1Q	Sep26	h	Grimsby Haycroft	W 3-0	Lowe,Maltby,Hall.	
2Q	Oct10	h	Cleethorpes Town	W 3-1	Birtles(2),Hall.	
3Q	24	a	Scunthorpe Utd	L 0-1		

All attendances are approximate

Midland Combination League 1915-16

No	Date	V	Opponents	F-A	Scorers	Att
1	Sep 4	a	Mexboro Town	W 1-0	Tilsley.	600
2	18	a	Sheff Utd res	L 2-4	Cook.Rippon(pen).	
3	25	h	Rotherham County	L 1-2	Royston.	1.000c
4	Oct 2	a	Rotherham County	L 2-3	Rippon.Wilkinson.	
5	9	h	Mexboro Town	W 3-1	Wright(2).Beevers.	
6	23	h	Sheff Utd res	D 1-1	Wright.	
7	30	a	Silverwood Colliery	L 1-3	Rippon.	
8	Nov 6	a	Chesterfield Town	L 1-3	Beevers.	
9	Dec25	h	Goole Town	L 1-2	Stockdale.	
10	Jan15	h	Worksop Town	D 0-0		
11	22	a	Worksop Town	L 0-1		
12	Feb 5	a	Halifax Town	L 1-2	Tench(pen).	
13	12	h	Chesterfield Town	L 1-2	Brown	600
14	26	h	Silverwood Colliery	W 9-2	Brown(5).Batey(3).Stevenson.	30
15	Apr22	h	Halifax Town	W 7-2	Brown(4).Stevenson.Batey(pen).O.G.	
16	24	h	Goole Town	W 7-0	Brown(5).Bruce.Jones.	

	HOME							AWAY							TOTAL						
P	W	D	L	F	A	PTS	P	W	D	L	F	A	PTS	P	W	D	L	F	A	PTS
8	4	2	2	29	10	10	8	0	0	8	8	19	0	16	4	2	10	37	29	10

c - attendances are approximate

Wharncliffe Charity League

	Date	V	Opponents	F-A	Scorers
	Nov13	a	Darfield	D 1-1	Unknown.
	20	h	Worksop Town	W 1-0	Beevers.
	27	a	Worksop Town	L 1-3	Watson.
	Jan 8	a	Hickelton Main	W 2-1	Bruce.Brown.
	Feb19	a	South Kirkby	L 2-3	Unknown.
	Mar 4	a	Dinnington Coll	W 2-0	Unknown.
	11	h	Kilnhurst Town	W 8-0	Stevenson(4).Naismith(2).Howson.Jones.
		a	Kilnhurst Town	W 6-1	Unknown.
	18	h	Rotherham County	W 5-0	Smith(2).Brown(2).Stevenson pen.
	25	h	South Kirkby	W 6-0	Brown(3).Scott(2).Stevenson.
	Apr 8	a	Rotherham County	L 2-4	Brown.Stevenson.
	8	h	Dinnington Coll	W 2-1	Mason.Armstrong.

	HOME							AWAY							TOTAL						
P	W	D	L	F	A	PTS	P	W	D	L	F	A	PTS	P	W	D	L	F	A	PTS
5	5	0	0	22	1	10	7	3	1	3	16	13	7	12	8	1	3	38	14	17

This League was used to supplement the Midland Combination

Midland League 1920-21

No	Date	V	Opponents	F-A	Scorers	Att
1	Aug28	h	Rotherham Town	L 1-2	Wainwright.	5.000c
2	Sep 4	h	Denaby Utd	W 3-1	McDonald(2).W Bromage.	6.000c
3	16	a	Rotherham Town	D 1-1	Mahon.	4.000c
4	18	a	Hull City res	D 1-1	Mahon.	
5	Oct 2	a	Scunthorpe Utd	L 0-1		4.000c
6	9	h	Barnsley res	D 0-0		5.000c
7	16	a	Halifax Town	L 0-2		
8	23	h	Notts Co res	L 0-5		5.000c
9	30	a	Denaby Utd	D 1-1	W Cowen.	
10	Nov 6	h	Hull City res	W 4-1	Kemp(2).W Cowen.Mahon(pen).	4.000c
11	13	a	Lincoln City	L 0-2		
12	18	a	Nottm For res	L 0-5		
13	20	h	Sheff Wed res	W 2-1	J Cowen.Docherty.	
14	27	h	Chesterfield	W 2-0	Sharpe(2).	
15	Dec 4	a	Leeds Utd res	L 1-3	W Cowen.	
16	18	h	Gainsboro Trinity	W 2-1	W Bromage.Sharpe.	
17	25	h	Worksop Town	W 3-6	Sharpe.Kemp.W Bromage.	4.000c
18	27	a	Mexboro Town	L 0-1		
19	28	h	Halifax Town	W 1-0	Scull O.G.	4.000c
20	Jan 1	a	Castleford Town	W 3-2	Cox.W Cowen.McDonald.	
21	22	h	Castleford Town	W 2-0	W Cowen(2).	5.000c
22	29	a	Sheff Wed res	D 0-0		10.000c
23	Feb 5	h	Nottm For res	W 3-1	Kemp(2).Mahon(pen).	5.000c
24	19	h	Leeds Utd res	D 0-0		5.000c
25	24	a	Notts Co res	L 0-1		
26	Mar 5	a	Sheff Utd res	D 2-2	W Bromage.Kemp.	6.000c
27	12	a	Gainsboro Trinity	L 0-2		3.000c
28	19	a	Rotherham Co res	L 0-2		3.000c
29	25	h	Rotherham Co res	D 0-0		7.000c
30	26	a	Barnsley res	D 0-0		
31	28	h	Mexboro Town	D 0-0		
32	29	h	Worksop Town	L 0-1		
33	Apr 2	h	Sheff Utd res	L 0-2		
34	9	h	Scunthorpe Utd	D 1-1	Kemp.	
35	16	a	Chesterfield	L 1-3	Tilsley.	
36	23	h	Grimsby Town res	L 0-2		
37	30	a	Grimsby Town res	W 1-0	Wainwright.	
38	May 5	h	Lincoln City	W 4-1	Wainwright.Cox.Docherty.Harris O.G.	4.000c

	HOME							AWAY							TOTAL						
P	W	D	L	F	A	PTS	P	W	D	L	F	A	PTS	P	W	D	L	F	A	PTS
19	9	5	5	25	19	23	19	2	5	12	13	35	9	38	11	10	17	38	54	32

F.A. Cup

	Date	V	Opponents	F-A	Scorers	Att
EP	Sep11	h	Atlas & Norfolk	W 6-0	McDonald(4).W Cowen.Newham.	4.000c
PR	25	h	Wombwell	L 0-1		6.000c

All attendances are approximate

Midland League 1921-22

No	Date	V	Opponents	F-A		Scorers	Att
1	Aug27	h	Gainsboro Trinity	L	1-2	Mcleod.	7,219
2	Sep 3	a	Gainsboro Trinity	D	2-2	Butler(2).	4,000c
3	12	h	Grimsby Town res	L	0-1		
4	17	h	Wakefield City	W	2-0	Butler(2pens).	
5	Oct 1	h	Harrogate	L	1-2	Copley.	4,000c
6	8	h	Barnsley res	L	0-3		3,000c
7	15	a	Lincoln City res	W	1-0	Hollins.	
8	22	a	Wath Athletic	L	2-3	Butler,Jackson.	
9	29	h	Rotherham Town	L	1-3	Williams.	
10	Nov 5	a	Wakefield City	W	1-0	Jackson.	4,000c
11	12	h	Wath Athletic	W	3-0	Butler(2),Harrison.	
12	19	a	Rotherham Town	D	0-0		
13	26	h	Rotherham Co res	W	2-1	Williams(pen),Black.	
14	Dec 8	h	Notts Co res	L	1-3	Naylor.	
15	17	h	Castleford Town	W	1-0	Reed.	
16	22	a	Nottm For res	W	2-0	Copley,Hollins.	
17	24	a	Mexboro Town	L	0-2		
18	26	h	Hull City res	W	1-0	Hollins.	
19	27	a	Hull City res	L	0-2		
20	31	a	Scunthorpe Utd	L	1-2	Smailes.	
21	Jan 2	h	Boston Town	W	3-2	Kemp,Harrison,Boardman.	3,000c
22	7	h	Scunthorpe Utd	L	0-1		
23	28	a	Castleford Town	L	1-3	Naylor.	
24	Feb 4	a	Barnsley res	L	0-8		
25	11	h	Mansfield Town	W	3-2	Cooper,Boardman,Copley.	
26	16	h	Worksop Town	W	3-1	Kemp(2),Boardman.	2,000c
27	18	a	Wombwell Town	D	2-2	Copley,Kemp.	
28	Mar 4	h	Lincoln City res	D	0-0		5,000c
29	11	h	Wombwell Town	W	3-1	Naylor,Boardman,Kemp.	4,000c
30	18	a	Rotherham Co res	W	4-1	Boardman(3)(1pen),Butler.	
31	23	a	Boston Town	D	2-2	Boardman(2).	
32	25	h	Sheff Wed res	L	0-3		
33	29	a	Harrogate	W	2-0	Copley,Boardman.	
34	Apr 1	a	Worksop Town	L	0-1		3,000c
35	8	h	Notts Co res	W	3-2	Copley(2),Boardman.	1,500c
36	14	h	Mexboro Town	W	1-0	Smithurst(pen).	6,000c
37	15	h	Denaby Utd	D	0-0		
38	17	a	Denaby Utd	W	1-0	Butler.	
39	18	a	Grimsby Town res	L	1-2	Boardman.	
40	22	a	Mansfield Town	L	1-3	Copley.	
41	27	h	Nottm For res	L	0-4		
42	29	a	Sheff Wed res	L	0-2		

HOME							AWAY							TOTAL						
P	W	D	L	F	A	PTS	P	W	D	L	F	A	PTS	P	W	D	L	F	A	PTS
21	11	2	8	29	28	24	21	6	4	11	24	38	16	42	17	6	19	53	66	40

F.A. Cup

EP	Sep10	h	Rotherham Town	W	2-0	Butler(2).	7,000c
PR	24	a	Wombwell	L	0-1		

c - attendances are approximate

Midland League 1922-23

No	Date	V	Opponents	F-A		Scorers	Att
1	Aug26	h	Gainsboro Trinity	W	1-0	Charlesworth.	10,000
2	28	h	Rotherham Town	W	3-0	Boardman(2),Bauchop.	5,000
3	Sep 2	h	Denaby Utd	D	1-1	Boardman.	7,000
4	9	a	Mexboro Town	D	0-0		5,000
5	11	h	Sheff Wed res	L	0-2		5,000
6	16	a	Denaby Utd	L	0-2		4,000
7	30	h	Rotherham Co res	W	3-0	Taylor(2),Bauchop.	4,000
8	Oct28	h	Wombwell	D	0-0		4,000
9	Nov11	a	Rotherham Co res	W	3-2	Haythorne,Taylor.	4,000
10	18	h	Boston Town	W	3-0	Boardman,Spencer,Taylor.	4,000
11	25	a	Boston Town	L	2-4	Boardman,Rintoul.	3,000
12	30	a	Nottm For res	L	0-1		
13	Dec 2	h	Mexboro Town	W	5-1	Boardman(3),Taylor,Shaw pen.	5,000
14	16	h	Notts Co res	W	2-0	Boardman,Picknet.	3,000
15	23	a	Gainsboro Trinity	W	4-1	Boardman(2),Picknett,Taylor.	
16	25	a	Scunthorpe Utd	D	2-2	Taylor,Charlesworth.	5,000
17	26	a	Mansfield Town	L	0-1		
18	30	h	Grimsby Town res	W	2-0	Boardman,Picknett.	
19	Jan 1	h	Lincoln City res	W	2-0	Picknett(2).	
20	6	a	Chesterfield res	W	2-0	Taylor,Boardman.	2,000
21	13	a	Rotherham Town	W	1-0	Shaw pen.	4,000
22	20	h	Nottm For res	W	2-1	Taylor,Picknett.	
23	27	a	Grimsby Town res	W	2-0	Boardman,Picknett.	
24	Feb 3	a	York City	W	2-0	Taylor,Shaw.	4,000
25	8	a	Hull City res	W	3-2	Boardman(2),Picknett.	
26	10	a	Castleford Town	W	2-0	Shaw pen,Slicer.	
27	17	a	Lincoln City res	W	4-0	Boardman(2),Spencer,Picknett.	
28	24	h	Hull City res	W	2-0	Boardman,Picknett.	4,000
29	Mar 3	a	Castleford res	D	1-1	Boardman.	
30	10	a	Worksop Town	L	1-3	White.	4,550
31	24	a	Barnsley res	D	0-0		
32	30	h	York City	W	3-1	Boardman(2),Picknett.	8,000
33	31	h	Wath Athletic	D	0-0		4,000
34	Apr 2	h	Scunthorpe Utd	D	0-0		
35	7	a	Wath Athletic	D	1-1	Picknett.	2,000
36	12	a	Sheff Wed res	W	1-0	Boardman.	1,000
37	14	a	Wombwell	W	2-0	Boardman,Taylor.	
38	21	h	Chesterfield res	W	3-0	Lumb(2),White.	
39	26	h	Barnsley res	W	2-0	Boardman,Lumb.	
40	28	h	Mansfield Town	W	2-0	Shaw pen,Ashmore.	3,000
41	May 3	a	Notts Co res	L	1-2	Spencer.	
42	5	h	Worksop Town	W	2-0	Shaw pen,Rintoul.	

HOME							AWAY							TOTAL						
P	W	D	L	F	A	PTS	P	W	D	L	F	A	PTS	P	W	D	L	F	A	PTS
21	16	4	1	40	6	36	21	10	5	6	32	22	25	42	26	9	7	72	28	61

F.A.Cup

Pr	Sep23	a	Cudworth Village	W	4-0	Taylor(2),Charlesworth,Rintoul.	3,000
1Q	Oct 7	a	Denaby Utd	D	0-0		
1QR	12	h	Denaby Utd	W	4-1	Ashmore,Charlesworth,Boardman,Rintoul.	6,000
2Q	21	a	Mexboro Town	D	0-0		8,000
2QR	26	h	Mexboro Town	W	2-0	Boardman,Taylor.	5,000
3Q	Nov 4	h	Wath Athletic	D	0-0		6,000
3QR	8	a	Wath Athletic	L	1-2	Bauchop.	6,200

All attendances are approximate

League Division 3 North 1923-24

No	Date	V	Opponents	F-A	Scorers	Att
1	Aug25	h	Wigan Borough	D 0-0		10,923
2	27	a	Ashington	L 1-3	Robertson.	6,000c
3	Sep 1	a	Wigan Borough	L 0-1		10,000c
4	3	h	Ashington	W 2-1	T Keetley,Parker.	6,000c
5	8	a	Chesterfield	L 1-2	T Keetley.	9,549
6	15	h	Chesterfield	L 0-3		7,029
7	22	a	Rotherham County	L 0-3		12,000c
8	29	h	Rotherham County	L 0-1		8,200
9	Oct 6	h	Wrexham	W 1-0	Robertson.	6,700c
10	13	a	Wrexham	D 2-2	T Keetley,Boardman.	6,000c
11	20	h	Darlington	W 1-0	Loughran.	7,200
12	27	a	Darlington	D 1-1	Robertson.	4,414
13	Nov 3	h	Rochdale	D 0-0		6,565
14	10	a	Rochdale	L 0-2		6,000c
15	24	a	Southport	D 2-2	Poyntz(2).	6,000c
16	Dec 1	h	Barrow	D 2-2	Robertson,Sissons.	5,000c
17	8	a	Barrow	D 0-0		
18	15	h	Durham City	W 2-1	McLean,T Keetley.	6,000c
19	22	a	Durham City	L 1-2	Boardman.	3,000c
20	25	h	Bradford PA	D 1-1	T Keetley.	6,000c
21	26	a	Bradford PA	L 2-4	Poyntz(2).	10,000c
22	29	h	Lincoln City	W 3-2	Cowan,Boardman,T Keetley.	6,000c
23	Jan 5	a	Lincoln City	D 1-1	Boardman.	6,000c
24	12	h	Southport	W 3-0	Poyntz,Cowan,T Keetley.	5,500c
25	19	h	Walsall	W 3-0	T Keetley(2),Cowan.	6,500c
26	26	a	Walsall	L 2-5	White,T Keetley.	5,000c
27	Feb 9	a	Wolverhampton Wan	L 0-1		10,000c
28	16	h	New Brighton	W 2-0	T Keetley,Poyntz.	5,000c
29	23	a	New Brighton	L 0-2		5,000c
30	Mar 1	h	Grimsby Town	W 2-1	Boardman,White.	4,500c
31	8	a	Grimsby Town	D 1-1	T Keetley.	4,000c
32	15	a	Halifax Town	W 1-0	T Keetley.	4,000c
33	22	h	Halifax Town	W 7-0	T Keetley(3),Cowan(3),Boardman(pen)	7,000c
34	29	a	Hartlepools Utd	D 1-1	White.	4,000c
35	Apr 5	h	Hartlepools Utd	W 3-1	T Keetley(2),Cowan.	6,500c
36	12	h	Accrington Stanley	L 1-2	T Keetley	
37	18	h	Tranmere Rovers	L 0-3		10,000c
38	19	a	Accrington Stanley	D 0-0		
39	21	h	Tranmere Rovers	W 4-0	Poyntz(2),Cowan,White.	7,000c
40	26	a	Crewe Alex	W 2-0	Poyntz,Boardman.	3,000c
41	May 1	h	Wolverhampton Wand	L 0-2		11,080
42	3	h	Crewe Alex	W 4-1	T Keetley(2),Cowan,Poyntz.	5,000c

Players: Jacklin, Wrigglesworth, Shaw, McLean, Cowan, Lowson, Sissons, Robertson, Keetley, Boardman, Palmer, Shears, Ashmore, Harris, Parker, Loughran, White, Poyntz, Russell, Gaffney, Benzie, McEachrane, Pennan, Smith, Notton, Bailey.

App: 24 42 26 41 33 18 29 16 40 41 2 3 4 11 3 10 25 29 18 2 24 16 1 1 1 2

Gls: 1 9 1 4 21 7 1 1 1 7

	P	W	D	L	F	A	PTS
HOME	21	13	4	4	35	17	30
AWAY	21	2	8	11	18	36	12
TOTAL	42	15	12	15	53	53	42

Season 1921/22

Players: (Back) Wigglesworth, Williams, Cooper, Hendry, Thorpe, Ashwood.
(Front) Wainwright, Butler, McLeod, Copley, Naylor

1926/27 Season

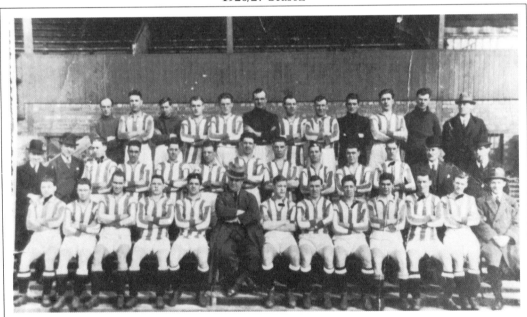

(Back): Stuart(Trainer), J.Smith, Harrison, Buckley, Bowman, Farmery, Milne, Joyce, Down, Bussingham, Holbrey (Asst.Trainer), Crowcroft (Dir.).
(Middle): Howard (Director), Barkhouse (Asst.Sec.), Sissons, Underwood, McLean, Brown, Morgan, Oxley, Emery,
Whitelaw, Christopher, Payne (Dir.), Ray (Sec.Manager).
(Front): Wilks, Telford, Longden, F.Keetley, Thomson (Chair.), Hall, McConnell, Campbell, Walker, Boardman, Hargreaves, Morris (Dir.).

League Division 3 North 1924-25

No	Date	V	Opponents	F-A	Scorers	Att
1	Aug30	h	Barrow	D 0-0		9,000
2	Sep 1	a	Ashington	L 0-2		
3	6	a	Lincoln City	L 0-2		9,000
4	8	h	Ashington	W 7-3	T.Ktley(2).Miller(2).Cowan.Hwell.Gcoign	6,000
5	9	a	Nelson	L 0-3		4,000
6	13	h	Tranmere Rovers	W 2-0	T.Keetley.Cowan.	5,000
7	20	a	Walsall	L 0-4		7,000
8	27	h	Wigan Borough	W 5-0	T.Keetley(2.1pen).Sissons.Cowan.Hanwell	7,000
9	Oct 4	a	Crewe Alex	D 1-1	Boardman.	
10	11	h	Durham City	D 0-0		6,000
11	18	a	Wrexham	L 1-2	H.Keetley	5,000
12	25	h	Rotherham County	W 4-1	T.Keetley(2.1pen).Bailey.Boardman.	6,000
13	Nov 1	a	Chesterfield	L 1-2	Campbell	6,000
14	8	h	Accrington Stanley	W 4-1	T.Keetley(2).Campbell(2).	6,000
15	22	h	New Brighton	W 1-0	Boardman.	6,000
16	Dec 6	h	Hartlepools Utd	W 1-0	Cowan.	6,000
17	20	h	Darlington	L 0-2		7,500
18	25	a	Bradford PA	L 1-4	T.Keetley.	15,000
19	26	h	Bradford PA	W 1-0	T.Keetley.	9,000
20	27	a	Barrow	L 0-4		
21	Jan 1	a	Grimsby Town	D 1-1	T.Keetley.	5,000
22	3	h	Lincoln City	W 2-1	Campbell.T.Keetley.	5,000
23	17	a	Tranmere Rovers	W 2-1	Boardman.T.Keetley.	6,000
24	24	h	Walsall	W 2-1	T.Keetley.McLean.	6,000
25	26	a	Halifax Town	L 0-2		
26	31	a	Wigan Borough	D 2-2	T.Keetley(2).	3,000
27	Feb 7	h	Crewe Alex	D 1-1	Campbell.	5,000
28	14	a	Durham City	L 0-1		
29	21	h	Wrexham	W 1-0	T.Keetley.	5,000
30	24	a	Rochdale	L 2-5	T.Keetley.Gascoigne.	
31	28	a	Rotherham County	L 0-3		
32	Mar 7	h	Chesterfield	L 0-1		8,000
33	14	a	Accrington Stanley	L 2-3	Boardman(2).	5,000
34	21	h	Halifax Town	L 0-1		4,000
35	28	h	New Brighton	W 2-0	Campbell.T.Keetley.	
36	Apr 4	h	Grimsby Town	D 2-2	T.Keetley(pen).Lambert.	5,000
37	10	h	Southport	L 0-1		4,000
38	11	a	Hartlepools Utd	D 2-2	T.Keetley.Campbell.	2,500
39	13	a	Southport	L 0-3		
40	14	h	Nelson	D 1-1	Lambert.	6,000
41	18	h	Rochdale	W 2-1	McLean.T.Keetley.	
42	25	a	Darlington	D 1-1	Boardman	7,000

Players (columns): A.Smith, Bowman, Rees, Buckley, Lambert, Warburton, F.Smith, Rankin, Emery, Campbell, H.Keetley, Russell, Bailey, Miller, Gascoigne, Boardman, White, T.Keetley, Hanwell, Sissons, Benzie, Cowan, McLean, Horsman, Wigglesworth, Jacklin

App: 30 24 38 36 15 33 40 7 41 5 34 34 5 15 9 3 31 11 6 2 9 18 9 1 3 3

Gls: 2 4 1 2 23 7 2 2 1 5 34 11 1 7

* All League game attendances are approximate

HOME								AWAY								TOTAL						
P	W	D	L	F	A	PTS		P	W	D	L	F	A	PTS		P	W	D	L	F	A	PTS
21	12	5	4	36	17	29		21	2	5	14	16	47	9		42	14	10	18	52	64	38

F.A. Cup

No	Date	V	Opponents	F-A	Scorers	Att
4Q	Nov15	h	Mansfield Town	W 3-2	T.Keetley.Cowan.Brelsford O.G..	9,011
5Q	29	a	Rotherham County	W 3-2	T.Keetley(2).Boardman.	14,734
6Q	Dec13	h	Southport	W 1-0	T.Keetley.	10,581
R1	Jan10	h	Norwich City	L 1-2	Campbell.	13,042

League Division 3 North 1925-26

No	Date	V	Opponents	F-A	Scorers	Att
1	Aug 29	a	Grimsby Town	L 0-3		9,012
2	31	h	Crewe Alex	W 5-2	T Keetley(2),Taylor,Lambert,Gascoigne	4,640
3	Sep 5	h	Wrexham	D 1-1	Taylor.	5,628
4	7	a	Crewe Alex	D 2-2	T Keetley.McConnell.	4,507
5	12	a	Coventry City	L 0-4		11,274
6	19	h	Nelson	D 1-1	Lambert.	3,088
7	24	h	New Brighton	W 2-0	Taylor.Boardman.	3,518
8	26	a	Barrow	W 2-0	Morgan.Lambert.	2,861
9	Oct 3	h	Ashington	W 2-1	F L Smith.Lambert.	6,517
10	10	a	Wigan Borough	W 1-0	Lambert.	4,457
11	17	a	Rotherham Utd	D 1-1	Lambert.	10,187
12	24	h	Halifax Town	D 2-2	Boardman.Taylor.	7,066
13	31	h	Chesterfield	D 2-2	Lambert.T Keetley(pen)	7,154
14	Nov 7	h	Bradford PA	L 0-3		3,880
15	14	a	Hartlepools Utd	L 1-2	T Keetley.	4,221
16	21	h	Rochdale	D 2-2	T Keetley(2).	4,831
17	Dec 5	h	Walsall	D 1-1	T Keetley.	4,054
18	19	h	Durham City	W 4-1	H Keetley(3).Hargreaves.	2,397
19	25	a	Southport	D 3-3	Hargreaves.H Keetley(2).	5,728
20	26	h	Southport	W 6-1	H Ktley(3).T Ktley.Hargreaves.Taylor	5,463
21	Jan 1	a	New Brighton	L 1-2	H Keetley.	3,019
*	Jan 2	h	Grimsby Town	W 1-0	McConnell (* Abandoned)	3,112
22	9	a	Tranmere Rovers	L 0-1		4,500
23	16	a	Wrexham	W 2-0	Hargreaves.T Keetley(pen)	3,442
24	23	h	Coventry City	W 8-1	T.Ktly(3.1pen).H.Ktly(2).Emry.Bman.McCn	4,963
25	30	a	Nelson	L 3-5	T Keetley(2.1pen).McConnell.	6,402
26	Feb 6	h	Barrow	L 0-1		5,478
27	13	a	Ashington	L 1-6	H Keetley.	3,778
28	20	h	Wigan Borough	D 1-1	H Keetley.	6,117
29	27	h	Rotherham Utd	D 0-0		7,198
30	Mar 6	a	Halifax Town	W 3-0	Boardman.T Keetley.Dransfield.	5,086
31	13	a	Chesterfield	W 3-0	Boardman(pen).Dransfield.Lambert.	7,922
32	20	a	Bradford PA	L 0-2		12,766
33	27	h	Hartlepools Utd	W 2-1	McLean.T Keetley.	4,694
34	Apr 2	h	Lincoln City	W 1-0	F L Smith.	9,418
35	3	a	Rochdale	L 1-4	H Keetley.	6,792
36	5	h	Lincoln City	L 1-3	T Keetley.	5,866
37	10	h	Tranmere Rovers	W 4-0	T Keetley(2).H Keetley.McConnell.	4,786
38	14	a	Accrington Stanley	W 3-2	T Keetley(2).H Keetley.	1,701
39	17	a	Walsall	L 1-2	T Keetley.	3,228
40	22	h	Grimsby Town	L 1-4	Lambert.	9,711
41	24	h	Accrington Stanley	W 6-2	Lbert(2).T Ktley.H Ktley.Emery.McCon	4,215
42	May 1	a	Durham City	L 0-3		1,522

Player appearances / goals (totals):

Player	App	Gls
Dransfield	9	
C.Smith	1	
J.Keetley	39	1
Varney	33	
H.Keetley	21	24
Hargreaves	38	5
F.Smith	11	
Morgan	26	
Bowman	40	
Down	10	
McConnell	37	5
Bromage	2	
Ashford	4	
Taylor	19	10
Warburton	25	
Holland	3	
Boardman	28	3
Campbell	28	
T.Keetley	13	2
Lambert	33	4
Sissons	5	17
Emery	7	2
Gascoigne	24	
McLean	1	1
Buckley	2	1
Wigglesworth	1	
Jacklin	2	2

	P	W	D	L	F	A	PTS
HOME	21	11	7	3	52	25	29
AWAY	21	5	4	12	28	47	14
TOTAL	42	16	11	15	80	72	43

F.A. Cup

	Date	V	Opponents	F-A	Scorers	Att
R1	Nov28	h	Wellington Town	W 2-0	H Keetley,Hargreaves.	5,458
R2	Dec12	h	Rotherham Utd	L 0-2		13,764

F.A. Cup goals: Gls 3

League Division 3 North 1926-27

No	Date	V	Opponents	F-A	Scorers	Att
1	Aug 28	h	Walsall	D 2-2	Boardman.T Keetley.	6,566
2	30	a	Stockport County	L 0-1		7,397
3	Sep 4	a	Nelson	L 1-5	Whitfield.	6,982
4	6	h	Stockport County	L 1-2	F Keetley pen.	4,597
5	11	h	Chesterfield	L 0-3		4,001
6	18	a	Ashington	D 1-1	F Keetley.	1,672
7	25	h	New Brighton	D 2-2	F Keetley.Hargreaves.	4,260
8	Oct 2	a	Wrexham	W 1-0	T Keetley.	5,126
9	9	h	Wigan Borough	W 4-1	H Keetley(3).Hall.	3,783
10	16	h	Crewe Alex	L 0-2		4,994
11	23	a	Hartlepools Utd	L 0-3		2,681
12	30	h	Southport	W 3-1	Hall(2).T Keetley.	3,764
13	Nov 6	a	Rochdale	L 2-7	H Keetley.T Keetley.	3,654
14	13	h	Tranmere Rovers	W 4-1	T Keetley(3.2pens).Hall.	3,325
15	20	a	Durham City	D 2-2	Wilks.H Keetley.	1,344
*	27	h	Desboro Town	D 0-0	(* Abandoned)	2,376
16	Dec 4	a	Lincoln City	D 0-0		4,487
17	18	a	Barrow	W 1-0	Telford.	2,840
18	25	a	Bradford PA	L 3-7	Morgan.T Keetley.McConnell.	17,533
19	27	h	Bradford PA	W 4-1	T Keetley(3).Fell O.G.	8,107
20	Jan 1	a	Rotherham Utd	W 3-1	F Keetley(2).Longden.	8,159
21	8	a	Wigan Borough	D 1-1	F Keetley.	2,441
22	15	a	Walsall	L 0-1		4,484
23	22	h	Nelson	W 6-0	Wilks.Hargreaves.McCon.T.Keetley(3)	4,977
24	29	a	Chesterfield	D 1-1	T Keetley pen.	4,788
25	Feb 5	h	Ashington	W 3-1	Wilks.Hargreaves.T Keetley pen.	6,336
26	12	a	New Brighton	W 2-0	T Keetley.Jones O.G.	3,677
27	19	h	Wrexham	D 2-2	Hargreaves.T Keetley pen.	7,153
28	Mar 5	a	Crewe Alex	W 3-1	F Keetley.H Keetley.Pringle O.G.	3,744
29	12	h	Hartlepools Utd	W 2-0	McConnell.Hargreaves.	5,136
30	19	a	Southport	L 0-2		3,712
31	26	h	Rochdale	W 3-2	T Keetley(3).	5,779
32	Apr 2	a	Tranmere Rovers	D 1-1	T Keetley.	4,350
33	4	h	Halifax Town	W 2-0	Hargreaves.T Keetley	3,964
34	9	h	Durham City	W 5-1	T Keetley(3).H Keetley.Hargreaves.	2,402
35	15	a	Stoke City	W 3-1	F Keetley.T Keetley Hargreaves.	18,069
36	16	a	Accrington Stanley	L 0-2		3,644
37	18	a	Stoke City	D 0-0		15,705
38	19	h	Rotherham Utd	D 2-2	T Keetley(2).	5,611
39	23	h	Lincoln City	L 1-3	McConnell.	4,366
40	25	h	Accrington Stanley	W 2-0	T Keetley(2).	15,000*
41	30	a	Halifax Town	L 1-2	McConnell.	4,299
42	May 7	h	Barrow	W 7-0	T Keetley(4).Longden(3).	3,580

Player appearances (App) and goals (Gls):

Player	App	Gls
Down	22	
Buckley	18	
Milne	40	
Underwood	36	
Morgan	32	1
Emery	37	
T.Keetley	36	35
F.Keetley	35	8
Boardman	10	1
McConnell	34	5
McDonald	9	
Whitfield	6	1
McLean	15	
Bowman	15	
Wilks	14	3
Longden	11	4
H.Keetley	20	7
Hargreaves	29	8
Campbell	3	
Hall	6	4
Whitelaw	7	
Farmery	20	
Joyce	4	
Telford	1	1
Gordon	1	
Bott	1	

+ 3 og

	P	W	D	L	F	A	PTS
HOME	21	13	4	4	58	27	30
AWAY	21	5	7	9	23	38	17
TOTAL	42	18	11	13	81	65	47

F.A. Cup

	Date	V	Opponents	F-A	Scorers	Att
R1	Dec 2	h	Desborough Town	W 3-0	F Keetley(2).T Keetley.	2,583
R2	11	h	Chesterfield	L 0-1		10,915

* Attendance given is approximate

League Division 3 North 1927-28

No	Date	V	Opponents	F-A	Scorers	Att
1	Aug 27	h	Lincoln City	W 3-0	T.Keetley(2).Emery.	8,451
2	31	a	New Brighton	L 1-3	T.Keetley(pen)	5,715
3	Sep 3	a	Hartlepools Utd	L 0-1		5,314
4	5	h	New Brighton	W 5-1	T.Ktley(2).Iden.McNestry.Phillipson	5,432
5	10	h	Accrington Stanley	D 0-0		6,143
6	17	a	Wigan Borough	D 1-1	Phillipson.	3,325
7	24	h	Rotherham Utd	W 2-0	T.Keetley.Morgan.	7,764
8	Oct 1	h	Darlington	W 5-0	F.Keetley(2).Hall(2).T.Keetley.	5,989
9	8	a	Ashington	W 2-1	F.Keetley.Hall.	2,655
10	15	h	Crewe Alex	W 3-1	T.Keetley(2.1pen).McConnell.	6,973
11	22	a	Wrexham	W 2-1	Hall(2).	3,536
12	29	h	Durham City	W 5-0	Hall(3).F.Keetley.Emery.	7,176
13	Nov 5	a	Southport	W 2-1	T.Keetley(2).	2,840
14	12	h	Chesterfield	W 4-0	Hall(2).T.Keetley.Underwood.	8,373
15	19	a	Bradford PA	W 2-0	F.Keetley.T.Keetley.	22,202
16	Dec 3	a	Stockport County	L 1-2	T.Keetley.	9,760
17	17	a	Nelson	W 1-0	T.Keetley.	3,410
18	24	h	Rochdale	W 5-2	T.Keetley(2.1pen).Phillipson(2).Hall	5,291
19	26	h	Halifax Town	D 1-1	Hall.	11,380
20	27	a	Halifax Town	W 1-0	Hall.	12,909
21	31	a	Lincoln City	L 0-2		8,631
22	Jan 7	h	Hartlepools Utd	D 1-1	McConnell.	7,641
23	14	h	Barrow	W 4-0	F.Keetley(2).Bott.Hall.	6,120
24	21	a	Accrington Stanley	W 3-1	Hall(2).T.Keetley.	4,931
25	28	h	Wigan Borough	W 4-1	T.Keetley(2.1pen).Hall.Morgan.	6,264
26	Feb 4	a	Rotherham Utd	L 1-2	T.Keetley(pen)	11,530
27	11	a	Darlington	L 0-3		6,714
28	18	h	Ashington	W 3-2	Hall.Bott.Patterson.	6,553
29	25	a	Crewe Alex	L 1-4	Patterson.	4,861
30	Mar 3	h	Wrexham	D 1-1	T.Keetley.	8,519
31	10	a	Durham City	W 3-1	T.Keetley(2).F.Keetley.	1,408
32	17	h	Southport	L 0-1		6,622
33	24	a	Chesterfield	L 0-1		4,696
34	31	h	Bradford PA	W 2-0	T.Keetley(2).	14,176
35	Apr 6	h	Bradford City	W 2-1	T.Keetley(2).	16,134
36	7	a	Barrow	D 0-0		7,989
37	9	a	Bradford City	L 0-1		13,375
38	14	h	Stockport County	L 0-2		5,872
39	21	a	Tranmere Rovers	D 0-0		4,072
40	28	h	Nelson	W 4-2	T.Keetley(4).	4,117
41	May 1	h	Tranmere Rovers	W 5-2	T.Keetley(4).F.Keetley.	4,056
42	5	a	Rochdale	L 0-1		1,768

Appearances and Goals

Player	App	Gls
Maughan	40	
Buckley	30	
Milne	27	
Underwood	30	1
Morgan	41	2
Emery	40	2
McNestry	6	1
F.Keetley	37	9
T.Keetley	42	36
McConnell	35	2
Phillipson	28	4
Longden	7	
Hall	24	18
Bowman	27	
McLean	6	
Whitelaw	8	
Bott	13	2
Patterson	6	2
Fawcett	1	
Tippett	12	
Farmery	2	

Summary

	P	W	D	L	F	A	PTS
HOME	21	15	4	2	59	18	34
AWAY	21	8	3	10	20	26	19
TOTAL	42	23	7	12	79	44	53

F.A. Cup

	Date	V	Opponents	F-A	Scorers
R1	Nov 26	a	Carlisle Utd	L 1-2	McConnell.

* Attendance given is approximate

League Division 3 North 1928-29

No	Date	V	Opponents	F-A	Scorers	Att
1	Aug25	a	Rochdale	W 3-1	Longden,Tippett,T.Keetley.	4,275
2	27	h	Southport	W 4-2	T.Keetley(3),Longden.	6,905
3	Sep 1	h	New Brighton	L 1-2	T.Keetley.	8,595
4	8	a	Wrexham	L 2-4	Binns,T.Keetley(pen)	5,498
5	15	h	Chesterfield	W 2-0	T.Keetley,F.Keetley.	7,143
6	22	a	Barrow	D 2-2	T.Keetley(2).	6,947
7	29	h	Lincoln City	D 0-0		6,727
8	Oct 1	a	Nelson	W 4-2	Longden(2),Tippett,F.Keetley.	3,297
9	6	h	Ashington	W 2-1	F.Keetley,T.Keetley.	6,783
10	13	a	South Shields	L 0-1		4,913
11	20	a	Bradford City	L 0-3		21,515
12	27	h	Accrington Stanley	W 4-1	T.Keetley(3),McConnell.	3,808
13	Nov 3	a	Hartlepools Utd	D 2-2	T.Keetley(2).	3,175
14	10	h	Carlisle Utd	W 3-0	T.Keetley(2,1pen),Emery.	6,371
15	17	a	Rotherham Utd	W 2-1	T.Keetley(2).	7,347
16	Dec 1	a	Crewe Alex	D 1-1	T.Keetley.	2,815
17	8	h	Crewe Alex	L 0-1		4,835
18	15	a	Stockport County	L 1-4	Patterson.	8,629
19	22	h	Halifax Town	L 0-3		3,574
20	26	h	Nelson	D 2-2	F.Keetley.McConnell.	7,369
21	29	h	Rochdale	W 4-2	T.Keetley(2).Bott.Patterson.	4,191
22	Jan 1	a	Southport	D 3-3	Bott.Patterson(2)	4,977
23	5	a	New Brighton	D 1-1	Patterson.	3,800
24	19	h	Wrexham	W 1-0	F.Keetley.	8,717
25	26	a	Chesterfield	W 1-0	F.Keetley.	5,201
26	Feb 2	h	Barrow	W 1-0	F.Keetley.	4,349
27	9	a	Lincoln City	L 1-2	T.Keetley.	5,168
28	16	a	Ashington	W 7-4	T.Keetley(6).Bott.	729
29	23	h	South Shields	W 2-1	T.Keetley(2,1pen).	7,206
30	Mar 2	h	Bradford City	D 1-1	Wilkinson.	14,574
31	9	a	Accrington Stanley	L 0-6		4,177
32	16	h	Hartlepools Utd	W 4-1	T.Keetley(4,1pen).	5,111
33	23	a	Carlisle Utd	W 2-1	T.Keetley(2).	7,358
34	29	h	Darlington	W 3-1	T.Keetley(3).	11,698
35	30	h	Rotherham Utd	W 1-0	Wilkinson.	7,891
36	Apr 1	a	Darlington	L 0-1		4,579
37	2	h	Tranmere Rovers	W 2-1	T.Keetley.Patterson.	3,842
38	6	a	Wigan Borough	L 2-4	McConnell.Emery.	6,741
39	20	a	Tranmere Rovers	D 1-1	Price.	4,012
40	27	h	Stockport County	L 0-2		9,453
41	May 1	h	Wigan Borough	L 1-2	Patterson.	2,242
42	4	a	Halifax Town	D 2-2	Tippett(2).	2,862

Appearances and Goals

Player	App	Gls
Maughan	29	
Buckley	41	
Bowman	40	
Underwood	35	
Morgan	29	
Emery	42	2
Tippett	19	4
F.Keetley	30	7
T.Keetley	32	41
Longden	14	4
Bott	29	3
Binns	1	1
Atkin	32	
McNestry	2	
McConnell	27	3
Whitelaw	9	
Milne	2	
Nelson	1	
Patterson	21	7
Farmery	11	
Bussingham	4	
McLean	8	
Wilkinson	8	2
Price	3	1

Summary

	P	W	D	L	F	A	PTS	POS
HOME	21	14	3	4	39	19	31	
AWAY	21	6	7	8	37	43	19	
TOTAL	42	20	10	12	76	62	50	5th

F.A. Cup

	Date	V	Opponents	F-A	Scorers	Att
R1	Nov24	a	Bradford City	L 1-4	T.Keetley	9,785

THE ROVERS OF 1927-28.

Back row—Mr. D. L. Menzies (Manager), J. Stewart (Trainer), ————, Smith (J.), Farmery, Buckley, Bowman, Maughan, Milne, Bussingham, Mr. A. Thomson (Chairman), and Holbrey (Asst. Trainer).
Middle row—Mr. A. E. Porter (Secretary), McLean, Emery, Morgan, Underwood, Whitelaw, Patterson.
Front row—McNestry, Keetley (F.), Longden, Keetley (T.), Hall, McConnell, Bott (W.), Phillipson.

Season 1931/32

(Back): Scott, Smith, Moody, Tate, Vickers, Hatton. (2nd Row): McLean (Trainer), Harvey, Shaw, C.Price, Flowers, Bowman, Carr, Adams. (3rd Row): Emery, Buckley, Dr.Ashforth, Hibbert, Menzies, J.Price, ? . (Front): Atkin, Wadsworth, Lievesley, R.Smith, Bott.

League Division 3 North 1929-30

No	Date	V	Opponents	F-A	Scorers	Att	No	Tate	Buckley	Bowman	Robinson	Morgan	Emery	Atkin	Keetley	Livesley	McConnell	Bott	Martin	Price	Glidden	Patterson	Wilkinson	Scott	McLean	Milne	Whitelaw	Gregory	Wadsworth	J.Smith	R.Smith	Flowers	Alcock	Harvey	Roe	Hatton
1	Aug31	h	Accrington Stanley	W 3-1	Bott(2),F Keetley.	4.794	1	1	2	3	4	5	6	7	8	9	10	11																		
2	Sep 2	h	South Shields	W 1-0	Bott(pen)	5.824	2	1	2	3	4	5	6	7	8		10	11	9																	
3	7	a	Darlington	L 2-6	Patterson,Price.	6.958	3	1	2	3	4	5	6	7					9	8	10	11														
4	11	a	South Shields	L 1-2	Patterson.	4.235	4		2	3	4	5	6	11			10			8		9	1						7							
5	14	h	Hartlepools Utd	D 0-0		5.194	5		2	3	4		6	7	8			11		10		9	1	5												
6	16	a	Halifax Town	L 0-1		2.668	6		2		6	5	9	7				11		10		8	1		4	3										
7	21	a	Crewe Alex	L 0-4		4.601	7		2		4		6	7			10	11		8		9	1	5		3										
8	23	h	Halifax Town	W 1-0	Patterson.	1.921	8	1	2		4		6	7			10	11		8		9		5		3										
9	28	a	Chesterfield	L 1-2	R Smith.	6.701	9	1	2	3	4	5	6	7				11		8		9									10					
10	Oct 5	h	Lincoln City	D 0-0		4.467	10	1	2	3	4	5	6	7	8			11				10					9									
11	12	a	Tranmere Rovers	L 1-2	McConnell.	5.587	11	1	2	3		5	6	7	9		10	11				8					4									
12	19	h	Southport	W 3-1	F Keetley,McConnell,Little O.G.	4.179	12	1	2	3		5	6	7	8		10	11									4	9								
13	26	a	Nelson	L 1-4	Bott.	4.324	13	1	2	3		5	6	7	8		10	11									4	9								
14	Nov 2	h	Carlisle Utd	L 1-4	McConnell.	3.966	14	1	2	3	4	5	6		8		10	11											7		9					
15	9	a	Wigan Borough	L 2-3	Patterson,Wadsworth.	4.481	15	1	2		4	5	6				10	11				9							7	3	8					
16	16	h	Wrexham	W 4-2	McConnell(2),Patterson,R Smith.	2.809	16	1	2		4	5	6				10	11				9							7	3	8					
17	23	a	Barrow	L 0-1		3.282	17	1	2		4	5	6				10	11				9							7	3	8					
18	Dec 7	a	New Brighton	L 0-1		1.785	18		2		4		6	7				11				10		5					8	3			9		1	
*	12	a	Accrington	D 1-1	Atkin. (*Abandoned - 40mins)	3.205																														
19	21	a	York City	D 2-2	Whitelaw,Patterson.	2.654	19	1	2				6					11				8					4	5	7	3	10		9			
20	25	a	Rochdale	W 4-2	Patterson(2),Smith R,Bott.	2.996	20		2	6								11				8					4	5	7	3	10		9		1	
21	26	h	Rochdale	W 3-1	Gregory,Wadsworth,Patterson.	7.799	21	1	2	4			6	8				11				9						5	7	3	10					
22	Jan 4	h	Darlington	W 3-1	Emery,Patterson,R Smith.	5.466	22	1	2	4			6	7				11				9						5	8	3	10					
*	11	h	Stoke City	L 2-3	Bott,Bowman (*Abandoned - 75mins)	13.221																														
23	18	a	Hartlepools Utd	L 0-3		5.555	23	1	2	4			6	7				11										5	8	3	10			9		
24	Feb 1	h	Chesterfield	W 2-1	Harvey,R Smith.	6.386	24	1	2	4			6					11				10						5	7	3	8			9		
25	8	a	Lincoln City	L 1-3	Wadsworth.	5.914	25	1	2				6					11				10				3	4	5	7		8			9		
26	15	h	Tranmere Rovers	D 1-1	Patterson.	4.489	26	1	2	4			6			9		11				10				3		5	7		8					
27	22	a	Southport	D 1-1	Gregory.	2.723	27	1	2	3			6			9		11				10						5	7		8	4				
28	24	a	Accrington Stanley	D 3-3	Lievesley(2),Bowman.	2.143	28	1	2	3	4		6			9		11				10						5	7		8					
29	Mar 1	h	Nelson	W 3-0	Lievesley(2),Gregory.	4.445	29	1	2	3			6			9		11				10						5	7		8	4				
30	8	a	Carlisle Utd	D 1-1	Lievesley.	4.850	30	1	2	3			6			9		11		10				5					7		8	4				
31	15	h	Wigan Borough	W 4-2	Scott,Price,Emery(pen),Lievesley.	1.931	31	1	2	3			6			9		11		10				5					7		8	4				
32	20	h	Stockport County	D 1-1	Bott.	2.952	32	1	2	3			6			9		11				10		5					7		8	4				
33	22	a	Wrexham	W 2-0	Emery,Lievesley.	4.205	33	1	2	3			6			9		11				10		5					7		8	4				
34	29	h	Barrow	W 4-0	Lievesley(2),Bott,Wadsworth.	4.416	34	1	2				6			9		11				10		5					7	3	8	4				
35	Apr 5	a	Port Vale	L 1-2	Lievesley.	9.905	35	1	2	3			6			9		11				10		5					7		8	4				
36	10	h	Crewe Alex	W 2-1	Bott(2,1pen).	3.072	36	1	2	3			6			9		11				10		5					7		8	4				
37	12	h	New Brighton	D 1-1	Bott.	4.502	37	1	2	3			6			9		11				10		5					7		8	4				
38	18	h	Rotherham Utd	W 2-0	Lievesley(2).	9.451	38	1	2	3			6			9		11		10				5					7		8	4				
39	19	a	Stockport County	L 0-3		7.877	39	1	2		6							11		10				5					7	3	8	4		9		
40	21	a	Rotherham Utd	L 0-1		6.749	40	1	2	3		6						11		10				5					7		8	4		9		
41	26	h	York City	L 0-3		4.322	41	1	2				6	7			10	11						5						3	8	4		9		
42	May 1	h	Port Vale	L 0-2		5.313	42	1	2	3			6	7				11		10				5								4		9		8
							App	36	42	30	17	15	39	19	8	14	13	40	2	13	1	29	4	17	1	5	7	13	28	13	28	15	3	7	2	1
							Gls			1			3		2	12	5	10		2		11		1			1	3	4		5			1		

HOME							AWAY							TOTAL						
P	W	D	L	F	A	PTS	P	W	D	L	F	A	PTS	P	W	D	L	F	A	PTS
21	13	5	3	39	22	31	21	2	4	15	23	47	8	42	15	9	18	62	29	39

F.A. Cup

	Date	V	Opponents	F-A	Scorers	Att		Tate	Buckley	Bowman	Robinson	Morgan	Emery	Atkin	Keetley	Livesley	McConnell	Bott	Martin	Price	Glidden	Patterson	Wilkinson	Scott	McLean	Milne	Whitelaw	Gregory	Wadsworth	J.Smith	R.Smith	Flowers	Alcock	Harvey	Roe	Hatton
R1	Nov30	h	Shildon	D 0-0		4.693	R1	1	2		10	5	6					11				9					4		7	3	8					
R1R	Dec 4	a	Shildon	D 1-1	Wadsworth. (after extra time)	4.000*	R1R	1	2		8	5	6					11				9					4		7	3		10				
R1R	9	a	Shildon	W 3-0	Patterson(2),R Smith. (at York)		R1R	1	2			5	6	7				11				9					4		8	3	10					
R2	14	h	New Brighton	W 1-0	Whitelaw.	6.545	R2	1	2			5	6				10	11				8					4		7	3			9			
R3	16	h	Stoke City	W 1-0	Emery.	7.748	R3	1	2	4			6	7				11				9						5	8	3	10					
R4	25	a	Millwall	L 0-4		30.440	R4	1	2	3			6				8	11				9					4	5	7		10					

* Attendance given is approximate

League Division 3 North 1930-31

No	Date	V	Opponents	F-A	Scorers	Att
1	Aug30	a	Gateshead	L 1-2	Lievesley.	15.545
2	Sep 1	h	Darlington	L 1-2	R.Smith.	4.915
3	6	h	Rotherham Utd	D 3-3	Bott(pen).Turner O.G.,Jackson O.G.	6.660
4	8	a	Halifax Town	W 2-0	J.Price.Atkin.	7.764
5	13	h	Hull City	L 0-2		6.238
6	18	h	Halifax Town	D 3-3	Lievesley(2),J.Price.	2.079
7	20	a	Lincoln City	L 0-1		6.722
8	27	h	Hartlepools Utd	D 1-1	Bott.	3.927
9	Oct 4	a	Wigan Borough	L 0-3		8.548
10	11	h	Nelson	W 2-0	Bott(2).	3.542
11	18	a	Chesterfield	L 1-2	Bott.	6.485
12	25	h	York City	L 0-2		4.331
13	Nov 1	a	Southport	L 1-2	Lievesley.	2.321
14	8	h	Accrington Stanley	W 6-1	Lievesley(3).Emery.Bott(pen).Law O.G.	3.331
15	15	a	Rochdale	W 5-3	Bott(3).Gladwin.R.Smith.	2.985
16	22	h	Crewe Alex	W 2-0	R.Smith(2).	4.273
17	Dec 6	h	Tranmere Rovers	W 6-0	Bott(3).Emery.R.Smith.Lievesley.	3.931
18	20	h	Barrow	D 0-0		3.954
19	25	h	New Brighton	D 0-0		3.717
20	26	a	New Brighton	L 1-2	Flowers.	4.389
21	27	h	Gateshead	D 1-1	R.Smith.	4.528
22	Jan 1	a	Carlisle Utd	D 1-1	Barber.	8.073
23	3	a	Rotherham Utd	L 0-3		4.132
24	14	a	Wrexham	L 1-4	Wadsworth	2.788
25	17	a	Hull City	L 2-8	Bott(2.pen).	5.575
26	24	h	Lincoln City	L 0-1		5.137
27	31	h	Hartlepools Utd	W 2-0	Bott.Atkin.	2.835
28	Feb 7	h	Wigan Borough	W 5-1	Castle(3).Bott.Emery.	3.241
29	14	a	Nelson	L 0-2		2.304
30	21	h	Chesterfield	W 1-0	Gladwin.	5.937
31	28	a	York City	L 2-4	Bott.Lievesley.	3.921
32	Mar 7	h	Southport	D 0-0		3.241
33	14	a	Accrington Stanley	L 0-2		2.571
34	21	h	Rochdale	W 4-0	Vickers(2).R.Smith.Atkin.	2.997
35	28	a	Crewe Alex	L 1-2	Atkin.	2.531
36	Apr 3	h	Stockport County	W 2-0	Gladwin.R.Smith.	4.306
37	4	h	Wrexham	D 1-1	R.Smith.	4.824
38	6	a	Stockport County	D 2-2	Emery(pen).Gladwin.	3.707
39	11	a	Tranmere Rovers	W 2-1	C.Price(2).	8.680
40	18	h	Carlisle Utd	W 2-0	R.Smith.(2).	2.528
41	25	a	Barrow	L 1-3	Gladwin.	4.638
42	May 2	a	Darlington	D 0-0		2.408

Players: Tate, Buckley, Bowman, Flowers, Scott, Emery, Atkin, R.Smith, Livesley, J.Price, Bott, J.Smith, Vickers, Carr, Wadsworth, Gladwin, C.Price, Moody, Spargo, Shaw, Miller, Blackburne, Barber, Castle, Foster

	Buckley	Bowman	Flowers	Scott	Emery	Atkin	R.Smith	Livesley	J.Price	Bott	J.Smith	Vickers	Carr	Wadsworth	Gladwin	C.Price	Moody	Spargo	Shaw	Miller	Blackburne	Barber	Castle	Foster
App	40	35	24	12	33	28	42	26	9	28	7	22	3	20	31	8	30	23	1	3	4	6	8	7
Gls			1		4	5	11	9	2	17	2		1	5	2				3	1		11	9	5

(plus 3 og)

HOME	P	W	D	L	F	A	PTS
	21	9	8	4	40	18	26

AWAY	P	W	D	L	F	A	PTS
	21	3	4	14	23	47	10

TOTAL	P	W	D	L	F	A	PTS
	42	12	12	18	63	65	36

F.A. Cup

							Att
R1	Nov29	a	Rochdale	W 2-1	Bott.R.Smith.		6.000*
R2	Dec13	h	Notts County	L 0-1			17.589

* Attendance given is approximate

League Division 3 North 1931-32

Player columns (across the top, reading down):
Critchley, Shaw, Rorrison, Yeardley, Vickers, Halliday, Potter, Beresford, Martin, Flowers, Tate, Pattison, Wadsworth, Foster, Parker, Gladwin, Atherton, R.Smith, Atkin, Emery, Spargo, Livesley, Bowman, Buckley, Moody

No	Date	V	Opponents	F-A	Scorers	Att
1	Aug 29	h	Stockport County	D 1-1	R.Smith.	6,264
2	31	a	Tranmere Rovers	W 1-0	Atherton.	6,701
3	Sep 5	a	Accrington Stanley	L 2-3	Wadsworth.Emery.	4,854
4	12	h	Wrexham	L 2-4	R.Smith.Atkin.	4,717
5	14	a	Rotherham Utd	L 3-6	Wadsworth.R.Smith.Jackson O.G.	5,011
6	19	a	Carlisle	L 1-5	R.Smith.	2,570
7	21	h	Rotherham Utd	W 2-0	Martin.Emery(pen).	3,845
8	26	h	Crewe Alex	W 2-1	Gladwin.Pattison.	4,614
9	Oct 3	a	Rochdale	L 1-3	Emery.	3,930
10	10	h	Halifax Town	W 3-1	Wadsworth(2).R.Smith.	3,859
11	17	a	Walsall	L 0-2		3,216
12	24	h	Gateshead	L 1-2	Martin.	2,381
13	31	a	New Brighton	L 0-1		3,041
14	Nov 7	h	Barrow	L 0-1		5,172
15	14	a	Hull City	L 1-4	Atherton.	5,856
16	21	h	Lincoln City	L 0-3		3,265
17	Dec 5	h	Hartlepools Utd	L 1-3	Gladwin.	2,352
18	19	h	Darlington	W 3-2	Flowers.Pattison.Potter.	4,896
19	25	h	York City	W 1-0	Halliday.	8,183
20	26	a	York City	W 2-1	Atkin.Pattison.	1,997
21	Jan 2	a	Stockport County	L 0-1	Halliday.	5,466
22	9	a	Chester	D 1-1	Halliday.	4,164
23	16	h	Accrington Stanley	W 3-1	Pattison.Halliday.Martin.	4,838
24	23	a	Wrexham	L 1-2	Halliday.	4,536
25	30	h	Carlisle	D 3-3	Pattison(2).Martin.	5,898
26	Feb 6	a	Crewe Alex	L 0-2	Pattison.Atherton.	2,856
27	13	h	Rochdale	W 2-0	Pattison.Atherton.	2,977
28	20	a	Halifax	L 0-4		3,066
29	27	h	Walsall	W 2-1	Atherton.R.Smith.	5,002
30	Mar 5	a	Gateshead	L 1-2	Atherton.	2,808
31	12	h	New Brighton	W 2-1	Atherton.Critchley.	4,485
32	19	a	Barrow	L 2-3	Atherton(2).	4,541
33	25	a	Southport	L 0-5		4,631
34	26	h	Hull City	W 2-1	Emery(pen).Atherton.	4,826
35	28	h	Southport	W 3-0	Wadsworth.Atherton(2).	7,551
36	Apr 2	a	Lincoln City	W 2-1	Potter.Wadsworth.	4,365
37	9	H	Chester	W 3-0	Potter(2).Gladwin.	3,520
38	16	a	Hartlepools Utd	L 0-5		1,721
39	30	a	Darlington	W 3-2	Potter(2).Atherton.	2,730
40	May 7	h	Tranmere Rovers	D 2-2	Potter(2).	

	P	W	D	L	F	A	PTS
HOME	20	12	3	5	38	27	27
AWAY	20	4	1	15	21	53	9
TOTAL	40	16	4	20	59	80	36

F.A. Cup

	Date	V	Opponents	F-A	Scorers	Att
R1	Nov28	a	Barrow	D 3-3	Gladwin.Flowers.Bowman(pen).	6,256
R1R	Dec 3	h	Barrow	D 1-1	Smith.R. (aet)	2,661
R1R	7	a	Barrow	D 1-1	Bowman.pen. (aet Maine Rd)	1,726
R1R	9	a	Barrow	W 1-0	Gladwin. (aet Elland Rd)	2,596
R2	12	a	Brighton	L 0-5		14,369

+ 1 og

League Division 3 North 1932-33

No	Date	V	Opponents	F-A	Scorers	Att
1	Aug27	a	Gateshead	L 0-4		6.780
2	29	h	Walsall	W 3-2	Waterston(2),Emery(pen).	4.346
3	Sep 3	a	Stockport County	D 1-1	Atherton.	4.530
4	5	a	Walsall	L 0-2		5.383
5	10	a	Darlington	D 2-2	Waterston,R.Smith.	2.222
6	17	h	Rochdale	W 1-0	Emery(pen).	4.094
7	24	h	Hull City	D 1-1	Beresford.	5.882
8	Oct 1	a	Barnsley	W 3-2	Parker,Beresford,Waterston.	6.333
9	8	h	Hartlepools Utd	W 4-1	Waterston(3),Beynon.	3.237
10	15	a	Halifax Town	D 0-0		6.238
11	22	a	Southport	L 0-1		4.289
12	29	h	Mansfield Town	D 2-2	Waterston(2).	5.767
13	Nov 5	a	Rotherham Utd	D 1-1	Flowers.	6.740
14	12	h	Accrington Stanley	D 2-2	Atherton(2).	3.780
15	19	a	New Brighton	D 4-4	Atherton,Hargreaves,Beynon,Waterston.	2.472
16	Dec 3	a	Barrow	L 0-3		2.801
17	17	a	York City	W 3-2	Parker,Beynon(2).	3.234
18	24	h	Crewe Alex	W 5-1	Beynon(2),Atherton,Waterston,Parker.	5.770
19	26	a	Tranmere Rovers	D 2-2	Beynon,Beresford.	7.813
20	27	a	Tranmere Rovers	L 2-3	Parker,Waterston.	5.179
21	31	h	Gateshead	W 3-1	Beynon(2),Waterston.	6.080
22	Jan 7	a	Stockport County	L 1-5	Waterston.	4.770
*	19	h	Chester	W 1-0	Beresford (*Abandoned - 40 mins)	1.574
23	21	h	Darlington	W 3-1	Beynon(2),Beresford.	3.770
24	28	a	Rochdale	W 3-2	Waterston(2),Armstrong O.G.	2.390
25	Feb 4	a	Hull City	L 1-6	Waterston.	7.985
26	11	h	Barnsley	W 3-1	Beynon(2),Waterston.	8.247
27	18	a	Hartlepools Utd	L 0-4		1.341
28	Mar 4	h	Southport	W 2-1	Emery(pen),R.Smith.	3.952
29	11	a	Mansfield Town	D 2-2	Waterston(2).	4.651
30	18	h	Rotherham Utd	W 1-0	Waterston.	6.565
31	25	a	Accrington Stanley	D 1-1	Waterston.	2.544
32	30	h	Halifax Town	W 5-1	Waterston(3),Parker,R.Smith.	3.118
33	Apr 1	h	New Brighton	W 2-0	Atherton,Burton.	4.287
34	8	a	Chester	L 0-2		5.669
35	14	h	Wrexham	D 1-1	Burton.	12.736
36	15	h	Barrow	D 1-1	Hargreaves.	4.546
37	17	a	Wrexham	L 0-3		8.225
38	22	a	Carlisle Utd	W 2-0	Kelly,Parker.	4.427
39	27	h	Chester	D 3-3	Burton,Kelly,Parker.	4.379
40	29	h	York City	W 3-2	Emery,Kelly,Renshaw.	4.275
41	May 4	a	Carlisle Utd	W 4-2	Atherton(2),Kelly,Emery.	3.324
42	6	a	Crewe Alex	L 0-4		2.003

Players: Walker, Hunter, Schofield, Galdwin, McHale, Emery, Kelly, Atherton, Waterson, R.Smith, Hargreaves, Beynon, Flowers, Parker, Tate, Beresford, Potter, Rodgers, Shaw, Martin, Critchley, Burton, Renshaw, Foster

App 20 37 42 29 31 38 10 30 36 20 8 23 23 28 22 26 2 2 3 6 4 11 3 8

Gls 5 4 9 24 3 2 13 1 7 5 6 2 2 3 1 + 1 og

HOME							
P	W	D	L	F	A	PTS	
21	13	8	0	52	26	34	

AWAY							
P	W	D	L	F	A	PTS	
21	4	6	11	25	53	14	

TOTAL							
P	W	D	L	F	A	PTS	
42	17	14	11	77	79	48	

F.C. Cup

	Date	V	Opponents	F-A	Scorers	Att
R1	Nov26	h	Gainsboro Trin	W 4-1	Beynon(2),Beresford,Atherton.	6.884
R2	Dec10	a	Northampton Town	W 1-0	Atherton.	10.008
R3	Jan14	h	Halifax Town	L 0-3		11.730

Cup App: R1 1 2 3 ... etc.

Season 1932/33

(Back): Wilkinson (Trainer), Hunter, France, Tate, Walker, Wilkins, Schofield, McLean (Trainer)
(Middle): Shaw, W.Smith, Flowers, Gladwin, Foster, McHale, Martin, Yeardley, Emery.
(Front): Beynon, Kelley, Renshaw, Atherton, Potter, Waterson, Beresford, R.Smith, Parker, Hargreaves.

Season 1933/34

(Back): MacLean, Hunter, Wilkins, Rodgers, Tate, Imrie, Schofield, Shaw, Wilkinson,
Capes, Morris, Menzies, Martin, Gladwin, Emery, Wass, Flowers, Smith, W.Smith, Ashforth, Green, McHale,
(3rd Row): Matthews, Kelly, Atherton, R.Smith, Dobb, Turner, Dixon, Tighe, Wayerson, Beresford.
(Front): Burton, Parker. (n.b. Renshaw absent)

League Division 3 North 1933-34

No	Date	V	Opponents	F-A	Scorers	Att
1	Aug26	h	New Brighton	W 1-0	Emery.	6,033
2	28	a	Stockport	L 3-4	R.Smith,Waterston,Emery.	6,428
3	Sep 2	a	Rotherham Utd	D 0-0		4,882
4	4	h	Stockport	L 0-2		4,933
5	9	h	Walsall	W 4-0	Emery pen.Dodd.Parker.Beresford.	4,374
6	16	a	York City	W 2-1	Parker(2).	6,708
7	23	h	Chester	W 3-1	R.Smith.Dodd(2).	6,057
8	30	a	Southport	D 0-0		2,355
9	Oct 7	a	Barrow	L 1-2	Dodd.	4,807
10	14	h	Carlisle Utd	W 2-1	Emery(pen).Beresford.	5,611
11	21	h	Wrexham	L 1-4	Beresford.	6,476
12	28	a	Hartlepools Utd	D 2-2	Dodd.Burton.	2,701
13	Nov 4	h	Mansfield Town	W 1-0	Burton.	5,786
14	11	a	Barnsley	D 2-2	Burton(2).	8,642
15	18	h	Tranmere Rovers	W 2-0	Waterston.Parker.	4,880
16	Dec 2	h	Chesterfield	L 1-3	Burton.	11,446
17	16	h	Gateshead	W 5-2	Dodd(4).Turner.	3,561
18	23	a	Darlington	L 0-4		2,444
19	25	h	Crewe Alex	W 4-0	Dodd(2).Beresford(2).	6,649
20	26	a	Crewe Alex	L 0-4		5,136
21	30	a	New Brighton	D 2-2	Turner.R.Smith.	2,033
22	Jan 3	a	Accrington Stanley	L 1-4	Beresford.	2,077
23	6	h	Rotherham Utd	W 2-1	Dodd(2).	5,038
24	13	a	Rochdale	W 2-0	Dodd(2).	3,186
25	20	a	Walsall	L 0-2		6,319
26	27	h	York City	W 3-1	Martin.Dodd.Burton.	4,879
27	Feb 3	a	Chester	L 1-3	Dodd.	4,012
28	10	a	Southport	W 3-0	Dodd(2).Emery.	4,882
29	17	h	Barrow	W 3-2	Turner.Burton.Dodd.	4,808
30	24	a	Carlisle Utd	W 1-0	Waterston.	3,074
31	Mar 3	a	Wrexham	D 1-1	Turner.	5,579
32	10	h	Hartlepools Utd	W 3-0	Gladwin.R.Smith.Turner.	3,770
33	17	a	Mansfield Town	D 1-1	Dodd.	4,524
34	24	h	Barnsley	D 4-4	Gladwin(2).Burton.Turner.	11,231
35	30	h	Halifax Town	W 3-0	Burton.	11,386
36	31	a	Tranmere Rovers	L 0-2		3,745
37	Apr 2	a	Halifax Town	W 1-0	Turner.	5,807
38	7	h	Rochdale	W 5-0	Turner(3).Dodd.Flowers.	4,873
39	14	a	Chesterfield	D 1-1	Mathews.	10,801
40	21	h	Accrington Stanley	W 5-1	R.Smith(2).Gladwin.Dodd.Turner.	5,005
41	28	a	Gateshead	W 4-2	Dodd.Gladwin.Burton.Turner.	552
42	May 5	h	Darlington	W 3-2	Flowers.Emery.Gladwin.	4,323

Appearances and Goals

Player	App	Gls
Renshaw	1	
Wright	1	
Turner	22	12
Tate	16	
Shaw	8	
Martin	2	1
Flowers	15	2
Atherton	1	
Green	20	
Schofield	21	
Mathews	8	1
Dodds	34	24
Kelly	3	
Parker	16	4
Beresford	29	6
Waterson	7	3
R.Smith	40	6
Burton	33	10
Emery	40	6
McHale	22	
Gladwin	34	6
Rodgers	21	
Hunter	26	
Imrie	42	

	P	W	D	L	F	A	PTS
HOME	21	17	1	3	58	23	35
AWAY	21	5	8	8	25	37	18
TOTAL	42	22	9	11	83	72	53

F.A. Cup

No	Date	V	Opponents	F-A	Scorers	Att
R1	Nov25	a	Barrow	L 2-4	Waterston,R.Smith.	4,929

League Division 3 North 1934-35

No	Date	V	Opponents	F-A	Scorers	Att
1	Aug25	a	Crewe Alex	D 1-1	Flowers.	5,793
2	28	a	Southport	W 2-1	Dodd,Seagrave O.G.	3,826
3	Sep 1	h	Stockport County	L 3-4	Dodd,R.Smith(2).	10,052
4	3	h	Southport	W 2-0	Gladwin,Turner.	4,743
5	8	a	Gateshead	D 0-0		5,943
6	15	h	Accrington Stanley	W 2-1	Dodd,Burton.	5,687
7	22	a	Darlington	D 1-1	Turner.	4,353
8	29	h	York City	W 4-1	R.Smith,Gladwin,Turner,Dodd.	5,041
9	Oct 6	a	New Brighton	D 1-1	Turner.	2,040
10	13	h	Chester	W 3-0	Burton,Turner,Dodd.	10,576
11	20	a	Walsall	W 2-0	Turner,Dodd.	6,062
12	27	h	Chesterfield	L 0-2		10,947
13	Nov 3	a	Mansfield Town	L 0-2		5,638
14	10	h	Barrow	W 2-0	Dodd,Gladwin.	6,390
15	17	a	Carlisle Utd	D 1-1	Dodd.	3,784
16	Dec 1	a	Lincoln City	W 2-0	Emery(pen),Bint.	4,871
17	15	a	Wrexham	W 2-1	Baines,Turner.	3,314
*	22	h	Halifax Town	2-1	Baines,Turner. (*Abandoned - 57mins)	3,452
18	25	a	Hartlepools Utd	L 1-2	Baines.	3,616
19	26	h	Hartlepools Utd	W 3-1	Emery,Turner,Flowers.	10,904
20	29	h	Crewe Alex	W 2-0	Baines,Turner.	7,479
21	Jan 5	a	Stockport County	W 2-3	Baines,Turner.	9,038
22	12	h	Rochdale	W 1-0	Turner.	5,895
23	19	h	Gateshead	W 5-0	Baines(3),Burton,Turner.	6,754
24	26	a	Accrington Stanley	W 5-1	Turner(3)Burton,Baines.	1,777
25	Feb 2	h	Darlington	W 2-0	Burton,Scott O.G.	9,143
26	9	a	York City	W 2-1	Baines(2).	6,517
27	16	h	New Brighton	W 7-1	Turner(5),Burton,Baines.	7,339
28	23	h	Chester	W 3-1	Baines(2),Burton.	9,685
29	Mar 2	h	Walsall	W 4-0	Baines(2),Burton,Turner.	12,743
30	9	a	Chesterfield	L 2-3	Burton,Baines.	14,284
31	16	h	Mansfield Town	W 2-1	Turner,Baines.	15,764
32	23	a	Barrow	L 1-2	Turner.	3,098
33	30	h	Carlisle Utd	W 3-0	Gladwin,Burton,Turner.	10,784
34	Apr 6	a	Rochdale	W 1-0	Baines.	7,154
35	11	h	Tranmere Rovers	W 2-0	Turner,R.Smith.	23,238
36	13	h	Lincoln City	L 1-3	Gladwin.	13,494
37	19	h	Rotherham Utd	L 3-5	Burton(2),Baines.	27,554
38	20	a	Tranmere Rovers	W 2-0	Baines,Dodd.	9,534
39	22	a	Rotherham Utd	W 3-1	Baines,Bint,Dodd.	20,357
40	27	h	Wrexham	W 2-1	Dodd,Rodgers.	13,342
41	May 2	h	Halifax Town	L 0-1		8,113
42	4	a	Halifax Town	L 0-1		8,653

HOME
P	W	D	L	F	A	PTS
21	16	0	5	53	21	37

AWAY
P	W	D	L	F	A	PTS
21	10	5	6	34	22	25

TOTAL
P	W	D	L	F	A	PTS
42	26	5	11	86	42	62

F.A. Cup
| R1 | Nov24 | h | Barrow | L 0-2 | | 8,983 |

(Back): McLean (Trainer), Shaw, Vaux, Tate, Imrie, Schofield, Rodgers, A.Wilkinson (Asst.Trainer).
(2nd Row): Tighe (Director), Menzies (Sec.Manager), Gladwin, Smith, Flowers, Fletcher, Hibbert (Chairman),
Lievesley, Green, Hall, Emery, Wass (Financial Sec.), Morris (Director).
(3rd Row): Caldwell, Allport, Smith, Harkin, Dodd, Rennie, Turner, Wright. (Front): Burton, Cave.

Season 1935/36

(Back):Tate(Asst.Trainer), Sharp, Shaw, Vaux, Wharton, Imrie, Jacobson, Rogers, McLean(Trainer).
(2nd Row): McLean, Flowers, Caldwell, Hibbert (Chairman), Green, Hall, Lievesley, Emery, Turner.
(3rd Row): Burton, Bott, Gladwin, Harkin, Baines, Dodd, R.Smith, Dutton, Turner.
(Front): Bint, Johnson.

League Division 2 1935-36

No	Date	V	Opponents	F-A	Scorers	Att
1	Aug 31	a	Blackpool	L 2-5	Burton(2).	20.649
2	Sep 2	h	Southampton	L 0-1		14.227
3	7	h	Charlton Ath	W 2-0	Baines.A.Turner.	13.263
4	9	a	Southampton	L 0-1		10.126
5	14	h	Bury	W 1-0	Baines.	12.625
6	16	h	Norwich City	W 3-0	Baines(2).A.Turner.	10.000
7	21	a	West Ham Utd	W 2-1	Burton.Baines.	26.431
8	28	h	Swansea Town	D 1-1	A.Turner.	16.914
9	Oct 5	a	Leicester City	L 0-6		16.672
10	12	h	Bradford PA	W 3-2	Dutton.Baines(2).	13.989
11	19	a	Hull City	W 3-2	Burton(3).	7.213
12	26	h	Barnsley	D 1-1	Dutton.	19.875
13	Nov 2	a	Plymouth Argyle	W 3-1	Baines.Bott.A.Turner.	16.734
14	9	h	Bradford City	W 2-1	A.Turner.McDermott O.G.	15.871
15	16	a	Newcastle Utd	L 1-2	Dutton.	26.845
16	23	h	Burnley	W 1-0	A.Turner.	12.999
17	30	a	Man Utd	D 0-0		23.569
18	Dec 7	h	Port Vale	W 2-0	Baines.Burton.	7.212
19	14	a	Fulham	W 3-1	Baines(2).Burton.	15.881
20	21	h	Tottenham Hotspur	W 2-1	Burton.A.Turner.	20.131
21	25	h	Nottm Forest	D 0-0		11.374
22	26	a	Nottm Forest	L 2-6	Baines(2).(1 pen)	16.897
23	28	h	Blackpool	L 0-3		12.373
24	Jan 1	a	Sheffield Utd	L 0-3		48.118
25	4	a	Charlton Ath	L 0-3		27.577
26	18	a	Bury	L 1-5	Burton.	6.176
27	25	h	West Ham Utd	L 0-2		10.551
28	Feb 1	a	Swansea Town	L 0-2		7.180
29	8	h	Leicester City	W 1-0	A.Turner.	15.479
30	22	h	Hull City	W 6-1	Baines(3).Johnston(2).A.Turner.	10.309
31	26	a	Bradford PA	L 1-3	Burton.	4.237
32	29	a	Port Vale	L 0-2		4.180
33	Mar 7	h	Newcastle Utd	D 2-2	Burton(2).	14.245
34	14	a	Bradford City	L 1-3	Baines.	7.709
35	21	h	Plymouth Argyle	L 1-2	Baines.	12.279
36	28	a	Burnley	D 1-1	Burton.	12.350
37	Apr 4	h	Man Utd	D 0-0		13.474
38	10	h	Sheffield Utd	D 0-0		28.560
39	11	a	Barnsley	L 1-2	Johnston.	13.323
40	18	h	Fulham	D 0-0		10.807
41	25	a	Tottenham Hotspur	L 1-3	Baines.	15.093
42	May 2	a	Norwich City	L 1-2	Burton.	12.464

App 37 37 37 24 11 24 37 37 39 38 40 3 22 19 4 3 5 14 8 8 5 4
Gls 1 2 15 19 9 3 1 3 10 4 5 6

+ 1 og

	P	W	D	L	F	A	PTS
HOME	21	10	7	4	28	17	27
AWAY	21	4	2	15	23	54	10
TOTAL	42	14	9	19	51	71	37

F.A. Cup

| R3 | Jan 11 | h | Nottm Forest | L 1-2 | A.Turner pen. | 19.409 |

League Division 2 1936-37

No	Date	V	Opponents	F-A	Scorers	Att
1	Aug 29	h	Coventry City	D 1-1	A.Turner.	15.495
2	31	h	Southampton	W 2-0	Dodd, R.Smith.	12.258
3	Sep 5	a	Plymouth Argyle	L 0-7		20.386
4	7	a	Southampton	L 0-1		9.329
5	12	h	Nottm Forest	L 0-2		11.201
6	19	a	Chesterfield	L 1-5	Baines.	15.174
7	26	h	Aston Villa	W 1-0	Gladwin.	23.426
8	Oct 3	a	Bradford City	D 0-0		12.191
9	10	h	Swansea Town	D 0-0		14.976
10	17	a	Bury	L 2-4	Baines(2).	6.739
11	24	h	Leicester City	D 0-0		14.434
12	31	h	West Ham Utd	L 0-1		12.814
13	Nov 7	h	Norwich City	L 1-2	Dutton.	11.235
14	14	a	Newcastle Utd	L 0-7		22.406
15	21	h	Bradford PA	L 1-3	Malam.	9.729
16	28	a	Barnsley	L 1-4	Malam.	11.707
17	Dec 5	h	Sheffield Utd	D 1-1	Gladwin.	14.752
18	12	a	Tottenham Hotspur	L 0-2		16.844
19	19	h	Blackpool	L 0-4		13.435
20	25	a	Burnley	L 0-3		21.295
21	26	a	Coventry City	D 1-1	Malam.	26.609
22	28	h	Burnley	W 2-0	Perry,A.Turner.	8.140
23	Jan 1	a	Blackburn Rovers	L 0-2		12.900
24	2	h	Plymouth Argyle	W 2-1	Perry(2).	12.883
25	9	a	Nottm Forest	L 1-2	Gladwin.	11.907
26	23	h	Chesterfield	L 0-4		5.419
27	30	a	Aston Villa	D 1-1	Perry.	13.252
28	Feb 6	h	Bradford City	D 1-1	Burton.	10.542
29	13	a	Swansea Town	W 1-0	Burton.	7.395
30	20	h	Bury	W 1-0	Perry.	10.725
31	27	a	Leicester City	L 1-7	Burton.	18.170
32	Mar 6	h	West Ham Utd	L 1-4	Perry.	8.079
33	13	a	Norwich City	L 1-2	A.Turner.	14.621
34	20	h	Newcastle Utd	L 1-2	Perry.	11.782
35	26	h	Fulham	W 2-1	Dutton.Burton.	14.014
36	27	a	Bradford PA	L 0-1		9.458
37	29	a	Fulham	L 0-1		16.050
38	Apr 3	h	Barnsley	L 0-1		12.716
39	10	a	Sheffield Utd	L 1-3	Dodd.	15.544
40	17	h	Tottenham Hotspur	D 1-1	Dutton(pen).	3.560
41	24	a	Blackpool	D 1-1	Dodd.	16.333
42	May 1	h	Blackburn Rovers	L 0-1		16.832

Appearances and Goals

Player	App	Gls
Sharp	3	
Wildsmith	34	
Dodsworth	28	
Bott	28	
Brooks	21	
Little	5	
Malam	38	3
Jacobson	6	
Button	14	3
C.Smith	18	
Perry	7	7
Bycroft	17	
Johnstone	9	
Keating	39	
Bradshaw	3	
L.Turner	22	
R.Smith	30	1
Dodd	25	3
A.Turner	27	3
Baines	16	3
Killourhy	21	
Burton	24	4
McMahon	6	
Hall	4	
Gladwin	4	3
Rodgers	8	
Shaw	4	
Imrie	1	

Summary

	P	W	D	L	F	A	PTS
HOME	21	6	9	6	18	29	18
AWAY	21	1	4	16	12	55	6
TOTAL	42	7	10	25	30	84	24

F.A. Cup

Round	Date	V	Opponent	Result	Att
R3	Jan 16	a	Chester	L 0-4	9.600

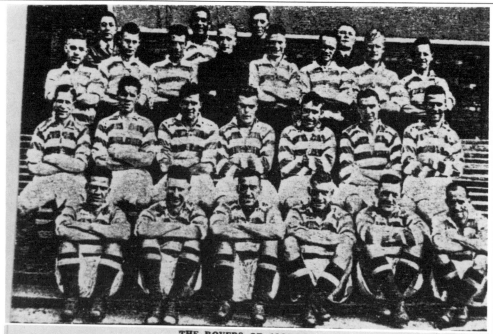

THE ROVERS OF 1936-37.

Back row—R. McLean (Trainer), Bycroft, Imrie, E. Wynter (Asst. Trainer).
Third row—Little, Payne, Dutton, Bradshaw, Bott (E.V.), Keating, Turner (L.), Sharp.
Second row—Burton, Rodgers, Kilhoury, Dodd, Gladwin, Dodsworth, Shaw.
Front row—Smith, McMahon, Hall, Turner (A.), Jacobson, Johnston.

DONCASTER ROVERS F.C., 1938-39.

Back Row: Shaw, McFarlane, Bycroft, Imrie, Smith, Walker.
Front Row: Little, Killourhy, Perry, Malam, Hiftle.

League Division 3 North 1937-38

No	Date	V	Opponents	F-A	Scorers	Att
1	Aug28	h	Bradford City	W 4-0	Pedwell(2).Malam.Perry.	13.144
2	Sep 1	a	York City	L 0-2		8.633
3	4	a	Southport	W 3-1	Burton.Perry.Killourhy.	7.014
4	11	h	Port Vale	W 3-2	Perry.Killourhy.Allen(pen).	11.538
5	13	a	Tranmere Rovers	L 0-2		7.228
6	18	h	Rochdale	W 5-0	Perry(3).Allen.Killourhy.	10.647
7	25	a	Rotherham Utd	D 2-2	Killourhy.Malam.	17.744
8	Oct 2	h	Chester	W 2-1	Perry(2).	16.391
9	9	a	Accrington Stanley	W 1-0	Perry.	6.542
10	16	a	Crewe Alex	D 0-0		4.786
11	23	h	Barrow	W 1-0	Malam.	9.378
12	30	a	Wrexham	L 0-2		4.019
13	Nov 6	h	Hartlepools Utd	D 3-3	Perry.Killourhy.C Smith.	10.538
14	13	a	Lincoln City	D 2-2	Burton.Dutton.	12.500
15	20	h	Hull City	W 2-1	Burton(2).	13.868
16	Dec 4	h	Gateshead	W 1-0	Dutton(pen).	10.359
17	18	h	Darlington	W 4-0	Killourhy(2).Malam.Dutton.	10.518
18	25	a	Carlisle Utd	D 2-2	Malam(2).	10.821
19	27	h	Carlisle Utd	L 1-3	Killourhy.	17.446
20	Jan 1	h	Bradford City	L 0-2		8.061
21	12	a	New Brighton	W 2-1	Perry.Malam.	2.460
22	15	h	Southport	W 3-0	Perry(2).Malam.	7.169
23	22	a	Port Vale	D 1-1	McFarlane.	7.153
24	29	a	Rochdale	W 5-4	McFarlane.Little.Killourhy.Malam(2).	5.069
25	Feb 1	a	Oldham Ath	L 1-2	Perry.	4.408
26	5	h	Rotherham Utd	L 0-1		20.618
27	12	a	Chester	L 0-4		5.188
28	19	a	Accrington Stanley	W 5-1	Killourhy(2).Perry(2).Morgan.	9.834
29	26	h	Crewe Alex	D 0-0		11.270
30	Mar 5	a	Barrow	D 1-1	Perry.	7.148
31	12	h	Wrexham	W 2-0	Bycroft.C Smith.	11.023
32	19	a	Hartlepools Utd	D 0-0		5.547
33	26	h	Lincoln City	W 3-0	Killourhy.Perry.Malam.	13.787
34	Apr 2	a	Hull City	L 1-2	Allen.	15.069
35	9	h	New Brighton	W 3-0	Perry.Malam.Allen.	9.169
36	15	h	Halifax Town	D 2-2	Killourhy.Perry.	19.356
37	16	a	Gateshead	W 3-2	Killourhy.Perry.Allen.	9.791
38	18	a	Halifax Town	W 1-0	Perry.	6.571
39	23	h	Oldham Ath	W 1-0	Perry.	18.274
40	30	a	Darlington	D 1-1	Burton.	6.914
41	May 2	h	York City	W 2-1	Burton.Allen(pen).	15.259
42	7	h	Tranmere Rovers	D 1-1	Perry.	14.249

Players (columns): Bradshaw, Shaw, Rodgers, McFarlane, Bycroft, R.Smith, Burton, Killourhy, Perry, Malam, Pedwell, Allen, Dutton, Vincent, Mitchel, Gold, Little, Morgan, Imrie, Sharp, Hiftle, Potts

App: 14 37 42 42 42 30 32 40 40 35 1 31 13 1 14 14 10 4 14 1 1 4

Gls: 2 1 2 6 14 24 12 2 6 3 — 1 14 14 10 4 14 1 1 4

	HOME							AWAY							TOTAL						
	P	W	D	L	F	A	PTS	P	W	D	L	F	A	PTS	P	W	D	L	F	A	PTS
	21	15	4	2	47	14	34	21	6	8	7	26	33	20	42	21	12	9	73	47	54

F.A. Cup

	Date		Opponents	F-A	Scorers	Att
R1	Nov27	h	Blyth Spartans	W 7-0	Killourhy(4).Morgan(2).Burton.	11.541
R2	Dec11	h	Guildford City	W 4-0	Burton.Dutton.Malam.Killourhy.	10.912
R3	Jan 8	h	Sheffield Utd	L 0-2		23.280

League Division 3 North 1938–39

No	Date	V	Opponents	F-A	Scorers	Att
1	Aug27	h	York City	W 1-0	Killourhy.	13.337
2	29	h	Southport	D 0-0		9.580
3	Sep 3	a	Wrexham	L 0-3		8.666
4	6	a	Rochdale	D 1-1	Perry.	4.469
5	10	h	Gateshead	L 2-3	Killourhy(2).	11.334
6	12	h	Rochdale	W 5-0	Little(2).Perry.Killourhy(2)(1pen).	5.530
7	17	a	Hartlepools Utd	W 3-1	Killourhy(2).Hiftle.	5.722
8	24	h	Darlington	W 4-1	Killourhy(2).Perry.Malam.	10.534
9	Oct 1	a	Carlisle Utd	W 3-2	Hiftle.Little.Malam.	5.258
10	8	h	Crewe Alex	L 1-2	Little.	13.555
11	15	a	Barnsley	D 1-1	Dell.	20.253
12	22	h	Oldham Ath	W 3-2	Dell(2).Malam.	15.094
13	29	a	Halifax Town	D 0-0		8.619
14	Nov 5	h	New Brighton	W 4-1	Dell(2).Perry.Little.	12.279
15	12	a	Barrow	D 4-4	Leyfield(2).Malam.Perry.	9.786
16	19	h	Chester	W 4-1	Little(3).Dell.	14.675
17	Dec 3	h	Hull City	W 1-0	Leyfield.	13.696
18	17	h	Stockport County	W 3-1	Dell.Malam.Leyfield.	8.217
19	24	a	York City	D 2-2	Malam.McFarlane.	6.562
20	26	h	Rotherham Utd	D 1-1	Perry.	17.868
21	27	a	Rotherham Utd	D 0-0		17.042
22	31	h	Wrexham	D 0-0		11.729
23	Jan14	a	Gateshead	L 0-2		2.460
24	26	h	Hartlepools Utd	W 3-1	Dell(2).Leyfield.	2.675
25	28	a	Darlington	W 2-1	Killourhy(2).	3.311
26	Feb 4	h	Carlisle Utd	W 1-0	Malam.	9.614
27	11	a	Crewe Alex	W 2-1	Little.Killourhy.	4.046
28	18	h	Barnsley	L 1-3	Malam.	34.046
29	25	a	Oldham Ath	D 0-0		6.010
30	Mar 4	h	Halifax Town	D 0-0		6.552
31	11	h	New Brighton	W 6-3	Perry(3).Killourhy.Malam(2)(1pen).	2.925
32	15	a	Bradford City	L 1-2	Killourhy.	3.472
33	18	h	Barrow	D 1-1	Hiftle.	6.843
34	25	a	Chester	W 4-0	Little.Owens.Perry.Leyfield.	4.982
35	Apr 7	a	Accrington Stanley	W 7-1	Owens(3).Perry(2).Dell(2).	12.257
36	8	a	Hull City	D 0-0		8.108
37	10	a	Accrington Stanley	D 0-0		2.819
38	15	h	Lincoln City	W 4-1	Owens.Perry.Dell.Leyfield.	6.585
39	20	h	Bradford City	L 1-2	Owens.	7.323
40	22	h	Stockport County	W 2-1	Owens.Leyfield.	4.857
41	29	a	Southport	W 4-0	Mitchell.McFarlane.Leyfield(2).	5.787
42	May 6	a	Lincoln City	W 5-2	Owens.Perry.Malam.Leyfield.Kirkaldie.	3.082

HOME

P	W	D	L	F	A	PTS
21	12	5	4	47	21	29

AWAY

P	W	D	L	F	A	PTS
21	9	9	3	40	26	27

TOTAL

P	W	D	L	F	A	PTS
42	21	14	7	87	47	56

F.A. Cup

Rd	Date	V	Opponents	F-A	Scorers	Att
R1	Nov26	h	New Brighton	W 4-2	Dell(2).Leyfield.Little.	11.006
R2	Dec10	a	Gainsboro Trin	W 1-0	Dell.	7.073
R3	Jan10	a	Southport	D 1-1	Potts.	11.145
R3R	12	h	Southport	W 2-1	Dell.Malam.	10.186
R4	21	a	Everton	L 0-8		41.115

Appearances (App) and Goals (Gls)

Player	App	Gls
R.Smith	11	
Brooks	1	
Morgan	2	
Little	32	10
Walker	37	
Dell	27	12
Kirkaldie	2	1
Owens	11	8
Hiftle	9	3
Shaw	16	
Leyfield	28	11
Imrie	20	
Barraclough	8	
Malam	36	11
Perry	33	14
Killourhy	17	14
Burton	4	
Mitchell	39	1
Bycroft	42	
McFarlane	34	2
Rodgers	8	
Potts	23	
Gold	22	

League Division 3 North 1939-40

No	Date	V	Opponents	F-A	Scorers	Att	1	2	3	4	5	6	7	8	9	10	11
1	Aug26	h	Rochdale	W 2-0	Leyfield(2).	10.453	GOLD	SHAW	A WALKER	MITCHELL	BYCROFT	MCFARLANE	KIRKALDIE	DELL	PERRY	MALAM	LEYFIELD
2	30	a	Chester	L 0-1		6.463	GOLD	SHAW	A WALKER	PHYPERS	BYCROFT	MCFARLANE	KIRKALDIE	DELL	PERRY	MALAM	LEYFIELD
3	Sep 2	a	New Brighton	L 2-4	Perry(2).	3.441	GOLD	SHAW	A WALKER	PHYPERS	BYCROFT	MCFARLANE	KIRKALDIE	OWENS	PERRY	MALAM	LEYFIELD

	P	W	D	L	F	A	PTS
HOME	1	1	0	0	2	0	2
AWAY	2	0	0	2	2	5	0
TOTAL	3	1	0	2	4	5	2

The 3rd division north was suspended due to the outbreak of the war:

East Midlands War League:

No	Date	V	Opponents	F-A	Scorers	Att	1	2	3	4	5	6	7	8	9	10	11
4	Oct21	h	Sheffield Wed	D 2-2	Killourhy(2)(1pen).	6.006	GOLD	SHAW	A WALKER	STIRLAND	BYCROFT	MITCHELL	BURTON	KILLOURHY	DODD	BERESFORD	BURBANKS
5	28	a	Nottm Forest	D 1-1	Barraclough.	3.030	GOLD	SHAW	A WALKER	STIRLAND	BYCROFT	MITCHELL	BARRACLOUGH	KILLOURHY	PERRY	BERESFORD	BURBANKS
6	Nov11	h	Notts County	W 2-1	Mitchell.Killourhy pen.	5.479	GOLD	SHAW	A WALKER	STIRLAND	BYCROFT	MITCHELL	BARRACLOUGH	KILLOURHY	OWENS	BERESFORD	BURBANKS
7	18	a	Mansfield Town	L 1-2	Burbanks.	2.500	GOLD	SHAW	A WALKER	STIRLAND	BYCROFT	MITCHELL	BURTON	KILLOURHY	OWENS	BERESFORD	BURBANKS
8	25	h	Chesterfield	L 2-4	Burbanks(2).	3.907	GOLD	SHAW	A WALKER	STIRLAND	BYCROFT	MITCHELL	BARRACLOUGH	KILLOURHY	OWENS	BERESFORD	BURBANKS
9	Dec 9	h	Barnsley	D 1-1	Owens.	3.866	GOLD	SHAW	A WALKER	STIRLAND	BYCROFT	MITCHELL	BARRACLOUGH	KILLOURHY	OWENS	BERESFORD	BAR'CLOUGH
10	Jan 1	h	Sheffield Utd	L 1-2	Barraclough.	2.723	GOLD	SHAW	A WALKER	PHYPERS	BYCROFT	MITCHELL	BARRACLOUGH	KILLOURHY	OWENS	BERESFORD	BURBANKS
11	6	h	Grimsby Town	W 2-0	Owens(2).	2.215	GOLD	SHAW	A WALKER	PHYPERS	BYCROFT	MITCHELL	BARRACLOUGH	KILLOURHY	OWENS	BERESFORD	BURTON
12	24	h	Nottm Forrest	W 4-3	B'clough(2).B'ford.Burb'ks.	2.849	GOLD	POTTS	A WALKER	PHYPERS	BYCROFT	MITCHELL	BARRACLOUGH	KILLOURHY	DEAKIN	BERESFORD	BURTON
13	Mar 2	h	Lincoln City	W 3-1	Barraclough(2).Killourhy.	2.289	GOLD	PHYPERS	A WALKER	STIRLAND	BYCROFT	PHYPERS	BARRACLOUGH	KILLOURHY	DEAKIN	BERESFORD	BURBANKS
14	9	a	Notts County	L 0-4		3.000	GOLD	SHAW	A WALKER	STIRLAND	VINCENT	MITCHELL	BARRACLOUGH	KILLOURHY	DEAKIN	BERESFORD	BURBANKS
15	16	h	Mansfield Town	W 4-2	Bycroft(4).	2.664	GOLD	SHAW	A WALKER	STIRLAND	BYCROFT	MITCHELL	BARRACLOUGH	RAYNOR	LIEVESLEY	BERESFORD	BURBANKS
16	23	a	Chesterfield	L 1-3	Beresford.	6.000	GOLD	POTTS	A WALKER	STIRLAND	BYCROFT	MITCHELL	BARRACLOUGH	RAYNOR	MILLERSHIP	BERESFORD	BURBANKS
17	26	a	Rotherham Utd	L 1-3	Beresford.	1.000	GOLD	SHAW	A WALKER	STIRLAND	BYCROFT	THOMPSON	BARRACLOUGH	RAYNOR	G.HENRY	BERESFORD	BURBANKS
18	Apr 6	a	Barnsley	D 1-1	Henry.	4.000	GOLD	SHAW	A WALKER	LIEVESLEY	BYCROFT	MITCHELL	BARRACLOUGH	G.HENRY	KILOURHY	BERESFORD	BURBANKS
19	20	a	Lincoln City	L 2-3	Henry.Barraclough.	1.000	GOLD	SHAW	A WALKER	PHYPERS	BYCROFT	STIRLAND	BARRACLOUGH	KILLOURHY	G.HENRY	BERESFORD	SINCLAIR
20	May 4	a	Sheffield Wed	W 3-1	Henry.Killourhy.Sinclair.	8.000	GOLD	SHAW	A WALKER	PHYPERS	BYCROFT	MITCHELL	BARRACLOUGH	G.HENRY	KILOURHY	BERESFORD	SINCLAIR
21	11	h	Rotherham Utd	W 2-1	Killourhy(2).	1.341	GOLD	SHAW	A WALKER	STIRLAND	BYCROFT	MITCHELL	BARRACLOUGH	KILLOURHY	JORDAN	BERESFORD	BURBANKS
22	25	h	Sheffield Utd	L 0-3		1.676	GOLD	SHAW	A WALKER	STIRLAND	PHYPERS	MITCHELL	BARRACLOUGH	KILLOURHY	JORDAN	BERESFORD	BURBANKS
23	Jun 1	a	Grimsby Town	L 4-7	Mit'l.Jor'n.Kil'hy(2)(1p).	500	GOLD	SHAW	A WALKER	CASSON	PHYPERS	MITCHELL	HEAVEY	KILLOURHY	JORDAN	BERESFORD	BURBANKS

	P	W	D	L	F	A	PTS	POS
HOME	11	6	2	3	24	20	14	
AWAY	9	1	2	6	13	25	4	
TOTAL	20	7	4	9	37	45	18	6th

League Cup:

No	Date	V	Opponents	F-A	Scorers	Att	1	2	3	4	5	6	7	8	9	10	11
R1	Apr13	h	Rotherham Utd	D 0-0		4.626	GOLD	SHAW	A WALKER	STIRLAND	S WALKER	MITCHELL	KIRKALDIE	RAYNER	BYCROFT	BERESFORD	BARRACLOUGH
R1R	15	a	Rotherham Utd	L 0-1 aet.		1.914	GOLD	SHAW	A WALKER	S WALKER	BYCROFT	MITCHELL	KIRKALDIE	RAYNER	JOHNSON	BERESFORD	BARRACLOUGH

War League North 1940-41

No	Date	V	Opponents	F-A	Scorers	Att	1	2	3	4	5	6	7	8	9	10	11
1	Aug31	h	Barnsley	W 2-1	Killourhy,Johnson.	3,104	GOLD	FORDE	WALKER	LIEVESLEY	BYCROFT	MITCHELL	BARR'GH	KILLOURHY	JOHNSON	MORALEE	SINCLAIR
2	Sep 7	a	Sheffield Utd	D 1-1	Bodle.	3,225	GOLD	FORDE	WALKER	LIEVESLEY	BYCROFT	MITCHELL	BARR'GH	KILLOURHY	JOHNSON	BODLE	BURTON
3	14	h	Bradford City	W 2-1	Bodle,Killourhy pen.	2,787	GOLD	FORDE	WALKER	STIRLAND	BYCROFT	MITCHELL	BARR'GH	KILLOURHY	JOHNSON	BODLE	BURTON
4	21	a	Barnsley	L 2-6	Bodle,Killourhy.	2,500	GOLD	FORDE	WALKER	STIRLAND	BYCROFT	MITCHELL	BARR'GH	KILLOURHY	JOHNSON	BODLE	BURTON
5	28	h	Sheffield Utd	W 1-0	Johnson	3,108	GOLD	FORDE	WALKER	STIRLAND	BYCROFT	MITCHELL	BURTON	BODLE	JOHNSON	KILL'Y	BRAY
6	Oct 5	a	Bradford City	L 1-5	Henry.	1,500	GOLD	FORDE	WALKER	STIRLAND	BYCROFT	MITCHELL	HENRY	KILLOURHY	JOHNSON	BODLE	BURTON
7	12	h	Hull City	W 4-2	Henry(2),Killourhy,Bodle.	2,413	GOLD	FORDE	WALKER	STIRLAND	BYCROFT	MITCHELL	JOHNSON	KILLOURHY	HENRY	BODLE	BURTON
8	19	a	Grimsby Town	L 2-3	Henry(2).	2,000	GOLD	FORDE	WOOLDRIDGE	STIRLAND	BYCROFT	MITCHELL	JOHNSON	KILLOURHY	HENRY	BODLE	BURTON
9	26	h	Huddersfield Town	D 1-1	Johnson.	2,500	GOLD	WALKER	WOOLDRIDGE	STIRLAND	BYCROFT	MITCHELL	BARR'GH	KILLOURHY	HENRY	JOHNSON	BURTON
10	Nov 2	h	Man City	L 0-4		2,184	GOLD	WALKER	WOOLDRIDGE	COPPING	BYCROFT	MITCHELL	JOHNSON	NIGHT'E	HENRY	BODLE	BURTON
11	9	h	Sheffield Wed	D 4-4	Henry(2),Night'e,Mitchell.	1,400	GOLD	WALKER	JONES	COPPING	BYCROFT	STIRLAND	BURTON	NIGHT'E	HENRY	BODLE	ORAM
12	16	a	Hull City	L 4-5	Henry(2),Bodle(2).	1,600	GOLD	WALKER	WOOLDRIDGE	MITCHELL	BYCROFT	COPPING	BURTON	NIGHT'E	HENRY	BODLE	ORAM
13	23	h	Grimsby Town	W 6-0	Burton(2),Oram(2),Henry(2)(1pen).	2,248	MAYB'Y	WALKER	MITCHELL	PHYPERS	BYCROFT	STIRLAND	BURTON	NIGHT'E	HENRY	BODLE	ORAM
14	30	a	Huddersfield Town	W 2-1	Bodle(2).	1,422	MAYB'Y	WALKER	MITCHELL	COPPING	BYCROFT	PHYPERS	BURTON	NIGHT'E	HENRY	BODLE	ORAM
15	Dec 7	a	Middlesbrough	D 2-2	Oram,Night'e.	1,000	MAYB'Y	MITC'L	WOOLDRIDGE	PHYPERS	BYCROFT	STIRLAND	BURTON	NIGHT'E	HENRY	BODLE	ORAM
16	14	a	York City	W 4-1	Burton(2),Henry,Night'e.	1,000	MAYB'Y	WALKER	MITCHELL	COPPING	BYCROFT	PHYPERS	BURTON	NIGHT'E	HENRY	BODLE	ORAM
17	21	h	York City	W 9-2	Henry(4),Bodle(2),Shaw(2),Night'e.	2,075	MAYB'Y	WALKER	MITCHELL	COPPING	BYCROFT	PHYPERS	BURTON	NIGHT'E	HENRY	BODLE	SHAW
18	25	h	Lincoln City	D 0-0		2,822	MAYB'Y	SHAW	MITCHELL	COPPING	BYCROFT	PHYPERS	BURTON	NIGHT'E	HENRY	BODLE	SINCLAIR
19	25	a	Lincoln City	L 1-3	Henry.	2,855	MAYB'Y	WALKER	MITCHELL	STIRLAND	BYCROFT	PHYPERS	BURTON	NIGHT'E	HENRY	BODLE	COPPING
20	28	h	Middlesbrough	W 5-0	Henry(2),Bodle,Night'e,Burbanks.	3,313	MAYB'Y	WALKER	MITCHELL	COPPING	BYCROFT	PHYPERS	BURTON	NIGHT'E	HENRY	BODLE	BURBANKS
21	Jan11	h	Sheff Wed	W 4-0	Bodle(3),Jordan.	3,000	MAYB'Y	WALKER	MITCHELL	STIRLAND	BYCROFT	PHYPERS	BURTON	NIGHT'E	JORDAN	BODLE	ORAM
22	18	h	Sheff Utd	W 5-1	Bodle92),Jordan,Night'e,Sinclair.	1,592	MAYB'Y	WALKER	WOOLDRIDGE	MITCHELL	BYCROFT	PHYPERS	BURTON	NIGHT'E	JORDAN	BODLE	SINCLAIR
23	Feb 8	h	Rotherham Utd	W 3-2	Bodle,Jordan,Sinclair.	2,101	MAYB'Y	WALKER	WOOLDRIDGE	MITCHELL	BYCROFT	PHYPERS	BURTON	NIGHT'E	JORDAN	BODLE	SINCLAIR
24	Mar 8	a	Rotherham Utd	W 2-1	Bodle(2).	600	MAYB'Y	WALKER	WOOLDRIDGE	STIRLAND	BYCROFT	PHYPERS	BURTON	NIGHT'E	ASQUITH	BODLE	MORRIS
25	15	a	Chesterfield	L 0-5		1,400	MAYB'Y	WALKER	WOOLDRIDGE	MORRIS	BYCROFT	MILLS	BURTON	NIGHT'E	ASQUITH	BODLE	SINCLAIR
26	22	h	Chesterfield	D 0-0		1,471	MAYB'Y	WALKER	WOOLDRIDGE	STIRLAND	BYCROFT	CARTE	BURTON	NIGHT'E	ASQUITH	BODLE	SINCLAIR
27	29	h	Rotherham Utd	W 3-2	Bodle pen,Jordan,Burton.	1,743	MAYB'Y	WALKER	WOOLDRIDGE	STIRLAND	BYCROFT	LIEVESLEY	BURTON	GLEDHILL	JORDAN	BODLE	SINCLAIR
28	Apr 5	h	Leeds Utd	L 1-4	Jordan.	4,000	MAYB'Y	WALKER	WOOLDRIDGE	STIRLAND	BYCROFT	LIEVESLEY	BURTON	GLEDHILL	JORDAN	BODLE	SINCLAIR
29	12	a	Halifax Town	L 1-8	Bodle.	2,000	MAYB'Y	SHAW	WALKER	STIRLAND	BYCROFT	WOOLDRIDGE	SINC'R	NIGHT'E	JORDAN	BODLE	MacLEAN
30	26	h	Halifax Town	D 2-2	Bycroft,Bodle.	1,164	MAYB'Y	WALKER	WOOLDRIDGE	JONES	MEENS	STIRLAND	BURTON	NIGHT'E	BYCROFT	BODLE	BARR'GH
31	May 3	h	Mansfield Town	W 2-1	Bodle pen,Sinclair.	1,241	MAYB'Y	WALKER	WOOLDRIDGE	STIRLAND	BYCROFT	MEENS	COUL'N	NIGHT'E	JORDAN	BODLE	SINCLAIR
32	17	a	Mansfield Town	L 1-6	Jones.	500	MAYB'Y	WALKER	WOOLDRIDGE	BECKWITH	VINCENT	LIEVESLEY	COUL'N	NIGHT'E	JONES	BODLE	SINCLAIR

War Cup:

No	Date	V	Opponents	F-A	Scorers	Att	1	2	3	4	5	6	7	8	9	10	11
33	Feb15	a	Grimsby Town	L 0-1		2,786	MAYB'Y	WALKER	WOOLDRIDGE	PHYPERS	BYCROFT	MITCHELL	BURTON	NIGHT'E	JORDAN	BODLE	SINCLAIR
34	Mar 1	h	Grimsby Town	D 0-0		3,608	MAYB'Y	WALKER	WOOLDRIDGE	STIRLAND	BYCROFT	PHYPERS	BURTON	NIGHT'E	JORDAN	BODLE	ORAM

HOME							AWAY							TOTAL							
P	W	D	L	F	A	PTS	P	W	D	L	F	A	PTS	P	W	D	L	F	A	PTS	POS
19	12	5	2	54	27	23	13	3	2	8	23	47	8	32	15	7	10	77	74	31	19th

Abbreviated names (where used): BARR'GH = BARRACLOUGH. COUL'N = COULSTON. KILL'Y = KILLOURHY. MAYB'Y = MAYBERRY. NIGHT'E = NIGHTINGALE.

War League North 1941-42

1st Championship

No	Date	V	Opponents	F-A	Scorers	Att	1	2	3	4	5	6	7	8	9	10	11
1	Aug30	a	Mansfield Town	L 1-4	Jordan.	2,000	MAYBERRY	WALKER A	WOOL'E	STIRLAND	MEENS	MITT'LL	BURTON	NIGHT'E	JORDAN	BODLE	SINCLAIR
2	Sep 6	h	Mansfield Town	W 4-1	Rogers(2),Nightingale,Bodle.	1,981	MAYBERRY	WALKER A	WOOL'E	STIRLAND	MEENS	MITT'LL	BURTON	NIGHT'E	KILLOURHY	BODLE	ROGERS
3	13	h	Chesterfield	W 3-1	Burton,Bodle,Nightingale.	2,533	MAYBERRY	WALKER A	WOOL'E	STIRLAND	MEENS	MITT'LL	BURTON	NIGHT'E	BYCROFT	BODLE	ROGERS
4	20	a	Chesterfield	L 1-3	Owens.	1,493	MAYBERRY	WALKER A	WOOL'E	LIEVESLEY	MEENS	MITT'LL	BURTON	NIGHT'E	OWENS	BODLE	FULLER
5	27	a	Barnsley	W 4-2	Bodle(3),Owens.	3,000	DANIELS	WALKER A	WOOL'E	STIRLAND	MEENS	LIEVESLEY	BURTON	NIGHT'E	OWENS	BODLE	FULLER
6	Oct 4	h	Barnsley	D 1-1	Owens.	3,678	DANIELS	WALKER A	WOOL'E	STIRLAND	BYCROFT	MITT'LL	BURTON	NIGHT'E	OWENS	BODLE	FULLER
7	11	h	Sheffield Wed	D 2-2	Burton,Nightingale.	2,554	DANIELS	WALKER A	WOOL'E	NIGHT'E	MITT'LL	HARSTON	BURTON	OWENS	DODD	BODLE	ROGERS
8	18	a	Sheffield Wed	L 2-5	Bodle,Burton.	940	GOLD	WALKER A	WOOL'E	HARSTON	MITT'LL	BROUGH	BURTON	NIGHT'E	OWENS	BODLE	ROGERS
9	25	a	Rotherham Utd	L 1-2	Fuller.	1,600	GOLD	WALKER A	WOOL'E	HARSTON	BYCROFT	BROUGH	BURTON	NIGHT'E	JORDAN	BODLE	FULLER
10	Nov 1	h	Rotherham Utd	W 5-1	Fuller(3),Bodle,Burton.	1,561	GIBSON	WALKER A	WOOL'E	HARSTON	MITT'LL	MITT'LL	BURTON	NIGHT'E	JORDAN	BODLE	FULLER
11	8	h	Grimsby Town	L 1-3	Bodle.	2,515	GIBSON	WALKER A	WOOL'E	HARSTON	BYCROFT	BROUGH	BURTON	NIGHT'E	MARSHALL	BODLE	ORAM
12	15	a	Grimsby Town	L 0-2		3,400	GIBSON	WALKER A	WOOL'E	HARSTON	BYCROFT	BROUGH	BURTON	NIGHT'E	JOHNSON	BODLE	FULLER
13	22	a	Lincoln City	L 1-3	Jordan.	3,844	GIBSON	SWALLOW	WOOL'E	STIRLAND	MITT'LL	BROUGH	BURTON	NIGHT'E	JORDAN	BODLE	FULLER
14	29	h	Lincoln City	L 1-3	Nightingale.		GIBSON	SWALLOW	SWALLOW	LIEVESLEY	BAILEY	BROUGH	BURTON	NIGHT'E	JORDAN	LITTLE	BARRA'GH
15	Dec 6	a	Gateshead	L 2-6	Hubbard,Nightingale pen.	3,000	FERGUSON	HEAD	WOOL'E	JONES G	BYCROFT	BROUGH	BURTON	NIGHT'E	HUBBARD	KILL'Y	BARRA'GH
16	13	h	Gateshead	W 5-1	Hubbard(2),Bodle,Burton,Barr'gh	1,783	FERGUSON	HEAD	WALKER A	BAILEY	BYCROFT	BROUGH	BURTON	NIGHT'E	HUBBARD	BODLE	BARRA'GH
17	20	h	Sheffield Utd	W 3-1	Bodle,Hubbard,Barber.	2,057	FERGUSON	HEAD	WALKER A	STIRLAND	BAILEY	BROUGH	BURTON	NIGHT'E	HUBBARD	BODLE	BARBER
18	25	a	Sheffield Utd	L 2-5	Bailey,Bodle.	9,234	POXTON	HEAD	WALKER A	MITT'LL	BAILEY	BROUGH	BURTON	NIGHT'E	HUBBARD	BODLE	BARBER

	P	W	D	L	F	A	PTS	POS
HOME	9	5	2	2	25	14	12	
AWAY	9	1	0	8	14	32	2	
TOTAL	18	6	2	10	39	46	14	27th

League Cup Qualifying Competition:

No	Date	V	Opponents	F-A	Scorers	Att	1	2	3	4	5	6	7	8	9	10	11
1	Dec27	a	Lincoln City	L 3-9	Nightingale,Bodle,Burton.	4,378	POXTON	HEAD	WALKER A	MITT'LL	BAILEY	LIEVESLEY	BURTON	NIGHT'E	HUBBARD	BODLE	BARBER
2	Jan 3	a	Huddersfield Town	L 1-3	Hubbard.	1,337	FERGUSON	BYCROFT	WOOL'E	STIRLAND	BAILEY	BROUGH	BURTON	WALKER C	HUBBARD	BODLE	BARRA'GH
3	10	h	Halifax Town	W 2-1	Bodle,Hubbard.	2,208	FERGUSON	MITT'LL	MITT'LL	GLADWIN	BYCROFT	BAILEY	BARBER	NIGHT'E	HUBBARD	BODLE	BURTON
4	Feb21	h	Grimsby Town	L 1-2	Mitchell pen.	871	FERGUSON	HEAD	WALKER A	NIGHT'E	MITT'LL	BROUGH	BURTON	HUBBARD	WADSWORTH	BERESFORD	BARBER
5	28	h	Huddersfield Town	L 1-6	Killourhy.	2,094	NICHOLLS	HEAD	WALKER A	JONES G	MITT'LL	BROUGH	KIRK'E	HUBBARD	HUBBARD	JORDAN	SINCLAIR
6	Mar14	h	Leeds Utd	L 1-6	Killourhy.	3,000	FERGUSON	JONES S	WOOL'E	HINDMARSH	MITT'LL	JONES G	JORDAN	KILLOURHY	HUBBARD	BROUGH	BURTON
7	21	a	Lincoln City	L 0-2		1,577	FERGUSON	HEAD	WALKER A	HINDMARSH	MITT'LL	BROUGH	GRAINGER	NIGHT'E	HUBBARD	JORDAN	BURTON
8	28	h	Leeds Utd	W 1-0	Brough.	1,225	FERGUSON	VAUX	WOOL'E	MITT'LL	MITT'LL	BROUGH	BURTON	JORDAN	JORDAN	LITTLE	SINCLAIR

	P	W	D	L	F	A	PTS	POS
HOME	5	2	0	3	5	9	4	
AWAY	4	0	0	4	5	21	0	
TOTAL	9	2	0	7	10	30	4	47th

Sheffield County Cup

No	Date	V	Opponents	F-A	Att	1	2	3	4	5	6	7	8	9	10	11
1	Apr18	a	Rotherham Utd	L 0-3	2,000	FERGUSON	SHAW W	MITT'LL	HINDMARSH	BYCROFT	BROUGH	BURTON	DRURY	HUBBARD	JORDAN	SINCLAIR

Abbreviated names (where used): BARR'GH = BARRACLOUGH. KILL'Y = KILLOURHY. KIRK'E = KIRKALDIE. MITT'LL = MITCHELL. NIGHT'E = NIGHTINGALE. WOOL'E = WOOLDRIDGE.

NOTE: A second championship was created by taking the League Cup Qualifying Competitions,and the Sheffield County Cup games.Thus the results counting as a second championship.

League Division North 1942-43

1st Championship:

No	Date	V	Opponents	F-A	Scorers	Att	1	2	3	4	5	6	7	8	9	10	11
1	Aug29 h	Sheffield Wed	L 1-3	Hubbard.	2.689	FERGUSON	HEAD	WALKER A	ALSFORD	BYCROFT	BROUGH	BURTON	DRURY	HUBBARD	NIGHT S	SINCLAIR
2	Sep 5 a	Sheffield Wed	L 2-3	Sutherland(2).	3.500	FERGUSON	WALKER	WOOL'E	ALSFORD	BYCROFT	ATTER	HUBBARD	DRURY	SUTHERLAND	BODLE	SINCLAIR
3	12 a	Chesterfield	L 1-3	Drury.		POXTON	SWALLOW	WALKER A	ALSFORD	BYCROFT	ATTER	HUBBARD	DRURY	SUTHERLAND	BODLE	SINCLAIR
4	19 h	Chesterfield	W 3-1	Hubbard pen,Suth'land,Drury.	2.191	FERGUSON	WALKER	WOOL'E	STIRLAND	ATTER	ATTWELL	HUBBARD	LEEMAN	SUTHERLAND	DRURY	SINCLAIR
5	26 h	Lincoln City	L 0-2		2.570	POXTON	WALKER	WOOL'E	STIRLAND	BYCROFT	ATTER	HUBBARD	LEEMAN	SUTHERLAND	DRURY	SINCLAIR
6	Oct 3 a	Lincoln City	L 0-3		3.000	FERGUSON	WALKER	WOOL'E	STIRLAND	ATTER	BROUGH	HUBBARD	DRURY	SOMERFIELD	BODLE	SINCLAIR
7	10 a	Leeds Utd	L 0-6		3.000	FERGUSON	WALKER	WOOL'E	STIRLAND	ATTER	ATTWELL	HUBBARD	DRURY	SUTHERLAND	BODLE	SINCLAIR
8	17 h	Leeds Utd	D 2-2	Hubbard(2).	2.000	POXTON	WALKER	WOOL'E	STIRLAND	BYCROFT	BROUGH	GRAINGER	DRURY	HUBBARD	BODLE	SINCLAIR
9	24 h	Sheffield Utd	L 2-4	Drury,Bodle.	2.300	FERGUSON	SHAW	WALKER A	GREGORY	BYCROFT	BROUGH	HUBBARD	DRURY	BODLE	SHERWOOD	SINCLAIR
10	31 a	Sheffield Utd	D 2-2	Walker,Sinclair.	6.400	POXTON	LAKING	BANNER	STIRLAND	BYCROFT	ATTWELL	WALKER C H	DRURY	SOMERFIELD	WOOL'E	SINCLAIR
11	Nov 7 h	Halifax Town	L 1-2	Hubbard.	2.451	FERGUSON	LAKING	BANNER	GREGORY	ATTER	ATTWELL	LEEMAN	NIGHT S	HUBBARD	SHERWOOD	SINCLAIR
12	14 a	Halifax Town	W 2-1	Hubbard(2).	4.000	FERGUSON	LAKING	WOOL'E	WILSON	ATTER	BROUGH	LEEMAN	KILLOURHY	HUBBARD	WALKER CH	SINCLAIR
13	21 h	Bradford City	L 0-2		1.829	FERGUSON	LAKING	McDER.	WOOL'E	BYCROFT	ATTER	GRAINGER	LEEMAN	HUBBARD	BROUGH	MITCHELL
14	28 a	Bradford City	W 4-1	Harkin(2),Hubbard(2).	2.000	FERGUSON	LAKING	WOOL'E	STIRLAND	ATTER	GLADWIN	BARRA	HARKIN	HUBBARD	BODLE	MITCHELL
15	Dec 5 a	Barnsley	D 1-1	Hubbard.	1.590	POXTON	LAKING	WOOL'E	STIRLAND	ATTER	MITCH	WALKER C H	HARKIN	HUBBARD	BODLE	SINCLAIR
16	12 h	Barnsley	L 0-2		2.996	POXTON	LAKING	WOOL'E	NIGHT	ATTER	MITCH	BYCROFT	HARKIN	HUBBARD	BODLE	NIGHT A
17	19 a	Grimsby Town	L 2-3	Bodle(2).	1.400	FERGUSON	LAKING	WOOL'E	STIRLAND	ATTER	BROUGH	SINCLAIR	HARKIN	HUBBARD	BODLE	THOROGOOD

	P	W	D	L	F	A	PTS
HOME	8	1	6	1	18	3	
AWAY	9	2	2	5	12	23	6
TOTAL	17	3	3	11	23	41	9	POS 47th

2nd Championship:

No	Date	V	Opponents	F-A	Scorers	Att	1	2	3	4	5	6	7	8	9	10	11
28	Mar 6 h	Rotherham Utd	D 1-1	Bodle.	2.040	POXTON	SWALLOW	CHALL'	STIRLAND	MITCH	BROUGH	SINCLAIR	HAINES	HUBBARD	WESTLAND	BODLE
29	13 a	Rotherham Utd	L 0-3			POXTON	SWALLOW	CHALL'	STIRLAND	BYCROFT	HARKIN	WALKER C H	HAINES	HUBBARD	BODLE	SINCLAIR
30	27 h	Grimsby Town	W 3-2	Jordan(3).	1.775	POXTON	LAKING	CHALL'	STIRLAND	ATTER	HARDY	SINCLAIR	HENRY	JORDAN	BODLE	THOROGOOD
31	Apr 3 a	Grimsby Town	L 0-2		700	POXTON	LAKING	CHALL'	STIRLAND	BYCROFT	HARDY	SINCLAIR	WESTLAND	JORDAN	BODLE	THOROGOOD
32	10 a	Nottm Forest	W 2-1	Burton,Thorogood.		POXTON	LAKING	WOOL'E	STIRLAND	BYCROFT	HARDY	BURTON	HARKIN	BARBER	BODLE	THOROGOOD

	P	W	D	L	F	A	PTS
HOME	4	1	3	0	16	14	9
AWAY	9	1	2	6	11	27	4
TOTAL	17	5	3	9	27	41	13	POS 42nd

NOTE: A second championship was created by adding the League
North Cup and the Sheffield County Cup games to the above 5 games.

League Cup North:

No	Date	V	Opponents	F-A	Scorers	Att	1	2	3	4	5	6	7	8	9	10	11
35	Dec26 a	York City	D 3-3	Hubbard(2),Thorogood.	4.552	POXTON	LAKING	WALKER A	STIRLAND	ATTER	GLADWIN	GRAINGER	SINCLAIR	HARKIN	HUBBARD	THOROGOOD
36	Jan 1 h	York City	L 3-5	Hubbard(2),Harkin.	2.500	POXTON	WALKER A	WOOL'E	STIRLAND	ATTER	MITCH	SINCLAIR	HARKIN	HUBBARD	BODLE	THOROGOOD
37	9 h	Barnsley	L 1-2	Bodle.	2.081	POXTON	LUNN	WOOL'E	STIRLAND	ATTER	LITTLE	SINCLAIR	HARKIN	HUBBARD	BODLE	THOROGOOD
38	16 a	Barnsley	D 1-1	Sinclair.	4.402	POXTON	WALKER A	WOOL'E	STIRLAND	ATTER	GLADWIN	SINCLAIR	HUBBARD	STEELE	BODLE	THOROGOOD
39	23 a	Grimsby Town	L 2-5	Steele(2).	2.000	POXTON	LAKING	CHALL'	STIRLAND	ATTER	GLADWIN	SINCLAIR	HUBBARD	STEELE	BODLE	THOROGOOD
40	30 h	Grimsby Town	W 1-0	Steele.	3.074	POXTON	LAKING	CHALL'	STIRLAND	ATTER	HARKIN	SINCLAIR	HUBBARD.	STEELE	BODLE	THOROGOOD
41	Feb 6 h	Chesterfield	L 1-2	Gladwin.	3.702	WILK	LAKING	CHALL'	STIRLAND	ATTER	GLADWIN	SINCLAIR	HUBBARD	STEELE	WESTLAND	THOROGOOD
42	13 a	Chesterfield	L 0-1		3.500	POXTON	LAKING	CHALL'	STIRLAND	ATTER	HARKIN	SINCLAIR	BODLE	HUBBARD	WESTLAND	THOROGOOD
43	20 a	Huddersfield Town	L 2-6	Harkin,Steele.	3.635	POXTON	LAKING	WOOL'E	STIRLAND	ATTER	BROUGH	HUBBARD	HARKIN	STEELE	BODLE	SINCLAIR
44	27 h	Huddersfield Town	W 3-1	Harkin,Hubbard,Westland.	4.374	POXTON	SWALLOW	CHALL'	STIRLAND	BYCROFT	BROUGH	SINCLAIR	HARKIN	HUBBARD	WESTLAND	BODLE

	P	W	D	L	F	A	PTS
HOME	5	2	0	3	9	10	4
AWAY	5	0	2	3	8	16	2
TOTAL	10	2	2	6	17	26	6	POS 43rd

Sheffield County Cup: 1942-43

No	Date	V	Opponents	F-A	Scorers	Att	1	2	3	4	5	6	7	8	9	10	11
45	April7 h	Rotherham Utd	W 3-1	Bodle,Jordan,Hanson O.G.	1.000	POXTON	LAKING	GREGORY	STIRLAND	BYCROFT	HARDY	BURTON	HARKIN	JORDAN	BODLE	THOROGOOD
46	24 a	Rotherham Utd	L 1-5	Gregory.	1.500	WILDMAN	LAKING	CHALL'	STIRLAND	BYCROFT	HARDY	BURTON	JORDAN	GREGORY	BODLE	THOROGOOD

Abbreviated names (where used): CHALL' = CHALLINOR. McDER. = McDERMOTT. MITCH = MITCHELL. NIGHT = NIGHTINGALE. WILK = WILKINSON. WOOLE = WOOLRIDGE.

League Division North 1943-44

1st Championship:

No	Date	V	Opponents	F-A	Scorers	Att	1	2	3	4	5	6	7	8	9	10	11
1	Aug28	a	Sheffield Utd	W 3-2	Gregory,Thorogood,Massarella.	7,568	ROBINSON	LAKING	BANNER	MACAULEY	BYCROFT	ATTWELL	MASSA'	BODLE	GREGORY	WESTLAND	THOROGOOD
2	Sep 4	h	Sheffield Utd	W 2-1	Steele.Thorogood pen.	5,880	ROBINSON	LAKING	BANNER	MACAULEY	GREGORY	MITCHELL	MASSA'	BODLE	STEELE	WESTLAND	THOROGOOD
3	11	a	Sheffield Wed	D 2-2	Massarella.Bodle.	8,365	ROBINSON	LAKING	BANNER	STIRLAND	GREGORY	MITCHELL	MASSA'	BODLE	STEELE	WESTLAND	THOROGOOD
4	18	h	Sheffield Wed	W 3-1	Steele.Thorogood.Massarella.	6,840	ROBINSON	LAKING	BANNER	MACAULEY	GREGORY	ATTWELL	MASSA'	BODLE	STEELE	WESTLAND	THOROGOOD
5	25	a	Lincoln City	L 1-2	Westland.	3,600	ROBINSON	ATTER	BANNER	STIRLAND	GREGORY	MITCHELL	MASSA'	BODLE	STEELE	WESTLAND	THOROGOOD
6	Oct 2	h	Lincoln City	W 3-1	Massarella.Bodle.Steele.	5,930	ROBINSON	LAKING	WOOL'E	MACAULEY	GREGORY	ATTWELL	MASSA'	BODLE	STEELE	WESTLAND	THOROGOOD
7	9	h	Chesterfield	W 4-0	Bodle(2).Westland.Thorogood pen.	8,307	ROBINSON	LAKING	BANNER	MACAULEY	GREGORY	ATTWELL	MASSA'	BODLE	STEELE	WESTLAND	THOROGOOD
8	16	a	Chesterfield	W 3-2	Bodle.Steele.Westland.	3,166	ROBINSON	GREGORY	BANNER	MACAULEY	BYCROFT	ATTWELL	MASSA'	BODLE	STEELE	WESTLAND	THOROGOOD
9	23	h	Leeds Utd	D 3-3	Steele(2).Bodle.	8,264	ROBINSON	LAKING	BANNER	MACAULEY	GREGORY	ATTWELL	MASSA'	BODLE	STEELE	WESTLAND	THOROGOOD
10	30	a	Leeds Utd	D 2-2	Massarella(2).	5,000	ROBINSON	LAKING	BANNER	MITCHELL	BYCROFT	STIRLAND	MASSA'	BODLE	JORDAN	MALAM	THOROGOOD
11	Nov 6	a	Halifax Town	L 0-1		4,000	ROBINSON	LAKING	GREGORY	MACAULEY	BYCROFT	STIRLAND	MASSA'	BODLE	STEELE	WESTLAND	THOROGOOD
12	13	h	Halifax Town	W 3-1	Bodle.Steele.MacCauley.	7,257	ROBINSON	GREGORY	BANNER	MITCHELL	BYCROFT	ATTWELL	MASSA'	MACAULEY	STEELE	BODLE	THOROGOOD
13	20	a	Bradford City	D 1-1	Bodle.	3,000	ROBINSON	LAKING	BANNER	MACAULEY	GREGORY	STIRLAND	MASSA'	STEELE	JORDAN	BODLE	THOROGOOD
14	27	h	Bradford City	W 3-1	Bodle.Gregory.Thorogood pen.	5,938	ROBINSON	LAKING	BANNER	MACAULEY	BYCROFT	ATTWELL	MASSA'	BODLE	GREGORY	WESTLAND	THOROGOOD
15	Dec 4	h	Barnsley	D 3-3	Thorogood.Westland.Steele.	7,446	POXTON	LAKING	BANNER	GREGORY	BYCROFT	MITCHELL	MASSA'	BODLE	STEELE	WESTLAND	THOROGOOD
16	11	a	Barnsley	W 4-0	Massarella(2).Bodle.Brough.	3,943	ROBINSON	LAKING	GREGORY	JONES	BYCROFT	ATTWELL	MASSA'	BODLE	JORDAN	BROUGH	THOROGOOD
17	18	h	Grimsby Town	W 2-1	Steele.Bodle.	2,914	ROBINSON	WOOL'E	GREGORY	JONES	BYCROFT	ATTWELL	MASSA'	BODLE	STEELE	WESTLAND	SINC'R
18	25	a	Grimsby Town	W 3-1	Massarella(2).Vincent og.	3,000	ROBINSON	LAKING	WOOL'E	GREGORY	BYCROFT	ATTWELL	MASSA'	BODLE	JORDAN	MITCHELL	THOROGOOD

	P	W	D	L	F	A	PTS	POS
HOME	9	7	2	0	26	12	16	
AWAY	9	4	3	2	19	13	11	
TOTAL	18	11	5	2	45	25	27	4th

War League Cup Qualifying Comp:

No	Date	V	Opponents	F-A	Scorers	Att	1	2	3	4	5	6	7	8	9	10	11
19	Dec27	h	Grimsby Town	W 1-0	Thorogood pen.	12,383	ROBINSON	GREGORY	BANNER	LAKING	BYCROFT	MITCHELL	SINC'R	JORDAN	STEELE	BODLE	THOROGOOD
20*	Jan 1	a	Grimsby Town	D 1-1	Bodle.	6,875	ROBINSON	LAKING	BANNER	MITCHELL	BYCROFT	BROUGH	MASSA'	BODLE	JORDAN	WESTLAND	SINC'R
21	8	a	Lincoln City	W 5-4	Steele(3).Bodle(2).	5,556	ROBINSON	LAKING	GREGORY	MITCHELL	BYCROFT	ATTWELL	MASSA'	BODLE	STEELE	WESTLAND	SINC'R
22	22	h	Rotherham Utd	L 1-2	Stirland.	8,284	ROBINSON	LAKING	BANNER	STIRLAND	BYCROFT	CATER	MASSA'	BODLE	JORDAN	BROUGH	THOROGOOD
23	29	a	Rotherham Utd	D 2-2	Jordan.Attwell.	13,000	ROBINSON	LAKING	BANNER	GREGORY	BYCROFT	ATTWELL	MASSA'	BODLE	JORDAN	BROUGH	THOROGOOD
24	Feb 5	a	Chesterfield	L 0-4		2,367	ROBINSON	LAKING	GREGORY	JONES	BYCROFT	STIRLAND	KIRK'	BODLE	STEELE	COURTIER	THOROGOOD
25	12	h	Chesterfield	W 3-2	Bodle(2).Massarella.	6,104	ROBINSON	LAKING	BANNER	JONES	BYCROFT	ATTWELL	MASSA'	BODLE	STEELE	GREGORY	THOROGOOD
26	19	h	Sheffield Utd	L 1-2	Massarella.	7,030	ROBINSON	WOOL'E	BANNER	JONES	BYCROFT	ATTWELL	MASSA'	BODLE	STEELE	GREGORY	THOROGOOD
27	26	a	Sheffield Utd	L 0-7		10,131	ROBINSON	LAKING	BANNER	HARTLEY	BYCROFT	ATTWELL	MASSA'	BODLE	WESTLAND	JONES	THOROGOOD

	P	W	D	L	F	A	PTS	POS
HOME	4	2	0	2	6	6	4	
AWAY	5	1	2	2	8	18	4	
TOTAL	9	3	2	4	14	24	8	

* This game was abandoned after 85 mins, but result allowed to stand.

2nd Championship:

2nd Championship:

No	Date	V	Opponents	F-A	Scorers	Att	1	2	3	4	5	6	7	8	9	10	11
28	Mar 4	h	Lincoln City	W 6-1	Th'good(2).Hart'y.Greg'y.Jor'n.Sinc'r	1,322	POXTON	LAKING	WOOL'E	GREGORY	BYCROFT	MITCHELL	SINC'R	JORDAN	HARTLEY	BODLE	THOROGOOD
29	11	a	Lincoln City	W 7-2	Hartley(4).Sinclair.Bodle.Thorogood.		POXTON	LAKING	BANNER	GREGORY	BYCROFT	ATTWELL	SINC'R	BODLE	HARTLEY	MITCHELL	THOROGOOD
30	Apr 1	h	Notts County	W 6-0	Sinclair(4).Thorogood.Massarella.		ROBINSON	LAKING	BANNER	STIRLAND	BYCROFT	MITCHELL	SINC'R	MASSA'	HARTLEY	JORDAN	THOROGOOD
31	8	a	Notts County	W 1-0	Jordan.		ROBINSON	LAKING	WOOL'E	GREGORY	BYCROFT	MITCHELL	SINC'R	BODLE	HARTLEY	JORDAN	THOROGOOD
32	15	a	Bradford PA	W 4-3	Bodle.Sinclair.Jordan.Thorogood.	6,970	POXTON	LAKING	WOOL'E	GREGORY	BYCROFT	STIRLAND	SINC'R	BODLE	JORDAN	WALKER	THOROGOOD
33	22	h	Bradford PA	W 3-1	Westland(3).		POXTON	LAKING	WOOL'E	STIRLAND	BYCROFT	GREGORY	SINC'R	BODLE	MASSA'	WESTLAND	THOROGOOD

	P	W	D	L	F	A	PTS	POS
HOME	8	5	1	2	22	9	11	
AWAY	9	4	2	3	20	24	10	
TOTAL	17	9	3	5	42	33	21	22nd

NOTE: A second championship was created by adding the League North Cup, and the Sheffield County Cup games to the above games.

Sheffield County Cup: 1943-44

No	Date	V	Opponents	F-A	Scorers	Att	1	2	3	4	5	6	7	8	9	10	11
34	Mar18	h	Barnsley	D 1-1	Attwell.	3,866	POXTON	LAKING	WOOL'E	GREGORY	BYCROFT	ATTWELL	SINC'R	QUINN	HARTLEY	MITCHELL	THOROGOOD
35	25	a	Barnsley	L 0-1		6,359	ROBINSON	LAKING	WOOL'E	GREGORY	BYCROFT	STIRLAND	SINC'R	BERESFORD	HARTLEY	MITCHELL	THOROGOOD

Abbreviated names (where used): KIRK' = KIRKALDIE. MASSA' = MASSARELLA. SINCL'R = SINCLAIR. WOOLE = WOOLDRIDGE.

War League North 1944-45

1st Championship:

No	Date	V	Opponents	F-A	Scorers	Att	1	2	3	4	5	6	7	8	9	10	11
1	Aug26	h	Hull City	W 8-1	Jor'n(3).Bodle(2).Tin'l.Quinn.Thoro'	6.980	POXTON	STEV'N	WOOL'E	STIRLAND	BYCROFT	BROUGH	TINDILL	QUINN	JORDAN	BODLE	THORO'
2	Sep 2	h	Hull City	W 2-1	Tindill.Bodle.	6.108	POXTON	STEV'N	WOOL'E	STIRLAND	BYCROFT	BROUGH	TINDILL	QUINN	JORDAN	BODLE	THORO'
3	9	h	Grimsby Town	L 1-3	Alberry.	5.981	POXTON	STEV'N	BANNER	STIRLAND	BYCROFT	BROUGH	TINDILL	QUINN	ALBERRY	BODLE	THORO'
4	16	a	Grimsby Town	L 1-2	Tindill.	5.000	POXTON	STEV'N	WOOL'E	STIRLAND	BYCROFT	ATTWELL	TINDILL	QUINN	ALBERRY	BODLE	THORO'
5	23	h	Derby County	L 1-4	Bodle.	8.029	POXTON	STEV'N	WOOL'E	STIRLAND	BYCROFT	BROUGH	TINDILL	BODLE	ALBERRY	PETERS	THORO'
6	30	a	Derby County	L 1-4	Mitcheson.	9.594	ROBINSON	POTTS	SWALLOW	STIRLAND	BYCROFT	BROUGH	TINDILL	BODLE	MITCHESON	PETERS	THORO'
7	Oct 7	a	Sheffield Utd	L 1-3	Mitcheson.	10.000	POXTON	STEV'N	SWALLOW	STIRLAND	BYCROFT	WOODBURN	TINDILL	MITCHESON	JORDAN	BODLE	THORO'
8	14	h	Sheffield Utd	W 3-0	Bodle.Jordan.Tindill.	3.831	POXTON	STEV'N	WOOL'E	STIRLAND	BYCROFT	HEYDON	TINDILL	WILLIAMS	JORDAN	BODLE	THORO'
9	21	h	Notts County	W 3-1	Bodle(2).Masserella.	4.361	ROBINSON	STEV'N	WOOL'E	BEEDALL	BYCROFT	MITCHELL	JORDAN	WILLIAMS	MASSA'	BODLE	THORO'
10	28	a	Notts County	W 2-0	Jordan.Pomphrey og.	2.000	POXTON	STEV'N	WOOL'E	STIRLAND	BYCROFT	MITCHELL	TINDILL	WILLIAMS	JORDAN	BODLE	THORO'
11	Nov 4	a	Chesterfield	W 2-1	Jordan.Thorogood.	3.500	ROBINSON	STEV'N	WOOL'E	STIRLAND	BYCROFT	MITCHELL	TINDILL	WILLIAMS	JORDAN	BODLE	THORO'
12	11	h	Chesterfield	L 0-1		5.429	ROBINSON	STEV'N	WOOL'E	STIRLAND	BYCROFT	MITCHELL	TINDILL	PETERS	JORDAN	BODLE	THORO'
13	18	h	Mansfield Town	W 2-1	Jordan,Heydon.	4.976	ROBINSON	TOM'N	WOOL'E	STIRLAND	BYCROFT	HEYDON	TINDILL	WILLIAMS	JORDAN	BODLE	THORO'
14	25	h	Mansfield Town	W 2-0	Thorogood.Tindill.	3.000	ROBINSON	TOM'N	WOOL'E	STIRLAND	BYCROFT	MITCHELL	TINDILL	MITCHESON	WILLIAMS	BODLE	THORO'
15	Dec 2	a	Bradford City	W 3-2	Jordan(2),tindill.	3.382	ROBINSON	TOM'N	WOOL'E	STIRLAND	BYCROFT	HEYDON	TINDILL	MITCHESON	JORDAN	BODLE	THORO'
16	9	h	Bradford City	W 4-1	Jordan(2),Thorogood.Bodle.	6.000	ROBINSON	TOM'N	WOOL'E	STIRLAND	BYCROFT	HEYDON	TINDILL	MITCHESON	JORDAN	BODLE	THORO'
17	16	h	Lincoln City	W 9-2	Bodle(4).Tin'l(2).Thoro'(2).Mitch'n.	2.252	ROBINSON	TOM'N	WOOL'E	STIRLAND	BYCROFT	MITCHELL	TINDILL	MITCHESON	JORDAN	BODLE	THORO'
18	23	a	Lincoln City	W 3-0	Jordan(2),tindill.	2.500	ROBINSON	TOM'N	WOOL'E	MITCHELL	BYCROFT	EVERY	TINDILL	MITCHESON	JORDAN	BODLE	THORO'

	P	W	D	L	F	A	PTS	POS
HOME	9	6	0	3	25	14	12	
AWAY	9	6	0	3	23	13	12	
TOTAL	18	12	0	6	48	27	24	7th

2nd Championship:

No	Date	V	Opponents	F-A	Scorers	Att	1	2	3	4	5	6	7	8	9	10	11
11	Mar 3	h	Chesterfield	W 2-1	Bodle(2).	7.531	POXTON	TOM'N	WOOL'E	BRITTON	BYCROFT	ATTWELL	TINDILL	MITCHESON	JORDAN	BODLE	THORO'
13	17	a	Chesterfield	L 0-2			POXTON	TOM'N	WOOL'E	STIRLAND	BYCROFT	STIRLAND	HEYDON	MITCHESON	MARRIOTT	BODLE	MASSA'
16	Apr 2	a	Rotherham Utd	W 2-0	Marriott.Tindill.	6.365	POXTON	STEV'N	WOOL'E	STIRLAND	BYCROFT	MITCHELL	MASSA'	QUINN	MARRIOTT	BODLE	TINDILL

	P	W	D	L	F	A	PTS	POS
HOME	9	5	1	3	21	12	11	
AWAY	10	6	1	4	23	14	13	
TOTAL	20	11	2	7	44	26	24	23rd

NOTE: A second championship was created by adding the League North cup (Qualifying and Proper) and also the Sheffield County Cup games to the above games.

War League Cup Qualifying Matches:

No	Date	V	Opponents	F-A	Scorers	Att	1	2	3	4	5	6	7	8	9	10	11
1	Dec26	h	Rotherham Utd	D 0-0		4.450	ROBINSON	STEV'N	WOOL'E	STIRLAND	BYCROFT	MITCHELL	TINDILL	MITCHESON	JORDAN	HEYDON	THORO'
2	30	a	Rotherham Utd	L 0-3		10.200	POXTON	TOM'N	WOOL'E	STIRLAND	BYCROFT	MITCHELL	TINDILL	MITCHESON	JORDAN	PETERS	THORO'
3	Jan 6	h	Lincoln City	W 6-1	Bodle(4).Mitcheson.Thorogood.	5.935	ROBINSON	TOM'N	WOOL'E	BRITTON	BYCROFT	STIRLAND	TINDILL	MITCHESON	JORDAN	BODLE	THORO'
4	13	a	Lincoln City	W 3-1	Thorogood(2).Mitcheson.	2.336	ROBINSON	TOM'N	WOOL'E	BRITTON	BYCROFT	ATTWELL	TINDILL	MITCHESON	JORDAN	BODLE	THORO'
5	20	a	Grimsby Town	W 2-1	Bodle.Jordan.	4.000	ROBINSON	TOM'N	BANNER	BRITTON	BYCROFT	ATTWELL	TINDILL	MITCHESON	JORDAN	BODLE	THORO'
6	27	h	Grimsby Town	W 5-1	Jordan(3).Bodle.Tindill.	5.272	ROBINSON	TOM'N	WOOL'E	BRITTON	BYCROFT	ATTWELL	TINDILL	MITCHESON	JORDAN	BODLE	THORO'
7	Feb 3	h	Sheffield Wed	L 1-3	Jordan.	9.340	ROBINSON	TOM'N	WOOL'E	BRITTON	BYCROFT	STIRLAND	TINDILL	MITCHESON	JORDAN	BEEDALL	MITCHELL
8	10	a	Sheffield Wed	W 6-1	Jordan(4).Tindill.Thorogood.	13.804	ROBINSON	TOM'N	WOOL'E	BRITTON	BYCROFT	ATTWELL	TINDILL	MITCHESON	JORDAN	BODLE	THORO'
9	17	a	Sheffield Utd	W 4-0	Bodle(2).Mitcheson(2).	16.905	ROBINSON	TOM'N	WOOL'E	BRITTON	BYCROFT	ATTWELL	TINDILL	MITCHESON	JORDAN	BODLE	THORO'
10	24	h	Sheffield Utd	W 3-2	Tindill.Attwell.Jordan.	13.127	ROBINSON	TOM'N	WOOL'E	BRITTON	BYCROFT	STIRLAND	TINDILL	BODLE	JORDAN	ATTWELL	THORO'

	P	W	D	L	F	A	PTS	POS
HOME	5	3	1	1	15	7	7	
AWAY	5	4	0	1	15	6	8	
TOTAL	10	7	1	2	30	13	15	7th

Doncaster qualified for the first round proper:

League Cup

	Date	V	Opponents	F-A	Scorers	Att	1	2	3	4	5	6	7	8	9	10	11
R11L	Mar24	a	Bradford PA	D 1-1	Bodle.	16.007	ROBINSON	TOM'N	WOOL'E	BRITTON	BYCROFT	ATTWELL	TINDILL	MITCHESON	JORDAN	BODLE	THORO'
R12L	31	h	Bradford PA	W 2-0	Jordan.Bodle.	19.549	ROBINSON	TOM'N	WOOL'E	BRITTON	BYCROFT	ATTWELL	TINDILL	MITCHESON	JORDAN	BODLE	THORO'
R21L	Apr 7	h	Derby County	L 1-2	Masserella.	23.899	ROBINSON	TOM'N	WOOL'E	BRITTON	BYCROFT	ATTWELL	TINDILL	MITCHESON	JORDAN	BODLE	MASSA'
R22L	14	a	Derby County	W 4-1	Jordan(2).Bodle(2).	19.062	ROBINSON	TOM'N	WOOL'E	BRITTON	BYCROFT	ATTWELL	TINDILL	MITCHESON	JORDAN	BODLE	THORO'
R31L	Apr21	h	Man Utd	L 1-2	Jordan.	29.177	ROBINSON	TOM'N	WOOL'E	STIRLAND	BYCROFT	ATTWELL	TINDILL	MITCHESON	JORDAN	BODLE	THORO'
R32L	28	a	Man Utd	L 1-3	Bodle.	31.728	ROBINSON	TOM'N	WOOL'E	STIRLAND	BYCROFT	ATTWELL	TINDILL	MITCHESON	JORDAN	BODLE	THORO'

Sheffield County Cup: 1944-45

	Date	V	Opponents	F-A	Scorers	Att	1	2	3	4	5	6	7	8	9	10	11
	Mar10	a	Sheffield Wed	L 0-1		8.827	ROBINSON	TOM'N	WOOL'E	STIRLAND	LIGHT'T	MITCHELL	TINDILL	MITCHESON	MARRIOTT	JORDAN	THORO'

Abbreviated names (where used): LIGHT'T = LIGHTFOOT. MASSA' = MASSERELLA. STEVN = STEVENSON. TOM'N = TOMLINSON. THORO' = THOROGOOD. WOOL'E = WOOLDRIDGE.

League Division 3 North East Region 1945-46

No	Date	V	Opponents	F-A	Scorers	Att	1	2	3	4	5	6	7	8	9	10	11
1	Aug25	a	Hartlepools Utd	D 1-1	Gregory.	5.997	ROB'N	SWALLOW	WOOD'E	ATTWELL	BAYNHAM	STIRLAND	TINDILL	GREGORY	JORDAN	MITCH'N	THORO'
2	Sep 1	h	Hartlepools Utd	W 2-0	Gregory,Thorogood.	6.658	ROB'N	STARBUCK	WOOD'E	STIRLAND	BYCROFT	ATTWELL	TINDILL	MITCH'N	JORDAN	GREGORY	THORO'
3	8	h	Darlington	L 1-2	Tindill.	7.044	ROB'N	TOMLINSON	WOOD'E	STIRLAND	BYCROFT	ATTWELL	JORDAN	MITCH'N	BURDITT	TODD	TINDILL
4	15	a	Darlington	L 1-2	Todd.	5.766	ROB'N	SWALLOW	WOOD'E	HEYDON	BYCROFT	ATTWELL	ROBY	MITCH'N	MARRIOTT	TODD	TINDILL
5	22	h	Rotherham Utd	L 0-3		8.665	HARD'K	SWALLOW	WOOD'E	EADES	LIGHTFOOT	EADES	TINDILL	MITCH'N	JORDAN	TODD	THORO'
6	29	a	Rotherham Utd	L 1-7	Jordan.	10.296	HARD'K	SWALLOW	WOOD'E	STIRLAND	BAYNHAM	HEYDON	TINDILL	MITCH'N	JORDAN	TODD	THORO'
7	Oct 6	a	Bradford City	D 3-3	Jordan(2),Thorogood.	9.252	ROB'N	STEVENSON	WOOD'E	HEYDON	BAYNHAM	EADES	TINDILL	MITCH'N	JORDAN	TODD	THORO'
8	13	h	Bradford City	W 3-1	Todd,Thorogood(2).	5.948	HARD'K	STEVENSON	WOOD'E	HEYDON	BAYNHAM	EADES	TINDILL	MITCH'N	JORDAN	TODD	THORO'
9	20	h	Carlisle Utd	W 3-0	Tindill,Jordan,Todd.	6.666	HARD'K	STEVENSON	WOOD'E	STIRLAND	ARCHER	HEYDON	TINDILL	MITCH'N	JORDAN	TODD	THORO'
10	27	a	Carlisle Utd	W 4-2	Jordan(2),Tindill,Mitcheson.	5.403	HARD'K	STEVENSON	WOOD'E	HEYDON	ARCHER	EADES	TINDILL	MITCH'N	JORDAN	TODD	WHITE
11	Nov 3	a	Gateshead	L 1-3	Jordan.	4.860	BRID'N	SWALLOW	WOOD'E	STIRLAND	ARCHER	EADES	TINDILL	MITCH'N	JORDAN	TODD	WHITE
12	10	h	Gateshead	D 2-2	Mitcheson,Archer pen.	6.959	BRID'N	ARCHER	WOOD'E	HEYDON	BYCROFT	EADES	TINDILL	CORK	MARRIOTT	TODD	STAN'H
13	Dec 1	h	York City	D 1-1	Todd.	5.523	HARD'K	STEVENSON	WOOD'E	STIRLAND	ARCHER	EADES	KIRKALDIE	MITCHESON	JORDAN	TODD	STAN'H
14	15	h	Halifax Town	W 3-0	Jordan(2),Todd.	4.301	HARD'K	SWALLOW	WOOD'E	HEYDON	ARCHER	EADES	LITTLE	MITCHESON	JORDAN	TODD	STAN'H
15	22	a	Halifax Town	W 3-2	Todd(2),Jordan.	2.190	HARD'K	SWALLOW	WOOD'E	HEYDON	ARCHER	McFARLANE	TINDILL	MITCHESON	JORDAN	TODD	STAN'H
16	25	h	Lincoln City	W 3-1	Todd(3).	6.302	ROB'N	SWALLOW	WOOD'E	HEYDON	ARCHER	McFARLANE	MARRIOTT	MITCHESON	JORDAN	TODD	STAN'H
17	26	a	Lincoln City	L 0-4		7.977	ROB'N	STEVENSON	WOOD'E	HEYDON	ARCHER	EADES	MARRIOTT	MITCHESON	JORDAN	TODD	STAN'H
18	29	a	York City	W 2-1	Marriott(2).	5.972	HARD'K	SWALLOW	WOOD'E	HEYDON	ARCHER	McFARLANE	EADES	MITCHESON	MARRIOTT	JORDAN	STAN'H

		HOME							AWAY							TOTAL							
P	W	D	L	F	A	PTS		P	W	D	L	F	A	PTS		P	W	D	L	F	A	PTS	POS
9	5	2	2	18	10	12		9	2	2	5	16	25	8		18	8	4	6	34	35	20	4th

League Division 3 North Eastern Region Cup:

No	Date	V	Opponents	F-A	Scorers	Att	1	2	3	4	5	6	7	8	9	10	11
19	Jan12	a	Lincoln City	W 3-2	Jordan(2),Kirkaldie	6.619	HARD'K	SWALLOW	WOOD'E	HEYDON	ARCHER	McFARLANE	KIRKALDIE	MITCHESON	JORDAN	TODD	MADD'N
20	19	h	Lincoln City	W 3-0	Kirkaldie,Jordan,Todd.	3.987	HARD'K	SWALLOW	WOOD'E	HEYDON	ARCHER	McFARLANE	KIRKALDIE	MITCHESON	JORDAN	TODD	MADD'N
21	26	h	Gateshead	W 4-2	Mitcheson(2),Jordan,Todd.	7.495	HARD'K	SWALLOW	WOOD'E	HEYDON	ARCHER	McFARLANE	MARRIOTT	MITCHESON	JORDAN	TODD	MADD'N
22	Feb 2	a	York City	W 3-1	Jordan(2),Maddison.	4.029	HARD'K	SWALLOW	WOOD'E	HEYDON	ARCHER	McFARLANE	MARRIOTT	KILLOURHY	JORDAN	TODD	MADD'N
23	9	a	Halifax Town	L 1-4	Todd.	4.139	HARD'K	SWALLOW	WOOD'E	HEYDON	ARCHER	McFARLANE	MARRIOTT	KILLOURHY	JORDAN	TODD	MADD'N
24	16	h	Halifax Town	D 1-1	Marriott.	9.070	HARD'K	SWALLOW	WOOD'E	HEYDON	ARCHER	McFARLANE	MARRIOTT	MITCHESON	JORDAN	TODD	MADD'N
25	23	h	Rotherham Utd	D 0-0		9.551	HARD'K	SWALLOW	WOOD'E	HEYDON	ARCHER	McFARLANE	KIRKALDIE	MITCHESON	MITCHESON	TODD	MADD'N
26	Mar 2	a	Rotherham Utd	W 3-1	Maddison,Kirkaldie,Marriott.	9.848	HARD'K	SWALLOW	WOOD'E	STIRLAND	ARCHER	McFARLANE	KIRKALDIE	MITCHESON	MARRIOTT	TODD	MADD'N
27	9	a	Gateshead	D 3-3	Marriott(2),Jordan.	5.000	HARD'K	SWALLOW	WOOD'E	STIRLAND	ARCHER	McFARLANE	LITTLE	JORDAN	MARRIOTT	TODD	MADD'N
28	16	h	York City	W 3-1	Jordan,Archer(2 pens).	8.226	HARD'K	SWALLOW	WOOD'E	STIRLAND	ARCHER	McFARLANE	KIRKALDIE	JORDAN	MARRIOTT	TODD	MADD'N

		HOME							AWAY							TOTAL							
P	W	D	L	F	A	PTS		P	W	D	L	F	A	PTS		P	W	D	L	F	A	PTS	POS
5	3	2	0	11	4	8		5	3	1	1	13	17	7		10	6	3	1	24	15	15	1st

Doncaster Qualified:

League Cup North.

	Date	V	Opponents	F-A	Scorers	Att	1	2	3	4	5	6	7	8	9	10	11
R1L	Mar23	h	Stockport County	D 2-2	Marriott,Todd.	12.026	HARD'K	SWALLOW	WOOD'E	HEYDON	ARCHER	McFARLANE	LITTLE	JORDAN	MARRIOTT	TODD	MADD'N
R2L	30	a	Stockport County	D 2-2	Todd,Maddison. *	12.634	HARD'K	SWALLOW	WOOD'E	STIRLAND	ARCHER	McFARLANE	LITTLE	JORDAN	MARRIOTT	TODD	MADD'N
R2L	Apr 3	h	Stockport County	W 4-0	Maddison(3),Todd.	13.056	HARD'K	SWALLOW	WOOD'E	HEYDON	ARCHER	McFARLANE	KIRKALDIE	JORDAN	MARRIOTT	TODD	MADD'N
R1L	6	h	Rotherham Utd	D 0-0		16.527	HARD'K	SWALLOW	WOOD'E	STIRLAND	ARCHER	McFARLANE	KIRKALDIE	JORDAN	MARRIOTT	TODD	MADD'N
R2L	13	a	Rotherham Utd	L 0-2		13.313	HARD'K	SWALLOW	WOOD'E	STIRLAND	ARCHER	McFARLANE	KIRKALDIE	KILLOURHY	JORDAN	TODD	MADD'N

* After extra time. Abandoned after 203 mins.

Division 3 North - 2nd Championship:

No	Date	V	Opponents	F-A	Scorers	Att	1	2	3	4	5	6	7	8	9	10	11
29	Apr19	a	York City	L 1-5	Todd		FERG'N	SWALLOW	WOOD'E	HEYDON	ARCHER	STIRLAND	LITTLE	MITCHESON	JORDAN	TODD	MADD'N
30	22	h	York City	D 1-1	Heydon		FERG'N	SWALLOW	WOOD'E	STIRLAND	ARCHER	STIRLAND	TINDILL	MITCHESON	OWEN	TODD	MADD'N
31	27	a	Oldham Ath	L 1-2	Jordan.	c.3.000	FERG'N	SWALLOW	WOOD'E	STIRLAND	ARCHER	McFARLANE	LITTLE	MITCHESON	JORDAN	TODD	MADD'N
32	May 4	h	Oldham Ath	W 5-1	Kill'y(2),Jordan,McFar'e,Stirland.	4.816	FERG'N	SWALLOW	WOOD'E	STIRLAND	ARCHER	McFARLANE	LITTLE	KILLOURHY	JORDAN	TODD	MADD'N

F.A.Cup

	Date	V	Opponents	F-A	Scorers	Att	1	2	3	4	5	6	7	8	9	10	11
R1lL	Nov17	h	Rotherham Utd	L 0-1		13.055	HARD'K	STEVENSON	WOOL'E	HEYDON	ARCHER	EADES	MITCHESON	OWENS	JORDAN	TODD	GREGORY
R1l2L	24	a	Rotherham Utd	L 1-2	Todd.	14.362	HARD'K	STEVENSON	WOOL'E	STIRLAND	ARCHER	HEYDON	TINDILL	MITCHESON	JORDAN	TODD	GREGORY

Abbreviated names (where used): FERG'N = FERGUSON. HARD'K = HARDWICKE. MADD'N = MADDISON. ROB'N = ROBINSON. STAN'H = STANIFORTH. THORO' = THOROGOOD. WOOLE = WOOLRIDGE.

League Division 3 1946-47

No	Date	V	Opponents	F-A	Scorers	Att
1	Aug31	h	Rochdale	W 2-1	Maddison(2).	8.279
2	Sep 4	a	Chester	W 3-1	Tindill,Jordan,Thompson (pen).	4.637
3	7	a	New Brighton	W 5-2	Tindill(3).Thompson,Jordan.	10.242
4	9	a	Stockport County	W 3-1	Jordan(2).Maddison.	12.830
5	14	h	Halifax Town	W 2-0	Thompson.Tindill.	13.765
6	16	h	Stockport County	L 1-3	Owens.	11.582
7	21	a	Carlisle United	W 3-2	Jordan.Tindill.Maddison.	12.888
8	28	h	Accrington Stanley	W 5-0	Jordan(3).Todd.Tindill.	12.873
9	Oct 5	a	Barrow	W 1-0	Jordan.	11.371
10	12	h	Bradford City	W 4-3	Jordan(3).Maddison.	13.054
11	19	a	York City	W 4-1	Jordan(3).Todd.	15.504
12	26	h	Tranmere Rovers	W 2-0	Thompson.Jordan.	14.008
13	Nov 2	a	Darlington	D 1-1	Todd.	9.989
14	9	h	Hull City	W 4-1	Kirkaldie(2).Jordan.Maddison.	17.820
15	16	a	Gateshead	W 3-1	Jordan(2).Todd.	7.646
16	23	h	Hartlepools United	W 5-1	Jordan(2).Thompson.Todd.Maddison.	13.093
17	Dec 7	a	Lincoln City	W 5-3	Bycroft.Owens.Jordan.Todd.Maddison.	10.917
18	21	h	Rotherham United	D 1-1	Owens.	21.297
19	25	h	Wrexham	W 5-0	Todd.Jdan.K.aldie.Tudor O.G.,Json O.G.	17.987
20	28	a	Wrexham	W 2-0	Maddison.Todd.	19.354
21	28	a	Rochdale	W 3-2	Todd.Maddison.Kirkaldie.	13.555
22	Jan 4	h	New Brighton	D 0-0		14.482
23	18	a	Halifax Town	L 2-4	Maddison.Todd.	8.814
24	22	a	Crewe Alex	W 3-0	Todd(2).Jordan.	4.331
25	25	h	Carlisle Utd	W 9-2	K.aldie(2).Tpson(2).Jdan(3).Todd.Mison.	14.051
26	Feb 1	a	Accrington Stanley	W 1-0	Jordan.	14.114
27	Mar 1	a	Tranmere Rovers	W 5-3	Todd(2).Kirkaldie.Jordan.Maddison.	15.150
28	8	h	Darlington	W 5-0	Todd(2).Kirkaldie.Jordan.Maddison.	14.787
29	13	h	Barrow	W 8-0	Todd.Mdson.Jdan(2).Kdie(2).Tson.Ogly.OG	6.998
30	15	a	Hull City	W 1-0	Jordan.	29.579
31	22	h	Gateshead	W 3-0	Jordan(2).Thompson.	15.481
32	29	h	Hartlepools Utd	W 2-0	Jordan.Todd.	8.310
33	Apr 4	h	Oldham Ath	W 4-2	Thompson(2).Jordan.Kirkaldie.	25.366
34	5	h	Crewe Alex	D 1-1	Kirkaldie.	18.142
35	7	a	Oldham Ath	W 1-0	Todd.	16.621
36	12	h	Lincoln City	D 1-1	Jordan.	19.221
37	19	a	Southport	W 5-0	Jordan(2).Kirkaldie.Todd.Maddison.	6.566
38	26	a	Rotherham Utd	L 2-3	Todd.Thompson (pen).	20.247
39	May 3	h	Chester	W 3-0	Thompson.Jordan.Todd.	17.015
40	10	h	Southport	W 2-0	Kirkaldie.Jordan.	17.401
41	24	a	Bradford City	W 1-0	Maddison.	15.631
42	Jun 7	h	York City	D 0-0		15.070

Players: Marriott, Lambton, Heydon, Mitcheson, Owens, Tomlinson, Corbett, Kirkaldie, Bycroft, Maddison, Todd, Jordan, Thompson, Tindill, McFarlane, Archer, Stirland, Woolridge, Swallow, Ferguson.

App: 39 24 18 38 1 42 9 32 41 40 42 41 33 24 18 7 5 4 3 1

Gls: 7 13 42 23 17 1 14 3

+ 3 O.G.

	HOME							AWAY							TOTAL						
	P	W	D	L	F	A	PTS	P	W	D	L	F	A	PTS	P	W	D	L	F	A	PTS
	21	15	5	1	67	16	35	21	18	1	2	56	22	37	42	33	6	3	123	38	72

F.A.Cup

	Date	V	Opponents	F-A	Scorers	Att
R1	Nov30	h	Accrington Stanley	D 2-2	Thompson.Todd.	15.223
R1R	Dec 4	a	Accrington Stanley	W 5-0	Kirkaldie(3).Todd.Jordan.	25.036
R2	14	a	Oldham Ath	W 2-1	Jordan.Maddison.	24.129
R3	Jan11	h	Portsmouth	L 2-3	Kirkaldie.Todd.	

Season 1946/47

THEY TOOK THE ROVERS INTO THE SECOND DIVISION

These are the players who brought Second Division football back to Doncaster. Names (left to right): front row: Mr. J. G. Bestall (manager), Archer, Owens, Thompson (J), Jordan, Todd, Maddison, Bycroft and R. McLean (trainer); back row: Tomlinson, Stirland, Heydon, MacFarlane, Ferguson, Corbett, Wooldridge and Swallow.

Season 1949/50

(Back): Lowes, Hodgson, Bycroft, Hardwick, Hainsworth, Goodfellow.
(Front): Tindill, Todd, Bennett, Doherty, Calverley

League Division 2 1947-48

Player columns (across the top): Stevenson, Little, Gillespie, Miller, Haydon, Owens, Livesley, Marriott, Mitcheson, Lowes, McFarlane, Archer, Corbett, Bennett, Tomlinson, Hodgson, Sterland, Kirkaldie, Calverley, Hardwick, Maddison, Todd, Jordan, Thompson, Tindill, Squires, Bycroft, Wands, Woolridge, Swallow, Ferguson

No	Date	V	Opponents	F-A	Scorers	Att
1	Aug23	h	Southampton	D 1-1	Maddison.	23.991
2	25	a	Cardiff City	L 0-3		44.415
3	30	a	Bury	L 2-4	Thompson,Jordan.	19.574
4	Sep 4	h	Cardiff City	D 2-2	Kirkaldie,Thompson.	27.760
5	6	h	West Ham Utd	W 1-0	Yeomanson O.G.	21.198
6	10	a	Bradford PA	L 0-4		18.942
7	13	a	Chesterfield	W 3-0	Jordan(2),Thompson.	17.791
8	18	h	Bradford PA	W 3-0	Todd(2),Maddison.	22.207
9	20	h	Millwall	D 2-2	Jordan,Tindill.	23.315
10	27	a	Tottenham H	L 0-2		46.011
11	Oct 4	h	Sheff Wed	L 0-1		29.446
12	11	a	Leeds Utd	D 0-0		34.775
13	18	h	Fulham	L 0-1		22.183
14	25	a	Coventry City	L 0-1		26.049
15	Nov 1	h	Newcastle Utd	L 0-3		29.601
16	8	a	Birmingham City	L 0-3		31.052
17	15	h	West Brom Alb	W 2-1	Mitcheson(2).	19.609
18	22	a	Barnsley	L 0-2		24.017
19	29	h	Plymouth Arg	W 2-0	Mitcheson,Todd.	16.710
20	Dec 6	a	Luton Town	L 1-2	Calverley.	15.556
21	13	h	Brentford	D 0-0		16.916
22	20	a	Southampton	L 1-6	Gillespie.	17.925
23	26	h	Nottm Forest	W 2-0	Jordan(2).	20.129
24	27	a	Nottm Forest	L 2-4	Todd,Kirkaldie.	22.201
25	Jan 3	h	Bury	L 1-3	Todd.	18.104
26	24	a	West Ham Utd	L 1-2	Armstrong O.G.	17.082
27	31	h	Chesterfield	W 1-0	Bennett.	23.527
28	Feb 7	a	Millwall	L 0-1		19.427
29	14	h	Tottenham	D 1-1	Bennett.	24.033
30	28	h	Leeds Utd	W 3-0	Todd(2),Bennett.	26.569
31	Mar 6	a	Fulham	D 0-0		17.153
32	13	h	Coventry City	D 0-0		22.677
33	20	a	Newcastle Utd	L 0-2		48.724
34	26	h	Leicester City	D 1-1	Todd.	24.044
35	27	h	Birmingham City	D 0-0		25.370
36	29	a	Leicester City	L 2-3	Lowes,Bennett.	30.107
37	Apr 3	a	West Brom Alb	W 3-1	Tindill(2),Bennett.	22.076
38	5	h	Sheff Wed	L 0-2		51.137
39	10	h	Barnsley	L 1-2	Thompson.	24.011
40	17	a	Plymouth Arg	D 2-2	Bennett(2).	21.528
41	24	h	Luton Town	L 0-2		7.263
42	May 1	a	Brentford	L 0-2		16.939

Average attendance: 16.162

	P	W	D	L	F	A	PTS
HOME	21	7	8	6	22	19	22
AWAY	21	2	3	16	17	46	7
TOTAL	42	9	11	22	39	65	29

F.A. Cup
R3 Jan10 a Fulham L 0-2

League Division 3 North 1948–49

No	Date	V	Opponents	F-A	Scorers	Att
1	Aug 21	a	Mansfield Town	D 2-2	Bennett,Calverley.	16,749
2	26	h	Tranmere Rovers	W 2-0	Reeve,Bennett.	17,740
3	28	h	Barrow	D 0-0		16,291
4	31	a	Tranmere Rovers	L 0-2		4,971
5	Sep 4	a	Wrexham	L 0-2		14,586
6	6	h	Oldham Ath	W 3-0	Reeve(2),Goodfellow.	10,998
7	11	a	Halifax Town	L 0-1		8,884
8	14	a	Oldham Ath	W 2-0	Mitcheson(2)	11,531
9	18	a	Bradford City	W 1-0	Reeve.	8,875
10	23	h	Crewe Alex	L 0-1		9,337
11	25	h	Carlisle Utd	W 2-0	Calverley,Hodgson (pen).	11,934
12	30	h	Stockport County	W 3-1	Tindill,Reeve,Todd.	10,460
13	Oct 2	h	Hull City	D 0-0		37,099 *
14	9	a	Gateshead	W 3-0	Bennett,Calverley,Reeve.	8,552
15	16	h	Hartlepools Utd	D 0-0		14,766
16	23	a	Darlington	W 5-1	Reeve(3),Todd,Antonio	15,326
17	30	h	Rochdale	W 1-0	Tindill.	18,866
18	Nov 6	a	New Brighton	W 1-0	Tindill.	6,030
19	13	h	Chester	D 0-0		10,658
20	20	a	Southport	W 2-0	Reeve,Antonio.	7,254
21	Dec 18	h	Mansfield Town	D 1-1	Reeve.	10,541
22	25	h	Accrington Stanley	D 0-0		12,220
23	27	a	Accrington Stanley	L 0-2		9,105
24	Jan 1	a	Barrow	L 1-3	Tindill.	8,237
25	8	a	York City	W 3-2	Tindill(2),Reeve.	11,230
26	15	h	Wrexham	W 4-2	Todd(2),Tindill,Tunney O.G.	9,281
27	22	h	Halifax Town	L 1-2	Todd.	14,374
28	Feb 5	h	Bradford City	W 2-0	Barritt,Antonio.	9,539
29	19	a	Carlisle Utd	L 0-3		10,378
30	Mar 5	h	Gateshead	W 2-1	Bennett,Hodgson (pen).	6,273
31	12	a	Hartlepools Utd	L 1-2	Todd.	6,925
32	19	h	Darlington	D 1-1	Todd.	9,548
33	26	a	Rochdale	W 2-0	Barritt,Tindill.	8,637
34	Apr 2	h	New Brighton	W 2-1	Todd,Barritt.	9,463
35	9	a	Chester	D 0-0		6,220
36	15	h	Rotherham Utd	D 0-0		32,322
37	16	h	Southport	L 1-2	Tindill.	11,918
38	18	a	Rotherham Utd	L 0-2		14,337
39	23	a	Crewe Alex	D 0-0		5,581
40	30	h	York City	W 1-0	Bennett.	7,709
41	May 4	a	Hull City	W 1-0	Barritt.	46,725
42	7	a	Stockport County	L 1-5	Bennett.	7,166

Appearances / Goals:

Player	App	Gls
Hardwick	31	
Tomlinson	24	
Hodgson	41	2
Goodfellow	32	1
Bycroft	41	
Miller	28	
Jones	6	
Reeve	30	12
Bennett	20	6
Todd	41	9
Calverley	37	3
Hainsworth	1	
Tindill	36	8
Stirland	6	
Lowes	14	2
Spedding	1	
Antonio	24	4
Graham	3	
Barritt	10	5
Mitcheson	6	2
Stevenson	13	2
Rouse	6	
Brown	4	
Gillespie	7	

+ 1 O.G.

	P	W	D	L	F	A	PTS
HOME	21	10	8	3	26	12	28
AWAY	21	10	2	9	27	28	22
TOTAL	42	20	10	12	53	40	50

F.A. Cup

			F-A	Scorers	Att
R1	Dec 4	a Bradford City	L 3-4	Calverley,Antonio,Reeve.	20,602

* Record attendance

League Division 3 North 1949–50

No	Date	V	Opponents	F-A	Scorers	Att
1	Aug20	a	Bradford City	W 2-1	Doherty.Antonio.	21,338
2	25	h	Rochdale	D 0-0		21,756
3	27	h	Chester	W 2-0	Todd(2).	16,945
4	30	a	Rochdale	W 1-0	Doherty (pen).	11,271
5	Sep 3	a	Southport	D 3-3	Goodfellow.Doherty.Antonio.	9,222
6	8	h	Darlington	W 2-1	Todd.Antonio.	16,188
7	10	a	Stockport County	W 1-0	Staniforth O.G.	15,550
8	14	a	Darlington	L 1-2	Tindill.	9,383
9	17	a	Rotherham Utd	W 2-0	Tindill.Antonio.	15,217
10	24	a	Gateshead	D 1-1	Calverley.	14,973
11	Oct 1	h	Hartlepools Utd	D 0-0		16,155
12	8	h	Carlisle Utd	D 0-0		17,342
13	15	a	Mansfield Town	W 2-1	Doherty(2).	19,446
14	22	h	Accrington Stanley	W 4-1	Todd(2).Dubois.Tindill.	14,109
15	29	a	Wrexham	W 1-0	Dubois.	12,022
16	Nov 5	h	Oldham Ath	D 1-1	Doherty.	14,328
17	12	a	York City	W 3-0	Doherty(2).Calverley.	12,952
*	19	h	Tranmere Rovers	W 1-0	Todd. (* Abandoned 5" mins - fog)	16,825
18	Dec 3	h	Barrow	W 1-0	Doherty (pen).	14,065
19	17	h	Bradford City	D 1-1	Doherty.	13,284
20	24	a	Chester	L 1-3	Bennett.	6,763
21	26	a	New Brighton	D 2-2	Doherty(2).	7,698
22	27	h	New Brighton	D 0-0		23,381
23	31	h	Southport	W 5-1	Todd(2).Doherty(2).Harrison.	21,941
24	Jan14	h	Stockport County	W 3-0	Doherty(3).	23,363
25	21	h	Rotherham Utd	W 1-0	Harrison.	30,893
26	Feb 4	h	Gateshead	D 1-1	Doherty.	22,207
27	11	a	Lincoln City	L 0-1		20,306
28	18	a	Hartlepools Utd	D 1-1	Tindill.	9,523
29	25	a	Tranmere Rovers	W 4-2	Lowes.Tindill.Harriscn.Doherty.	10,697
30	Mar 4	h	Crewe Alex	L 0-2		19,166
31	11	a	Accrington Stanley	D 2-2	Harrison.Doherty.	8,963
32	18	h	Wrexham	W 2-0	Doherty (pen).Todd.	15,114
33	25	a	Oldham Ath	W 4-1	Harrison(2).Doherty.Tindill.	22,204
34	Apr 1	h	York City	D 1-1	Tindill.	15,866
35	7	h	Halifax Town	W 4-0	Doherty(2).Calverley Tindill.	20,981
36	8	a	Carlisle Utd	D 0-0		11,503
37	10	a	Halifax Town	D 2-2	Harrison.Doherty.	8,709
38	15	h	Mansfield Town	L 0-1		19,567
39	19	a	Crewe Alex	W 2-0	Todd.Harrison.	8,325
40	22	a	Barrow	D 1-1	Daley.	6,716
41	29	h	Lincoln City	L 1-4	Daley.	11,712
42	May 3	h	Tranmere Rovers	D 1-1	Doherty.	15,107

Appearances / goals totals (by player column):

	Hardwick	Hainsworth	Hodgson	Lowes	Bycroft	Goodfellow	Tindill	Antonio	Todd	Doherty	Calverley	Harrison	Dubois	Miller	Bennett	L.Graham	Barritt	R.Graham	Sarson	Williams	Daley
App	42	42	35	34	42	42	10	42	35	39	20	11	12	4	10	3	2	1	1	1	11
Gls				1		1	9	4	10	27	3	9	2		1						6

+ 1 O.G.

	P	W	D	L	F	A	PTS
HOME	21	9	3		30	15	27
AWAY	21	10	8	3	36	23	28
TOTAL	42	19	17	6	66	38	55

F.A. Cup

	Date	V	Opponents	F-A	Scorers	Att
R1	Nov26	h	New Brighton	W 5-1	Tindill(2).Calverley.Todd.Doherty.	13,330
R2	Dec10	h	Mansfield Town	W 1-0	Todd.	22,569
R3	Jan 7	a	Reading	W 3-2	Todd(2).Doherty.	25,050
R4	28	a	Blackpool	L 1-2	Doherty (pen).	31,362

League Division 2 1950-51

No	Date	V	Opponents	F-A	Scorers	Att
1	Aug19	a	Leeds Utd	L 1-3	Harrison.	40.208
2	23	a	Southampton	D 1-1	Tindill.	24.579
3	26	h	West Ham Utd	W 3-0	Lowes.Doherty.Harrison.	22.804
4	30	h	Southampton	D 0-0		23.444
5	Sep 2	a	Swansea Town	D 2-2	Graham.Harrison.	20.076
6	9	a	Hull City	W 2-1	Doherty(pen).Lawlor.	40.218
7	11	a	Sheffield Utd	D 0-0		34.897
8	16	a	Notts County	W 2-1	Tindill.Doherty.	39.719
9	23	a	Brentford	D 1-1	Doherty.	21.544
10	30	h	Blackburn Rovers	L 0-1		23.973
11	Oct 7	h	Man City	W 4-3	Doherty(2)(1pen).Lawlor.Harrison.	32.937
12	14	a	Leicester City	L 0-2		33.782
13	21	h	Cardiff City	D 0-0		26.356
14	28	a	Coventry City	L 1-3	Doherty.	32.757
15	Nov 4	h	Grimsby Town	W 3-1	Doherty(2).Giles.	23.197
16	11	a	Birmingham City	W 2-0	Doherty(2).	26.779
17	18	h	Chesterfield	L 1-2	Giles.	21.696
18	25	a	Q.P.R.	W 2-1	Martin.Heath O.G.	16.861
19	Dec 2	h	Bury	D 1-1	Tindill.	20.339
20	9	a	Preston North End	L 1-6	Lawlor.	27.024
21	16	h	Leeds Utd	D 4-4	Doherty(3).Martin.	16.745
22	23	h	West Ham Utd	D 0-0		16.186
23	25	h	Barnsley	W 3-2	Lawlor.Harrison.Calverley.	28.995
24	26	a	Barnsley	W 1-0	Lawlor.	33.867
25	Jan13	h	Hull City	L 2-4	Doherty.Tindill.	30.604
26	20	h	Notts County	W 3-2	Lawlor(2).Tindill.	26.045
27	27	a	Swansea Town	W 1-0	Tindill.	21.878
28	Feb 3	h	Brentford	L 0-3		20.733
29	17	a	Blackburn Rovers	L 2-4	Calverley.Miller.	21.605
30	24	a	Man City	D 3-3	Lawlor(2).Brannagan O.G.	38.691
31	Mar 3	h	Leicester City	D 2-2	Harrison.Tindill.	22.403
32	10	a	Cardiff City	D 0-0		27.724
33	17	h	Coventry City	W 2-1	Harrison.Miller.	18.464
34	23	h	Luton Town	W 5-2	Harrison(2).Tindill(2).Lawlor.	32.613
35	24	a	Grimsby Town	L 0-1		18.754
36	26	a	Luton Town	L 1-3	Tindill.	14.486
37	31	h	Birmingham City	L 0-1		16.091
38	Apr 7	a	Chesterfield	W 4-1	Harrison(2).Tindill.Herbert.	13.832
39	14	h	Q.P.R.	L 0-2		16.344
40	21	a	Bury	L 1-3	Harrison.	13.586
41	26	h	Preston North End	W 2-0	Harrison.Tindill.	29.327
42	May 5	h	Sheffield Utd	D 1-1	Tindill.	14.557

Appearances and Goals

Player	App	Gls
Hardwick	41	
Rouse	4	
Graham	38	1
Lowes	13	1
Bycroft	41	
Miller	38	2
Tindill	42	13
Martin	26	2
Harrison	29	13
Doherty	23	14
Calverley	32	3
Lawlor	33	10
Makepeace	14	
Hainsworth	24	
Jones	28	
Giles	11	2
Dubois	8	
Herbert	6	1
Anderson	2	
Hodgson	2	
Holmes	2	
Adey	1	
Teasdale	1	
Patterson	1	
Wakeman	1	
Sarson	1	

+ 2 O.G.

Summary

	P	W	D	L	F	A	PTS
HOME	21	9	6	6	37	32	24
AWAY	21	6	7	8	27	36	19
TOTAL	42	15	13	14	64	68	43

F.A. Cup

	Date	V	Opponents	F-A	Scorers	Att
R3	Jan 6	a	Rotherham Utd	L 1-2	Miller.	22.000

League Division 2 1951-52

No	Date	V	Opponents	F-A	Scorers	Att
1	Aug18	a	Sheffield Wed	L 1-3	Lawlor.	41.452
2	22	h	Blackburn Rovers	W 1-0	Tindill.	23.793
3	25	h	Leeds Utd	W 2-0	Tindill.Lawlor.	22.222
4	27	a	Blackburn Rovers	D 3-3	Tindill.Martin.Calverley.	16.516
5	Sep 1	a	Rotherham Utd	L 0-2		21.252
6	5	h	Brentford	L 1-2	Tindill.	21.154
7	8	h	Cardiff City	W 1-0	Adey.	19.676
8	12	a	Southampton	L 0-2		16.649
9	15	a	Birmingham City	D 2-2	Martin(pen).Green O.G.	16.220
10	22	h	Leicester City	D 2-2	Dubois.Harrison.	19.732
11	29	a	Nottm Forest	D 1-1	Martin.	26.713
12	Oct 6	h	Q.P.R.	W 4-0	Harrison(2).Dubois.Martin.	17.673
13	13	a	Notts County	L 0-1		23.087
14	20	h	Luton Town	D 1-1	Docherty.	18.801
15	27	a	Bury	D 1-1	Docherty.	14.521
16	Nov 3	h	Swansea Town	W 3-0	Docherty(2).Tindill.	17.797
17	10	a	Coventry City	W 2-1	Tindill.Harrison.	19.367
18	17	h	West Ham Utd	W 4-1	Doherty(3).Tindill.	18.956
19	24	a	Sheffield Utd	L 1-2	Harrison.	30.108
20	Dec 1	h	Barnsley	L 1-2	Dubois.	20.902
21	8	a	Hull City	L 0-2		28.533
22	15	h	Sheffield Wed	D 1-1	Tindill.	27.763
23	22	a	Leeds Utd	D 0-0		21.793
24	25	h	Everton	W 3-1	Tindill.Doherty.Harrison.	23.526
25	26	a	Everton	D 1-1	Martin.	47.234
26	29	h	Rotherham Utd	L 0-3		29.267
27	Jan 5	a	Cardiff City	L 1-2	Harrison.	28.404
28	19	h	Birmingham City	L 0-5		20.282
29	26	a	Leicester City	L 1-2	Lawlor.	30.405
30	Feb 9	h	Nottm Forest	L 0-1		25.470
31	16	a	Q.P.R.	W 2-0	Tindill.Adey.	14.783
32	Mar 1	h	Notts County	L 1-5	Adey.	22.467
33	12	a	Luton Town	W 4-1	Lawlor.Adey.Jones.Tindill.	5.635
34	15	h	Bury	D 1-1	Lawlor.	17.453
35	22	a	Swansea Town	W 2-1	Lawlor.Doherty.	17.150
36	29	h	Coventry City	W 1-0	Lawlor.	8.575
37	Apr 5	a	West Ham Utd	D 3-3	Lawlor.Giles.Doherty.	18.140
38	12	h	Sheffield Utd	W 2-1	Lawlor(2).	22.870
39	14	h	Southampton	L 0-1		19.784
40	19	a	Barnsley	D 1-1	Giles.	17.327
41	26	h	Hull City	L 0-1		24.476
42	30	a	Brentford	L 0-1		10.243

No	Hardwick	Makepeace	Graham	Jones	Bycroft	Miller	Tindill	Martin	Adey	Lawlor	Giles	Harrison	Patterson	Brown	Doherty	Rouse	Calverley	Dubois	Docherty	Herbert	Teasdale	Wakeman	Ewing	Hall	Hodgson	Anderson
1	1	2	3	4	5	6	7	8		10		9						11								
2	1	2	3	4	5	6	7	8		10		9						11								
3	1	2	3		5	6	7	8		10		9		4				11								
4	1	2	3		5	6	7	8		10		9		4				11								
5	1	2	3		5	6	7	8	9					4				11	10							
6	1	2	3		5	6	7	8	9		11			4	10											
7	1	2	3	4	5	6	7	8	9	10	11															
8	1	2			5	6		9	8	10	11			4				7							3	
9		2	3		5	6	9		8	10	11			4				7			1					
10		2	3	4	5	6	11		8	10		9						7			1					
11	1	2	3		5			11	8			9		4				7	10	6						
12	1	2			5			11	8			9		4				7	10	6					3	
13	1	2	3		5			11	8			9		4				7	10	6						
14	1	2	3	4	5			7	8			11	9						10	6						
15	1	2	3	4	5	6		7	10			11	9					8								
16	1	2	3	4			6	7	10			11	9	5				8								
17	1	2	3	4			6	11	10				9	5		7		8								
18	1	2	3	4			6	11	10				9	5		7		8								
19		2	3	4			6	11	10				9	5				7	8		1					
20	1	2	3	4			6		10				9	5				7	8	11						
21	1	2	3	4			6	11	8				9	5				7	10							
22	1	2	3	4			6	11	10				9	5				7	8							
23	1	2	3	4			6	11	10				9	5				7	8							
24	1	2	3	4	5		6	11	8				9		10				7							
25	1	2	3	4	5		6	11	8				9		10				7							
26	1	2	3	4			5	11	8				9						7	10	6					
27	1	2	3	4			6	11	8	10		9	5						7							
28	1	2	3	4			6	11	7	10		9	5		8											
29	1	2	3	4			6	11	7	10		9	5		8											
30	1		3	4			6	11		8		9	5		10	2	7									
31	1		3	4			6	11	9	8			5		10	2	7									
32	1		3	4			6	10	9			8	11		5		2	7								
33	1		3	4			6	11	9	8			5		10	2	7									
34			3	4			6	11	9	8			5		10	2	7				1					
35	1		3				7		9	8	11		5	4	10	2			6							
36	1		3				7		9	10	11		5	4	8	2			6							
37	1		3			6	7		9	10	11		5	4	8	2										
38	1		3	6			7		9	10	11		5	4	8	2										
39	1		3				7		9	10	11		5	4	8	2							6			
40	1	3					7	8		10	11		5	4		2							6	9		
41	1		3				7	10		8	11		5	4		2							6	9		
42	1		3			6		10	9	8	11		5	4		2	7									
App	38	30	39	26	17	32	40	32	13	24	16	25	24	17	16	13	12	12	11	9	5	4	3	2	1	1
Gls				1			11	5	4	10	2	7			6			1	3	4						

	HOME						AWAY						TOTAL					
	P	W	D	L	F	A	PTS	P	W	D	L	F	A	PTS	P	W	D	L	F	A	PTS
	21	9	4	8	29	28	22	21	4	8	9	26	32	16	42	13	12	17	55	60	38

+ 1 O.G.

F.A. Cup

R3	Jan12	h	Buxton	W 2-0	Harrison(2).	20.322
R4	Feb 6	a	Middlesbrough	W 4-1	Lawlor(2).Harrison.Tindill.	41.560
R5	23	a	Portsmouth	L 0-4		45.391

R	Hardwick	Makepeace	Graham	Jones	Miller	Tindill	Martin	Lawlor	Harrison	Patterson	Brown	Doherty	Docherty	Herbert
R3	1	2	3	4	6	11	8	10		5		7	9	
R4	1		3	4	6	11	8		9	5		2	7	10
R5	1		3	4	6	11	8		9	5	10	2	7	

League Division 2 1952-53

No	Date	V	Opponents	F-A	Scorers	Att		Hardwick	Makepeace	Graham	Brown	Patterson	Miller	Doherty	Tindill	Harrison	Herbert	Walker	Adey	Lawlor	Jones	Teasdale	Martin	McMorran	Rouse	Gregg	Calverley	Kingshott	Harvey	Ewing	Robinson
1	Aug23 h		Barnsley	D 1-1	Tindill.	19.662	1	1		3	4	5	6		7		10		9				8	2		11					
2	27 h		Swansea Town	L 2-3	Martin,Adey.	16.164	2			3	4	5	6	7	10				9				8	2		11					
3	30 a		Lincoln City	L 0-2		20.775	3			3	4	5		10	7		6	11	9				8	2							
4	Sep 4 a		Swansea Town	L 1-2	Harrison.	19.531	4	1	2	3			5		7	11	10		9		4	6	8								
5	6 h		Hull City	W 3-1	Tindill,Harrison,Doherty(pen).	21.150	5	1	2	3			5		7	11	10		9		4	6	8								
6	9 h		Huddersfield Town	D 1-1	Adey.	27.614	6	1	2	3			5		7	11	10		9		4	6	8								
7	13 a		Blackburn Rovers	L 1-2	Tindill.	25.081	7	1	2	3			5		7	11	10		9		4	6	8								
8	17 a		Huddersfield Town	L 1-3	Walker.	26.504	8	1	2	3			5		7	11		10	9		4	6	8								
9	20 h		Nottm Forest	W 1-0	Adey.	16.645	9	1	2	3			5		7	11		10	9		4	6	8								
10	27 a		Everton	L 1-7	Tindill.	34.344	10	1	2	3			5		7	11		10	9		4	6	8								
11	Oct 4 h		Brentford	L 0-2		13.465	11	1	2	3	4	5	6		7			10	11	9			8								
12	11 h		Bury	D 1-1	Martin.	12.173	12	1	2	3	4	5	6	7	11			10		9			8								
13	18 a		Southampton	D 3-3	Herbert,Brown,Doherty.	14.579	13	1	2	3	4	5	6	7	11			10		9			8								
14	Nov 1 a		Leicester City	L 2-4	Walker,Doherty(pen).	29.719	14	1	2	3	4	5	6	7	8			10	11	9											
15	8 h		West Ham Utd	D 1-1	Walker.	10.612	15	1	2	3	4	5	6	7	8	9	10	11													
16	15 a		Fulham	W 3-1	Herbert,Tindill,Harrison.	20.717	16	1	2	3	4	5	6	7	8	9	10	11													
17	22 h		Rotherham Utd	W 2-1	Herbert,Doherty.	21.561	17	1	2	3	4	5	6	7	8	9	10	11													
18	29 a		Plymouth Argyle	D 0-0		12.989	18	1	2	3	4	5	6	7	8	9	10	11													
19	Dec 6 h		Leeds Utd	D 0-0		15.774	19	1	2	3	4	5	6		7	9	10	11		8											
20	13 a		Luton Town	W 2-1	Herbert(2).	15.258	20	1	2	3	4	5	6		7	9	10	11		8											
21	20 a		Barnsley	D 2-2	Tindill,Lawlor.	9.747	21	1	2	3	4	5	6		7	9	10	11		8											
22	25 a		Sheffield Utd	D 2-2	Doherty,Harrison.	41.216	22	1	2	3	4	5	6	7	11	9	10			8											
23	26 h		Sheffield Utd	L 0-2		27.656	23	1	2	3	4	5	6	7	11		10		9	8											
24	Jan 3 h		Lincoln City	W 2-0	Harrison(2).	14.206	24	1	2	3	4	5	6	7	10	9		11		8											
25	17 a		Hull City	D 1-1	Miller.	28.481	25	1	2	3	4	5	6	7	11	9	10			8											
26	24 h		Blackburn Rovers	D 3-3	Jones,Doherty,Harrison.	15.010	26		2	3		5	6	7	11	9	10			8	4					1					
27	31 h		Fulham	D 0-0		10.721	27	1	2	3		5	6	7	11	9	10			8	4										
28	Feb 7 h		Nottm Forest	D 2-2	Harrison,Lawlor.	16.857	28	1	2	3		5	6		7	9	10			8	4										11
29	18 h		Everton	W 3-0	Lawlor,Herbert,Harrison.	8.951	29		2	3	4	5		7	11	9	10			8	6					1					
30	21 a		Brentford	L 0-1		16.716	30		2	3	4	5		7	11	9	10			8	6					1					
31	28 a		Bury	L 1-2	Adey.	13.887	31	1	2	3	4	5		7	11	9			8		6						10				
32	Mar 7 h		Southampton	W 1-0	Doherty.	16.787	32	1	2	3	4	5		7	11	9				8			6	10							
33	14 a		Notts County	L 3-4	Harrison(2),Doherty(pen).	17.906	33	1	2	3	4	5		7	11	9				8			6	10							
34	21 h		Leicester City	D 0-0		15.141	34	1	2	3	4	5		7	11	9				8			6	10							
35	28 a		West Ham Utd	W 3-1	Doherty,Tindill,Lawlor.	13.435	35	1	2		4	5		7	11	9				8			6	10	3						
36	Apr 3 h		Birmingham City	W 1-0	Lawlor.	18.056	36		2		4	5	6		7	9		11		8				10	3	1					
37	6 a		Birmingham City	L 1-2	Walker.	12.055	37		2		6	5			7	9		11		8	4			10	3	1					
38	11 a		Rotherham Utd	L 2-4	Tindill,McMorran.	14.574	38		2		4	5			7		11	9	8		6			10	3	1					
39	18 h		Plymouth Argyle	D 1-1	Harrison.	12.286	39		2		6	5			7	9		11		8	4			10	3	1					
40	22 h		Notts County	W 2-0	Tindill,Lawlor.	10.063	40		2		6	5			7	9		11		8	4			10	3	1					
41	25 a		Leeds Utd	D 1-1	Tindill.	12.715	41		2		6	5			7			11	9	8	4			10		1			3		
42	30 h		Luton Town	W 1-0	McMorran.	9.415	42		2		6	5			7			11	9	8	4			10		1			3		

HOME						AWAY							TOTAL						
P	W	D	L	F	A	PTS	P	W	D	L	F	A	PTS	P	W	D	L	F	A	PTS
21	9	9	3	26	17	27	21	3	7	11	32	47	13	42	12	16	14	58	64	40

	App	32	39	34	32	35	28	29	42	28	21	21	21	21	15	15	13	11	9	8	2	2	2	1	1
	Gls							1		1	9	10	12	6	4	4	6	1		2	2				

F.A. Cup

		Date	V	Opponents	F-A		Att																	
R3		Jan10 a		Arsenal	L 0-4		57.440	R3	1	2	3	4	5	6	7	11	9	10			8			

League Division 2 1953-54

No	Date	V	Opponents	F-A	Scorers	Att		Hardwick	Makepeace	Graham	T.Brown	Patterson	Teasdale	Tindill	Lawlor	Harrison	McMorran	Robinson	Walker	Herbert	Adey	Mooney	Gavin	Hunt	Donnelly	R.Brown	Gregg	Rouse	Rushby
1	Aug19	a	Swansea Town	W 1-0	Harrison.	20.041	1	1	2	3	4	5	6	7	8	9			11	10									
2	22	h	Lincoln City	D 1-1	Lawlor.	16.531	2	1	2	3	4	5	6	7	8	9			11	10									
3	24	a	Bristol Rovers	W 1-0	McMorran.	28.117	3	1	2	3	4	5	6	11	8	9	10					7							
4	29	a	Notts County	W 5-1	Robinson(2),Harrison,Lawlor,Tindill.	10.117	4	1	2	3	4	5		6	7	8	9	10	11										
5	Sep 2	h	Bristol Rovers	W 1-0	Lawlor.	20.337	5	1	2	3	4	5	6	7	8	9	10	11											
6	5	h	Hull City	W 4-1	Robinson,Harrison,McMorran,Lawlor.	21.226	6	1	2	3	4			6	7	8	9	10	11										5
7	10	a	Brentford	W 4-1	Robinson,Tindill,Harrison,Lawlor.	14.047	7	1	2	3	4	5		6	7	8	9	10	11										
8	12	a	Everton	L 1-4	McMorran.	58.110	8	1	2	3	4	5	6	7	8			10	11		9								
9	16	h	Brentford	W 3-0	Robinson,Tindill,McMorran.	19.463	9	1	2	3	4	5	6	7	8		9	10	11										
10	19	h	Oldham Ath	W 1-0	Robinson.	21.335	10	1	2	3	4	5	6	7	8	9		10	11										
11	26	a	Bury	L 1-2	Tindill.	15.999	11	1	2	3	4	5	6	7	8	9		10	11										
12	Oct 3	h	Rotherham Utd	L 1-2	Tindill.	29.380	12	1	2	3	4	5	6	7	8	9		10	11										
13	10	a	Leicester City	L 0-2		31.299	13	1	2	3	4	5	6	7	8			10	11		9								
14	17	h	Stoke City	W 1-0	McMorran.	17.187	14	1	2	3	4	5	6	7	8			10	11		9								
15	24	a	Fulham	W 2-1	McMorran,Lawlor.	25.238	15	1	2	3	4	5	6	7	8			10	11		9								
16	31	h	West Ham Utd	W 2-0	Lawlor,Robinson.	15.118	16	1	2	3	4	5	6	7	8			10	11		9								
17	Nov 7	a	Leeds Utd	L 1-3	Lawlor.	26.830	17	1	2	3	4	5	6	7	8			10	11		9								
18	14	h	Birmingham City	W 3-1	Tindill,Harrison,Lawlor.	16.586	18	1	2	3	4	5	6	7	8	9	10		11										
19	21	a	Nottm Forest	D 2-2	Tindill,Lawlor.	28.491	19	1	2	3	4	5	6	7	8	9	10		11										
20	28	h	Luton Town	L 1-3	Lawlor.	18.273	20	1	2	3	4	5	6	7	8	9	10		11										
21	Dec 5	a	Plymouth Argyle	D 0-0		18.729	21	1	2	3	4	5	6	7	8	9	10		11										
22	12	h	Swansea Town	W 1-0	Tindill.	14.438	22	1	2	3	4	5	6	9	8			10		11			7						
23	19	a	Lincoln City	W 2-0	McMorran,Lawlor.	12.904	23	1	2	3	4	5	6	9	8			10		11			7						
24	25	a	Blackburn Rovers	L 0-2		27.337	24		2	3	4	5	6			8	9	10		11			7				1		
25	26	h	Blackburn Rovers	L 0-2		21.481	25		2	3	4	5	6			8	9	10		11			7				1		
26	Jan 2	h	Notts County	W 4-2	Harrison(2),McMorran,Herbert.	14.233	26	1	2	3	4	5	6				9	10		11	8		7						
27	16	a	Hull City	L 1-3	Lawlor.	23.828	27	1	2	3	4	5	6	7	8	9	10		11										
28	23	h	Everton	D 2-2	McMorran,Walker.	21.203	28	1	2	3	4	5	6	7	8	9	10		11										
29	Feb 6	a	Oldham Ath	D 2-2	McMorran,Walker.	16.149	29	1	2	3	4	5	6	9	8			10		11			7						
30	13	h	Bury	L 0-1		16.175	30	1	2		4	5	6	9	10			8		11			7	3					
31	27	h	Leicester City	L 0-2		18.766	31	1	2		4	5		7	10	9		8		11	6			3					
32	Mar 6	a	Stoke City	D 2-2	Tindill,Walker.	13.662	32	1	2		4	5		7	10			8		11	6	9		3					
33	13	h	Fulham	D 2-2	Adey,Lawlor.	10.025	33	1			4	5		7	8			10		11	6	9		3					2
34	20	a	West Ham Utd	L 1-2	Lawlor(pen).	14.665	34	1	2		4	5	6	7	8					11	10	9		3					
35	27	h	Nottm Forest	L 1-3	Tindill.	13.441	35	1	2		4	5	6	7				10	11		8	9		3					
36	Apr 3	a	Luton Town	L 0-2		10.838	36	1	2	3	4	5		7	10			8	11			9	6						
37	10	h	Leeds Utd	D 0-0		12.472	37	1	2	3	4	5	6	7	8			11	10	6	9								
38	16	h	Derby County	L 1-3	Tindill.	11.688	38	1	2	3		5		8		7		11	10	6	9				4				
39	17	a	Birmingham City	W 1-0	Donnelly.	15.266	39	1	2	3		5			7	8	9	10		6					4	11			
40	19	a	Derby County	L 0-2		14.012	40	1	2	3		5			7	8	9	10		6					4	11			
41	24	h	Plymouth Argyle	D 3-3	Lawlor(2),Tindill.	7.313	41	1	2	3		5			7	8		10		6					4	11	9		
42	29	a	Rotherham Utd	L 0-4		13.017	42	1	2	3		5			7	8		10		11	6				4		9		

HOME						AWAY							TOTAL								App	40	41	36	37	41	32	39	39	24	37	18	22	14	13	8	7	5	3	2	2	1	1
P	W	D	L	F	A	PTS	P	W	D	L	F	A	PTS	P	W	D	L	F	A	PTS																								
21	9	5	7	32	28	23	21	7	4	10	27	35	18	42	16	9	17	59	63	41	Gls							12	17	7	10	7	3	1	1			1					

F.A. Cup

R1	Jan 9	a	Sunderland	W 2-0	McMorran(2).	49.435	R3	1	2	3	4	5	6	7	8	9	10		11										
R2	30	a	Plymouth Argyle	W 2-0	Tindill(2).	24.293	R4	1	2	3	4	5	6	7	10	9	8		11										
R3	Feb20	a	Leyton Orient	L 1-3	McMorran.	29.191	R5	1	2	3	4	5	6	7	10	9	8		11										

Season 1953/54

An informal 'Team group' (en route to the F.A.Cup match at Plymouth)
Graham, Rouse, Patterson, McMorran, Tindill, Brown, Makepeace, Hardwick, Teasdale, Harrison and Lawlor.

Season 1955/56

(Back): Brown, Rodgers, Arnold, Wallace, Graham, Gregg, Hardwick, Makepeace, Roose, R.Walker
(Middle): Bycroft (Coach), Connelly, Palin, Gavin, Young, Williams, Hunt, Mordue, Ewing, Hodgson (Trainer).
(Front): Anderson, Wood, Mooney, Tindill, J.Walker, Jeffrey, G.Walker, McMorran, Nicholson, Bryceland.

League Division 2 1954-55

No	Date	V	Opponents	F-A	Scorers	Att
1	Aug21	a	Liverpool	L 2-3	Lawlor C (2).	49.751
2	25	h	Swansea Town	W 2-1	Walker J (2).	15.504
3	28	h	Bristol Rovers	D 2-2	Tindill.McMorran.	16.399
4	Sep 2	a	Swansea Town	L 0-3		20.602
5	4	a	Plymouth Argyle	W 2-1	Mooney.Walker J.	22.306
6	8	a	Fulham	L 2-5	Brown.Herbert.	19.997
7	15	h	Fulham	W 4-0	McMorran.Mooney.Tindill.Brown.	15.098
8	18	a	Rotherham Utd	W 3-2	Tindill.Brown.Lawlor C.	20.207
9	25	a	Derby County	L 0-5		14.056
10	27	h	Port Vale	W 1-0	McMorran.	12.818
11	Oct 2	h	West Ham Utd	W 2-1	Herbert(2)(1pen).	13.841
12	9	h	Bury	W 1-0	Brown.	15.902
13	16	a	Lincoln City	L 1-5	Tindill.	13.737
14	30	a	Ipswich Town	L 1-5	Lawlor C.	17.866
15	Nov 6	h	Nottm Forest	L 0-3		6.553
16	13	a	Leeds Utd	L 0-1		15.757
17	27	a	Middlesbrough	L 1-3	Walker J.	21.373
18	Dec 4	h	Hull City	D 2-2	Walker J.Tindill.	8.372
19	11	a	Luton Town	L 0-3		14.541
20	18	h	Liverpool	W 4-1	Tindill(2).McMorran.Mooney.	9.655
21	25	h	Blackburn Rovers	L 1-3	Mooney.	15.754
22	26	a	Blackburn Rovers	L 2-7	Walker J(2).	36.272
23	Jan 1	a	Bristol Rovers	L 0-1		19.154
24	15	h	Plymouth Argyle	W 3-2	Jeffrey.Herbert.Tindill.	5.471
25	22	a	Port Vale	D 1-1	McMorran.	16.323
26	Feb 5	h	Rotherham Utd	L 0-4		16.580
27	12	h	Derby County	W 2-0	Mooney.Walker G.	9.150
28	24	a	West Ham Utd	W 1-0	Walker J.	4.373
29	26	a	Bury	W 4-1	Tindill(2).Walker J.Jeffrey.	11.976
30	Mar 5	h	Lincoln City	D 1-1	Walker J.	11.772
31	16	a	Birmingham City	L 1-4	Walker J.	6.441
32	19	h	Ipswich Town	D 1-1	Walker J.	8.137
33	26	a	Nottm Forest	L 1-3	Tindill.	6.560
34	Apr 2	h	Leeds Utd	L 0-1		12.470
35	8	h	Notts County	W 4-2	Tindill(2).Jeffrey.Mooney.	12.223
36	9	a	Stoke City	L 0-3		20.239
37	11	a	Notts County	L 0-4		13.144
38	16	h	Middlesbrough	W 3-1	Walker G.Walker J.Jeffrey.	9.925
39	20	h	Stoke City	D 1-1	Jeffrey.	10.292
40	23	a	Hull City	D 1-1	Jeffrey.	12.270
41	30	h	Luton Town	L 0-3		12.585
42	May 4	h	Birmingham City	L 1-5	Walker J.	21.305

	Hardwick	Makepeace	Graham	Teasdale	Patterson	Herbert	Mooney	Brown	McMorran	Jeffery	Tindill	J.Walker	Williams	Hunt	G.Walker	Gavin	Lawlor	R.Walker	Nicholson	Lawlor	Young	Gregg	Rouse	Dale
1	1	2	3	4	5	6	7			10		11	9				8							
2	1	2	3	4	5	6	7		8	10		11	9											
3	1	2	3	4	5	6	7		9	10		11					8							
4	1	2	3	4	5	6	7			10		11	9				8							
5	1	2	3	4	5	6	7			10		11	9				8							
6	1	2	3	4	5	6	7		9	10							8							
7	1	2	3	4	5	6	7	8	9	10	11													
8	1	2		4	5	6	7	10	9			11					3			8				
9	1	2		4	5	6	7	10	9			11					3			8				
10	1	2	3	4	5	6	7	10	9			11							8					
11	1			4	5	6	7	10	9			11					3		8		2			
12	1		2	4	5	6	7	8	9	10	11						3							
13		2	3	4		6	7	8			11	9					5	10			1			
14		2	3	4		6	7				11	9					5		10		1			
15	1	2	3			6	7	10			11	9	4		5		8							
16	1	2	3			6	7	10			11	9	4		5		8							
17	1	2	3			6	7	8	10		11	9			5									
18	1	2	3	4		6		8	10	7	9			11	5									
19	1	2	3	4		6		8	10	7	9			11	5									
20	1	2		4		6	7		9	10	8			11	3	5								
21	1	4	3			6	7		9	10	8			11	2	5								
22	1	2	3	4		6	7		9		8	10		11	5									
23	1	2	3			6	7		10		8	9			11	4	5							
24	1	2	3			6	7		9	10	8		5		11	4								
25	1	2	3			6	7		9	10	8		5		11	4								
26	1	2	3			6			10		8	9	5	4	7		11							
27	1	2	3			6	7				10	9	5	4	11		8							
28	1	2	3			6	7				10	8	9	5	4	11								
29	1		2			6			8	9	10	5		4	11	3		7						
30	1	2	3			6					10	9	5	4	11		7	8						
31	1	2	3			6			8	10	9	5			11	4		7						
32	1	2	3			6					10	8	9	5	4	11		7						
33	1	2	3			6					8	10	9	5	4	11		7						
34	1	2	3			6	7		8	10			9	5	4		11							
35	1	2	3			6	7				10	8	9	5	4	11								
36	1	2	3				7			10		8	9	5	4	11					6			
37	1	2	3				7				10	8	9	5	4	11					6			
38	1		2			6	7				10	8	9	5	4	11	3							
39	1					6	7			9	10	8		5	4	11	3						2	
40	1	2		4			6			8	10		9	5		11	3				6			7
41	1	2		4			6			10	8	7	9	5		11	3							
42	1	2				6	7			10	8		9	5	4	11	3							

App	40	37	34	21	12	39	32	14		28	21	39	29	19	16	24	17	10	8	4	10	3	2	1
Gls						4	6	4		5		6	13	14			2				4			

HOME							AWAY							TOTAL						
P	W	D	L	F	A	PTS	P	W	D	L	F	A	PTS	P	W	D	L	F	A	PTS
21	10	5	6	35	34	25	21	4	2	15	23	61	10	42	14	7	21	58	95	35

F.A. Cup

	Date	V	Opponents	F-A	Scorers		Att
R3	Jan 8	a	Watford	W 2-0	Tindill(2).		17.130
R4	29	h	Aston Villa	D 0-0			27.767
R5	Feb 2	a	Aston Villa	D 2-2	Tindill.Mooney.		36.522
R5R	7	a	Aston Villa	D 1-1	Jeffrey.	(at Maine Road)	15.047
R52R	14	a	Aston Villa	D 0-0		(at Hillsboro')	16.117
R53R	15	a	Aston Villa	W 3-1	Jeffrey(2).Walker G.	(at Hawthorns)	18.177
R6	19	a	Birmingham City	L 1-2	Mooney.		57.830

	Hardwick	Makepeace	Graham	Teasdale	Patterson	Herbert	Mooney	Brown	McMorran	Jeffery	Tindill	J.Walker	Williams	Hunt	G.Walker	Gavin	Lawlor	R.Walker	Nicholson	Lawlor	Young	Gregg	Rouse	Dale
R3	1	2	3			6	7	10	9		8				11	4	5							
R4	1	2	3			6	7		10	8	9		5		11	4								
R5	1	2	3			6	7		10	8	9		5	4	11	3								
R5R	1	2	3			6	7		8	10	11	9	5	4										
R52R	1	2	3			6	7			10	8	9	5	4	11									
R53R	1	2	3			6	7			10	8	9	5	4	11									
R6	1	2	3			6	7			9	8	5	4	11					10					

League Division 2 1955-56

No	Date	V	Opponents	F-A	Scorers	Att
1	Aug20	h	Stoke City	L 2-4	Mooney(2).	13,087
2	22	a	Plymouth Argyle	D 2-2	Tindill,Walker J.	21,344
3	27	a	Bristol Rovers	L 2-4	Tindill,Herbert.	20,804
4	Sep 1	h	Plymouth Argyle	W 3-1	Walker G.Tindill,Jeffrey.	9,374
5	3	h	Rotherham Utd	D 1-1	Jeffrey.	15,284
6	5	h	Leicester City	W 6-2	Jeffrey(2),Walker J(2),Mooney,Herbert	11,840
7	10	h	Sheffield Wed	D 2-2	Tindill,Mooney.	26,790
8	17	a	Nottm Forest	L 0-5		13,067
9	24	h	Hull City	W 3-0	Tindill,Mooney,Walker G.	12,629
10	Oct 1	a	Blackburn Rovers	D 1-1	Walker J.	24,493
11	8	a	Swansea Town	L 0-2		20,871
12	15	h	Notts County	D 1-1	Jeffrey.	10,170
13	22	a	West Ham Utd	L 1-6	Walker G.	13,303
14	29	h	Fulham	W 4-2	Tindill,Mooney,Jeffrey,Herbert.	14,121
15	Nov 5	a	Bury	L 1-5	Tindill.	8,921
16	12	h	Barnsley	D 1-1	Walker J.	12,517
17	19	a	Middlesbrough	L 1-4	Mooney.	15,360
18	26	h	Bristol City	W 3-2	Mooney.McMorran(2).	11,144
19	Dec 3	a	Leeds Utd	L 0-3		21,769
20	10	h	Port Vale	W 3-0	Tindill.Walker G.Mooney.	7,351
21	17	a	Stoke City	L 2-5	Tindill,Jeffrey.	15,527
22	24	h	Bristol Rovers	W 2-1	Mooney.Jeffrey.	12,018
23	26	a	Lincoln City	D 1-1	Mooney.	18,083
24	27	h	Lincoln City	W 2-0	Tindill,Gavin(pen).	18,323
25	31	a	Rotherham Utd	D 3-3	Tindill,Jeffrey.Mooney.	15,427
26	Jan14	a	Sheffield Wed	L 2-5	Jeffrey,McMorran.	17,853
27	21	h	Nottm Forest	L 1-3	Walker R.	10,477
28	Feb11	h	Blackburn Rovers	D 2-2	McMorran.Tindill.	9,503
29	25	a	Notts County	L 2-3	Walker G.Jeffrey.	13,762
30	Mar10	a	Port Vale	L 0-2		16,389
31	17	h	Bury	L 2-3	McMorran.Tindill.	8,553
32	24	a	Barnsley	D 2-2	Walker R.Williams.	9,892
33	26	h	West Ham Utd	W 2-1	Walker R.Jeffrey.	6,272
34	30	h	Liverpool	W 1-0	Jeffrey.	15,308
35	31	h	Swansea Town	W 3-1	Tindill.McMorran(2).	11,864
36	Apr 2	a	Liverpool	W 2-1	Tindill.Brown.	49,659
37	7	a	Bristol City	L 1-4	Tindill.	20,777
38	10	a	Hull City	D 1-1	Tindill.	8,155
39	14	h	Leeds Utd	L 1-2	Tindill.	18,404
40	21	a	Fulham	L 0-4		17,755
41	28	a	Leicester City	L 0-3		18,267
42	May 3	h	Middlesbrough	L 0-1		5,670

			HOME					AWAY						TOTAL						
P	W	D	L	F	A	PTS	P	W	D	L	F	A	PTS	P	W	D	L	F	A	PTS
21	11	5	5	45	32	27	21	1	6	14	24	66	8	42	12	11	19	69	98	35

F.A. Cup

No	Date	V	Opponents	F-A	Scorers	Att
43	Jan 7	h	Nottm Forest	W 3-0	McMorran(2),Jeffrey.	18,717
44	28	a	Bristol Rovers	D 1-1	McMorran.	35,259
45	31	h	Bristol Rovers	W 1-0	Tindill.	22,093
46	Feb18	h	Tottenham	L 0-2	30,436

Appearances / Goals

Player	App	Gls
Gregg	21	
Makepeace	42	
Graham	31	
Teasdale	39	
Williams	42	1
Herbert	19	3
Mooney	41	12
Jeffrey	37	13
Tindill	38	18
Wood B.	2	
Walker G.	36	5
McMorran	24	7
Hardwick	21	
Walker J.	15	5
Kilkenny	14	
Gavin	12	1
Hunt	11	
Walker R.	7	3
Brown	5	1
Ewing	2	
Bell	1	
Staton	1	
Nicholson	1	

League Division 2 1956-57

No	Date	V	Opponents	F-A	Scorers	Att
1	Aug18	a	Leicester City	L 1-3	Jeffrey.	26.165
2	20	h	Rotherham Utd	D 1-1	Jeffrey.	14.720
3	25	h	Bristol Rovers	L 2-4	Mooney,Ewing(pen).	9.314
4	27	a	Rotherham Utd	W 1-0	Jeffrey.	8.816
5	Sep 1	a	Notts County	W 2-1	Jeffrey,O.G.	14.412
6	3	a	Stoke City	D 1-1	Jeffrey.	14.990
7	8	h	Liverpool	D 1-1	Jeffrey.	13.580
8	10	h	Stoke City	W 4-0	Jeffrey(2),Tindill(2).	14.659
9	15	a	Leyton Orient	D 1-1	Mooney.	19.923
10	22	h	Huddersfield Town	W 4-0	Walker R.Gavin,Mooney,Jeffrey.	19.692
11	29	a	Bury	D 4-4	Jeffrey(2),Ewing.	10.788
12	Oct 6	h	Lincoln City	W 3-1	Jeffrey(2),Walker R.	16.497
13	13	a	Swansea Town	L 2-4	Jeffrey,Cavanagh.	15.790
14	20	h	Barnsley	W 5-2	McMorran,Ewing,Mooney,Tindill(2).	14.971
15	27	a	Nottm Forest	L 1-2	Walker R.	24.512
16	Nov 3	h	West Ham Utd	W 3-0	McMorran,Mooney,Walker R.	13.071
17	10	a	Blackburn Rovers	D 2-2	Mooney,Gavin(pen).	16.588
18	17	h	Bristol City	W 4-1	Walker R,Walker G(2),McMorran.	12.472
19	24	a	Sheffield Utd	L 0-4		24.088
20	Dec 1	h	Fulham	W 4-0	Mooney(3),Tindill.	13.143
21	8	a	Port Vale	L 1-4	Tindill.	12.330
22	15	h	Leicester City	L 0-2		13.987
23	22	h	Bristol Rovers	L 1-6	Walker R.	11.692
24	25	a	Middlesbrough	L 2-3	Cavanagh.Walker R.	16.515
25	26	a	Middlesbrough	W 2-1	Cavanagh,Tindill.	8.975
26	29	h	Notts County	W 4-2	McMorran(2),Walker R,Walker G.	11.911
27	Jan12	a	Liverpool	L 1-2	Tindill.	35.954
28	19	h	Leyton Orient	W 6-1	Cvngh.Gvin(p).McMrrn.Tndll.Mney.R.Wlkr	10.069
29	Feb 2	a	Huddersfield Town	W 1-0	Cavanagh.	17.888
30	9	h	Bury	D 1-1	Tindill.	12.570
31	16	a	Lincoln City	L 1-4	Gavin.	9.204
32	23	h	Swansea Town	L 0-1		5.113
33	Mar 2	a	Barnsley	L 1-3	Tindill.	16.928
34	9	h	Nottm Forest	D 1-1	Nicholson.	14.128
35	16	a	West Ham Utd	D 1-1	Hunt.	15.336
36	23	h	Blackburn Rovers	D 1-1	Tindill.	12.476
37	30	a	Bristol City	L 0-4		18.848
38	Apr 6	h	Sheffield Utd	W 1-0	Brown.	12.219
39	13	a	Fulham	L 0-3		14.417
40	19	h	Grimsby Town	L 2-4	Tindill.McMorran	15.618
41	20	h	Port Vale	W 4-0	Tindill(2).Cavanagh.Kilkenny.	7.626
42	22	h	Grimsby Town	L 0-1		8.981

Player Appearances and Goals

Player	App	Gls
Gregg	40	
Makepeace	41	
Graham	41	
Gavin	38	4
Williams	40	
Ewing	23	3
Mooney	37	10
Jeffrey	13	15
Brown	5	1
Cavanagh	42	6
G.Walker	17	3
Tindill	31	15
R.Walker	28	9
McMorran	25	7
Kilkenny	13	1
Hunt	12	1
Nicholson	3	1
Walker	3	
Donnelly	3	
Hardwick	2	
Connolly	3	
Station	2	

+ 1 og.

Summary

	P	W	D	L	F	A	PTS
HOME	21	12	5	4	51	21	29
AWAY	21	3	5	13	26	56	11
TOTAL	42	15	10	17	77	77	40

F.A. Cup

Round	Date	V	Opponents	F-A	Scorers	Att
R3	Jan 5	h	West Brom Alb	D 1-1	Cavanagh.	24.627
R4	9	a	West Brom Alb	L 0-2		18.043

DONCASTER ROVERS, 1956-57

Back Row—Collinson, Twynehan, Gavin, Mordue, Gregg, Hardwick, Graham, Kilkenny and Taylor.
Second Row—Ewing, White, Hunt, Donnelly, Makepeace, Walker, R., Williams, Rushby and J. Spink ("A" team trainer).
Third Row—S. Bycroft (reserve team trainer), Mooney, Bell, McMorran, Walker, J., Cavanagh, Jeffrey, Wood, and J. Hodgson (trainer).
Front Row—Connolly, Bryceland, Tony Haries (mascot), Walker, C., and Burden.

Season 1957/58

DONCASTER ROVERS F.C.

B. Makepeace, J. Teasdale, H. Gregg, C. Williams,
R. Herbert.
J. Mooney, H. Tindill, L. Graham, J. Walker, A. Jeffrey.
G. Walker.

League Division 2 1957-58

No	Date	V	Opponents	F-A	Scorers	Att
1	Aug24	a	Rotherham Utd	L 1-2	Tindill.	12,923
2	28	h	Leyton Orient	W 2-0	Cavanagh.Walker.	12,877
3	31	h	Huddersfield Town	L 0-3		14,631
4	Sep 5	a	Leyton Orient	L 0-2		13,192
5	7	a	Grimsby Town	L 1-3	Kelly.	16,906
6	11	a	Middlesbrough	L 0-5		24,758
7	14	h	Stoke City	L 0-1		9,157
8	18	h	Middlesbrough	W 3-2	Ewing.Kelly.Mooney.	9,237
9	21	a	Bristol City	D 2-2	Walker.Kelly.	21,476
10	28	h	Cardiff City	L 0-1		9,909
11	Oct 5	a	Liverpool	L 0-5		33,701
12	12	h	Sheffield Utd	D 2-2	Tindill.Kelly.	12,045
13	19	a	West Ham Utd	D 1-1	McMorran.	20,216
14	28	h	Barnsley	D 1-1	Ewing.	18,971
15	Nov 2	a	Fulham	L 1-4	Cavanagh(pen)	21,280
16	9	h	Swansea Town	W 3-0	Walker.Cavanagh(pen).Ewing.	9,256
17	16	a	Derby County	L 0-1		20,129
18	23	h	Bristol Rovers	W 3-2	Tindill(2).Nicholson.	9,158
19	30	a	Lincoln City	D 1-1	Kelly.	10,017
20	Dec 7	h	Notts County	W 4-0	Nicholson.Mooney.Walker.Cavanag(pen)	8,674
21	14	a	Ipswich Town	L 0-2		13,576
22	21	h	Rotherham Utd	W 3-2	Nicholson(2).Tindill.	10,860
23	25	a	Charlton Ath	L 0-2		17,417
24	26	h	Charlton Ath	L 1-2	Nicholson.	15,563
25	28	a	Huddersfield Town	D 2-2	Callan(2).	16,682
26	Jan1	h	Grimsby Town	D 3-3	Nicholson.Walker.Callan.	10,817
27	18	a	Stoke City	D 0-0		21,443
28	Feb 1	h	Bristol City	W 2-1	Tindill.Callan.	9,752
29	8	a	Cardiff City	L 1-3	Mooney.	13,277
30	19	h	Liverpool	D 1-1	Cavanagh.	6,093
31	22	a	Bristol Rovers	L 1-2	Nicholson.	17,821
32	Mar 1	h	West Ham Utd	L 1-1	Kelly.	12,411
33	8	a	Barnsley	D 1-1	Reeson.	11,569
34	15	h	Fulham	L 1-6	Higham.	15,189
35	22	a	Swansea Town	L 3-4	Reeson.Walker.Higham.	13,961
36	29	h	Derby County	L 1-2	Reeson.	8,119
37	Apr 4	h	Blackburn Rovers	L 1-5	Hunt.	14,487
38	5	a	Sheffield Utd	L 0-3		20,370
39	7	h	Blackburn Rovers	L 2-3	Walker.Reeson.	23,853
40	12	h	Lincoln City	L 1-3	Higham.	9,459
41	19	a	Notts County	W 5-0	Jones.Walker.Higham.Fletcher(2).	16,102
42	26	h	Ipswich Town	D 1-1	Walker.	7,046

Att (average): 19,858

	P	W	D	L	F	A	PTS
HOME	21	7	5	9	34	40	19
AWAY	21	1	6	14	22	48	8
TOTAL	42	8	11	23	56	88	27

FAC: 1957-58:
R3 Jan 4 h Chelsea L 0-2

League Division 3 1958-59

No	Date	V	Opponents	F-A		Scorers	Att
1	Aug23	a	Tranmere Rovers	L	0-3		12.477
2	28	h	Brentford	W	1-0	Cavanagh.	10.654
3	30	h	Stockport County	W	4-1	Graham(pen).Mooney.Cavanagh.Fletcher.	10.447
4	Sep 2	a	Brentford	W	1-0	Fletcher.	14.845
5	6	a	Reading	L	0-2		14.791
6	9	h	Q.P.R.	W	2-0	Higham.Walker R.	10.725
7	15	a	Q.P.R.	L	1-3	Jones.	10.118
8	20	a	Bournemouth & B.A.	L	0-1		11.551
9	22	a	Plymouth Argyle	L	0-4		24.829
10	27	h	Norwich City	L	0-1		8.998
11	Oct 2	h	Plymouth Argyle	L	4-6	Walker R(2).Meredith.Graham(pen)	5.345
12	4	a	Southend Utd	L	0-5		11.889
13	9	h	Bury	L	0-1		4.202
14	11	h	Mansfield Town	L	0-2		10.672
15	16	h	Colchester Utd	W	2-1	Walker R.Sharp.	2.786
16	18	a	Notts County	D	2-2	Fletcher.Sharp.	9.341
17	25	a	Chesterfield	L	0-2		7.760
18	Nov 1	a	Newport County	L	1-3	Walker R.	7.316
19	8	h	Halifax Town	L	1-2	Higham.	6.796
20	22	h	Bradford City	L	0-3		7.244
21	29	a	Wrexham	L	1-2	Sharp.	9.749
22	Dec13	a	Hull City	L	1-5	Walker R.	10.411
23	26	h	Tranmere Rovers	W	2-0	Minton.Walker R(pen).	5.050
24	26	a	Rochdale	L	0-1		4.075
25	27	h	Rochdale	D	1-1	Callan.	7.237
26	Jan 1	a	Bury	L	0-5		10.120
27	3	a	Stockport County	L	0-2		7.573
28	24	h	Southampton	W	3-2	Sharp(2).Cavanagh.	6.251
29	31	a	Colchester Utd	L	0-1		18.056
30	Feb 4	a	Norwich City	L	0-3		14.457
31	7	h	Bournemouth	W	5-0	Fernie(2).Stephens(2)(1pen).Minton.	4.457
32	21	h	Southend Utd	W	2-1	Walker R.Fernie.	5.727
33	24	h	Reading	L	2-5	Walker R.Cavanagh.	9.345
34	28	a	Mansfield Town	L	1-3	Sharp.	8.111
35	Mar 7	h	Notts County	W	2-1	Reeson(2).	4.663
36	11	a	Accrington Stanley	L	0-2		3.892
37	14	h	Chesterfield	W	2-1	Cavanagh.Fletcher.	4.651
38	21	h	Newport County	W	1-0	Fletcher.	3.907
39	27	h	Swindon Town	W	2-0	Fletcher(2).	6.435
40	28	a	Halifax Town	L	1-5	Fletcher.	5.110
41	30	a	Swindon Town	D	0-0		9.502
42	Apr 4	h	Accrington Stanley	W	3-0	Callan.Meredith(2).	5.290
43	11	a	Bradford City	L	0-3		10.160
44	18	h	Wrexham	D	1-1	Sharp.	3.526
45	23	h	Hull City	L	0-2		8.881
46	25	a	Southampton	D	1-1	Fletcher.	5.782

Appearances / Goals:

Player	App	Gls
Nimmo	44	1
Makepeace	24	3
Graham	13	2
Cavanagh	38	5
Williams	20	
Kilkenny	40	
Mooney	23	1
Jones	11	1
Higham	13	2
Fletcher	27	9
Walker	45	9
Sharp	29	7
Gavin	31	
Minton	11	2
White	27	
Fernie	25	3
Mordue	20	
Callan	17	2
Meredith	12	3
Reeson	10	2
Stephens	10	2
Cope	5	
Station	5	
McIntosh	2	
Rodgers	1	1
Clifton	3	3

HOME								AWAY								TOTAL						
P	W	D	L	F	A	PTS		P	W	D	L	F	A	PTS		P	W	D	L	F	A	PTS
23	13	2	8	40	31	28		23	1	3	19	10	58	5		46	14	5	27	50	89	33

F.A. Cup

R1	Nov15	h	Consett	W	5-0	Mooney(2).Sharp.Reeson.Stephens.
R2	Dec 6	a	Tranmere Rovers	W	2-1	Cavanagh.Kilkenny.
R3	Jan19	h	Bristol City	L	0-2	

Season 1958/59

(Back): Fletcher, Makepeace, White, Brough, McIntosh, Nimmo, Graham, Rodgers.
(Middle): Jones, Jeffrey, Cavanagh, ? , ? , Williams, ? , Morave, Kilkenny, Gavin.
(Front): Ardron, Mooney, Stephens, ? , ? , Higham, ? , Reeson, Meredith, Walker, Bycroft.

DONCASTER ROVERS 1959-60
Back Row—Makepeace, Darby, Mordue, Nimmo, Broadbent, Kilkenny, Gavin, Clark, W. Ardron (Trainer), Staton, Wheatley, Swallow, Hymers, White, Mason and Lunn
Front Row—Sharp, Fernie, Leighton, Walker, Fletcher, Benson, Meredith, Bowskill and Cope.

League Division 4 1959-60

No	Date	V	Opponents	F-A	Scorers	Att		Nimmo	Makepeace	Gavin	Kilkenny	Mordue	Walker	Leighton	Fernie	Chappell	Broadbent	Sharp	Marshall	Meredith	Lunn	White	Hymers	Clarke	Staton	Fletcher	Cope
1	Aug22	a	Torquay Utd	L 1-2	Fernie.	8.608	1	1	2	3	4	5	11		8	9	10	7						6			
2	27	h	Millwall	D 0-0		7.967	2	1	2	3	4	5	6	7	8	9	10	11									
3	29	h	Northampton Town	W 3-2	Fernie(2).Chappell.	7.033	3	1	2	3	4	5	6	7	8	9	10	11									
4	31	a	Millwall	D 1-1	Fernie.	15.326	4	1	2	3	4	5	6	7	8		10	11							9		
5	Sep 5	h	Watford	W 1-0	Sharp.	7.168	5	1	2	3	4	5	6	7	8	9	10	11									
6	8	h	Barrow	L 1-4	Leighton.	7.649	6	1	2	3	4	5	6	7	8	9	10	11									
7	12	a	Workington	L 0-2		4.927	7	1	2			5	6		8	9	10	11			4	3			7		
8	14	h	Barrow	D 1-1	Fletcher.	6.332	8	1	2			5	6	7	8	10		11			4	3			9		
9	19	h	Rochdale	W 2-1	Fernie.Walker R(pen).	5.066	9	1	2			5	6	7	8	10		11			4	3			9		
10	24	h	Southport	W 5-0	Fernie(2).Chappell(2).Fletcher.	4.155	10	1	2			5	6	7	8	10		11			4	3			9		
11	26	a	Gateshead	L 0-5		4.318	11	1	2			5	6	10	8	9		11			4	3			7		
12	Oct 3	h	Darlington	L 0-1		5.643	12	1	2			5	6		10	9	11	7			4	3				8	
13	7	a	Aldershot	D 1-1	Walker R(pen)	5.621	13	1	5		6	2	10		8	9				11						7	
14	10	a	Carlisle Utd	L 0-2		7.019	14	1	5		6	2	10		8	9				11	4	3				7	
15	15	h	Aldershot	L 1-2	Fernie.	1.359	15	1	5		6	2	10		8	9	7			11	4	3					
16	17	h	Notts County	L 0-4		4.705	16	1	5	3			10		8	9			7	4	11		2		6		
17	24	a	Walsall	L 2-5	Fernie.Clark.	9.294	17	1	5	3			11		8	9			7	4	10		2		6		
18	31	h	Hartlepools Utd	W 5-1	Shrp.Fltcher,Broadent,Wlker R,Meredth	4.149	18	1	2				10			8	7	4	11				3	6	5	9	
19	Nov 7	a	Crewe Alex	L 0-2		5.866	19	1	2				10			8	7	4	11				3	6	5	9	
20	21	a	Crystal Palace	L 0-4		15.563	20	1	2				11		10	9	8	7	4		6		3		5		
21	28	h	Bradford PA	W 2-0	Chappell.Sharp.	4.229	21	1	2				11		10	9	8	7	4		6		3		5		
22	Dec12	h	Exeter City	L 0-1		3.754	22	1	2	6			11	9	10		8	7	4		5		3				
23	19	h	Torquay Utd	L 1-3	Fletcher.	2.312	23	1	2				11		10		8	7	4		6		3		5	9	
24	26	a	Oldham Ath	D 1-1	Sharp.	5.058	24	1	2	6			10		9		8	7	4	11	5	3					
25	28	h	Oldham Ath	D 0-0		4.574	25	1	2	6			10		9		8	7	4	11	5	3					
26	Jan 2	a	Northampton Town	L 1-3	Walker R.	6.253	26	1	2	6			10		9		8	7	4	11	5	3					
27	16	a	Watford	W 2-1	Fernie(2).	9.153	27	1	2	6			10		8	9	11	7	4		5	3					
28	23	h	Workington	W 2-0	Chappell.Fernie.	4.680	28	1	2	6			10		8	9	11	7	4		5	3					
29	30	a	Stockport County	L 0-2		4.337	29	1	2	6			10		8	9	11	7	4		5	3					
30	Feb 6	a	Rochdale	L 0-2		3.740	30	1		3	6		10		8	9	11	7	4		2				5		
31	13	h	Gateshead	W 1-0	Leighton.	2.710	31	1		6			10	9	8		11	7	4		2		3		5		
32	27	h	Carlisle Utd	W 4-1	Leighton(3).Broadbent.	4.426	32	1	2	6			10	9	7		11		4				3	8	5		
33	Mar 5	a	Notts County	W 4-3	Leighton(2).Fernie(2).	16.469	33	1	2	6	5	11	9	7			10		4				3	8			
34	8	h	Chester	W 2-0	Clark,Broadbent.	4.909	34	1	2	6	5	4	9	7			10			11			3	8			
35	12	h	Walsall	D 1-1	Clark.	8.720	35	1	2		4	5	6	9	10			7		11			3	8			
36	19	a	Hartlepools Utd	W 6-2	Clark(4).Leighton.Broadbent.	2.893	36	1	2		4	5	6	9	7		10			11			3	8			
37	26	a	Crewe Alex	W 4-0	Fernie(2).Clark.Broadbent.	7.446	37	1	2		4	5	6	9	7		10			11			3	8			
38	Apr 2	a	Chester	L 0-2		3.862	38	1	2		4	5	6	9	7		10			11			3	8			
39	9	h	Crystall Palace	L 1-2	Walker R.	6.105	39	1	2		4	5	6	9	7		10			11			3	8			
40	15	h	Gillingham	W 3-0	Fernie(2).Leighton.	7.048	40	1	2	6	5	10	9	7			8		4	11			3				
41	16	a	Bradford PA	D 3-3	Leighton.Walker R.Broadbent.	8.032	41	1	2	6	5	10	9	7			8		4	11			3				
42	18	a	Gillingham	L 1-2	Walker R.	6.966	42	1	2	6	5	10	9	7			8		4	11			3				
43	23	h	Stockport County	W 1-0	Leighton.	4.873	43	1	2	6	5	10	9	7			8		4	11			3				
44	30	a	Exeter City	L 2-4	Leighton(2).	5.038	44	1	2	6	5		9	7	8	10			4	11					3		
45	May 2	a	Southport	D 1-1	Fernie.	2.847	45	1	2			5	6	9	7	8	10		4	11					3		
46	4	a	Darlington	D 2-2	Leighton(2).	2.752	46	1	2	6	5	11	9	7	8	10			4						3		

HOME						AWAY						TOTAL						
P	W	D	L	F	A	PTS	P	W	D	L	F	A	PTS	P	W	D	L	F	A	PTS
23	13	3	7	40	23	29	23	3	7	13	29	53	13	46	16	10	20	69	76	42

App: 46 44 9 32 29 44 26 44 25 37 29 25 22 19 19 19 13 11 9 3

Gls: 7 15 19 5 6 4   1   8   4

F.A. Cup

No	Date	V	Opponents	F-A	Scorers	Att		Nimmo	Makepeace	Gavin	Kilkenny	Mordue	Walker	Leighton	Fernie	Chappell	Broadbent	Sharp	Marshall	Meredith	Lunn	White	Hymers	Clarke	Staton	Fletcher	Cope
R1	Nov14	h	Gainsborough Trin	D 3-3	Fernie(2).Chappell.	6.181	R1	1	2					7	10	9	8	11	4		6		3		5		
R1R	18	a	Gainsborough Trin	W 1-0	Walker R.	4.000	R1R	1	2			11			10	9	8	7	4		6		3		5		
R2	Dec 5	h	Darlington	W 3-2	Sharp(2).Chappell.	6.688	R2	1	2	4		11			10	9	8	7			6		3		5		
R3	Jan 9	a	Bristol Rovers	D 0-0		15.541	R3	1	2	6			10		8	9	11	7	4		5	3					
R3R	12	h	Bristol Rovers	L 1-2	Chappell.	15.217	R3R	1	2	6			10		8	9	11	7	4		5	3					

League Division 4 1960-61

No	Date	V	Opponents	F-A	Scorers	Att
1	Aug 20	a	Darlington	L 0-1		7,890
2	23	h	Southport	L 0-1		8,062
3	27	h	Crystal Palace	L 1-5	Fernie.	6,511
4	30	a	Southport	D 1-1	Walker R.	5,188
5	Sep 3	a	York City	D 1-1	Leighton.	7,758
6	6	h	Exeter City	W 2-1	Leighton(2).	5,121
7	10	a	Hartlepools Utd	L 1-2	Leighton.	4,711
8	14	a	Exeter City	L 0-2		5,015
9	17	h	Wrexham	W 3-1	Fernie(2),Senior.	4,607
10	20	h	Peterborough Utd	L 1-2	Curtis(pen).	9,644
11	24	a	Carlisle Utd	L 1-2	Wilson.	5,340
12	26	a	Peterborough Utd	L 2-6	Fernie,Broadbent.	16,290
13	Oct 1	h	Rochdale	W 3-2	Broadbent(2),Walker R.	3,798
14	8	h	Millwall	W 3-0	Fernie,Broadbent,Meredith.	3,449
15	15	a	Barrow	L 1-2	Fernie.	4,584
16	22	h	Gillingham	L 2-3	Fernie,Broadbent.	5,029
17	29	a	Bradford PA	D 1-1	Meredith.	8,422
18	Nov 2	a	Aldershot	L 0-5		5,994
19	19	h	Oldham Ath	W 2-1	Senior,Haigh.	3,400
20	Dec 3	h	Chester	W 2-1	Senior,Haigh.	2,584
21	10	a	Crewe Alex	L 1-2	Curtis(pen).	6,973
22	17	h	Darlington	W 4-0	Swallow(2),Haigh,Meredith.	3,083
23	26	h	Stockport County	W 3-1	Senior,Swallow,Curtis(pen).	7,203
24	27	a	Stockport County	L 0-1		7,204
25	31	a	Crystal Palace	L 1-5	O.G.	17,911
26	Jan 7	a	Workington	W 3-1	Fernie(2),Broadbent.	2,528
27	14	h	York City	L 0-2		5,330
28	21	h	Hartlepools Utd	W 5-3	Wilson,Leighton,Meredith,Broadbent(2).	2,771
29	28	h	Northampton Town	L 0-2		3,028
30	Feb 4	a	Wrexham	D 2-2	Leighton(2).	4,293
31	11	h	Carlisle Utd	W 1-0	Haigh.	3,818
32	18	a	Rochdale	L 1-2	Brettell.	3,173
33	25	a	Millwall	W 1-0	Ballagher.	7,990
34	Mar 4	h	Barrow	W 3-0	Ballagher,Broadbent,Leighton.	4,477
35	11	a	Gillingham	L 0-2		4,871
36	18	h	Bradford PA	W 2-0	Veall,Broadbent.	6,494
37	25	a	Northampton Town	L 0-3		8,604
38	31	h	Accrington Stan	W 1-0	Broadbent.	5,901
39	Apr 1	h	Aldershot	W 3-1	Leighton,Ballagher,Swallow.	3,520
40	3	a	Accrington Stan	D 2-2	Leighton(2).	3,631
41	8	a	Oldham Ath	D 1-1	Ballagher.	13,554
42	15	h	Workington	L 3-4	Leighton(2),Haigh.	4,257
43	17	a	Mansfield Town	W 2-1	Veall,Swallow.	4,748
44	22	a	Chester	W 2-1	Leighton,Ballagher.	2,466
45	25	h	Mansfield Town	L 2-3	Leighton(2).	3,574
46	29	h	Crewe Alex	W 6-0	Ballagher(3),Broadbent(2),Senior.	3,684

+ 1 O.G.

Appearances and Goals

Player	App	Gls
Nimmo	45	
Makepeace	11	
Curtis	40	3
Mordue	24	
Staton	26	
Lunn	43	
Fernie	20	9
Haigh	45	5
Leighton	28	16
Broadbent	46	13
Meredith	25	4
Chappell	8	
Swallow	29	5
Ballagher	16	8
Walker	22	2
Veall	14	2
Wilson	15	2
Senior	12	5
Brettell	9	1
Kilkenny	10	
Marshall	7	
White		
Hymers		
Darby		
Wales		

Summary

	P	W	D	L	F	A	PTS
HOME	23	15	0	8	52	33	30
AWAY	23	4	7	12	24	45	15
TOTAL	46	19	7	20	76	78	45

F.A. Cup

	Date	V	Opponents	F-A	Scorers	Att
R1	Nov 5	a	Chesterfield	D 3-3	Curtis(2),Swallow.	6,341
R2	9	h	Chesterfield	L 0-1		8,972

League Cup

	Date	V	Opponents	F-A	Scorers	Att
R1	Oct 18	h	Stoke City	W 3-1	Walker R(2),Meredith.	5,694
R2	Nov 16	a	Chelsea	L 0-7		9,951

DONCASTER ROVERS - 1960-61

Back Row Mr. W. J. Crayston (Secretary-Manager), Fernie, Haigh, Leighton, Chappell,
Broadbent, Meredith, Walker, Senior, Swallow, Lunn, Mr. J. G. Bestall (Team
Manager), W. Ardron (Trainer)

Front Row Wilson, Nimmo, Makepeace, White, Staton, Hymers, Marshall, Mordue,
Kilkenny, Wales.

DONCASTER ROVERS 1961-62

Back Row Fairhurst, Haigh, Nimmo, Broadbent, Hildreth, Wales, Cope, Marshall
Centre Row Taylor, Bratt, Wright, Garnett, Staton, Lunn, Swallow, Hinton, Wall, Ardron
(Trainer)
Front Row Lodge, Leighton, Malloy, Ballagher, Veall.

League Division 4 1961-62

No	Date	V	Opponents	F-A	Scorers	Att
1	Aug19	a	Gillingham	D 2-2	Broadbent,Veall.	6,516
2	22	h	Workington	D 1-1	Leighton.	8,610
3	26	h	Millwall	L 1-2	Leighton.	6,134
4	30	a	Workington	D 0-0		5,905
5	Sep 2	a	Mansfield Town	L 0-4		7,885
6	5	h	Colchester Utd	L 1-4	Robinson.	3,705
7	16	a	Rochdale	W 3-2	Veall,Ballagher,Leighton.	5,138
8	19	h	Chester	W 2-0	Ballagher,Veall.	6,779
9	23	h	Crewe Alex	W 3-0	Swallow,Veall,Leighton.	7,131
10	27	a	Chester	W 3-2	Leighton,Swallow,Lodge.	6,671
11	30	a	Exeter City	W 5-1	Haigh,Robinson,Swallow,Lodge,Broadbent	6,427
12	Oct 7	h	Tranmere Rovers	W 6-1	Swallow(2),Leighton(2),Lodge,King O.G.	8,003
13	10	h	Wrexham	L 0-2		8,597
14	14	a	Southport	L 1-3	Robinson.	5,312
15	18	a	Wrexham	L 1-3	Leighton.	8,927
16	21	a	Hartlepools Utd	L 0-1		4,621
17	28	a	Darlington	L 0-1		5,202
18	Nov11	a	Oldham Ath	L 1-3	Larkin.	9,329
19	18	h	Stockport County	D 1-1	Larkin.	4,056
20	Dec 2	h	Bradford City	W 2-0	Larkin,Ballagher.	4,501
21	9	a	Carlisle Utd	L 0-1		4,639
22	16	h	Gillingham	W 2-1	Larkin(2).	3,710
23	26	h	York City	L 1-2	Anderson.	6,321
24	Jan 1	a	Barrow	L 1-4	Robinson.	4,130
25	12	h	Mansfield Town	L 0-1		2,966
26	20	h	Barrow	W 3-2	Larkin(pen),Ballagher,Younger.	2,944
27	26	a	Aldershot	L 1-3	Anderson.	6,597
28	Feb 3	h	Rochdale	L 1-2	Bonson.	4,032
29	10	a	Crewe Alex	L 0-2		4,563
30	16	a	Exeter City	W 3-1	Anderson,Larkin(pen),Bonson.	2,089
31	23	a	Tranmere Rovers	L 2-3	Ballagher,Bonson.	7,214
32	Mar 3	h	Southport	L 1-1	McCarthy O.G.	2,982
33	5	a	Millwall	L 0-2		8,856
34	10	h	Hartlepools Utd	D 2-2	Leighton,Larkin.	2,291
35	17	h	Darlington	L 1-2	Larkin.	3,055
36	30	a	Oldham Ath	D 0-0		3,032
37	Apr 2	a	York City	L 2-5	Leighton(2).	6,264
38	6	a	Stockport County	L 1-2	Leighton.	4,144
39	13	h	Aldershot	W 2-1	Leighton,Lodge.	3,055
40	20	a	Chesterfield	L 0-3		7,236
41	23	h	Chesterfield	D 0-0		4,502
42	25	a	Bradford City	L 0-2		10,036
43	28	h	Carlisle Utd	L 1-2	Larkin.	2,349
44	30	a	Colchester Utd	L 3-5	Larkin(2),Bonson.	6,012

+ 2 O.G.

Doncaster only played 44 games, due to Accrington dropping out of the league.

	HOME							AWAY							TOTAL						
	P	W	D	L	F	A	PTS	P	W	D	L	F	A	PTS	P	W	D	L	F	A	PTS
	22	8	5	9	34	29	21	22	3	2	17	26	56	8	44	11	7	26	60	85	29

App 44 15 39 3 42 36 34 27 30 17 23 1 25 25 23 22 18 16 14 5 14 5 4 1 1

F.A. Cup

R1	Nov 4	h	Chesterfield	L 0-4		6,984

League Cup 1961-62

R1	Sep13	h	Grimsby Town	W 3-2	Broadbent(pen),Leighton,Haigh.	4,466
R2	Oct 4	a	Rochdale	L 0-4		5,476

League Division 4 1962-63

No	Date	V	Opponents	F-A		Scorers	Att
1	Aug18	h	Brentford	L	0-2		8,247
2	20	a	Chesterfield	L	1-3	Booth.	7,494
3	25	a	York City	L	0-1		5,585
4	28	h	Chesterfield	D	0-0		7,725
5	Sep 1	h	Chester	L	1-2	Booth.	6,506
6	8	a	Crewe Alex	L	0-3		5,058
7	12	a	Exeter City	W	1-0	Booth.	3,885
8	15	h	Gillingham	W	1-0	Booth.	4,709
9	22	a	Stockport County	L	1-2	Booth.	3,650
10	29	h	Oxford Utd	W	4-2	Booth(2).Nibloe.Johnson.	6,007
11	Oct 3	a	Bradford City	W	3-2	Nibloe.Hale.Storton O.G.	5,214
12	6	a	Tranmere Rovers	W	3-2	Hale.Billings.Nibloe.	8,272
13	9	h	Bradford City	D	1-1	Nibloe.	7,811
14	13	h	Torquay Utd	W	2-0	Booth.Hale pen.	8,592
15	19	a	Lincoln City	W	2-1	Booth.Billings	10,265
16	23	a	Rochdale	L	1-3	Booth.	3,534
17	27	h	Oldham Ath	D	1-1	Billings.	12,762
18	30	h	Rochdale	D	2-2	Booth.Rooney.	9,764
19	Nov10	h	Hartlepools Utd	L	2-3	Booth.Johnson.	7,640
20	17	a	Darlington	L	1-5	Hale.	2,422
21	Dec 1	a	Aldershot	L	1-3	Booth.	4,765
22	8	h	Newport County	D	2-2	Hale pen.Booth.	3,829
23	15	a	Brentford	L	0-1		9,589
24	22	h	York City	W	3-2	Nibloe.Robinson.Booth.	4,030
25	26	a	Workington	W	2-0	Booth.Hale.	5,063
26	Feb 9	h	Stockport County	L	1-2	Windross.	5,756
27	Mar 2	a	Torquay Utd	D	2-2	Ripley.Billings.	4,706
28	9	h	Lincoln City	W	3-0	Ripley.Booth.Broadbent.	4,041
29	16	a	Oldham Ath	L	0-4		9,407
30	20	a	Oxford Utd	D	3-3	Booth(2).Hale.	5,902
31	23	h	Barrow	D	2-2	Hale.Booth.	5,672
32	28	h	Workington	L	0-1		2,541
33	30	a	Southport	L	1-2	Booth.	1,799
34	Apr 2	h	Exeter City	D	1-1	Booth.	5,206
35	6	h	Darlington	W	2-0	Windross.Hale.	4,493
36	13	a	Hartlepools Utd	D	1-1	Booth.	2,666
37	15	h	Mansfield Town	D	1-1	Booth.	8,017
38	16	a	Mansfield Town	L	2-4	Booth(2).	11,657
39	20	h	Aldershot	W	2-1	Booth.Wallace.	3,406
40	25	h	Tranmere Rovers	W	4-2	Booth(3).Windross.	5,928
41	27	a	Newport County	W	4-2	Booth(2).Windross.	2,242
42	May 1	a	Gillingham	L	0-1		5,359
43	4	h	Southport	D	0-0		5,305
44	6	a	Barrow	L	0-4		4,042
45	11	a	Chester	D	1-1	Booth.	2,935
46	18	h	Crewe Alex	D	1-1	Booth.	4,452

Players (column headers): Mansell, Fairhurst, Purvis, Rooney, Hellewell, Wallace, Billings, Johnson, Nibloe, Broadbent, Meadows, Robinson, Taylor, White, Sambrook, Windross, Ripley, Booth, Hale, Bratt, Thompson, Raine, Conwell, Wales, Potter.

App: 40 9 17 44 9 18 9 44 41 45 44 31 8 40 11 29 26 20 16 15 14 14 6 5 1

Gls: 9 34 3 2 3 1 1 5 2 4 1 1 + 1 O.G.

	P	W	D	L	F	A	PTS
HOME	23	9	10	4	36	26	28
AWAY	23	5	4	14	28	51	14
TOTAL	46	14	14	18	64	77	42

F.A. Cup

	Date	V	Opponents	F-A		Scorers	Att
R1	Nov 3	a	South Shields	D	0-0		6,721
R1R	8	h	South Shields	W	2-1	Booth.Billings.	5,854
R2	24	h	Tranmere Rovers	L	1-4	Booth.	9,557

League Cup

	Date	V	Opponents	F-A		Scorers	Att
R1	Sep 5	a	Bradford City	D	2-2	Booth.Johnson.	4,731
R1R	18	h	Bradford City	W	2-0	Booth.Billings.	5,591
R2	26	a	Birmingham City	L	0-5		11,384

DONCASTER ROVERS F.C., 1962-63
(Back): Wales, McCall, Brain, Myers, Cornwell.
(Middle): Clayton (Trainer), Fairhurst, Raine, White, Thompson, Ripley, Bratt, Marshall (Asst.Trainer).
(Front): Johnson, Ramshaw, Robinson, Carwright, Windross, Billings, Taylor, Airey, Sambrook, Wright.

DONCASTER ROVERS, 1963-64
Back Row Fairhurst, Crompton, Machin, Hodgewell, Potter, Westlake, Mansell, Billing, Fecht
Centre Row Marshall (Trainer), Moore, Lambton, Raine, White, Ripley, Conwel, Meadow, Johnson, Clayton (Trainer)
Front Row Robinson, Hale, Booth, Nibloe, Haspell, Broadbent
On Ground McMinn, Lovell, Elliott, Stirling

League Division 4 1963-64

No	Date	V	Opponents	F-A	Scorers	Att
1	Aug24	h	Newport County	D 1-1	Booth.	6,040
2	28	a	Oxford Utd	W 1-0	Hale.	9,401
3	31	a	Stockport County	W 3-1	Booth.Raine.Robinson.	7,901
4	Sep 7	h	Bradford PA	W 3-2	Hale.Nibloe.Booth.	6,484
5	10	h	Oxford Utd	L 0-1		9,096
6	14	a	Chesterfield	D 3-3	Booth.Westlake.Broadbent.	9,684
7	17	h	Workington Town	L 1-2	Robinson.Raine.	9,031
8	21	a	Exeter City	L 1-3	Booth.	5,777
9	28	h	Brighton & H.A	D 1-1	Taylor.	5,085
10	Oct 1	a	Workington	L 1-4	Booth.	4,192
11	5	a	Chester	D 1-1	Hale.	6,214
12	8	h	Barrow	W 3-1	Hale.Ripley.Robinson.	4,422
13	12	h	Gillingham	L 1-2	Robinson.	6,670
14	14	a	Barrow	W 2-0	Booth(2).	5,420
15	19	a	Lincoln City	L 1-3	Booth.	6,932
16	22	h	York City	D 0-0		4,974
17	25	h	Bradford City	W 2-1	Broadbent.Hale.	6,245
18	28	a	York City	L 1-3	Hale.	4,981
19	Nov 2	a	Aldershot	L 2-4	Hale.Booth.	4,379
20	9	a	Carlisle Utd	D 1-1	Hale.	5,397
21	23	h	Halifax Town	W 3-1	Booth.Nibloe.Hale.	5,119
22	29	a	Tranmere Rovers	L 0-3		3,781
23	Dec14	a	Newport County	W 4-1	Booth(2).Hale.Robinson.	2,344
24	21	h	Stockport County	L 0-3		4,142
25	26	a	Southport	W 3-0	Booth(3).	3,276
26	28	h	Southport	L 1-3	Booth.	11,719
27	Jan 1	a	Bradford PA	L 1-3	Booth.	6,963
28	18	h	Chesterfield	D 1-1	Hale.	6,000
29	25	h	Darlington	W 10-0	Hle(4).Booth(2).Rply(2).Wndrss.Brdbnt	6,150
30	Feb 1	h	Exeter City	W 1-0	Booth.	8,083
31	8	a	Brighton & H.A	L 0-4		7,429
32	15	h	Chester	W 3-2	Hale.Broadbent(pen).Ripley.	6,554
33	22	h	Gillingham	D 1-1	Hale.	7,681
34	29	h	Lincoln City	D 0-0		9,474
35	Mar 7	a	Bradford City	L 1-2	Broadbent(pen).	5,848
36	14	h	Aldershot	L 1-2	Booth.	3,407
37	21	a	Carlisle Utd	L 0-6		4,753
38	24	h	Rochdale	W 2-0	Hale.Thompson.	5,160
39	28	h	Hartlepools Utd	D 2-2	Hale.Jeffrey.	5,816
40	31	a	Rochdale	D 2-2	Jeffrey.Hale.	2,181
41	Apr 4	a	Halifax Town	W 2-0	Jeffrey.Booth.	5,255
42	8	a	Torquay Utd	L 0-1		6,316
43	11	h	Tranmere Rvers	L 1-2	Taylor.	6,840
44	18	a	Darlington	L 0-2		2,556
45	20	a	Hartlepools Utd	L 1-2	Booth.	4,385
46	25	h	Torquay Utd	W 1-0	Jeffrey.	4,262

App 33 43 39 6 23 36 37 43 20 44 39 20 20 17 17 16 9 7 6 5 3 1 1 1
Gls 2 4 5 23 2 4 2 20 1 4 2

	P	W	D	L	F	A	PTS
HOME	23	11	8	4	46	23	30
AWAY	23	4	4	15	24	52	12
TOTAL	46	15	12	19	70	75	42

F.A. Cup

R1	Nov16	h	Tranmere Rovers	W 3-0	Robinson,Nibloe,Ripley.	5,622
R2	Dec 7	h	Notts County	D 1-1	Booth.	8,810
R2R	10	a	Notts County	W 2-1	Broadbent(pen),Hale.	10,607
R3	Jan 4	h	Bristol City	D 2-2	Taylor,Ripley.	18,050
R3R	7	a	Bristol City	L 0-2		20,285

League Cup

R1	Sep 4	h	York City	D 0-0		8,020
R1R	23	a	York City	L 0-3		5,343

League Division 4 1964-65

Player columns (left-hand stack): Williams, McMinn, Marsden, Fairhurst, Barlow, Henderson, Kelly, Tait, Leivers, Potter, Grainger, Broadbent, Taylor, Jeffrey, Hale, Billings, Robinson, Ricketts, Ripley, Wylie, Watton, Raine, Oxford.

No	Date	V	Opponents	F-A	Scorers	Att
1	Aug22	a	Bradford PA	L 2-5	Tait,Jeffrey.	7,293
2	25	h	Southport	L 1-2	Jeffrey.	8,984
3	29	h	Aldershot	W 1-0	Jeffrey.	6,449
4	31	a	Southport	W 5-3	Jeffrey(2),Hale(2),Robinson.	5,196
5	Sep 5	h	Torquay Utd	W 2-0	Ricketts,Robinson.	9,084
6	8	h	Wrexham	D 1-1	Robinson.	12,087
7	12	a	Chesterfield	L 0-1		9,427
8	16	a	Wrexham	W 2-0	Jeffrey,Robinson.	7,947
9	18	h	Notts County	D 0-0		11,362
10	26	a	Halifax Town	W 4-2	Broadbent(2),Hale,Grainger.	4,917
11	29	h	Darlington	W 6-3	Jeffrey(4),Broadbent,Morgan O.G.	14,103
12	Oct 3	h	Newport County	W 1-0	Jeffrey.	14,402
13	5	a	Darlington	D 2-2	Hale,Jeffrey.	5,979
14	9	a	York City	L 2-4	Hale,Jeffrey.	11,898
15	17	h	Lincoln City	L 1-2	Jeffrey.	9,635
16	19	a	Tranmere Rovers	L 0-3		12,699
17	24	a	Brighton & H A	D 1-1	Jeffrey.	16,323
18	31	h	Oxford Utd	D 2-2	Hale(pen),Tait.	7,645
19	Nov 7	a	Barrow	W 2-1	Robinson,Jeffrey.	2,442
20	21	a	Rochdale	L 1-2	Tait.	4,752
21	28	h	Millwall	W 4-0	Broadbent(3),Jeffrey.	7,063
22	Dec12	h	Bradford PA	D 1-1	Robinson.	8,446
23	19	a	Aldershot	L 0-3		2,948
24	26	h	Stockport County	W 3-0	Tait,Jeffrey,Ricketts.	8,497
25	28	a	Stockport County	L 0-2		3,083
26	Jan 2	a	Torquay Utd	W 4-2	Broadbent(2),Grainger,Jeffrey.	4,696
27	16	a	Chesterfield	W 2-0	Jeffrey(2).	6,414
28	23	a	Notts County	L 2-5	Jeffrey,Hale.	8,045
29	30	h	Hartlepools Utd	W 0-1		6,383
30	Feb 3	a	Bradford City	W 3-0	Hale(3).	4,080
31	6	h	Halifax Town	W 4-0	Jeffrey(3),Hale.	6,034
32	13	a	Newport County	L 0-1		2,605
33	20	h	York City	W 4-3	Jeffrey,Hale,Ricketts,Robinson.	8,578
34	27	a	Lincoln City	W 2-0	Jeffrey,Robinson.	5,193
35	Mar 6	h	Brighton & H A	W 2-1	Jeffrey(2).	10,345
36	13	a	Oxford Utd	L 0-3		7,901
37	20	h	Barrow	W 4-2	Jeffrey(2),Tait(2).	4,399
38	29	a	Hartlepools Utd	D 1-1	Broadbent.	5,935
39	Apr 3	h	Rochdale	D 2-2	Jeffrey,Grainger.	7,842
40	6	h	Chester	L 1-4	Tait.	8,007
41	10	a	Millwall	D 1-1	Hale.	10,462
42	16	a	Crewe Alex	W 4-4	Jeffrey(2),Wylie,Leivers.	6,029
43	17	h	Bradford City	D 0-0		7,097
44	19	h	Crewe Alex	W 3-1	Jeffrey,Ricketts,Broadbent.	5,560
45	24	a	Chester	L 0-3		6,405
46	27	h	Tranmere Rovers	W 1-0	Jeffrey.	8,675

App: 16 24 46 44 29 42 40 1 34 46 2 39 35 31 19 19 18 10 3 3 3 2 1

Gls: 1 4 8 13 36 46 10 3 1 7 2   + 1 O.G.

	P	W	D	L	F	A	PTS
HOME	23	13	6	4	46	25	32
AWAY	23	7	5	11	38	47	19
TOTAL	46	20	11	15	84	72	51

F.A. Cup

	Date	V	Opponents	F-A	Scorers	Att
R1	Nov14	h	Bradford PA	W 3-2	Jeffrey(2),Ricketts.	12,372
R2	Dec 5	h	Scarborough	D 0-0		10,535
R2R	9	a	Scarborough	W 2-1	Hale,Robinson.	7,802
R3	Jan 9	h	Huddersfield Town	L 0-1		19,914

League Cup

	Date	V	Opponents	F-A	Scorers	Att
R1	Sep 2	h	Bradford PA	W 1-0	Henderson.	7,684
R2	23	h	Preston N.E.	W 1-0	Jeffrey.	13,399
R3	Oct14	h	Bradford City	L 2-3	Barlow O.G.	11,373

Season 1964/65

(Back): Lovell, Stirling, Ricketts, Raine, Billings, McMinn.
(Middle): Clayton (Trainer), Fairhurst, Walton, Oxford, Elliott, Potter, Marsden, Ripley, Marshall (Trainer)
(Front): Robinson, Tait, Hale, Henderson, Lievers (Player/Manager), Jeffrey.

Season 1966/67

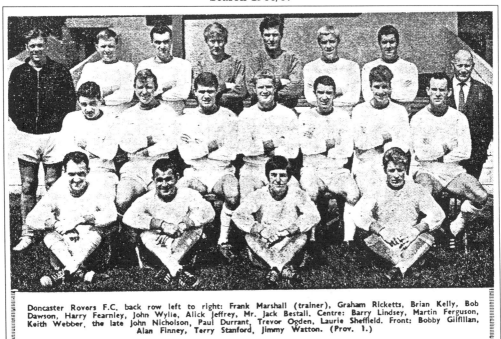

Doncaster Rovers F.C. back row left to right: Frank Marshall (trainer), Graham Ricketts, Brian Kelly, Bob Dawson, Harry Fearnley, John Wylie, Alick Jeffrey, Mr. Jack Bestall. Centre: Barry Lindsey, Martin Ferguson, Keith Webber, the late John Nicholson, Paul Durrant, Trevor Ogden, Laurie Sheffield. Front: Bobby Gilfillan, Alan Finney, Terry Stanford, Jimmy Watton. (Prov. 1.)

League Division 4 1965-66

No	Date	V	Opponents	F-A	Scorers	Att		Poter	Kelly	Nicholson	Wylie	Ripley	Ricketts	Robinson	Sheffield	Ogden	Jeffrey	Grainger	Finney	Coleman	Watton	Gillilan	Fearnley	Wilson	Durrant	Broadbent	Dawson	Lewers	Chapman	Fairhurst	Lovell	McMinn
1	Aug21	h	Lincoln City	W 4-0	Sheffield(2),Jeffrey,Ricketts.	11.566	1	1	2		4		6	7	9		8			3					11	10			5			
2	24	h	Hartlepools Utd	W 4-0	Jeffrey(2),Sheffield,Ashworth O.G.	10.851	2	1	2		4		6	7	9		8			3					11	10			5			
3	28	a	Southport	L 1-2	Robinson.	3.824	3	1	2		4	12	6	7	9*		8			3					11	10			5			
4	Sep 4	h	Wrexham	W 2-0	Broadbent(2).	9.109	4	1	2			4	5	6	7		9			3					11	8	10					
5	11	a	Bradford PA	W 1-0	Ricketts.	7.257	5	1	2			4	5	6	7		9		11	3						8	10					
6	13	a	Hartlepools Utd	L 0-2		5.324	6	1	2		5		6	7	8	9				3					11	10				4		
7	17	h	Aldershot	W 3-2	Sheffield(2),Broadbent.	10.839	7	1	2		4	12	6	7*	8	9				3					11	10			5			
8	25	a	Newport County	L 0-4		2.970	8	1		5	4		6	7	9		8*								11		10		2		3	12
9	Oct 2	h	Torquay Utd	L 0-1		9.913	9	1	2	5	4	12	6		9*		8	11							7	10					3	
10	7	a	Luton Town	L 3-4	Jeffrey,Ogden,Sheffield.	5.020	10	1	2	3	4	5	6	7	8	9	10	11														
11	9	h	Stockport County	W 1-0	Ripley.	8.237	11		2	3	4	5	6	7	8	9	10	11								1						
12	15	a	Tranmere Rovers	L 0-1		9.281	12		2	3	4	5	6	7	8	9	10	11								1						
*	22	h	Colchester Utd	L 0-1	* Abandoned fog 36 mins.	4.263																									
13	29	a	Barnsley	W 5-1	Jeffrey(2)(1pen),Sheffield(2),Ricketts	13.358	13		2	3	4	5	6	7	9		8								11		1		10			
14	Nov 6	h	Bradford City	D 1-1	Jeffrey.	7.929	14		2	3	4	5	6	7	9		8								11		1		10			
15	19	h	Port Vale	W 1-0	Alcock O.G.	6.065	15	1	2	3	4	5	6			9	8				11		10	7								
16	23	h	Luton Town	D 1-1	Jeffrey.	4.134	16	1	2	3	4	5	6		9		8				11		10	7								
17	Dec 4	h	Colchester Utd	W 2-0	Jeffrey,Sheffield.	6.035	17	1	2	3	4	5	6		9		8				11		10	7								
18	11	a	Notts County	W 2-1	Sheffield,Smith O.G.	5.049	18		2	3	4	5	6		9		8				11		10	7			1					
19	18	h	Tranmere Rovers	W 3-1	Jeffrey(3).	8.106	19		2	3	4	5	6		9		8				11		10	7			1					
20	27	a	Barrow	L 1-2	Sheffield.	6.712	20		2	3	4	5	6		9		8				11	12	10	7			1*					
21	28	h	Barrow	D 1-1	Gilfillan.	9.458	21		2	3	4	5	6		9		8				11		10	7			1					
22	Jan 1	a	Stockport County	D 1-1	Sheffield.	7.120	22		2	5	4		6		9		8				11	3	10	7			1					
23	8	h	Crewe Alex	W 4-1	Sheffield(2),Gilfillan,Coleman.	7.330	23		2	5	4		6		9		8				11	3	10	7			1					
24	15	a	Colchester Utd	L 1-2	Jeffrey.	3.778	24		2	5	4		6		9		8				7	11	3	10			1					
25	28	a	Lincoln City	W 3-0	Sheffield(2),Jeffrey.	7.499	25	1	2	5	4		6		9		8				7	11	3	10								
26	Feb 5	h	Southport	D 1-1	Ricketts.	9.471	26	1	2	5	4		6		9		8				7	11	3	10								
27	12	a	Rochdale	W 1-0	Jeffrey.	2.542	27	1	2	5	4		6	7	9		8				11	10										
28	15	h	Chesterfield	W 1-0	Finney.	8.349	28	1	2	5	4		6	7	9		8				11	10	3									
29	19	a	Wrexham	L 3-4	Jeffrey,Sheffield,Coleman(pen).	6.201	29		2	5	4		6	7	9		8				11	10	3				1					
30	25	h	Bradford PA	W 6-2	Shffld(2).Jffry.Rckts.Flflln.McClmn.OG	10.252	30		2	5	4		6		9		8				11	10	3	7	1							
31	Mar 4	h	Rochdale	W 2-0	Sheffield(2).	12.255	31		2	5	4		6		9		8				11	10	3	7	1							
32	8	a	Halifax Town	W 3-2	Jeffrey,Sheffield,Gilfillan.	6.849	32		2	5	4		6		9		8				11	10	3	7	1							
33	12	a	Aldershot	D 1-1	Dawes O.G.	3.486	33		2	5	4		6		9		8				11	10	3	7	1							
34	19	h	Newport County	W 1-0	Coleman.	12.364	34		2	5	4		6		9		8				11	10	3	7	1							
35	26	a	Torquay Utd	D 0-0		8.645	35		2	5	4		6		9		8				11	10	3	7	1							
36	Apr 9	h	Chester	D 1-1	Jeffrey.	11.443	36		2	5	4	12	6		9		8				11*	10	3	7	1							
37	11	a	Darlington	L 2-3	Jeffrey,Coleman(pen).	12.181	37		2	5	4	12	6	7	9		8*				10		3	11	1							
38	12	h	Darlington	W 6-3	Sheffield(2),Ogden(3),Kelly.	15.572	38	1	2	5	4		6		9	8					10	7		11								
39	16	a	Port Vale	W 1-0	Sheffield.	6.669	39	1	2	5	4		6		9	8					10		3	7	11							
40	22	h	Halifax Town	D 2-2	Gilfillan,Wylie.	16.998	40		2	5	4		6		9	8					10*	3	7	1	11	12						
41	25	a	Chesterfield	D 1-1	Ricketts.	8.541	41		2	5	4		6		9		8				10	3	7	1	11							
42	30	a	Chester	W 4-1	Sheffield(2),Gilfillan,Jeffrey.	9.831	42		2	5	4		6		9		8				11*	10	3	7	1	12						
43	May 3	h	Barnsley	W 2-1	Sheffield,Jeffrey.	16.494	43		2	5	4*		6		9		8				11	3	10	1	7	12						
44	6	h	Notts County	L 0-3		16.389	44		3	5	4		6		9		8				11		10	1	7							2
45	11	a	Crewe Alex	W 1-0	Coleman.	3.927	45	1	2	5	4		6		9		8				10	3	11	1	7							
46	16	a	Bradford City	D 1-1	Durrant.	7.812	46		2	5	4		6		9						10	3	11	1	7	8						

	HOME						AWAY							TOTAL												
	P	W	D	L	F	A	PTS	P	W	D	L	F	A	PTS	P	W	D	L	F	A	PTS						
	23	15	6	2	49	21	36	23	9	5	9	36	33	23	46	24	11	11	85	54	59						

	Poter	Kelly	Nicholson	Wylie	Ripley	Ricketts	Robinson	Sheffield	Ogden	Jeffrey	Grainger	Finney	Coleman	Watton	Gillilan	Fearnley	Wilson	Durrant	Broadbent	Dawson	Lewers	Chapman	Fairhurst	Lovell	McMinn
App	19	45	39	46	14	46	17	43	11	38			5	14	32	31	29	15	20	11	8	7	5	5	3	2	1
Sub					5									1				1	2						1
Gls		1		1	1	6	1	28	4	22			1	5		6			1	3					

+ 5 O.G.

F.A. Cup

| R1 | Nov13 | h | Wigan Ath | D 2-2 | Ricketts,Kelly. | 10.005 | R1 | | 2 | 3 | 4 | 5 | 6 | 7 | 9 | | 8 | | | | | | | | 11 | 10 | | 1 | | | | |
| R1R | 17 | a | Wigan Ath | L 1-3 | Ogden. | 7.113 | R1R | 1 | 2 | 3 | 4 | 5 | 10 | 11 | | 9 | 8 | | | | | | | | 7 | | | 6 | | | | |

League Cup

R1	Sep 1	H	Barnsley	D 2-2	Ogden(2).	14.307	R1		2		4		6	7	9	8				3					11	10						
R1R	8	a	Barnsley	W 2-1	Broadbent(pen),Robinson.	11.946	R1R	1	2		4	5	6	7		9		11		3						8	10					
R2	22	h	Burnley	L 0-4		24.988	R2	1	2		4		6		9	8				3					7	11	10		5			

League Division 3 1966-67

Player columns (appearance/goal grid): Nicholson, Ashmore, Durrant, Ferguson, Crowmack, Warboys, Leigh, Flowers, Mottershead, Sykes, Lindsay, Webber, Jeffrey, Dawson, Kettleboro', Ogden, Gilfillan, Coleman, Sheffield, Watson, Finney, Ricketts, Robertson, Wylie, Watton, Kelly, Fearnley

No	Date	V	Opponents	F-A	Att	Scorers
1	Aug20	a	Peterborough Utd	D 3-3	7,321	Jeffrey,Sheffield,Crowe O.G.
2	27	h	Torquay Utd	W 2-1	11,539	Sheffield,Jeffrey.
3	Sep 3	a	Brighton & H A	D 0-0	10,753	
4	6	h	Oxford Utd	W 2-1	11,906	Ricketts(pen),Ogden.
5	9	h	Darlington	L 0-4	14,207	
6	17	a	Q.P.R.	L 0-6	8,090	
7	23	h	Watford	D 0-0	13,040	
8	28	a	Oxford Utd	L 1-6	7,382	Sheffield.
9	Oct 1	a	Swindon Town	W 1-0	7,940	Sheffield.
10	7	h	Bristol Rovers	W 3-2	11,614	Sheffield(2),Coleman.
11	15	a	Colchester Utd	L 0-5	6,461	
12	17	a	Mansfield Town	L 1-3	8,257	Gilfillan.
13	21	h	Shrewsbury Town	W 2-1	10,558	Ogden(2).
14	29	a	Middlesborough	L 0-2	12,082	
15	Nov 5	h	Swansea Town	W 4-1	7,882	Sheffield(2),Gilfillan,Watson.
16	12	a	Bournemouth & B A	L 1-4	4,273	Ogden.
17	15	h	Mansfield Town	L 4-6	7,188	Ogden(3),Watson.
18	18	a	Leyton Orient	D 2-2	6,992	Webber,Ogden.
19	Dec 3	h	Workington	W 2-1	4,515	Ricketts,Finney.
20	9	a	Scunthorpe Utd	L 1-2	6,400	Ricketts.
21	17	h	Peterborough Utd	W 3-1	7,035	Jeffrey(3).
22	23	h	Grimsby Town	W 3-2	9,185	Coleman,Ricketts,Ogden.
23	26	a	Grimsby Town	L 1-4	9,182	Finney.
24	31	a	Torquay Utd	L 0-4	5,743	
25	Jan14	a	Darlington	L 2-3	5,963	Coleman,Webber.
26	21	h	Q.P.R.	D 1-1	12,062	Gilfillan.
27	Feb 4	a	Watford	L 1-4	11,747	Webber.
28	11	h	Swindon Town	W 1-0	7,935	Coleman.
29	18	a	Oldham Ath	L 0-1	9,737	
30	25	a	Bristol Rovers	L 2-4	9,012	Watson.Coleman.
31	Mar 3	h	Colchester Utd	L 1-4	8,481	Coleman(pen).
32	10	h	Oldham Ath	D 1-1	6,985	Jeffrey.
33	18	a	Shrewsbury Town	L 1-2	4,875	Jeffrey.
34	25	h	Middlesborough	L 0-4	9,628	
35	27	a	Walsall	L 0-4	6,696	
36	28	h	Walsall	W 2-1	4,831	Gilfillan(2).
37	Apr 1	a	Swansea Town	L 0-6	6,292	
38	8	h	Bournemouth & B A	D 1-1	2,918	Gilfillan.
39	12	a	Reading	L 0-4	4,729	
40	15	a	Leyton Orient	L 1-4	6,393	Kelly.
41	21	h	Gillingham	L 2-3	3,364	Gilfillan,Lindsey(pen).
42	25	h	Reading	L 0-2	3,066	
43	29	a	Workington	L 1-3	1,310	Ogden.
44	May 5	h	Scunthorpe Utd	W 3-0	3,948	Gilfillan,Ricketts(pen),Warboys.
45	13	a	Gillingham	L 1-3	4,179	Warboys.
46	16	h	Brighton & H A	D 1-1	3,039	Leigh.

```
        P  W  D  L  F  A  PTS
(home) 23 11  6  6 40 40  28
(away) 23  1  2 20 18 77   4
        46 12  8 26 58 117 32
```

App 17 39 39 29 29 38 16 21 15 26 38 28 22 21 20 18 16 15 13 11 11 7 8 3 2 2

Sub 1

Gls 1 5 2 3 8 6 10

+ 1 O.G.

F.A. Cup

						Att	
R1	Nov26	a	Halifax Town	D 2-2		8,336	Gilfillan,Ogden.
R1R	29	h	Halifax Town	L 1-3	(aet)	9,191	Ogden.

League Cup

						Att	
R1	Aug24	a	Bradford City	D 1-1		4,603	Kelly.
R1R	30	h	Bradford City	W 5-2		8,790	Sheffield(2),Jeffrey(2),Gilfillan.
R2	Sep14	a	Darlington	D 1-1		7,701	Sheffield.
R2R	19	h	Darlington	W 2-0		9,719	Sheffield,Webber.
R3	Oct 4	h	Swindon Town	D 1-1		9,190	Watson.
R3R	11	a	Swindon Town	L 2-4	(aet)	8,147	Sheffield(2).

League Division 4 1967-68

No	Date	V	Opponents	F-A	Scorers	Att
1	Aug19	a	Barnsley	L 0-1		11,305
2	26	h	Swansea Town	L 1-2	Jeffrey(pen).	6,127
3	Sep 2	a	Hartlepools Utd	D 0-0		7,669
4	5	h	Wrexham	D 2-2	Warboys,Jeffrey.	5,884
5	9	h	Newport County	D 1-1	Gilfillan.	6,207
6	16	a	York City	W 2-1	Warboys,Watson.	5,679
7	23	h	Rochdale	W 2-0	Gilfillan,Jeffrey(pen).	6,530
8	25	a	Wrexham	D 0-0		9,733
9	30	a	Brentford	L 2-4	Jeffrey(2).	7,308
10	Oct 3	h	Luton Town	W 2-0	Gilfillan,Watson.	5,529
11	7	a	Port Vale	L 2-4	Gilfillan,Warboys.	5,436
12	14	h	Chester	D 0-0		6,002
13	21	a	Chesterfield	L 0-2		11,097
14	25	a	Luton Town	L 3-5	Watson,Warboys,Kelly.	13,925
15	28	h	Exeter City	W 3-1	Webber(2),Hamilton O.G.	6,204
16	Nov 4	a	Darlington	D 1-1	Webber.	5,221
17	11	h	Aldershot	W 3-0	Jeffrey(pen),Webber,Renwick O.G.	6,054
18	14	h	Hartlepools Utd	L 0-1		7,818
19	17	a	Workington	D 2-2	Watson,Webber.	1,873
20	25	h	Lincoln City	D 0-0		5,627
21	Dec 2	a	Halifax Town	W 3-2	Watson(2),Aiken.	4,359
22	15	h	Barnsley	L 1-2	Gilfillan.	9,364
23	23	a	Swansea Town	L 1-3	Webber.	5,556
24	26	h	Crewe Alex	D 2-2	Watson,Webber.	9,060
25	30	a	Crewe Alex	D 2-2	Webber,Flowers.	4,711
26	Jan19	h	York City	W 2-0	Watson,Warboys.	7,921
27	Feb 3	a	Rochdale	L 0-2		1,728
28	10	h	Brentford	W 2-0	Warboys,Gilfillan.	7,183
29	17	a	Bradford PA	D 1-1	Jeffrey.	4,813
30	24	h	Workington	W 3-0	Warboys,Webber,Jeffrey.	6,513
31	27	a	Newport County	L 1-2	Ricketts.	4,661
32	Mar 2	a	Chester	W 3-2	Johnson,Warboys,Gilfillan.	2,484
33	8	h	Notts County	W 3-1	Johnson(2),Wilcockson.	9,765
34	15	h	Chesterfield	W 1-0	Webber.	14,047
35	23	a	Exeter City	W 1-0	Webber.	3,323
36	29	h	Darlington	W 2-1	Johnson,Peverell O.G.	12,660
37	Apr 6	a	Aldershot	L 1-2	Warboys.	4,050
38	8	a	Southend Utd	W 2-1	Webber,Jeffrey.	13,804
39	13	h	Port Vale	D 0-0		10,782
40	16	h	Southend Utd	W 2-1	Johnson,Jeffrey.	8,898
41	20	a	Lincoln City	W 1-0	Jeffrey.	7,793
42	23	h	Bradford City	D 2-2	Clish(2).	8,969
43	26	h	Halifax Town	D 0-0		7,917
44	May 4	h	Notts County	W 2-0	Jeffrey(pen),Wilcockson.	4,070
45	4	a	Bradford City	D 1-1	Jeffrey.	12,478
46	10	h	Bradford PA	W 2-0	Johnson(2).	5,526

Players: Mason, Ashmore, Wylie, Watton, Gray, Bird, Gavan, Aiken, Johnson, Rabjohn, Clish, Wilcockson, Warboys, Flowers, Webber, Gilfillan, Watson, Jeffrey, Kettleboro', Mottershead, Leigh, Robertson, Ricketts, Shaw, Kelly, Morritt.

+ 3 O.G.

	App	Sub	Gls
Mason	1		
Wilcockson	15	2	2
Warboys	32		9
Flowers	33	1	1
Webber	31		12
Gilfillan	37	3	7
Watson	26	1	9
Jeffrey	41	1	14
Kettleboro'	13	1	
Leigh	21	5	
Robertson	42		
Ricketts	17	6	1
Shaw	22	1	
Kelly	28	1	1
Morritt	39	1	

(Appearance figures per player: App 39 28 22 17 42 23 21 13 41 26 37 31 33 32 18 17 15 14 7 7 7 7 1; Sub 1 1 1 6 1 5 1 1 3 1 1 2 2 1; Gls 1 1 1 12 8 7 12 1 9 2 7 2 1 9 2 1)

	HOME							AWAY							TOTAL						
	P	W	D	L	F	A	PTS	P	W	D	L	F	A	PTS	P	W	D	L	F	A	PTS
	23	12	8	3	36	16	32	23	6	7	10	30	40	19	46	18	15	13	66	56	51

F.A. Cup

	Date		Opponents	F-A	Scorers	Att
R1	Dec 9	a	York City	W 1-0	Jeffrey.	6,364
R2	Jan 6	h	Workington	D 1-1	Gilfillan.	9,496
R2R	10	a	Workington	W 2-1	Webber,Watson.	4,740
R3	27	h	Swansea Town	L 0-2		12,379

League Cup

	Date		Opponents	F-A	Scorers	Att
R1	Aug23	h	Scunthorpe Utd	L 1-2	Jeffrey.	8,666

DONCASTER ROVERS F.C. 1967-68

Photo — Maurice Thompson

Standing: Mr. Geo Raynor (Team Manager); W. Barker (Physiotherapist); Robertson, Flowers, Ricketts, Leigh, Gavan, Wylie, Bird, Watton, F. Marshall (Trainer), Mr. Tom Garnett (Secretary/General Manager); Seated: Kettleborough, Jeffrey, Warboys, Kelly, Watson, Mottershead, Gilfillan, Webber; On the Ground: Golze, Mitchell, Gray, Shone.

1968/69 Season
(Back): Flowers, Robertson, Wilcockson, Morritt, Clis, Gray, Stainwright.
(Front): Gilfillan, Usher, Rabjohn, Johnson, Jeffrey, Webber.

League Division 4 1968-69

Player columns (left to right): Stainwright, Morritt, Barratt, Harrity, Alken, Bird, Gray, Webber, Gavan, Briggs, Watson, Flowers, Usher, Johnson, Jeffery, Regan, Gilfillan, Haselden, Robertson, Rabjohn, Clish, Wilcockson, Ogston

No	Date	V	Opponents	F-A	Scorers	Att
1	Aug10	h	Bradford City	D 1-1	Gilfillan.	10,130
2	17	a	York City	D 1-1	Jeffrey.	5,559
3	23	h	Scunthorpe Utd	W 4-3	Rabjohn,Webber,Jeffrey(2).	10,474
4	31	a	Colchester Utd	W 2-1	Webber,Johnson.	3,199
5	Sep 3	a	Chester	L 1-2	Jeffrey.	6,564
6	7	h	Exeter City	W 3-1	Jeffrey(3).	8,590
7	14	a	Port Vale	W 2-0	Gilfillan,Jeffrey.	4,616
8	17	h	Rochdale	W 2-0	Gilfillan,Johnson.	12,183
9	20	h	Peterborough Utd	W 1-0	Johnson.	12,965
10	28	a	Chesterfield	W 1-0	Gilfillan.	9,756
11	Oct 4	h	Darlington	L 0-1		22,268
12	8	H	Chester	W 4-3	Regan(2),Jeffrey(pen),Rabjohn.	10,171
13	12	a	Wrexham	L 1-3	Jeffrey(pen).	8,130
14	18	h	Bradford PA	W 4-1	Johnson,Flowers,Usher,Jeffrey.	11,007
15	26	a	Halifax Town	L 1-4	Jeffrey.	6,634
16	Nov 2	h	Lincoln City	L 0-2		5,497
17	6	h	Swansea Town	D 0-0		6,216
18	9	a	Southend Utd	L 0-2		8,691
19	23	a	Aldershot	W 2-1	Regan,Haselden.	4,556
20	29	h	Grimsby Town	W 2-1	Johnson,Rabjohn.	8,935
21	Dec14	h	Wrexham	D 0-0		6,950
22	21	a	Bradford PA	L 1-2	Webber.	3,911
23	26	a	Darlington	D 0-0		8,343
24	Jan 1	a	Lincoln City	D 1-1	Gilfillan.	9,794
25	14	h	Halifax Town	D 0-0		8,656
26	18	h	Southend Utd	W 2-0	Gilfillan,Regan.	7,357
27	25	a	Swansea Town	W 1-0	Watson.	5,714
28	Feb 1	a	Notts County	D 1-1	Gilfillan.	6,587
29	4	h	Newport County	D 2-2	Watson,Regan.	8,321
30	25	h	Aldershot	W 7-0	Watson(2),Clish,Usher,Rgn,Briggs,Rbtsn	9,312
31	Mar 1	a	Bradford City	D 1-1	Johnson.	8,932
32	3	a	Newport County	D 0-0		2,649
33	7	h	York City	W 2-1	Watson,Johnson.	12,482
34	11	h	Notts County	D 0-0		10,255
35	14	a	Scunthorpe Utd	W 2-0	Regan,Briggs.	6,650
36	19	a	Workington	D 1-1	Johnson.	2,512
37	22	h	Colchester Utd	W 1-0	Robertson.	10,799
38	29	a	Exeter City	D 0-0		6,746
39	Apr 5	h	Chesterfield	D 0-0		12,162
40	7	a	Rochdale	D 0-0		12,647
41	8	h	Brentford	W 5-0	Regan(2),Briggs,Watson,Gelson O.G.	11,561
42	12	a	Peterborough Utd	W 1-0	Clish.	5,173
43	14	a	Brentford	L 0-1		4,222
44	19	h	Port Vale	W 2-0	Watson.	9,795
45	22	h	Workington	D 0-0		8,787
46	May 5	a	Grimsby Town	W 3-1	Briggs,Watson,Robertson.	5,003

	App	Sub	Gls

	P	W	D	L	F	A	PTS
HOME	23	13	8	2	42	16	34
AWAY	23	8	9	6	23	22	25
TOTAL	46	20	18	8	65	38	59

+ 1 O.G.

F.A. Cup

	Date	V	Opponents	F-A	Scorers	Att
R1	Nov16	h	Notts County	W 1-0	Jeffrey.	8,318
R2	Dec 7	h	Southport	W 2-1	Regan(2).	9,285
R3	Jan 4	a	Liverpool	L 0-2		48,330

League Cup

	Date	V	Opponents	F-A	Scorers	Att
R1	Aug14	h	Peterborough Utd	D 0-0		7,765
R1R	19	a	Peterborough Utd	L 0-1		8,241

League Division 3 1969-70

No	Date	V	Opponents	F-A	Scorers	Att		Ogston	Wilcockson	Clish	Flowers	Robertson	Bird	Watson	Regan	Briggs	Johnson	Usher	Haselden	Gray	Branfoot	Irvine	Gilfillan	Rabjohn	Sheffield	Marsden	Wesson	Clarke
1	Aug 9	a	Torquay Utd	L 1-2	Watson.	9.575	1	1	2		4	5		7	8		10	11	6	3						9		
2	16	h	Mansfield Town	W 2-0	Regan(2).	10.960	2	1	2		3	4	5	6	7	8	9	10	11									
3	23	a	Rotherham Utd	W 1-0	Regan.	13.909	3	1	2	3	4	5	6	7	9		10	11					8					
4	27	a	Shrewsbury Town	D 0-0		4.912	4	1	2	3*	4	5	6	7	8	9		11	12				10					
5	30	h	Barnsley	W 1-0	Regan(pen).	16.671	5	1	2		4	5	6	7	8	9	10	11	3									
6	Sep 6	a	Reading	L 0-1		6.631	6	1	2		4	5	6	7*	8	9	10	11	3				12					
7	13	h	Tranmere Rovers	W 2-1	Regan.Marsden.	9.977	7		2		4	5		7	8		10	11	6	3					9			1
8	16	h	Bury	D 1-1	Regan.	10.677	8		2		4	5		7	8		10	11	6	3					9			1
9	20	a	Halifax Town	D 1-1	Johnson.	5.875	9		2		4	5		12	8		10	11	6	3				7	9*			1
10	27	h	Southport	W 1-0	Usher.	10.042	10	1	2		4	5		12	8			11	6	3			10*	7				
11	30	h	Brighton & H A	W 2-0	Watson(2).	10.799	11	1	2		4	5		7	8	9		11	6	3			10					
12	Oct 4	a	Fulham	D 1-1	Wilcockson.	13.535	12	1	2		4	5		7	9		10	11	6	3			8					
13	6	a	Mansfield Town	W 2-1	Usher.Briggs.	9.452	13	1	2		4	5		7	8	9	10	11	6	3								
14	11	h	Luton Town	W 2-0	Briggs,Slough O.G.	17.380	14	1	2		4	5		7	8	9	10	11	6	3								
15	18	a	Orient	L 0-2		9.660	15	1	2		4	5		7*	8	9	10	11	6	3			12					
16	24	h	Stockport County	L 0-1		12.199	16	1	2		4	5				9	10	11	6	3			7		8			
17	31	a	Walsall	W 3-1	Gilfillan.Sheffield.Haselden.	7.319	17	1	2		4	5		8				11	6	3			10	7	9			
18	Nov 8	h	Bristol Rovers	W 3-1	Rabjohn,Haselden,Flowers.	10.065	18	1	2		4	5		8			10	11	6	3				7	9			
19	21	h	Plymouth Argyle	D 1-1	Sheffield.	8.195	19	1	2		4	5		8			10	11	6	3				7	9			
20	26	a	Bournemouth & B A	L 1-3	Johnson.	3.806	20	1	2		4	5		8			10	11	6	3				7	9			
21	Dec13	a	Tranmere Rovers	W 3-1	Regan.Flowers.Briggs.	2.906	21	1	2	3	4	5*		8	9	10	11		6	12			7					
22	26	h	Rotherham Utd	L 1-2	Briggs.	19.742	22	1		3	4			8	9	10	11				2	7						
23	27	a	Barnsley	L 1-2	Briggs.	17.395	23	1		3	4	5*12		8	9	10	11				2	7						
24	Jan 3	a	Brighton & H A	L 0-1		10.845	24	1		3	4		5			9	10	11	6		2	7	8					
25	10	h	Halifax Town	L 0-1		6.365	25	1		3	4*		5			9	10	11	6		2	7	8	12				
26	17	a	Southport	D 2-2	Regan(2).	2.346	26	1			4		5		10	9		11	6	3	2	7	8					
27	20	h	Reading	L 2-3	Regan(2).	6.483	27	1			4		5		8	9	10	11	6	3	2	7						
28	23	h	Rochdale	W 3-1	Regan.Briggs.Harker O.G.	6.237	28	1			4				10	9	8	11	5	3	2	7	6					
29	31	h	Fulham	L 0-1		8.180	29	1			4				8		10	11	5	3	2	7	6		9			
30	Feb 7	a	Luton Town	L 0-4		12.828	30				4	5			11		9	10	6	3	2	7	8					1
31	18	a	Gillingham	L 1-2	Sheffield.	4.621	31			3	4			11*	9				5	2		7	8	6	12	10	1	
32	21	a	Stockport County	L 1-3	Irvine.	2.662	32			3	4				10					5	6	2	7	11	12	9	8*	1
33	28	h	Walsall	D 0-0		4.378	33			3*	4	5			8	9		11	6	10	2	7	12				1	
34	Mar 3	h	Bradford City	D 1-1	Johnson.	4.454	34				4	5			8	9	10	11	6	3	2	7					1	
35	7	a	Plymouth Argyle	D 0-0		6.460	35	1			4	5			8	9	10	7	6	3	2		11					
36	9	a	Barrow	D 1-1	Johnson.	3.949	36	1			4	5			8	9	10	7*	6	3	2	12	11					
37	14	h	Gillingham	W 1-0	Briggs(pen).	4.282	37	1			4	5			8	9	10	11	6	3	2	7						
38	16	a	Rochdale	L 0-2		4.496	38	1			4	5			8	9	10			3	2	7	11	6				
39	21	a	Bradford City	L 0-3		6.962	39	1			4	5			8	9	11		6	3	2	7	10					
40	28	h	Barrow	W 3-2	Sheffield.Briggs.Johnson.	3.196	40	1			4	5			8	10	11		6	3	2	7			9			
41	30	h	Orient	L 0-1		5.536	41	1			4	5			12	8	10	11	6	3*	2	7			9			
42	31	a	Bristol Rovers	L 1-3	Sheffield.	19.053	42	1			4	5			8*10		11	6			2	7	3	12	9			
43	Apr 4	h	Shrewsbury Town	W 2-1	Regan.Haselden.	3.984	43	1			4	5*			12	8	10	11	6		2	7	3		9			
44	7	h	Bournemouth & B A	W 2-1	Johnson(2).	3.732	44	1			5					8	10	11		6	2	7	3	4	9			
45	9	h	Torquay Utd	W 1-0	Sheffield.	3.381	45	1			4	5					10	11	6		2	7	3	8	9			
46	14	a	Bury	D 1-1	Johnson.	3.011	46	1			4	5					10	11	6		2	7	3	8	9			

HOME							AWAY							TOTAL						
P	W	D	L	F	A	PTS	P	W	D	L	F	A	PTS	P	W	D	L	F	A	PTS
23	13	4	6	31	19	30	23	4	8	11	21	35	16	46	17	12	17	52	54	46

		Ogston	Wilcockson	Clish	Flowers	Robertson	Bird	Watson	Regan	Briggs	Johnson	Usher	Haselden	Gray	Branfoot	Irvine	Gilfillan	Rabjohn	Sheffield	Marsden	Wesson	Clarke
App		38	21	11	46	37	9	14	35	30	38	43	39	34	24	23	21	15	13	7	5	3
Sub							1	2	2	4			2			1	1	4	2	1	
Gls			1		2			3	13	8	8	2	3			1	1	1	6	1		+ 2 O.G.

F.A. Cup

	Date	V	Opponents	F-A	Scorers	Att		Ogston	Wilcockson	Clish	Flowers	Robertson	Bird	Watson	Regan	Briggs	Johnson	Usher	Haselden	Gray	Branfoot	Irvine	Gilfillan	Rabjohn	Sheffield	Marsden	Wesson	Clarke
R1	Nov15	h	Crewe Alex	D 1-1	Sheffield.	9.390	R1	1	2		4	5		8			10	11	6	3			7	9				
R1R	19	a	Crewe Alex	W 1-0	Robertson.	5.085	R1R	1	2		4	5		8			10	11	6	3			7	9				
R2	Dec 6	a	Chester	D 1-1	Johnson.	7.705	R2	1	2	3	4	5		8			10	11	6			7		9				
R2R	9	h	Chester	L 0-2		10.822	R2R	1	2	3	4	5		8	12	10	11	6			7*		9					

League Cup

	Date	V	Opponents	F-A	Scorers	Att		Ogston	Wilcockson	Clish	Flowers	Robertson	Bird	Watson	Regan	Briggs	Johnson	Usher	Haselden	Gray	Branfoot	Irvine	Gilfillan	Rabjohn	Sheffield	Marsden	Wesson	Clarke
R1	Aug13	a	Grimsby Town	W 2-0	Robertson,Watson.	6.664	R1	1	2	3	4	5	6	7	8	9	10	11										
R2	Sep 3	a	Blackburn Rovers	L 2-4	Briggs,Robertson.	10.024	R2	1	2		4	5	6	7	8	9	10	11		3								

League Division 3 1970-71

No	Date	V	Opponents	F-A	Scorers	Att		G.Johnson	Branfoot	Adamson	Flowers	Bird	Haselden	Rabjohn	Watson	Regan	Usher	Gilfillan	Robertson	Briggs	R.Johnson	Clish	Irvine	Kitchen	Chatterley	Marsden	Young	Harris	Martin	Gray	Ogston
1	Aug15 h	Mansfield Town	L 1-2	Irvine.	8.147	1	1	2				6	4	11	8	12	3	5	9	10*		7							
2	22 a	Rotherham Utd	L 0-2		8.693	2	1	2				6	4	11	8*		3	5	9	10		7			12				
3	29 h	Tranmere Rovers	D 2-2	Rabjohn.Haselden.	3.720	3	1	2			5	6	4			11	3		9	10		7			8				
4	31 a	Rochdale	L 0-1		3.551	4	1	2				6		4	10		11		5	9		7			8			3	
5	Sep 5 a	Aston Villa	L 2-3	Briggs.Irvine.	23.619	5	1	3			2	6	4			11		5	9	10		7			8				
6	11 h	Halifax Town	L 1-2	Briggs.	4.570	6	1	2			4	6	12			11		5*	9	10		7			8	3			
7	19 a	Fulham	D 1-1	Briggs.	13.642	7	1	4			5	6				8	11		9	10	3	7				2			
8	22 a	Bristol Rovers	L 0-2		11.048	8	1	4			5	6				8	11		9	10	3	7				2			
9	26 h	Torquay Utd	L 0-1		3.653	9	1	2			4	6				8	11		5	9	10	7				3			
10	29 h	Brighton & H A	W 2-0	Bird.Rabjohn.	3.447	10	1		2	3	4	5	6	10	8	9	7	11											
11	Oct 3 a	Bury	W 3-2	Regan.Watson.Gilfillan.	2.772	11	1		2	3	4	5	6	10	8	9	7	11											
12	10 h	Reading	W 2-0	Regan.Haselden.	4.936	12	1		2	3	4	5	6	9	8	9	10	11											
13	17 a	Mansfield Town	L 1-2	Marsden.	7.580	13	1		2	3	4	5	6*10	8	9	7	11							12				
14	21 a	Plymouth Argyle	D 1-1	Branfoot.	8.425	14	1		2	3		5		10		9		11				8		7		6	4		
15	23 h	Walsall	L 1-2	Evans O.G.	4.762	15	1		2	3	4	5		10	12	9*	7	11				8			6				
16	31 a	Barnsley	W 1-0	Irvine.	9.480	16	1		2		4	5		10	7	9				6		8	3	11					
17	Nov 6 h	Preston North End	D 1-1	Bird.	5.300	17	1		2		4	5		10	7	9				6		8	3	11					
18	10 h	Chesterfield	W 2-1	Watson(2).	6.393	18	1		2		4	5		10	11	9	12			6			3	7					
19	14 a	Wrexham	D 0-0		8.441	19	1		2		4	5		8	11	9				6*		10	3	7	12				
20	27 h	Shrewsbury Town	W 3-0	Kitchen.Robertson.Irvine.	5.184	20	1		2		4		6	10	11	9				5			3	7	8				
21	Dec 5 h	Swansea Town	L 1-2	Kitchen.	4.174	21	1		2		4		6	10	11	9*				5	12		3	7	8				
22	12 a	Halifax Town	L 0-4		3.175	22	1			2	4		6	10	11	12				5	9*		3	7	8				
23	19 h	Rotherham Utd	L 0-2		6.471	23	1		2	3	4	5	6	10	7		11			9				8					
24	26 a	Bradford City	L 0-3		5.031	24	1			4	5			12	10	8	11			6	9		3	7*			2		
25	Jan 2 h	Port Vale	L 1-2	Briggs(pen).	2.997	25	1	2*		4	6				10	8	11			5	9		3	12		7			
26	9 a	Brighton & H A	L 0-3		7.811	26	1		2	10	6			11	8					5	9		3	7			4		1
27	16 h	Plymouth Argyle	D 0-0		2.868	27	1	2	5	4		6			10		11			9	8		3	7					
28	23 a	Gillingham	W 1-0	Irvine.	3.209	28	1	2	5	4		6			10		11			9	8		3	7					
29	30 h	Shrewsbury Town	D 1-1	Robertson.	2.416	29	1	2		4	5	6			10		11			9	8		3	7					
30	Feb 5 a	Swansea City	D 1-1	Robertson.	9.260	30	1	2	4		5	6			10		11			9	8		3	7					
31	13 h	Gillingham	D 2-2	Bird.Watson.	2.735	31	1	2	4		5	6		8			11			9			3	7	10				
32	20 a	Chesterfield	L 0-4		8.042	32	1	2	4*		5	6			10		11			9	12		3	7	8				
33	26 h	Barnsley	W 1-0	Briggs.	4.792	33	1	2	4			6			10		11		8	5	9			7					
34	Mar 6 a	Walsall	W 2-1	Gilfillan.Briggs.	3.054	34	1	2	3	4		6*12		8			11	10		5	9			7					
35	9 h	Bristol Rovers	L 0-1		4.000	35	1	2	3	4			12	10			11	8	5	9			7*		6				
36	13 h	Wrexham	W 2-1	Gilfillan.Briggs.	3.109	36	1	2		4				10			11	8	5	7				6		9			
37	15 a	Port Vale	L 0-1		4.782	37	1	2		4				10			11	8	5	7			3	12	6		9*		
38	20 a	Preston North End	L 0-4		14.613	38	1	2	9	4		3		10			11	8	5				7		6				
39	26 h	Aston Villa	W 2-1	Robertson.Kitchen.	7.879	39	1	2	3	4		6	12	10			11	9	5*				7	8					
40	Apr 2 a	Tranmere Rovers	L 0-1		3.015	40	1	2	3	4		6		10			11	9	5				7	8					
41	10 h	Bradford City	W 3-1	Briggs.Gilfillan(2).	4.361	41	1	2	3	4		6		10*			11	9	5	7				12	8				
42	13 h	Bury	W 2-0	Kitchen(2).	4.974	42	1	2	3	4		6			11*	9		7					12	8	5				
43	17 a	Reading	L 0-1		5.570	43	1	3		4		6			11*	9	5	7					12	8	10		2		
44	24 h	Fulham	L 0-1		4.399	44	1	2	4	3	12			6		8		11	10	5			7*	9	4				
45	27 h	Rochdale	L 1-2	Kitchen.	2.884	45	1	2	3			6*		10			11	9	5				7	8	4	12			
46	May 1 A	Torquay Utd	L 1-2	Briggs.	3.196	46	1	2	3			6		10			11		5	9			7	8	4				

	HOME						AWAY						TOTAL							App	45	44	24	30	25	33	19	37	20	35	22	34	28	13	20	34	13	9	7	6	4	2	1	1
P	W	D	L	F	A	PTS	P	W	D	L	F	A	PTS	P	W	D	L	F	A	PTS	Sub			1			5	1	1	2			1	1		4	1		3	1					
23	8	5	10	27	37	21	23	5	4	14	17	39	14	46	13	9	24	45	66	35	Gls		1		3	2	2	4	2		5	4	9		5	6		1						+ 1 O.G.

F.A. Cup

					Att			G.Johnson	Branfoot	Adamson	Flowers	Bird	Haselden	Rabjohn	Watson	Regan	Usher	Gilfillan	Robertson	Briggs	R.Johnson	Clish	Irvine	Kitchen	Chatterley
R1	Nov21 a	Crewe Alex	D 0-0		5.784	R1	1	2		4	5		10	11	9				6		8	3	7		
R1R	24 h	Crewe Alex	L 1-3	Watson.	6.201	R1R	1	2		4	5		10*11	9				6		8	3	7	12	

League Cup

					Att			G.Johnson	Branfoot			Bird	Haselden	Rabjohn	Watson	Regan	Usher	Gilfillan	Robertson	Briggs	R.Johnson	Clish	Irvine	Kitchen
R1	Aug19 h	Darlington	D 1-1	Briggs.	4.498	R1	1	2			6	4	11	8	7	3	5	9	10					
R1R	24 a	Darlington	L 1-3	Irvine.	4.784	R1R	1	2			6	4	11	12		3	5*	9	10		7		8	

League Division 4 1971-72

No	Date	V	Opponents	F-A	Scorers	Att
1	Aug14	h	Newport County	W 4-2	Watson.Branfoot.Briggs(2).	4.797
2	21	a	Workington	L 0-2		2.394
3	28	h	Barrow	L 0-1		3.696
4	31	a	Grimsby Town	L 1-3	Rabjohn.	10.400
5	Sep 4	a	Scunthorpe Utd	D 0-0		5.234
6	11	h	Exeter City	D 2-1	Watson.Briggs(pen).	3.616
7	17	a	Stockport County	W 2-1	Briggs.McMillan O.G.	2.894
8	25	h	Southend Utd	L 0-2		3.884
9	29	a	Crewe Alex	W 1-0	Gilchrist.	2.271
10	Oct 2	a	Gillingham	L 0-2		4.899
11	9	h	Cambridge Utd	D 1-1	Briggs.	3.521
12	16	a	Newport County	W 3-1	Elwiss(2).Gilchrist.	2.720
13	19	h	Lincoln City	W 2-0	Branfoot.Elwiss.	5.272
14	22	h	Northampton Town	D 1-1	Elwiss.	5.988
15	30	a	Southport	L 0-3		4.595
16	Nov 6	h	Darlington	W 4-0	Gilchrist.Wilcockson.Haselden(2).	4.297
17	13	a	Hartlepool	D 0-0		2.129
18	27	a	Chester	D 1-1	Elwiss.	2.716
19	Dec 4	h	Peterborough Utd	W 3-2	Elwiss.Briggs(2).	3.258
20	18	h	Scunthorpe Utd	L 0-2		5.534
21	27	a	Reading	L 1-3	Watson.	7.123
22	Jan 1	h	Stockport County	D 2-2	Gilchrist(2).	3.241
23	8	a	Barrow	W 2-1	Gilchrist(2).	1.806
24	15	h	Colchester Utd	W 2-0	Elwiss.Haselden.	3.047
25	21	h	Crewe Alex	D 0-0		3.992
26	29	a	Lincoln City	L 0-2		7.568
27	Feb 5	h	Aldershot	W 2-1	Elwiss.Usher.	2.703
28	12	a	Northampton Town	D 1-1	Elwiss.	3.565
29	19	h	Southport	W 2-1	Elwiss(2).	3.531
30	26	a	Darlington	L 1-4	Irvine.	2.330
31	Mar 4	h	Hartlepool	W 2-1	Irvine(pen).Gilchrist.	2.571
32	11	a	Cambridge Utd	D 1-1	Irvine.	3.207
33	13	a	Colchester Utd	W 2-1	Irvine.Elwiss.	5.004
34	18	h	Workington	D 0-0		4.214
35	21	h	Brentford	L 0-3		5.256
36	25	a	Exeter City	L 0-1		3.370
37	31	h	Southend Utd	L 1-2	Kitchen.	16.073
38	Apr 1	h	Reading	D 1-1	Robertson.	2.875
39	4	h	Gillingham	D 1-1	Elwiss.	2.769
40	8	a	Aldershot	L 0-3		2.152
41	11	a	Bury	D 3-3	Irvine.Watson.Elwiss.	4.141
42	15	h	Chester	D 0-0		2.370
43	17	a	Brentford	L 1-2	Watson.	13.484
44	22	a	Peterborough Utd	L 0-2		4.737
45	25	h	Grimsby Town	W 2-1	Watson.Briggs.	12.320
46	29	h	Bury	W 4-1	Watson.Usher.Haselden.Elwiss.	2.126

+ 1 O.G.

Appearances and Goals

Player	App	Sub	Gls
Johnson	43		
Branfoot	44		2
Clish	7		
Wilcockson	35		1
Robertson	40		1
Brookes	19		
Watson	32		7
Rabjohn	24		1
Briggs	44		8
Irvine	44		5
Usher	40		2
Elwiss	35		15
Uzelac	31		
Haselden	25		4
Gilchrist	22		8
Moore	18		
Beardsley	10		
Kitchen	6		1
Adamson	4		
Book	3		

Summary

	P	W	D	L	F	A	PTS
HOME	23	11	8	4	35	24	30
AWAY	23	5	6	12	21	39	16
TOTAL	46	16	14	16	56	63	46

F.A. Cup

	Date	V	Opponents	F-A	Scorers	Att
R1	Nov20	h	Stockport County	L 1-2	Uzelac.	4.590

League Cup

	Date	V	Opponents	F-A	Scorers	Att
R1	Aug17	a	Grimsby Town	L 3-4	Watson.Branfoot.Irvine.	8.882

DONCASTER ROVERS 1971-72

(Back): Gilchrist, Watson, Usher, Branfoot, Wilcockson, Clish. (Middle): Marshall (Trainer), Briggs, Robertson, Rabjohn, Elwiss, Finch, Johnson, Uzelac, Bird, Adamson, Reed, Barker (Physio). (Front): Wilson, Simm, Haselden, Gallagher, Kitchen, Setters (Manager), Irvine, Young, Brookes, Straw,

DONCASTER ROVERS F.C.

DIVISION FOUR—1972-73

Back row (left to right): JOHN QUIGLEY (Trainer-coach) STAN BROOKES STEVE BRIGGS STEVE WIGNALL CHRIS RABJOHN KIM BOOK GLENN JOHNSON GRAHAM MOORE JOHN HASELDEN MIKE ELWISS HAROLD WILCOCKSON

Front row (left to right): IAN BRANFOOT MIKE KITCHEN BRIAN JOY ARCHIE IRVINE STEVE UZELAC BRIAN USHER

League Division 4 1972-73

No	Date	V	Opponents	F-A	Scorers	Att		Book	Branfoot	Haselden	Irvine	Brookes	Uzelac	Moore	Elwiss	Kitchen	Rabjohn	Usher	Joy	Wignall	Briggs	Hunt	Johnson	Roberts	Reed	Morrison	Watson	McLuckie	Wilcockson
1	Aug12	a	Workington	L 0-2		2.032	1		2	3*	6	8	4	7		9	10		11	5			1			12			
2	19	h	Mansfield Town	L 0-1		3.540	2		2	3	6	8	4	7		10				5	11		1			9			
3	26	a	Cambridge Utd	L 1-3	Watson.	2.941	3		2		6	3	4	8		10	7			5			1		12	9*11			
4	29	a	Barnsley	L 2-4	Kitchen.Irvine(pen).	3.377	4		2		4	5	6	8		9	7	11					1			3	10		
5	Sep 1	h	Stockport County	D 2-2	Kitchen.Hart O.G.	2.222	5		2		4	5	6	8		9		7*11	12				1			3	10		
6	8	a	Gillingham	L 0-3		1.575	6		2		8	3	4	7		9	11			6						5	10		
7	15	h	Southport	W 2-0	Irvine.Elwiss.	2.055	7	1	2		3	4	5	6	7	8	9	10	11										
8	20	a	Crewe Alex	W 1-0	Kitchen.	1.820	8	1	2		5	6	3	4	7	9	10	8	11										
9	23	a	Lincoln City	L 1-2	Elwiss.	6.455	9	1	2		5*	6	3	4	7	9	10	8	11	12									
10	26	h	Hereford Utd	D 0-0		3.111	10	1	2		3	4	5	6	7	8	9	10	11										
11	29	h	Bradford City	W 1-0	Branfoot.	2.511	11	1	2		3	4	5	6	7	8	9	10	11										
12	Oct 6	h	Northampton Town	W 3-0	Kitchen.Elwiss(2).	2.489	12	1	2		3	7	5	4	6	10	9	8	11										
13	11	a	Torquay Utd	L 0-1		1.952	13	1	2		4	5	6	7	8	9	10*11	12											
14	14	a	Peterborough Utd	L 1-3	Uzelac.	4.237	14	1	2	3	10	4	5	6	8	9	7	11*12											
15	21	h	Aldershot	W 1-0	Kitchen.	1.997	15	1	2	9	11	4	5	6	8	10	7*12	3											
16	24	h	Chester	D 0-0		2.240	16	1	2	10	6	3	4	7	11	9	8		5										
17	28	h	Darlington	W 1-0	Haselden.	1.544	17	1	2	10			3	4	7	9	11	8	6	5									
18	Nov 4	a	Hereford Utd	L 2-3	Haselden(2).	8.332	18	1	2	9	4	5		6*	7	8	10	11	12	3									
19	11	h	Crewe Alex	L 0-2		1.687	19	1	2	9	4	5		7	8	10			11	3	6								
20	25	h	Bury	W 4-1	Haselden(2).Irvine.Kitchen.	1.739	20	1	2	9	4	5		6	8	10	7	11	3										
21	Dec 2	a	Hartlepool	D 0-0		2.964	21	1	2		4	5	6	8	10	9	7	11	3										
22	16	h	Colchester Utd	W 1-0	Elwiss.	1.880	22	1	2		6	4	5	10	8	9	7	11	3										
23	23	a	Reading	L 0-1		4.762	23	1	2		4	10	5		8	9	7		3	6	11								
24	26	h	Lincoln City	D 1-1	Branfoot.	3.325	24	1	2		4	7	6*		8	9	10		3	5	11							12	
25	30	a	Mansfield Town	D 0-0		5.187	25	1	2	10*	4	6			8	9	7	11	3	5	12								
26	Jan 6	h	Cambridge Utd	D 0-0		1.735	26	1	2	9	4	5			8	11	10		3	6	7								
27	19	a	Stockport County	L 1-2	Haselden.	2.586	27	1	2	9	4	3	6	7		10			11	5	8								
28	26	h	Gillingham	L 0-1		3.059	28	1	2	9	4	11	5		7	8			3	6		10							
29	Feb 3	h	Torquay Utd	W 1-0	Haselden.	1.594	29	1	2	5	4			6		8	10	7	3		9							11	
30	9	a	Southport	D 2-2	Briggs.Joy.	3.566	30	1	2	6	4			5		8	10	11	3		7	9							
31	16	h	Workington	D 1-1	Hunt.	2.026	31	1	2	12	4	3	6*			8	11			5	7	10	9						
32	20	a	Chester	W 2-1	Brookes.Briggs.	2.701	32	1	2	7	8	5	4			6				3	9	11	10						
33	24	h	Colchester Utd	D 1-1	Briggs.	2.550	33	1	2	10	6	3	5		12		11*			4	7	8	9						
34	Mar 2	a	Northampton Town	W 2-0	Brookes,Haselden.	4.509	34	1	2	8	6	5	4			7				3	9	11	10						
35	6	a	Newport County	L 0-1		6.374	35	1	2	7		5	4	6			8			3	11	9	10						
36	9	h	Peterborough Utd	D 1-1	Elwiss.	2.633	36	1	2	7	8	5	4		6					12	3	9	11*	10					
37	17	a	Aldershot	L 0-1		3.435	37	1	2	10	4*	3	6			8	11	7		12	5		9						
38	20	h	Exeter City	W 5-1	Elwiss(2),Irvine,Brookes,Haselden.	1.823	38	1	2	10	6	5	3*			11	9	8		7	4	12							
39	23	h	Darlington	W 2-0	Briggs,Elwiss.	2.506	39	1	2	9	6	5			7		11		10	3	8				4				
40	31	a	Bury	L 0-5		2.039	40	1		9	6	3	5			8	7		11	4	10								2
41	Apr 7	h	Hartlepool	W 2-1	Briggs,Haselden.	1.488	41	1	2	9	6	3	5			10	7		11	4	8								
42	14	a	Exeter City	W 1-0	Rabjohn.	3.609	42	1	2	9	6	3			8	7	10		11	4					5				
43	21	h	Newport County	L 1-5	Elwiss.	1.942	43	1	2	9	6	3			8	10	7*		11	5	12				4				
44	23	a	Bradford City	L 3-4	Moore(2),Elwiss.	2.278	44	1	2	9	4	7			8	10			11	3	6				5				
45	24	h	Reading	L 0-2		1.623	45		2	9	6	7	4		8	10			11		3			1	5				
46	27	h	Barnsley	D 0-0		2.721	46			9	6	7	4		8	10	12		11*	2	3			1	5				

HOME							AWAY							TOTAL									App	39	44	37	44	44	39	26	34	37	36	20	28	23	15	9	7	7	6	5	4	1	1
P	W	D	L	F	A	PTS	P	W	D	L	F	A	PTS	P	W	D	L	F	A	PTS			Sub		1						1	1		2	6		3				1	1	1		
23	10	8	5	28	19	28	23	5	4	14	21	39	14	46	15	12	19	49	58	42			Gls		2	10	4	3	1	11	11	6	1		1		5	1			1					+ 1 O.G.

F.A. Cup

R1	Nov18	h	Bury	W 3-1	Kitchen,Elwiss,Rabjohn.	2.630	R1	1	2*	9	4	5	6		7	10	8	11	3	12									
R2	Dec 9	a	Scarborough	W 2-1	Kitchen,Elwiss.	7.109	R2	1	2	9	4	5	6	11	7	10	8		3										
R3	Jan17	a	Reading	L 0-2		10.361	R3	1	2	9	4	5		8*	7	11	10		3	6	12								

League Cup

R1	Aug16	a	Hartlepool	L 0-1		6.752	R1		2	3	6	8	4	7*10	9		11	5				1			12				

League Division 4 1973-74

Players (columns): McLuckie, Talkes, Turner, Haselden, Pritchet, Reed, Carver, Curran, Moore, Irvine, Higgins, Kitchen, O'Callaghan, Elwiss, Woods, Uzelac, Brookes, Murray, Wignall, Ternent, Book

No	Date	V	Opponents	F-A	Scorers	Att
1	Aug 25	h	Stockport County	D 1-1	Higgins.	2,851
2	Sep 1	a	Bradford City	D 1-1	Higgins.	4,123
3	7	h	Torquay Utd	L 0-1		3,313
4	11	h	Barnsley	W 1-0	O'Callaghan.	3,070
5	15	a	Brentford	L 0-2		4,957
6	17	a	Peterborough Utd	L 1-5	Murray(pen).	6,648
7	22	h	Workington	W 5-2	Kitchen(2),O'Callaghan(2),Higgins.	1,517
8	29	a	Gillingham	L 1-5	Kitchen.	3,864
9	Oct 2	h	Peterborough Utd	W 3-1	Elwiss,Kitchen,Ternent.	2,383
10	6	h	Reading	D 0-0		2,516
11	13	a	Chester	L 0-3		2,150
12	20	h	Hartlepool	D 2-2	Kitchen,Uzelac.	1,676
13	23	a	Barnsley	L 0-2		3,301
14	27	a	Darlington	L 0-1		2,057
15	Nov 3	h	Swansea City	W 3-1	Kitchen,O'Callaghan,Elwiss.	1,523
16	10	a	Newport County	L 1-3	Uzelac.	2,852
17	14	a	Exeter City	W 2-1	Murray,O'Callaghan.	5,259
18	17	h	Bury	D 1-1	O'Callaghan.	2,088
19	Dec 8	a	Crewe Alex	L 0-4		1,360
20	22	h	Gillingham	L 1-2	Kitchen.	1,878
21	26	a	Scunthorpe Utd	L 1-2	Kitchen.	5,775
22	29	a	Torquay Utd	L 0-3		3,487
23	Jan 1	h	Bradford City	D 2-2	Murray,Elwiss.	3,480
24	12	h	Brentford	L 1-2	Elwiss.	3,009
25	20	a	Stockport County	D 0-0		4,050
26	27	h	Colchester Utd	W 2-0	Ternent,Kitchen.	4,285
27	Feb 3	h	Rotherham Utd	L 1-2	O'Callaghan.	5,955
28	10	a	Workington	L 1-3	Walker O.G.	1,667
29	17	h	Chester	L 1-2	Brookes.	2,472
30	24	a	Reading	L 0-5		9,187
31	Mar 2	h	Scunthorpe Utd	W 1-0	Murray(pen).	1,587
32	10	h	Darlington	D 0-0		1,467
33	17	a	Hartlepool	L 0-3		3,502
34	19	a	Rotherham Utd	W 2-1	Higgins,Murray.	2,804
35	22	h	Newport County	W 2-0	Higgins,Curran.	1,163
36	26	h	Mansfield Town	D 0-0		1,894
37	30	a	Swansea City	L 0-3		1,855
38	Apr 2	a	Colchester Utd	L 0-3		5,124
39	6	h	Exeter City	W 1-0	Irvine(pen).	1,373
40	13	a	Bury	L 1-3	Moore.	3,951
41	15	a	Lincoln City	D 3-3	O'Callaghan,Kitchen(pen),Higgins.	2,863
42	16	h	Lincoln City	W 2-0	Woods,O'Callaghan.	2,385
43	20	h	Crewe Alex	L 0-2		1,640
44	23	h	Northampton Town	W 2-1	O'Callaghan,Curran.	1,561
45	27	a	Northampton Town	L 1-3	Brookes.	3,137
46	29	a	Mansfield Town	L 0-2		2,474

App: 42 38 38 38 43 29 28 27 35 37 30 32 23 21 15 13 6 3 4 3 1
Sub: 2 5 2 2 1 4 10 10 6 1 1 2
Gls: 1 2 5 2 2 1 6 3 5 7 3 6 1 1 2

+ 1 O.G.

	HOME							AWAY							TOTAL						
	P	W	D	L	F	A	PTS	P	W	D	L	F	A	PTS	P	W	D	L	F	A	PTS
	23	10	7	6	32	22	27	23	2	4	17	15	58	8	46	12	11	23	47	80	35

F.A. Cup

R	Date	V	Opponents	F-A	Scorers	Att
R1	Nov 24	h	Lincoln City	W 1-0	Murray(pen).	3,628
R2	Dec 15	h	Tranmere Rovers	W 3-0	Kitchen,Elwiss,Woods.	2,444
R3	Jan 5	a	Liverpool	D 2-2	O'Callaghan,Kitchen.	31,483
R3R	8	h	Liverpool	L 0-2		22,499

League Cup

R	Date	V	Opponents	F-A	Scorers	Att
R1	Aug 28	a	Notts County	W 4-3	Kitchen(3),Elwiss.	7,735
R2	Oct 8	a	Newcastle Utd	L 0-6		16,065

Doncaster Rovers 1973-74

Back row (left to right): John Quigley (coach), Bill Gold (physiotherapist), Steve Uzelac, Keith Pritchett, Mike Elwiss, Steve Wignall, Kim Book, Brendan O'Callaghan, Stan Brookes, John Haselden, Graham Moore, Maurice Setters (team manager).

Front row (left to right): Steve Reed, Archie Irvine, Alan Murray, Peter Kitchen, Peter Woods, Ray Ternent, Terry Curran, Peter Higgins, Robert McLuckie

DONCASTER ROVERS 1975-76

BACK ROW — John Quigley (Trainer), Carver, Curran, Uzelac, O'Callaghan, Brookes, Reed, Wroe, Stan Anderson (Team Manager)

MIDDLE ROW — Wignall (S), Ternent, Murray, Chappell, Kitchen, Woods, Higgins

FRONT ROW — Jones, Yates, Lee, McConville, Jeffrey, Woodhouse, Bennett, Wignall (D)

League Division 4 1974-75

No	Date	V	Opponents	F-A	Scorers	Att
1	Aug17	h	Stockport County	W 2-1	Higgins(2).	2,383
2	24	a	Exeter City	L 1-2	Lee R.G.	3,819
3	31	h	Newport County	L 0-2		2,157
4	Sep 7	a	Swansea City	D 3-3	Kitchen(2).Uzelac.	1,554
5	13	h	Rochdale	W 4-1	Murray(3).Kitchen.	1,928
6	17	h	Scunthorpe Utd	D 1-1	Markham O.G.	3,116
7	21	a	Crewe Alex	L 1-2	Lee.	4,102
8	24	a	Northampton Town	L 0-2		4,269
9	28	h	Rotherham Utd	D 0-0		4,710
10	Oct 2	a	Chester	L 0-3		2,922
11	5	h	Brentford	W 2-1	Lee R.G.Woolgar.	1,692
12	12	a	Bradford City	L 0-2		3,128
13	15	h	Lincoln City	D 2-2	Lee R.G.Kitchen.	2,034
14	19	h	Darlington	L 1-3	Murray.	1,649
15	26	a	Workington	W 3-0	Kitchen.O'Callaghan.Higgins.	1,256
16	Nov 2	a	Torquay Utd	L 0-2		2,492
17	5	h	Chester	D 1-1	Murray.	1,286
18	8	h	Shrewsbury Town	L 1-3	O'Callaghan.	1,673
19	13	a	Lincoln City	L 0-4		5,300
20	16	a	Mansfield Town	L 2-5	Curran.Higgins.	5,634
21	30	a	Reading	L 0-2		4,243
22	Dec 7	h	Hartlepool	W 3-0	O'Callaghan(2).Kitchen.	1,357
23	21	h	Cambridge Utd	L 0-1		1,677
24	26	a	Rochdale	L 0-2		1,077
25	28	h	Southport	D 1-1	Chappell.	1,356
26	Jan 4	a	Scunthorpe Utd	D 0-0		2,472
27	11	a	Hartlepool	L 1-2	Uzelac.	2,950
28	18	h	Reading	D 1-1	O'Callaghan.	1,505
29	24	h	Barnsley	D 1-1	Kitchen.	4,153
30	Feb 1	a	Shrewsbury Town	L 4-7	Kitchen(2).Curran.Reed.	3,632
31	8	h	Torquay Utd	W 3-0	O'Callaghan.Curran.Murray.	2,166
32	15	a	Barnsley	W 1-0	O'Callaghan.	6,451
33	22	h	Mansfield Town	W 4-3	Kitchen(2).Uzelac.Curran.	7,278
34	28	a	Newport County	W 2-0	Kitchen.O'Callaghan.	2,252
35	Mar 8	h	Northampton Town	W 2-0	Kitchen(2).	5,319
36	15	a	Rotherham Utd	L 0-1		8,049
37	17	a	Stockport County	W 2-0	Curran.Murray.	1,995
38	21	h	Swansea City	W 3-2	Curran.Wignall.Kitchen.	5,011
39	28	a	Cambridge Utd	L 1-4	Kitchen.	4,159
40	31	a	Southport	L 1-2	Kitchen.	1,515
41	Apr 1	h	Crewe Alex	W 2-1	O'Callaghan(2).	4,845
42	5	h	Workington	D 0-0		3,232
43	12	a	Brentford	L 0-1	Kitchen.	5,147
44	19	h	Bradford City	W 4-1	Kitchen(2).Chappell(2).	3,640
45	22	h	Exeter City	D 3-3	Curran.Kitchen.Chappell.	4,251
46	26	a	Darlington	L 1-4	O'Callaghan.	2,647

+ 1 O.G.

Players: Miller, R.Lee, Long, Crabtree, Crellin, Woolgar, Wood, Chappell, R.G.Lee, Reed, Uzelac, Wood, Higgins, Kitchen, O'Callaghan, Murray, Curran, Wignall, Brookes, Irvine, Carver, Ternent, Brown

	App	Sub	Gls
Totals	40 25 14 43 41 34 44 29 31 42 29 13 37 32 14 24	1 1 1 1 1	4 2 4 5 1

	P	W	D	L	F	A	PTS
HOME	23	10	9	4	41	29	29
AWAY	23	4	3	16	24	50	11
TOTAL	46	14	12	20	65	79	40

F.A. Cup

	Date	V	Opponents	F-A	Scorers	Att
R1	Nov23	a	Oswestry Town	W 3-1	Kitchen(2).O'Callaghan.	2,000
R2	Dec14	a	Chesterfield	L 0-1		5,267

League Cup

	Date	V	Opponents	F-A	Scorers	Att
R1	Aug20	h	Mansfield Town	W 2-1	Kitchen.Irvine.	5,078
R2	Sep10	a	Bury	L 0-2		4,587

League Division 2 1975-76

No	Date	V	Opponents	F-A	Scorers	Att
1	Aug16	h	Cambridge Utd	L 0-2		2.999
2	22	a	Tranmere Rovers	D 2-2	Curran(2).	2.013
3	30	h	Crewe Alex	W 3-1	Chappell,O'Callaghan,Alesinoye.	2.467
4	Sep 6	a	Bournemouth	W 1-0	Kitchen.	3.511
5	15	h	Brentford	D 1-1	Uzelac.	6.353
6	20	a	Watford	L 1-2	Murray.	4.228
7	24	a	Barnsley	W 1-0	O'Callaghan.	6.681
8	27	h	Southport	W 5-2	Kitchen(3)(1pen),O'Callaghan(2).	5.219
9	Oct 3	a	Northampton Town	L 1-2	Chappell.	6.155
10	10	a	Stockport County	W 2-1	Kitchen,O'Callaghan.	3.159
11	18	h	Swansea City	W 2-1	Kitchen,O'Callaghan.	6.640
12	22	a	Bradford City	W 4-3	O'Callaghan(3),Chappell.	3.687
13	25	a	Darlington	D 2-2	Chappell,Murray.	3.725
14	Nov 1	h	Reading	D 1-1	Uzelac.	7.293
15	4	h	Huddersfield Town	W 4-1	Kitchen,O'Callaghan,Miller,Ternent.	10.650
16	8	a	Hartlepool	L 1-2	Murray.	3.592
17	15	h	Newport County	W 5-1	Miller(3),O'Callaghan(2).	7.793
18	28	a	Exeter City	L 0-1		2.848
19	Dec 6	h	Torquay Utd	L 0-1		7.667
20	13	a	Tranmere Rovers	W 3-0	Murray,Kitchen,O'Callaghan.	5.684
21	20	a	Workington	L 1-3	Kitchen.	1.642
22	26	h	Lincoln City	L 2-4	Kitchen,Miller.	14.353
23	27	a	Scunthorpe Utd	W 1-2	Kitchen.	5.969
24	Jan10	a	Crewe Alex	W 2-1	Kitchen,O'Callaghan.	2.501
25	17	h	Watford	L 1-2	Kitchen.	5.845
26	20	h	Rochdale	W 1-0	O'Callaghan.	3.586
27	24	a	Brentford	D 1-1	Miller.	4.885
28	30	h	Bradford City	D 1-1	Miller.	4.484
29	Feb 7	a	Huddersfield Town	W 2-1	O'Callaghan,Murray.	6.305
30	14	h	Hartlepool	W 3-0	O'Callaghan,Kitchen(2).	5.035
31	21	a	Newport County	W 3-2	Kitchen,O'Callaghan(2).	1.543
32	24	h	Barnsley	D 2-2	O'Callaghan,Miller.	8.250
33	27	h	Darlington	W 3-2	O'Callaghan,Kitchen(2)(1pen).	5.587
34	Mar 6	a	Reading	L 0-4	Chappell.	6.637
35	9	h	Northampton Town	W 3-1	Kitchen,Chappell,Balderstone.	8.737
36	13	h	Stockport County	L 1-2	Miller.	4.231
37	16	a	Swansea	D 0-0		3.128
38	20	h	Exeter City	D 2-2	Kitchen,Murray.	4.149
39	27	a	Torquay Utd	W 1-0	Miller.	2.121
40	30	h	Workington	D 3-3	Kitchen,Robinson,Wignall D.	1.633
41	Apr 3	a	Cambridge Utd	D 1-1	O'Callaghan.	1.599
42	6	a	Southport	D 1-1	Taylor.	4.097
43	10	h	Bournemouth	L 0-1		4.097
44	16	a	Rochdale	L 0-5		1.462
45	17	a	Lincoln City	L 0-1		14.096
46	19	h	Scunthorpe Utd	L 0-1		4.097

	P	W	D	L	F	A	PTS
HOME	23	10	6	7	42	31	26
AWAY	23	9	5	9	33	38	23
TOTAL	46	19	11	16	75	69	49

F.A. Cup

	Date	V	Opponents	F-A	Scorers	Att
R1	Nov22	a	Bury	L2-4	Uzelac(2).	7.094

League Cup

	Date	V	Opponents	F-A	Scorers	Att
R1 1L	Aug20	h	Grimsby Town	W 3-1	O'Callaghan(3).	3.218
R1 2L	25	a	Grimsby Town	D 0-0		5.552
R2	Sep 9	h	Crystal Palace	W 2-1	Chappell,O'Callaghan.	6.268
R3	Oct 8	a	Torquay Utd	D 1-1	Reed.	2.785
R3R	13	h	Torquay Utd	W 3-0	O'Callaghan(2),Balderstone.	9.784
R4	Nov11	h	Hull City	W 2-1	Kitchen,Ternent.	20.476
R5	Dec 3	a	Tottenham Hotspur	L 2-7	Murray,Kitchen.	25.702

League Division 4 1976-77

No	Date	V	Opponents	F-A	Scorers	Att
1	Aug21	a	Southport	D 2-2	Laidlaw.Sibbald O.G.	1,964
2	28	h	Torquay Utd	L 0-4		4,382
3	Sep 4	a	Brentford	D 2-2	Laidlaw.Taylor.	3,804
4	10	h	Newport County	W 1-0	O'Callaghan.	3,739
5	14	h	Aldershot	L 1-2	Kitchen.	5,017
6	18	a	Swansea City	D 1-1	Kitchen.	3,504
7	25	h	Darlington	W 4-0	Woodcock.O'Callaghan.Kitchen(2).	3,618
8	Oct 1	a	Stockport County	L 1-2	Kitchen.	7,132
9	9	h	Barnsley	W 2-1	O'Callaghan.Kitchen.	6,707
10	16	a	Huddersfield Town	L 1-2	Kitchen.	7,494
11	22	h	Bradford City	L 2-3	Woodcock.O'Callaghan.	6,816
12	25	h	Colchester Utd	W 3-2	Taylor.Kitchen.Laidlaw.	3,856
13	30	a	Rochdale	L 0-1		2,436
14	Nov 2	a	Halifax Town	L 0-1		2,350
15	5	h	Hartlepool	W 2-1	Kitchen(2).	2,631
16	27	h	Crewe Alex	W 3-0	Kitchen(2).Laidlaw.	3,465
17	Dec 4	a	Exeter City	W 2-0	O'Callaghan(2).	2,891
18	18	h	Bournemouth	D 0-0		3,485
19	27	a	Scunthorpe Utd	D 1-1	Brookes.	7,128
20	28	h	Southend Utd	L 0-3		5,605
21	Jan 1	a	Hartlepool	D 0-0		2,206
22	8	h	Cambridge Utd	W 2-0	Kitchen.Miller.	3,682
23	11	h	Rochdale	L 0-1		3,008
24	15	a	Aldershot	L 0-1		3,462
25	22	h	Southport	W 3-1	Taylor(2).Brookes.	3,441
26	29	a	Workington	D 1-0	O'Callaghan.	1,350
27	Feb 5	a	Torquay Utd	W 1-0	O'Callaghan.	2,642
28	12	h	Brentford	W 5-0	Kitchen.Taylor.O'Callaghan(2).Smith.OG.	4,095
29	26	h	Swansea City	W 2-1	Murray.Taylor.	4,359
30	Mar 1	a	Newport County	W 2-1	O'Callaghan.Kitchen.	1,724
31	5	a	Darlington	W 3-1	O'Callaghan.Robinson.Murray.	3,407
32	11	h	Stockport County	W 1-0	Uzelac.	6,340
33	19	a	Barnsley	D 1-1	Miller.	10,180
34	25	h	Huddersfield Town	W 2-0	O'Callaghan.Taylor.	11,042
35	29	a	Watford	L 1-5	Robinson.	5,476
36	Apr 2	a	Bradford City	L 1-3	Laidlaw.	6,882
37	9	a	Southend Utd	L 1-2	Kitchen(pen).	4,691
38	11	a	Scunthorpe Utd	W 3-0	Kitchen(2).O'Callaghan.	4,676
39	12	h	Halifax Town	W 3-0	Kitchen.Miller.Laidlaw.	4,840
40	15	a	Colchester Utd	W 0-1		4,668
41	19	h	Workington	W 6-3	Kitchen(3).Miller.Taylor.Laidlaw.	3,782
42	23	h	Watford	W 1-0	Taylor.	4,476
43	30	a	Crewe Alex	W 2-1	Murray.Kitchen.	2,359
44	May 3	a	Cambridge Utd	L 0-3		5,219
45	7	h	Exeter City	L 0-3		3,447
46	14	a	Bournemouth	L 1-3	Miller.	2,981

+ 2 O.G.

Appearance / Goals grid players (columns): McConnville, S.Wignall, Boden, Reed, Binch, Olney, Snodin, D.Wignall, Bowden, Jones, Ternent, Woodcock, Walker, Creamer, Laidlaw, Kitchen, O'Callaghan, Murray, Miller, Taylor, Uzelac, Robinson, Bailey, Brookes, Peacock.

	Reed	D.Wignall	Jones	Ternent	Creamer	Laidlaw	Kitchen	O'Callaghan	Murray	Miller	Taylor	Uzelac	Robinson	Bailey	Brookes	Peacock
App	46	17	1	2	5	44	43	46	36	46	46	21	37	9	42	46
Sub		5	1	1	1				1			1	2	2	2	
Gls						7	23	15	3	5	9	1	2		2	

HOME							
P	W	D	L	F	A	PTS	
23	16	2	5	47	25	34	

AWAY							
P	W	D	L	F	A	PTS	
23	5	7	11	24	40	17	

TOTAL							
P	W	D	L	F	A	PTS	
46	21	9	16	71	65	51	

F.A. Cup

R1	Nov20	h	Shrewsbury Town	D 2-2	Kitchen(2).	5,232
R1R	23	a	Shrewsbury Town	L 3-4	Kitchen.Reed.Miller.	6,134

League Cup

R1 1L	Aug14	h	Lincoln City	D 1-1	Taylor.	5,594
R1 2L	18	a	Lincoln City	D 1-1	O'Callaghan.	7,089
R1R	24	a	Lincoln City	D 2-2	O'clighn(2).(At Nottm F.aet-won on pens	3,726
R2	31	h	Derby County	L 1-2	Kitchen.	14,888

Doncaster Rovers F.C. 1976-77

BACK ROW — John Quigley (Trainer), David Binch, Stephen Reed, Brendan O'Callaghan, Stephen Uzelac, Peter Creamer, Dennis Peacock, Stan Brookes, Mark Jones, Brian Taylor, Stan Anderson (Team Manager)

MIDDLE ROW — Ian Miller, David Wignall, Joe Laidlaw, Tony Phillips (Chairman), Ray Ternent, Ian Jones (Director), Alan Murray, Fred Robinson, Peter Kitchen

FRONT ROW — Douggie Maillie, Malcolm Duncan, Mark Gascoigne, Alick Jeffrey, Ian McConville

Doncaster Rovers F.C. 1977-78

Back Row: Owen, Miller, Taylor, Jones (M), Maillie, Peacock, Biggins, O'Callaghan, Reed, Wignall (S), Bentley.

Seated: McConville, Jones (C), Laidlaw, Robinson, Wignall (D). Front Row: Duncan, Bowden (P), Snodin, Meaghan.

League Division 4 1977-78

No	Date	V	Opponents	F-A	Scorers	Att		Peacock	Olney	Robinson	Laidlaw	Owen	Taylor	Miller	M.Jones	O'Callaghan	C.Jones	Bentley	Bowden	Bailey	Biggins	Gray	Carnell	Meagan	Reed	Habbin	Snodin	Wignall	McConville	Hemsley	O'Riordan	S.Wignall
1	Aug20	h	Newport County	2-2	Laidlaw(2)(1pen).	3.041	1		5	12	4	8*	6	7		9	10	11			1			2					3			
2	23	a	Swansea City	0-3		6.285	2		5		8	4	12	6	7		9	10*	11			1			2					3		
3	27	a	Aldershot	0-1		3.128	3	1	2*	3	4	5	6	7	8	9	10	11	12													
4	Sep 3	h	Watford	0-1		2.963	4	1	2	3	4	5	6	7	8	9	10*	11							12							
5	9	a	Stockport County	1-1	Owen.	3.614	5	1		3	4	5	6	7		9	10	11							2	8						
6	17	h	Brentford	3-1	McConville,Habbin,O'Callaghan.	3.044	6	1		3	4	5	6	7		9	12	11							10			2	8*			
7	20	h	Southport	2-1	Habbin(2).	3.686	7	1		3	8	5	6	7		9	12	11*	4						10			2				
8	24	a	Grimsby Town	0-0		4.983	8	1		11	8	5	6	7		9			4						10			2	3			
9	27	h	Southend Utd	2-0	Laidlaw(2)(1pen).	5.103	9	1		4	8	5	6	7		9		11							3	10		2				
10	Oct 1	a	Huddersfield Town	1-4	Habbin.	4.592	10	1		4	8	5	6*	7		9	12	11							3	10		2				
11	5	a	Bournemouth	1-0	O'Callaghan.	2.632	11	1		4	8	5	6	7		9		11							3	10		2				
12	8	h	Barnsley	2-1	O'Callaghan,Laidlaw(pen).	7.971	12	1		4	8	5	6	7*		9	12	11							3	10		2				
13	15	a	Rochdale	1-3	Hemsley.	1.963	13	1		4	8	5	6	7		9		11*							12	10		2		3		
14	21	h	Darlington	1-2	O'Callaghan.	4.215	14	1		4	8	5*	6	7		9	12								2	10	11			3		
15	28	a	York City	1-0	Laidlaw(pen).	3.023	15	1		2	8	5	6	7		9	11						4			10	12			3*		
16	Nov 5	a	Halifax Town	1-0	Jones C.	1.815	16	1	3	2	8	5	6	7		9	11						4*			10	12					
17	12	h	Northampton Town	4-2	Laidlaw,Habbin,Bowden,O'Callaghan.	2.688	17	1	3*	2	8	5	6	7		9	11						4			10	12					
18	19	a	Hartlepool Utd	2-0	Laidlaw,Jones C.	2.309	18	1	3	2	8	5	6	7		9	11						4*			10	12					
19	Dec 3	h	Crewe Alex	2-0	O'Callaghan,Bevan O.G.	2.854	19	1	3	2	8	5	6	7		9		11	4							10*	12					
20	10	a	Reading	0-3		4.321	20	1	3	2	8	5	6	7		9		11	4*							10	12					
21	26	h	Scunthorpe Utd	1-1	Snodin G.	5.097	21	1		3	4	5	6	7		9		11							2	8	10					
22	28	a	Wimbledon	3-3	Laidlaw(pen),Snodin G,O'Callaghan.	2.032	22	1		2	4	5	6	7		9	12	11							3	8	10*					
23	31	h	Halifax Town	1-1	Habbin.	3.913	23	1	2		4	5		7		9		11*	12				6			8	10	3				
24	Jan 2	a	Torquay Utd	0-2		3.376	24	1	8*	2	4	5		7		9	8	12					6			10	11					
25	10	h	Swansea City	1-1	Habbin.	2.509	25	1		3	4	5	6			9		11	7						2	10	8*	12				
26	14	a	Newport County	0-1		4.029	26	1	3		4	5			8	9		11						7	6	10				2		
27	28	a	Watford	0-6		11.816	27	1		2	4	5	12	7	8*	9		11								10				3	6	
28	Feb 4	h	Stockport County	1-0	Owen.	2.147	28	1		2	4	8	5	7		9		11								10				3	6	
29	25	h	Huddersfield Town	4-3	Owen(3),Laidlaw(pen).	4.712	29	1	5	2	4	8	6	7		9		11								10				3		
30	28	h	Grimsby Town	0-1		4.280	30	1	5	2	4	8	6	7		9		11								10	12			3*		
31	Mar 4	a	Barnsley	0-0		7.575	31	1		2	4	8	6	7			11					5				9	10			3		
32	7	a	Southport	1-1	Owen.	1.455	32	1		2	4	8	6	7			11					5				9	10			3		
33	10	h	Rochdale	1-1	Owen.	2.755	33	1		2	4	8	6	7			11					5				9	10			3		
34	18	a	Darlington	1-1	Owen.	1.772	34	1	10	2		8	6			4*		11	7			5	12			9				3		
35	25	h	Wimbledon	0-2		2.484	35	1	10	2	4	9	6		8*			7								5	11	12		3		
36	27	a	Scunthorpe Utd	0-0		3.724	36	1	10		4	8	6					7				5	2			9	11			3		
37	28	h	York City	1-1	Owen.	2.385	37	1	10	3	4	8	6					7				5	2			9	11					
38	Apr 1	h	Torquay Utd	1-0	Habbin.	1.440	38	1	7	3	4	9	6					11	12			5	2			10	8*					
39	3	a	Southend Utd	0-4		5.890	39	1	10	2	4	9	6					11*	12			5	7			9				3		
40	8	a	Northampton Town	0-0		2.793	40	1		2	4	8	6					7				5	10			9		11	3			
41	11	h	Aldershot	4-3	Laidlaw(pen),Owen,Meagan,Habbin.	1.595	41	1	10	2	4	8						12				5*	6	7		9		11	3			
42	15	h	Hartlepool Utd	2-0	Owen(2).	2.040	42	1	5	2	4		6					10					12	7*		9		11	3			
43	18	a	Brentford	2-2	Habbin,Taylor.	11.512	43	1	5	2	4	8	6	7				10					12			9		11*	3			
44	22	a	Crewe Alex	0-2		2.126	44	1	5	2	4	8	6	7				10					12			9		11*	3			
45	25	h	Bournemouth	0-0		1.654	45	1	5	3	11	8	6	7				4*							2	9	10	12				
46	29	h	Reading	2-2	Laidlaw(2)(1pen).	1.670	46	1	5	3	4	8*	6	7	12			11					10			2	9					

								Peacock	Olney	Robinson	Laidlaw	Owen	Taylor	Miller	M.Jones	O'Callaghan	C.Jones	Bentley	Bowden	Bailey	Biggins	Gray	Carnell	Meagan	Reed	Habbin	Snodin	Wignall	McConville	Hemsley	O'Riordan	S.Wignall
							App	44	26	42	45	45	41	35	6	30	10	28	16		3	2	6	11	5	41	13	10	7	23	2	
							Sub		1			1	1		1	6	1	5						3	1	1	9	1	1			
							Gls			13	11	1				7	2	1						1		10	2		1	1		

+ 1 O.G.

HOME
P W D L F A PTS
23 11 8 4 37 26 30

AWAY
P W D L F A PTS
23 4 9 10 15 37 17

TOTAL
P W D L F A PTS
46 15 17 14 52 63 47

F.A. Cup

| R1 | Nov26 | h | Shrewsbury Town | 0-1 | | 5.279 | R1 | 1 | 3 | 2 | 8 | 5 | 6 | 7 | | 9 | 11 | | 4* | | | | | | | | 10 | 12 | | | | |

League Cup

| 1R1L | Aug13 | a | Sheffield Wed | 2-5 | O'Callaghan,Jones C. | 7.602 | R11L | | 12 | 4 | 8 | 6 | 7 | | | 9 | 10 | 11 | | | 1 | | | 2 | | | | | | 3 | 5* |
| 1R2L | 16 | h | Sheffield Wed | 0-3 | | 7.303 | R12L | | | 2 | 4 | 8 | 6*| 7 | | 9 | 10 | 11 | | | 1 | | | 5 | | | 12 | | | 3 | |

League Division 4 1978-79

No	Date	V	Opponents	F-A	Scorers	Att
1	Aug19	a	Hartlepool Utd	W 4-3	Snodin G,French,Lewis,Habbin.	2,634
2	26	a	York City	D 1-1	Laidlaw.	3,654
3	Sep 1	h	Scunthorpe Utd	D 0-0		4,667
4	9	a	Huddersfield Town	L 1-2	Owen.	4,038
5	12	h	Port Vale	L 1-3	Owen.	3,405
6	16	a	Reading	L 0-3		5,394
7	23	h	Barnsley	D 2-2	French,Habbin.	9,380
8	26	h	Bournemouth	L 1-1	Taylor.	2,441
9	30	a	Northampton Town	L 0-3		3,011
10	Oct 7	h	Stockport County	W 2-0	Owen,Edwards O.G.	2,742
11	10	h	Torquay Utd	W 1-0	Owen.	2,507
12	14	a	Wigan Ath	L 0-1		5,788
13	17	h	Portsmouth	L 2-3	Laidlaw,Bentley.	2,480
14	21	h	Newport County	D 0-0		2,008
15	28	a	Wimbledon	L 2-3	Jones C(2).	3,252
16	Nov 4	h	Bradford City	W 2-0	Bradley,Owen.	2,981
17	11	a	Scunthorpe Utd	L 0-0		3,403
18	18	h	York City	L 1-2	Bradley.	2,479
19	Dec 2	h	Rochdale	W 1-0	Owen.	2,248
20	9	a	Aldershot	L 1-2	Reed.	3,030
21	26	h	Darlington	L 2-3	Bentley,Owen.	2,889
22	Jan16	a	Port Vale	W 3-1	Olney,Cork,Laidlaw.	3,381
23	30	h	Hereford Utd	W 1-0	Owen.	1,719
24	Feb 3	a	Bournemouth	L 1-7	Laidlaw.	2,986
25	10	h	Northampton Town	W 2-0	Bradley,Snodin G.	1,922
26	13	a	Crewe Alex	W 4-2	Laidlaw,Pugh,Owen(2).	1,532
27	21	a	Stockport County	W 1-0	Owen.	2,907
28	24	h	Wigan Ath	L 0-1		4,612
29	27	h	Huddersfield Town	L 0-2		3,419
30	Mar 3	a	Newport County	L 0-3		2,549
31	6	a	Halifax Town	D 0-0		1,658
32	9	h	Wimbledon	W 1-0	Cox.	1,927
33	20	h	Reading	D 2-2	French,Lewis.	2,487
34	23	h	Hartlepools Utd	D 0-0		2,552
35	28	a	Torquay Utd	L 1-2	French(pen).	1,694
36	31	h	Grimsby Town	L 0-1		4,707
37	Apr 3	a	Barnsley	L 0-2		12,082
38	7	a	Rochdale	L 0-2		1,606
39	14	a	Darlington	L 2-3	Snodin G,Packer.	1,967
40	16	h	Crewe Alex	W 2-0	Packer,Cox.	1,658
41	17	h	Halifax Town	D 1-1	Cox.	2,227
42	21	a	Hereford Utd	L 0-2		3,209
43	24	h	Portsmouth	L 0-4		5,863
44	28	h	Aldershot	D 1-1	French.	1,539
45	30	a	Bradford City	L 0-1		2,189
46	May 5	a	Grimsby Town	W 4-3	Lewis(3),Laidlaw.	10,423

	P	W	D	L	F	A	PTS
HOME	23	8	8	7	25	22	24
AWAY	23	5	3	5	25	51	13
TOTAL	46	13	11	22	50	73	37

Players: Cox, Gilligan, Reed, Flanagan, Ustin, Pugh, Lister, Lally, Bowden, Cannell, Jones, Cork, Packer, Robinson, Hemsley, Meagan, Lewis, French, G.Snodin, Lewis, Habbin, Taylor, Bradley, Olney, Bentley, Owen, Peacock

App: 46 29 32 32 42 13 16 24 28 36 38 27 9 6 4 7 4 7 4 11 5 33 9 16 3 14 11 1 10
Sub: 10 2 1 1 1 2 3 8 6 1 2 1 1 5 1 1
Gls: 10 12 11 6 5 7 8 3 5 7 4 2 1 2 8 2 2 1 3 5

+ 1 O.G.

F.A. Cup

R1	Nov25	h	Huddersfield Town	W 2-1	Lewis,Laidlaw.	4,330
R2	Dec16	a	Shrewsbury Town	L 0-3		2,724

League Cup

R1 1L	Aug12	h	Sheffield Wed	L 0-1		7,232
R1 2L	Aug15	a	Sheffield Wed	W 1-0	French.	8,055
1RR	Aug22	h	Sheffield Wed	L 0-1		8,462

DONCASTER ROVERS F.C. 1978/79

The Rovers team which played against Sheffield Wednesday in the replay of the 1st round of the Football League Cup.
Back row, Dave Bradley, Kevin Olney, Dennis Peacock, Brian Taylor, Bobby Owen, Micky French.
Front row, Dick Habbin, Jack Lewis, Joe Laidlaw, Glyn Snodin, Tommy Meagan, Fred Robinson.

DONCASTER ROVERS F.C. 1979/80

Back row, left to right, Les Cocker (Assistant Manager), Dave Bradley, Steve Lister, Ian Nimmo, Alan Warboys, Dennis Peacock, John Dowie, Les Packer, Tommy Meagan, David Cork, Billy Bremner (Team Manager)
Centre row, Left to right, Cyril Knowles (Coach), Pat Lally, Jack Lewis, Shaun Flanagan, Glyn Snodin, Dave Bentley, Billy Russell, Daral Pugh, Gerry Delahunt (Physiotherapist)
Front row, left to right, Apprentices, Tony Vaughan, Roy Banks, Gary Hatto, Ian Snodin, Steve Daniels, Steve Cork, Barry Culshaw. Dave Harle.

League Division 4 1979-80

No	Date	V	Opponents	F-A	Scorers	Att	No	Peacock	Russell	Ripley	Lister	Bradley	Dowd	Pugh	Nimmo	Warboys	Dowie	Bentley	Lewis	Mell	Bremner	Cork	Shipley	Daniels	Packer	Boyd	Harle	Lally	Riley	I.Snodin	Flanagan	Little	G.Snodin
1	Aug18	h	Northampton Town	W 2-1	Warboys(pen),Pugh.	4.402	1	1	2	3		5		7	8	9	10	11				4						6					
2	21	a	Halifax Town	D 1-1	Warboys.	2.519	2	1	2	3		5	6	7	8	9	10	11	12			4*											
3	25	a	Huddersfield Town	L 0-3		5.232	3	1	2	3		5	6	7	8	9	10	11	12									4*					
4	Sep 1	h	Bradford City	L 0-3		5.589	4	1	2	3	4	5		7	8*	9	10	11	12									6					
5	11	h	Torquay Utd	W 5-3	Lister,Pugh,Warboys,Lewis(2).	3.557	5	1	2		4	5	6	7		9	10*	11	8												3		12
6	15	a	Lincoln City	D 1-1	Nimmo.	4.834	6	1	2	3	5		6*	7	8	9	10	11	4									12					
7	17	a	Tranmere Rovers	L 0-1		3.024	7	1	2		5			7	8	9	10	11	4									6					3
8	22	h	Newport County	L 1-3	Warboys.	3.228	8	1	2		4		6	7	8	9	10	11	12									5					3*
9	28	a	Scunthorpe Utd	D 0-0		4.440	9		2		4	5		12	8	9		11	10				1					6			7*		3
10	Oct 2	h	Tranmere Rovers	D 1-1	Warboys.	2.973	10		2		4	5		7	8*	9		11	10				1					6			12		3
11	6	a	Crewe Alex	W 2-1	Dowd,Wilkinson O.G.	2.448	11		2		4		5	7	8	9		11	10				1					6					3
12	9	h	Halifax Town	W 2-1	Lister(2).	3.551	12		2		4		5	7	8	9		11*	10				1					6			12		3
13	13	h	Wigan Ath	W 3-1	Snodin G,Lewis,Nimmo.	4.169	13		2		4		5	7	8	9		11*	10				1					6			12		3
14	19	a	Stockport County	W 3-0	Nimmo(2),Dowd.	3.222	14	1	2		4*		5	7	8	9		11	10									6			12		3
15	23	a	York City	W 3-1	Lister(2),Lewis.	4.707	15	1	2		4		5	7	8	9		11	10									6*			12		3
16	26	h	Portsmouth	W 2-0	Lister,Warboys(pen).	9.801	16	1	2		4		5	7	8	9		11	10									6					3
17	Nov 3	a	Northampton Town	L 0-1		3.427	17	1	2		4		5	7	8	9		11*	10									6			12		3
18	6	h	York City	W 2-0	Nimmo(2).	6.653	18	1	2		4		5*	7	8	9		11	10									6			12		3
19	9	h	Peterborough Utd	W 2-1	Pugh,Lewis.	7.447	19	1	2		4		5	7	8	9		11*	10									6			12		3
20	17	a	Bournemouth	D 0-0		3.771	20	1	2		4		5	7	8	9			10									6			11		3
21	Dec 1	h	Aldershot	D 1-1	Nimmo.	6.210	21	1	2		4	6		7	8	9		11	10									6*			12		3
22	21	h	Darlington	L 0-1		3.909	22	1	2		4	5	6	7	8				10*						12						9	11	3
23	26	a	Walsall	L 1-3	Nimmo.	5.449	23	1	2		4	5	6*	7	8									12				11	9			10	3
24	29	h	Huddersfield Town	L 1-2	Little.	7.387	24	1	2		4	6		7*	8		10			12								5	9			11	3
25	Jan 5	a	Hereford Utd	D 2-2	Riley(2).	2.793	25	1	2		4	6		7	8													5	9		11	10	3
26	12	h	Port Vale	L 2-3	Pugh,Bentley O.G.	3.859	26	1	2		4*	6		12	8	9												5	11		7	10	3
27	19	a	Torquay Utd	D 2-2	Lister,Bradley.	3.403	27	1	2		4	6	7		8	9												5	11			10	3
28	26	a	Bradford City	L 1-3	Nimmo.	5.544	28	1	2		4	6	7	12	8*	9												5	11			10	3
29	Feb 2	h	Lincoln City	D 1-1	Lister.	3.627	29	1	2		4		6			9			12						8*			5	11		7	10	3
30	12	a	Rochdale	L 2-3	Lister,Little.	1.512	30	1	2		4		6	7	8	9				11*								5	12			10	3
31	16	h	Scunthorpe Utd	W 5-0	Bentley(2),Warboys(2),Mell.	3.304	31	1	2		4		6			9		11*	12	8								5			7	10	3
32	26	a	Newport County	L 1-2	Warboys.	4.652	32	1	2		4		6		12	9		11		8*								5			7	10	3
33	Mar 1	h	Stockport County	D 1-1	Lister.	3.332	33	1	2		4		6		12	9		11		8*								5			7	10	3
34	8	a	Portsmouth	L 0-2		14.382	34	1			4		6	12	8	9		11	7*									5			2	10	3
35	11	h	Hartlepool Utd	L 0-2		2.453	35	1	2*		4		6	12	8	9		11	7									5				10	3
36	22	a	Peterborough Utd	L 2-3	Mell,Lister.	4.107	36		2		4		6	12	8	9		10		11*						1		5			7		3
37	29	h	Bournemouth	W 1-0	Flanagan.	2.327	37		2		4	5	6		8	9		11*			10					1				12	7		3
38	Apr 4	a	Darlington	L 1-2	Warboys.	2.285	38		2		4	5	6	12	8	9										1		11*			7	10	3
39	5	h	Walsall	D 1-1	Bradley.	3.784	39				12	5	6	7		9			8							1		2		4*	11	10	3
40	8	a	Hartlepool Utd	W 2-1	Pugh,Flanagan.	2.228	40				2	5	6	7		9			8							1				4	11	10	3
41	11	h	Hereford Utd	W 1-0	Lister.	2.862	41				2	5	6	7	12	9			8							1				4	11	10	3*
42	19	a	Aldershot	D 1-1	Snodin I.	2.921	42		2		4	5	6	7					8	9*						1				12	11	10	3
43	22	h	Crewe Alex	D 1-1	Warboys.	2.498	43		12		2	5	6	7		9			8							1				4	11	10*	3
44	26	h	Rochdale	W 2-0	Nimmo,Bannon O.G.	2.493	44		2			5	6	7	8	9										1				4	11	10	3
45	30	a	Wigan Ath	D 0-0		4.740	45		2			5	6	7	8				12	9*						1				4	11	10	3
46	May 3	a	Port Vale	L 0-3		2.338	46		2			5	6	9	8				12	10						1	11			4	7*		3

HOME							AWAY							TOTAL						
P	W	D	L	F	A	PTS	P	W	D	L	F	A	PTS	P	W	D	L	F	A	PTS
23	11	6	6	37	27	28	23	4	8	11	25	36	16	46	15	14	17	62	63	44

	Peacock	Russell	Ripley	Lister	Bradley	Dowd	Pugh	Nimmo	Warboys	Dowie	Bentley	Lewis	Mell	Bremner	Cork	Shipley	Daniels	Packer	Boyd	Harle	Lally	Riley	I.Snodin	Flanagan	Little	G.Snodin	
App	30	41	5	39	25	37	33	36	39	9	27	24	8	1	2	5	0	1	11	1	34	7	7	22	22	40	
Sub		1		1			7	3				8	1				1	1			1	1	2	9		1	
Gls				12	2	2	5	10	11		2	5	2									2	1	2	2	1	+ 3 og

F.A. Cup

No	Date	V	Opponents	F-A	Scorers	Att	No	Peacock	Russell	Ripley	Lister	Bradley	Dowd	Pugh	Nimmo	Warboys	Dowie	Bentley	Lewis	Mell	Bremner	Cork	Shipley	Daniels	Packer	Boyd	Harle	Lally	Riley	I.Snodin	Flanagan	Little	G.Snodin
R1	Nov23	a	Port Vale	W 3-1	Pugh,Nimmo,Lewis.	4.973	R1	1	2		4		6	7	8	9			10									5			11		3
R2	Dec15	h	Mansfield Town	L 1-2	Nimmo.	7.952	R2	1	2		4	6		7	8	9									10			5			11		3

League Cup

No	Date	V	Opponents	F-A	Scorers	Att	No	Peacock	Russell	Ripley	Lister	Bradley	Dowd	Pugh	Nimmo	Warboys	Dowie	Bentley	Lewis	Mell	Bremner	Cork	Shipley	Daniels	Packer	Boyd	Harle	Lally	Riley	I.Snodin	Flanagan	Little	G.Snodin
1R1L	Aug11	a	Sheffield Utd	D 1-1	Dowie.	9.748	R11L	1	2	3		5	6	7	9	8	10	11	12			4*											
1R2L	14	h	Sheffield Utd	W 3-1	Nimmo,Pugh,Warboys(pen).	8.444	R12L	1	2	3		5	6	7	8	9	10	11				4											
2R1L	28	h	Exeter City	W 3-1	Lister,Ripley,Nimmo.	4.636	R21L	1	2	3	4*	5	6	7	8	9	10	11	12														
2R2L	Sep 5	a	Exeter City	L 1-5	Dowie. (aet)	3.129	R22L	1	2	3	4		6	7*		9	10	11	12									5					8

League Division 4 1980-81

No	Date	V	Opponents	F-A	Scorers	Att		Boyd	Russell	Dowie	Lister	Harle	Saunders	Pugh	Nimmo	Warboys	G.Snodin	Little	Aldridge	Shipley	Wilcox	I.Snodin	Bremner	Bates	Flanagan	Swan	Dowd	Bennett	Mell	Dawson	Lally	Humphries
1	Aug16	a	Port Vale	L 0-3		2.846	1	1	2		4		5	7	9		10	11*				12					6		8	3	
2	19	h	Darlington	W 2-0	Nimmo(2).	3.157	2	1	2		4			7	8	9	10						11	3				6			5	
3	23	h	Peterborough Utd	L 0-4		3.536	3	1	2		4			7	8	9	10						11*	3				6		12	5	
4	30	a	Hartlepool Utd	L 0-1		2.112	4	1	2		4		5	7		9	10	11					3					6		8		
5	Sep 6	h	Hereford Utd	W 5-1	Nimmo(2).Little.Warboys(2)(1pen).	2.186	5	1	2	3	4	5		7	8	9	10	11										6				
6	13	h	Northampton Town	W 2-0	Little,Pugh.	2.280	6	1	2	3	4	5	12	7	8	9	10	11										6*				
7	16	a	Torquay Utd	W 3-2	Nimmo(2),Snodin G.	2.442	7	1	2	3	4	5	6	7	8	9	10	11														
8	19	h	Southend Utd	W 1-0	Little.	6.044	8	1	2	3	4	5	6	7	8	9	10	11														
9	27	a	York City	W 1-0	Mell.	4.641	9	1	2	3		5	4	7	8		10	11					12					6*		9		
10	30	h	Torquay Utd	W 2-0	Lister,Warboys.	6.916	10	1	2	3	4	5	6	7	8	9	10	11														
11	Oct 4	h	Lincoln City	L 0-1		9.693	11	1	2	3	4	5*	6	7	8	9	10	11					12									
12	8	a	Wigan Ath	L 0-3		3.068	12	1	2		3	5	4*	7	8	9	10	11					12					6				
13	11	a	Crewe Alex	D 0-0		4.033	13		2	3	4	5			12	9	10	11*	1		7							6		8		
14	18	h	Halifax Town	D 0-0		4.044	14	1	2	3	4	5		7*	8	9		11			12			10		6						
15	21	h	Bury	W 1-0	Warboys(pen).	3.529	15	1	2		4	12	5		8	9	10*	11			7					6			3			
16	25	a	Aldershot	L 0-1		2.988	16	1	2		4	3	5	12		9	10	11			7*					6			8			
17	28	a	Scunthorpe Utd	D 1-1	Nimmo.	4.058	17	1	2	5	4	12			8	9	10	11								6			7		3*	
18	Nov 1	h	Wimbledon	W 2-1	Mell,Brown O.G.	3.245	18	1	2	5	4			12	8	9*	10	11								6			7		3	
19	4	h	Wigan Ath	D 1-1	Little.	3.625	19	1	2	5	4			12	8	9*	10	11								6			7		3	
20	7	a	Stockport County	L 1-2	Nimmo.	2.474	20	1	2		4	5		7*	8		10	11					12			6			9		3	
21	11	a	Darlington	L 0-5		2.094	21	1	2		4	9*	5		8		10	11			7					6			12		3	
22	15	h	Port Vale	W 2-0	Harle,Flanagan.	2.422	22	1	2		4	5		7		9	10	11*					12		8	6					3	
23	29	h	Rochdale	L 1-2	Snodin G.	2.502	23	1	2	3				7	12	9	10	11			5				8*	4					6	
24	Dec 6	a	Bournemouth	W 2-1	Swan.Nimmo.	2.495	24	1	2					7	8	9	10	11			4				5	6			12		3*	
25	19	h	Mansfield Town	W 2-1	Little.Pugh.	3.650	25	1	2			12		7	8	9	10*	11			4				5	6			3			
26	26	a	Bradford City	D 1-1	Mell.	4.356	26	1	2	10	12			7	8	9		11			4				5	6*			3			
27	27	h	Tranmere Rovers	W 1-0	Little.	5.530	27	1	2		6	12		7	8	9	10*	11			4				5				3			
28	Jan10	h	Aldershot	W 3-1	Saunders.Lister.Little(pen).	4.502	28	1	2		6			9	7	8		10	11		4				5				3			
29	17	a	Rochdale	D 2-2	Pugh.Snodin I.	3.021	29	1	2		6			9	7	8		10	11		4				5						3	
30	24	h	Hartlepool Utd	L 1-2	Nimmo.	6.814	30	1	2		6*			3	7	8	9	10	11		4				5						12	
31	31	a	Peterborough Utd	W 1-0	Nimmo.	6.146	31	1	2			6		5	7	8	9	10	11		4										3	
32	Feb 6	h	Northampton Town	D 1-1	Nimmo.	5.680	32	1	2		9	6		5	7	8		10	11*		4					12					3	
33	14	a	Hereford Utd	W 3-1	Nimmo(2),Snodin I.	2.835	33	1	2	12	6*	5		7	8		10	11			4									9	3	
34	20	h	York City	W 3-2	Nimmo,Russell,Dawson.	5.839	34	1	2		12	5		7	8		10	11			4					6*				9	3	
35	27	a	Southend Utd	D 0-0		6.422	35	1	2		6	5		7	8	9	10	11			4									3	
36	Mar 7	a	Lincoln City	D 1-1	Nimmo.	8.832	36	1	2		6	5		7	8	9	10	11			4									12	3*
37	13	h	Crewe Alex	D 1-1	Dawson.	7.207	37	1	2	12	6*	5		7	8	9	10	11			4									3	
38	21	a	Halifax Town	W 3-0	Saunders,Nimmo,O'Neill O.G.	3.762	38	1	2	12				5	7	8*	9	10	11		4									3	6
39	27	h	Scunthorpe Utd	W 1-0	Dawson.	8.001	39	1	2		8	12		5	7		9	10	11*		4									3	6
40	31	a	Bury	L 0-2		3.394	40	1	2		9	11		5	7	8		10			4									3	6
41	Apr 4	a	Wimbledon	L 0-1		3.595	41	1	2		6	11			7	8*	9	10			4	3				5				12	
42	10	h	Stockport County	W 2-1	Dawson(2).	6.120	42	1	2		6	11*		7		9	10		8		4	12				5				3	
43	17	a	Tranmere Rovers	D 1-1	Warboys(pen).	2.921	43	1	2		5	11		7	8	9	10				4					12	6*			3	
44	21	h	Bradford City	W 2-0	Lister,Snodin G.	8.856	44	1	2		8	11		5	7		9	10			4					6				3	
45	May 2	h	Bournemouth	W 2-1	Warboys.Nimmo.	11.373	45	1	2		11	12		5	7	8	9	10			4*					6				3	
46	6	a	Mansfield Town	D 1-1	Dawson.	4.506	46	1	2		8	11		5	7		9	10			4*					6				3	12

HOME						AWAY							TOTAL						
P	W	D	L	F	A	PTS	P	W	D	L	F	A	PTS	P	W	D	L	F	A	PTS
23	15	4	4	36	20	34	23	7	8	8	23	29	22	46	22	12	12	59	49	56

	Boyd	Russell	Dowie	Lister	Harle	Saunders	Pugh	Nimmo	Warboys	G.Snodin	Little	Aldridge	Shipley	Wilcox	I.Snodin	Bremner	Bates	Flanagan	Swan	Dowd	Bennett	Mell	Dawson	Lally	Humphries
App	45	46	12	36	26	27	39	37	36	44	37	1	1	1	27	1	3	5	12	24	0	14	11	21	0
Sub			3	8	1	3	2							5	2	1	1		1	3	2	1	1		
Gls		1		3	1	2	3	18	6		3	7			2			1	1			3	6		+ 2 O.G.

F.A. Cup

	Date	V	Opponents	F-A	Scorers	Att		Boyd	Russell	Dowie	Lister	Harle	Saunders	Pugh	Nimmo	Warboys	G.Snodin	Little	Aldridge	Shipley	Wilcox	I.Snodin	Bremner	Bates	Flanagan	Swan	Dowd	Bennett	Mell	Dawson	Lally	Humphries
R1	Nov22	a	Sutton Coldfield	W 2-0	Lally,Dowd.	2.250	R1	1	2		4	8		11		10		7					5			9	3				6	
R2	Dec13	h	Blackpool	W 2-1	Little,Mell.	6.398	R2	1	2		5			7	8	9	10	11			4						6		3			
R3	Jan 3	a	Hull City	L 0-1		10.709	R3	1	2		4		5	7	8	9	10	11			6								3			

League Cup

	Date	V	Opponents	F-A	Scorers	Att		Boyd	Russell	Dowie	Lister	Harle	Saunders	Pugh	Nimmo	Warboys	G.Snodin	Little	Aldridge	Shipley	Wilcox	I.Snodin	Bremner	Bates	Flanagan	Swan	Dowd	Bennett	Mell	Dawson	Lally	Humphries
1R1L	Aug 9	h	Mansfield Town	D 1-1	Snodin G.	4.201	R11L		2		4*	5	7		9	11	10		1			12	3			6	8					
1R2L	12	a	Mansfield Town	L 1-2	Nimmo. (aet)	3.400	R12L	1	2		4		5	7	9		11	10								6	8		3			

League Division 3 1981-82

Player columns (top to bottom): Bremner, Allanson, Little, Cawthorne, Nimmo, Cooper, Bennett, Wiggington, I.Snodin, Parkinson, S.Humphries, Swan, G.Humphries, Liddell, Mell, Douglas, Lister, Warboys, Harle, Pugh, Dowd, Lally, G.Snodin, Dawson, Russell, Boyd

No	Date	V	Opponents	F-A	Scorers	Att
1	Aug29	h	Reading	L 0-1		4,192
2	Sep 5	a	Bristol City	D 2-2	Mell.Dawson.	6,996
3	11	h	Exeter City	W 3-0	Warboys.Harle.Dowd.	4,369
4	19	a	Wimbledon	W 1-0	Warboys(pen).	2,364
5	22	a	Burnley	W 1-0	Dawson.	3,799
6	26	h	Brentford	W 1-0	Warboys.	5,494
7	29	h	Preston North End	W 1-0	Pugh.	7,513
8	Oct10	a	Newport County	L 0-1		4,571
9	17	h	Millwall	W 1-0	Russell.	6,466
10	20	h	Lincoln City	W 4-1	Dawson(2).Pugh.Mell.	8,261
11	24	a	Swindon Town	D 2-2	Russell.Lister.	7,024
12	31	h	Bristol Rovers	W 4-2	Pugh.Lister.Douglas.Snodin G.	6,694
13	Nov 3	a	Carlisle Utd	L 0-2		3,725
14	6	h	Huddersfield Town	L 1-2	Warboys(pen).	11,319
15	14	a	Gillingham	L 0-3		8,189
16	28	a	Plymouth Argyle	L 2-4	Snodin I.Nimmo.	4,341
17	Dec 2	a	Chester	D 1-1	Snodin G.	1,740
18	5	h	Portsmouth	D 0-0		5,912
19	Jan16	a	Southend Utd	D 1-1	Pugh.	5,029
20	29	h	Wimbledon	D 1-1	Dawson.	5,849
21	Feb 2	a	Chesterfield	L 1-3	Snodin G.	6,157
22	6	a	Exeter City	L 1-2	Lister(pen).	3,193
23	9	h	Burnley	L 0-1		5,638
24	13	h	Chester	W 4-3	Little.Lister.Pugh.Snodin G.	4,098
25	17	a	Reading	D 3-3	Little.Pugh.Dawson.	2,596
26	20	a	Preston North End	L 1-3	Dawson.	5,840
27	27	h	Newport County	D 0-0		4,190
28	Mar 6	a	Millwall	W 2-0	Mell.Douglas.	4,055
29	10	a	Lincoln City	L 0-5		5,227
30	12	h	Swindon Town	D 0-0		3,532
31	16	h	Carlisle Utd	D 1-1	Lister.	3,431
32	20	a	Bristol Rovers	L 0-3		4,957
33	23	h	Oxford Utd	D 1-1	Lister.	3,800
34	27	a	Huddersfield Town	W 2-1	Cawthorne.Harle.	6,871
35	Apr 3	h	Gillingham	D 1-1	Wigginton.	3,902
36	6	a	Fulham	L 1-3	Snodin I.	5,081
37	10	h	Chesterfield	D 0-0		5,221
38	12	a	Oxford Utd	L 1-3	Russell.	8,493
39	17	a	Portsmouth	D 0-0		8,657
40	20	h	Walsall	W 1-0	Liddell.	3,903
41	24	h	Plymouth Argyle	D 2-2	Dawson.Douglas.	3,894
42	May 1	a	Brentford	D 2-2	Snodin G.Lister(pen).	4,124
43	4	h	Southend Utd	D 1-1	Mell.	3,734
44	8	h	Fulham	W 2-1	Mell(2).	4,729
45	15	h	Walsall	D 0-0		3,799
46	18	h	Bristol City	D 2-2	Snodin G(2).	4,252

Totals row: App 33, Sub 35 28 40 30 27 42 21 14 40 38 12 13 12 1 13 5 33 13 0 20 4 12 19 1 0

HOME								AWAY								TOTAL					
P	W	D	L	F	A	PTS		P	W	D	L	F	A	PTS		P	W	D	L	F	A	PTS
23	9	9	5	31	24	36		23	4	8	11	24	44	20		46	13	17	16	55	68	56

F.A. Cup

R1	Nov21	a	Mansfield Town	W 1-0	Douglas.	5,456
R2	Dec12	h	Penrith	W 3-0	Warboys(2).Little.	6,282
R3	Jan 2	h	Cambridge Utd	W 2-1	Warboys.Reilly O.G.	6,741
R4	23	a	Norwich City	L 1-2	Dawson.	17,311

League Cup

1R1L	Sep 1	h	Chesterfield	D 0-0		3,801
1R2L	15	a	Chesterfield	D 1-1	Douglas. (aet)	4,962
2R1L	Oct10	h	Crystal Palace	W 1-0	Mell.	7,783
2R2L	27	a	Crystal Palace	L 0-2		7,476

DONCASTER ROVERS F.C. 1981/82

Back row (left to right): David Pugh (coach), Steve Lister, Hugh Dowd, Carl Swan, Willie Boyd, Steve Humphries, Alan Warboys, Pat Lally, Alan Little, Dave Bentley (coach).
Middle row: Gerry Delahunt (physiotherapist), Glynn Snodin, David Harle, Ian Snodin, Ian Nimmo, Richard Dawson, Daral Pugh, Stewart Mell, Billy Russell, Billy Bremner (Manager).
Front row: Philip Kyle, Russell Wilcox, Brett Foster, Paul Maxted, Glenn Humphries, Patrick Dyson.

ROVERS squad with their CIL-sponsored new red and white hooped colours. Back row: Carl Swan, Steve Lister, Alan Warboys, Dennis Peacock, Willie Boyd, Hugh Dowd, Ian Nimmo, Colin Douglas, Graham Cawthorne. Front row: Glenn Humphries, Alan Little, Garry Liddell, Stewart Mell, Glyn Snodin, Ian Snodin (capt.), Daral Pugh and Billy Russell.

1982/83 Season

League Division 3 1982–83

No	Date	V	Opponents	F-A		Scorers	Att
1	Aug 28	h	Newport County	D	0-0		3.471
2	Sep 4	a	Bristol Rovers	L	0-2		3.471
3	8	a	Oxford Utd	L	0-3		4.661
4	10	h	Exeter City	W	6-1	Lster(p),Grhm,Lddll,Sndn G,Dgls,Vney.OG	3.205
5	18	a	Southend Utd	L	2-3	Russell,Lister.	2.944
6	25	h	Reading	W	7-5	Snodin I(3)(2p),Dglas,Rssll,Sndn G,Grhm	3.118
7	28	h	Wigan Ath	L	3-6	Snodin G,Douglas,Snodin I.	4.457
8	Oct 2	a	Orient	L	0-1		1.846
9	9	a	Lincoln City	L	1-5	Douglas.	4.785
10	16	h	Brentford	D	4-4	Snodin G,Humphries,Austin,Liddell.	3.266
11	19	h	Wrexham	D	1-1	Snodin G(pen).	3.420
12	23	a	Bradford City	L	0-1		5.526
13	30	h	Chesterfield	D	0-0		4.065
14	Nov 2	a	Huddersfield Town	L	0-3		6.848
15	8	h	Plymouth Argyle	D	2-2	Russell,Austin.	2.942
16	13	a	Gillingham	D	1-1	Austin.	4.451
17	27	a	Portsmouth	L	1-2	Humphries.	9.468
18	Dec 4	h	Cardiff City	D	2-2	Douglas,Snodin G.	3.078
19	18	h	Millwall	W	2-1	Mell,Snodin G.	2.568
20	27	a	Sheffield Utd	L	1-3	Mell.	16.139
21	28	h	Preston N E	W	2-0	Mell,Austin.	3.895
22	Jan 1	a	Walsall	L	0-1		3.859
23	3	h	Bournemouth	W	2-1	Snodin G(2)(1pen).	3.297
24	8	h	Bristol Rovers	L	1-2	Snodin G.	3.234
25	15	a	Newport County	W	2-1	Lister,Humphries.	3.482
26	22	h	Southend Utd	D	0-0		3.242
27	29	a	Wigan Ath	W	3-0	Snodin I,Snodin G(2)(1pen).	4.387
28	Feb 5	a	Reading	L	0-2		2.092
29	15	a	Wrexham	L	0-5		1.899
30	19	h	Lincoln City	D	2-2	Douglas,Russell.	4.667
31	26	a	Brentford	L	0-4		4.413
32	Mar 1	h	Huddersfield Town	L	0-4		6.078
33	5	h	Bradford City	L	1-2	Walker.	3.473
34	12	a	Chesterfield	D	3-3	Walker,Austin,Russell.	2.875
35	19	a	Plymouth Argyle	W	2-1	Walker(2).	3.406
36	25	h	Gillingham	L	0-2		2.528
37	Apr 2	a	Preston N E	L	1-4	Humphries.	5.285
38	5	h	Sheffield Utd	W	2-0	Walker,Humphries.	9.006
39	9	a	Cardiff City	L	0-3		5.456
40	12	h	Orient	L	0-3		2.355
41	16	h	Oxford Utd	L	0-1		1.592
42	23	a	Millwall	L	0-2		4.288
43	30	h	Portsmouth	L	0-2		2.974
44	May 2	a	Bournemouth	D	2-2	Douglas,Lister.	3.995
45	7	a	Exeter City	L	0-3		3.110
46	14	h	Walsall	L	1-3	Liddell.	1.507

Players (appearance grid columns): Watson, G.Snodin, Dowd, Meagan, Mann, Boyd, Austin, Little, Robertson, Owen, Campbell, Walker, Allason, Swan, Woods, Johnson, Wiggington, Lister, Graham, Douglas, Liodell, Pugh, Humphries, Cawthorne, I.Snodin, Mell, Russell, Peacock

App: 39 40 28 34 21 38 6 12 33 9 39 18 12 3 9 12 3 6 30 7 13 2 6 38 13

Sub: 5 3 5 5 7 2 2 1 1 5 4 3

Gls: 9 2 5 6 2 12 3 9 11 27 57 97 38 + 1 O.G.

	HOME							AWAY							TOTAL						
P	W	D	L	F	A	PTS		P	W	D	L	F	A	PTS		P	W	D	L	F	A	PTS
23	6	8	9	38	44	26		23	3	3	17	19	53	12		46	9	11	27	57	97	38

F.A. Cup

						Scorers	Att
R1	Nov 20	a	Workington	W 2-1		Owen,Little.	1.336
R2	Dec 11	a	Peterborough Utd	L 2-5		Mell,Snodin I.	4.012

Milk Cup (League Cup)

						Scorers	Att
1R1L	Aug 31	a	Huddersfield Town	D 1-1		Graham.	4.430
1R2L	Sep 14	h	Huddersfield Town	L 0-1			4.690

League Division 4 1983-84

Player columns (top headers, right side):
Buckovina, Gregory, Dobbin, Buckley, Saddington, Mutrie, Brown, Allason, Philliben, Woods, Tomlinson, Green, Boyd, Yates, Harle, G.Snodin, Kowalski, Douglas, Moss, Miller, Humphries, Lister, I.Snodin, Beckin, Russell, Peacock

No	Date	V	Opponents	F-A	Scorers	Att
1	Aug27	h	Wrexham	W 3-0	Douglas,Humphries,Moss.	2,189
2	Sep 3	a	Mansfield Town	W 2-1	Moss,Snodin ..	2,962
3	7	a	Reading	L 2-3	Miller.Moss.	3,888
4	11	h	Hereford Utd	W 3-0	Moss,Douglas,Russell.	3,970
5	17	a	Hartlepool Utd	L 0-1		1,611
6	24	h	Bury	W 3-1	Douglas,Lister,Moss.	2,777
7	27	h	York City	D 2-2	Moss,Douglas.	4,996
8	Oct 1	a	Torquay Utd	L 1-4	Green.	1,723
9	8	a	Peterborough Utd	D 1-1	Snodin I.	4,400
10	15	h	Aldershot	W 3-1	Humphries,Harle,Douglas.	2,299
11	18	a	Chesterfield	D 0-0		6,488
12	21	h	Halifax Town	W 3-2	Russell,Snodin G(2).	3,365
13	29	a	Tranmere Rovers	D 1-1	Snodin G.	2,787
14	Nov 1	h	Colchester Utd	D 3-3	Snodin I(pen),Douglas,Miller.	3,491
15	5	a	Bristol City	W 2-1	Harle.Kowalski.	6,145
16	12	h	Blackpool	W 2-1	Douglas(2).	4,604
17	26	h	Chester City	D 0-0		2,967
18	Dec 3	a	Swindon Town	L 1-2	Snodin I(pen).	3,733
19	17	a	Crewe Alex	D 1-1	Moss.	2,515
20	26	h	Northampton Town	W 1-0	Douglas.	3,827
21	27	a	Darlington	W 2-1	Mutrie.Moss.	2,457
22	31	h	Stockport County	W 2-1	Moss(2).	3,736
23	Jan 2	a	Rochdale	D 3-3	Moss,Douglas,Higgins O.G.	2,001
24	7	h	Mansfield Town	W 3-1	Russell,Miller,Snodin G.	3,804
25	14	a	Wrexham	W 2-1	Lister,Snodin G.	2,266
26	28	a	Hereford Utd	W 3-0	Harle,Miller,Russell.	2,554
27	Feb 4	h	Torquay Utd	D 1-1	Snodin G(pen).	3,727
28	11	a	Bury	W 3-2	Harle,Moss,Snodin G(pen).	2,400
29	14	a	Colchester Utd	D 1-1	Snodin G.	2,821
30	18	h	Tranmere Rovers	D 1-1	Harle.	3,781
31	25	h	Halifax Town	W 2-1	Woods,Snodin I.	2,408
32	Mar 3	h	Chesterfield	W 2-1	Russell.Yates.	4,162
33	6	h	Bristol City	W 1-0	Douglas.	4,954
34	10	a	Blackpool	L 1-3	Russell.	6,062
35	17	h	Peterborough Utd	D 1-1	Douglas.	3,672
36	24	a	Aldershot	L 1-2	Dobbin(pen).	5,636
37	Apr 8	a	York City	D 1-1	Snodin G.	11,297
38	14	h	Swindon Town	W 3-0	Snodin G.Snodin I(pen).Russell.	3,804
39	21	a	Northampton Town	W 4-1	Harle.Douglas.Dobbin,Snodin G.	1,912
40	24	h	Darlington	W 3-2	Snodin G(2).Snodin I(pen).	4,741
41	28	a	Chester	L 0-1		1,696
42	May 1	h	Reading	L 2-3	Brown A.Douglas.	4,972
43	5	h	Rochdale	W 3-0	Snodin I.Brown A.Moss.	3,396
44	7	a	Stockport County	W 2-0	Snodin I.Moss.	2,993
45	12	h	Crewe Alex	W 1-0	Moss.	3,879
46	15	h	Hartlepool Utd	L 0-1		3,770

App 38 41 17 39 30 44 21 41 44 34 41 28 27
Sub   1 1   1 2 2 4 15 15   3 2 1 6 1
Gls   6   2 3 4 5 6 7 8* 9 10 11

HOME
P W D L F A PTS
23 15 6 2 45 22 36

AWAY
P W D L F A PTS
23 9 7 7 36 31 25

TOTAL
P W D L F A PTS
46 24 13 9 81 67 61

F.A. Cup
R1 Nov19 a Mansfield Town   L 0-3   5,261 R1

Milk Cup (League Cup)
1R1L Aug30 a Scunthorpe Utd   D 1-1 Moss.   4,295 R11L
1R2L Sep 9 h Scunthorpe Utd   W 3-0 Humphries,Douglas,Snodin I(pen).   4,377 R12L
2R1L Oct 5 h Fulham   L 1-3 Douglas.   4,843 R21L
2R2L   26 a Fulham   L 1-3 Moss.   3,891 R22L

+ I.O.G.

Season 1983/84

(Back): G.Snodin, Kowalski, Boyd, Peacock, Breckin, Allanson.
(Middle): Lister, Woods, Moss, Green, Douglas, Russell.
(Front): McIlver (Youth Physio), Bukovina, I.Snodin, Hunphries, Miller, Bentley (Asst.Manager)

Season 1986/87

(Back): Russell, Redfearn, Rhodes, Nesbitt, Deakin.   (Middle): Stead (Player/Coach),
Humphries, Woods, Deane, Holmes, Clayton, Rushbury, Boersma (Trainer).
(Front): Dobbin, Brown, Cusack (Player/Manager), Philliben, Joyce.

League Division 3 1984-85

No	Date	V	Opponents	F-A	Scorers	Att
1	Aug25	a	Preston N E	L 0-2		3.748
2	31	h	Burnley	W 2-0	Snodin G,Brown A.	3.368
3	Sep 8	a	Reading	W 4-1	Brown A(3),Snodin G.	4.050
4	14	h	Lincoln City	W 3-2	Snodin G,Harle,Douglas.	4.962
5	18	h	Millwall	L 0-1		4.241
6	22	a	Bournemouth	W 3-1	Snodin G(2),Butterworth.	3.662
7	29	h	Bolton Wand	W 2-0	Snodin G(2).	4.850
8	Oct 2	a	Brentford	D 1-1	Douglas.	4.901
9	7	h	Rotherham Utd	L 0-1		10.389
10	13	a	Hull City	L 2-3	Woods,Snodin G(pen).	7.071
11	20	a	Bristol Rovers	D 1-1	Dobbin.	5.621
12	23	h	Cambridge Utd	W 3-2	Snodin I(2)(1pen),Buckley.	3.873
13	26	h	Plymouth Argyle	W 4-3	Butterworth(2),Harle,Philliben.	4.488
14	Nov 6	h	Bristol City	D 1-1	Harle.	3.947
15	11	a	York City	L 1-3	Douglas.	8.540
16	24	h	Swansea City	W 4-1	Snodin G(2),Douglas,Buckley.	3.575
17	28	a	Derby County	L 1-3	Butterworth.	10.901
18	Dec 1	a	Newport County	L 1-2	Snodin G.	1.816
19	14	h	Wigan Ath	D 1-1	Snodin G.	3.278
20	22	h	Gillingham	L 0-1		3.035
21	26	a	Bradford City	W 1-0	Snodin I.	9.440
22	29	a	Orient	L 1-2	Douglas.	2.323
23	Jan 1	h	Walsall	W 4-1	Harle,Snodin I,Parker,Snodin G.	3.485
24	19	h	Reading	L 0-4		3.556
25	Feb 2	a	Bolton Wand	L 1-3	Harle.	5.810
26	9	h	Bournemouth	W 3-0	Douglas(2),Snodin I.	2.338
27	16	h	Brentford	D 2-2	Snodin I,Snodin G(pen).	3.129
28	22	h	Derby County	W 2-1	Douglas,Butterworth.	5.713
29	Mar 2	a	Plymouth Argyle	L 1-2	Snodin I.	4.619
30	5	a	Cambridge Utd	D 1-1	Woods.	1.682
31	8	h	Bristol Rovers	D 2-2	Harle,Buckley.	3.651
32	12	a	Burnley	W 1-0	Deans.	3.020
33	16	h	Hull City	L 1-2	Snodin G.	5.942
34	23	a	Rotherham Utd	W 3-2	Douglas,Buckley,Deans.	5.087
35	26	h	Preston N E	L 1-2	Lister.	2.784
36	30	a	Bristol City	L 0-1		7.965
37	Apr 6	h	Bradford City	L 0-3		5.959
38	8	a	Walsall	L 0-1		3.706
39	14	h	York City	W 3-0	Harle,Deans,Snodin G.	3.816
40	19	a	Swansea City	L 1-3	Deans.	3.707
41	24	a	Lincoln City	W 2-0	Douglas,Snodin I(pen).	1.824
42	27	h	Newport County	W 3-2	Buckley,Lister,Deans.	1.885
43	30	a	Millwall	L 1-2	Buckley.	6.918
44	May 3	a	Wigan Ath	L 2-5	Snodin I,Harle.	2.660
45	6	h	Orient	D 1-1	Snodin G.	2.114
46	11	a	Gillingham	L 1-2	Harle.	2.332

	Gregory	Russell	Humphries	I.Snodin	Yates	Dobbin	Buckley	Douglas	A.Brown	Butterworth	G.Snodin	Kowalski	Peacock	Saddington	Harle	Travis	Berry	Parker	Allen	Deans	Lee	Woods	T.Brown	Philliben	Lister
1				4		5		7	9		8*	11	12	1		10		5						6	
2	1	2	3	4		5	6	7	8	9	10*	11	12												
3			3	4		5	6		8	9		11		1		10								2	7
4			5	4	3	7	12	8	9*			11		1		10								2	6
5			5	4	3	7	12	8			9	11		1		10								2*	6
6		2	6	4	3	7		9		8		11		1		10								5	
7		2	6	4	3	7		9		8		11		1		10								5	
8		2	6	4	3	7		9		8*		11		1		10								5	
9		2	6*	4	3	7	12	9		8		11		1		10								5	
10		2	6	4		7		8		9		11		1		10						12		5	3
11		2	6	4		7	12	9		8				1		10	11*							5	3
12		2		4	3	7	11	9	8*12					1		10								5	6
13		2		4	3		7	9		8	11*12			1		10								5	6
14		2		4	3		7	9		8		11		1		10							6	5	
15		2			3	4*	7	9		8	11	12		1		10							6	5	
16		2		4			7	9		8		11		1		10							6	5	3
17		2		4		12	7	9		8		11		1		10							6	5*	3
18		2	5	4	3	7	12	9		8		11	10*	1									6		
19		2	6	4			7	9			12	11		1		10						8*		5	3
20		2	6*	4	3		7	9				11	12	1		10								5	
21		2	6	4			7*	9			12	11	5	1		10		8							3
22		2	6	4			12	7	9			11	5	1		10		8*							3
23		2	6	4			7	9				11	5	1		10		8							3
24		2		6			7	9				11	5	1	4	10*		8						12	3
25		2	6	4		5*	7	9			12	11		1		10								8	3
26		2	6	4			7	9				11	10	1								8		5	3
27		2	6	4			7	9*		8		11	10	1					5	12				5	3
28		2		4			7	9		8		11	6	1	5	10									3
29		2		4			7	9		8		3	11	1		10								5	6
30		2		4	5		7	9				3		1		10		8	11						6
31		2	6	4			7	9				11		1		10		8						5	3
32		2	5	4			7*	9				11	12	1		10		8						3	6
33		2	6	4			7*	9		10		11	12	1				8						5	3
34		2	6	4			7	9				3		1		10		8						5	11
35		2	6	4			7	9				11		1		10		8						5	3
36		2		4				9			7	3*	6	1		10		8					5	12	11
37		2		4			7*	9		8		11		1		5	10						6	12	3
38		2	6	4				9		12		3		1		7*10							5		11
39		2						7	9			11	6	1		4	10	8						5	3
40			2				7*	9				11	6	1		4	10	8				12		5	3
41				4			7	9				11		1	5	10		8					6	2	3
42				4			7	9				11		1	5	10		8					6	2	3
43							7	9				12	11	4	1	5	10	8*					6	2	3
44				4			7	9				11		1	5	10		8					6	2	3
45		2		4			7	9				5	11	1		10		8					6		3
46		2	5	4			8	7	9			11				10			1				6*	3	12

				App	1	38	27	41	17	15	34	46	4	23	43	13	44	6	37	10	1	5	1	14	1	3	14	33	35
				Sub				2		5			6		7				9			1		5		3		3	1
				Gls			8		1	6	10	4	5	18					9		1		5		2		1	2

HOME | AWAY | TOTAL
P	W	D	L	F	A	PTS		P	W	D	L	F	A	PTS		P	W	D	L	F	A	PTS
23	11	5	7	42	32	27		23	6	3	14	29	40	15		46	17	8	21	71	72	42

F.A. Cup

	Date		Opponents	F-A	Scorers	Att
R1	Nov 17	a	Rochdale	W 2-1	Snodin G,Philliben.	2.319
R2	Dec 8	a	Altrincham	W 3-1	Douglas(2), O.G.	4.195
R3	Jan 5	h	Q.P.R.	W 1-0	Harle.	10.583
R4	26	a	Everton	L 0-2		37.535

	Gregory	Russell	Humphries	I.Snodin	Yates	Dobbin	Buckley	Douglas	A.Brown	Butterworth	G.Snodin	Kowalski	Peacock	Saddington	Harle	Travis	Berry	Parker	Allen	Deans	Lee	Woods	T.Brown	Philliben	Lister
1R		2		4			7	9				11		1		10						8	5	6	3
2R		2	6	4			7	9				11		1		10						8		5	3
3R		2	6	4			7	9				11	5	1		10									3
4R		2	6	4			5	7	9		8	11		1		10									3

Milk Cup (League Cup)

	Date		Opponents	F-A	Scorers	Att
1R1L	Aug28	h	York City	L 2-3	Brown A,Douglas.	4.632
1R2L	Sep 4	a	York City	L 0-5		5.550

	Gregory	Russell	Humphries	I.Snodin	Yates	Dobbin	Buckley	Douglas	A.Brown	Butterworth	G.Snodin	Kowalski	Peacock	Saddington	Harle	Travis	Berry	Parker	Allen	Deans	Lee	Woods	T.Brown	Philliben	Lister
1R1	1	2	5	4	3		7	9*	8	12	11				10									6	
1R2		2		6	10*		9	8	12	11	7	1		4	5									3	

League Division 3 1985-86

No	Date	V	Opponents	F-A	Scorers	Att		Peacock	Caswell	Rushbury	Dobbin	T.Brown	Humphries	Buckley	Nesbitt	Douglas	Woods	Deakin	Butterworth	Peatie	Stead	Flynn	Phillben	Rhodes	Wakenshaw	Deans	Cusack	Swinburne	Joyce	Holmes	Deane	A.Brown	Harle	Allen	Travis	Walker	Wadsworth
1	Aug17	a	Newport County	D 2-2	Nesbitt,Woods.	2.396	1	1	2	3	4	5	6	7	8	9	10	11																			
2	24	h	Bolton Wand	D 1-1	Douglas.	2.990	2	1		3	4	5	11	7		9	10							2			8*	6					12				
3	26	a	Notts County	D 1-1	Buckley.	3.922	3	1	2	3	8	5	4	7		9	10										6					11				
4	31	h	Darlington	W 2-0	Woods,Douglas.	2.671	4	1	2	3	8	5	4	7		9	10										6					1				
5	Sep 8	a	Lincoln City	D 3-3	Caswell,Woods,Dobbin.	3.205	5		2	3*	8	5	4	7	12	9	10	11									6						1			
6	13	h	Brentford	D 0-0	Douglas.	2.831	6		2	3	8	5	4	7		9	10	11									6						1			
7	17	h	Plymouth Argyle	W 1-0	Woods.	2.904	7	1	2	3	8	5	4	7		9	10*	11									6					12				
8	21	a	Rotherham Utd	L 1-2	Brown T.	5.189	8	1	2	3	10	5	4*	7	12	9		11									6					8				
9	28	h	Reading	L 0-1		4.012	9		2	3	8	5	4	7		9		12								10*	6	1				11				
10	Oct 1	a	Blackpool	L 0-4		4.121	10		2	3	12	5	4	7		9	8	11*									6	1				10				
11	5	h	Walsall	W 1-0	Harle(pen).	2.901	11		2	3	8		4	7		9	10*	12		5							6	1				11				
12	12	a	Wolverhampton Wand	W 2-1	Douglas(2).	4.324	12		2	3		4	7		9	8*	12			5							6	1				11	10			
13	19	h	Bristol Rovers	L 0-2		3.032	13		2	3	12	4		7		9	8				5						6					11*	10	1		
14	22	a	Swansea City	W 2-0	Douglas,Dobbin.	3.827	14		2	3	11	5		7		9			8							4	1					6	10			
15	26	a	Chesterfield	D 0-0		3.746	15		2	3	11	5		7		8			9*							4	1		12	6			10			
16	Nov 2	h	Bristol City	D 1-1	Brown T.	2.871	16		3	11	5		4	7		9			8								2*	6				10	12			
17	5	h	Wigan Ath	D 2-2	Dobbin(2).	2.069	17		3	11	5	4*	7	12	8			9						1						2		10				
18	8	a	Cardiff City	W 1-0	Caswell.	1.894	18		2	3	11	5*	4	7		8			9					1			6			2		10				
19	23	h	Bournemouth	D 1-1	Harle.	2.390	19		3	11		4	7		8		9*	12					5	1			6			2		10				
20	30	a	Gillingham	L 0-4		3.592	20		3	11		4	7		8		9*			2	5			1			6					10		12		
21	Dec 8	a	Darlington	W 2-0	Woods(2).	3.370	21		3	11*		4	7		8	10	12			2	5			1			6							9		
22	15	h	Derby County	L 0-3		4.617	22		3			4	7*		8	10	11	9		2	5			1			6							12		
23	21	a	Bolton Wand	L 0-2		4.546	23		3			4	7		8	10	11*12			2	5			1			6		9							
24	26	a	York City	W 1-0	Buckley(pen).	5.472	24		3		11	4	7		8	*10	12			2	5			1			6		9							
25	28	h	Notts County	W 2-1	Cusack,Buckley(pen).	3.673	25		3		11	4	7			10				2	5			1			6		9					8		
26	Jan 1	h	Bury	W 1-0	Douglas.	3.283	26		3		11	4	7		12	10				2	5			1			6		9					8*		
27	7	a	Bristol City	L 1-4	Douglas.	5.385	27			12	11	4	7		8	10				2	5			1			6		9	3*						
28	18	h	Newport County	D 1-1	Buckley.	2.336	28		3	12	11	4	7						8	2	5			1		9	6		10*							
29	24	a	Brentford	W 3-1	Dobbin,Joyce,Cusack.	3.568	29		3	7	11	4							9	8	2	5		1			6		10							
30	Feb 1	h	Lincoln City	D 1-1	Douglas.	2.723	30	1		3	4	11		7		8			12	9*	2	5					6		10							
31	4	h	Swansea City	D 0-0		2.029	31	1		3	12	11		7		8				2	5	4					6		10		9*					
32	8	a	Bristol Rovers	L 0-1		3.894	32	1		3	9		4	7		8				12	2	5	11*				6		10							
33	15	a	Plymouth Argyle	W 1-0	Douglas.	4.827	33		3	9	11	4	7		8					2	5	10					6									
34	Mar 4	h	Blackpool	D 0-0		2.316	34		3		11	4*	7	9	8				12	2	5	10	1				6									
35	8	a	Walsall	L 0-1		4.801	35		3		11		7		8				12	2	5	4	1				6		10							9*
36	15	h	Wolverhampton Wand	L 0-1		2.656	36		3		11		7		8					2	5	4	1	9			6		10*						12	
37	21	h	Chesterfield	W 2-0	Wakenshaw(2).	1.989	37		3		11		7		8	10	4				5	2	1	9			6									
38	29	a	Bury	W 2-1	Wakenshaw,Woods.	2.294	38		3		11		7		8	10	4				5	2	1	9			6									
39	31	h	York City	D 1-1	Holmes.	3.319	39		3		11		7			10*	4				5	2	1	9					6	8	12					
40	Apr 5	a	Wigan Ath	L 1-2	Buckley(pen).	4.143	40		3		11		7		8	12	4				5	2	1	9			10*	6								
41	12	h	Cardiff City	L 0-2		2.051	41		3	10	11		7		8	12	4*				5	2	1	9			6									
42	15	h	Rotherham Utd	D 0-0		3.159	42		3		11		7		8	10	4				5	2	1						9							
43	19	a	Bournemouth	D 1-1	Douglas.	2.796	43		3*		11		7		8	10	4			12	5	2	1	9			6									
44	25	h	Gillingham	L 2-3	Douglas,Dobbin.	1.659	44		3	12	11		7*		8	10	4				5	2	1	9			6									
45	May 3	a	Derby County	D 1-1	Douglas.	12.030	45		3	9	11		7		8	10	4			2	5*12	1					6									
46	5	a	Reading	L 0-2		8.388	46		3	9	11		7		8	10	5			2		12	1				6*	4								

	HOME							AWAY							TOTAL								App	9	15	45	25	38	29	45	2	41	28	13	12	3	19	27	20	30	8	4	43	4	15	5	2	15	3	0	3	1
	P	W	D	L	F	A	PTS	P	W	D	L	F	A	PTS	P	W	D	L	F	A	PTS		Sub			6					3	1		2	1	9	1	1		2		1			1		1	2			2	2	1
	23	7	10	6	20	21	24	23	9	6	8	25	30	24	46	16	16	14	45	51	48		Gls		2		6	2		5	1	13	7								3		2		1	1		2					

F.A. Cup

| R1 | Nov16 | a | Wigan Ath | L 1-4 | Douglas. | 3.315 | 1R | | 2 | 3 | 11 | | 4 | 7 | | 8 | | 12 | | | | | | 1 | | | 6 | | 9 | | | 10 | 5 | | | |

Milk Cup (League Cup)

| 1R1 | LAug20 | a | Notts County | L 0-1 | | 2.425 | 1R1 | 1 | 2 | 3 | 4 | 5 | 6 | 7 | | 9 | 10 | 12 | | | | | | | | | 8* | | | | | | | 11 | | | |
| 1R2 | LSep 3 | h | Notts County | W 2-1 | Dobbin,Douglas. (aet) | 2.679 | 1R2 | 1 | 2 | 3 | 8 | 5 | 4 | 7 | | 9 | 10* | | | | | | | | | 12 | | | 6 | | | | 11 | | | | |

League Division 3 1986-87

No	Date	V	Opponents	F-A	Scorers	Att
1	Aug23	a	Mansfield Town	L 1-2	Dobbin(pen).	3,969
2	30	h	Brentford	W 2-0	Dobbin,Redfearn.	1,675
3	Sep 6	a	Walsall	W 3-1	Woods,Dobbin,Burke.	4,939
4	14	h	Blackpool	D 2-2	Woods(2).	3,335
5	17	h	Bristol City	W 1-0	Dobbin.	2,236
6	20	a	Newport County	L 2-3	Redfearn,Rushbury.	2,392
7	27	h	York City	W 3-1	Clayton(2),Rushbury.	3,501
8	Oct 1	a	Chester City	L 0-1		2,590
9	11	a	Bury	L 0-2		2,578
10	14	h	Carlisle Utd	W 2-0	Russell,Redfearn(pen).	2,134
11	18	h	Darlington	D 0-0		2,500
12	21	a	Bournemouth	L 2-3	Clayton,Whitlock O.G.	4,195
13	25	a	Notts Coutny	L 1-3	Burke.	4,179
14	Nov 1	h	Fulham	W 2-1	Redfearn,Woods.	2,258
15	4	a	Wigan Ath	D 1-1	Deane.	2,388
16	7	h	Gillingham	W 2-0	Russell,Woods.	2,691
17	22	h	Port Vale	W 2-1	Woods,Burke.	2,455
18	Dec13	a	Middlesborough	L 0-1		8,001
19	21	h	Swindon Town	D 2-2	Burke,Russell.	2,936
20	26	a	Chesterfield	L 1-4	Cornforth.	3,741
21	27	h	Bolton Wand	W 3-0	Cornforth(2),Humphries.	3,301
22	Jan 1	h	Rotherham Utd	W 3-0	Gaynor,Redfearn(2).	4,652
23	24	h	Walsall	D 1-1	Redfearn(pen).	2,613
24	Feb 3	a	Port Vale	L 2-4	Russell,Clayton.	2,835
25	7	a	Bristol City	L 0-5		8,982
26	14	h	Newport County	L 0-1		1,811
27	17	h	Mansfield Town	W 1-0	Redfearn.	1,563
28	21	a	York City	D 1-1	Redfearn.	2,807
29	27	h	Chester City	D 1-1	Cusack.	2,166
30	Mar 3	a	Fulham	D 0-0		4,168
31	7	h	Notts County	L 1-2	Clayton.	2,564
32	14	a	Darlington	D 2-2	Burke,Gaynor.	1,559
33	17	h	Bournemouth	D 0-3		1,777
34	21	h	Bury	D 0-0		1,439
35	28	a	Carlisle Utd	L 0-1		2,002
36	Apr 4	a	Gillingham	L 1-2	Russell.	3,501
37	14	a	Brentford	D 1-1	Redfearn.	3,426
38	18	a	Rotherham Utd	D 0-2		3,687
39	20	h	Chesterfield	D 1-1	Miller.	1,545
40	22	h	Wigan Ath	D 1-1	Kinsella.	1,470
41	25	a	Swindon Town	D 1-1	Redfearn.	8,218
42	28	a	Blackpool	D 1-1	Redfearn(pen).	1,638
43	May 2	h	Bristol Rovers	W 2-0	Miller,Gaynor.	1,206
44	4	a	Bolton Wand	W 1-0	Redfearn.	4,838
45	6	a	Bristol Rovers	L 0-2	Gaynor,Deane,Redfearn(pen).	3,003
46	9	h	Middlesborough	L 0-2		4,500

	P	W	D	L	F	A	PTS
HOME	23	11	8	4	32	19	30
AWAY	23	3	6	14	21	41	12
TOTAL	46	14	14	18	53	60	42

F.A. Cup

R1	Nov15	a	Whitby Town	D 2-2	Russell,Deane.	2,387
R1R	18	h	Whitby Town	W 3-2	Woods,Stead,Redfearn(pen).	3,140
R2	Dec 6	a	Chester City	L 1-3	Woods.	3,821

Littlewoods Cup (League Cup)

R11L	Aug26	h	Rotherham Utd	D 1-1	Russell.	1,434
R12L	Sep 2	a	Rotherham Utd	L 1-4	Woods.	2,958

+ 1 O.G.

League Division 3 1987/88

No	Date	V	Opponents	F-A	Scorers	Att		Rhodes	Stead	R.Robinson	Humphries	Flynn	Cusack	Russell	Chamberlain	Deane	Gaynor	Burke	Kinsella	Holmes	Joyce	Beattie	Raffell	Miller	Rankine	Brevett	Kimble	Gaughan	Gorman	Harbottle	Brannigan	Peckett	James	Buckley	Stubbs	Nesbitt	Raven	Turnbull	Mendonca	Samways	L.Robinson	Hall
1	Aug15 h		Grimsby Town	W 1-0	Chamberlain.	2.857	1	1	2	3		4	5	6	7	8	9			14	11+			10																		
2	22 a		Fulham	L 0-4		4.157	2	1	2	3		4	5	6	7	8*	9	12	14	11		10+																					
3	29 h		Sunderland	L 0-2		2.740	3	1	2	3			5	6	7+12	14	10	9	11*					4											8								
4	31 a		Aldershot	L 1-2	Deane.	2.595	4	1	2	3			5	6	7	12	9	10	11					8*	4																		
5	Sep 5 h		Northampton Town	L 0-2		1.869	5	1	2	3			5	6	7		9	10	12		8			11*																			
6	12 a		Wigan Ath	L 1-2	Deane.	2.764	6	1+	2	3		4	5	6	7		9	12			14			8	11									10*								
7	15 h		Blackpool	W 2-1	Gaynor(2).	1.558	7	1	2	3		4	5	6			9	12			8			11*							7		10								
8	18 h		Chesterfield	W 1-0	Deane.	1.952	8	1	2	3		4	5	6			9	11			8										7		10								
9	26 a		York City	D 1-1	Burke.	2.702	9	1	2	3			5	6			9	7	11		4	8												10								
10	29 a		Mansfield Town	L 0-2		3.159	10	1	2	3			5	6			9	7		11	4	8									14			10+								
11	Oct 3 h		Gillingham	W 4-2	Gay'r.Miller.Stubbs.Kin'a.	1.747	11	1	2	3			5	6			9	7		11	4	8												10								
12	17 h		Notts County	L 0-1		2.645	12	1	2	3	4	11	6				9				5	8									14			7	10+							
13	20 h		Walsall	L 0-2		1.387	13	1	2	3	4	5	6				9					8				11		14						7	10+							
14	24 a		Bristol Rovers	L 0-4		2.817	14	1	2	3		12	6*				9				4	5	8			11		10+						7	14							
15	31 h		Bury	L 1-2	Deane.	1.403	15	1	2	3		4	6				9				7*		8			11	12						10		5						
16	Nov 4 a		Brighton & H.A.	L 0-2		7.145	16	1	2	3			6				9				4	5	8			11								7		10						
17	7 h		Port Vale	D 1-1	Deane.	1.365	17	1	2	3	12						9				6	4	5			8	11						7*		10						
18	21 a		Preston N.E.	W 2-1	Kimble.Cusack.	5.178	18	1	2	3			5	6			9				4	7				8	11								10							
19	28 h		Brentford	L 0-1		1.360	19	1	2*	3			5				9				4	12				8	11						7+		14	6	10					
20	Dec 5 a		Chester City	D 1-1	Flynn.	1.591	20	1				4				10+				14	6	2			8	3	11						7			5	9					
21	11 a		Southend Utd	L 1-4	Kinsella.	2.258	21	1				4										2			3*	8	12	11						7		10+	5	9				
22	19 h		Bristol City	L 1-2	Deane.	1.819	22	1	2			12				14	9+			5*	8				4	3	11				6		7			10						
23	26 h		York City	W 2-0	Deane.Raven.	2.409	23	1	2+							14	9			5	8					3	11				6		7		4	10						
24	28 a		Rotherham Utd	L 0-1		5.740	24	1	2			12				14	9			5	8					3	11*				6		7+		4	10						
25	Jan 1 a		Sunderland	L 1-3	Burke.	19.419	25	1	2			12				14	9			5	8					3	11+				6		7*		4	10						
26	2 h		Wigan Ath	L 3-4	Brannigan.Raven.Kinsella.	2.464	26	1		12		*+			7	9			5	8*	2				3		11				6	14+			4	10						
27	9 h		Fulham	D 2-2	Turnbull.Raven.	1.827	27	1					7	9					5		2					3	14	11			10+	6				4	8					
28	16 a		Chesterfield	W 1-0		2.715	28	1	5				7	9							2					3		4	11		10	6					8					
29	31 h		Aldershot	D 0-0		1.908	29	1	5				7	9							2				3	12	4	11		10*	6				2	8					
30	Feb 6 a		Northampton Town	L 0-1		4.381	30	1	5				7	9					2				12	3	14	4	11		10+	6				8*							
31	13 h		Rotherham Utd	D 2-2	Deane.Burke.	2.751	31	1	5				7*	9		12			2				3	10	4	11			6					8							
32	20 a		Grimsby Town	D 0-0		3.890	32	1	5					9		7			2				3	8	4	11			6					10							
33	27 a		Gillingham	L 1-3	Rankine.	4.049	33	1					14	9		7+			2				4	8	3	11*			6					5	12	10					
34	Mar 1 h		Mansfield Town	L 0-2		1.987	34	1	5				7*	9					2				3	8	4	11			6					12	10						
35	5 a		Notts County	L 0-2		5.816	35	1	5				7						2	10*		14	4	8	3+	11	12		6					9							
36	11 h		Chester City	D 2-2	Rankine. Langley O.G.	1.482	36		5				7*	10		4			12				3	8		11	14		6					2	9+		1					
37	19 a		Bury	L 1-2	Robinson R.	2.431	37		5				7	10		4*			2	9		6	3	8		11+	14							12			1					
38	25 h		Bristol Rovers	L 0-1		1.311	38		5				10*	9					6	2	7		3	8		11								4	12		1					
39	Apr 2 a		Port Vale	L 0-5		3.680	39		5				10	9					2*	7		12	3	8		11+	14							6			1	4				
40	4 h		Preston N.E.	W 3-2	Chamberlain(3).	2.167	40		5				10	9*					7	2			3	8		11								6	12		1	4				
41	9 a		Walsall	L 1-2	Deane.	6.631	41		5				10	9					7*	2			3	8		11								6	12		1	4				
42	15 a		Blackpool	L 2-4	Joyce.Gorman.	2.291	42		5				10	9*					8	2+	7		3			11	12							6			1	4	14			
43	23 h		Brighton & H.A.	L 0-2		1.683	43		5				10	9					7	14			6	2	8	3	11							4+			1					
44	30 a		Brentford	D 1-1	Robinson L.	3.122	44		5				10	9					7	2			3			11								6	8		1	4				
45	May 2 h		Southend Utd	L 0-1		1.306	45		5				10	9					7*	2	12		6	3		11+	14							8			1	4				
46	7 a		Bristol City	L 0-1		18.373	46		5				10	9					7+	14			6	2	12	3	11*							8			1	4				

HOME							AWAY							TOTAL								
P	W	D	L	F	A	PTS	P	W	D	L	F	A	PTS	P	W	D	L	F	A	PTS	App	
23	6	5	12	25	35	17	23	2	4	17	15	48	8	46	8	9	29	40	83	25	Sub	
																					Gls	

App: 35 23 37 8 18 17 6 22 42 7 14 21 22 10 2 11 41 14 16 34 0 1 4 15 2 7 6 8 2 17 24 2 11 7 0
Sub: 6 7 1 3 6 4 2 3 4 1 4 6 1 1 6
Gls: 1 1 1 4 10 3 3 3 1 2 1 1 1 1 3 1 1
+1 O.G.

F.A. Cup

R1	Nov14 h		Rotherham Utd	D 1-1	Holmes.	3.359	R1	1	2	3		6			9			7	4		8			11							5	10	
R1R	17 a		Rotherham Utd	L 0-2		4.530	R1R	1	2*	3	12	6			9			7	4		8			11+	14							5	10	

Littlewoods Cup (League Cup)

1R1L	Aug19 a		Scarborough	L 0-1		3.128	1R1L	1	2	3	4	5	6	7	8*	9	12		11	10															
1R2L	25 h		Scarborough	W 3-1	Gaynor,Kinsella,Stead.	2.370	1R2L	1	2	3		5	6	7	9+	10	8	11			4										14				
2R1L	Sep22 h		Arsenal	L 0-3		5.469	2R1L	1	2	3		5	6		9	11			4	8					7*				10	12				
2R2L	Oct 6 a		Arsenal	L 0-1		18.321	2R2L	1	2	3		5	6		7*	9		11+		4	8	12		14				10						

League Division 4 1988-89

No	Date	V	Opponents	F-A	Scorers	Att		Malcolm	Douglas	R.Robinson	Turnbull	Beatie	Raven	L.Robinson	Daly	Rankine	Dobson	Kimble	Gorman	Gaughan	Raffel	Peckett	Samways	Stewart	Hall	Ashurst	Trotter	Brockie	Ward	Brevett	Jones	Powell
1	Aug27	a	Rotherham Utd	L 0-3		4.489	1	1	2	3	4		6	7	8+	9	10*11	12	14	5											
2	Sep 3	h	Exeter City	W 2-1	Dobson(2)(1pen).	1.515	2	1	2	3	4	5	6	7	8*	9	10	11		12												
3		a	Colchester Utd	W 1-0	Rankine.	1.726	3	1	2	3		5	6	7		9	10	11		8	4											
4	16	h	Torquay Utd	L 1-2	Robinson R.	2.220	4		2	3	8	5	6	7		9	10	11+12	14		4*		1									
5	20	a	Rochdale	L 0-2		1.645	5		2	3		5*	6	7		9	10	11	12	8	4+14		1									
6	24	h	Wrexham	D 2-2	Beattie,Rankine.	1.631	6		2	3		5	6	7	8	9	10*11		12	4		1										
7	Oct 1	a	Stockport County	L 0-2		1.959	7	1	2	6		5	4	7	8	9		11	12		3			10*								
8	4	h	Hereford Utd	W 3-2	Rankine.Robinson R.Douglas.	1.281	8	1	10	3	4	5*	6	7	8	9		11	12		2											
9	8	h	Hartlepool Utd	W 1-0	Rankine.	2.091	9	1	2	3	4	5	6	7	8	9	10	11														
10	15	a	Crewe Alex	W 2-0	Dobson(2).	2.180	10	1	2	3	4	5	6	7	8	9	10	11														
11	21	h	Halifax Town	L 1-4	Robinson R.	3.037	11	1	2	3	4	5	6	7	8	9	10+11*12		14													
12	25	a	York City	D 1-1	Dobson(pen).	2.957	12	1	2	3	4	5	6	7	8	9	10	11														
13	29	h	Leyton Orient	W 1-0	Rankine.	2.182	13	1	2	3	4	5	6	7	8*	9	10+11	14	12													
14	Nov 5	a	Darlington	W 3-1	Daly,Raven,Gorman.	1.625	14	1	2	3	4	5*	6	7	8	9	10+11	14	12													
15	8	a	Grimsby Town	L 0-5		3.382	15	1	2	3	4	5	6	7	8	9	10	11														
16	12	h	Peterborough Utd	L 2-3	Dobson(2).	2.224	16	1	10	3	4*	2	6	7		9		12	11	14	8+			5								
17	26	h	Burnley	W 1-0	Douglas.	2.724	17	1	11	3		2	6	7	8*	9	10		12					5	4							
18	Dec 2	a	Tranmere Rovers	D 2-2	Rankine,Dobson.	3.412	18	1	11	3		2	6	7*	8	9	10		12					5	4							
19	17	h	Scunthorpe Utd	D 2-2	Dobson(pen),Daly.	3.381	19	1	11	3			6		8	9	10		7*	12				5	4		2					
20	26	a	Cambridge Utd	D 0-0		2.673	20	1	11	4			6	7	8	9	12							5			2	10*	3			
21	28	a	Lincoln City	L 1-3	Dobson.	5.213	21	1	4				6	7	8	9	10*			12				5		2	11					
22	Jan 2	h	Scarborough	W 3-1	Robinson R,Robinson L,Rankine.	3.053	22	1	11	3			6	7	8	9	10							5		2	4					
23	10	h	Carlisle Utd	L 1-3	Dobson.	2.128	23	1	11	3			6	7	8+	9	10			12				5		2	4*14					
24	14	a	Exeter City	L 0-3		2.540	24	1	5				6	7	8	9	10		11	12		2*		4	3							
25	21	h	Rotherham Utd	W 1-0	Gaughan.	4.432	25	1	2				6	7	8	9	10*		11	12				5	4		3					
26	28	a	Torquay Utd	L 2-3	Ashurst,Gaughan.	2.103	26	1	2				6	7	8	9	10+		11					5	4		3	14				
27	Feb 4	h	Rochdale	D 1-1	Brockie(pen).	1.868	27	1		2	12	14	6	7	8+	9			11*					5	4		3	10				
28	11	a	Wrexham	D 1-1	Brockie(pen).	3.238	28		2		10		6	7	8	9			11		1			5	4		3					
29	18	a	Hartlepool Utd	L 1-2	Jones.	1.919	29		2		10		6	7	8*	9			11		1			5	4		3	12				
30	24	h	Crewe Alex	L 0-1		1.713	30		2	12	10		6		8*	9		14	11		1			5	4		3	7+				
31	28	h	York City	L 1-2	Turnbull.	1.526	31		2	4	10		6		8	9		14	11		1			5			3	7+				
32	Mar 3	a	Halifax Town	L 0-2		1.675	32		2*	4	10		6	7	8+	9		14	11		1			5			3	12				
33	10	h	Darlington	W 1-0	Daly(pen).	1.538	33		2	4	10		6	7	8	9		3	11		1			5								
34	14	a	Leyton Orient	L 0-4		2.824	34		2	3*10			6	7	8	9			11		12			1			5	4				
35	18	h	Colchester Utd	W 3-1	Rankine(2),Jones.	1.237	35	1	2		10		6	7	8+	9			11		3			5	4				14			
36	25	a	Scarborough	L 0-2		2.792	36	1	6		10			7		9			11*	12				5	4		3	8	2			
37	27	h	Cambridge Utd	D 1-1	Daly.	1.937	37	1	6			4		7	8	9			11	10+				5	2		3	14				
38	Apr 1	a	Scunthorpe Utd	L 1-2	Rankine.	5.334	38	1	6		10			7	8	9			11+	4				5	2		3	14				
39	4	a	Carlisle Utd	W 1-0	Rankine.	2.991	39	1	6		10			7	8	9			11					5	4		3		2			
40	8	h	Lincoln City	L 0-1		2.124	40	1	6		10			7	8*	9			11					5	4		3	12	2			
41	14	h	Stockport County	D 2-2	Turnbull,Robinson L(pen).	1.363	41	1	6		10			7	8*	9		11		12	14			5			3	4	2+			
42	22	a	Hereford Utd	L 1-3	Turnbull.	1.804	42	1	6		10			7	8+	9		11		4				5			3	14				
43	29	a	Burnley	L 0-3		4.211	43	1	2		8			7	12	9		14		11+	6			5	4		3	10*				
44	May 1	h	Grimsby Town	L 2-3	Turnbull,Robinson L(pen).	2.183	44	1+	2		8			7	14	9		12		11*	6			5			3	10				
45	6	h	Tranmere Rovers	D 0-0		2.268	45		2		8			7		9		11			1			5	4		3	10				
46	13	a	Peterborough Utd	L 0-2		2.984	46		2		8			7		9		11+		12	6	14	1		5			4	3	10*		

HOME						AWAY							TOTAL						
P	W	D	L	F	A	PTS	P	W	D	L	F	A	PTS	P	W	D	L	F	A	PTS
23	9	6	8	32	32	24	23	4	4	15	17	45	12	46	13	10	23	49	77	36

		Malcolm	Douglas	R.Robinson	Turnbull	Beatie	Raven	L.Robinson	Daly	Rankine	Dobson	Kimble	Gorman	Gaughan	Raffel	Peckett	Samways	Stewart	Hall	Ashurst	Trotter	Brockie	Ward	Brevett	Jones	Powell
App		34	46	27	31	17	35	43	37	46	22	26	0	22	11	0	12	1	30	3	23	4	22	9	4	
Sub			2	1				2			2	5	9	12	2	7			1	1	8					
Gls		2	4	4		1	1	3	4	11	10		1	2							1		2		2	

F.A. Cup

	Date	V	Opponents	F-A	Scorers	Att		Malcolm	Douglas	R.Robinson	Turnbull	Beatie	Raven	L.Robinson	Daly	Rankine	Dobson	Kimble	Gorman	Gaughan	Raffel	Peckett	Samways	Stewart	Hall	Ashurst	Trotter	Brockie	Ward
R1	Nov19	h	Brandon Utd	D 0-0		2.139	1R	1		4		2	6	7		9	10		8*11					12		3	5		
R1R	22	h	Brandon Utd	W 2-1	Dobson(2). (at Doncaster)	1.832	1R1	1	8	4		2	6	7		9	10		12	11					3*	5			
R2	Dec11	h	Sheffield Utd	L 1-3	Daly.	6.556	2R	1	11	3		2	6	7*	8	9	10		12						5	4			

Littlewoods Cup (League Cup)

	Date	V	Opponents	F-A	Scorers	Att		Malcolm	Douglas	R.Robinson	Turnbull	Beatie	Raven	L.Robinson	Daly	Rankine	Dobson	Kimble	Gorman	Gaughan	Raffel	Peckett
1R1L	Aug30	h	Darlington	D 1-1	Rankine.	1.504	1R1	1	2	3	4		6	7	8	9	10	11+		14	5	
1R2L	Sep 6	a	Darlington	L 0-2		1.366	1R2	1	2	3		5	6+	7		9	10	11	12*	8	4	14+*

Season 1988/89

(Back): Brevett, Daly, Gaughan, Beattie, Samways, Malcolm, Robinson, Turnbull, Douglas, Gorman, Dobson.
(Front): Delahunt (Physio), Hall, Raven, Rankine, Raffell, Mackay (Manager),
Kinnear (Asst.Manager), Robinson, Peckett, Kimble, Beaglehole (Coach).

Season 1990/91

(Back): Blakey (Gen.Manager), Brailsford, Douglas, Holmes, Jones, Crichton, Samways, Muir, Ormsby,
Boyle, Golze (Youth Team Coach).   (Middle): Reddish, Noteman, Brevitt, Nicholson,
Beaglehole (Asst.Manager), Bremner (Manager), Turnbull, Harle, Gormley, Morrow.
(Front): Redhead, Rankine, Place, Brockie, Adams, Stiles.

League Division 4 1989-90

No	Date	V	Opponents	F-A	Scorers	Att		Sammways	Robinson	Brevett	Raffell	Ashurst	Douglas	McGinley	Stiles	Turnbull	Rankine	G.Jones	Summer	Gaughan	Brockie	Cusack	Gallagher	Adams	Nicholson	Cygan	D.Jones	Noteman	Morrow	Muir	McKay	Harle	Grayson	Reddish
1	Aug19 a		Exeter City	L 0-1		3.036	1	1	2	3	4	5	6	7+	8	9	10	11		14														
2	26 h		Gillingham	D 0-0		1.840	2	1	7	3	6	5	4	14	8	9	10			11+	2													
3	Sep 2 a		Lincoln City	L 1-2	Turnbull.	3.906	3	1	7	3	6	5	4		8	9	10		11		2													
4	9 h		Peterborough Utd	L 0-3		2.327	4	1	7	3	6	5	4		8	9	10		11+14		2													
5	16 a		Scarborough	W 2-1	Brockie(pen).Turnbull.	2.750	5	1	7	3	6	5	4		8	9	10			11	2													
6	22 h		Southend Utd	L 0-1		2.386	6	1	7	3	6	5	4		8	9	10			11	2													
7	26 h		Aldershot	L 0-1		1.960	7	1	7	3	6	5	4	12	8	9	10			11	2*													
8	30 a		Hartlepool Utd	W 6-0	Turnbull(3).Gaughan.Robinson L(2).	1.757	8	1	7	3	6	5	4		8	9	10			11	2													
9	Oct 7 a		Torquay Utd	L 0-2		2.059	9	1	7	3	6	5	4	12	8	9	10	14		11+	2*													
10	14 h		Carlisle Utd	D 1-1	Brockie(pen).	2.419	10	1	7	3	6	5	4+14		8	9	10			12	2*		11											
11	17 a		Cambridge Utd	L 0-1		2.483	11	1	7	3	6	5	4	14	8	9	10			2+			11											
12	21 h		Burnley	L 2-3	Robinson(pen).Eli O.G.	2.900	12	1	7	3	6	5	4+	8*	9	10	12			14			11											
13	28 a		York City	L 1-2	Stiles.	2.978	13	1	7	3	6	5	2	14	8		10			4			11	9+									
14	31 h		Maidstone Utd	D 1-1	Douglas.	1.806	14	1	7	3	6		2		5	8	9	10		4			11											
15	Nov 4 h		Scunthorpe Utd	L 1-2	Rankine.	3.274	15	1	7	3	6+		2		5	8	9	10		4*			11	12	14									
16	11 a		Rochdale	W 3-1	Jones D(3).	1.716	16	1	2	3		5	6		8	9	4						7			10	11							
17	25 h		Hereford Utd	W 1-0	Jones D.	2.167	17	1	2	3		5	6		8	9	4						7			10	11							
18	Dec 2 h		Stockport County	W 2-1	Jones D.Robinson L(pen).	3.023	18	1	2	3	4	5	6		9					8			7			10	11							
19	15 a		Halifax Town	W 2-0	Noteman.Adams.	1.233	19	1	2	3		5	6		8	9				4			7			10	11							
20	26 h		Wrexham	D 2-2	Noteman.Jones D.	3.668	20	1	2	3		5	6		8	14				10+			7			9	11							
21	30 h		Colchester Utd	W 2-0	Robinson L(pen).Turnbull.	2.982	21	1	2	3		5	6		8	9	4			14			7			10	11+							
22	Jan 1 a		Chesterfield	W 1-0	Robinson L(pen).	5.620	22	1	2	3		5	6		8	9	4			14			7			10	11+							
23	13 a		Gillingham	L 1-3	Douglas.	3.817	23	1	2		3	12		5	6			8	10*	4			9			7		11						
24	16 h		Grimsby Town	D 0-0		4.336	24	1	2			5	6		8	9	4			9			7			10	11							
25	20 h		Exeter City	W 2-1	Rankine.Robinson L(pen).	3.492	25	1	2	3		5	6		8		4			11			7+			10	9	14						
26	27 a		Peterborough Utd	L 1-2	Noteman.	4.080	26	1	2	3+12		5	6		8		4			11			7*			10	9	14						
27	Feb 2 a		Southend Utd	L 0-2		3.174	27	1	2	3	12	5	6		8		4			11			7*			10	9							
28	10 h		Scarborough	D 1-1	Turnbull.	2.899	28	1	2	3		5	6		8	9	4						7			10	11							
29	13 h		Lincoln City	L 0-1		3.079	29	1		3	2+	5	6		8	9	4			7	14					12		10	11*					
30	16 a		Stockport County	L 1-3	Morrow.	3.609	30	1		3	2	5	6		8					11	10		12	7*				9						
31	25 h		Hereford Utd	L 0-1		2.958	31	1	2	3		6	5		8+	9	4			12	7*			14			11	10						
32	Mar 3 a		Grimsby Town	L 1-2	Jones D.	5.536	32	1	2	3		5	6		8	12	4*				14			7+		10	11	9						
33	6 h		Hartlepool Utd	D 2-2	Turnbull.Robinson L(pen).	2.518	33	1	2	3		5	6		8+	7	4				14			12		10	11	9*						
34	10 a		Aldershot	D 1-1	Jones D.	1.512	34	1	2+	3	7*	5	6		8	9	4				14					10	11	12						
35	17 h		Torquay Utd	W 2-1	Stiles.Brockie(pen).	1.887	35	1		3	14		6		8	10	4			12	2		11+			5	7	9*						
36	20 a		Carlisle Utd	L 0-1		3.970	36	1		3		5	6		8	9	4				2					10	11	7						
37	25 h		Cambridge Utd	W 2-1	Daish O.G..Turnbull.	2.147	37	1		3		5	6		8	9					2					10	11	7		4				
38	31 a		Burnley	W 1-0	Jones D.	5.066	38	1				5	6		8	9	11				2					10	3		7	12	4*			
39	Apr 7 h		York City	L 1-2	Muir.	2.185	39	1	12			5	6		8+	9*	11				2					10	3	14	7	4				
40	11 a		Maidstone Utd	L 0-1		1.375	40	1		3	10+	5	6		8	9					2		14			11	12	7*		4				
41	14 h		Chesterfield	W 1-0	Jones D.	3.737	41	1		3		5	6		8	9					12					10	11	7		4	2*			
42	16 a		Wrexham	D 0-0		4.210	42	1		3		5	6		8	9					12					10	11	14	7+	4	2*			
43	21 h		Halifax Town	L 3-4	Turnbull.Muir.Grayson.	2.232	43	1		3+		5	6		9					14	2					10	11	7		4	8*			
44	24 a		Colchester Utd	L 0-2		2.631	44	1			3	5	6		8	9					12		2*			10	11	7+		4	14			
45	28 h		Rochdale	W 4-0	Muir(2).Jones D(2).	2.191	45	1			3	5	6		9	8					2*					10	11	7		4	12			
46	May 5 a		Scunthorpe Utd	L 1-4	Morrow.	3.020	46	1				5	6		9	8+					2					10	11	12	7		4	3*14		

HOME						AWAY							TOTAL								App	46	32	41	23	43	45		4	42	40		36	1		2	20	19	1		23	1		27	30	1	15		10	4	
P	W	D	L	F	A	PTS	P	W	D	L	F	A	PTS	P	W	D	L	F	A	PTS	Sub		1	4					6		2			2		9	5		1	7	1	1			6	1	1		2	1
23	7	7	9	29	29	28	23	7	2	14	24	28	23	46	14	10	22	53	57	51	Gls		8			2			2	10	2		1	3			1			12	3	2	4		1	+ 2 O.G.

F.A. Cup

								Sammways	Robinson	Brevett	Raffell	Ashurst	Douglas	McGinley	Stiles	Turnbull	Rankine	G.Jones	Summer	Gaughan	Brockie	Cusack	Gallagher	Adams	Nicholson	Cygan	D.Jones	Noteman	Morrow
R1	Nov18 h	Notts County	W 1-0	Noteman.	3.817	R1	1	2	3		5	6		8	9	4			7					10	11			
R2	Dec 9 a	Grimsby Town	L 0-1		6.623	R2	1	2	3	4	5	6	8		9				7					10	11			

Littlewoods Cup (League Cup)

1R1L	Aug22 a	Huddersfield Town	D 1-1	Turnbull.	3.983	1R1L	1	7	3	4	5	2		8	9	10			11	12	6*							
1R2L	29 h	Huddersfield Town	L 1-2	Turnbull.	3.583	1R2L	1	7	3	6	5	4	14	8*	9	10	11+		12	2								

League Division 4 1990-91

Player columns (left header, rotated): Nicholson · Holland · Limber · Cillen · Bennett · Smalley · Whitehurst · Parsley · Reddish · Samways · Rowe · Ashurst · M.Jones · Grayson · Adams · Morrow · Turnbull · Marden · Harle · Borckie · Place · Noteman · D.Jones · Muir · Stiles · Gormley · Douglas · Ormsby · Holmes · Brevett · Rankine · Chrichton

No	Date	V	Opponents	F-A	Scorers	Att
1	Aug 25	a	Carlisle Utd	W 3-2	Noteman.Jones.D.Muir.	4,218
2	Sep 1	h	Wrexham	W 3-1	Muir.Noteman.Ormsby	2,101
3	8	a	Halifax Town	W 1-0	Jones D.	2,394
4	15	a	Rochdale	W 3-0	Muir(2).Gormley.	2,607
5	18	h	Walsall	W 2-0	Muir(2).	4,026
6	22	a	York City	L 1-3	Noteman.	3,742
7	29	h	Darlington	L 0-1		3,695
8	Oct 2	a	Torquay Utd	L 0-1		3,312
9	7	a	Scarborough	L 1-2	Brockie(pen).	2,160
10	13	h	Hartlepool Utd	D 2-2	Muir(2).	2,801
11	20	h	Lincoln City	W 1-0	Grayson.	2,866
12	23	a	Cardiff City	W 2-0	Gormley(pen).Grayson.	3,891
13	27	a	Chesterfield	L 1-2	Muir.	4,389
14	Nov 3	h	Gillingham	D 1-1	Rankine.	2,500
15	10	a	Peterborough	D 1-1	Grayson.	4,691
16	24	h	Blackpool	W 1-0	Grayson.	2,113
17	Dec 1	h	Aldershot	W 3-0	Turnbull(3).	2,093
18	15	a	Scunthorpe Utd	D 1-1	Turnbull.	3,963
19	21	a	Stockport County	D 0-0		3,347
20	26	h	Maidstone Utd	W 3-0	Brevett(2)(1pen).Grayson.	2,717
21	29	h	Hereford United	W 3-1	Noteman.Ormsby.Muir.	3,171
22	Jan 1	a	Northampton Town	D 0-0		5,270
23	12	a	Wrexham	D 1-1	Harle.	1,850
24	19	h	Carlisle Utd	W 4-0	Gormley(2).Morrow.Brevett.	2,447
25	25	h	Rochdale	W 1-0	Noteman.	3,433
26	Feb 2	a	Walsall	L 0-1		3,805
27	16	h	York City	D 2-2	Turnbull(2)(1pen).	2,916
28	16	a	Blackpool	L 0-2		3,533
29	22	h	Peterborough Utd	L 0-2		2,995
30	26	h	Burnley	W 2-1	Brockie(pen).Muir.	3,080
31	Mar 2	a	Aldershot	D 1-1	Harle(pen).	1,728
32	8	h	Scunthorpe Utd	L 2-3	Whitehurst.Muir.	4,244
33	16	a	Darlington	D 1-1	Smith O.G.	4,410
34	24	h	Scarboro	L 0-2		2,734
35	30	a	Maidstone Utd	W 1-0	Rankine.	1,512
36	Apr 1	h	Stockport Co	W 1-0	Ashurst.	3,372
37	6	a	Hereford Utd	D 1-1	Noteman.	2,013
38	13	h	Northampton Town	W 2-1	Gormley.Muir.	2,939
39	16	a	Hartlepool Utd	D 1-1	Ormsby.	3,363
40	20	a	Lincoln City	D 0-0		3,363
41	23	h	Halifax Town	L 1-2	Ormsby(pen).	2,360
42	27	h	Cardiff City	D 1-1	Noteman.	2,227
43	30	a	Burnley	L 0-1		10,456
44	May 4	h	Chesterfield	L 0-1		2,649
45	7	h	Torquay Utd	D 1-1	Adams.	1,642
46	11	a	Gillingham	L 0-2		2,656

	P	W	D	L	F	A	PTS
HOME	23	12	5	6	36	21	41
AWAY	23	5	9	9	20	24	24
TOTAL	46	17	14	15	56	45	65

F.A. Cup

R1	Nov17	a	Chester City	D 2-2	Gormley.Rankine.		1,749
R1R	20	h	Chester City	L 1-2	Noteman.	(aet)	3,543

Rumbelows Cup (League Cup)

1R1L	Aug28	h	Rotherham Utd	L 2-6	Muir.Jones D.	3,665
1R2L	Sep 4	a	Rotherham Utd	L 1-2	Brockie(pen).	3,448

League Division 4 1991-92

No	Date	V	Opponents	F-A	Scorers	Att
1	Aug 17	h	Carlisle Utd	L 0-3		2,634
2	24	a	Scunthorpe Utd	L 2-3	Kerr,Tynan.	3,505
3	31	h	Burnley	L 1-4	Noteman.	2,980
4	Sep 3	a	Northampton Town	L 1-3	Noteman.	2,742
5	7	h	Wrexham	W 3-1	Noteman(2),Rankine.	1,464
6	14	a	Barnet	L 0-1		3,762
7	18	a	Scarborough	L 0-1		1,506
8	20	h	Blackpool	L 0-2		2,428
9	28	a	Rochdale	D 1-1	Milner O.G.	2,653
10	Oct 5	h	Crewe Alex	L 1-3	Rankine.	1,879
11	12	a	Maidstone Utd	D 2-2	Rankine,McKenzie.	1,255
12	19	h	Gillingham	D 1-1	Limber.	1,468
13	26	a	Cardiff City	L 1-2	Gormley.	2,491
14	Nov 2	a	Mansfield Town	D 2-2	Harle,Noteman.	4,186
15	6	h	Rotherham Utd	D 1-1	Gormley.	3,507
16	8	h	York City	L 1-5	Ormsby.	2,144
17	30	h	Lincoln City	L 1-5	Ormsby.	1,999
18	Dec 20	h	Scunthorpe Utd	L 1-2	Gormley.	1,825
19	26	a	Carlisle Utd	L 1-2	Noteman.	3,174
20	28	a	Burnley	L 1-3	Muir,Gormley,Noteman.	9,604
21	Jan 1	h	Northampton Tn	L 0-3		1,973
22	4	a	Walsall	W 3-1	Muir,Gormley,Noteman.	3,444
23	11	h	Halifax Town	D 0-2		2,067
24	18	a	Chesterfield	L 1-2	Ormsby.	3,372
25	Feb 1	a	Gillingham	L 1-2	Ormsby.	2,366
26	8	h	Cardiff City	L 1-2	Noteman.	2,094
27	12	a	Lincoln City	W 2-0	Noteman.Gormley.	2,011
28	18	h	Hereford Utd	D 0-0		1,270
29	22	a	Halifax Town	L 0-1		1,275
30	29	h	Walsall	L 0-1		1,919
31	Mar 3	h	Chesterfield	W 1-0	Jeffrey.	2,385
32	7	a	Hereford Utd	W 1-0	Noteman.	1,782
33	10	a	Rotherham Utd	L 1-3	Jeffrey.	4,883
34	14	h	Mansfield Town	L 0-1	Jeffrey.	2,846
35	21	a	York City	D 1-1	Jeffrey.	2,127
36	31	h	Barnet	W 1-0	Jeffrey.	1,247
37	Apr 3	a	Wrexham	W 2-1	Nicholson.Reddish.	2,769
38	11	h	Scarborough	W 3-2	Warboys.Jeffrey.Nicholson.	1,638
39	14	a	Blackpool	W 1-0	Jeffrey.	4,353
40	20	h	Rochdale	W 2-0	Warboys.Jeffrey.	2,255
41	24	a	Crewe Alex	L 0-1	Jeffrey.	3,639
42	May 2	h	Maidstone Utd	W 3-0	Reddish.Ormsby(pen).Jeffrey.	1,680

	P	W	D	L	F	A	PTS
HOME	21	6	2	13	21	35	20
AWAY	21	3	6	21	3	19	30
TOTAL	42	9	8	25	40	65	36

Pld 42 Sub Gls

+ 1 O.G.

F.A. Cup

R1	Nov16	a	Burnley	D 1-1	Rankine.	7,976
R2	27	h	Burnley	L 1-3	Whitehurst.	4,207

Rumbelows Cup (League Cup)

1R1L	Aug20	a	Crewe Alex	L 2-5	Whitehurst(2)	2,900
1R2L	27	h	Crewe Alex	L 2-4	Cullen,Noteman.	1,376

League Division 3 1992-93

No	Date	V	Opponents	F-A		Scorers	Att
1	Aug15	h	Bury	L	2-3	Jeffrey(2)(1pen)	3,350
2	22	a	Shrewsbury Town	L	1-2	Jeffrey.	1,867
3	29	h	Torquay Utd	L	2-3	Gormley,Heritage.	1,969
4	Sep 1	h	Barnet	W	2-1	Gormley,Jeffrey.	1,727
5	5	a	Wrexham	D	1-1	Jeffrey.	2,389
6	12	a	Crewe Alex	L	0-4		3,127
7	15	h	Colchester Utd	W	1-0	Jeffrey.	1,719
8	18	h	Lincoln City	D	0-0		2,936
9	25	a	Scarborough	D	1-1	Jeffrey.	1,859
10	Oct 3	a	York City	D	1-1	Morrow.	4,611
11	10	h	Gillingham	W	1-0	Jeffrey.	2,477
12	17	a	Northampton Town	W	1-0	Prindiville.	2,137
13	23	h	Hereford Utd	W	2-1	Morrow,Brady(pen).	2,614
14	31	a	Walsall	L	1-3	Brady(pen).	3,525
15	Nov 7	a	Scunthorpe Utd	W	1-0	Brady.	4,451
16	21	h	Carlisle Utd	L	1-2	Hine.	2,149
17	28	a	Rochdale	D	1-1	Morrow.	2,094
18	Dec11	h	Cardiff City	L	0-1		2,023
19	19	a	Chesterfield	D	0-0		3,319
20	26	a	Halifax Town	D	2-2	Richards(2).	1,854
21	28	h	Darlington	L	0-1		2,876
22	Jan 2	h	Rochdale	D	1-1	Richards.	2,559
23	8	a	Colchester Utd	L	0-2		4,402
24	16	h	Scarborough	W	4-3	Douglas,Prindiville,White,W.Gormley.	2,009
25	23	h	Lincoln City	L	1-2	Gormley.	3,269
26	26	a	Torquay Utd	W	2-1	Gormley(pen),W.White	1,771
27	29	h	Shrewsbury Town	L	0-1		2,227
28	Feb 6	a	Bury	L	0-3		2,496
29	13	h	Wrexham	D	1-1	Morrow.	2,693
30	16	h	Crewe Alex	D	1-1	Rowe.	1,844
31	20	a	Barnet	L	0-2		3,458
32	27	a	Gillingham	D	1-1	O'Connor O.G.	2,975
33	Mar 5	h	York City	L	0-1		3,188
34	13	h	Scunthorpe Utd	L	0-1		2,760
35	27	a	Carlisle Utd	D	1-1	Moss.	2,939
36	Apr 6	a	Cardiff City	D	1-1	Jeffrey(pen).	9,938
37	10	h	Halifax Town	L	0-1		2,160
38	12	a	Darlington	W	2-1	Moss,Jeffrey(pen).	2,318
39	17	h	Chesterfield	W	2-1	Reddish,Heritage.	2,341
40	24	h	Northampton Town	D	2-2	Moss,Colkin O.G.	2,111
41	May 1	a	Hereford Utd	W	2-0	Gormley,Jeffrey.	2,352
42	8	h	Walsall	L	0-3		2,900

Summary

HOME
P	W	D	L	F	A	PTS
21	6	5	10	22	28	23

AWAY
P	W	D	L	F	A	PTS
21	5	9	7	20	29	24

TOTAL
P	W	D	L	F	A	PTS	POS
42	11	14	17	42	57	47	16

F.A. Cup

R1	Nov14	h	Hartlepool Utd	L	1-2	Quinlan.	4,513

Coca-Cola Cup (League Cup)

R1l1	Aug18	h	Lincoln City	L	0-3			2,507
R12L	25	a	Lincoln City	D	1-1	Hewitt.	(agg 4-1)	1,996

Player Totals

Player	App	Sub	Gls
Crichton	41		
Douglas	12	9	1
Prindiville	42		1
Hine	18	7	1
Hicks	36		
Crosby	26	3	
Hewitt	27		
Gormley	41	6	6
Morrow	17	4	4
Jeffrey	29	11	9
Rowe	21	1	1
Richards	36	3	3
Quinlan	7	6	
Heritage	25	1	2
Hodder	1		
Hodson	15	1	
Reece	1		
Reddish	3		1
Falana	2		
Brady	4		2
Roberts	6	1	
C.White	5		
W.White	4	2	1
Kabia	5		
Gilzean	3	1	
Masefield	8		
Taylor	2	1	
Moss	9	2	3
Bennett	1		

+ 2 og

ADVANCED SUBSCRIBERS

John Treleven
Dave McPherson, Colchester
J. Motson
David Earnshaw, Belper, Derbyshire
Raymond Shaw
Mr. K.P. Wood
J.A. Harris
David Keats, Thornton Heath
Moira and Frederick Furness
Alan Davies
Stewart Fell
David Jowett
John Byrne
Graham Spackman
David Downs
L.A. Zammit
Fred Lee, Plymouth Argyle
J. Ringrose
Mark Tyler
Peter Kirby, Maidstone
G.D. Painter
Philip H. Whitehead
Derek Hyde
Phil Hollow
M.J. Cripps
Geoffrey Wright
Willy Østby – Norway
Jonny Stokkeland, Kvinesdal, Norway
Terje Ovrebo, Norway
Duncan Watt
Peter Baxter
Peter Cogle
A.H. Atkins, Toronto, Canada
W.D. Phillips
Martin Simons, Belgium
Lars–Olof Wendler, Sweden
Terry Frost
A.N. Other
Steve Emms
G.S. Briggs
B.H. Standish
Harry Kay
Geoff Allman
Jonathan Hall
Donald Noble, Dunkeld
Richard Stocken
Peter Pickup (Trinity Fan)
Michael McConkey, Luton, Beds.
A. & J.A. Waterman
David Helliwell
Dave Smith
Mr. L. Burgess
Chris Hooker, Ontario, Canada
Göran Schönhult, Sweden

Christer Svensson
Karen Ann Giblin
Andrew Anderson
Brian Tabner
Gordon Small
Bob Lilliman
Allen Bolton
David and William Evans
Alan Hindley
Trond Isaksen, Norway
John Draper– PNE Programmes
John Coyle, Solihull
Paul James Gibbs, Northampton
Tom Beardsley, U.S.A.
Mr. Richard Wells
Stephen Kieran Byrne
Roger Wash
Derek Wheatcroft
Michael Grayson
Dennis Wood
R.V. Calmels
David Lumb
Paul Gilligan
Ivor Valerie Jones – Eggborough
Colin Heath of Bentley
Steve Wood
Kathleen Davies, Auckley
Jim and Andrew Briggs
J. Boylan, Warmsworth
Clifford Binns, Balby, Doncaster
Wayne Armstrong,Outwood,Wakefield
Graham Garnett, Balby, Doncaster
Henry Butler – Balby
Doreen & Jack Watson, Balby
Gordon Hunter, Balby
S.J. Orford, Balby
Neil Marks, Thorne
John Barker, Balby, Doncaster
John W.S. Cullinane
Basil Wilson Godley
L.Briars
Craig Robin Elliott
James Gibblin, Balby, Doncaster
Mark Hollingsworth,Cantley,Doncaster
Gordon Ramsey
Paul Watson, Balby, Doncaster
George & Carole Bartram, Doncaster
Gordon King, Leeds
John Ellis
John New
Stephen Pritchard, Doncaster
T.B. Revitt, Hatfield, Doncaster
Richard Mycock, Truro, Cornwall
Robert Newsome, Balby, Doncaster

David Newsome, Hanwell, London
Paul Seaton, Doncaster
Kenneth Marshall, Sprotborough
Mr. Christopher Daffern, Doncaster
Tim Neill
Ken Avis
Betty,Des,Gillian Shepherd of Tickhill
John Hinchcliffe Thornton–Cleveleys
Wally Lamb, Gainsborough
Paul Joll, Moorends
Paul Cook, Doncaster
Tony Walker, Upton, W. Yorks.
Tracy Jane Nadolny
Bill Hemmings, Balby, Doncaster
A.N. Patching, Norwich
Graham Hardy, Doncaster
Chas Walker
Bill Rollitt, Knaresborough
Brian Aspinall, Burnley
Paul Richards, Bentley, Doncaster
Peter Duffield, Balby, Doncaster
John Starbuck, Doncaster
Craig Robert Hendry
Malcolm John Smith
J. Darton
Brian C. Smith
Karl Hawkridge, Conisbrough
David Littleford, Balby, Doncaster
Mellony Ann Shepard
Dr. W. Erskine, Sprotbrough
Allan Maxey
Nigel Atkins, Doncaster
Gordon Kirby, Bentley, Doncaster
Daniel Bond, Balby
Christopher Rumley, Balby
Barry Phillips, Kirk Sandall
Malcolm Hoyle
Ken Magson, Doncaster
A.R. Cutmore, Carterton, Oxon
Steve Fell, Haxey
Basil Burns
S.G. Lawton, Finningley
Matthew Rush, Wheatley
Paul Mayfield, N.Leverton, Retford
R.H. White, Saudi Arabia
J.A. Ellis
Barry Jackson, Fort Worth, Texas
Dave & Mandy Frost, Bradford
R. White
C. Brown, London
A. Griffin
D. Phillips, Bucks.
Arran Matthews
F.F.Wheeler

The Final Word......
By Alick Jeffrey

I am delighted and honoured to have been asked by Barry and Tony to write this closing piece to the history of Doncaster Rovers F.C.

I have only known Barry and Tony for a short time, but I know that it has taken them a painstaking fifteen years of research to compile this much awaited book. The book has been a labour of love for both of them.

I will always be indebted to the late, and great, P.D.Doherty for signing me as a young fifteen year old. Apart from a few hiccups with injuries, I spent my whole footballing career with the Rovers, and enjoyed every moment of it.

I will always remember the fans, the players, and the staff of the Rovers, and all the people who loved the great club. My one wish is that in my lifetime I will see the Rovers in the Premier Division, or maybe win The Cup at Wembley.

I hope the Doncaster fans and public have enjoyed reading this book, as much as Barry and Tony enjoyed writing it.

Who knows!

A. J. Jeffrey

(N.B. Alick and his wife Sheila now run 'The Black Bull' Hotel, in the Doncaster market place. Call in and have a natter about the old days ...... they will be glad to see you.)

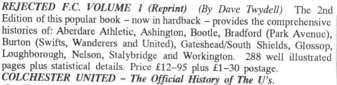

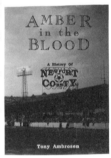